terra australis 29

Terra Australis reports the results of archaeological and related research within the south and east of Asia, though mainly Australia, New Guinea and island Melanesia — lands that remained *terra australis incognita* to generations of prehistorians. Its subject is the settlement of the diverse environments in this isolated quarter of the globe by peoples who have maintained their discrete and traditional ways of life into the recent recorded or remembered past and at times into the observable present.

Since the beginning of the series, the basic colour on the spine and cover has distinguished the regional distribution of topics as follows: ochre for Australia, green for New Guinea, red for South-East Asia and blue for the Pacific Islands. From 2001, issues with a gold spine will include conference proceedings, edited papers and monographs which in topic or desired format do not fit easily within the original arrangements. All volumes are numbered within the same series.

List of volumes in *Terra Australis*

Volume 1: Burrill Lake and Currarong: Coastal Sites in Southern New South Wales. R.J. Lampert (1971)

Volume 2: Ol Tumbuna: Archaeological Excavations in the Eastern Central Highlands, Papua New Guinea. J.P. White (1972)

Volume 3: New Guinea Stone Age Trade: The Geography and Ecology of Traffic in the Interior. I. Hughes (1977)

Volume 4: Recent Prehistory in Southeast Papua. B. Egloff (1979)

Volume 5: The Great Kartan Mystery. R. Lampert (1981)

Volume 6: Early Man in North Queensland: Art and Archaeology in the Laura Area. A. Rosenfeld, D. Horton and J. Winter (1981)

Volume 7: The Alligator Rivers: Prehistory and Ecology in Western Arnhem Land. C. Schrire (1982)

Volume 8: Hunter Hill, Hunter Island: Archaeological Investigations of a Prehistoric Tasmanian Site. S. Bowdler (1984)

Volume 9: Coastal South-West Tasmania: The Prehistory of Louisa Bay and Maatsuyker Island. R. Vanderwal and D. Horton (1984)

Volume 10: The Emergence of Mailu. G. Irwin (1985)

Volume 11: Archaeology in Eastern Timor, 1966–67. I. Glover (1986)

Volume 12: Early Tongan Prehistory: The Lapita Period on Tongatapu and its Relationships. J. Poulsen (1987)

Volume 13: Coobool Creek. P. Brown (1989)

Volume 14: 30,000 Years of Aboriginal Occupation: Kimberley, North-West Australia. S. O'Connor (1999)

Volume 15: Lapita Interaction. G. Summerhayes (2000)

Volume 16: The Prehistory of Buka: A Stepping Stone Island in the Northern Solomons. S. Wickler (2001)

Volume 17: The Archaeology of Lapita Dispersal in Oceania. G.R. Clark, A.J. Anderson and T. Vunidilo (2001)

Volume 18: An Archaeology of West Polynesian Prehistory. A. Smith (2002)

Volume 19: Phytolith and Starch Research in the Australian-Pacific-Asian Regions: The State of the Art. D. Hart and L. Wallis (2003)

Volume 20: The Sea People: Late-Holocene Maritime Specialisation in the Whitsunday Islands, Central Queensland. B. Barker (2004)

Volume 21: What's Changing: Population Size or Land-Use Patterns? The Archaeology of Upper Mangrove Creek, Sydney Basin. V. Attenbrow (2004)

Volume 22: The Archaeology of the Aru Islands, Eastern Indonesia. S. O'Connor, M. Spriggs and P. Veth (2005)

Volume 23: Pieces of the Vanuatu Puzzle: Archaeology of the North, South and Centre. S. Bedford (2006)

Volume 24: Coastal Themes: An Archaeology of the Southern Curtis Coast, Queensland. S. Ulm (2006)

Volume 25: Lithics in the Land of the Lightning Brothers: The Archaeology of Wardaman Country, Northern Territory. C. Clarkson (2007)

Volume 26: Oceanic Explorations: Lapita and Western Pacific Settlement. Stuart Bedford, Christophe Sand and Sean P. Connaughton (2007)

Volume 27: Dreamtime Superhighway: Sydney Basin Rock Art and Prehistoric Information Exchange, Jo McDonald (2008)

Volume 28: New Directions in Archaeological Science, edited by Andrew Fairbairn and Sue O'Connor

terra australis 29

ISLANDS OF INQUIRY

Colonisation, seafaring and the archaeology of maritime landscapes

Edited by Geoffrey Clark, Foss Leach and Sue O'Connor

ANU

THE AUSTRALIAN NATIONAL UNIVERSITY

E PRESS

ANU
E PRESS

© 2008 ANU E Press

Published by ANU E Press
The Australian National University
Canberra ACT 0200 Australia
Email: anuepress@anu.edu.au
Web: http://epress.anu.edu.au

National Library of Australia Cataloguing-in-Publication entry

Title: Islands of inquiry : colonisation, seafaring and the archaeology of maritime landscapes /
         editors: Sue O'Connor, Geoffrey Clark, Foss Leach.

ISBN: 9781921313899 (pbk.) 9781921313905 (PDF)

Series: Terra Australis ; 29

Notes: Bibliography.

Subjects: Coastal archaeology.
             Coastal settlements--History.
            Island archaeology.
            Underwater archaeology.

Other Authors/Contributors:
            O'Connor, Sue.
            Clark, Geoffrey R. (Geoffrey Richard), 1966-
            Leach, B. Foss (Bryan Foss), 1942-

Dewey Number:
            930.109146

Series Editor: Sue O'Connor

Typesetting and design: Rachel Lawson

Cover photograph: Palau rock island. Photograph by David Sanger. Gettyimages 200514730-001.
Back cover map: *Hollandia Nova*. Thevenot 1663 by courtesy of the National Library of Australia.
Reprinted with permission of the National Library of Australia.

Papers in honour of Atholl Anderson

'Aye,' said the Captain, reverentially; 'it's a almighty element. There's wonders in the deep, my pretty. Think on it when the winds is roaring and the waves is rowling. Think on it when the stormy nights is so pitch dark,' said the Captain, solemnly holding up his hook, 'as you can't see your hand afore you, excepting when the wiwid lightning reweals the same; and when you drive, drive, drive through the storm and dark, as if you was a driving, head on, to the world without end,'

Charles Dickens, *Dombey and Son* (1848:252). Philadelphia: Lea and Blanchard

Preface

The impetus for this volume is the pending retirement of Professor Atholl Anderson from the Department of Archaeology and Natural History in the Australian National University in June 2008, after a distinguished and brilliant career in academic archaeology. In geographic range, Atholl's field research has extended over large swathes of the Pacific Ocean, from the west coast of South America to Western Micronesia, to Island Southeast Asia, and west to the Indian Ocean. Few prehistorians of Oceania have seen as much of their subject matter at such close quarters. The variety and span of his study areas are matched, and quite possibly exceeded, by the prodigious variety of subjects he has tackled in numerous scientific publications, which are outlined by Foss Leach in Chapter 1.

As a colleague, mentor and friend to fellow archaeologists, Atholl has been hugely influential in the development of archaeology in Australasia and further afield, and his intense interest in prehistory has been propelled by both a love of history and a desire to see the past with fresh eyes – even if that means upsetting long-established and often cherished conceptual frameworks in the process. This bent for revisionism aimed squarely at improving the historical realism of the discipline has led him to engage with new scientific techniques and theoretical orientations, along with instituting field projects in remote places to recover the essential data. Such an unusually high level of intellectual enthusiasm recalls Samuel Johnson's comment about the prolific Edmund Burke that: 'His stream of mind is perpetual', and throughout his career, numerous prehistorians have benefited from Atholl's generous sharing of ideas, information and contacts.

In putting together this volume, our aim was to honour Atholl's contribution to archaeology by soliciting papers on subjects which have been at the core of his research endeavours over several decades. The title *Islands of Inquiry: Colonisation, seafaring and the archaeology of maritime landscapes* reflects Atholl's abiding intellectual interest and fascination with the way people reached, occupied and transformed diverse, and often extreme, insular environments. Both 'colonisation' and 'seafaring' are well-established themes in island archaeology, but the concept of 'maritime landscapes' might at first glance appear incongruous. However, island peoples, in the past as well as in the present, have a strong and visceral connection with the seas and oceans in which they live. Maritime influences, whether they be situated in subsistence, trade or ritual domains, permeate the social life of island communities, and are amenable to archaeological study. Thus, a major aim of the volume is to highlight the importance of an archaeologically informed history of landmasses in the oceans and seas of the world.

Contributors were asked to write on a relevant theme, and to eschew valediction and sentiment in favour of scholarly writing. All papers were refereed and we are grateful to the authors for their participation, and the referees and the manuscript reader, Professor Tim Murray. We also thank Lorena Kanellopoulos, Duncan Beard, Laticia Wedhorn and Rachel Lawson for their generous help with volume production. Publication was possible with financial assistance from the Department of Archaeology and Natural History and the College of Asia and the Pacific (ANU).

Geoffrey Clark, Foss Leach and Sue O'Connor

Contents

Island environments: Theory, biological introductions and transformations

Ethnohistory, cross-cultural contact and archaeology in Australasia and the Pacific

Archaeological science and taphonomy

1

Atholl John Anderson:
No ordinary archaeologist

Foss Leach

Honorary Research Associate, Museum of New Zealand Te Papa Tongarewa, Wellington, New Zealand

Foss.Leach@University-of-Ngakuta.ac.nz

Atholl Anderson first ventured into serious archaeological research in 1966, when he carried out an extensive survey of archaeological sites in the Tasman Bay area at the northern end of the South Island of New Zealand. The main objective was 'a complete coverage of all the sites of prehistoric settlement, including mapping, stratigraphical analysis, and sampling of contents'. The completed study was submitted to the Geography Department at Canterbury University as a thesis for the MA degree in 1966 (*Maori occupation sites in back beach deposits around Tasman Bay*). This was a bold initiative for a budding archaeologist, aged 23, working alone, with no formal training in archaeology – that came later. The degree was awarded with Honours. Like many other young students of the time, he had a Teachers Training College studentship. This was a scheme which provided financial assistance for those bent on a teaching career to attend university. After being awarded the MA degree, he was obliged to attend Training College for a year to complete the requirements for a Diploma in Teaching and thereafter to be placed in a school somewhere in New Zealand. So in 1968, Atholl became the assistant headmaster at the small rural school of Karamea, from time to time doubling as the publican of the local hotel. Karamea, at the northernmost end of the West Coast of the South Island, is famous for its forest and fishing, and provided ample opportunities for his great love of the outdoors. He was married by this time to Sandy, with a daughter Rachel.

In spite of the wonderful attractions of West Coast life, Atholl's burning ambition in life was professional archaeology, and a career in teaching was not leading in the right direction. I first met Atholl late in 1969, when he walked into the Anthropology Department at Otago University to seek advice on how to obtain the necessary qualifications to join mainstream professional archaeology. I was a junior lecturer at the time. He was accepted into the MA course in Anthropology in 1970 and became part of a group of young students the like of which had never been seen before at Otago, and arguably has not been seen since. There was a strong spirit of friendship, collaboration and healthy competition between them, and several have excelled academically, with international reputations. Atholl joined a small team of research students in the Palliser Bay archaeological project 1969–1972 and carried out groundbreaking research combining the analysis of a rocky-shore marine environment with high-quality excavation of nearby midden sites and detailed laboratory analysis (1979e, 1981c). This set a standard of maritime economic archaeology which has not been matched in New Zealand since. During this research, he first ventured into archaeometry, greatly improving a novel method of conchiolin dating, which clarified the chronology of the midden sites he excavated (1973b). At this time, he also took his first steps in what was to become one of his strongest academic attributes, archaeological theory, publishing an insightful reappraisal of sampling theory relating to midden excavations. He strongly rejected concepts of cluster, random and column sampling as having fundamental misconceptions. He commented 'leaving the choice of excavation areas to chance is clearly likely to produce results of the same status as those obtained by mixing chemicals at random: A puzzling if not dangerous mess' (1973a:123). He argued that a 'more sensible approach is to ... excavate on the basis of research objectives rather than chance, and to restrict interpretations, in the main, to the results of a full and careful analysis of everything excavated' (1973a:124). Throughout his career, Atholl has been exemplary in this regard. He was awarded his second MA degree in 1973 with First Class Honours (*Archaeology and behaviour: Prehistoric subsistence behaviour at Black Rocks peninsula, Palliser Bay*).

Following the end of the Palliser Bay project, Atholl applied for a Commonwealth scholarship at Cambridge University with a proposal for doctoral research based in the Chatham Islands, and began fieldwork there early in 1973. During the site survey, a letter from Cambridge University was delivered on horseback during torrential rain while he was digging an underground sauna at the field camp. This contained welcome news of acceptance at Cambridge. After returning to mainland New Zealand, he travelled to England and took up residence in Cambridge with his family. Carrying out further research in the Chatham Islands, on the other side of the world, without research grants was impossible, so he decided to focus on archaeological problems closer at hand. He initially carried out fieldwork in France, before turning attention to northern Sweden. He became sufficiently competent in Swedish to do detailed library research, as well as intensive fieldwork. This was not without the usual calamities which accompany archaeological fieldwork. On one occasion, out in the mountains in South Lapland on a very hot day, he took a short cut through a large swamp. When he was half way across, the thick layer of sphagnum moss gave way and he very nearly disappeared in deep liquid mud underneath. In one of the wonderful newsy letters which he frequently wrote from abroad, he described this close encounter thus:

I was waist deep in less than a second then slowed to a sinking rate of about 3 inches a second as I frantically clawed moss under my chest and arms. This stopped me going entirely under, but I would not have lasted more than a few hours. What saved me was the fact that I had by the greatest good fortune gone through by a small raft of peat and moss with several small willows growing on it. I managed to very gingerly work my way close enough to it and ease myself out, which was very difficult, and then crawled, like the monster from the black lagoon, back to the edge of the swamp. I was very lucky; if I had gone through several yards either way of that little patch of willows I would never have been able to hold on long enough to be found, especially since I was nearly two hours from the end of the nearest logging track.

Figure 1. A whimsical portrayal of Atholl as the bow-piece of a canoe (courtesy of Murray Webb, 1987).

When he returned to the closest township, he learned that a man had gone missing in the same general area three weeks earlier. Atholl is a person with a strong sense of adventure, brimming with self-confidence and with good survival instincts, and his career has continued to be punctuated with occasional close shaves.

Following the research in Lapland, he submitted his doctoral dissertation in 1976 (*Prehistoric competition and economic change in northern Sweden*). This helped him to obtain his first academic post, at Auckland University during the 1977 academic year. At this time, he took his first steps into the tropical Pacific, to the southern Tongan island of 'Ata, as a member of the Royal Society of New Zealand's Southwest Pacific Expedition (1979b).

In 1978, he took up an appointment in the Anthropology Department, University of Otago, where he remained until 1993, progressing from assistant lecturer to a personal chair. He remarried soon after returning to Dunedin and Rosanne has been a staunch supporter of his research ever since, often accompanying him to remote parts of the Pacific. He and Rosanne have two children (Kirsten and John). He is a strong family man, devoted to his wife, three children and grandchildren.

The Otago period was an extremely productive one, not only as a researcher, but also as a teacher, supervising many thesis students and taking them on his own fieldwork expeditions. A great deal of Atholl's energy during this period was devoted to the Southern Hunters Project, which was focused on archaeological research in southern New Zealand, an area occupied by hunter-gatherers. However, he continued his Pacific interests with an expedition to the Kermadec Islands in 1978 (1981i). He later commented that this was his first experience of leading a team to a Pacific Island. His account of the crisis which arose when one of his assistants ate a poisonous plant makes hilarious reading, despite the gravity of the event (2004a:56–57).

The Southern Hunters Project involved excavations in no fewer than 20 archaeological

Figure 2. Atholl in the foreground at Shag River Mouth discussing strategy for excavation of the high-dune sequence, 1988–1989 (courtesy of Angela Boocock).

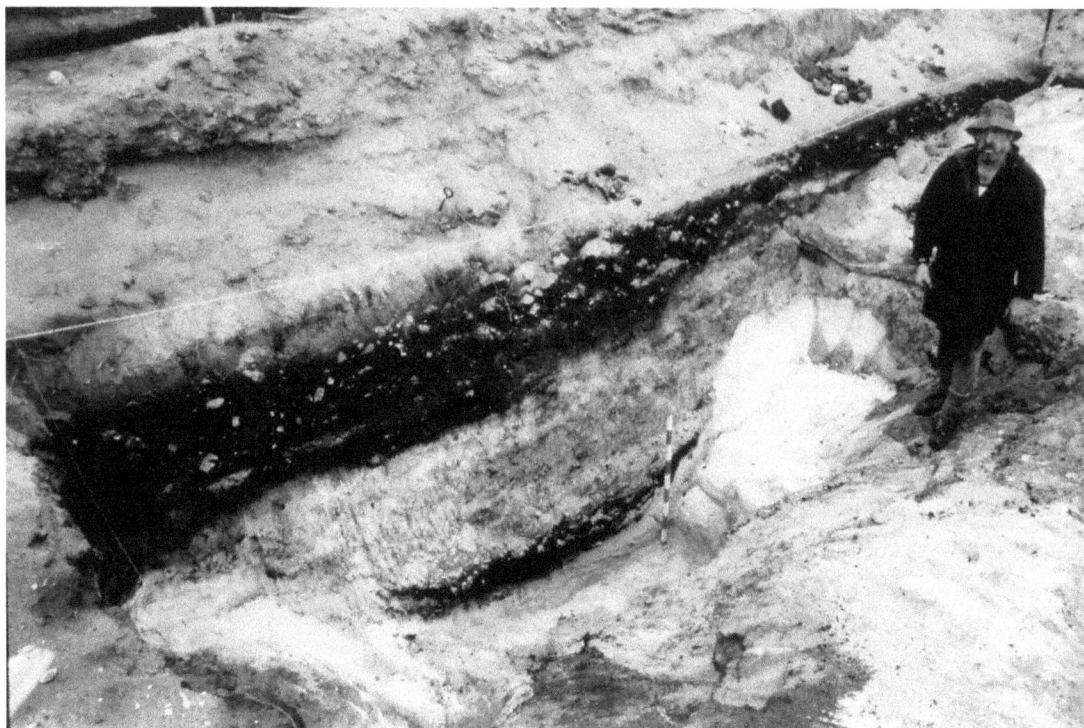

Figure 3. Atholl during excavation of the high dune at Shag River Mouth 1988–1989 (courtesy of Ian Smith).

sites, revisiting places which had earlier seen excavation, and in many cases fossicking, as well as previously untouched sites. Arguably the most significant of these were Purakanui, Lee Island and Shag River Mouth, but they all contributed to a far better understanding of prehistoric life in southern New Zealand. The Purakanui excavations (1981a) took place close to his seaside home at the time. This research built on his interests in economic prehistory and the exploitation of the marine environment, begun earlier at Palliser Bay.

The three rock shelters on Lee Island in Lake Te Anau in Fiordland were newly discovered and contained a wealth of bird bones, fibre artefacts and other perishable remains. His analysis of the fibre remains involved a pioneering study of cordage and knots (Anderson *et al.* 1991b). The publication that resulted from the Lee Island excavations was his first major multi-authored work representing collaborative research (Anderson and McGovern-Wilson eds 1991), something that characterises much of his subsequent work. Atholl has always been a great team leader, inspiring others with the depth of his knowledge, good humour and personal charisma.

The excavations at Shag River Mouth, spread over four years, and subsequent analyses were once again collaborative, involving large numbers of students. Numerous uncontrolled excavations had been carried out at this site for more than a century, producing large quantities of artefacts and moa bones. It is a great credit to Atholl that he managed to find untouched stratigraphy, establish a chronology for this major southern site, and produce a substantive monograph (Anderson *et al.* eds 1996).

The Southern Hunters Project explored many aspects of prehistoric economics, but a major focus was inevitably on moa. During this period, Atholl produced his classic book *Prodigious Birds: Moas and moa-hunting in prehistoric New Zealand* (1989a), which has been reprinted as a paperback. This was a masterly and much-needed synthesis, covering historical, biological, chronological and cultural aspects of this famous New Zealand megafauna. It was a start to Atholl's ongoing interest in Pacific megafauna and extinctions. This work covered the whole of New Zealand and required a careful reappraisal of evidence from radiocarbon dating. The

Figure 4. Atholl pondering the complexities of the high-dune excavation at Shag River Mouth 1988–1989 (courtesy of Ian Smith).

deficiencies which were uncovered led him to review the chronology of colonisation in New Zealand and later to undertake re-dating of major moa-hunting sites, such as Houhora (Anderson and Wallace 1993) and Wairau Bar (Higham *et al.* 1999). Issues of chronology and dating have been of interest to him ever since.

Archaeology and polemics are no strangers to each other, and Atholl has never shied away from reasoned debate on controversial issues. His first major encounter arose when a colleague published an argument that New Zealand had been occupied at least twice the length of time of current orthodoxy. Atholl responded to this with a well-reasoned argument to the effect that if anything, the New Zealand chronology should be shortened, not lengthened (1991c). He carefully re-examined the entire history of radiocarbon dating in New Zealand, and re-evaluated the dating of many archaeological sites, not only for New Zealand, but for East Polynesia (Spriggs and Anderson 1993).

In all this, Atholl has displayed a dogged determination to get to the truth of any issue by focusing on quality of evidence and interpretation. Since the initial foray with moa chronology, refinement in dating has become a major preoccupation in Atholl's research. Probably the best-known example of this is the controversy over radiocarbon dates of the small Polynesian rat, *Rattus exulans*, in New Zealand. Suggestions that this rat came to New Zealand with or without humans 2000 years ago have seen intensive research both for and against. Atholl has left no stone unturned to get to the truth and has been responsible for uncovering serious deficiencies in the initial accelerator dates. His publications on this topic have spanned eight years (1996h, 1997c, 1998d, 2000b, 2004h; Smith and Anderson 1998; Anderson and Higham 2004; Higham *et al.* 2004), again showing his determination to resolve this matter. The issue of short and long chronology is one which frequently arises in archaeology, most famously perhaps with the problem of Glozel in France, but the Pacific region has had its fair share of similar debate. In stressing the need for the highest quality of dating throughout the process, from sample selection from secure provenance and close documentation, to the finest laboratory methodology, Atholl has set aside the spectacular and been the champion of good scholarship. Throughout his career, he has steadfastly stressed the importance of interpretations arising from primary high-quality data and vigorously opposed speculative scenario building.

He has always been careful to distinguish what can and cannot be established by archaeological methods and by other disciplines which contribute to prehistory. A good example is his insistence that hypotheses based on one line of evidence must be tested against all available archaeological information. A typical case of this arose when it was proposed on the basis of pollen evidence that humans had arrived on Mangaia in the Cook Islands by the surprisingly early date of 2500 BP. Atholl showed that the pollen evidence alone could be interpreted in a number of ways, but was insufficient to overturn existing unambiguous archaeological evidence for a much shorter time scale (1994e).

Atholl has Scottish ancestry from his father, and through his mother he is descended from a branch of Ngai Tahu Maori from Rakiura (Stewart Island). When the Ngai Tahu placed a claim before the Waitangi Tribunal about historical grievances endured by their people from actions and inactions by the Crown, Atholl became a key researcher for the Ngai Tahu iwi (tribe). He gave a great deal of important evidence to the Waitangi Tribunal, clarifying difficult, highly contentious, historical issues. He has earned the greatest respect from both the Crown and Maori tribal authorities, not just for the depth of scholarship he brought to these hearings, but also for his balance and scrupulous honesty, even at times when his evidence ran counter to some tribal submissions. As a result, he has become a foremost authority on the ethnohistory of southern Maori, marshalling diverse historical documents into publishable form. An excellent example of this is *Traditional lifeways of the southern Maori* (1994 ed), an enormous task of

Figure 5. Atholl taking notes during the excavations at Emily Bay, Norfolk Island, 1996 (courtesy of Ian Smith).

editorial work definitely not for the faint hearted. In these endeavours, Atholl also managed to bridge the gap between deep scholarship and publications for a wider audience, such as *When all the moa ovens grew cold* (1983a), *Te Puoho's last raid: the battle of Tuturau, 1836–1837* (1986d), and *The welcome of strangers* (1998a). The Ngai Tahu settlement with the Crown following the Waitangi Tribunal hearings has been among the most successful of recent times, and Atholl made an important contribution towards this outcome. He also contributed a number of biographies of southern Maori to the *Dictionary of New Zealand Biography*, including one on his ancestress Anne Wharetutu Newton (1990f).

In 1993, Atholl and his family moved to Canberra, where he took up the Establishment Chair of Prehistory at the Research School of Pacific and Asian Studies, Australian National University. This post offered new opportunities for research throughout the Pacific basin and rim, both for himself and for students under his supervision. His numerous fieldwork expeditions have taken him to Niue, Fiji, Norfolk, Lord Howe, Tuvalu, Maupiti, Kiritimati Island (Kiribati), Palau, Taiwan, Philippines, Juan Fernandez, Mangareva, Rapa, Christmas Island (Indian Ocean), New Caledonia, Yaeyama Islands (Japan), Galapagos Islands, Mocha Island (Chile), and Huahine. Some of these are extremely isolated places and reflect Atholl's desire to investigate the remotest limits of prehistoric exploration of the Pacific.

These expeditions took place within the framework of two major projects: the Indo-Pacific Colonisation Project, and the Asian Fore-Arc Project, and have resulted in many scholarly publications and lecture series. Collaborative monographs have been produced on Norfolk Island (Anderson and White eds 2001), Niue (Walter and Anderson 2002) and Kiritimati (Anderson *et al.* 2000c). Volumes on Rapa (Anderson and Kennett eds nd) and Fiji (Clark and Anderson eds nd) are forthcoming.

This period of research in Canberra has been immensely productive. Besides carrying out and publishing fundamental archaeological research in various parts of the Pacific, Atholl has pursued a number of interrelated themes centering on colonisation and the sustainability of settlement on small islands. Island sequences and the chronology of initial settlement of islands have been continuing concerns (2000e, 2005a; Spriggs and Anderson 1993; Anderson and Clark 1999; Anderson and Sinoto 2002; Anderson *et al.* 2003a; Phear *et al.* 2004). He has made major contributions not just towards the facts of migration and dispersal, but towards suggestions of causes for these events (1995a, 2001a, 2003b, 2004b, 2006b), and has highlighted issues of isolation, remoteness and abandonment (2001b, 2005b).

Atholl's interest in birds, megafauna and extinctions has resulted in reports of fossil fauna and new bird species from Niue (Steadman *et al.* 2000; Worthy *et al.* 2002), and the important discovery of extinct megafauna in Fiji (Worthy *et al.* 1999; Anderson *et al.* 2001a). His excavations in the Volivoli caves inland from Sigatoka in 1998 uncovered a previously unknown extinct crocodile, which was named after him – *Volia athollandersoni* – and features on the Fijian 50c stamp. He has also considered wider issues of faunal collapse and landscape change on Pacific islands (2002b, 2007a).

A keen yachtsman himself, Atholl has contributed significantly to discussion of voyaging strategies (1996a) and the development and capabilities of Pacific voyaging canoes (2000d, 2001d), and considered the effects of La Niña and El Niño on Pacific migrations (Anderson *et al.* 2006a).

Throughout this period in Canberra, he has continued to publish extensively on New Zealand archaeological topics. In 1998, he launched the Southern Margins Project, organising expeditions to Rakiura (Stewart Island), New Zealand's Subantarctic Islands, and Whenua Hou (Codfish Island) off Stewart Island. This project built on Atholl's earlier research in the

Figure 6. Atholl wet sieving during excavations in Palau, 2000 (courtesy of Geoffrey Clark).

Kermadecs and Norfolk Island, as well as New Zealand, and showed that Polynesian voyaging had extended into the sub-polar region some 700 years ago (Anderson and O'Regan 2000; Anderson 2005d). Atholl was thus able to extend his definition of 'South Polynesia' to include not only Norfolk, the Kermadecs, the two main islands of New Zealand, the Chatham Islands and Rakiura, but also the Auckland Islands.

One might think that someone who has devoted so much energy to his own personal research and publications would have had little time for advancing the careers of others. The opposite is the case with Atholl. He has been a dedicated teacher throughout his career, supervising many thesis students at both the University of Otago and Australian National University, and has helped students from other countries too. But his generosity towards others does not stop there – over the years, he has also accepted the thankless task of serving on a variety of university committees, the New Zealand Historic Places Trust, and many editorial boards, and acted as advisor to Te Runanga o Ngai Tahu, and as a referee for diverse granting agencies. He has always been a prompt and insightful referee of manuscripts submitted for publication in journals and books. He has helped numerous colleagues over the difficult hurdles of promotion in academic institutions by giving personal and professional assistance, and has gone out of his way to promote people for awards, honorary positions and degrees.

A typical example of his generosity towards others was the festschrift for Ron Scarlett, which he initiated in 1976 before his doctorate was completed. Ron was a person whose contribution behind the scenes, identifying bird bones from archaeological sites, might otherwise have gone unnoticed (ed 1979). Not all those he approached for contributions felt that such an accolade was justified, but Atholl correctly recognised that people like Ron provided extremely important

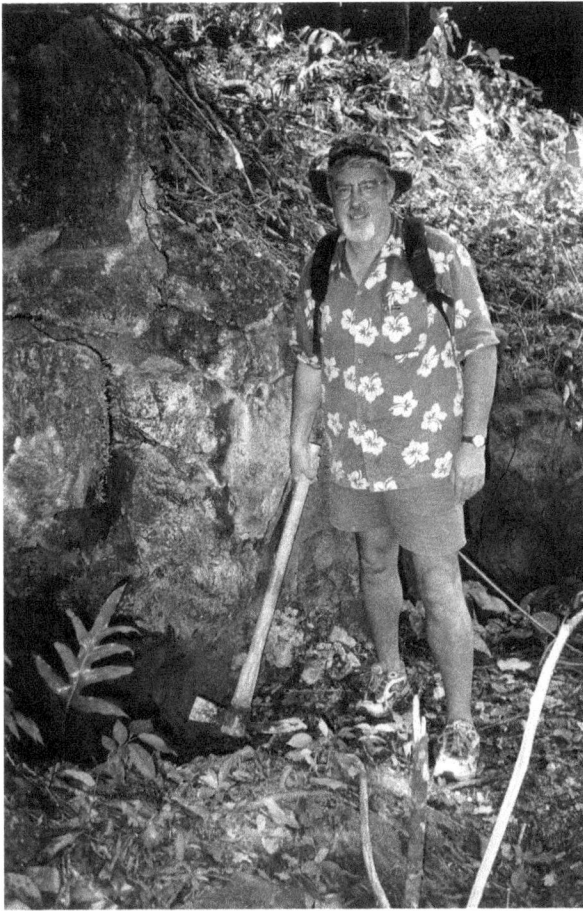

Figure 7. Atholl during fieldwork in Palau 2000 (courtesy of Geoffrey Clark).

basic data, without which archaeology would be the poorer. The volume was well supported and a valuable contribution to knowledge resulted. This was the first of several festschrifts of which he was an invaluable organiser, and was followed by those for Jim Allen (Anderson and Murray eds 2000), Rhys Jones (Anderson *et al.* eds 2001), and Janet Davidson (Anderson *et al.* eds 2007).

Not surprisingly, his own contributions to knowledge have been widely recognised. His awards include Fellow of the Royal Society of New Zealand (1991), Fellow of the Australian Academy of the Humanities (1996), Fellow of the Society of Antiquaries of London (2002), Doctorate of Science University of Cambridge (2002), Federation Medal of Australia for services to archaeology (2001), and Companion of the New Zealand Order of Merit for services to archaeology and anthropology (2005). He has often been invited to give keynote addresses and has held visiting fellowships at numerous academic institutions around the world.

From a very young age, Atholl displayed enthusiasm for many outdoor pursuits: tramping in the forests of New Zealand, hunting deer, skiing, sailing and mountaineering. On one spectacular occasion, he had a near miss on Mount Windward at 2000 m, slithering 500 m down a near-vertical ice slope in winter before coming to a halt on the brink of a bluff. He was 17 years old at the time, but this event did not put him off mountaineering. He went on to conquer some quite demanding peaks as an adult. He also developed an abiding interest in diverse fishing activities: scuba diving, spear fishing, dragging nets for flounders, whitebaiting, surf casting and fly fishing. Not all of his professional colleagues may fully appreciate just how strong the 'call of the wild' is for him, so this sketch of 'Atholl the academic' should be rounded off with some comments on this other side to his character.

Figure 8. Atholl has been a keen mountaineer since school days. Here, he is with Barry Clark on the summit of Mt Cupola, Nelson Lakes National Park, 1998 (courtesy of Barry Clark).

In whatever part of the world he travels, he characteristically seeks out every opportunity to explore the nearby environment, whether mountain, forest, river or sea: fly fishing for grayling in the ice lakes of Alaska, long-line fishing in the cold Subantarctic waters of the Auckland Islands, catching halibut in the seas around Kachemak Bay (Alaska), sailing chartered yachts around the Stockholm archipelago in the Baltic Sea, the inner Hebrides of Scotland, or Tuvalu in the tropical Pacific, and sailing his own yacht *Cepheus* in the Marlborough Sounds in New Zealand. When he lived in Dunedin, he was often seen windsurfing on the harbour, especially when high winds forced all but the bravest off the water. This lifestyle has not been without its mix of adventures, including breaking an arm skiing in Japan, and breaking a foot site-surveying at Murdering Beach in Otago. In another life, Atholl may well have been an explorer. As it is, he has combined the best things of two worlds, academic and outdoors, equally at home in both.

Atholl is due to retire in 2008 and take up residence in a property right in the centre of the richest vineyards of the Wairau Valley in New Zealand, surrounded on all sides by grapes of one of his favourite wines, Marlborough sauvignon blanc. One corner of his property adjoins the icy cold waters of Spring Creek, famous for prize-winning brown trout. What better way to fill out the years ahead than by writing books close to the very best things of life – mountains, forest, clear rivers, and the sea.

Figure 9. Atholl's deep knowledge of all aspects of fishing follows a lifetime's interest in fly fishing in remote parts of the world. Maruia River, New Zealand, 2002 (courtesy of Barry Clark).

Figure 10. For Atholl, one of the great pleasures of life is unwinding by the camp fire at the end of a day's tramping. Taken at Downie's hut, Matakitaki River, Nelson Lakes National Park, 1993 (courtesy of Barry Clark).

Publications of Atholl John Anderson

Excluding book reviews, consultancy reports, unpublished seminars and public lectures, conference papers and reprints.

1972   Anderson, A.J. and N.J. Prickett. Radiocarbon dates for the Wairarapa IV. *New Zealand Archaeological Association Newsletter* 15:164.

1973a   Anderson, A.J. A critical evaluation of the methodology of midden sampling. *New Zealand Archaeological Association Newsletter* 16:119–127.

1973b   Anderson, A.J. The conchiolin dating method. *New Zealand Journal of Science* 16:553–558.

1973   Anderson, A.J. and D.G. Sutton. Archaeology of Mapoutahi Pa, Otago. *New Zealand Archaeological Association Newsletter* 16:107–118.

1974   Leach, B.F. and A.J. Anderson. The transformation of an estuarine to a lacustrine environment in the lower Wairarapa. *Journal of the Royal Society of New Zealand* 4:267–275.

1978   Anderson, A.J. The role of a competition model in the archaeological explanation of economic change, in D. Green, C. Hazelgrove and M. Spriggs (eds), *Social Organisation and Settlement: contributions from anthropology, archaeology and geography*, pp. 31–45. British Archaeological Reports (Oxford) International Series 47.

1978   Leach, B.F. and A.J. Anderson. The prehistoric sources of Palliser Bay obsidian, *Journal of Archaeological Science* 5:301–307.

1979   Anderson, A.J. (ed), *Birds of a Feather: osteological and archaeological papers from the South Pacific in honour of R.J. Scarlett*. British Archaeological Reports (Oxford) International Series 62.

1979a   Anderson, A.J. Introduction, in A.J. Anderson (ed), *Birds of a Feather: osteological and archaeological papers from the South Pacific in honour of R.J. Scarlett*, pp. i–v. British Archaeological Reports (Oxford) International Series 62.

1979b   Anderson, A.J. Archaeological explorations on Ata Island, Tonga, in Lau-Tonga 1977. *Royal Society of New Zealand Bulletin* 17:1–21.

1979c   Anderson, A.J. Excavations at the Archaic site at Waianakarua Mouth, north Otago, *New Zealand Archaeological Association Newsletter* 22:156–162.

1979d   Anderson, A.J. Excavations at the Hawksburn moa-hunting site: an interim report, *New Zealand Archaeological Association Newsletter* 22:48–59.

1979e   Anderson, A.J. Prehistoric exploitation of marine resources at Black Rocks point, Palliser Bay, in B.F. Leach and H.M. Leach (eds), *Prehistoric Man in Palliser Bay*, pp. 49–65. National Museum Bulletin 21.

1979f   Anderson, A.J. The 1978 Raoul Island archaeological expedition: an interim report, *New Zealand Archaeological Association Newsletter* 22:76–82.

1979a   Leach, B.F. and A.J. Anderson. Prehistoric exploitation of crayfish in New Zealand, in A.J. Anderson (ed), *Birds of a Feather: osteological and archaeological papers from the South Pacific in honour of R.J. Scarlett*, pp. 141–161. British Archaeological Reports (Oxford) International Series 62.

1979b   Leach, B.F. and A.J. Anderson. 1979 The role of labrid fish in the prehistoric economies of New Zealand, *Journal of Archaeological Science* 6:1–15.

1980a   Anderson, A.J. Re-discovery of a moa-hunting site in the Old Man Range, *New Zealand Archaeological Association Newsletter* 23:169–172.

1980b   Anderson, A.J. Towards an explanation of prehistoric social organisation and settlement patterns amongst the southern Ngai Tahu, New Zealand *Journal of Archaeology* 2:3–23.

1981a   Anderson, A.J. A fourteenth century fishing camp at Purakanui Inlet, Otago, *Journal of the Royal Society of New Zealand* 11:201–221.

1981b   Anderson, A.J. A lure hook shank from Shag River Mouth, Otago, *New Zealand Archaeological Association Newsletter* 24:280–282.

1981c   Anderson, A.J. A model of prehistoric collecting on the rocky shore, *Journal of Archaeological Science* 8:109–120.

1981d   Anderson, A.J. Archaeological sites at Aramoana, Otago Harbour, *New Zealand Archaeological Association Newsletter* 24:92–97.

1981e   Anderson, A.J. Economic change and the prehistoric fur trade in northern Sweden: the relevance of a Canadian model, *Norwegian Archaeological Review* 14:1–38.

1981f   Anderson, A.J. Pre-European hunting dogs in the South Island, New Zealand, *New Zealand Journal of Archaeology* 3:15–20.

1981g   Anderson, A.J. Radiocarbon dates for Archaic sites at Purakanui and Hawksburn, *New Zealand Archaeological Association Newsletter* 24:63–64.

1981h   Anderson, A.J. The archaeology of moa-hunting in southern New Zealand, *Calgary Archaeologist* 8/9:8–10.

1981i   Anderson, A.J. The archaeology of Raoul Island and its place in the settlement history of Polynesia, *Archaeology and Physical Anthropology in Oceania* 15:131–141.

1981j   Anderson, A.J. The value of high-latitude models in south Pacific archaeology: a critique, *New Zealand Journal of Archaeology* 3:143–160.

1981   Anderson, A.J. and N.A. Ritchie. Excavations at the Dart bridge site, Upper Wakatipu region, *New Zealand Archaeological Association Newsletter* 24:5–10.

1982a   Anderson, A.J. A review of economic patterns during the Archaic phase in southern New Zealand, *New Zealand Journal of Archaeology* 4:45–75.

1982b   Anderson, A.J. Barracouta fishing in prehistoric and protohistoric New Zealand, *Journal de la Société des Océanistes* 72–73:145–158.

1982c   Anderson, A.J. Central Norrland. In M. Jarman, G. Bailey and H. Jarman (eds), *Early European Agriculture: its foundation and development*, pp. 114–120. Cambridge University Press.

1982d   Anderson, A.J. Comment on convergent cultural adaptation in the subantarctic zone. *Current Anthropology* 23:87.

1982e   Anderson, A.J. Further comment and reply to Selinge. *Norwegian Archaeological Review* 15:124–125.

1982f   Anderson, A.J. Habitat preferences of moa in central Otago, A.D. 1000–1500 according to palaeobotanical and archaeological evidence. *Journal of the Royal Society of New Zealand* 12:321–336.

1982g   Anderson, A.J. Maori settlement in the interior of southern New Zealand from the early eighteenth to the late nineteenth centuries A.D. *Journal of the Polynesian Society* 91:53–80.

1982h   Anderson, A.J. North and Central Otago. In N.J. Prickett (ed), *The First Thousand Years: Regional perspectives in New Zealand archaeology*, pp. 114–120. Dunmore Press, Palmerston North.

1982i   Anderson, A.J. The Otokia mouth site at Brighton Beach, Otago. *New Zealand Archaeological Association Newsletter* 25:47–52.

1982j   Anderson, A.J. West Coast, South Island. In N.J. Prickett (ed), *The First Thousand Years: Regional perspectives in New Zealand archaeology*, pp. 103–112. Dunmore Press, Palmerston North.

1983a   Anderson, A.J. *When All the Moa Ovens Grew Cold: Nine centuries of changing fortune for the southern Maoris*. Otago Heritage Books, Dunedin.

1983b   Anderson, A.J. Analysis of fish remains from southern Fiordland and Stewart Island. *New Zealand Archaeological Association Newsletter* 26:264–270.

1983c   Anderson, A.J. Excavations at Mapoutahi Pa, Otago. University of Otago Anthropology Department Working Papers No. 1.

1983d   Anderson, A.J. Faunal depletion and subsistence change in the early prehistory of southern New Zealand. *Archaeology in Oceania* 18:1–10.

1983e   Anderson, A.J. Maori wooden bowls from Central Otago. In S. Bulmer, G. Law and D. Sutton (eds), *A Lot of Spadework to be Done: essays in honour of Lady Aileen Fox*, pp. 129–142. New Zealand Archaeological Association Monograph 14.

1983f   Anderson, A.J. Moa-hunting in the high country of southern New Zealand. In J. Clutton-Brock and C. Grigson (eds), *Animals and Archaeology* Volume 2, pp. 33–52. British Archaeological Reports (Oxford) International Series 83.

1984   Anderson, A.J. The extinction of moa (Aves: Dinornithidae) in southern New Zealand. In P.S. Martin and K.G. Klein (eds), *Quaternary Extinctions*, pp. 728–740. University of Arizona Press.

1984   Anderson, A.J. and N.A. Ritchie. Preliminary report on test excavations at a newly discovered moahunting site at Coal Creek, Central Otago. *New Zealand Archaeological Association Newsletter* 27:174–180.

1985   Anderson, A.J. The Scandinavian colonisation of the north Swedish interior, 500–1500 A.D. In S. Dyson (ed), *Comparative Studies in the Archaeology of Colonialism*, pp. 38–52. British Archaeological Reports (Oxford) International Series 233.

1986   Anderson, A.J. (ed), Traditional Fishing in the Pacific: Ethnographical and archaeological papers from the 15th Pacific Science Congress. *Pacific Anthropological Records* 37. Bishop Museum, Honolulu.

1986a   Anderson, A.J. Introduction. In A.J. Anderson (ed), *Traditional Fishing in the Pacific: Ethnographical and archaeological papers from the 15th Pacific Science Congress*, pp. ix–xi. Pacific Anthropological Records 37. Bishop Museum, Honolulu.

1986b   Anderson, A.J. Mahinga ika o te moana: selection in the pre-European fish catch of southern New Zealand. In A.J. Anderson (ed), *Traditional Fishing in the Pacific: Ethnographical and archaeological papers from the 15th Pacific Science Congress*, pp. 151–165. Pacific Anthropological Records 37. Bishop Museum, Honolulu.

1986c   Anderson, A.J. Makeshift structures of little importance: a reconsideration of Maori dwellings with reference to the round hut. *Journal of the Polynesian Society* 95:91–114.

1986d   Anderson, A.J. *Te Puoho's Last Raid: the battle of Tuturau, 1836–1837*. Otago Heritage Books, Dunedin.

1986e   Anderson, A.J. The Maori in Fiordland. In C. McMillan and B. Turner (eds), *Mountains of Water: the story of Fiordland National Park*, pp. 82–85. Lands and Survey Department, Wellington.

1986   Anderson, A.J. and N.A. Ritchie. Pavements, pounamu and ti: the Dart Bridge site, western Otago. *New Zealand Journal of Archaeology* 8:115–141.

1986   Leach, F., A. Anderson, D. Sutton, R. Bird, P. Duerden and E. Clayton. The origin of prehistoric obsidian artefacts from the Chatham and Kermadec Islands. *New Zealand Journal of Archaeology* 8:143–170.

1987a   Anderson, A.J. Hunting and fishing. In J. Wilson (ed), *From the Beginning: the archaeology of the Maori*, pp. 73–84. Penguin Books, Auckland.

1987b   Anderson, A.J. Recent developments in Japanese prehistory; a review. *Antiquity* 61:270–281.

1987c   Anderson, A.J. Recent uplift at Raoul Island, Kermadec Group, Southwest Pacific. *New Zealand Journal of Geology and Geophysics* 30:325–327.

1987d   Anderson, A.J. Supertramp science: some thoughts on archaeometry and archaeology in Oceania. In W.R. Ambrose and J.M.J. Mummery (eds), *Archaeometry: Further Australasian studies*, pp. 3–18. Research School of Pacific Studies, Australian National University, Canberra.

1987e   Anderson, A.J. The first recorded name for Moa. *Journal of the Royal Society of New Zealand* 17:421–422.

1988a   Anderson, A.J. Coastal subsistence economies in prehistoric coastal New Zealand. In G.N. Bailey and J.E. Parkington (eds), *The Archaeology of Hunter-Gatherer Subsistence Economies in Coastal Environments*, pp. 93–101. Cambridge University Press.

1988b   Anderson, A.J. Moa extinctions in Southern New Zealand: a reply to Sutton. *Archaeology in Oceania* 23:98–99.

1988c   Anderson, A.J. Prehistoric fowling in the Nothofagus forest of southern New Zealand. *Archaeozoologia: Revue Internationale d'Archéologie* II(1/2):201–207.

1988d   Anderson, A.J. The art of concealment: Maori rock art in the South Island. *Ka Tuhituhi o Nehera*, pp. 4–8. National Museum Publication, Wellington.

1988   Anderson, A.J. and B. McFadgen. Return voyaging from New Zealand to East Polynesia. In C. Cristino, P. Vargas, R. Izaurieta and R. Budd (eds), *First International Congress, Easter Island and East Polynesia, Volume 1: Archaeology*, pp. 13–23. Universidad de Chile.

1989a   Anderson, A.J. *Prodigious Birds: moas and moa-hunting in prehistoric New Zealand*. Cambridge University Press.

1989b   Anderson, A.J. A diary discovered: Bayard Booth on Shag Mouth. In D.G. Sutton (ed), *Saying So Doesn't Make It So: Essays in honour of B. Foss Leach*, pp. 64–75. New Zealand Archaeological Association Monograph 17.

1989c   Anderson, A.J. Mechanics of overkill in the extinction of New Zealand Moas. *Journal of Archaeological Science* 16:137–151.

1989d   Anderson, A.J. On evidence for the survival of moa in European Fiordland. *New Zealand Journal of Ecology* 12(Supplement):39–44.

1989e   Anderson, A.J. The beast without: moa as colonial frontier myths in New Zealand. In R. Willis (ed), *Signifying Animals: human meaning in the natural world*, pp. 236–245. One World Archaeology Series. Unwin and Hyman, London.

1990a   Anderson, A.J. A record of 1000 years of the unwritten past. *Historic Places* 28:5–10.

1990b   Anderson, A.J. Comment on T.F. Flannery: Pleistocene Faunal Loss. *Archaeology in Oceania* 25(2):63–64.

1990c   Anderson, A.J. Kuri. In C.M. King (ed), *The Handbook of New Zealand Mammals*, pp. 280–287. Oxford University Press, Auckland.

1990d   Anderson, A.J. The Last Archipelago: 1000 years of Maori settlement in New Zealand. In A. Anderson, J. Binney, D. Hamer, R. Dalziel, E. Olsen, W.H. Oliver and J. Phillips, *Towards 1990: Seven leading historians examine significant aspects of New Zealand history*, pp. 1–19. Government Printer, Wellington.

1990e   Anderson, A.J. Edward Shortland 1812–1893. In W. Oliver (ed), *Dictionary of New Zealand Biography, Volume One 1769–1869*, pp. 394–397. Allen and Unwin and Department of Internal Affairs, Wellington.

1990f   Anderson, A.J. Anne Wharetutu Newton fl.1827–1870. In W. Oliver (ed), *Dictionary of New Zealand Biography, Volume One 1769–1869*, pp. 308–309. Allen and Unwin and Department of Internal Affairs, Wellington.

1990g   Anderson, A.J. Te Puoho-o-te-rangi ?–1836/1837. In W. Oliver (ed), *Dictionary of New Zealand Biography, Volume One 1769–1869*, pp 483–484. Allen and Unwin and Department of Internal Affairs, Wellington.

1990h   Anderson, A.J. Te Huruhuru ?–1861. In W. Oliver (ed), *Dictionary of New Zealand Biography, Volume One 1769–1869*, pp. 454–455. Allen and Unwin and Department of Internal Affairs, Wellington.

1990i   Anderson, A.J. Topi Patuki 1810-20–1900. In W. Oliver (ed), *Dictionary of New Zealand Biography, Volume One 1769–1869*, pp. 337–338. Allen and Unwin and Department of Internal Affairs, Wellington.

1990j   Anderson, A.J. Te Whakataupuka fl. 1826–1834. In W. Oliver (ed), *Dictionary of New Zealand Biography, Volume One 1769–1869*, pp. 520–521. Allen and Unwin and Department of Internal Affairs, Wellington.

1990k   Anderson, A.J. Hone Tuhawaiki ?–1844. In W. Oliver (ed), *Dictionary of New Zealand Biography, Volume One 1769–1869*, pp. 553–555. Allen and Unwin and Department of Internal Affairs, Wellington.

1990   Anderson, A.J. and B. McFadgen. Prehistoric two-way voyaging between New Zealand and East Polynesia: Mayor Island obsidian on Raoul Island and possible Raoul Island obsidian in New Zealand. *Archaeology in Oceania* 25:37–42.

1990   Anderson, A.J. and R. McGovern-Wilson. The pattern of prehistoric colonisation in New Zealand. *Journal of the Royal Society of New Zealand* 20:41–63.

1991a   Anderson, A.J. Current research issues in the study of moas and moa-hunting. In B. McFadgen and P. Simpson (eds), *Research Directions for Conservation Science*, pp. 17–29. Science and Research Series 37. Department of Conservation, Wellington.

1991b   Anderson, A.J. *Race Against Time: the early Maori-Pakeha families and the development of the mixed-race population in southern New Zealand. Hocken Lecture 1990.* Hocken Library, University of Otago.

1991c   Anderson, A.J. The chronology of colonization in New Zealand. *Antiquity* 65:767–795.

1991d   Anderson, A.J. Rockshelter excavations and radiocarbon chronology. In A.J. Anderson and R. McGovern-Wilson (eds), *Beech Forest Hunters: the archaeology of Maori rockshelter sites on Lee Island, Lake Te Anau, in southern New Zealand*, pp. 9–17. New Zealand Archaeological Association Monograph 18.

1991e   Anderson, A.J. Implements in stone and bone. In A.J. Anderson and R. McGovern-Wilson (eds), *Beech Forest Hunters: the archaeology of Maori rockshelter sites on Lee Island, Lake Te Anau, in southern New Zealand*, pp. 18–28. New Zealand Archaeological Association Monograph 18.

1991   Anderson, A.J. and M. McGlone. Living on the edge: prehistoric land and people in New Zealand. In J. Dodson (ed), *The Naive Lands: Human-environmental interactions in Australia and Oceania*, pp. 199–241. Longman Cheshire, Sydney.

1991   Anderson, A.J. and R. McGovern-Wilson (eds), *Beech Forest Hunters: the archaeology of Maori rockshelter sites on Lee Island, Lake Te Anau, in southern New Zealand.* New Zealand Archaeological Association Monograph 18.

1991   Anderson, A.J. and R. McGovern-Wilson. Maori settlement on Lee Island. In A.J. Anderson and R. McGovern-Wilson (eds), *Beech Forest Hunters: the archaeology of Maori rockshelter sites on Lee Island, Lake Te Anau, in southern New Zealand*, pp. 76–88. New Zealand Archaeological Association Monograph 18.

1991a   Anderson, A.J., D. Foster and R. Wallace. Woodchips and wooden artefacts. In A.J. Anderson and R. McGovern-Wilson (eds), *Beech Forest Hunters: the archaeology of Maori rockshelter sites on Lee Island, Lake Te Anau, in southern New Zealand*, pp. 29–42. New Zealand Archaeological Association Monograph 18.

1991b   Anderson, A.J., J. Goulding and M. White. Bark and fibre artefacts. In A.J. Anderson and R. McGovern-Wilson (eds), *Beech Forest Hunters: the archaeology of Maori rockshelter sites on Lee Island, Lake Te Anau, in southern New Zealand*, pp. 43–55. New Zealand Archaeological Association Monograph 18.

1991c   Anderson, A.J., R. McGovern-Wilson and S. Holdaway. Identification and analysis of faunal remains. In A.J. Anderson and R. McGovern-Wilson (eds), *Beech Forest Hunters: the archaeology of Maori rockshelter sites on Lee Island, Lake Te Anau, in southern New Zealand*, pp. 56–66. New Zealand Archaeological Association Monograph 18.

1991   Morrison, K. and A.J. Anderson. Lee Island and its environment. In A.J. Anderson and R. McGovern-Wilson (eds), *Beech Forest Hunters: the archaeology of Maori rockshelter sites on Lee Island, Lake Te Anau, in southern New Zealand*, pp. 3–8. New Zealand Archaeological Association Monograph 18.

1992   Anderson, A.J. and I.W.G. Smith. The Papatowai Site: new evidence and interpretations. *Journal of the Polynesian Society* 101:129–158.

1993   Anderson, A.J. Thomas Rangiwahia Ellison 1867–1904. *The Dictionary of New Zealand Biography, Volume 2 (1870–1900)*, pp. 131–132. Department of Internal Affairs, Wellington.

1993   Anderson, A.J. and R.T. Wallace. Radiocarbon chronology of the Houhora site, Northland, New Zealand. *New Zealand Journal of Archaeology* 15:5–16.

1993   Spriggs, M. and A.J. Anderson. Late colonization of East Polynesia. *Antiquity* 67:200–217.

1994   Anderson, A.J. (ed), *J.H. Beattie Traditional Lifeways of the Southern Maori: The Otago University Museum Ethnological Project, 1920*. Otago University Press, Dunedin.

1994a   Anderson, A.J. Introduction: James Herries Beattie and the 1920 Project. In A. Anderson (ed), *J.H. Beattie Traditional Lifeways of the Southern Maori: The Otago University Museum Ethnological Project, 1920*, pp. 9–32. Otago University Press, Dunedin.

1994b   Anderson, A.J. Comment on J. Peter White's paper. Site 820 and the evidence for early human occupation of Australia . *Quaternary Australasia* 12:30–31.

1994c   Anderson, A.J. Moahunting in New Zealand. In G. Burenhult (ed), *The Illustrated History of Humankind, Volume 4: New World and Pacific Civilizations*, p. 163. Harper Collins, New York.

1994d   Anderson, A.J. The occupation of the Pacific Islands, 50,000 BC–AD 1500: voyagers and fisherfolk. In G. Burenhult (ed), *The Illustrated History of Humankind, Volume 4: New World and Pacific Civilizations*, pp. 143–162. Harper Collins, New York.

1994e   Anderson, A.J. Palaeoenvironmental evidence of island colonization: a response. *Antiquity* 68:845–847.

1994f   Anderson, A.J. Thomas Rangiwahia Ellison 1866-68?–1904: Ngai Tahu and Te Atiawa; rugby player and lawyer. In C. Orange (ed), *The Turbulent Years 1870–1900*, pp. 18–20. Bridget Williams Books, Wellington.

1994   Anderson, A.J. and T.F.G. Higham. Radiocarbon dating of oyster shell midden from beside the Dart Bridge site in western Otago. *Archaeology in New Zealand* 37:182–184.

1994   Anderson, A.J., H. Leach, I.W.G. Smith and R. Walter. Reconsideration of the Marquesan sequence in East Polynesian prehistory, with particular reference to Hane (MUH1). *Archaeology in Oceania* 29:29–54.

1994   McGlone, M.S., A.J. Anderson and R. Holdaway. An ecological approach to the early settlement of New Zealand. In D.G. Sutton (ed), *The Origins of the First New Zealanders*, pp. 136–163. Auckland University Press.

1995a   Anderson, A.J. Current approaches in East Polynesian colonization research. *Journal of the Polynesian Society* 104:110–132.

1995b   Anderson, A.J. Historical and archaeological aspects of muttonbirding in New Zealand. *New Zealand Journal of Archaeology* 17:35–55.

1995c   Anderson, A.J. Kuri, Maori Dog. In C.M. King (ed), *The Handbook of New Zealand Mammals*, pp. 281–287. Oxford University Press, Auckland. Second edition.

1995   Jones, K.L., R. Hooker and A.J. Anderson. Bruce Bay Revisited: Archaic Maori Occupation and Haast's 'Palaeolithic'. *New Zealand Journal of Archaeology* 17:111–124.

1995   Walter, R. and A.J. Anderson. Archaeology of Niue Island: initial results. *Journal of the Polynesian Society* 104:471–481.

1996a   Anderson, A.J. Adaptive voyaging and subsistence strategies in the early settlement of East Polynesia. In T. Akazawa and E. Szathmary (eds), *Prehistoric Dispersal of Mongoloids*, pp. 359–374. Oxford University Press.

1996b   Anderson, A.J. An Early Maori village at Waihemo. *Te Karaka* 4.

1996c   Anderson, A.J. Discovery of a prehistoric habitation site on Norfolk Island. *Journal of the Polynesian Society* 105:479–486.

1996d   Anderson, A.J. Origins of Procellariidae hunting in the Southwest Pacific. *International Journal of Osteoarchaeology* 6:1–8.

1996e   Anderson, A.J. Rat colonisation and Polynesian voyaging: another hypothesis. *Rapa Nui Journal* 10:31–35.

1996f   Anderson, A.J. Te Whenua hou: prehistoric Polynesian colonisation of New Zealand and its impact on the environment. In T. Hunt and P. Kirch (eds), *Historical Ecology in the Pacific Islands*, pp. 271–283. Yale University Press.

1996g   Anderson, A.J. Wakawaka and mahinga kai: models of traditional land management in southern New Zealand. In J. Davidson, G. Irwin, F. Leach, A. Pawley and D. Brown (eds), *Oceanic Culture History: essays in honour of Roger Green*, pp. 631–640. New Zealand Journal of Archaeology Special Publication.

1996h   Anderson, A.J. Was *Rattus exulans* in New Zealand 2000 years ago? AMS radiocarbon ages from Shag River Mouth. *Archaeology in Oceania* 31:178–184.

1996   Anderson, A.J. and B. Allingham. The high dune and swamp excavations. In A. Anderson, B. Allingham and I. Smith (eds), *Shag River Mouth: the archaeology of an early southern Maori village*, pp. 39–50. Research Papers in Archaeology and Natural History 27. ANH Publications, Australian National University, Canberra.

1996   Anderson, A.J. and W. Gumbley. Fishing gear. In A. Anderson, B. Allingham and I. Smith (eds), *Shag River Mouth: the archaeology of an early southern Maori village*, pp. 148–160. Research Papers in Archaeology and Natural History 27. ANH Publications, Australian National University, Canberra.

1996a   Anderson, A.J. and I. Smith. Introduction and history of investigations. In A. Anderson, B. Allingham and I. Smith (eds), *Shag River Mouth: the archaeology of an early southern Maori village*, pp. 1–13. Research Papers in Archaeology and Natural History 27. ANH Publications, Australian National University, Canberra.

1996b   Anderson, A.J. and I. Smith. Fish remains. In A. Anderson, B. Allingham and I. Smith (eds), *Shag River Mouth: the archaeology of an early southern Maori village*, pp. 237–244. Research Papers in Archaeology and Natural History 27. ANH Publications, Australian National University, Canberra.

1996c   Anderson, A.J. and I. Smith. Shag River Mouth as an early Maori village. In A. Anderson, B. Allingham and I. Smith (eds), *Shag River Mouth: the archaeology of an early southern Maori village*, pp. 276–291. Research Papers in Archaeology and Natural History 27. ANH Publications, Australian National University, Canberra.

1996d   Anderson, A.J. and I. Smith. The transient village in southern New Zealand. *World Archaeology* 27:359–371.

1996   Anderson, A.J., B. Allingham and I. Smith (eds), *Shag River Mouth: the archaeology of an early southern Maori village*. Research Papers in Archaeology and Natural History 27. ANH Publications, Australian National University, Canberra.

1996a   Anderson, A.J., I. Smith and T. Higham. Radiocarbon chronology. In A. Anderson, B. Allingham and I. Smith (eds), *Shag River Mouth: the archaeology of an early southern Maori village*, pp. 60–69. Research Papers in Archaeology and Natural History 27. ANH Publications, Australian National University, Canberra.

1996b   Anderson, A.J., T. Worthy and R. McGovern-Wilson. Moa remains and taphonomy. In A. Anderson, B. Allingham and I. Smith (eds), *Shag River Mouth: the archaeology of an early southern Maori village*, pp. 200–213. Research Papers in Archaeology and Natural History 27. ANH Publications, Australian National University, Canberra.

1996c   Anderson, A.J., J. Head, R. Sim and D. West. Radiocarbon dates on shearwater bones from Beeton shelter, Badger Island, Bass Strait. *Australian Archaeology* 42:17–19.

1996   Allingham, B. and A.J. Anderson. Preliminary excavations. In A. Anderson, B. Allingham and I. Smith (eds), *Shag River Mouth: the archaeology of an early southern Maori village*, pp. 35–38. Research Papers in Archaeology and Natural History, 27. ANH Publications, Australian National University, Canberra.

1996   Boyd, B., M. McGlone, A.J. Anderson and R. Wallace. Late Holocene vegetation history at Shag River Mouth. In A. Anderson, B. Allingham and I. Smith (eds), *Shag*

River Mouth: the archaeology of an early southern Maori village, pp. 257–275. Research Papers in Archaeology and Natural History 27. ANH Publications, Australian National University, Canberra.

1996   Leach, B.F., J.M. Davidson, L.M. Horwood and A.J. Anderson. The estimation of live fish size from archaeological cranial bones of the New Zealand barracouta *Thyrsites atun*. *Tuhinga: Records of the Museum of New Zealand Te Papa Tongarewa* 6:1–25.

1996   Smith, I. and A.J. Anderson. Collection, identification and quantification strategies. In A. Anderson, B. Allingham and I. Smith (eds), *Shag River Mouth: the archaeology of an early southern Maori village*, pp. 70–73. Research Papers in Archaeology and Natural History 27. ANH Publications, Australian National University Canberra.

1997a   Anderson, A.J. Uniformity and regional variation in marine fish catches from prehistoric New Zealand. *Asian Perspectives* 36:1–26.

1997b   Anderson, A.J. Seasonality and subsistence: Hunting and gathering in Murihiku. In M. McKinnon (ed), *New Zealand Historical Atlas*, plate 16. David Bateman in association with Department of Internal Affairs.

1997c   Anderson, A.J. The dating of Rattus exulans bones — further discussion. *Journal of the Polynesian Society* 106:312–313.

1997   Anderson, A.J. and M. McGlone. A forceful impact: The East Polynesians' effect on fauna and flora. In M. McKinnon (ed), *New Zealand Historical Atlas*, plate 12. David Bateman in association with Department of Internal Affairs.

1997   Anderson, A.J., W. Ambrose, F. Leach and M. Weisler. Material sources of basalt and obsidian artefacts from a prehistoric settlement site on Norfolk Island, South Pacific. *Archaeology in Oceania* 32:39–46.

1998a   Anderson, A.J. *The Welcome of Strangers: an ethnohistory of southern Maori AD 1650–1850*. University of Otago Press, Dunedin.

1998b   Anderson, A.J. James Herries Beattie 1881–1972. In C. Orange (ed), *Dictionary of New Zealand Biography, Volume Four 1921–1940*, pp. 42–43. Auckland University Press and Department of Internal Affairs, Wellington.

1998c   Anderson, A.J. Rating the Dating? *New Zealand Science Monthly* 9:2.

1998d   Anderson, A.J. Reply to comments on "A production trend in AMS ages on *Rattus exulans* bone". *Archaeology in New Zealand* 41:231–234.

1998   Dickinson, W.R., D.V. Burley, P.D. Nunn, A.J. Anderson, G. Hope, A. De Biran, C. Burke and S. Matararaba. Geomorphic and archaeological landscapes of the Sigatoka Dune Site, Viti Levu, Fiji: Interdisciplinary investigations. *Asian Perspectives* 37:1–31.

1998   Holdaway, R.N. and A.J. Anderson. [14]C AMS dates on *Rattus exulans* bones from natural and archaeological contexts on Norfolk Island, South-west Pacific. *Archaeology in New Zealand* 41:195–198.

1998   Smith, I.W.G. and A.J. Anderson. Radiocarbon dates from archaeological rat bones: the Pleasant River case. *Archaeology in Oceania* 33:88–91.

1998   Worthy, T.H., R. Walter and A.J. Anderson. Fossil and archaeological avifauna of Niue Island, Pacific Ocean. *Notornis* 45:177–190.

1999   Anderson, A.J. Moas and moa-hunting. In T. Akimichi (ed), *Ethnobiology of the Austronesians*, pp. 325–338. Heibonsha, Tokyo.

1999   Anderson, A.J. and G. Clark. The Age of Lapita Settlement in Fiji. *Archaeology in Oceania* 34:31–39.

1999   Higham, T.F.G., A.J. Anderson and C. Jacomb. Dating the First New Zealanders: the chronology of Wairau Bar. *Antiquity* 73:420–427.

1999   White, J.P. and A.J. Anderson. Prehistory of Norfolk Island. *Nature Australia* Spring 1999:26–29.

1999   Worthy, T.H., A.J. Anderson and R.E. Molnar. Megafaunal expression in a land without mammals — the first fossil faunas from terrestrial deposits in Fiji (Vertebrata: Amphibia, Reptilia, Aves). *Senckenbergiana biologica* 79:237–242.

2000a   Anderson, A.J. Defining the period of moa extinction. *Archaeology in New Zealand* 43:195–200.

2000b   Anderson, A.J. Differential reliability of ^{14}C AMS ages of *Rattus exulans* bone gelatin in south Pacific prehistory. *Journal of the Royal Society of New Zealand* 30:243–261.

2000c   Anderson, A.J. Implications of prehistoric obsidian transfer in South Polynesia. *Bulletin of the Indo-Pacific Prehistory Association* 20:117–123.

2000d   Anderson, A.J. Slow boats from China: issues in the prehistory of Indo-Pacific seafaring. In S. O'Connor and P. Veth (eds), *East of Wallace's Line: studies of past and present maritime cultures of the Indo-Pacific region*, pp. 13–50. Balkema, Rotterdam.

2000e   Anderson, A.J. The advent chronology of south Polynesia. In P. Wallin and H. Martinsson-Wallin (eds), *Essays in honour of Arne Skjolsvold 75 years*, pp. 73–82. Occasional Papers of the Kon-Tiki Museum 5.

2000f   Anderson, A.J. Skinner, H. Devenish 1886–1978. In C. Orange (ed), *Dictionary of New Zealand Biography, Volume Four 1921–1940*, pp. 479–480. Auckland University Press and Department of Internal Affairs, Wellington.

2000   Anderson, A.J. and T. Murray (eds), *Australian Archaeologist: Collected papers in honour of Jim Allen*. Coombs Academic Publishing, Australian National University, Canberra.

2000   Anderson, A.J. and T. Murray. J. Allen: Australian archaeologist. In A.J. Anderson and T. Murray (eds), *Australian Archaeologist: Collected papers in honour of Jim Allen*, pp. 8–20. Coombs Academic Publishing, Australian National University, Canberra.

2000   Anderson, A.J. and G. O'Regan. To the final shore: prehistoric colonisation of the Subantarctic islands in South Polynesia. In A.J. Anderson and T. Murray (eds), *Australian Archaeologist: Collected papers in honour of Jim Allen*, pp. 440–454. Coombs Academic Publishing, Australian National University, Canberra.

2000a   Anderson, A.J., G.R. Clark and T.H. Worthy. An inland Lapita site in Fiji. *Journal of the Polynesian Society* 109:311–316.

2000b   Anderson, A.J., E. Conte, G. Clark, Y. Sinoto and F. Petchey. Renewed excavations at Motu Paeao, Maupiti Island, French Polynesia: preliminary results. *New Zealand Journal of Archaeology* 21(1999):47–65.

2000c   Anderson, A.J., P. Wallin, H. Martinsson-Wallin and G. Hope. Towards a first prehistory of Kiritimati (Christmas) Island, Republic of Kiribati. *Journal of the Polynesian Society* 109:273–294.

2000   Leach, B.F., J.M. Davidson, K. Fraser and A.J. Anderson. Pre-European catches of barracouta, *Thyrsites atun*, at Long Beach and Shag River Mouth, Otago, New Zealand. *Archaeofauna* 8:11–30.

2000   Steadman, D.W., T.H. Worthy, A.J. Anderson and R. Walter. New species and records of birds from prehistoric sites on Niue, Southwest Pacific. *Wilson Bulletin* 112:165–186.

2001a   Anderson, A.J. Mobility models of Lapita migration. In G.R. Clark, A.J. Anderson and T. Vunidilo (eds), *The Archaeology of Lapita Dispersal in Oceania: papers from the Fourth Lapita Conference, June 2000, Canberra, Australia*, pp. 15–23. Terra Australis 17.

2001b   Anderson, A.J. No meat on that beautiful shore: the prehistoric abandonment of subtropical Polynesian islands. In A.J. Anderson and B.F. Leach (eds), *Zooarchaeology of Oceanic Coasts and Islands: Papers from the 8th International Congress of the International Council of Archaeozoology, 23–29 August 1998, Victoria B.C., Canada*, pp. 14–23. Special Issue of the International Journal of Osteoarchaeology 11.

2001c   Anderson, A.J. The chronology of prehistoric colonization in French Polynesia. In C.M. Stevenson, G. Lee and F.J. Morin (eds), *Pacific 2000: Proceedings of the Fifth International conference on Easter Island and the Pacific*, pp. 247–252. Easter Island Foundation, Los Osos.

2001d   Anderson, A.J. Towards the sharp end: the form and performance of prehistoric Polynesian voyaging canoes. In C.M. Stevenson, G. Lee and F.J. Morin (eds), *Pacific 2000: Proceedings of the Fifth International conference on Easter Island and the Pacific*, pp. 29–36. Easter Island Foundation, Los Osos.

2001e   Anderson, A.J. The origins of muttonbirding in New Zealand. *New Zealand Journal of Archaeology* 22(2000):5–14.

2001   Anderson, A.J. and G.R. Clark. Advances in New Zealand mammalogy 1990–2000: Polynesian dog or kuri. *Journal of the Royal Society of New Zealand* 31:161–163.

2001   Anderson, A.J. and R.C. Green. Domestic and religious structures in the Emily Bay settlement site, Norfolk Island. In A.J. Anderson and J.P. White (eds), *The Prehistoric Archaeology of Norfolk Island, Southwest Pacific*, pp. 43–52. Supplement 27, Records of the Australian Museum.

2001   Anderson, A.J. and B.F. Leach (eds), *Zooarchaeology of Oceanic Coasts and Islands: Papers from the 8th International Congress of the International Council of Archaeozoology, 23–29 August 1998, Victoria B.C., Canada*. Special Issue of the International Journal of Osteoarchaeology 11.

2001   Anderson, A.J. and B.F. Leach. Introduction. In A.J. Anderson and B.F. Leach (eds), *Zooarchaeology of Oceanic Coasts and Islands: Papers from the 8th International Congress of the International Council of Archaeozoology, 23–29 August 1998, Victoria B.C., Canada*, pp. 2–3. Special Issue of the International Journal of Osteoarchaeology 11.

2001   Anderson, A.J. and J.P. White (eds), *The Prehistoric Archaeology of Norfolk Island, Southwest Pacific*. Supplement 27, Records of the Australian Museum.

2001a   Anderson. A.J. and J.P. White. Approaching the prehistory of Norfolk Island. In A.J. Anderson and J.P. White (eds), *The Prehistoric Archaeology of Norfolk Island, Southwest Pacific*, pp. 1–9. Supplement 27, Records of the Australian Museum.

2001b   Anderson, A.J. and J.P. White. Prehistoric settlement on Norfolk Island and its Oceanic context. In A.J. Anderson and P.J. White (eds), *The Prehistoric Archaeology of Norfolk Island, Southwest Pacific*, pp. 135–141. Supplement 27, Records of the Australian Museum.

2001   Anderson, A.J., I. Lilley and S. O'Connor (eds), *Histories of Old Ages: essays in honour of Rhys Jones*. Pandanus Books, Australian National University, Canberra.

2001a   Anderson, A.J., L. Ayliffe, D. Questiaux, T. Sorovi-Vunidilo, N. Spooner, and T. Worthy. The terminal age of the Fijian megafauna. In A.J. Anderson, I. Lilley and S. O'Connor (eds), *Histories of Old Ages: essays in honour of Rhys Jones*, pp. 251–264. Pandanus Books, Australian National University, Canberra.

2001b   Anderson, A.J., S. Bedford, G.R. Clark, I. Lilley, C. Sand, G. Summerhayes and R. Torrence. An inventory of Lapita sites containing dentate-stamped pottery. In G.R. Clark, A.J. Anderson and T. Vunidilo (eds), *The Archaeology of Lapita Dispersal in Oceania: papers from the Fourth Lapita Conference, June 2000, Canberra, Australia*, pp. 1–13. Terra Australis 17.

2001c   Anderson, A.J., T.F.G. Higham, and R. Wallace. The radiocarbon chronology of the Norfolk Island archaeological sites. In A.J. Anderson and J.P. White (eds), *The Prehistoric Archaeology of Norfolk Island, Southwest Pacific*, pp. 33–42. Supplement 27, Records of the Australian Museum.

2001d   Anderson, A.J., I.W.G. Smith and J.P White. Archaeological fieldwork on Norfolk Island. In A.J. Anderson and J.P. White (eds), *The Prehistoric Archaeology of Norfolk Island, Southwest Pacific*, pp. 11–32. Supplement 27, Records of the Australian Museum.

2001   Clark, G.R. and A.J. Anderson. The age of the Yanuca Lapita site, Viti Levu, Fiji. *New Zealand Journal of Archaeology* 22(2000):15–30.

2001   Clark, G.R., A.J. Anderson and T. Vunidilo (eds), *The Archaeology of Lapita Dispersal in Oceania: papers from the Fourth Lapita Conference, June 2000, Canberra, Australia*. Terra Australis 17.

2001   Clark, G.R., A.J. Anderson and S. Matararaba. The Lapita site at Votua, northern Lau Islands, Fiji. *Archaeology in Oceania* 36:134–143.

2001   Holdaway, R.N. and A.J. Anderson. Avifauna from the Emily Bay settlement site, Norfolk Island: a preliminary account. In A.J. Anderson and J.P. White (eds), *The Prehistoric Archaeology of Norfolk Island, Southwest Pacific*, pp. 85–100. Supplement 27, Records of the Australian Museum.

2001   MacPhail, M.K., G.S. Hope and A.J. Anderson. Polynesian plant introductions in the southwest Pacific: initial pollen evidence from Norfolk Island. In A.J. Anderson and J.P. White (eds), *The Prehistoric Archaeology of Norfolk Island, Southwest Pacific*, pp. 123–134. Supplement 27, Records of the Australian Museum, Sydney.

2001   Matisoo-Smith, E., K.A. Horsburgh, J.H. Robins and A.J. Anderson. Genetic variation in archaeological *Rattus exulans* remains from the Emily Bay settlement site, Norfolk Island. In A.J. Anderson and J.P. White (eds), *The Prehistoric Archaeology of Norfolk Island, Southwest Pacific*, pp. 81–84. Supplement 27, Records of the Australian Museum.

2001   Schmidt, L., A.J. Anderson and R. Fullagar. Shell and bone artefacts from the Emily Bay settlement site, Norfolk Island. In A.J. Anderson and J.P. White (eds), *The Prehistoric Archaeology of Norfolk Island, Southwest Pacific*, pp. 67–74. Supplement 27, Records of the Australian Museum.

2001   Turner, M., A.J. Anderson and R. Fullagar. Stone artefacts from the Emily Bay settlement site, Norfolk Island. In A.J. Anderson and P.J. White (eds), *The Prehistoric Archaeology of Norfolk Island, Southwest Pacific*, Supplement 27, Records of the Australian Museum.

2001   Walter, R. and A.J. Anderson. Fishbone from the Emily Bay settlement site, Norfolk Island. In A.J. Anderson and J.P. White (eds), *The Prehistoric Archaeology of Norfolk Island, Southwest Pacific*, pp. 101–108. Supplement 27, Records of the Australian Museum.

2002a   Anderson, A.J. A fragile plenty: pre-European Maori and the New Zealand environment. In E. Pawson and T. Brooking (eds), *Environmental Histories of New Zealand*, pp. 19–34. Oxford University Press, Melbourne.

2002b   Anderson, A.J. Faunal collapse, landscape change and settlement history in Remote Oceania. *World Archaeology* 33:375–390.

2002c   Anderson, A.J. Rat bone, recollection and record. *Archaeology in New Zealand* 45:216–219.

2002   Anderson, A.J. and Y.H. Sinoto. New radiocarbon ages of colonization sites in East Polynesia. *Asian Perspectives* 41:242–257.

2002   Anderson, A.J. and R.K. Walter. Landscape and culture change on Niue Island, West Polynesia. In T. Ladefoged, T. and M. Graves (eds), *Pacific Landscapes: archaeological approaches*, pp. 153–172. Easter Island Foundation, Los Osos.

2002a   Anderson, A.J., S. Haberle, G. Rojas, A. Seelenfreund, I.W.G. Smith and T. Worthy. An archaeological exploration of Robinson Crusoe Island, Juan Fernandez Archipelago, Chile. In S. Bedford, C. Sand and D. Burley (eds), *Fifty Years in the Field: essays in honour and celebration of Richard Shutler Jr's archaeological career*, pp. 239–249. New Zealand Archaeological Association Monograph 25.

2002b   Anderson, A.J., H. Martinsson-Wallin and P. Wallin. *The Prehistory of Kiritimati (Christmas) Island, Republic of Kiribati: Excavations and Analyses*. Occasional Papers of The Kon-Tiki Museum 6.

2002   Sheppard, P.J., A.J. Anderson and R.K. Walter. Geochemical analysis and sourcing of archaeological stone from Niue. In R. Walter and A.J. Anderson The Archaeology of Niue Island, West Polynesia. *Bishop Museum Bulletin in Anthropology* 10.

2002   Walter, R. and A.J. Anderson. The Archaeology of Niue Island, West Polynesia. *Bishop Museum Bulletin in Anthropology* 10.

2002   Worthy, T., A.J. Anderson and R.K. Walter. Fossil fauna from Niue island. In R. Walter and A.J. Anderson The Archaeology of Niue Island, West Polynesia. *Bishop Museum Bulletin in Anthropology* 10.

2003a   Anderson, A.J. Investigating early settlement on Lord Howe Island. *Australian Archaeology* 57:98–102.

2003b   Anderson, A.J. Uncharted waters: colonization of remote Oceania. In M. Rockman and J. Steele (eds), *Colonization of Unfamiliar Landscape*, pp. 169–189. Routledge, London.

2003a   Anderson, A.J., E. Conte, P.V. Kirch and M. Weisler. Cultural chronology in Mangareva (Gambier Islands), French Polynesia: evidence from recent radiocarbon dating. *Journal of the Polynesian Society* 112:119–140.

2003b   Anderson, A.J., E. Conte, P.V. Kirch and M. Weisler. Recherches archéologiques aux îles Gambier (2001). In H. Marchesi (ed), *Bilan de la recherche archéologique en Polynésie Française. Dossier d'Archéologie Polynésienne 2*, pp. 137–146. Service de la Culture et du Patrimoine, Punaauia.

2003   Bellwood, P., J. Stevenson, A. Anderson and E. Dizon. Archaeological and palaeoenvironmental research in Batanes and Ilocos Norte provinces, northern Philippines. *Bulletin of the Indo-Pacific Prehistory Association* 23:141–162.

2003   Conte, E. and A.J. Anderson. Radiocarbon ages for two sites on Ua Huka, Marquesas. *Asian Perspectives* 42:155–160.

2003   Kennett, D.J., A.J. Anderson, M. Prebble and E. Conte. La colonization et les fortifications de Rapa. In H. Marchesi (ed), *Bilan de la recherche archéologique en Polynésie Française. Dossier d'Archéologie Polynésienne 2*, pp. 165–170. Service de la Culture et du Patrimoine, Punaauia.

2003   Szabo, K., H. Ramirez, A. Anderson and P. Bellwood. Prehistoric subsistence strategies on the Batanes Islands, Northern Philippines. *Bulletin of the Indo-Pacific Prehistory Association* 23:163–172.

2004a   Anderson, A.J. Fear and loathing on desert islands. In M. Campbell (ed), Digging into History: 50 years of the New Zealand Archaeological Association, pp. 55–57. *Archaeology in New Zealand* Special Issue.

2004b   Anderson, A.J. Initial human dispersal in Remote Oceania: pattern and explanation. In C. Sand (ed), *Pacific Archaeology: assessments and prospects. Proceedings of the International Conference for the 50th anniversary of the first Lapita excavation, Koné-Nouméa 2002*, pp. 71–84. Le cahiers d'Archéologie en Nouvelle-Calédonie 15.

2004c   Anderson, A.J. Islands of ambivalence. In S. Fitzpatrick (ed), *Voyages of Discovery: The archaeology of islands*, pp. 251–274. Praeger, London.

2004d   Anderson, A.J. It's about time: the Indo-pacific colonization project. In T. Murray (ed), *Archaeology from Australia*, pp. 3–17. La Trobe University, Melbourne.

2004e   Anderson, A.J. Maori. *Enciclopedia Archeologica*, pp. 941–942. Instituto della Enciclopedia Italiana, Roma.

2004f   Anderson, A.J. Shag River Mouth. *Enciclopedia Archeologica*, p.977. Instituto della Enciclopedia Italiana, Roma.

2004g   Anderson, A.J. Wairau Bar. *Enciclopedia Archeologica*, pp. 989–990. Instituto della Enciclopedia Italiana, Roma.

2004h   Anderson, A.J. The age disconformity in AMS radiocarbon results on *Rattus exulans* bone. *New Zealand Journal of Archaeology* 24(2002):149–156.

2004   Anderson, A.J. and T. Higham. The age of rat introduction in New Zealand: further evidence from Earthquakes #1, North Otago. *New Zealand Journal of Archaeology* 24(2002):135–147.

2004   Anderson, A.J., E. Conte, P.V. Kirch and M. Weisler. Archaeological investigations in the Gambier Islands, French Polynesia. In C. Sand (ed), *Pacific Archaeology: assessments and prospects. Proceedings of the International Conference for the 50th anniversary of the first Lapita excavation, Koné-Nouméa 2002*, pp. 343–352. Le cahiers d'Archéologie en Nouvelle-Calédonie 15.

2004   Burley, D., D. Steadman and A.J. Anderson. The volcanic outlier of 'Ata in Tongan prehistory: reconsideration of its role and settlement chronology. *New Zealand Journal of Archaeology* 25 (2003):89–106.

2004   Conte, E., P.V. Kirch, M.I. Weisler and A.J. Anderson. Archaeological field investigations. In E. Conte and P.V. Kirch (eds), *Archaeological investigations in the Mangareva Islands (Gambier Archipelago), French Polynesia*, pp. 33–93. Archaeological Research Facility Contribution 62, University of California at Berkeley.

2004   Higham, T.F.G., R.E.M. Hedges, A.J. Anderson, C. Bronk Ramsey and B. Fankhauser. New AMS radiocarbon determinations of *Rattus exulans* bone from Shag River Mouth, New Zealand. *Radiocarbon* 46:207–218.

2004   Kennett, D.J., A.J. Anderson, M.J. Cruz, G.R. Clark and G. Summerhayes. Geochemical characterization of Lapita pottery via inductively-coupled plasma-mass spectrometry. *Archaeometry* 46:35–46.

2004   Kirch, P.V., J. Coil, M.I. Weisler, E. Conte, and A.J. Anderson. Radiocarbon dating and site chronology. In E. Conte and P.V. Kirch (eds), *Archaeological investigations in the Mangareva Islands (Gambier Archipelago), French Polynesia*, pp. 94–105. Archaeological Research Facility Contribution 62, University of California at Berkeley.

2004   Phear, S., G. Clark and A.J. Anderson. A radiocarbon chronology for Palau. In C. Sand (ed), *Pacific Archaeology: assessments and prospects. Proceedings of the International Conference for the 50th anniversary of the first Lapita excavation, Koné-Nouméa 2002*, pp. 255–263. Le cahiers d'Archéologie en Nouvelle-Calédonie 15.

2005a   Anderson, A.J. Crossing the Strait: archaeological chronology in the Batanes Islands, Philippines and the regional sequence of Neolithic dispersal. *Journal of Austronesian Studies* 1:27–48.

2005b   Anderson, A.J. Keynote address: Distance looks our way. Remoteness and isolation in early East and South Polynesia. In C.M. Stevenson, J.M. Ramirez, E.J. Morin and N. Barbacci (eds), *The Renaca papers: VI International Conference on Rapa Nui and the Pacific*, pp. 1–12. Easter Island Foundation, Los Osos.

2005c   Anderson, A.J. Settlement of the Pacific. *Berkshire Encyclopaedia of World History*.

2005d   Anderson, A.J. Subpolar settlement in South Polynesia. *Antiquity* 79:791–800.

2005a   Anderson, A.J., J. Chappell, G. Clark and S. Phear. Comparative radiocarbon dating of lignite, pottery and charcoal samples from Babeldaob Island, Republic of Palau. *Radiocarbon* 47:1–9.

2005b   Anderson, A.J., T. Higham and N. Ritchie. The chronology and interpretation of Italian Creek rockshelter, Central Otago. *Archaeology in New Zealand* 48:242–247.

2005c   Higham, T.F.G., A.G. Anderson, C. Bronk Ramsey and C. Tompkins. Diet-derived variations in radiocarbon and stable isotopes: a case study from Shag River Mouth, New Zealand. *Radiocarbon* 47:367–375.

2006a   Anderson, A.J. Alternative interpretations of structural evidence at Rakaia Mouth, New Zealand. *Archaeology in Oceania* 41:123–126.

2006b   Anderson, A.J. Islands of Exile: ideological motivation in maritime migration. *Journal of Island and Coastal Archaeology* 1:33–47.

2006c   Anderson, A.J. Polynesian seafaring and American horizons: a response to Jones and Klar. *American Antiquity* 71: 759–764.

2006d   Anderson, A.J. Retrievable time: prehistoric colonization of South Polynesia from the outside in and the inside out. In T. Ballantyne and B. Moloughney (eds), *Disputed Histories: imagining New Zealand's pasts*, pp. 25–41. University of Otago Press, Dunedin.

2006   Anderson, A.J. and T.F.G. Higham. Response to Beavan Athfield's comment on "Diet-derived variations in radiocarbon and stable isotopes: a case study from Shag River Mouth, New Zealand". *Radiocarbon* 48:1–2.

2006a   Anderson, A.J., J. Chappell, M. Gagan, and R. Grove. Prehistoric maritime migration in the Pacific Islands: an hypothesis of ENSO forcing. *The Holocene* 16:1–6.

2006b   Anderson, A.J., R. Roberts, W. Dickinson, G. Clark, D. Burley, A. De Biran, G. Hope and P. Nunn. Times of sand: sedimentary history and archaeology at the Sigatoka dunes, Fiji. *Geoarchaeology* 21:131–154.

2006   Clark, G., A.J. Anderson and D. Wright. Human colonization of the Palau Islands, Western Micronesia. *Journal of Island and Coastal Archaeology* 1:215–232.

2006a   Kennett, D., A.J. Anderson and B. Winterhalder. The ideal free distribution, agricultural origins and the colonization of the Pacific. In D. Kennett and B. Winterhalder (eds), *Behavioural Ecology and the Transition to Agriculture*, pp. 265–288. University of California Press, Berkeley.

2006b   Kennett, D., A.J. Anderson, M. Prebble, E. Conte and J. Southon. Prehistoric human impacts on Rapa, French Polynesia. *Antiquity* 80:1–15.

2007a   Anderson, A.J. Chapter 7: Island archaeology: with a case study of colonization and anthropogenic change in the Pacific Islands. In G. Baldaccino (ed), *A World of Islands: an island studies reader*, pp. 237–266. Agenda Academic, Luqa, Malta and Institute of Island Studies, Charlottetown, PEI, Canada.

2007b   Anderson, A.J. Colonial illusion and reality at the Old World's end. In B. Hardh (ed), *On the Road: Studies in honour of Lars Larsson*. Almqvist and Wiksell International.

2007c   Anderson, A.J. Discussion: Middens of the sea people. In N. Milner, O.E. Craig and G.N. Bailey (eds), *Shell Middens in Atlantic Europe*. Oxbow Press.

2007   Anderson, A.J., K. Green and F. Leach (eds), *Vastly Ingenious: The archaeology of Pacific material culture in honour of Janet M. Davidson*. Otago University Press, Dunedin.

2007   Anderson, A.J., H. Martinsson-Wallin and K. Stothert. Ecuadorian sailing rafts and Oceanic landfalls. In A.J. Anderson, K. Green and F. Leach (eds), *Vastly Ingenious, The archaeology of Pacific material culture in honour of Janet M. Davidson*. Otago University Press, pp. 117–133.

2007   Anderson, A.J. Short and sometimes sharp: human impacts on marine resources in the archaeology history of South Polynesia. In T.C. Rick and J.M. Erlandson (eds), *Human Impacts on Ancient Marine Environments: a global perspective*. University of California Press.

2007   Anderson, A.J. Maori Land and Livelihood, AD 1250–1850. In R. Scott (ed), *The Natural History of Canterbury*. Canterbury University Press.

2007   Anderson, A.J. Origins, settlement and society of South Polynesia. In G. Burns (ed), *The New Oxford History of New Zealand*. In press.

2007   Anderson. A.J., M. Gagan and J. Shulmeister. Mid-Holocene cultural dynamics and climatic change in the western Pacific. In D. Anderson, K. Maasch and D. Sandweiss (eds), *Climatic Change and Cultural Dynamics: a global perspective on Holocene transitions*. Academic Press.

2007   O'Connor, S. and A.J. Anderson (eds), Maritime migration and colonization in Indo-Pacific prehistory. *Asian Perspectives* 47(1).

2008   Tau, Te.M. and A.J. Anderson (eds), *Ngai Tahu: A Migration History: The Carrington Text*. Bridget Williams Books, Wellington.

n.d.   Anderson, A.J. and D. Kennett (eds), *The Prehistory of Rapa Island, French Polynesia*. New Zealand Archaeological Association Monograph. In prep.

n.d.   Clark, G. and A.J. Anderson (eds), *The Early Prehistory of Fiji*. Terra Australis, Australian National University. In prep.

2

Getting from Sunda to Sahul

Jim Allen

Department of Archaeology, La Trobe University, Australia

jjallen8@bigpond.net.au

James F. O'Connell

Department of Anthropology, University of Utah, USA

Introduction

The level of intentionality in the behaviour of early modern humans is a continuing debate that we have had with Atholl over the years. For our part, we argue that the cognitive abilities of early modern humans, reflected in the patterns of the late Pleistocene archaeological records, are qualitatively different from their predecessors and not vastly different from our own. This being the case, we feel able to assume purpose in past human behaviour that Atholl does not. Presented with evidence that is often meagre, indirect or ambiguous, Atholl counters with explanations that require little or no intent on the part of these humans. Nowhere has our debate crystallised as clearly as in the case of early watercraft and their use in colonising Sahul, a milestone modern-human achievement for which no direct evidence is or is likely to become available. We all accept without question that it happened, that watercraft were involved and that this water crossing was only achieved by modern humans. Despite some continuing debate, it is increasingly likely that first colonisation occurred about 45,000 years ago. Beyond this, we do not know where people stepped off the Asian continent, what routes to Sahul may have been taken, what length of time elapsed between humans leaving Sunda and arriving in Sahul (Figure 1), what viable population sizes might have been needed to form successful colonisations, where first Sahul landfall was, whether the first successful entry was preceded by unsuccessful ones, whether there were multiple successful entries at different locations, and so on. But one can engage in constructive, theoretically driven, potentially testable speculation on all of these points.

This paper was first presented at an ANU seminar in 2005 to draw attention to these questions, largely untouched since Birdsell's (1977) seminal paper. It provoked useful discussion between Atholl and us and was a focus for subsequent work (Bulbeck 2007; O'Connell *et al.* 2007; O'Connor 2007), and we offer it here to acknowledge our intellectual debt to Atholl Anderson.

Since direct evidence to answer questions concerning the initial colonisation of Sahul is

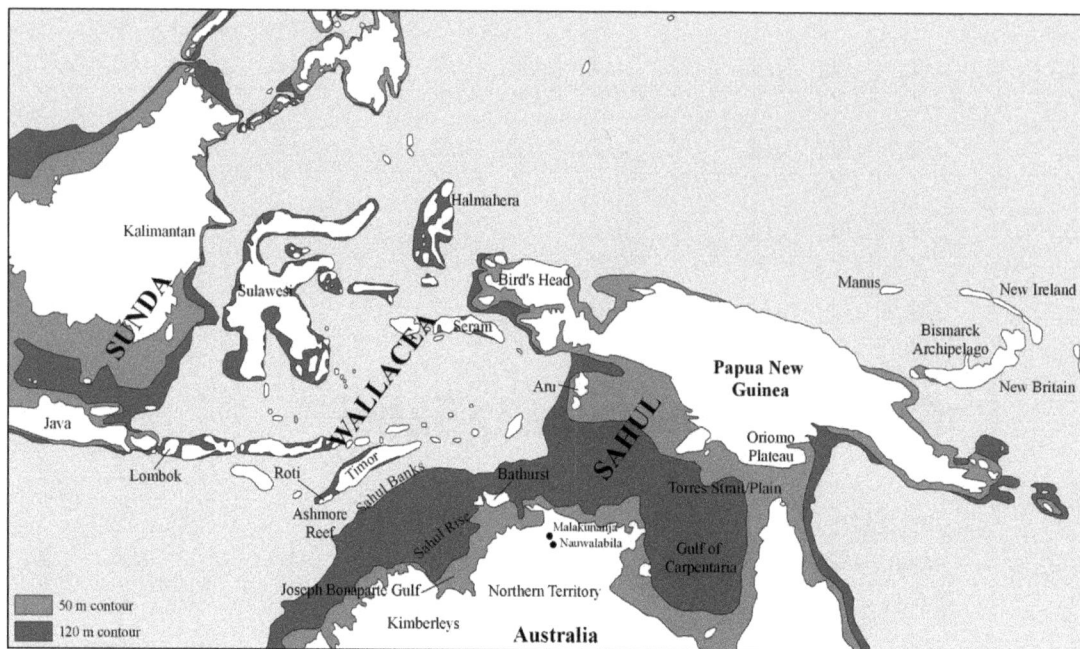

Figure 1. Map of Wallacea showing places referred to in the text.

unlikely to be forthcoming in the archaeological record, alternative approaches are limited. For us, inductive approaches are currently unsatisfactory, relying as they do on arguable interpretations of sketchy data that are frequently date-driven. For example, O'Connor (2007) predicates her entire argument on a human arrival date in Sahul of 60,000 BP. This date, mooted 18 years ago (Roberts *et al.* 1990), has received no compelling support in the intervening years and today only a tiny minority defend it. The incorrect argument of Chappell *et al.* (1996) and Fifield *et al.* (2001) that our appeals to a younger chronology were the result of blind adherence to radiocarbon has been continuously weakened by the increasing use of luminescence and improved radiocarbon pre-treatment (ABOX-SC). To date, neither technique has produced an archaeologically associated date approaching 50,000 BP, outside the two original Northern Territory claims of Nauwalabila and Malakunanja. Regardless of what calibration is applied to available radiocarbon dates, a current 'best-estimate' date for human arrival is c. 45,000 years ago, or a little earlier (Allen and O'Connell 2003; O'Connell and Allen 2004; O'Connell *et al.* 2007).

A better alternative is to develop models for this colonisation that will throw up testable hypotheses to approach these questions. This paper offers one such model that assumes that the first successful human colonisation of Sahul was the consequence of many small but deliberate decisions that involved conscious and continuing risk assessment of behaviours intended to maximise reproductive fitness. People crossed from Sunda to Sahul as a consequence of these behaviours, rather than with conscious intent, like the chicken, to get to the other side. Even so, the colonisation of Sahul was not accidental.

Background

The first public recognition that human entry into Australia and New Guinea at any time in the past required the crossing of a significant water barrier might be attributed to Grafton Elliot Smith at the meeting of the British Association for the Advancement of Science in Sydney in 1914 (Elkin 1978:99). Although a glacio-eustatic explanation of relative sea-level changes had first appeared in 1842, and occasionally later in the 19th century, it was not until 1910 that a paper by R.A. Daly revived the theory and finally dismissed previously accepted models of sunken land bridges and lost continents (Daly 1910; Baulig 1935).

Today, we take for granted that this water barrier, with all routes having at least one crossing of about 90 km whatever the sea level, has always confronted humans moving into Sahul. It is this barrier that kept *Homo erectus* west of Timor and Sulawesi for more than a million years, and it is the ability to overcome this barrier that has been and continues to be a principal hallmark of the behavioural modernity of the initial human colonists into Sahul.

So commonplace is this understanding that with a few exceptions, most notably Joseph Birdsell in 1977, no close attention has been paid to how or where the initial crossing may have been achieved. A route from Timor to northwest Australia has sometimes been favoured (e.g. Butlin 1993), although on arguable evidence. Indeed, recently both Australianists (e.g. Chappell 2000; O'Connor and Chappell 2003) and European scholars (e.g. Foley and Lahr 1997) have posited distinctly separate colonisations of Australia and New Guinea even though these countries comprised a single landmass at the time of colonisation, regardless of which chronology is favoured for that event. Instead, models of Australian colonisation have mostly discussed how people spread through the continent after they landed (e.g. Bowdler 1977; Horton 1981; Rindos and Webb 1992).

However, the question of *how* landfall was made is fundamental in considering how Australia and New Guinea might subsequently have been settled, because understanding the processes of successfully establishing a foothold in Sahul directly informs the strategies that eventually took people to Tasmania and into the nearer western Pacific islands.

Past studies have called up a diverse range of questions, from the motivation(s) of first colonists and the nature of watercraft involved, to the relative inputs of biology, culture and adaptability, speed of settlement and technological inventiveness. We take as a useful starting point Joseph Birdsell's 1977 paper 'The recalibration of a paradigm for the first peopling of Greater Australia'.

The Birdsell model

Birdsell's larger model was primarily biological in nature and paid scant attention to culture as a contributing factor. In large part, it was concerned with population events after arrival in Australia, whether people remained coastally oriented or moved inland, the time needed to infill the continent, and so on.

However, Birdsell's enduring contribution to modelling Sahul colonisation concerned his detailed treatment of probable routes for watercraft between the Sunda and Sahul continental shelves. Like many before and since, Birdsell favoured minimalist assumptions and sought to define those routes that provided the fewest, safest and shortest sea crossings. He isolated three pertinent variables concerning each target island, the next island to be reached from home base. These were distance to the target island, target height (and thus visibility from the home island) and target width, the notion being that wider targets could be more readily reached with limited navigation and other sailing capabilities. These three variables taken together were seen to indicate preferred options, apart from distance alone. A high and wide target, for example, could offset a longer distance.

Birdsell defined three variants for a northern route through Sulawesi and two variants for a southern route through Timor. The two northernmost routes arrived in present-day New Guinea in the vicinity of the Bird's Head; two middle routes arrived, depending on sea level, at Aru and further south on the Torres Plain; while the southernmost route via Timor reached Sahul west of the present-day Kimberley region. These routes variously took from eight to 18 stages and each involved from one to four stages of more than 30 km. From north to south, the longest crossings of the five routes, based on a sea level of -150 m, were, respectively, 93 km, 69 km, 103 km, 98 km and 87 km.

Birdsell explored a mid-range scenario by raising the sea level to -50 m. At this level, all routes increased some inter-island distances, but such a sea-level change had little real effect on the three northern routes, apart from the problem of reaching Sulawesi in the first place, where, by Birdsell's reckoning, the gap doubles to 87 km. Mulvaney and Kamminga (1999:108) indicated that Birdsell favoured the southern route through Timor, but this was the case only when the sea was at its lowest point. Birdsell (1977:130) noted that during periods of higher sea level, the Timor route would have been 'excessively formidable' and 'of no great importance'. Birdsell believed there was 'a constant if somewhat straggling trickle of small groups of human beings over all or most of the routes' and given the limitations of potential watercraft, group sizes were likely to have consisted of small families. He also accepted that these were staged journeys, arguing that when each new target island was reached, there would be a long period of adaptation to local wind, water and tides, and that the crossing from Sunda to Sahul may have taken centuries (1977:147).

Some authors have rejected this view. For example, Thiel (1987:238–239) reckoned that by drifting on the longest possible route from Sunda to Sahul, people could have made the crossing in 14 days. In our view, such speculations are obfuscating, since such a journey does not conform to the normal known behaviour of hunter-gatherers, ignores the geographic and ecological potentials of Wallacea, and makes unwarranted assumptions about weather, fresh-water requirements and long-term biological viability, just to name a few. At any given time, a bird in the hand on Sulawesi may well have been worth two potential birds in the Kimberleys.

On routes

Many commentators after Birdsell have preferred the shortest routes and assumed minimalist conditions such as the most basic watercraft and smallest biologically viable colonist group size. As well, most have assumed a continuous west-to-east movement, with few westward returns, except where water gaps were short. Birdsell's colonising routes covered most available options, and these routes have been reproduced mostly uncritically by subsequent commentators.

One exception is Butlin (1993:16–25), who determined that the Timor to Kimberley route offered the best chance of success and was probably the route most regularly used. Butlin also based his judgement on minimalist assumptions, pointing out that Timor was more easily reached during the Pleistocene than was Borneo/Sulawesi (his assumed point of departure to reach New Guinea) and that the Kimberley route required less navigational skill because Australia had huge target width compared with the target islands of Wallacea.

Butlin used newer data, unavailable to Birdsell, and noted that if the sea level fell to 60 m below present levels (and in many cases a lesser amount of -30 m to -40 m), a long chain of shoal islands, running roughly parallel to Timor and Roti, would appear on the eastern side of the Timor Trough. These are now known as the Sahul Banks (Figure 1). If viable, these islands would reduce the single crossing to the Australian shore considerably. Butlin estimated some of these islands might be as close as 90 km from Timor/Roti and he believed they would be visible from Timor. East of these islands, the Sahul Rise is a low formation of limestone outcrops cut by tidal channels that were exposed by sea levels between -60 m and -80 m (Figure 1). Butlin saw these as stepping stones that would have led in the north on to Bathurst Island and in the south on to the southern side of Joseph Bonaparte Gulf.

To bolster his case, Butlin (1993:33–41) offered an additional series of 'pull' and 'push' factors. For Timor–Australia, pull factors included smoke, bushfire glow and migratory birds, and more generally for Island Southeast Asia, inter-island visibility. Push factors were more strictly Malthusian, centred on population increase and consequent reductions in resource availability.

A modelling approach

In contrast to this inductivism, we believe there are alternative ways to look at the question of how Sahul was settled, by developing theoretical models that may refocus arguments about sea levels, marine technological capabilities, motivations to move, and the like. Ideally, these should be testable in the data (available or potentially gatherable), or minimally make sensible appeal to uniformitarian principles of human behaviour, well beyond notions like exploration being a fundamental component of the human spirit. We also take the view here that there is no imperative to assume minimalist conditions a priori. Regardless of whether the behaviourally modern-human move eastwards began in Africa or Southwest Asia or even Southeast Asia, it is reasonable to assume that the adaptive ability that carried modern humans through and beyond the previous range of *Homo erectus* was capable of sufficient invention to reach Sahul as a part of a process involving conscious assessment of the risks and the minimisation of those risks, rather than as an accident.

The question of sea levels

Contrary to the minimalist views of many commentators who have favoured lower sea-level periods for the initial colonisation of Sahul on the grounds of shorter distances, Thiel (1987) proposed that this colonisation was the result of rising seas reducing land area and drowning islands, with the resulting pressures leading to human migration. The central tenet of this argument had been shown already to be probably wrong, when Dunn and Dunn (1977) demonstrated that rising sea levels significantly increased the length of coastline in Sundaland, thus catering for higher populations in this important ecotone (see also Bellwood 1990). However, Thiel may have been right for the wrong reasons. Chappell (1993:45–47; 2000:89–90) has argued that the earliest voyages to Sahul probably occurred during phases of sea-level rise or during relative maximum levels because rising seas favour the development of coral reefs and lagoons; rivers and streams develop estuaries and mangroves and trap sediments that can move landwards, contributing to backwater swamp and inland waterway expansion and the formation of deltaic plains. Such sedimentary 'aquatic coastal environments' favour the regular use of watercraft, as opposed to the rocky coastal environments associated with falling and low sea levels, especially on precipitous coasts. Under these conditions, corals form only a narrow fringing reef and lagoons become dry land. Rivers are entrenched in narrow valleys and discharge their sediment directly into the ocean; coastlines are likely to be steep and simple with few offshore islands. Areas of sedimentary coast 'would have been small and uncommon on the islands from Lombok to Timor, the Moluccas, much of northern New Guinea and the Bismarks' during falling-sea periods (Chappell 2000:90).

If, as Chappell suggests, watercraft usage fluctuated with sea-level rises, it would seem likely Sahul was reached first during a high sea-level/high-usage phase. Chappell (1993:45) notes that for levels between -20 m and -75 m, inter-island distances do not vary very much, with three exceptions, Kalimantan to Sulawesi, Tanimbar to the Aru shelf, and especially Timor to the Kimberley. At -75 m, Butlin's stepping-stone islands are 'small and sparse', and they disappear at -30 m. The Timor route is the most problematic in terms of distances at all lowerings less than

-75 m. Distances between target islands during the time of probable landfall (even allowing this to be as wide a margin as 60 kya years to 40 kya) were most favourable along the northern route from Sulawesi to New Guinea.

The Lambeck and Chappell (2001) sea-level curve constructed from Huon Peninsula (Papua New Guinea) data indicates there were four occasions during the 60–40 kya period when the sea levels rose and peaked, before falling again (Figure 2). These oscillations ranged between c. -80 m and -42 m, with the four maxima varying between -53 m and -42 m. While we favour the last of these high stands, at c. 44 kya, as a probable arrival time, for reasons argued elsewhere (Allen and O'Connell 2003; O'Connell and Allen 2004), the model put forward here holds for any of these options, given that the high-stand maxima vary by only c. 11 m.

Working from maps published by Voris (2000), there are few differences in land exposed by the -40 m and -50 m contours. In both cases, the Gulf of Carpentaria is open to the sea and the Aru Islands are part of the mainland. But at -75 m, the Torres Plain is greatly extended and the gulf has become Lake Carpentaria. At intermediate times, fluctuating salinities suggest this was a complex estuarine embayment (Torgersen *et al.* 1985).

This leads to three other questions concerning lowered sea levels. Somewhat contrary to his own argument, Butlin (1993:24) notes that the islands of the Sahul Banks rose out of a part of the ocean frequently more than 150 m in depth. With sea levels at c. -40 m these islands were probably small atolls, but at lower sea levels they would have presented sheer coral cliffs with heights proportional to sea level fall below -40 m, thus suggesting their usefulness as stepping stones during periods of very low sea level would be minimal. In the Pacific, similar islands are known as makatea islands, formed there by tectonic uplift at plate margins. Many lack surface water, with rainwater disappearing into the karst. Whether the Sahul Banks comprised makatea islands or coral atolls is unclear but of little consequence; both are precarious for settlement (Kirch 2002:49–50).

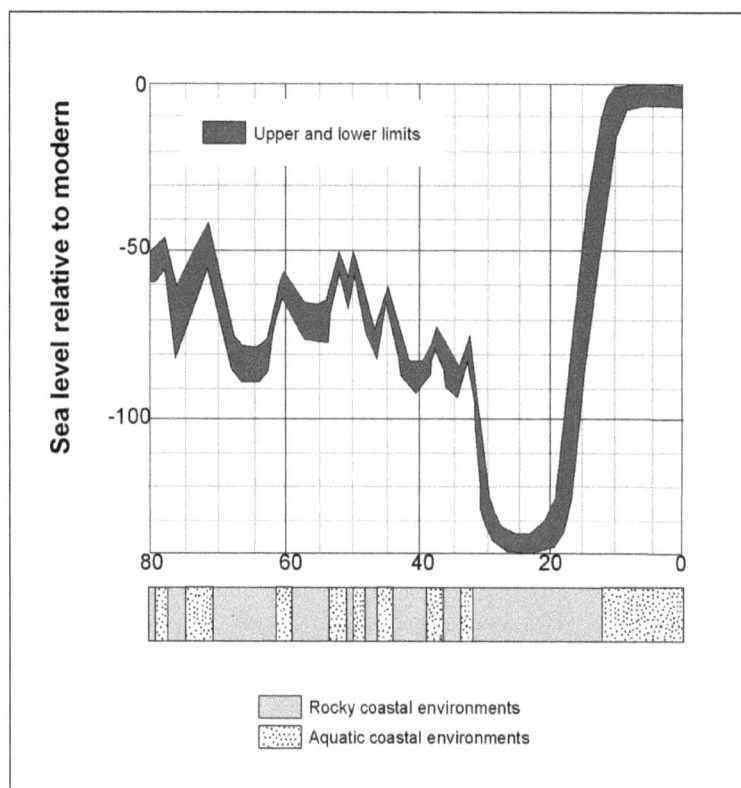

Figure 2. Pleistocene sea-level fluctuations following Lambeck and Chappell (2001). Data for periods of rocky versus estuarine coasts from Chappell (2000).

The second question follows directly. What might have been the propensity of such islands to provide food and especially fresh water in any quantity? Birds, birds' eggs and marine foods would support seafarers in transit, but might not assist any longer-term settlement. Fresh water may have been more difficult to obtain, even in the short term. The Ashmore Reef, about 100 km south of Roti, consists of three small vegetated islands on a large area of reef. Currently, fresh water is available from wells that tap into fresh-water lenses (the Ghyben-Herzberg aquifer) beneath the surface of the islands. The sizes and salinity distributions of such acquifers are dependent on many factors, including rainfall, the amount and nature of surface vegetation, the nature and distribution of soils and the size of an island, particularly the width from sea to lagoon. It is thus uncertain that such low islands anywhere in Wallacea would have greatly assisted movements towards Sahul, apart from providing fishing and birding grounds.

The third question concerns the viability of different coasts for hunter-gatherer settlers beyond the general parameters outlined by Chappell, who himself noted exceptions to them (Chappell 1993:46). Remnant 'aquatic' coastal environments may have supported some human movement at periods of lower sea level. Demonstrating this possibility seems to require better data than are currently available. In particular, it is reasonable to ask whether the greatly expanded Sahul plain west of the Kimberley Plateau would have had a sufficient number of streams and rivers to facilitate successful settlement by chance arrivals, especially in periods when lower sea levels were accompanied by lower precipitation.

Watercraft and seafaring

Almost all commentators have assumed a minimalist position when speculating about what marine technology was employed in the successful colonisation of Sahul. While such a position makes the fewest assumptions, it should not deny the possibility that greater technological inventiveness was involved, given that such inventiveness is one hallmark of modern humans (O'Connell and Allen 2007) and that the speed with which distant parts of Australia were colonised strongly suggests initial colonisation was inventive and systematic. Added to this, we now recognise that watercraft had to be of sufficient size or number to get founding populations into Sahul (see also Irwin 1992:27). The sizes and compositions of such populations are considered in more detail below.

Anderson (2002:13–19) has most recently summarised the minimalist case. Along with many commentators, he favours bamboo rafts for their buoyancy, speed and ease of construction, and light displacement which would allow such a craft to be propelled by wind, even without sails. If bamboo rafts were used, however, there are interesting implications, for Birdsell (1977:144, following Munro 1868) argued that while suitable bamboos are nearly continuous along the northern route, they do not occur along the southern route beyond Java, and that if the southern route was used, different materials would have been demanded. Although the Pleistocene distribution of bamboo is unknown, if drier and cooler conditions pertained we might expect its Pleistocene distribution to have been even narrower than today. Understanding distributions of bamboo 45,000 years ago is also complicated by the likelihood that its usefulness to humans caused them to move this plant to locations beyond its natural distribution at that time.

Anderson also considers initial settlement required no more than occasional drift voyaging and he suggests systematic voyaging in Pleistocene Near Oceania remains improbable. Whether he includes coastal voyaging in this dismissal is unclear. But while people reached Manus by at least 20,000 years ago, involving a crossing of at least 180 km including some 60 km out of the sight of land, Anderson argues this could have been achieved by a drifting or paddled raft.

Anderson (2000:16–17) is critical of both the term and the concept of Irwin's proposed 'voyaging nursery', extending from Island Southeast Asia to the Bismarcks. Regardless, we continue to find utility in Irwin's data and arguments, particularly as they pertain to Wallacea. Whether or not earlier watercraft were in use still further west is unimportant here; it is no leap of faith to suppose that once the larger landforms of the Sunda shelf had been left behind, the technological sophistication and use of watercraft, even bamboo rafts, increased among the large and small islands of Wallacea.

Irwin (1992:18–30) initially followed Birdsell in examining questions of distance, angle of target and intervisibility, adding data and comment on climate and weather, watercraft and navigation, passages in the voyaging corridor, and voyaging intent and frequency. He observed that even with sea levels at -40 m to -70 m, distances between high islands – those islands visible at a distance – were much the same when sea levels were lowest, so that the distances and angles he calculated were similar to Birdsell's.

By translating island heights into the specific distances that land might be ahead, Irwin demonstrated that Birdsell's northern route through Halmahera provides unbroken intervisibility; his two other northern routes are on the borders of intervisibility; but the two southern routes, through Tanimbar and to the Kimberley coast, are both blind. Again, this intervisibility remains essentially constant, whatever the sea level. Moving westwards from New Guinea in the reverse direction (an important consideration, see below), the Halmahera route is just beyond the limits of intervisibility, but the route through Seram has continuous intervisibility, which it did not have moving eastwards (Irwin 1992:21–22).

Given the equatorial position of Wallacea, Irwin (1992:24–25) argues that there would have been no wholesale latitudinal displacement of weather patterns during the period of interest. As is the case today, the southern winters would have been dominated by the southeasterly trade winds and the summers by the northwest monsoon winds. Currents followed the wind patterns, such that seasonal reversals of winds and currents would have been predictable. In particular, their equatorial position would have placed both the voyaging corridor and the settled islands between northern and southern tropical-cyclone belts. While elsewhere sailors may avoid adverse cyclonic weather, frequently their settlements do not. This seems likely to have been a further advantage of the corridor for first settlers.

Thus, seasonal two-way sea journeys would have been facilitated by winds and currents. The most likely exception is again the Timor–Kimberley coast route. A computer simulation by Wild (1985:69, cited in Irwin 1992:28) found that most watercraft drifting from Timor during the monsoon season reached the Australian coast, but the reverse voyage was difficult, even during the southeasterly trades, when most craft were blown back on to the Australian coast or south into the Indian Ocean.

Ideal free distribution (IFD) and optimal foraging theory

Questioning whether the human settlement of Sahul was deliberate or accidental may be missing the point altogether. If a group leaves familiar territory, food-procurement success will decline and the probability of failure due to unpredictable events will increase (Wobst 1974:152–153). Long-distance moves will lower the population density and increase instability in social networks. Thus, large-scale or long-distance migrations are improbable; in Wobst's view 'colonisation would take place gradually and randomly by small breakaway groups along the fringes of the settled area'. In modelling the colonisation of the New World by 25 people, Wobst calculated a maximum migration speed would be only 5 km/year, a speed that could not be conceptualised as a conscious process of migration.

We agree with this general position. Even so, reaching Sahul was only a matter of time once humans first moved beyond the Sunda mainland.

Watercraft were essential to move east from Sundaland, and whether or not watercraft sufficient to the task had been invented before or after the edges of the Sunda shelf had been reached is immaterial here. While it is currently impossible to calculate the costs and benefits for the first people of moving beyond this 'edge of the world', it is still a more effective way to consider the problem for hypothesis building than are appeals to the adventurous spirit. Humans do not take risks without some understanding of an eventual return that will justify such risks. We can assume reasonably that leaving the edge represented an increase in investment in marine technology, even if this technology was simple and unsophisticated. We can then only assume the benefits would fall into some of those categories that Butlin termed 'push' and 'pull' factors. Within the current argument, it is unimportant to specify these, be they crowding from population increase, declining returns from existing territories, or what Hiatt (2001) called colonisation by elopement.

What is important is to recognise that the investment in marine technology is a calculated response to some set of conditions that propels people into Wallacea. Once there, the probable imbalance between terrestrial and marine resources in relatively impoverished island habitats would demonstrate the possibility of increasing returns from marine resources as a function of improving technology, of which watercraft were a part. This is the way any distinctive material-cultural assemblages were developed in past cultural groups. In our view, the use of marine resources and increasing familiarity with them on the islands of Wallacea over time demanded a concomitant response in improved watercraft technology. This may still have been bamboo rafts. The notion does not demand canoes, outriggers, sails, or other more complex technology, but it does not deny them either.

In modelling the movements of behaviourally modern humans, we thus appeal to the ideal free distribution model (hereafter IFD). This was developed by Fretwell (1972) to account for distributions of dispersive birds in new habitats. It proposes that the way individuals occupy new territories is set up via habitat selection. Each habitat within a territory will have a different suitability, dependent on the number of occupants. The model suggests that in an empty landscape, the 'best' habitats, that is, those that optimise evolutionary success, will be occupied first.

But since optimality is density-dependent, there comes a point when optimal evolutionary success is threatened by population increase within the habitat. If habitat suitability declines with an increase in population density, then optimum distribution may become an unstable function of population size, where slight increases in population may cause major changes in distribution. When the suitabilty of the best habitat declines, as a function, for example, of increasing population depressing the availability of resources, and falls to the level of suitability of the next-most-suitable habitat, this second habitat will be occupied – and so on, in a cascading demographically driven pattern of habitat occupation where all occupied habitats have the same level of suitability, or in other words, all individuals have the same level of reproductive fitness. But this can occur only if all individuals are free to choose where they settle; that is, this is the pattern that settlement will ideally follow if no other constraints are applied.

The IFD model is not without its critics. Lima and Zollner (1996:132–133) point out that a dispersing animal will have little information about the distribution or number of living sites within a habitat or the greater landscape. They point out that IFD models mostly deal with small spatial scales that have high levels of available information and that opportunities for learning at large scales are minimal, since they involve the repeated abandonment and location of habitats that might be widely spaced, thus increasing risk. While such criticisms are valid, they might apply less to human groups that can disperse and regroup during exploration phases and exchange information via language, thus minimising risk.

While we perceive IFD as an overarching model that is useful in conceptualising how and why groups might occupy pristine territories, Fretwell was anxious to emphasise that the model only predicted the equalising of reproductive fitness if all individuals were free to occupy whatever territory they chose, and it is probable that in the face of finite resources at any particular location, those in possession moved to exclude other groups. At this more specific level, we model behaviour by appealing to optimal-foraging theory, a set of models for assessing food acquisition (Stephens and Krebs 1986; for a review of archaeological applications, see Bird and O'Connell 2006), a primary concern among hunter-gatherers and archaeologists reconstructing their past behaviour.

One of these models, the diet-breadth model, ranks available foods according to their potential to maximise nutritional-return rates, by assessing not only nutritional value, but also time spent in search, capture and processing. Marginal-value theory, on the other hand, determines the point in time when foragers should abandon one location for the greater benefits of another. As understood, this mostly means that higher foraging returns at the new location will compensate for lower present returns plus costs associated with moving. However, these costs may also include social costs, and at this point, we perceive how IFD and optimal-foraging models begin to meld.

Taken in conjunction, IFD and optimal-foraging theory provide us with a way to understand how Wallacea might have been crossed as part of a conscious foraging strategy that involved neither accidental castaways, nor deliberate colonisations. Under the diet-breadth model, technologies that reduce search and capture time and expand the list of available foods will be favoured. Thus, we would expect watercraft and fishing technologies to improve once people moved into the island world of Wallacea. We have expanded on these ideas elsewhere (O'Connell *et al.* 2007).

How might this operate on the ground? Let us assume that a behaviourally modern hunter-gatherer group exploits a territory that borders the Sunda shelf coast, the same barrier that has restricted earlier humans for more than a million years. Like these earlier humans, members of the group know islands exist to their east because they can see them from sea level; but unlike these earlier humans, they have (or develop) sufficient technology to occasionally reach these islands, utilise new sets of resources and return to their group. Even if the natural resources of the new location rival those in the existing group territory, this does not of itself make it a preferred habitat. Provided the suitability of the existing territory does not diminish, the social advantages of the established population there, from territorial knowledge to cultural association, from security from predators to marriage partners, maintains the original territory as the preferred location of the group.

Under Fretwell's IFD model, this balance is ultimately upset by population increase. However, the upset might equally be caused by diminishing resources in the territory, competition with neighbouring groups, or even short-term climate change such that the suitability of the habitat diminishes. While internal group conflict might cause fission, the decision to establish a new settlement on a peripheral island need not involve expulsion, nor indeed any conscious decision to go. A family or two may merely spend longer and longer periods away from their original group territory and in the new one; others might gradually join them until a new foraging territory comes into existence. The assumption here is that the initial group will settle in the habitat where diet breadth maximises its reproductive fitness (Beaton 1991). While the group remains small, all people joining it will settle in the same place because suitability is highest there. Since humans are gregarious, the variation to IFD known as Allee's principle will apply (Fretwell 1972:90–91). Initially, the suitability of the new habitat increases with an increase in the density of human groups, for the cooperative and social advantages already outlined. If at the same time the suitability in the original territory continues to decrease, it becomes advantageous to move into the new territory, until the suitability of the new territory approximates that in the former territory. Although the new territory will be different in its resources and their deployment, and human densities will differ in each, the IFD model suggests the reproductive fitness of both groups will equalise. As discussed in the next section, it may be necessary for the new group to maintain social and economic ties with its ancestral group for the exchange of different resources (a mutual benefit) and the exchange of genes (perhaps mainly a benefit to the new group).

The important point is that under the model, a small change in conditions, be it population increase, competitive increase, or resource downturn, can occasion a relatively large change in the distribution of the humans involved.

Some islands, such as Suluwesi, are large and would likely contain multiple territories, while smaller islands might be bypassed altogether for more suitable habitats. It may be instructive that today, with high populations and an agricultural base, only 6000 of Indonesia's 17,000 islands are inhabited. When multiple hunter-gatherer groups are operating entirely within island environments, some islands will have much greater natural suitability than others, whether this is a product of island size, reef size, resource diversity and productivity, availability of water, or combinations of all these things. Water sources, or equivalents such as coconuts, perhaps a less crucial variable on the Sunda mainland, will likely become a more critical one on islands with restricted catchments, making some islands or groups of islands preferred habitats and others very peripheral.

One implication of this is that the next-most-suitable habitat need not be adjacent to the first. Not all islands will be occupied in longitudinal turn and some may be never occupied nor even utilised. As such, our model is neither strictly a diffusionist wave-of-advance model, nor a streaming linear point-and-arrow model (Rockman 2003). While our interest is in a general east-to-west advance, specific islands may have been initially colonised from any direstion.

Thus our model leads us to conclude that the earliest Wallacean colonists selected the most suitable habitats, and when fission occurred, similarly suitable habitats were occupied, even at a distance. We refer to this model as the 'sweet-spot' model, a term coined by Robert Elston (e.g. Elston 1992) to mean a place in a landscape that, given particular hunter-gather technology, diet and population, is optimally located with regard to procuring a suite of resources, including food, water, fuel and shelter. While moving from sweet spot to sweet spot may well have been also the prevailing mode that propelled modern behavioural humans to the edge of Sunda, we believe the nature of the island world of Wallacea refined and intensified it as a strategy for colonising it. Eventually, Sahul loomed on the horizon.

The magic number

The demographic parameters of successfully colonising Wallacia and Sahul appear to be the missing pages of most such histories. Exceptions include Birdsell's (1957) early modelling that indicated a founding group expanding at ethnographically observed rates might fill Australia to carrying capacity in only several thousand years. Jones (1989:753–756) favoured chance castaway landings that were occasionally successful in establishing viable small populations, but he recognised no account had been taken of the genetic shortcomings of such models.

Frequently quoted, but least likely, is Calaby's (1976:23–24) imaginative but biologically improbable suggestion that a single pregnant female caught in a flood and swept to sea on a fallen tree or raft of vegetation could have been the Aboriginal Eve.

The general absence of the demographic parameter in the settlement of Sahul is understandable, given that the scales at which archaeology or genetics operate are unlikely to directly inform the problem. As with voyaging simulations in the Indo-Pacific region, demographic simulations of small colonising populations appear to offer the best illumination at present.

An early important attempt in Australia at simulating small founding populations was made by McArthur (1976). McArthur recognised that unlike modelling large populations, the demographic fate of each individual in a small group is of great significance to the fate of the group, but that by assessing the fate of each individual year by year, and introducing birth and marriage (monogamous vs polygamous) and incest rules, the capacity of the 1976 CSIRO computer was rapidly strained. Thus, these simulations ended when any population included either 500 men and women who had ever lived, and/or the maximum timespan for any of the populations generated was 500 years. The simulations were run for groups of three, five and seven couples and whatever the size of the group, groups with younger members had significantly lower probabilities of extinction than those with older couples, but the smaller groups had higher likelihoods of extinction.

McArthur found the slowing down or reversal of a group's demographic increase was traceable to distortions in the sex ratios, either the predominance of one sex among the births, or the failure of some to survive and reproduce. However, under the constraints of the experiment, McArthur was unable to indicate what demographic threshold needed to be achieved for long-term viability.

The problem has recently been re-examined by Moore (2001), who notes that in bands of 25–50 individuals, people are frequently organised around co-resident lineages that restrict potential spouses from marrying opposites who are closely related. In ethnographically described small-scale foraging societies, such marriage restrictions are almost universal. Thus, in small groups, eligible spouses rapidly become rare. Four demographic factors – birth rates, death rates, sex ratio and distribution of sibship size – appear to determine the success of an isolated colonising band. The stochastic nature of birth and death rates can devastate small groups, as can an unbalanced sex ratio, even if women outnumber men and polygyny is adopted, since, other things being equal, the average completed fertility in polygynous marriages is often lower than in monogamous ones. Even if economically viable, such a band will almost inevitably die out unless members either commit incest, a solution with its own fitness costs, or recruit suitable spouses from outside the group.

Again using computer simulations, Moore (2001:400) proposed that unbalanced sex ratios might be more damaging for the long-term viability of a group than fertility issues, especially if long runs of male offspring occur. More telling is the clear indication that lower starting population sizes produce more variable and less predictable results than larger starting populations. Whereas the fate of small groups might turn on a few specific births or deaths, these small events are buffered in larger groups.

Most telling in Moore's simulations is that while the longevity of the group increases with size, no groups of any of the tested sizes up to 60 people avoid extinction, and only rarely do they remain extant for 1000 years in isolation. Such an incursion into Sahul might well remain archaeologically invisible. However, the potential for viability increases significantly if the group exchanges spouses with one other group of equal size. This suggests that if we model the crossing of Wallacea in a 'string-of-pearls' formation, the lead group in the string is as biologically viable in its reproductive ability as a group further towards the centre of the string, provided contact with the second group is maintained.

Stemming directly from Moore's analysis (see also Wobst 1974:170–173) is the conclusion that there is no magic number that will assure viability for any isolated small group of hunter-gatherer colonists crossing Wallacea or entering an empty landscape. While, equally, every small group has some minimal chance of survival, if it arrived as a biologically unbalanced group of castaways on Sahul, its ultimate biological success would seem to be miniscule and dependent on soon being overtaken by subsequent castaway colonists to add to the gene pool. Such an event is probably rare, and even if it did occur, success would require some minimum complementarity in age and gender, as Crusoe realised when he met Friday. The alternate strategy whereby deliberate contact is maintained to bolster potential long-term reproductive success seems to us more probable.

The discussion here has centred on the biological requirements for small pioneering groups entering empty landscapes. We have considered only what Moore refers to as the period of stochastic crisis when extinction might result from the magnified effects of only one or two deaths in a small group. However, if the small group can attain a size at which these critical stochastic events are buffered by the co-occurrence of benevolent events, it may reach the point of 'Malthusian takeoff', when the group begins to increase its population geometrically. At this point, while the threat of extinction recedes, it is replaced by the opposite problem of too many people for the mode of production. While less suitable habitats previously bypassed may now be filled in, or economic intensification might increase the productivity of a habitat, other social solutions, such as infanticide, might also be introduced.

The Timor route

None of the variables discussed here offers much support for the Timor to the Kimberley coast route. While the target was wide, it was a blind crossing and its value could not be determined by scouting, its location only surmised on the basis of smoke, migrating birds and bushfire glow. It required sufficient technology to cover a longer journey at times of higher sea level, the opportune times to utilise coasts and islands, but from a starting point that may have lacked bamboo, the favoured watercraft-building material. If people could not return to Timor, no new information about what lay ahead was available to subsequent intending colonists. The nature of the Kimberley coast at various lower sea levels is uncertain, but extensive mud flats and lack of fresh water may have been a problem. Lastly, the long-term reproductive viability of colonists taking this route would seem to have depended on being overtaken by subsequent gender- and age-compatible colonists.

Alternatively, these deficiencies appear not to attend the northern route that eventually brought people on to or near the Bird's Head of western New Guinea. This is the most likely route of entry into Sahul.

Conclusion

We intend to pursue the corollary to this paper, the dispersal of people through Sahul, in another place. However, we note that if people did enter through the Bird's Head, as we suggest, then dispersal eastwards was controlled in large part by geography. The central cordillera running the length of New Guinea, and in places reaching 4000 m above sea level, is thought to have been shrouded in cloud and inhospitable. This mountain chain formed an effective wedge, isolating people moving along the northern coast towards the Bismarck Archipelago from those moving southwards into Australia. On either side, the catchment of the cordillera provided numerous rivers, the basis for coastal and lowland sweet spots. But to the north, the coastline channelled people in string-of-pearls fashion towards the immediate dead-end of the Bismarcks, while to the south, a different scenario was played out.

Despite decades of biological research in Australia and New Guinea that has emphasised the differences between the two regions, recent genetic research has begun to change this situation. There are now three or four shared haplogroups, P3, S, Q2, and possibly P4, that indicate ancient mtDNA linkages (Friedlaender *et al.* 2005; Friedlaender *et al.* 2007; Hudjashov *et al.* 2007). Interestingly, one of these, Group S, is in Papua on the Oriomo Plateau (Figure 1), and thus is south of the cordillera, supporting the view of an early incursion along the southern New Guinea coast towards what is now Australia. The others are from the Bismarck Archipelago. This genetic evidence is more fully considered in O'Connell *et al.* (2007).

In keeping with our understanding of the ability of behaviourally modern humans to solve problems with technology and determine the costs and benefits of their actions and decisions, we see little to recommend the parsimony of minimalist views that wash the first Australians and New Guineans ashore as helpless castaways. We find equally unpersuasive views that invoke long-distance migration and voyages of exploration in the style of Magellan and Cook. People crossed Wallacea as a consequence of specialised foraging behaviour, in much the same manner as they had travelled from Africa to the edge of Sunda.

References

Allen, J. and J.F. O'Connell 2003. The long and the short of it: archaeological approaches to determining when humans first colonized Australia and New Guinea. *Australian Archaeology* 57:5–19.

Anderson, A. 2000. Slow boats from China: issues in the prehistory of Indo-Pacific seafaring. In S. O'Connor and P. Veth (eds), *East of Wallace's Line. Studies of Past and Present Maritime Cultures of the Indo-Pacific Region*, pp. 13–50. Published as *Modern Quaternary Research in South East Asia* 16. Rotterdam: Balkema.

Baulig, H. 1935. *The Changing Sea Level.* The Institute of British Geographers, Publication No. 3. London: George Philip and Son.

Beaton, J.B. 1991. Colonizing continents: some problems from Australia and the Americas. In T.D. Dillehay, and D.J. Meltzer (eds), *The First Americans: Search and Research*, pp. 209–230. Baton Rouge: CRC Press.

Bellwood, P. 1990. From Late Pleistocene to Early Holocene in Sunderland. In C. Gamble and O. Soffer (eds), *The World at 18,000 BP. Vol. 2. Low Latitudes,* pp. 255–263. London: Unwin Hyman.

Bird, D.W. and J.F. O'Connell 2006. Behavioral ecology and archaeology. *Journal of Archaeological Research* 14:143–188.

Birdsell, J.B. 1957. Some population problems involving Pleistocene man. *Cold Springs Harbor Symposia on Quantitative Biology* 22:47–69.

Birdsell, J.B. 1977. The recalibration of a paradigm for the first peopling of Greater Australia. In J. Allen, J. Golson and R. Jones (eds), *Sunda and Sahul. Prehistoric Studies in Southeast Asia, Melanesia and Australia*, pp.113–67. London: Academic Press.

Bowdler, S. 1977. The coastal colonisation of Australia. In J. Allen, J. Golson and R. Jones (eds), *Sunda and Sahul. Prehistoric Studies in Southeast Asia, Melanesia and Australia*, pp.205–245. London: Academic Press.

Bulbeck, D. 2007. Where river meets sea: a parsimonious model for *Homo sapiens* colonization of the Indian Ocean Rim and Sahul. *Current Anthropology* 48:315–321.

Butlin, N.G. 1993. *Economics and the Dreamtime. A Hypothetical History.* Cambridge: Cambridge University Press.

Calaby, J.H. 1976. Some biogeographical factors relevant to the Pleistocene movement of man in Australasia. In R.L. Kirk and A.G. Thorne (eds), *The Origin of Australians,* pp. 23–28. Human Biology Series No. 6, Canberra: Australian Institute of Aboriginal Studies.

Chappell, J. 1993. Late Pleistocene coasts and human migrations in the Austral region. In M. Spriggs, D.E. Yen, W. Ambrose, R. Jones, A. Thorne and A. Andrews (eds), *A Community of Culture. The People and Prehistory of the Pacific,* pp. 43–48. Occasional Papers in Prehistory, No. 21. Canberra: Department of Prehistory, Research School of Pacific Studies, The Australian National University.

Chappell, J. 2000. Pleistocene seedbeds of western Pacific maritime cultures and the importance of chronology. In S. O'Connor and P. Veth (eds), *East of Wallace's Line. Studies of Past and Present Maritime Cultures of the Indo-Pacific Region,* pp. 77–98. Published as *Modern Quaternary Research in South East Asia* 16. Rotterdam: Balkema.

Chappell, J., J. Head and J. Magee 1996. Beyond the radiocarbon limit in Australian archaeology and Quaternary research *Antiquity* 70:543–552.

Daly, R.A. 1910. Pleistocene glaciation and the coral reef problem. *American Journal of Science* (4th series) 30:297–308.

Dunn, F.L. and D.F. Dunn 1977. Maritime adaptations and the exploration of marine resources in Sundaic Southeast Asian prehistory. *Modern Quaternary Research in Southeast Asia* 3:1–28.

Elkin, A.P. 1978. N.W.G. Macintosh and his work. *Archaeology and Physical Anthropology in Oceania* 13(2 & 3):85–142.

Elston, R.G. 1992. Economics and strategies of lithic procurement at Tosawihi. In R.G. Elston and C. Raven (eds), *Archaeological Investigations at Tosawihi, a Great Basin Quarry. Part 1: The Periphery,* pp. 775–802. Report to Ivanhoe Gold Company, Winnemucca, Nevada by Intermountain Research, Silver City, Nevada.

Fifield, L.K., M.I. Bird, C.S.M. Turney, P.A. Hausladen, G.M. Santos and M.L. di Tada 2001. Radiocarbon dating of the human occupation of Australia prior to 40 ka BP – successes and pitfalls. *Radiocarbon* 43:1139–1145.

Foley R. and M.M. Lahr 1997. Mode 3 technologies and the evolution of modern humans. *Cambridge Archaeological Journal* 7(1):3–36.

Fretwell, S.D. 1972. *Populations in a Seasonal Environment.* Princeton: Princeton University Press.

Friedlaender, J.S., T.G. Schurr, F. Gentz, G. Koki, F.R. Friedlaender, G. Horvat, P. Babb, S. Cerchio, F. Kaestle, M. Schanfield, R. Deka, R. Yanagihara and D.A. Merriwether 2005. Expanding Southwest Pacific Mitochondrial Haplogroups P and Q. *Molecular Biology and Evolution* 22:1506–1517.

Friedlaender, J. S., F.R. Friedlaender, J.A. Hodgson, M. Stoltz, G. Koki, G. Horvat, S. Zhadonov, T.G. Schurr, and D.A. Merriwether 2007. Melanesian mtDNA Complexity. *PLoS ONE* 2(2): e248.doi:10.1371/journal.pone.0000248.

Hiatt, L.R. 2001. *Homo Mobilis.* In A. Anderson, I. Lilley and S. O'Connor (eds), *Histories of Old Ages. Essays in honour of Rhys Jones,* pp. 111–21. Canberra: Pandanus Books.

Horton, D.R. 1981. Water and woodland; the peopling of Australia. *Australian Institute of Aboriginal Studies Newsletter* 16:21–27.

Hudjashov, G., T. Kivisild, P.A. Underhill, P. Endicott, J.J. Sanchez, A.A. Lind, P. Shen, P. Oefner, C. Renfrew, R. Villems and P. Forster 2007. Revealing the prehistoric settlement of Australia by Ychromosome and mtDNA analysis. *Proceedings of the National Academy of Science* 104(21): 8726–8730.

Irwin, G. 1992. *The Prehistoric Exploration and Colonisation of the Pacific.* Cambridge: Cambridge University Press.

Jones, R. 1989. East of Wallace's Line: issues and problems in the colonisation of the Australian continent. In P. Mellars and C. Stringer (eds), *The Human Revolution. Behavioural and Biological*

Perspectives on the Origins of Modern Humans, pp. 743–782. Edinburgh: Edinburgh University Press.

Kirch, P.V. 2002. *On The Road of the Winds: An Archaeological History of the Pacific Islands before European Contact.* Berkeley: University of California Press.

Lambeck, K. and J. Chappell 2001. Sea level change through the last glacial cycle. *Science* 292:679–686.

Lima, S.L. and P.A. Zollner 1996. Towards a behavioural ecology of ecological landscapes. *Trends in Ecology and Evolution* 11:131–135.

McArthur, N. 1976. Computer simulations of small populations. *Australian Archaeology* 4:53–57.

Moore, J.H. 2001 Evaluating five models of colonization. *American Anthropologist* 103:395–408.

Mulvaney, J. and J. Kamminga 1999. *Prehistory of Australia.* St. Leonards, Sydney: Allen and Unwin.

Munro, W. 1868. *A Monograph of the Bambusaceae Including Description of All the Species.* London: The Linnean Society.

O'Connell, J.F. and J. Allen 2004. Dating the colonization of Sahul (Pleistocene Australia–New Guinea): a review of recent research. *Journal of Archaeological Science* 31:835–853.

O'Connell, J.F. and J. Allen 2007. Pre-LGM Sahul (Australia–New Guinea) and the archaeology of early modern humans In P. Mellars, K. Boyle, O. Bar-Yosef and C. Stringer (eds), *Rethinking the Human Revolution,* pp. 395–410. Cambridge: McDonald Institute for Archaeological Research.

O'Connell, J.F., J. Allen and K. Hawkes 2007. Modeling Sahul colonization: implications for the origins of seafaring. Paper presented at the workshop 'Origins of Seafaring.' MacDonald Institute, Cambridge University. August 2007.

O'Connor, S. 2007. Pleistocene Migration and Colonisation in the Indo-Pacific Region. Paper presented at the workshop 'Origins of Seafaring.' MacDonald Institute, Cambridge University. August 2007.

O'Connor, S. and J. Chappell 2003. Colonisation and coastal subsistence in Australia and Papua New Guinea: different timing, different modes? In C. Sand (ed), *Pacific Archaeology: assessments and prospects,* pp. 17–32. Le Cahiers de l'Archéologie en Nouvelle-Calédonie 15. Nouméa: Departement Archéologie, Service des Musées et du Patrimoine de Nouvelle-Calédonie.

Roberts, R.G., R. Jones and M.A. Smith 1990. Thermoluminescence dating of a 50,000 year old human occupation site in northern Australia. *Nature* 345:153–156.

Rindos, D. and E. Webb 1992. Modelling the initial colonisation of Australia: perfect adaptation, cultural variability and cultural change. *Proceedings of the Australasian Society for Human Biology* 5:441–454.

Rockman, M. 2003. Knowledge and learning in the archaeology of colonization. In M. Rockman and J. Steele (eds), *Colonization of Unfamiliar Landscapes: The Archaeology of Adaptation,* pp. 3–24. London: Routledge.

Stephens, D.W. and J.R. Krebs 1986. *Foraging Theory.* Princeton: Princeton University Press.

Thiel, B. 1987. Early settlement of the Philippines, Eastern Indonesia, and Australia–New Guinea: a new hypothesis. *Current Anthropology* 28(2):236–241.

Torgersen, T., J. Luly, P. De Deckker, M.R. Jones, D.E. Searle, A.R. Chivas and W.J. Ullman 1988. Late quaternary environments of the Carpentaria Basin, Australia. *Palaeogeography, Palaeoclimatology, Palaeoecology* 67(3–4): 245–261.

Voris, H.K. 2000. Maps of Pleistocene sea levels in Southeast Asia: Shorelines, river systems and time durations. *Journal of Biogeography* 27:1153–1167.

Wild, S. 1985. Voyaging to Australia: 30,000 years ago. *Proceedings of Ausgraph* 85. Brisbane: Third Australasian Conference on Computer Graphics.

Wobst, H.M. 1974. Boundary conditions for Palaeolithic social systems: a simulation approach. *American Antiquity* 39:147–178.

3

Seafaring simulations and the origin of prehistoric settlers to Madagascar

Scott M. Fitzpatrick
Department of Sociology and Anthropology, North Carolina State University, USA
scott_fitzpatrick@ncsu.edu

Richard Callaghan
Department of Archaeology, University of Calgary, Canada

Introduction

How and when islands in the Pacific and Indian Oceans were colonised by Austronesian speakers has been of great interest to archaeologists for decades. Few people, however, have gone to such great lengths to answer the questions from so many different methodological and theoretical perspectives as Atholl Anderson. Atholl probably also has the distinction of having stepped on more islands in the Pacific than any other archaeologist and his efforts to understand Oceanic prehistory have influenced and will continue to inspire future generations of archaeologists. Given that his research has been so varied and spanned several oceans, dozens of islands and thousands of years in prehistory, we felt it appropriate to write a paper for Atholl's festschrift that embodied one of the core questions regarding Austronesian expansion – how did peoples reach these islands?

Using computer simulations of voyaging, we examine the prehistoric colonisation of Madagascar. This approach to studying ancient seafaring is increasingly used worldwide to investigate colonisation, migration and culture contact (Levison *et al.* 1973; Irwin 1992; Callaghan 2001, 2003a, 2003b, 2003c; Montenegro *et al.* 2006; Avis *et al.* 2007; Callaghan and Fitzpatrick 2007, 2008). The results of these simulations can be coupled with other data to develop more robust hypotheses regarding the possible routes of migration to Madagascar by Austronesian speakers, illustrating the extent to which peoples were willing to travel to colonise new islands.

The colonisation of Madagascar

Madagascar, one of the world's largest islands (587,000 km^2), is located in the Indian Ocean about 420 km from the southeast African coast and 5600 km west of the Indonesian archipelago.

Archaeological and paleoenvironmental evidence suggests Madagascar was first colonised by peoples about 2000 BP (Dewar and Wright 1993), although its settlement history thereafter appears to have been more complex, with people voyaging from around the Indian Ocean, including Southeast Asia, East Africa, South Asia and the Near East (Dewar and Wright 1993:418). What makes the Madagascar case particularly intriguing is that it lies relatively close to the African mainland, but was settled initially by Austronesian speakers from much further away. The most widely spoken language on the island is Malagasy, of Austronesian origin, which has its closest affinity to Borneo (Dhal 1951, 1977). There is also evidence of extended contact with the Bantu language, but it seems to have diverged from Island Southeast Asian languages 1000 to 2000 years ago (Dewar and Wright 1993:419). Genetic analysis also indicates major migrations to Madagascar from both Indonesia and East Africa (Pigache 1970).

A computer-simulated approach

Migrations from East Africa would have required sea crossings of about 400 km (215 nautical miles). Direct migrations crossing the Indian Ocean from Indonesia to Madagascar, however, were 15 times further, requiring sea crossings of about 6000 km (3200 nautical miles). It is the latter crossings which are of interest here, since this is where the first colonists originated. In this paper, we use computer simulations to investigate migration routes, strategies and seasonality. These simulations take advantage of detailed oceanographic, anemological and climatological data to determine how watercraft will move or react to ocean conditions at a given time of the year.

A number of voyaging strategies can be investigated using computer simulations. The two basic divisions are between simple downwind sailing and directed voyages. In this analysis, we investigate both strategies. The first is downwind sailing, or sailing before the wind. In this strategy, vessels are simply sailed before the wind with little or no attempt to navigate in a particular direction. This allows close to the maximum distance to be covered in a given time. The initial discovery of Madagascar may have involved this type of strategy. It is consistent with, but not limited to, situations where sailors are lost at sea. Dening (1963:138–153) notes that the limited empirical evidence of voyagers lost at sea in Polynesia suggests a common pattern of behaviour in which sailors conclude they are lost early in the voyage and respond by allowing the vessel to sail before the wind, with no further attempt to navigate in a particular direction.

The second strategy used in the simulations is one in which sailors intentionally try to sail in a particular direction. This requires vessels that have some capability to sail to windward. During the period from 1000 to 2000 years ago, it is well known that Indonesian and other vessels sailing in the Indian Ocean had such capabilities. McGrail (2001:301) notes that vessels carved into the eighth-ninth century temple of Borobudur on Java carry lug sails and canted rectangular sails. La Baron Bowen Jr (1954:201) refers to the canted rectangular sails at Borobudur as a form of lug sail. Lug sails are one of the most powerful rigs for sailing to windward that can be made using fairly simple technology (Bolger 1984:42). We also simulated return trips from Madagascar to Indonesia as linguistic evidence suggests contact was maintained between Malagasy speakers and languages on the eastern side of the Indian Ocean (Adalaar 1989).

One possible route is described in the *Periplus of the Erythraean Sea* (Schoff 1912). The *Periplus* was probably written about AD 60 (Schoff 1912:15) and overlaps the period of interest here. The *Periplus* describes the timing of trading voyages from about 10° S along the East African coast around the Indian Ocean and through the Straits of Malacca to about 5° S off the east coast of Sumatra. There is a description of the goods traded along what is largely a coastal

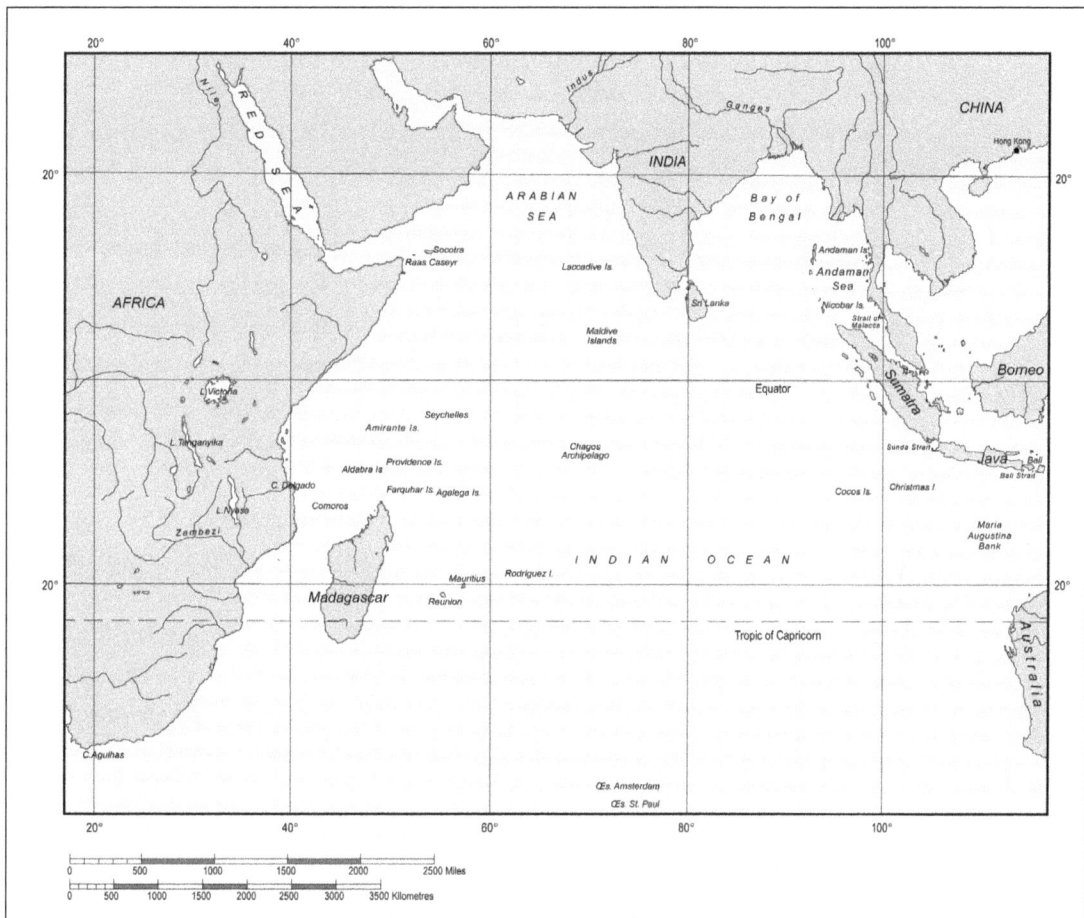

Figure 1. Map of the Indian Ocean.

route. However, seasons for two open-sea crossings are given. One is for crossing the Arabian Sea, and the other for crossing the Bay of Bengal. The crossings make use of the seasonal monsoonal shifts. Overall, the coastal route from the Straits of Malacca to just north of Madagascar would involve sailing more than 11,000 km, or 6000 nautical miles. As this route is well documented and is primarily a coastal trading route, we did not simulate migration voyages along it. Rather, we investigate alternative, more direct routes to the south.

The simulation program

The problem of establishing alternative migration routes, durations and seasonality is addressed here using computer simulations based on the known patterns of winds and currents throughout the year. When running downwind-sailing simulations, four main *variables* are considered: (1) current patterns; (2) wind patterns; (3) vessel type; and (4) propulsion. The *structure* of the simulation is the actual mechanics of the program – for example, how data are selected, and success as a percentage of all voyages calculated. *Parameters* include such factors as the starting position of the vessel, whether it is a downwind or directed voyage, the duration at sea, and what constitutes a successful voyage.

Currents will affect objects caught in them in a 1:1 ratio. That is, the object will have the same speed and set as the current unless other forces are operating. Any object floating with an appreciable part above the water will be more affected by winds than currents unless a current is exceptionally strong. The effect of wind on objects floating high in the water was used by traditional navigators in Kiribati to determine the direction of land when recent winds differed from the flow of the current (Lewis 1972:212). The source of wind and current data is the CD-ROM version of the US Navy *Marine Climatic Atlas of the World* (Version 1.1 1995).

The type of vessel and how it is propelled make up the final variables of the problem, as the shape of an object above and below the waterline will respond to the effects of wind. However, in this problem, we do not know what types of vessels were used. Some form of Indonesian sailing vessel from the period of interest is most likely, as Indonesian-style outriggers are still used in some parts of Madagascar (Dewar and Wright 1993:419). Recently, a replica of a first-millennium Indonesian vessel based on one depicted on the temple of Borobudur <http://www.borobudurshipexpedition.com/index.htm> made a direct crossing of the Indian Ocean to Madagascar. However, there are 11 vessels depicted at Borobudur, not all of which are the same design (McGrail 2001:301). Because we do not know precisely what types of vessels were involved in migrations to Madagascar, and it is likely multiple designs were used, we have used generalised sailing speeds derived from a number of vessel types. Speeds at which the vessels used in this simulation can travel under various wind conditions are taken from figures provided by Levison *et al.* (1973).

The program itself is also based on the United States Navy *Marine Climatic Atlas* (US Navy 1995), which includes all of the world's seas and oceans, except Arctic waters. The data are organised in a resolution of one degree Marsden squares (one degree of longitude by one degree of latitude). In particular, this resolution allows the effects of smaller and more variable currents to be accurately reflected in the outcomes. The program randomly selects wind and current data that are frequency-weighted according to the compiled observations of the *Marine Climatic Atlas*. These forces are allowed to operate on vessels for a 24-hour period before a new selection is made (see Levison *et al.* 1973 for a justification of the period length).

The distance and direction travelled are based on the wind and current data, combined with the speeds from Levison *et al.* (1973:19) and parameters selected by the program operator. Examples of parameters here include the use of sails, sea anchors to keep a vessel oriented into the wind during storms, or droques to slow the vessel and prevent following seas from swamping it. It is also possible to include changes of heading when under sail. This last feature is important when assessing the level of navigational skill required to reach a selected target during directed voyages. The program automatically shifts to the database for the following month after the month originally selected has expired. This feature better reflects the reality of changing wind and current conditions over long voyages. The result of the simulations is expressed as the percentage of successes for a particular vessel type from selected points.

Parameters of the simulation are choices made by the program operator in order to set up the simulation to answer a particular question. These include the following information: (1) points of origin and destination; (2) crew strategy; (3) performance characteristics; (4) duration of voyages; (5) time of year; and (6) number of simulations.

Four points of origin were used, with Madagascar as the destination. These were the Bali Straits between Bali and Java; the Sunda Straits between Java and Sumatra; the north end of the Malacca Straits off the northwestern tip of Sumatra; and just west of Sri Lanka and south of India. One point of origin off the northeastern tip of Madagascar was used for return voyages to Indonesia.

The second parameter is the strategy used by the crew. As noted above, in this analysis, we have chosen to investigate two strategies. The first is downwind sailing or sailing before the wind. In this strategy, vessels are simply sailed before the wind with no attempt to navigate, allowing close to the maximum distance to be covered in a given time. The second strategy is one in which sailors intentionally try to sail in a particular direction.

The duration of the downwind voyages was set at 200 days, after which it was assumed the crew perished. Two hundred days would approach the longest voyage in an open boat due to shipwreck or other misfortunes documented in the Pacific (Howay 1944; Levison *et al.* 1973:20–21; Callaghan 2003c). The longest recorded shipwreck voyage in an open boat seems to be in the order of seven to eight months, and several of these have been documented in the past few decades. A number of these recorded voyages covered distances of about 5500 km over six to 10 weeks, and more travelled slightly shorter distances. For the purposes of this study, 100 downwind voyages were simulated for all 12 months of the year from each of the points of origin.

Survival

Survival of the crew in long open-ocean voyages is an important consideration. The three main factors affecting survival at sea are the surface temperature, the availability of water and the availability of food. These factors are all related to the duration of the voyage. Sea surface temperature is not a significant factor here, as the surface temperatures of the equatorial Indian Ocean, 28C–29C (Heikell 1999:209), are well above temperatures that would present a significant problem (McCance *et al.* 1956).

Water is probably the greatest problem on long ocean voyages. Lee (1965:96, 99) states that the maximum time an individual can be deprived of water under survival conditions is 10 days. The availability of water, however, is very difficult to calculate. As stated by Levison *et al.* (1973:20), 'between the extremes of no water and ample water the whole range of unpredictable situations makes it impractical to construct a separate risk table for this factor' in a simulation program. Aside from what is stored on board, water can be obtained from precipitation, especially in the tropics, and it is not difficult to retrieve from sails (Heikell 1999:5). Even in the dry season, some regions of the Indian Ocean have showers in the afternoon (1999:214–215). There are several other sources of drinking water at sea, besides precipitation. Bombard (1986:61) was, at times, able to collect nearly a pint of water from dew during survival experiments in the Mediterranean. While displacement vessels have an advantage over rafts in that the hull will collect dew, almost any material (including cloth, matting and leather) can be used to collect water particles. Lee and Lee (1980:139–160) cite instances in which water has been obtained by shipwreck survivors from fish and barnacles, or in which blood was a viable substitute. Bombard (1986:212–213) demonstrated that one can survive by drinking seawater, as long as small amounts are drunk before dehydration sets in.

Given that the voyages investigated here are not shipwreck situations, it is expected that vessels are well provisioned. A wide variety of dried fruits and nuts are available in the lands around the Indian Ocean (Heikell 1999:11) and rice and other grains have considerable storability. Fish are currently abundant and easy to catch in the equatorial Indian Ocean (Heikell 1999:18) and should have been more so in the past. In emergencies, a number of resources may have been available. Lee and Lee (1980:139–160) describe instances of survivors eating everything from non-vegetable plankton to toredo borers. One report (Lee and Lee 1980:110–111) describes barracuda leaping on to a life-raft, though they were perceived more as a threat than a food source. Sharks, often too small to be a threat, are commonly reported following small vessels. Turtles and sea birds are other food sources not necessarily requiring specialised technology to capture that are often reported available to survivors.

Results

Downwind sailing from the Bali Straits would not allow voyagers to reach Madagascar at any time of the year. However, from April to August, it would be possible with some knowledge to use the technique to sail significant distances to the west and to reach 88° E, particularly in June. Similarly, downwind sailing is not a feasible strategy for reaching Madagascar from the Sunda Straits. From the Bali Straits, significant progress westward can be made from April to August, especially in June when voyagers using downwind sailing could reach as far west as about 83° E.

From the northwest tip of Sumatra, downwind sailing could allow voyagers to reach as far west as about 72° E from December to March, before they would be driven back to the east. However, in November and December, downwind sailing could be used to reach Sri Lanka in as few as 40 days, making no attempt to navigate other than keeping the wind at the stern. From the India/Sri Lanka position in January (Figure 2), and to a lesser extent in February, the pattern for downwind sailing is interesting. Vessels would move to the southwest through the Maldives before the pattern bifurcates, with vessels moving either to Madagascar or Java. Downwind voyages to Madagascar using this route would take as few as 81 days. The route to Java could take as few as 73 days. In March, November and December, vessels move through the Maldives before travelling east to Indonesia. During the rest of the year, vessels are pushed back to Sri Lanka.

The final set of downwind simulations was from Madagascar to Indonesia. From August through April, most vessels were simply blown back to the island, with a few in March and April, and August through December moving to the west, and landing on the adjacent African coast. The majority of vessels setting sail from May to July moved to the northwest, landing along the Somali coast, with a smaller number reaching the west coasts of India and Sri Lanka.

The second set of simulations assumed a moderate ability to sail to windward, averaging 1 knot when sailing across or into the wind. These voyages were directed, in that a heading towards Madagascar was selected. Other than choosing an initial heading, no attempt was made to steer the vessels. From the Bali Straits, it was not possible to reach Madagascar. From August to March and in May, vessels were forced to Java. In June and July, vessels could sail west to a position south of Sri Lanka before being forced back to the east. However, 18 percent of vessels setting out in April reached Sri Lanka in an average of 157 days.

Sailing west from the Sunda Straits from December through March, a number of voyages either reached Madagascar or passed north of the island. Vessels passing north would have had little trouble making landfall on Madagascar. In December, five percent of vessels passed to the north of Madagascar, reaching Africa in 103 to 115 days. In January, eight percent of vessels reached Madagascar or the nearby Seychelles or Amirante Islands. On average, the voyages took 163 days, but they could be as short as 109 days. In February, 18 percent of vessels landed in Madagascar or the Seychelles and Amirante Islands. On average, the voyages took 142 days, with a minimum of 99 days. Vessels starting out in March (Figure 3) had the greatest chance of reaching Madagascar, or they passed to the north, landing on the coast of Africa in a total of 53 percent of voyages. The average voyage duration was 152 days, with the shortest being 100 days. In April and October, vessels made headway south of Sri Lanka before being swept eastward. Approximately 25 percent of vessels landed on Sri Lanka and the west coast of India. From May to September, vessels sailed west to a position south of Sri Lanka before being blown back eastward to the coasts of Thailand and Burma. Vessels setting sail in November primarily were forced back to Java, although two landed on Sri Lanka and two on the Somali coast.

Simulations of voyages westward from the northwest tip of Sumatra in January (Figure 4)

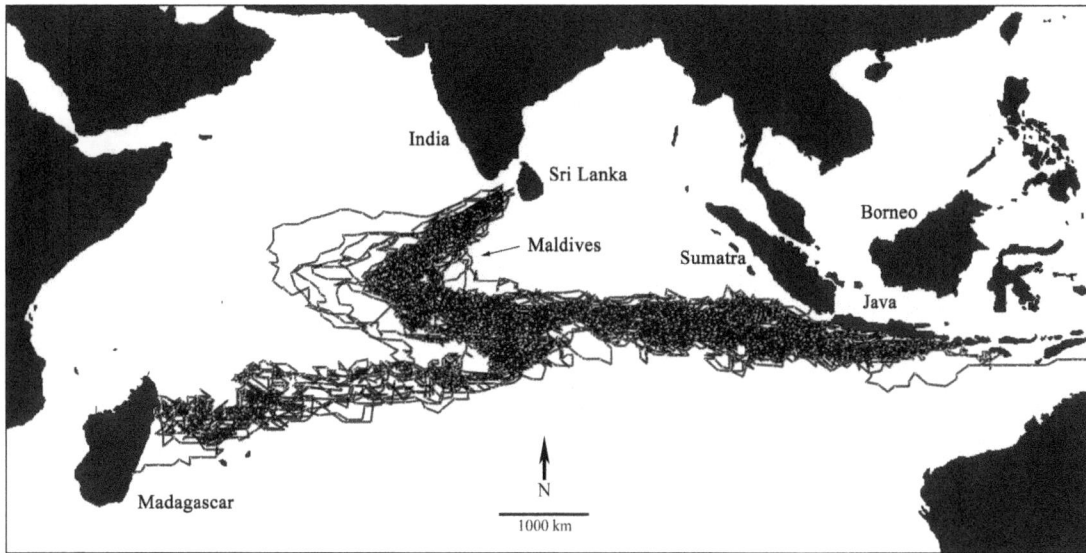

Figure 2. Downwind sailing from South India/Sri Lanka in January.

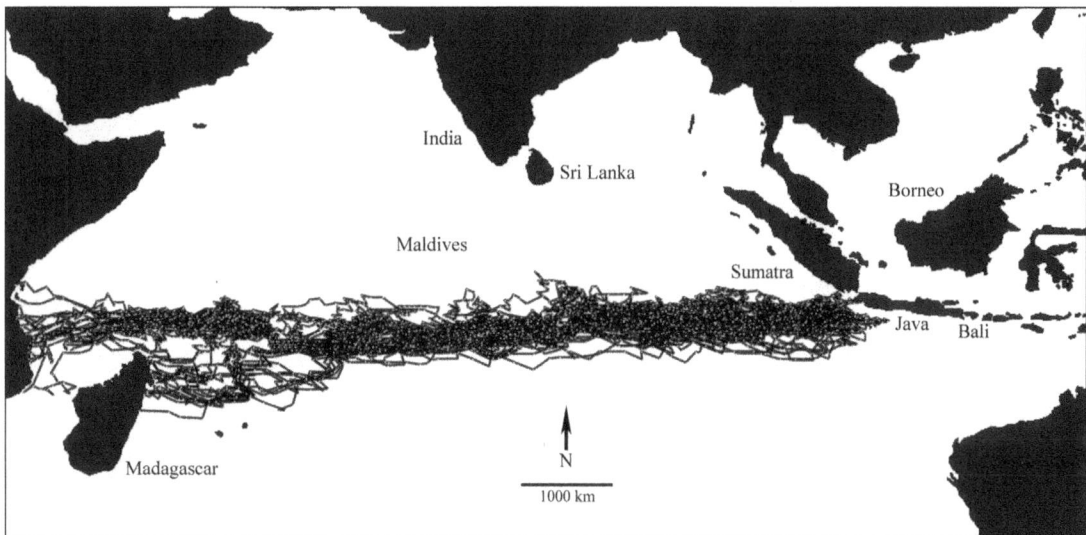

Figure 3. Directed sailing from the Sunda Straits in March.

and February all reached Madagascar in 93 and 72 days respectively. In December and March, a few vessels reached Madagascar, but most passed to the north, landing on the African coast. Vessels starting in December reached Madagascar in a minimum of 111 days, while those beginning in March took a minimum of 180 days. Vessels starting in October were forced to the west coast of India in a minimum of 40 days, while vessels starting in November were mostly forced to Sri Lanka in a minimum of 21 days. In April, vessels were all forced to Sri Lanka in a minimum of 23 days.

Simulations from the India/Sri Lanka position were given a southwest heading. From December through March, all voyages passed through the Maldives, making landfall on Madagascar. The minimum durations were as follows: December: 60 days; January: 44 days; February: 43 days; March: 61 days. Vessels in April were first swept towards Sumatra and then to the west past northern Madagascar, landing on the African coast in a minimum of 110 days. A similar pattern was found for October, with vessels landing on the Somali coast in minimum of 95 days.

The final set of simulations was from Madagascar to Indonesia. A heading of due east was given to the vessels. From November through April, there were successful voyages between Madagascar and Indonesia. However, the percentage of successful voyages and their durations varied considerably. Success ranged from 50 percent for vessels setting out in March, to 100 percent for those setting out in April. Durations ranged from 113 days in January, to 55 days in November. Overall, April (Figure 5) proved the most favourable time to begin voyages to Indonesia, with 100 percent success rates and durations as low as 63 days. In May, most vessels landed in Sri Lanka, with a minimum duration of 38 days. From May through August, most vessels landed on the west coast of India and Sri Lanka. Minimal durations were from 23 to 38 days. In September, about half of the vessels landed in India and Sri Lanka, with a minimum duration of 29 days, while the rest landed on the east coast of Africa. In October, virtually all vessels were swept west to Africa.

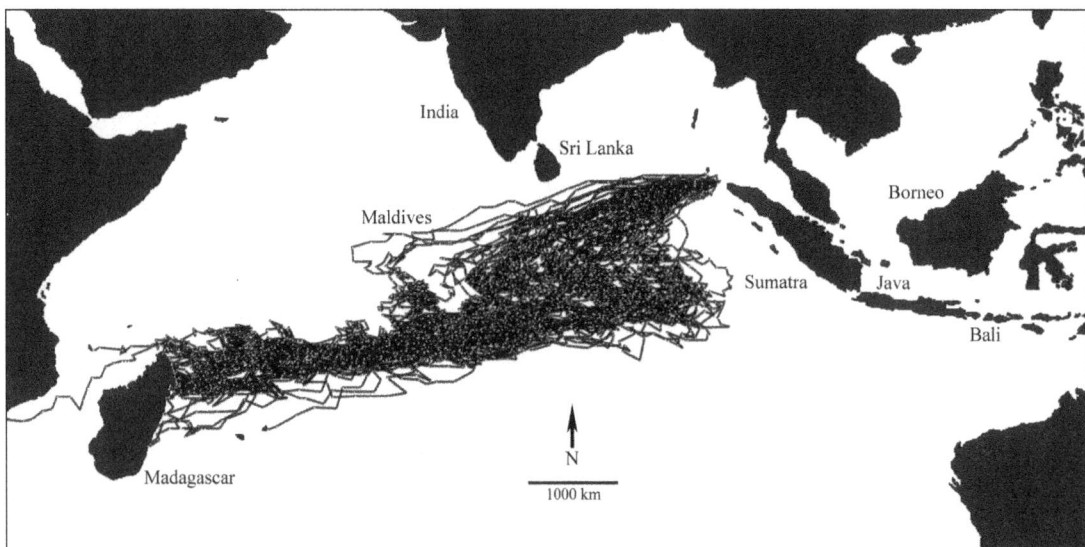

Figure 4. Directed sailing from northwest Sumatra in January.

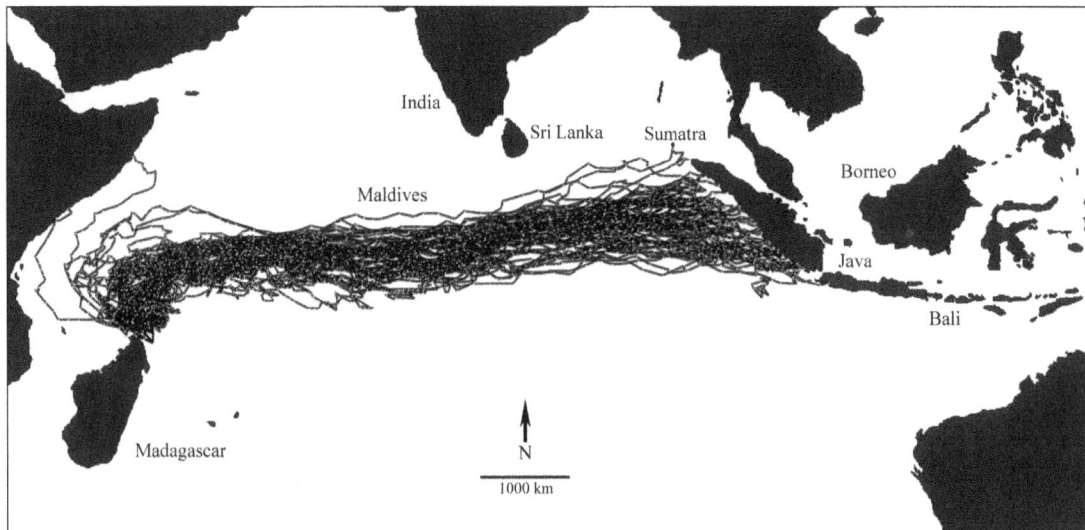

Figure 5. Directed sailing from Madagascar to Indonesia in April.

Discussion and conclusions

Computer simulations of seafaring between Indonesia and Madagascar have provided insight into the challenges facing prehistoric settlers. Our findings indicate that downwind sailing from the Bali or Sunda Straits did not result in reaching Madagascar. Some vessels would have made it as far to the west as 88° E from the Bali Straits and 83° E from the Sunda Straits during the months of April through August. After reaching those positions, vessels are forced back to Indonesia. Using a downwind strategy from these positions does not result in the discovery of any islands. Downwind sailing from off the northwest tip of Sumatra proves more intriguing. From December through March, vessels could reach as far west as 72° E before being swept back to the east. The ability to sail this far to the west would bring vessels to the Maldives and the Chagos Archipelago. In the months of November and December, downwind sailing could bring vessels from off Sumatra to Sri Lanka in about 40 days. Downwind sailing from the India/ Sri Lanka position is also interesting, particularly in January, when vessels pass through the Maldives before sailing on to either Madagascar or Indonesia. At other times of the year, vessels also pass through the Maldives, but only move to Indonesia.

The pattern of downwind simulations suggests the Maldives, and to a lesser extent the Chagos Archipelago, may have been important stopping points on the voyage to Madagascar from either the India/Sri Lanka or Sumatra positions. They may also have been important for travel from India/Sri Lanka to Indonesia. The Maldives and the Chagos Archipelago are not well known archaeologically, however. Although Maldivians were aware of the Chagos Archipelago (Ramiro-Frias 1999:19), the archipelago was not permanently settled until the French arrived in the second half of the 18th century. According to Maloney (1980:75), Buddhists arrived in the Maldives in the first few centuries AD. The islands were occupied at the time (1980:49–70), but the antiquity of occupation has not yet been determined. That the Maldivians were capable sailors at the time of the initial settlement of Madagascar from Indonesia is suggested by the record of Ammianus Marcellinus (1980:72) writing in the fourth century AD, who provides a list of emissaries sent to Rome, including Maldivians.

People voyaging from Indonesia to Madagascar by simply using a strategy of downwind sailing and starting from December to March could have broken the journey in the Maldives. There, they could have resupplied and provisioned, and sailed to a favourable position for continuing on to Madagascar, particularly in January. However, there does appear to have been two-way contact between the two regions. Downwind sailing from Madagascar to Indonesia is not possible at any time of the year, nor can the Maldives be reached. From May to July, it would have been possible to use the route described in the *Periplus of the Erythraean Sea* to travel along the African coast and then on to southern India and Sri Lanka, and from there to Indonesia.

Sailing with a heading towards Madagascar, and with the ability to sail across and to windward, is more complex. From a position in the Bali Straits, some vessels could make it to the Maldives in June and July, but the numbers are too low to make this a viable route for regular contact. A fairly large number of vessels would reach Sri Lanka if starting out in April, but the durations would be rather long. March would be the most favourable month for westward sailing to Madagascar. While just over half of the vessels were successful in the simulations, the numbers would be much greater if the Maldives were used as a waypoint. As with sailing from the Bali Straits seasonally, a significant number of vessels would have landed in Sri Lanka. Vessels starting out during January and February from off the northwest tip of Sumatra would all arrive in Madagascar, most in a reasonable length of time. The Maldives would once again be strategic in the voyages. As with the other Indonesian starting points, a significant number of vessels made landfall in Sri Lanka in the simulations. From December through March, vessels simply heading to the southwest from Sri Lanka would reach Madagascar via the Maldives in a fairly reasonable length of time. Sailing from Madagascar to Indonesia with an eastward heading is possible from December through April. The April success rate is 100 percent. The Maldives are also strategic to these voyages.

Durations for the simulations with a heading are considerably longer than is likely in reality. Only a single heading was chosen and maintained throughout the voyages. Sailors would have had the flexibility to change their heading throughout the voyage, moving out of areas with unfavourable winds and considerably shortening the duration of the voyage. Still, the patterns shown by the simulations do reveal the possibilities for direct contact between Indonesia and Madagascar. They also show the interconnectedness of sea routes in the Indian Ocean.

Simple downwind sailing could account for westward voyages from the northwest tip of Sumatra if the voyages were begun in November and December, but such voyages would have required use of the Maldives as a waypoint. The voyages would be lengthy, with a large number of failures. Unsuccessful voyages would not necessarily be disastrous for the crews, as most vessels would end up back in Indonesia or in Sri Lanka. The strategy of using downwind sailing to reach Madagascar from Indonesia seems unlikely, even using the Maldives as a stopping point. Downwind voyages from Madagascar are ruled out to Indonesia, but not to western India and Sri Lanka. In both instances, downwind sailing would need to follow a primarily coastal route, similar to that of the *Periplus of the Erythraean Sea*. Downwind sailing to either Madagascar or Indonesia from Sri Lanka in January and February is an interesting possibility, but the durations are rather long. The Maldives would again figure prominently in such voyages. Sailing on a westward heading from Indonesia would be most successful from off the northwestern tip of Sumatra starting in January and February, with most vessels passing through the Maldives. From the India/Sri Lanka position, with a southwest heading, starting in December through March, success in reaching Madagascar is high, and also would involve the Maldives. If leaving Madagascar in April with an eastward heading, the success rate for reaching Indonesia is 100 percent. Once again, the Maldives would be encountered.

In conclusion, if the weather patterns were followed, direct contact from northern Indonesia with Madagascar, and in the reverse direction, is feasible. However, it seems likely the Maldives, in such a strategic position, would have been relied on for resupplying and waiting for favourable conditions to continue the voyage. It might be expected that evidence of these stopovers will be found archaeologically in the Maldives, particularly if these voyages were repeated over time.

Acknowledgments

We would like to thank the editors for inviting us to contribute a paper to this important volume. Thanks also to reviewers who provided useful comments and especially to Atholl who has helped inspire a new generation of archaeologists.

References

Adalaar, K.A. 1989. Malay influence on Malagasy: linguistic and culture–historical implications. *Oceanic Linguistics* 28:1–46.

Avis, C., Á. Montenegro and A. Weaver 2007. The discovery of Western Oceania: a new perspective. *Journal of Island and Coastal Archaeology* 2:197–209.

Bolger, P.C. 1984. *100 Small Boat Rigs*. Camden Maine: International Marine.

Bombard, A. 1986. *The Bombard Story*. London: Grafton Books.

Breen, C. and Lane, P.J. 2003. Archaeological approaches to East Africa's changing seascapes. *World Archaeology* 35:469–489.

Burney, D.A., L. Pigott Burney, L.R. Godfrey, W.L. Jungers, S.M. Goodman, H.T. Wright and A.J.T. Jull 2004. A chronology for late prehistoric Madagascar. *Journal of Human Evolution* 47:25–63.

Callaghan, R.T. 2001. Ceramic age seafaring and interaction potential in the Antilles: a computer simulation. *Current Anthropology* 42:11–22.

Callaghan, R.T. 2003a. Comments on the mainland origins of the Preceramic cultures of the Greater Antilles. *Latin American Antiquity* 14:323–338.

Callaghan, R.T. 2003b. Prehistoric trade between Ecuador and west Mexico: a computer simulation of coastal voyages. *Antiquity* 77:796–804.

Callaghan, R.T. 2003c. The use of simulation models to estimate frequency and location of Japanese Edo period wrecks along the Canadian Pacific Coast. *Canadian Journal of Archaeology* 27:62–82.

Callaghan, R.T. and S.M. Fitzpatrick 2007. On the relative isolation of a Micronesian archipelago during the historic period: the Palau case study. *International Journal of Nautical Archaeology* 36:353–364.

Callaghan, R.T. and S.M. Fitzpatrick 2008. Examining prehistoric migration patterns in the Palauan archipelago, western Micronesia: A Computer Simulated Analysis of Drift Voyaging. *Asian Perspectives* 47:28–44.

Clark, C.D., S.M. Garrod and M. Parker Pearson 1998. Landscape archaeology and remote sensing in southern Madagascar. *African Archaeological Review* 19:1461–1477.

Dahl, O.C. 1951. *Malgache et Maanyan: Une comparision linguistique*. Oslo: Egede Institutett.

Dahl, O.C. 1977. La subdivision de la famille Barito et la place du Malgache. *Acta Orientalia* 34:77–134.

Dening, G.M. 1963. The geographical knowledge of the Polynesians and the nature of inter-island contact, *Polynesian Navigation*. J. Golson (ed), *Polynesian Society Memoir* No. 34:138–153.

Dewar, R.E. 1997. Does it matter that Madagascar is an island? *Human Ecology* 25:481–489.

Dewar, R.E. 1995. Of nets and trees: untangling the reticulate and dendritic in Madagascar's prehistory. *World Archaeology* 26:301–318.

Dewar, R.E. and T.W. Henry 1993. The culture history of Madagascar. *Journal of World Prehistory* 7:417–466.

Heikell, R. 1999. *Indian Ocean Cruising Guide*. St. Ives Cambridgeshire: Imray Laurie Norie and Wilson Ltd.

Hingston, M., S.M. Goodman, J.U. Ganzhorn and S. Sommer 2005. Reconstruction of the colonization of southern Madagascar by introduced *Rattus rattus*. *Journal of Biogeography* 32:1549–1559.

Howay, F.W. 1944. Some lengthy open-boat voyages in the Pacific Ocean. *American Neptune* 4:53–57.

Hurles, M.E., B.C. Sykes, M.A. Jobling and P. Forster 2005. The dual origin of the Malagasy in Island Southeast Asia and East Africa: evidence from maternal and paternal lineages. *American Journal of Human Genetics* 76:894–901.

Irwin, G. 1992. *The Prehistoric Exploration and Colonization of the Pacific*. Cambridge: Cambridge University Press.

LeBaron B. R. Jr 1954. Eastern sail affinities, Part II. *American Neptune* 13:185–211.

Lee, E.C.B. 1965. *Survival at Sea*. Rome: Centro Internazionale Radio Medico.

Lee, E.C.B. and K. Lee. 1980. *Safety and Survival at Sea*. New York: Norton.

Levison, M., R.G. Ward and J.W. Webb. 1973. *The Settlement of Polynesia, a Computer Simulation*. Canberra: Australian University Press.

Lewis, D. 1972. *We, the Navigators*. Honolulu: University of Hawaii Press.

McCance, R.A., C.C. Ungley, J.W.L. Crosfill and E.M. Widdowson 1956. *The Hazards to Men Lost at Sea, 1940-44*. Medical Research Council Special Report No. 291. London: Medical Research Council.

McGrail, S.. 2001. *Boats of the World: From the Stone Age to Medieval Times*. Oxford: Oxford University Press.

Maloney, C. 1980. *People of the Maldive Islands*. Bombay: Orient Longman.

Montenegro, Á., M.E. Reneé Hetherington and A.J. Weaver 2006. Modelling pre-historic transoceanic crossings into the Americas. *Quaternary Science Reviews* 25:1323–1338.

Parker Pearson, M. 1997. Close encounters of the worst kind: Malagasy resistance and colonial disasters in Southern Madagascar. *World Archaeology* 28:393–417.

Pigache, J.P. 1970. La problème anthropobiologique à Madagascar. *Taloha* 3:175–177.

Romero-Frias, X. 1999. *The Maldive Islanders, a Study of an Ancient Ocean Kingdom*. Barcelona: Nova Ethnographia Indica.

Schoff, W.H. 1912. *The Periplus of the Erythraean Sea*. New York: Longmans, Green and Co.

United States Navy 1995. *Marine Climatic Atlas of the World*. Asheville: National Climatic Data Center.

4

Friction zones in Lapita colonisation

Geoffrey Clark

Department of Archaeology and Natural History, Australian National University, Australia
geoffrey.clark@anu.edu.au

Stuart Bedford

Department Archaeology and Natural History, Australian National University, Australia

Introduction

A landscape can be conceived as composed of aggregates of factors that either impede or facilitate the movement of living organisms (Lee 1996). Landscapes that are hostile, fragmented, unfamiliar or difficult to reach are resistant to settlement and are colonisation 'friction zones', while those that are familiar, continuous, easy to reach and resource rich support species establishment. In this paper, we examine Lapita colonisation using the ecological concept of friction landscapes (i.e. Joly *et al.* 2003). We begin by reviewing the major points in the Lapita distribution where colonisation is argued to have been negatively impacted by the properties of a particular environment. To evaluate these, we examine, first, how colonisation 'patchiness' has in several cases been proposed and later modified during the course of Lapita studies, as a result of improved sampling and better understanding of the palaeolandscape. Second, we construct a simple friction model of Lapita colonisation to identify points where Neolithic settlement may have been difficult, and compare these 'friction zones' with those indicated by the known distribution of Lapita sites.

Neolithic colonisation of the Indo-Pacific region is conventionally partitioned into three geographic areas. The oldest movement from mainland Asia is suggested to have spread first through the Philippines and northern Borneo–Sulawesi, with another branch (based on differences in the earliest ceramic assemblages) occupying eastern Indonesia (Bellwood 2005; Spriggs 2007). At some point – palaeoecological opinion suggests human arrival at 4500 BP, while archaeological sites are more recent at 3500 BP – one or more of these groups ventured into the Pacific Ocean and colonised Palau, the Marianas and probably Yap (Dodson and Intoh 1999; Athens *et al.* 2004; Clark 2005). Another movement brought Austronesian speakers, known to archaeologists under the Lapita rubric, to the Bismarck Archipelago by 3400–3300 BP and as far east as Samoa by 2850 BP (Green 2002; Specht 2007).

The Lapita colonisation of the Bismarck Archipelago–Samoa area (Figure 1) is interesting as its geography includes elements common to both of the other Neolithic colonisation events, with in situ non-Austronesian populations in the large and mostly intervisible islands of the Bismarck Archipelago–Solomon Islands, and uninhabited and generally smaller and increasingly remote landmasses at the eastern extent of Lapita in Fiji–West Polynesia. Archaeologically, Lapita is the best known of the Neolithic migrations and the combination of a comparatively rich material record and a diverse colonisation landscape could provide insight into the structure and pattern of the other prehistoric dispersals.

This is plausible, as Neolithic expansions in island Asia and the Pacific share a punctuated dispersal chronology (Anderson 2001), represented archaeologically by the spread of new types and styles of material culture over large areas. Similarly, the distribution of the three prehistoric expansions in each area is not geographically uniform, and they exhibit colonisation 'patchiness' at large and small scales. For example, the avoidance of small islands within an archipelago is proposed for Palau (Wickler 2001; cf. Clark *et al.* 2006), the avoidance of an archipelago is suggested by Sheppard and Walter (2006, cf. Felgate 2007) for the main Solomon Islands by early Lapita groups, and Austronesian colonisation either failed in, or avoided, Australia and inland New Guinea.

The reality of 'patchiness' in a colonisation distribution is important to evaluate, as the 'gaps', if real, point to the limits of Neolithic demographic, economic and transportation systems, and it informs whether maritime expansion and migration, for instance, proceeded mainly by long-distance leapfrogging, or demic wave-of-advance movement, or some combination of the two (Burley and Dickinson 2001; Anderson 2003; Diamond and Bellwood 2003; Fort 2003).

Lapita gaps: Past and present

Understanding of the geographic distribution of Lapita emerged gradually in the early 20th century with the discovery of distinctive 'dentate' ceramics at Watom in the west (Meyer 1909), New Caledonia in the centre (Piroutet 1917) and Tonga in the east (McKern 1929). The investigation of Lapita sites became an increasing focus of archaeological activity through the 1960s and 1970s, resulting in the discovery of sites in new archipelagos, including Reef/Santa Cruz (Green and Cresswell 1976), and Vanuatu (Hébert 1965; Hedrick and Shutler 1968; Garanger 1971), and additional Lapita deposits in Island New Guinea, New Caledonia and Fiji. The western and eastern margins of Lapita were extended to their current limits by the discovery of Lapita pottery on Aitape (Terrell and Welsch 1997), Manus (Kennedy 1981) and Samoa (Jennings 1974).

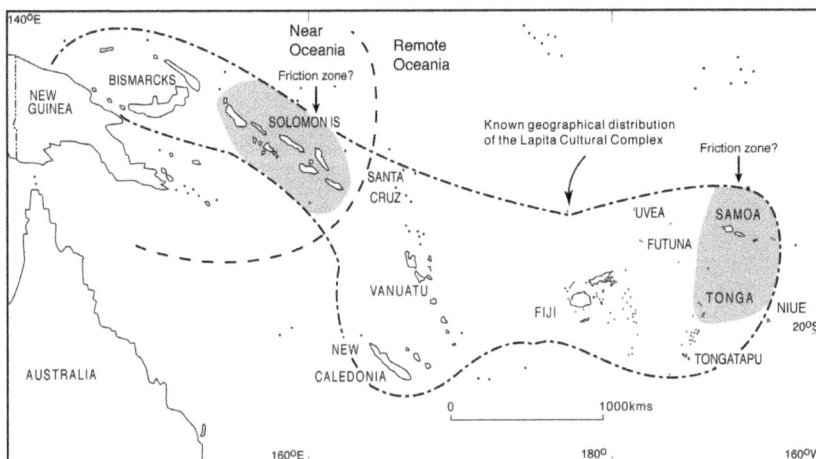

Figure 1. Map of the Lapita distribution and location of potential 'friction zones'.

By the 1980s, Lapita was not only recognised as a widespread cultural complex that stretched from Island New Guinea in the west to Samoa in the east (Golson 1971), but significantly was seen to represent the first population to occupy Remote Oceania (Spriggs 1984). Before the primacy of Lapita was established, there were several other ceramic styles (i.e. paddle impressed and incised and applied relief) that represented potentially different waves of prehistoric migration (Golson 1968:10). With such a crowded field of colonising groups, geographic gaps in the Lapita distribution could be explained by the initial settlement of an area by one of the 'non-Lapita' ceramic cultures. Once the chronological position of Lapita was clarified, such an explanation was no longer tenable. However, the presence of non-Austronesians in Near Oceania (Bismarck Archipelago–Solomon Islands) since the late-Pleistocene presents an analogous situation in which the success of Lapita colonisation might have been controlled by the strength of the indigenous response to incoming migrants.

Nonetheless, ongoing research has tended to diminish the size and extent of gaps in the Lapita distribution, with new sites recorded in Vanuatu (Bedford 2006), the Loyalty Islands (Sand 1995) and the Western Province of the Solomon Islands (Felgate 2003). At the same time, more Lapita sites were also being found in Fiji and Tonga (Burley *et al.* 2001; Clark and Anderson 2001), and the tally of Lapita sites in Island New Guinea has continued to grow (Specht and Torrence 2007; Summerhayes 2007).

A key to much of this success has been the recognition of factors that have transformed palaeolandscapes, particularly tectonic and volcanic activity, along with sea-level change (Dickinson and Burley 2007). The exemplar is Samoa which has a single Lapita site removed by tectonic subsidence 4 m below its original position, so that it is now underwater (Dickinson and Green 1998). Groube (1971:279) had earlier claimed that the absence of Lapita in Samoa after 'thorough archaeological examination' was real, although he did not discuss why Lapita colonisation should have failed to reach Samoa.

The increasing number of Lapita sites, coupled with improved understanding of the palaeolandscape, provides fertile ground for refining models of colonisation, since variability in the size, number and location of sites across an island or archipelago might well result from landscapes that were unfamiliar and difficult to occupy prehistorically (Rockman and Steel 2003). Such 'friction zones' or 'gaps' in the Lapita geography have been recently proposed for the central Solomons and the northern Tonga–Samoa region (Figure 1).

Sheppard and Walter (2006:48) argue that during the earliest phase of Lapita expansion, the main Solomons were entirely leapfrogged, with migrants travelling directly from Island New Guinea to the Reef/Santa Cruz Islands. The 'leapfrogging' pattern of movement of early Lapita colonists is thought to be the result of negative and positive factors. On the one hand, the already established population in the Solomons inhibited early Lapita occupation, and on the other, the discovery that uninhabited islands east of the main Solomons held dense and easily accessible marine and terrestrial resources encouraged long-distance movement and avoidance of the main Solomon Islands.

In northern Tonga and Samoa, the number of recorded Lapita sites is much lower than in southern Tonga (Burley 2007). The western end of 'Upolu has a single Lapita site, Mulifanua, that is submerged from flexural subsidence of the lithosphere under volcanic loading. Active volcanism during the late Holocene has also affected site preservation and visibility on the large islands, as has colluvial infilling of valley floors (Green 2002:132). Subsidence is much less on other islands in the Samoa group (e.g. Tutuila), but except for Mulifanua, no other Lapita settlements have been found, despite large-scale investigations associated with development (Addison and Morrison In press).

Across the 71 islands of Vava'u in northern Tonga, only five Lapita sites have been identified, and all are small and cover no more than 1500 m² (Burley 2007). The distribution of late-ceramic plainware sites is also relatively sparse in northern Tonga. This scenario is in striking contrast to central and southern Tonga, where the density of ceramic sites suggests rapid population expansion during Lapita and post-Lapita phases (Burley *et al.* 2001; Burley 2007). Burley (2007:196) notes that the fading Lapita presence in Vava'u, and by extension Samoa, reflects the fact that these islands are the 'frontier periphery' of Lapita colonisation (Burley 2007:196). Addison and Morrison (In press) go further and suggest that colonisation of Samoa was beyond the sustainable limits of Lapita expansion, and the archipelago was not settled permanently until c. 2400 cal. BP.

In the following sections we explore the geographic relationship between islands in the Lapita sphere to identify which island groups might have been 'unfamiliar' friction environments that could have slowed, restricted or redirected migrant movement.

The geography of Lapita expansion

Migrant frequency and volume have been shown to decrease as distance increases (Ravenstein 1882; Lee 1996). Translated to oceanic settings, large islands separated from one another by small water gaps should be colonised more quickly than small and remote islands. This might not happen when the coastal niches of large islands are already occupied by in situ populations, or where landscapes are subject to frequent natural catastrophes (tsunamis, volcanic eruption), or where environments are associated with high mortality from diseases, such as malaria. In such cases, large islands might still be occupied to some extent, settled by colonies in peripheral locations – for instance, on small islands adjacent to the mainland.

As simulation of colonisation indicates that inter-group contact, particularly for non-related marriage partners, was essential to demographic success (Moore 2001), it is important to note that the existence of non-Austronesian groups in the Bismarck Archipelago–Solomons region might well have been a 'positive', rather than a 'negative factor' in the establishment of at least some Lapita colonies. Integration between migrants and indigenous groups would provide both demographic support for the generational growth of migrant communities and access to coastal and inland resources. The almost complete absence of archaeological knowledge about the nature of Lapita and non-Lapita interaction anywhere in the Bismarcks–Solomon Islands means that we cannot yet estimate either the significance or the sign (positive or negative) of prehistoric interaction in relation to Lapita colonisation (Pawley 2007:40–42).

The facility with which prehistoric people could reach new lands is a function, among other factors, of island number, size, height, distance, seafaring skills and technology, and the particular wind, current and seasonal weather patterns around each landmass.

As a first step to modelling Lapita friction zones, a total of eight physical and distance variables were calculated. The definition of 'large island' and small 'water gap' is naturally problematic (e.g. Specht 2007). For the purpose of our analysis, an island area of 250 sq km was considered 'large'. Tongatapu, for example, has an area of 260 sq km and was the focus of an early Lapita occupation (Burley 2007). We know that Lapita groups occupied islands with an area less than 250 sq km, but in the West Pacific, where the earliest Lapita sites are found, many such islands were either close to, or were part of, an archipelago with an island area of 250 sq km or more.

'Large' islands as defined above are common across the known Lapita distribution and its margins, with the area from southeastern New Guinea to Niue having some 52 'large' islands (Table 1). The total includes those where a Lapita presence has not yet been recorded, but which lie on either the western (Karkar, Umboi, Long) or eastern (Niue) fringes of the current distribution (Table 1).

The latitude and longitude of the 'large' islands was recorded using the Google Earth program using the approximate island centre as a reference point. Land area (square kilometres) and maximum height (metres above sea level) were also recorded (Kennedy 1974; Carter 1984; Douglas and Douglas 1989), as these values correlate approximately with geological and environmental diversity (Table 1). For instance, Rennell, Tongatapu and Niue are in relative terms, small (260–630 sq km) and low (73–154 m asl) limestone islands.

To estimate the degree of landscape 'fragmentation', we counted the total number of 'large' islands within c. 200 nautical miles (370 km) of each of the 52 'large' islands (measured from any point on the coastline of an island using the 'ruler' function in Google Earth), and the number of separate archipelagos with an island of 250 sq km area within 200 nm of a large island. A value of 200 nm for practical Lapita voyaging in the Indo-Pacific is a reasonably conservative figure, based on Neolithic long voyages in excess of 400 nm to reach Palau from the Philippines, and to reach Fiji from southern Vanuatu (440 nm), but it does not take into account specific wind and current conditions, which would require a more detailed analysis (i.e. Irwin 1992; Di Piazza *et al.* 2007). The Mariana Islands are greater than 1000 nm from the Philippines and suggest the possibility of Neolithic voyages much longer than 400 nm, but they may have been settled by island hopping from Palau to Yap (230 nm), and then from Yap to Guam (420 nm), which spans the practical-to-difficult voyaging range suggested here. The 200 nm value is also within the approximate voyaging distance needed to reach Ndende (Santa Cruz) from the Solomon Islands (San Cristobel), and to travel from Ndende to northern Vanuatu.

The success of human colonisation lies ultimately in occupying terrestrial territory, with the great majority of habitable land in the Pacific Ocean contained in archipelago clusters (geologically, island arcs or volcanic hot spots). Locations from which it was feasible to reach several new island groups within a 200 nm zone could represent important migrant dispersal 'nodes'. In contrast, islands that could only be reached by voyages substantially greater than 200 nm are likely to have been harder to colonise in terms of seafaring and its demographic consequence – the transport of adequate numbers of migrants to ensure colony success. Therefore, the shortest distance separating a 'large' island from its closest 'large' neighbour was measured, as was the shortest distance separating each island from the closest distinct archipelago.

Variables were standardised by taking the raw value and subtracting the mean, and dividing the total by the standard deviation. The standardised variables were analysed with multidimensional scaling (MDS) and the results evaluated with hierarchical cluster analysis (HCA) using SPSS 13.0 software. MDS attempts to find the structure in a set of distance measures between cases so that the Euclidean distance between points in an MDS plot reflects the actual dissimilarities between cases. The effectiveness of the procedure in representing the variance of the scaled data against the inter-point distance is measured by the RSQ (squared correlation index) statistic. RSQ values are the proportion of variance in the scaled data that is accounted for by the corresponding distance between cases in the MDS plot. RSQ values ≥ 0.6 are considered acceptable. In short, the distance between islands in the MDS plots reflects their similarity/dissimilarity.

Three MDS analyses were run. The first examined the relationship between location (latitude and longitude), land area and maximum height above sea level to explore island variability. The second MDS examined landmass fragmentation and archipelago accessibility using four variables (number of large islands within 200 nm, number of distinct island groups within 200 nm of a large island, distance from a large island to the nearest 'large' island, and distance from a

Table 1. Islands with an area greater than 250 sq km used in the statistical analysis.

Name	Region	Area (sq km)	Latitude (S)	Longitude (W)	Height (m)
Mussau	Mussau	400	1.257	149.353	650
Manus	Admiralty	1639	2.56	146.582	720
Karkar	PNG-Coast	400	4.381	145.585	1660
Long	PNG-Coast	500	5.209	147.703	1158
Umboi	PNG-Coast	777	5.392	147.563	1655
New Britain	New Britain	37736	5.441	150.431	2500
New Hanover	New Hanover	1190	2.328	150.162	957
New Ireland	New Ireland	9600	3.198	151.598	2150
Fergusson	Entrecasteaux	1437	9.313	150.394	2072
Goodenough	Entrecasteaux	687	9.204	150.146	2566
Normanby	Entrecasteaux	1040	10.126	151.114	1100
Tagula	Entrecasteaux	866	11.310	153.283	806
Trobriand	Entrecasteaux	267	8.366	151.834	55
Woodlark	Entrecasteaux	873	9.743	152.469	225
Bougainville	Solomons	9317	6.115	155.188	2792
Buka	Solomons	682	5.155	154.381	365
Choisel	Solomons	2538	7.456	156.598	1067
Guaudalcanal	Solomons	6475	9.369	160.100	2447
Kolombangara	Solomons	688	7.592	157.446	1768
Malaita	Solomons	3885	9.060	161.051	1433
Maramasike	Solomons	481	9.341	161.281	518
New Georgia	Solomons	3365	8.197	157.396	860
Rendova	Solomons	411	8.330	157.182	1060
Rennell	Solomons	630	11.385	160.169	154
San Cristobel	Solomons	3191	10.358	161.529	1250
Santa Isabel	Solomons	4660	8.036	159.674	1219
Vangunu	Solomons	509	8.383	157.598	1082
Vella Lavella	Solomons	629	7.446	156.391	808
Ndende	Reef/Santa Cruz	506	10.436	165.565	550
Ambrym	Vanuatu	678	16.151	168.711	1270
Aoba	Vanuatu	402	15.236	167.501	1496
Efate	Vanuatu	900	17.406	168.243	647
Epi	Vanuatu	445	16.437	168.137	833
Erromango	Vanuatu	881	18.509	169.869	886
Gaua	Vanuatu	328	14.171	167.316	797
Maewo	Vanuatu	304	15.111	168.810	811
Malakula	Vanuatu	2041	16.223	167.323	879
Pentacost	Vanuatu	491	15.456	168.114	947
Santo	Vanuatu	3885	15.225	166.571	1879
Tanna	Vanuatu	550	19.302	169.199	1084
Vanua Lava	Vanuatu	334	13.505	167.291	946

continued on facing page

Name	Region	Area (sq km)	Latitude (S)	Longitude (W)	Height (m)
Grande Terre	New Caledonia	16750	21.229	165.272	1618
Lifou	New Caledonia	1150	20.582	167.139	85
Mare	New Caledonia	650	21.322	167.592	129
Kandavu	Fiji	407	19.052	178.134	660
Taveuni	Fiji	268	16.508	179.576	1241
Viti Levu	Fiji	5534	16.346	179.133	1032
Vanua Levu	Fiji	10390	17.486	178.088	1224
Tongatapu	Tonga	260	21.111	175.116	82
Upolu	Samoa	1100	13.560	171.448	1143
Savai'i	Samoa	1820	13.377	172.247	1858
Niue	Niue	264	19.403	169.520	73

See text for data sources. Note that the placement of Buka and Bougainville in the Solomons reflects their proximity to the islands of the Solomon group, rather than their contemporary political status.

large island to its closest inter-archipelago neighbour). The third MDS study combined all of the variables to assess which islands might have been particularly resistant to Lapita colonisation.

MDS results

1. Island location, area and height

The first MDS plot (RSQ=0.985) was largely influenced by latitude, longitude and island area, with New Britain as an outlier due to its large size, which is more than twice that of any other island (Figure 2). Islands with an area more than 1800 sq km are located through most of the Lapita distribution, including the Bismarcks, Solomons, Vanuatu, New Caledonia, Fiji and Samoa. The smallest of the 'large' islands in area and height are the uplifted limestone islands of Mare, Lifou, Tongatapu and Niue. Both Vanuatu and the Solomons have numerous islands of more than 250 sq km, including some very large islands such as Santo, Guadalcanal and

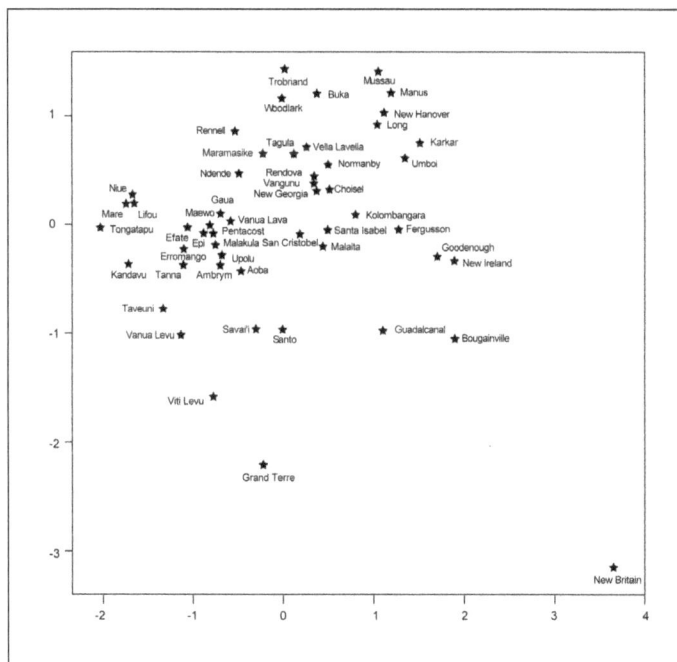

Figure 2. MDS plot of 'large' island location, area and height.

Bougainville (Buka and Bougainville are geographically part of the northern Solomon Islands). These two archipelagos are clearly 'rich' in substantial landmasses and might be expected to have a more complicated history of internal colonisation than islands that are smaller or more remote from neighbouring clusters of large islands.

2. Landscape fragmentation and relative accessibility

The second MDS analysis (RSQ=0.978) considered the fragmentation or accessibility of the different island landscapes encountered by Lapita colonisers by using a value of 200 nm as a nominal voyaging range within which colonisation could have proceeded rapidly given the availability of suitable 'large' islands.

The plot (Figure 3) shows three groups and three outliers (Ndende (Santa Cruz), Tongatapu and Niue). Group 1 is composed of islands within 200 nm of four to eight large islands, and predominantly within 130 nm of another archipelago. These islands should have been reached relatively quickly from adjacent landmasses during Lapita colonisation. Several of the western islands (New Ireland, New Britain, Buka, Woodlark and Manus) are within 200 nm of three different island groups. As these islands are connected potentially to almost as many external large islands as internal, they are likely to have had complicated exogenous migrant sequences.

The second group contains islands that are within 200 nm of nine to 13 other large islands and within 40 nm of another 250 sq km island. The group includes all of Vanuatu and most of the Solomons. These islands are reasonably distant, however, from other island groups (130–330 nm). Once reached, colonists were likely to have had frequent interactions within these two archipelagos and a lower frequency of external movements.

The only island in the 'large' category between the Solomon Islands and Vanuatu is Ndende, which is an outlier in the MDS plot, as it has only four large islands around the 200 nm radius (all are in adjacent island groups). From the Bismarcks to the end of the main Solomon Islands, any large island could be reached by a voyage of 100–150 nm, while the inter-archipelago distance to and from Ndende increases to 200–220 nm. If Ndende and nearby smaller islands were colonisation 'nodes' to which Lapita groups regularly travelled en route to Vanuatu, New Caledonia and islands further east, we should expect to find evidence of numerous large sites with evidence of abundant imports from the west.

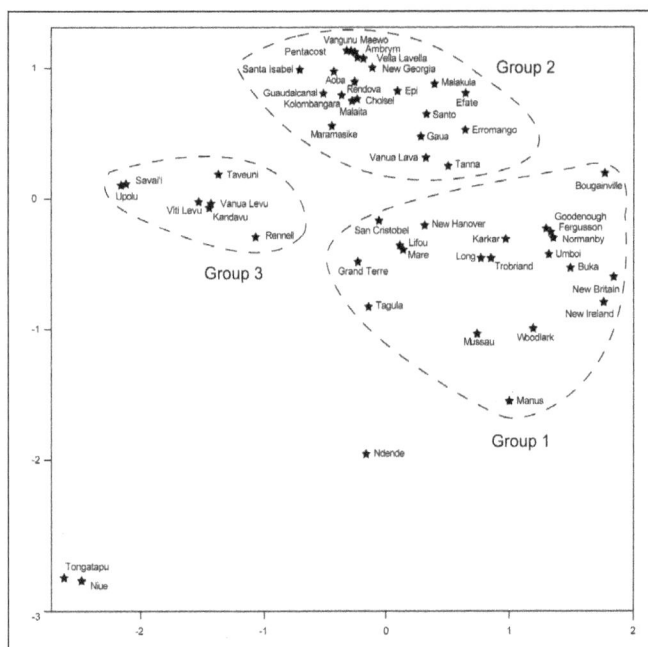

Figure 3. MDS plot of landscape fragmentation and archipelago accessibility. See text for discussion of Group 1, Group 2 and Group 3. Note the outlier position of Tongatapu and Niue.

A test of the argument advanced by Sheppard and Walter (2006) for Lapita avoidance of the Solomons would be a large-scale study of sherd composition from early Lapita assemblages in the Reef/Santa Cruz which demonstrated that imported pottery, like much of the obsidian, was only brought from locations west of the Solomon Islands. However, if a proportion of imported ceramics was found to have been made in the Solomons, that would support the possibility of incremental Lapita movement through the Solomon chain, rather than archipelago avoidance.

The third group consists of Fiji–Samoa and Rennell. These islands are within 100 nm of one to five 'large' islands, but are increasingly distant from any other island group (305–460 nm). Lapita colonists reaching these islands found themselves in an increasingly fragmented environment where there were fewer large islands and greater distances between island groups. Tongatapu and Niue are extreme outliers, as they are, in relative terms, remote from another large island, the closest more than 300 nm away. However, Tongatapu has numerous small islands in its vicinity, including several of volcanic origin, that give the archipelago greater environmental diversity and inter-island accessibility than Niue.

3. Familiar and unfamiliar landscapes

Combining the two sets of variables in the final MDS analysis (RSQ=0.954) shows that in island terms, the large area of New Britain and small dimensions of Niue and Tongatapu are highly anomalous compared with the islands typically encountered by Lapita colonists (Figure 4). A dispersed group (Group 1) contains islands to the west of the Solomons that can be reached from one or more adjacent island groups within 100–130 nm, highlighting the relative continuity of the island landscape for human colonisation. The tighter clustering in Group 2 emphasises the similarity between the Solomon Islands and Vanuatu as island-rich and internally accessible landscapes, the main difference being the sizeable water gap separating the southern Solomons from northern Vanuatu, and the presence of non-Austronesians in the Solomons. After Vanuatu, there are fewer large islands, and the Y-axis in the plot separates landmasses with a large area such as New Caledonia, Viti Levu, Savai'i and Vanua Levu that are nonetheless 'distant' (200 nm or more) from another archipelago.

Small and relatively remote islands include Ndende and the raised limestone islands of Rennell, Lifou and Mare. Niue and Tongatapu are extreme outliers, and they clearly represent

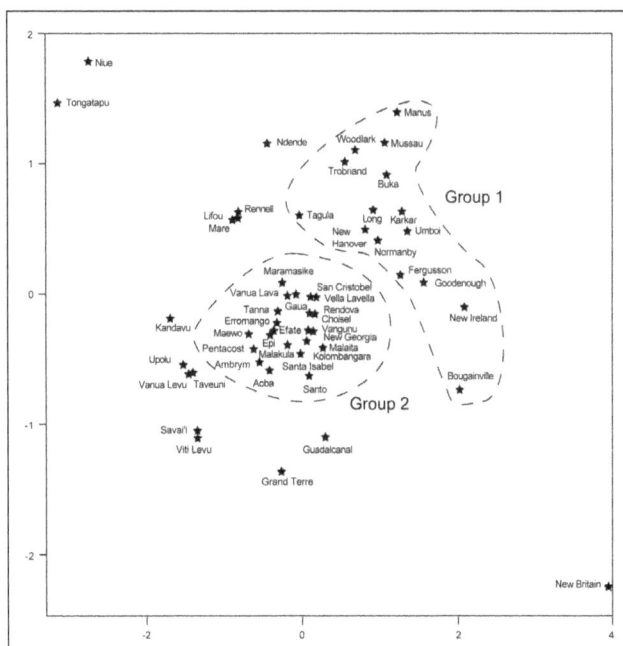

Figure 4. MDS plot of combined variables used in previous analyses. See text for discussion of Group 1 and Group 2. Note the outlier position of Tongatapu, Niue and New Britain.

environments that were in relative terms unfamiliar in their size, geology and level of 'remoteness' compared with islands in the west of the Lapita distribution. Such islands may have been potentially difficult landscapes for Lapita groups to initially colonise.

Discussion and conclusion

The pattern of Lapita colonisation taken from the existing distribution of sites suggests significant gaps in the Solomon Islands and in northern Tonga–Samoa (Figure 1). The absence of early occupation in the Solomon Islands has been taken to mean that poor relations with non-Austronesians were a factor that could not be surmounted by Lapita migrants. Thus, it is proposed that the establishment of Lapita colonists further east was made by leapfrogging the entire Solomon archipelago (Sheppard and Walter 2006) to reach the uninhabited Reef/ Santa Cruz (Ndende) islands – a canoe voyage of more than 800 nm. In contrast, the low density of Lapita sites in northern Tonga and their absence, except for Mulifanua, in Samoa suggests demographic exhaustion combined with the difficulties of voyaging in an increasingly fragmented environment.

The assumption of long-distance voyages implied by the avoidance of the Solomons is somewhat at odds with a proposed slowdown in colonisation in northern Tonga–Samoa, as the ability to make maritime journeys of c. 800 nm must to some extent counter the effects of a low population density. An effective maritime reach of c. 400 nm would, for instance, be sufficient to connect colonising groups across the entire Fiji–West Polynesian area.

In view of the uncertainty concerning the reliability of archaeological site distributions, we suggest three criteria be used to further evaluate distribution 'gaps' and 'friction zones'.

First, the reliability of Lapita site distributions should be further tested in archaeological and palaeoenvironmental investigations. Felgate (2007), for instance, has argued strongly against the leapfrogging model for the Solomons, and instead makes the case that the geomorphology of the region, along with an apparent preference for Lapita habitation in the inter-tidal zone, has made the discovery of early sites difficult. In northern Tonga, a pollen record from Avai'o'vuna swamp on Vava'u shows that charcoal from human fires was deposited at 2890–2460 cal. BP (Beta-114012, 2620±80 BP) and continues in the record afterwards (Fall 2005), suggesting a constant and perhaps low-density Lapita presence on Vava'u, about 300 nm from Samoa.

Second, 'anomalous' site distributions can be compared with those of neighbouring areas for consistency. Like the Solomon Islands, the Bismarck Archipelago was already occupied before the arrival of Lapita groups. As Lapita groups were able to co-exist in some manner with non-Austronesians in the Bismarcks, it is unclear why they were unable to do so anywhere in the island-rich Solomons. In the case of Samoa, islands such as Niuatoputapu to the south (140 nm from Samoa) and 'Uvea in the east (200 nm from Samoa) have continuous Lapita-to-post-Lapita records (Kirch 1988; Sand 2000). Why would these small islands be settled, but not the large landmasses of Samoa?

Third, colonisation should be modelled using demographic, environmental and voyaging variables. Computer simulation of canoe voyaging is well established (Irwin 1992; Di Piazza et al. 2007), and there have been useful attempts to model the population characteristics and behaviour of colonising groups (e.g. Wobst 1974; Moore 2001) Consideration of the environmental variation encountered by prehistoric colonists (at large and small scales) is less developed, but it has the advantage of identifying locations that were in relative, and perhaps actual, terms 'unfamiliar' and difficult for migrants to initially occupy.

Our model of Lapita geography based on the physical characteristics of islands with a land area greater than 250 sq km does not support the view that the Solomon Islands were entirely bypassed in early Lapita times, as in the archipelago 'leapfrogging' model (Sheppard and Walter 2006). The Solomons are an island-rich and diverse archipelago similar in many respects to Vanuatu. Analysis indicates that these two island groups are prime environments for internal colonisation, and therefore population mixing, because inter-island distances between the numerous large islands in them are generally much less than the distances required to reach a neighbouring archipelago. The avoidance of the Solomons in early Lapita times, if confirmed, would indicate a negative response to migrants that was both unusually strong and homogeneous across the entire archipelago. As noted above, the analysis of Lapita sites in the Reef/Santa Cruz group – especially the presence/absence of imported pottery sourced to the main Solomon Islands – will provide the key information to resolve the colonisation pattern and voyaging capacity of Lapita groups.

The geography of Fiji–West Polynesia was quickly established by Lapita migrants, as a pot sherd from the Mulifanua site in Samoa indicates transfer from the Udu Peninsula in Fiji, and obsidian from Tafahi in northern Tonga was taken to Lakeba in east Fiji (Best 1984; Dickinson 2006:119). The MDS analysis (Figure 4) adds further support to the idea that Lapita colonisation was slowed or redirected by the fragmented island landscape found when approaching the Andesite line. In comparative terms, Tongatapu, where the majority of Lapita sites in Tonga is found, is small, remote and unfamiliar. When Lapita colonists arrived c. 2900 years ago, sea levels were higher and land area would have been even less that of today (Dickinson and Burley 2007). Tongatapu is composed of limestone and although its soils have been enriched by deposits of volcanic ash, it has low relief, an absence of standing fresh water and depauperate terrestrial resources. Migrants could have responded to Tonga's 'unfamiliar' environment by travelling west to Fiji, or by engaging in long-distance voyages of exploration eastward. However, except for Niue, there are no 'large' islands within 1000 nm east of Tonga, and there is no archaeological evidence that Lapita people ever colonised Niue (c. 220 nm from Tonga). In contrast, return movement from Tonga to east Fiji (c. 200 nm) is archaeologically attested (Best 1984; Clark and Murray 2006).

The diminishing number of Lapita sites in northern Tonga and Samoa might result, then, from the reorganisation of migrant social and economic systems after reaching the 'unfamiliar' large island of Tongatapu – an event that we suggest resulted in a high rate of return movement to the more 'familiar' islands in the Fiji group (Figure 4). The demographic effect of a substantial rate of back migration could be countered by closer settlement spacing on Tongatapu. The numerous Lapita sites present along the old shoreline of the Fanga 'Uta lagoon may be consistent with such a settlement approach. The need for population connectivity during the early phase of Lapita arrival in southern Tonga would discourage, for a time, population fissioning and the permanent occupation of the Vava'u group and Samoa. In terms of material culture, a closer population spacing would facilitate the transmission of art styles, and it is notable that Lapita pottery designs in Tonga display strong continuity from early through to late sites (Burley et al. 2002:222). Rather than demographic exhaustion, our scenario favours the short-lived redistribution of migrants to the more 'familiar' environment of Fiji, followed by the gradual growth of permanent colonies on Tongatapu and Ha'apai and their spread to northern Tonga and Samoa. The presence of Lapita and post-Lapita populations on islands near to Samoa, such as 'Uvea, suggests a hiatus of 100–200 years before the permanent colonisation of Samoa. Thus, the relative 'unfamiliarity' of environments does appear to effect colonisation, but not by the 300–400 year interval proposed by Addison and Morrison (In press). Although our model does not directly inform us about the colonisation mode – whether it was by 'leapfrogging' or staged advance – the inference drawn from a delay in the occupation of Samoa is that colony establishment from Fiji (+400 nm) and southern Tonga (+400 nm) was difficult.

We have assessed the Lapita distribution using the recognised boundary based on site/ceramic locations, but there are important questions about how robust that boundary actually is. If we were to include islands and archipelagos further east than Samoa in our statistical analysis it would confirm their 'unfamiliar' status, and none of these islands has any evidence of Lapita occupation. While the eastern edge of Lapita appears to be firmly set, how secure is the boundary at its western and northern ends, with mainland New Guinea, the Torres Strait, Australia and Island Southeast Asia? The majority of archaeological expeditions in Island Southeast Asia has examined cave and rock-shelter sites, and these locations – if the general experience in the western Pacific is anything to go by – tend not to contain the oldest ceramic deposits. The south coast of New Guinea is thought to be devoid of Lapita sites (Summerhayes and Allen 2007), although 'red slip' pottery about 2500 years old has recently been identified in the Torres Strait (McNiven *et al.* 2006). In simulations of one-way voyages from the Solomons to Australia, Irwin recorded a 100 percent success rate (Irwin 1992:143), and concluded that Lapita sites might be found on the northern Australia coast. Felgate provides tantalising evidence for this in the form of anomalous quartz-calcite temper in late-Lapita sherds from the Solomons that hint at an Australian connection (Felgate and Dickinson 2001; Dickinson 2006:115). It appears likely that the Lapita distribution will be extended in the future, and further geographic and environmental modelling should be applied to understand its complicated colonisation history.

Acknowledgements

GC studied under Atholl at Otago University and did his first fieldwork with him as an undergraduate during the Shag Mouth excavations in 1988–1989. In 1995, when I began a PhD at the ANU supervised by Atholl, academic collaboration and friendship developed. During and after PhD research, I assisted and worked with Atholl on projects in Fiji, Maupiti (Society Islands), Norfolk Island, Palau and Christmas Island (Indian Ocean), enjoying immensely the adventures, work and camaraderie. Like many colleagues, I have only benefited from exposure to an intellect that is relentless (at times remorseless), focussed, crisp and keen. I hope that in his much-deserved retirement the fly rod does not entirely supplant the trowel.

SB first worked with Atholl Anderson in 1984 as a field assistant during mid-winter excavations at Coal Creek in Central Otago, southern New Zealand. There was a large gap before our paths crossed again at the ANU in 1995 when Atholl was roped in as a PhD advisor. His extraordinary capacity for placing regional issues in the wider context shone as he ploughed through, literally overnight, my final draft. My only regret was that I had not consulted with him more often. Collegial fieldwork was planned for more tropical climes in 2000, but was cancelled due to the military coup in Fiji. There is hope yet that other opportunities will arise during his so-called 'retirement'.

References

Addison, D.J. and A.E. Morrison In press. The Lapita settlement of Samoa: Is a continuous occupation model appropriate? In Proceedings of the VII International Conference on Easter Island and the Pacific Islands: Migration, identity, and cultural heritage, Gotland, Sweden.

Anderson, A.J. 2001. Mobility models of Lapita migration. In G.R. Clark, A.J. Anderson and T. Vunidilo (eds), *The Archaeology of Lapita Dispersal in Oceania. Papers from the Fourth Lapita Conference, June 2000, Canberra, Australia*, pp. 15–23. Terra Australis 17.

Anderson, A. 2003. Different mechanisms of Holocene expansion. *Science* (online) 9 May, 2003.

Athens, J.S., M.F. Dega and J. Ward 2004. Austronesian colonisation of the Mariana Islands: The palaeoenvironmental evidence. *Bulletin of the Indo-Pacific Prehistory Association* 24:21–30.

Bedford, S. 2006. *Pieces of the Vanuatu Puzzle: Archaeology of the North, South and Centre*. Terra Australis 23. Canberra: Pandanus Books, The Australian National University.

Bellwood, P. 2005. Coastal south China, Taiwan, and the prehistory of the Austronesians. In C-Y Chey and J-G Pan (eds), *The Archaeology of Southeast Coastal Islands of China Conference*, pp. 1–22, Executive Yuan, Council for Cultural Affairs, Taiwan.

Best, S. 1984. Lakeba: The prehistory of a Fijian Island. Unpublished PhD thesis, Department of Anthropology, University of Auckland.

Burley, D.V. 2007. In search of Lapita and Polynesian Plainware settlements in Vava'u, Kingdom of Tonga. In S. Bedford, C. Sand and S.P. Connaughton (eds), *Oceanic Explorations: Lapita and Western Pacific settlement*, pp. 187–198. Terra Australis 26. ANU E Press, Australian National University.

Burley, D. V., W.R. Dickinson, A. Barton and R. Shutler Jr. 2001. Lapita on the periphery: New data on old problems in the Kingdom of Tonga. *Archaeology in Oceania* 36:89–104.

Burley, D.V. and W.R. Dickinson 2001. Origin and significance of a founding settlement in Polynesia. *Proceedings of the National Academy of Sciences* 98:11829–11831.

Burley, D.V., A. Storey and J. Witt 2002. On the definition and implications of eastern Lapita ceramics in Tonga. In S. Bedford, C. Sand and D. Burley (eds), *Fifty years in the field. Essays in honour and celebration of Richard Shutler Jr's archaeological career*, pp. 213–225. New Zealand Archaeological Association Monograph 25.

Carter, J. 1984. *Pacific islands yearbook*, 15th edition. Sydney: Pacific Publications.

Clark, G. 2005. A 3000-year culture sequence from Palau, Western Micronesia. *Asian Perspectives* 44:349–380.

Clark, G. and A. Anderson 2001. The pattern of Lapita settlement in Fiji. *Archaeology in Oceania* 36:77–88.

Clark, G., A. Anderson and D. Wright 2006. Human colonisation of the Palau islands, western Micronesia. *Journal of Island and Coastal Archaeology* 1:215–232.

Clark, G. and T. Murray 2006. Decay characteristics of the eastern Lapita design system. *Archaeology in Oceania* 41:107–117.

Diamond, J. and P. Bellwood 2003. Farmers and their languages: The first expansions. *Science* 300:597–603.

Dickinson, W.R. 2006. *Temper sands in prehistoric Oceanian pottery: Geotectonics, sedimentology, petrography, provenance*. The Geological Society of America. Special Paper 406.

Dickinson, W.R. and R.C. Green 1998. Geoarchaeological context of Holocene subsidence at the Ferry Berth site. Mulifanua, Upolu, Western Samoa, *Geoarchaeology* 13:239–263.

Dickinson, W.R. and D.V. Burley 2007. Geoarchaeology of Tonga: Geotectonic and geomorphic controls *Geoarchaeology* 22:229–259.

Di Piazza, A., P. Di Piazza, and E. Pearthree 2007. Sailing virtual canoes across Oceania: Revisiting island accessibility. *Journal of Archaeological Science* 34:1219–1225.

Dodson, J.R. and M. Intoh. 1999. Prehistory and palaeoecology of Yap, Federated States of Micronesia. *Quaternary International* 59:17–26.

Douglas, N. and N. Douglas (eds) 1989. *Pacific islands yearbook*, 16th edition. Australia: Angus and Robertson.

Fall, P.L. 2005. Vegetation change in the coastal-lowland rainforest at Avai'o'vuna swamp, Vava'u, Kingdom of Tonga. *Quaternary Research* 64:451–459.

Felgate, M.W. 2003. Reading Lapita in Near-Oceania: Intertidal and shallow-water pottery scatters, Roviana Lagoon, New Georgia, Solomon Islands. Unpublished PhD thesis, University of Auckland.

Felgate, M. 2007. Leap-frogging or Limping? Recent evidence from the Lapita littoral fringe, New Georgia, Solomon Islands. In S. Bedford, C. Sand and S.P. Connaughton (eds), *Oceanic Explorations: Lapita and Western Pacific settlement*, pp. 123–140. Terra Australis 26. ANU E Press, Australian National University.

Felgate, M.W. and W.R. Dickinson 2001. Late-Lapita and Post-Lapita pottery transfers: Evidence from intertidal-zone sites of Roviana Lagoon, Western Province, Solomon Islands. In M. Jones and P.J. Sheppard (eds), *Proceedings of the 2001 Australasian Archaeometry Conference*, pp. 105–122. Auckland: Research Papers in Anthropology and Linguistics, Number 5.

Fort, J. 2003. Population expansion in the western Pacific (Austronesia): A wave of advance model. *Antiquity* 77:520–530.

Garanger, J. 1971. Incised and applied relief pottery, its chronology and development in southeastern Melanesia, and the extra areal comparisons. In R. Green and M. Kelly (eds), *Studies in Oceanic Culture History*, Volume 2, pp. 53–66. Honolulu: Pacific Anthropological Records Number 12.

Golson, J. 1968. Archaeological Prospects for Melanesia. In I. Yawata and Y.H. Sinoto (eds), *Prehistoric Culture in Oceania*, A Symposium, pp. 3–14. Honolulu; Bishop Museum Press.

Golson, J. 1971. Lapita Ware and Its Transformations. In R. Green and M. Kelly (eds), *Studies in Oceanic Culture History*, Volume 2, pp. 67–76. Pacific Anthropological Records Number 12. Honolulu: Bishop Museum.

Green, R.C. 2002. A retrospective view of settlement pattern studies in Samoa. In T. Ladefoged and M. Graves (eds), *Pacific Landscapes Archaeological Approaches*, pp. 125–152. California: The Easter Island Foundation, Bearsville Press.

Green, R.C. and M.M. Cresswell (eds) 1976. *Southeast Solomon Islands Cultural History: A Preliminary Survey*. Bulletin of the Royal Society of New Zealand 11. Wellington.

Groube, L.M. 1971. Tonga, Lapita pottery, and Polynesian origins. *Journal of the Polynesian Society* 80: 278–316.

Hébert, B. 1965. Nouvelles Hébrides. Contribution à l'Étude Archeologique de l'Île Éfaté et des Îles Avoisantes. *Études Mélanésiennes* 18–20:71–98.

Hedrick, J. and M.E. Shutler 1969. Report on "Lapita Style" pottery from Malo Island, Northern New Hebrides. *Journal of the Polynesian Society* 78(2):262–265.

Irwin, G. 1992. *The Prehistoric exploration and colonisation of the Pacific*. Cambridge: Cambridge University Press.

Jennings, J.D. 1974. The Ferry Berth site, Mulifanua District, Upolu. In R.C. Green and J.M. Davidson (eds), *Archaeology in Western Samoa*, Volume II, pp. 176–178. Bulletin of the Auckland Institute and Museum Number 7.

Joly, P., C. Morand and A. Cohas 2003. Habitat fragmentation and amphibian conservation: building a tool for assessing landscape matrix connectivity. *C.R. Biologies* 326:S123–S139.

Kennedy, J. 1981. Lapita colonisation of the Admiralty Islands? *Science* 213:757–759.

Kennedy, T.F. 1974. *A descriptive atlas of the Pacific islands*. Reed Education: Wellington.

Kirch, P.V. 1988. *Niuatoputapu: The prehistory of a Polynesian chiefdom*. Monograph 5. Seattle: Burke Museum.

Lee, E.S. 1996 [1965]. A theory of migration. In R. Cohen (ed), *Theories of migration*, pp. 14–57. United Kingdom: Edward Elgar.

Meyer, O. 1909. Funde Prähistorischer Töpferei und Steinmesser auf Vuatom, Bismarck Archipel. *Anthropos* 4:251–252.

Moore, J.H. 2001. Evaluating five models of colonisation. *American Anthropologist* 103:395–408.

McKern, W.C. 1929. *Archaeology of Tonga*. Bernice P. Bishop Museum Bulletin 60. Honolulu: The Bishop Museum.

McNiven, I., W.R. Dickinson, B. David, M. Weisler, F. von Gnielinski, M. Carter and U. Zoppi 2006. Mask cave: Red-slipped pottery and the Australian–Papuan settlement of Zenadh Kes (Torres Strait). *Archaeology in Oceania* 41:49–81.

Pawley, A. The origins of early Lapita culture: The testimony of historical linguistics. In S. Bedford, C. Sand and S.P. Connaughton (eds), *Oceanic Explorations: Lapita and Western Pacific settlement*, pp. 17–49. Terra Australis 26. ANU E Press, Australian National University.

Piroutet, M. 1917. *Étude Stratigraphique sur la Nouvelle Calédonie*. Macon: Imprimerie Protat Fréres.

Ravenstein, E.G. 1889. The laws of migration. *Journal of the Royal Statistical Society* 52:241–305.

Rockman, M. and J. Steele (eds) 2003. Colonisation *of unfamiliar landscapes; the archaeology of adaptation*. London: Routledge.

Sand, C. 1995. *"Le Temps d'Avant" la préhistoire de la Nouvelle-Calédonie*. Paris: L'Harmattan.

Sand, C. 2000. La datation du premier peuplement de Wallis et Futuna: Contribution a la définition de la chronologie Lapita en Polynésie occidentale. *Journal de la Société des Océanistes* 111:165–172.

Sheppard, P. and R. Walter 2006. A revised model of Solomon Islands culture history. *Journal of the Polynesian Society* 115:47–76.

Specht, J. 2007. Small islands in the big picture: The formative period of Lapita in the Bismarck Archipelago. In S. Bedford, C. Sand and S.P. Connaughton (eds), *Oceanic Explorations: Lapita and Western Pacific settlement*, pp. 51–70. Terra Australis 26. ANU E Press, Australian National University.

Specht, J. and R. Torrence 2007. Lapita all over: Land-use on the Willaumez Peninsula, Papua New Guinea. In S. Bedford, C. Sand and S.P. Connaughton (eds), *Oceanic Explorations: Lapita and Western Pacific settlement*, pp. 71–96. Terra Australis 26. ANU E Press, Australian National University.

Spriggs, M. 1984. The Lapita Cultural Complex: Origins, distribution, contemporaries and successors. *Journal of Pacific History* 19(4):202–223.

Spriggs, M. 2007. The Neolithic and Austronesian expansion within Island Southeast Asia and into the Pacific. In S. Chiu and C. Sand (eds), *From Southeast Asia to the Pacific. Archaeological Perspectives on the Austronesian Expansion and the Lapita Cultural Complex*, pp. 104–140. Taipei: Academia Sinica.

Summerhayes, G. 2007. The rise and transformations of Lapita in the Bismarck Archipelago. In S. Chiu and C. Sand (eds), *From Southeast Asia to the Pacific. Archaeological Perspectives on the Austronesian Expansion and the Lapita Cultural Complex*, pp. 141–184. Taipei: Academia Sinica.

Summerhayes, G. and J. Allen 2007. Lapita Writ Small? Revisiting the Austronesian Colonisation of the Papuan South Coast. In S. Bedford, C. Sand and S.P. Connaughton (eds), *Oceanic Explorations: Lapita and Western Pacific settlement*, pp. 97–122. Terra Australis 26. ANU E Press, Australian National University.

Terrell, J. and R. Welsch 1997. Lapita and the temporal geography of prehistory. *Antiquity* 71:548–572

Wickler S. 2001. The colonisation of western Micronesia and early settlement of Palau. In C.M. Stevenson, G. Lee and F.J. Morin (eds), *Pacific 2000. Proceedings of the Fifth International Conference on Easter Island and the Pacific*, pp. 185–196. California: The Easter Island Foundation, Bearsville Press.

Wobst, H.M. 1974. Boundary conditions for Palaeolithic social systems: A simulation approach. *American Antiquity* 39:147–178.

5

Flights of fancy: Fractal geometry, the Lapita dispersal and punctuated colonisation in the Pacific

Ian Lilley

ATSIS Unit, University of Queensland, Australia

i.lilley@uq.edu.au

Introduction

Atholl Anderson has long been interested in the big questions surrounding pre-European population movement in the Asia-Pacific. For the most part, though, his publications have concentrated on the initial settlement of Remote Oceania, and particularly Polynesia, rather than either the Austronesian progression through Southeast Asia or the Lapita spread through Near Oceania. In this chapter, I would like to return to his 2001 consideration of Lapita mobility, where he asked (Anderson 2001:21) whether the large-scale pattern of episodic movement he identified in Remote Oceania could be linked at a processual level with the Lapita spread through already-inhabited parts of Melanesia and preceding population movements in Asia.

I have two aims in addressing this question. The first is to begin to explore the potential of a new way of characterising and explaining the Lapita phenomenon. My focus is on a type of episodic movement known as a 'Lévy flight'. My second aim is to consider whether the patterns and processes I discuss in this connection can be meshed with Anderson's models concerning punctuated or episodic colonisation. The objective is to help test the processual links he proposes between varying patterns or cycles of mobility stretching all the way from South China to South Polynesia. I am particularly interested to know whether the presence of existing populations in northwestern Melanesia really made any difference to the process underlying the large-scale, long-term movement of people that eventually saw the colonisation of Remote Oceania, or whether there is, to put it in Anderson's words (2001:21), 'an inherent trajectory in island colonisation which is … self-sufficient in its processes and causes and which, if all islands were the same, would display a regular pattern of binary mobility phases?'.

Anderson's models

Atholl's evolving ideas about the settlement of the Pacific are detailed in a number of recent papers (Anderson 2001, 2003a, b, 2004). His proposals are rooted in the tenets and evidence of biogeography and his personal knowledge and experience of sailing and the sea. They also depend on adherence to the 'short' chronology of initial settlement in Polynesia, and especially East Polynesia, which not everyone accepts (Lilley 2006:19-21). Anderson argues on these bases that human dispersal into the Pacific was episodic rather than continuous and, if not the product of random movement, then certainly resulting from much less elaborate search strategies than the complex, risk-managing approach implicit in the now-orthodox 'against, across, then down the wind' model tendered by fellow ocean-sailor Geoff Irwin (1992).

Anderson includes Near Oceania and even Southeast Asia in his 2001 paper on Lapita mobility, but that discussion and his more recent writings on the topic draw a fundamental distinction between movement patterns in Near Oceania and Remote Oceania. As many readers will know, Remote Oceania was first settled by people with cultural and biological characteristics which derive from Near Oceania and in some cases ultimately from Asia (Spriggs 1995; Green 2000). This necessarily implicates these latter regions in any comprehensive consideration of the colonisation of the remote Pacific, as Anderson's 2001 paper and passing references in his later articles make clear. However, he is plainly concerned to achieve a certain level of analytical clarity concerning colonisation processes and so although his 2001 Lapita-mobility paper treated migration and dispersal interchangeably, his later work (2003a, b, 2004) distinguishes between the two processes, taking the 'social science view that … [the former] refers to movement between existing populations … [while the latter applies] to all other kinds of long-distance movements that resulted in colonisation' (2003a:71-72).

Anderson (2001:16-21) takes this view because his analysis of Lapita mobility identified 'four interesting implications' of the spatial and chronological data he examined. The last and most abstract of these implications is the prospect mentioned above that there might be an 'inherent trajectory in island colonisation'. The preceding three implications that build up to this 'conjecture' are that:

1. There appears to be a 'binary-state or dual-phase process' entailed at a large scale, with 'a stable phase which is relatively sedentary' in Near Oceania 'followed by an unstable phase of high mobility' in Remote Oceania.

2. The stable and unstable phases equate with different relationships between population and resource pressure (Keegan's (1995) K- and A-type colonising modes, respectively); and

3. There were 'significantly different' settlement and social patterns between the two phases and regions, with relatively long-lived and widely-spaced villages in Near Oceania and smaller, less-formal and only short-lived settlements in Remote Oceania.

I understand Anderson's reasoning in arriving at these conclusions, which align with conventional wisdom about the influence of existing populations on Lapita settlement and movement patterns (despite a recently reported date of 3100 cal BP for Lapita in Vanuatu, which if confirmed, reduces the 'stable phase' Near Oceania; Galipaud and Swete Kelly 2007). Of late, however, I have come to question this latter perspective, and to think that there might be another way of conceptualising the issue that minimises the impact of existing communities. The following discussion sketches an emerging position.

Fractals and Lapita in Near Oceania

Recent methodological developments within and beyond archaeology suggest there may be some value in exploring the application of a form of fractal geometry known as Lévy flights to the questions outlined above. Fractal geometry is the non-Euclidean geometry of complex non-linear systems. It is a branch of chaos theory that is based on the work of Benoit Mandelbrot. Apart from a couple of forward-looking contributions by the likes of Zubrow (1985) over the

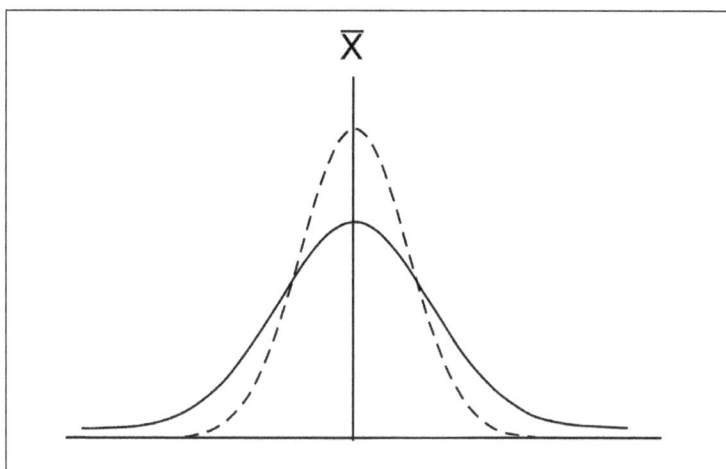

Figure 1. Gaussian or normal (broken line) and Lévy long- or heavy-tailed distributions (after Chakravarti 2004:51, Figure 1).

past two decades, fractals have only come to the attention of archaeologists over the past few years. To quote from one of the handful of papers on the matter:

> Fractal geometry is the study of the form and structure of complex, rough, and irregular phenomena. In the past, many fractal patterns were mistakenly treated as if they were non-fractal. In such cases, the patterns have typically been analysed using conventional statistics, which often assume that the variation in the pattern is caused by normally distributed (Gaussian) effects. When the patterns are really fractal, classical statistical modelling yields faulty results that do not properly characterize the data. (Brown *et al.* 2005:40)

Lévy flights are a form of fractal geometry named after the French mathematician Paul Lévy. They characterise certain uneven patterns of diffusion. To paraphrase Brown *et al.* (2005, 2007; also Ravilious 2006), they are a form of random walk. In Brownian motion, the best-known kind of random walk, the sizes of the steps are normally distributed (Figure 1). Over time, this gives an even, 'wave-of-advance' dispersal pattern like Ammerman and Cavalli-Sforza's (1971; also Ackland *et al.* 2007) well-known model for the expansion of agriculturalists into Europe, Keegan's (1995) 'K-type pattern' of settlement in the Caribbean, and, of most direct relevance here, Irwin's (1992) 'against, across and then down the wind' model of Pacific colonisation (Figure 2 and Figure 3).

In contrast, Lévy flights exhibit step lengths with distributions characterised by 'power-law tails' (Figure 1). Essentially, this means the distributions are characterised by groups of small steps indicative of intense, localised activity that are joined by occasional very large steps that jump across large areas in which no groups of small steps occur (Figure 4). This feature causes what is called anomalous diffusion or super diffusion; it results, in other words, in extremely rapid dispersal. Because of the power-law distribution of step lengths, Lévy flights produce fractal patterns in space. This has certain implications, the most important of which here is that they are 'scale invariant' and so exhibit what are called 'self-similar' patterns at all scales (i.e. local, regional, global).

Why is any of this relevant to the Lapita dispersal? I think it is pertinent to our consideration of three factors:

- the speed of the Lapita spread,
- its unevenness or patchiness at both regional and subregional scales, and

- the way it might link through scale-invariance with Anderson's models concerning the punctuated colonisation of the remote Pacific.

I will discuss the last point in a separate section towards the end of the chapter. Regarding speed, Anderson (2001:16) has pointed out that the Norse colonisation of the North Atlantic and the colonisation of East Polynesia were 'rather faster' than the Lapita dispersal. Yet as he concedes immediately after making that observation, it is still generally agreed that the Lapita spread was very rapid, archaeologically speaking.

By regional patchiness I mean the large gaps in the distribution of classic Lapita on the New Guinea mainland and in the Solomons. Anderson (2001:16) puts it well:

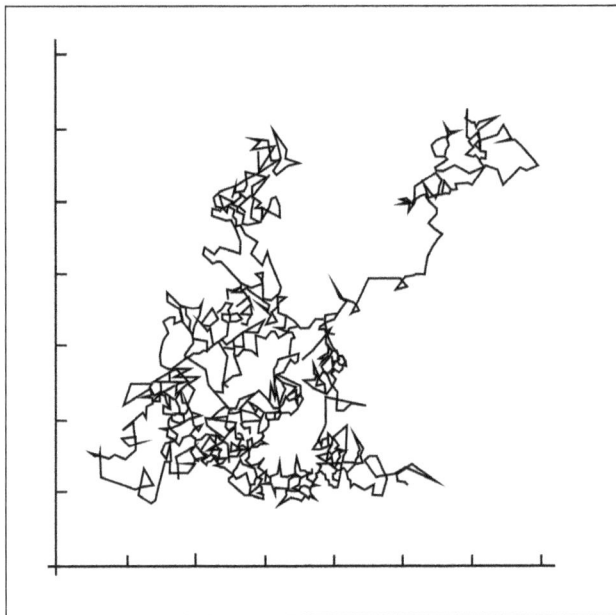

Figure 2. An example of 1000 steps of an approximate Brownian motion in two dimensions (after 'Lévy flight' Figure 1, Wikipedia electronic document http://en.wikipedia.org/wiki/L%C3%A9vy_flight last accessed 20 March 2008).

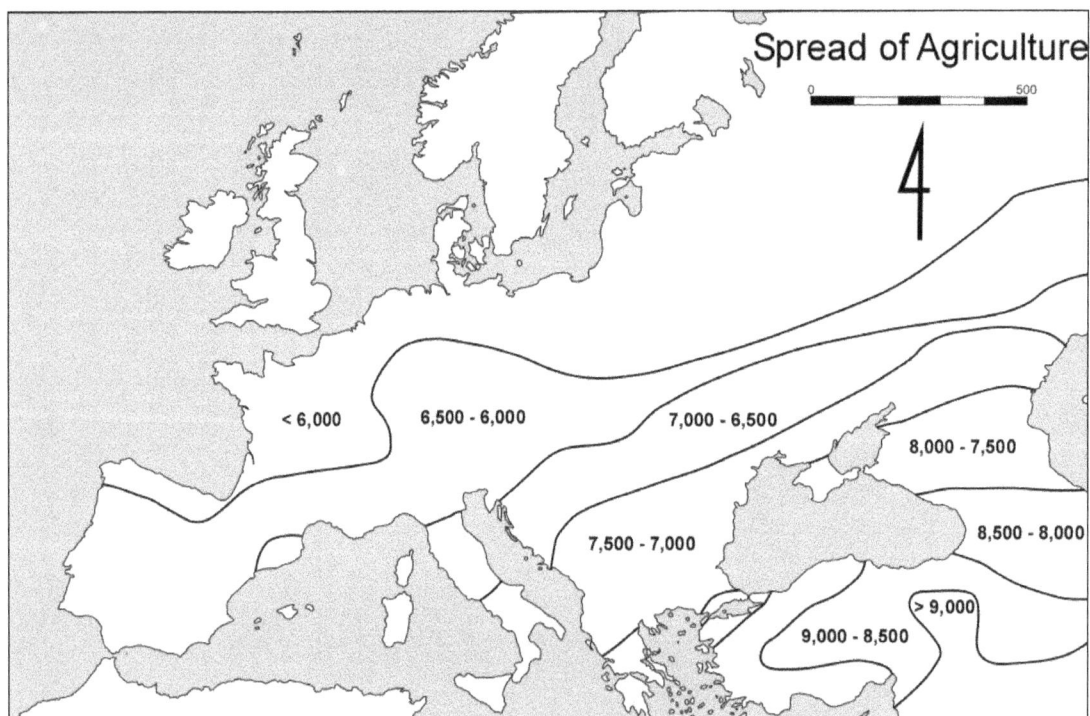

Figure 3. The wave of advance of agriculture through Europe (after Ammerman and Cavalli-Sforza 1971:685, Figure 6).

[T]he broad pattern of current distributional data has remained much the same for more than 20 years, suggesting that it is not just on grounds of relative site recording intensity that the density of sites on the coasts of large islands is lower than on small islands throughout the Lapita range, or that mainland New Guinea, and perhaps the main Solomon Islands, are largely bereft of Lapita sites (especially early Lapita sites).

More recently, and in contrast with the views of Felgate (2007), Sheppard and Walter (2006:67–68) have made it clear that on the basis of their current research, they also think the initial Lapita dispersal bypassed the main Solomons chain:

[T]here is no evidence for early Lapita settlement in the Solomon Islands outside the record in Remote Oceania – primarily that in the Reef/Santa Cruz Islands … Based on the archaeological, genetic and linguistic data, it seems evident that the Reef/Santa Cruz Islands were settled directly by populations from New Britain with whom on-going relations were retained, while leapfrogging the Solomon Islands.

To anticipate discussion below, it is interesting in this context to note that people from Vanuatu may have 'jumped' all the way to Tonga in West Polynesia, leapfrogging New Caledonia and Fiji (Dickinson 2006:119). With regard to leapfrogging mainland New Guinea, Terrell (Terrell and Schechter 2007) has this year indicated that after considerable long-term effort, he and his colleagues have found only one minute piece of classic Lapita on the north coast of New Guinea to add to the original Aitape piece that has intrigued Pacific scholars for so long. I think on that basis that we can maintain that the New Guinea mainland was avoided by Lapita makers and users.

To turn to subregional patchiness, by this term I mean the unevenness of Lapita site-distribution patterns within areas where Lapita sites are known. This is clear from the table in Anderson *et al.* (2001, which inadvertently excludes the KLK Lapita site on Tuam Island in Siassi; Lilley 2002). To take New Britain as an example, there are groups of substantial Lapita sites in the Arawe Islands, around Talasea, and in the Watom–Duke of Yorks area, as well as a group of Lapita sites around Kandrian yet to be examined and reported in detail, but there is very little Lapita elsewhere on New Britain or its immediate offshore islands. In some places, this might result from landscape change owing to volcanism, particularly at the western end of New Britain and along the north coast from Cape Hoskins to Rabaul. In other places, it

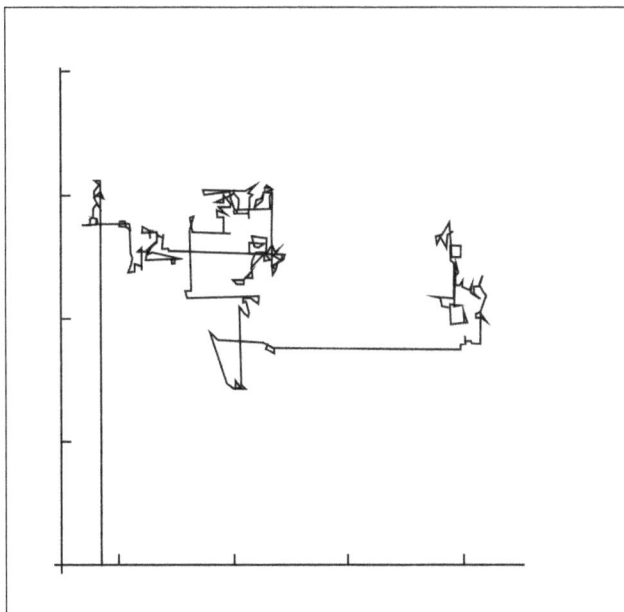

Figure 4. An example of 1000 steps of a Lévy flight in two dimensions: compare the large jumps with the Brownian pattern in Figure 2 (after 'Lévy flight' Figure 2, Wikipedia electronic document http://en.wikipedia.org/wiki/L%C3%A9vy_flight last accessed 20 March).

may result from a lack of archaeological research (the preliminary Lapita Homeland survey notwithstanding; Allen *et al.* 1984). However, Specht has surveyed parts of the coastline in the Cape Gloucester area (Specht 1967) and between Arawe and Kandrian (Specht 1991), and I have examined Umboi and the Siassi Islands, the Kove Islands and mainland New Britain immediately west of the Willaumez Peninsula (Lilley 1991), and the New Britain mainland around Gasmata and the offshore islands between there and Kandrian (Specht *et al.* 1992). I found only minor quantities of Lapita, and Specht found none around Gloucester and only one site (Kreslo) on the south coast.

Examining the distribution of Lapita sites in the New Ireland–Manus region and in Vanuatu suggests much the same sort of distribution. New Caledonia may be another matter, but even there, Lapita is far from continuously distributed. Fiji or West Polynesia definitely seem different, as suggested by Anderson's (2001:17, Table 1) demonstration that while overall Lapita site density is virtually identical in Near Oceania and Remote Oceania, and similar between Near Oceania on the one hand and Vanuatu and New Caledonia on the other, site density in Fiji–West Polynesia is twice that of Vanuatu–New Caledonia. I have yet to determine what, if anything, this difference might mean for the present modelling exercise.

For some years, numbers of Pacific researchers have been referring to Anthony's (1990) classic paper on migration in archaeology to 'explain' the rapid, leapfrogging dispersal of Lapita at the regional scale, though not, as far as I am aware, at the subregional scale considered immediately above. As Spriggs (1997:105) reminds us, Anthony noted that 'the archaeological signature of leapfrogging 'should resemble 'islands' of settlement in desirable or attractive locations, separated by significant expanses of unsettled, less desirable territory'. 'This,' Spriggs observed, 'is precisely the Lapita settlement pattern.' Like Spriggs and others including Anderson (e.g. 2001), I have found Anthony's work very useful (Lilley 2004). In the final analysis, however, it does not explain in any but the most general sense why the pattern of Lapita dispersal and settlement is as it is at any scale, rather than just giving us some terms in which to describe it.

This is where fractal geometry and especially Lévy flights come in. A considerable amount of work has been done by biologists relating foraging search patterns to Lévy flights. Brown *et al.* (2007:130; see also Hecht 2005) cite studies showing that Lévy flights:

> are optimal search patterns for foragers searching for scarce targets that are randomly placed and can be visited any number of times ... It has been proposed that animal and insect foragers may perform Lévy flights because the probability of returning to a previously visited site is lower than for Brownian walks. Consequently, the number of newly visited sites is higher for Lévy flight searchers.

These sorts of findings led Brown and colleagues (2007) to analyse foraging patterns among San hunter-gatherers in southern Africa. The research found that these people use Lévy flight searches in their subsistence routines, and on that basis, operate at near-maximum search efficiency.

This is not the place to wade into the 'strandlooper' debate surrounding Lapita colonisation (e.g. Anderson 2003a:76–78; Davidson and Leach 2001; Kirch and Green 2001:121; Valentin *et al.* 2007), though the implications of the San research for this question should be apparent. Here, I would note instead that Brown *et al.* (2007) also briefly discuss human migration and cultural diffusion in this and their 2005 paper (also Ravilious 2006), referring explicitly to Anthony's work and his questioning of the conventional wave-of-advance model for the European Neolithic. In this connection, they (2007:135) note that it is not just leapfrogging per se that makes Lévy flights relevant to certain cases of human dispersal, but also the fact that 'Lévy flights can produce faster long-distance migration than Brownian motion because the latter will have few long jumps and many medium-length jumps, whereas the former will produce some surprisingly long leaps'.

This is what I think might have been happening in the Lapita context in Near Oceania: People were using a pattern of movement we can now identify as a Lévy-flight distribution to search effectively and efficiently for particular sets of resources, moving in rapid and sometimes very long leaps between patches. These leaps occurred at the subregional as well as the regional levels, producing the subregional and regional patchiness sketched above. I hypothesize that this 'self-similarity' at regional and subregional levels is a reflection of the scale-invariance characteristic of fractal patterns. In the same vein, Anderson's two-part larger pattern distinguishing Lapita mobility in Near and Remote Oceania may be a supra-regional dimension of the same scale-invariant phenomenon. In this view, his initial 'stable … [and] relatively sedentary' phase in Near Oceania would equate with the intense 'close-quarters' searching in a defined area, while the following 'unstable phase of high mobility' in Remote Oceania would equate at this scale with the Lévy 'leap' that resulted in the leapfrogging evident at regional and subregional scales. In short, it can be argued that the same two-part pattern applies to the Lapita dispersal in its entirety and at all scales of analysis.

Larger patterns

Interestingly, Anderson notes that there are also pauses and 'leaps' (if not leapfrogging) within Polynesia as well. On this basis, he (2001:21) asks whether the large-scale Lapita and Polynesian pulses he identifies might not be part of 'a progression of cyclic variation in mobility'. He (Anderson 2001:21) painted the scenario in this way:

> Looking back … [along the entire] Austronesian expansion we see stable settlement in New Zealand preceded by rapid expansion into the outlying archipelagos, preceded by several hundred years of settlement stability in East Polynesia that had followed, in turn, a phase of rapid and far-reaching migration … Before that we had a long period of settlement stability in West Polynesia, preceded by the Lapita expansion and that in turn, perhaps, by an earlier cycle of expansion from the South China region.

Plainly, if my hypotheses are credible, there should be subregional pulses within the archipelagos of Polynesia (and indeed East and Southeast Asia and perhaps western Micronesia) of the same sort as those I have highlighted in Near Oceania. Considering this possibility in detail is beyond the scope of the present exploratory exercise, and I have not searched for any descriptions in the Polynesian literature of subregional movement that approximates a Lévy flight distribution. It should be borne in mind, though, that even if there are no such descriptions to be found, the quote from Brown *et al.* (2007) early in the chapter makes it clear that patterns that are actually fractal can be mistaken for Gaussian wave-of-advance distributions. The question thus remains open to empirical (re-)investigation. The same applies to East and Southeast Asia.

This is not to say that such analysis will be straightforward. Recent detailed research by Ackland *et al.* (2007:8716) on wave-of-advance models explicitly considers the question of leapfrogging in the early European Neolithic, 'in which small isolated enclaves of farming were formed by small-scale, long-distance migration'. They found that 'the same distribution can be produced' with a minor variation in some basic demographic parameters of the wave-of-advance scenario and 'enhanced migration rates along major rivers'. The researchers point out that there are other instances, including the settlement of Crete by 8000 BP, in which 'water-borne travel' produces long-distance leaps within an overall wave-of-advance pattern. This suggests that travelling by water, indeed, dispersing through an island world such as the Indo-Pacific, might produce a pattern of colonisation that appears to be a Lévy-flight distribution but in fact is still explicable as a Gaussian wave-of-advance.

This crucial point is a matter for empirical testing, to determine which dispersal model best fits the Pacific data. Of more interest to me at this tentative exploratory stage is not just that Lévy-flight research may give us a new label for particular distribution patterns, or even that it gives us the statistical tools to characterise them mathematically. Rather, as Brown and his colleagues put it (2005:67), Lévy-flight geometry also gives us the theory to 'understand the cultural dynamics that produced the patterns'. In other words, it has the potential to help us understand what might underlie the 'inherent trajectory of island colonisation' that Anderson has identified and I have discussed further in this paper.

Remember that fractal geometry is the geometry of complex non-linear systems. Non-linear dynamics of various different kinds can generate fractal patterns. Two important sorts of non-linear systems are especially well known for generating fractal patterns: chaotic systems and self-organised systems. A system is chaotic if endpoints of trajectories of change that have very similar initial conditions diverge substantially. This basic characteristic of chaos only occurs in strongly non-linear systems, and on reflection, seems unlikely to apply to Lapita and even post-Lapita change, given the readily discernible similarities among Lapita and post-Lapita societies (Kirch 1997; Spriggs 1997), interpretations like those of Bedford and Clark (2001) notwithstanding (see also Spriggs 2003).

'Self-organised criticality' underpins another sort of complex non-linear system. Such systems evolve without external interference and trend towards the temporarily stable state of 'criticality'. The classic exemplar of this phenomenon is a pile of sand to which more sand is added one grain at a time. The slope of the pile will ultimately reach a critical state, its 'angle of repose', after which the addition of even one more grain of sand causes an 'avalanche'. This radical shift in system state is the same as the long jump in a Lévy flight, and conceptually is not dissimilar to the sudden shifts in evolutionary trajectories described by both punctuated equilibrium and catastrophe theory. Dramatic change can periodically result from even a minor perturbation if it prompts an avalanche that ramifies all the way through the interconnected elements of a system in a chain reaction. This is the proverbial 'butterfly effect' of chaos theory. Avalanches allow the system to evolve back to a critical state, where the renewed addition of more sand will eventually cause more avalanches. In other words, the system evolves back to marginal stability following perturbation, only to be 'reset' for another avalanche.

Brown *et al.* (2005:69) note that the concept of self-organised criticality has been applied to various human social systems, particularly war and politics. Archaeologically, Bentley and Maschner (2001) have applied the idea to stylistic change in ceramics. This idea seems likely to repay application to questions to hand here. It may help explain how, when and why population 'jumps' occurred, prompted by variations in resource distribution/ecological pressure and/or sociopolitical perturbations such as internecine rivalries (e.g. Anderson 2003b:181–184, 2004). Analysis of the sort undertaken by Bentley and Maschner (2001) may also help identify and explain patterns of ceramic and perhaps other cultural change that would illuminate aspects of the Lapita and wider Austronesian dispersal through the Asia-Pacific. While they (Bentley and Maschner 2001:61) note that 'the process of 'lumping' archaeological types and the incompleteness of the archaeological record may make self-organised criticality difficult to test with strictly archaeological data', they also argue that 'Artifact styles have irreversible histories, and with enough data, their descent should be traceable in a hierarchical pattern – patterns that can be seen as avalanches of causally-connected change' (Bentley and Maschner 2001:50).

Specialist mathematical assessment will be required to distinguish between Lévy-flight distributions and the Gaussian waves of advance distorted by 'water-borne travel' suggested by Ackland *et al.* (2007). In considering this question, we must, of course, address the vital matter of Lapita sailing technology, a constant theme in Anderson's work. This is because the maximum distance of any 'leap' (or shape of any distorted Gaussian wave) will to a large extent be a function of the sophistication of the watercraft being used. In the right conditions, a canoe with a sail can travel much further in a given period than one without. However, we already have the tools to produce the data needed for analyses like those advocated by Bentley and Maschner (2001). For ceramics, we have research of the sort behind Dickinson's (2006) demonstration that some Lapita potters took what at first glance looks very much like a Lévy flight directly from Vanuatu to Tonga, despite the presence of the large and resource-rich islands of Fiji in between. Similar combinations of fine-grained stylistic analysis and petrographic sourcing should be able to link assemblages in the ramifying or hierarchical manner described by Bentley and Maschner, ultimately allowing us to very closely map the pattern of initial Lapita dispersal from the Bismarcks through Island Melanesia and West Polynesia. Similar studies should be possible with stone and perhaps certain other non-ceramic assemblages, too, deploying high-precision sourcing of the sort recently used in Collerson and Weisler's (2007) ground-breaking study of Polynesian trade. Appropriately applied, investigations such as these will help keep research into the Lapita dispersal at the forefront of studies of human population movement as the differences between fractal and Gaussian distributions are more thoroughly examined.

And the people behind the pot sherds?

There is one obvious implication of linking the process underlying Lapita dispersal through Near Oceania to that driving the initial movement of people through Remote Oceania, and then tying both to a larger process propelling the movement of Austronesian speakers out from East and Southeast Asia. This is that it 'dehumanises' our interpretation of Pacific prehistory by eliminating agency on the part of the colonisers and by denying the impact on the Lapita phenomenon of the populations that had lived in East and Southeast Asia and Near Oceania for tens of millennia before Austronesian speakers appeared on the scene. Such an implication may be thought to conflict with received archaeological wisdom. Propositions such as Green's (2000) influential 'intrusion, integration and innovation' ('Triple-I') model, for example, and my (1999, 2004) diaspora hypothesis hold that the Lapita phenomenon results directly from the interaction of new and existing populations in Near Oceania. Indeed, one of the most basic characteristics of the Lapita settlement pattern in the region, namely a predilection for small offshore islands, is seen to reflect the fact that the larger islands were already occupied (e.g. Spriggs 1995:126). Lévy flight and similar sorts of processual models might even appear to ignore seemingly incontrovertible genetic evidence that intercourse between locals and settlers was biological as well as social (e.g. Oppenheimer 2003).

In fact, modelling of the sort explored above, like that investigated elsewhere by Anderson, does none of these things. It is all a matter of analytical scale, as Murray has recently reminded us (Lucas 2007:161–162). It is inconceivable to me that existing populations in Near Oceania had no influence on short-to-medium-term events and processes at a local scale. Nor is it supportable at the level of the individual and the community to characterise Austronesian settlers as mindless automatons who were simply pushed and pulled around the place by large-scale biogeographical processes. It is clear to me, though, that the agency of individual social actors and the social relationships within and between particular communities are irrelevant at the level of geographical and chronological resolution we are dealing with here. We are considering the processes of population movement entailed in the settlement of vast areas over tens of generations. Recalling Braudel, I would argue in this context that intermediate-scale processes such as 'introduction, integration and innovation' or diaspora formation are what emerge when global processes impact on local events and individuals and communities have to contend with the impositions of the longue durée on everyday life. When dealing with the former rather than the latter, as Anderson usually does, the importance of any difference between migration and dispersal seems moot.

Acknowledgements

Different versions of the Levy flights part of this paper were presented at conferences in Honiara (Solomon Islands) and Gotland (Sweden) before being incorporated into the present piece. I thank all those who gave me feedback on those occasions, including Atholl, even if it looks as if I didn't listen to any of you! An anonymous reviewer also added some crucial insights. My research activity and conference travel is very generously supported by Michael Williams, Director of the ATSIS Unit at the University of Queensland.

References

Ackland, G., M. Signitzer, K. Stratford and M. Cohen 2007. Cultural hitchhiking on the wave of advance of beneficial technologies. *Proceedings of the National Academy of Sciences* 104(21):8714–8719.

Allen, J., W. Ambrose, J. Specht and D. Yen 1984. *Lapita Homeland Project: Report of the 1984 Field Season.* Canberra: Australian National University.

Ammerman, A. and L. Cavalli-Sforza 1971. Measuring the rate of spread of early farming in Europe. *Man NS* 6(4):674–688.

Anderson, A. 2001. Mobility models of Lapita migration. In G. Clark, A. Anderson and T. Vunidilo (eds), *The Archaeology of Lapita Dispersal in Oceania*, pp. 15–23. Canberra: Pandanus Press.

Anderson, A. 2003a. Initial human dispersal in Remote Oceania: pattern and explanation. In C. Sand (ed), *Pacific Archaeology: Assessments and Prospects*, pp. 71–84. Nouméa: Département Archéologie.

Anderson, A. 2003b. Entering uncharted waters: models of initial colonization in Polynesia. In M. Rockman and J. Steele (eds), *Colonization of Unfamiliar Landscapes*, pp. 169–189. London: Routledge.

Anderson, A. 2004. It's about time. In T. Murray (ed), *Archaeology from Australia*, pp. 3–17. Melbourne: Australian Scholarly Publishing.

Anthony, D. 1990. Migration in archaeology: the baby and the bathwater. *American Anthropologist* 92:895–914.

Bedford, S. and G. Clark 2001. The rise and rise of the incised and applied relief tradition: A review and reassessment, In G. Clark, A. Anderson and T. Vunidilo (eds), *The Archaeology of Lapita Dispersal in Oceania*, pp. 61–74. Canberra: Pandanus Books.

Bentley, A. and H. Maschner 2001. Stylistic change as a self-organized critical phenomenon: An archaeological study in complexity. *Journal of Archaeological Method and Theory* 8:35–66.

Brown, C., L. Liebovitch and R. Glendon 2007. Lévy flights in Dobe Ju/'hoansi foraging patterns. *Human Ecology* 35:129–138.

Brown, C., W. Witschey and L. Liebovitch 2005. The broken past: Fractals in archaeology. *Journal of Archaeological Method and Theory* 12:37–78.

Burley, D. and W. Dickinson 2001. Origin and significance of a founding settlement in Oceania. *Proceedings of the National Academy of Sciences* 98(20):11829–11831.

Collerson, K. and M. Weisler 2007. Stone adze compositions and the extent of ancient Polynesian voyaging and trade. *Science* 317:1907–1911.

Davidson, J. and F. Leach 2001. The strandlooper concept and economic naivety. In G. Clark, A. Anderson and T. Vunidilo (eds), *The Archaeology of Lapita Dispersal in Oceania*, pp. 115–123. Canberra: Pandanus Books..

Dickinson, W.R. 2006. *Temper sands in prehistoric Oceanian pottery: Geotectonics, sedimentology, petrography, provenance*. The Geological Society of America. Special Paper 406.

Felgate, M. 2007. Leap-frogging or Limping? Recent evidence from the Lapita littoral fringe, New Georgia, Solomon Islands. In S. Bedford, C. Sand and S.P. Connaughton (eds), *Oceanic Explorations: Lapita and Western Pacific settlement*, pp. 123–140. Terra Australis 26. ANU E Press, Australian National University.

Galipaud, J-C. and M.C. Swete Kelley 2007. Makue (Aore Island, Santo, Vanuatu): A new Lapita site in the ambit of New Britain obsidian. In S. Bedford, C. Sand and S.P. Connaughton (eds), *Oceanic Explorations: Lapita and Western Pacific settlement*, pp. 151–162. Terra Australis 26. ANU E Press, Australian National University.

Green, R. 2000. Lapita and the cultural model for intrusion, integration and innovation. In A. Anderson and T. Murray (eds), *Australian Archaeologist: Collected papers in honour of Jim Allen*, pp. 372–392. Canberra, Coombs: Academic Publishing.

Hecht, J. 2005. Animals forage with near-perfect efficiency. *New Scientist* http://www.newscientist.com/article.ns?id=dn7419.

Irwin, G. 1992. *The Prehistoric Exploration and Colonisation of the Pacific*. Cambridge: Cambridge University Press.

Keegan, W. 1995. Modeling dispersal in the prehistoric West Indies. *World Archaeology* 26(3):400–420.

Kirch, P.V. 1997. The Lapita Peoples. Oxford: Blackwell.

Kirch, P.V. and R.C. Green 2001. *Hawaiki, Ancestral Polynesia*. Cambridge: Cambridge University Press.

Lilley, I. 1991. Lapita and post-Lapita developments in the Vitiaz Strait–West New Britain Area. *Bulletin of the Indo-Pacific Prehistory Association* 11:313–322.

Lilley, I. 1999. Lapita as politics. In J-C. Galipaud and I. Lilley (eds), *Le Pacifique de 5000 à 2000 BP : Suppléments à l'histoire d'une colonisation*, pp. 21–30. Paris: Éditions de l'Institut de Recherche pour le Développement.

Lilley, I. 2002. Lapita and Type Y pottery in the KLK site, Siassi, Papua New Guinea. In S. Bedford, D. Burley and C. Sand (eds), *Fifty Years in the Field. Papers in Honour of Richard Shutler*, pp. 79–90. Auckland: New Zealand Archaeological Association.

Lilley, I. 2004. Diaspora and identity in archaeology: moving beyond the Black Atlantic. In L. Meskell and R. Preucel (eds), *A Companion to Social Archaeology*, pp. 287–312. Oxford: Blackwell.

Lilley, I. 2006. Archaeology in Oceania: Themes and issues. In I. Lilley (ed), *Archaeology of Oceania: Australia and the Pacific Islands*, pp. 1–28. Oxford: Blackwell.

Lucas, G. 2007. Visions of archaeology. An interview with Tim Murray. *Archaeological Dialogues* 14(2):155–177.

Oppenheimer, S. 2003. Austronesian spread into Southeast Asia and Oceania: Where from and when? In C. Sand (ed), *Pacific Archaeology: Assessments and Prospects*, pp. 54–70. Nouméa: Département Archéologie.

Ravilious, K. 2006. Locating, locating, locating. *New Scientist* 192(2579):44–47.

Sheppard, P. and R. Walter 2006. A revised model of Solomon Islands culture history. *Journal of the Polynesian Society* 115:47–76.

Specht, J. 1967. Preliminary report on visit to Kilenge, West New Britain District, T.P.N.G. Unpublished report. Sydney, Australian Museum.

Specht, J. 1991. Kreslo: a Lapita pottery site in south-west New Britain, Papua New Guinea, In J. Allen and C. Gosden (eds), *Report of the Lapita Homeland Project*, pp. 189–204. Canberra: Australian National University.

Specht, J., C. Gosden, J. Webb, W. Boyd and I. Lilley 1992. Report on archaeological research in West New Britain Province, P.N.G. January–February 1992. Unpublished report. Sydney, Australian Museum.

Spriggs, M. 1995. The Lapita Culture and Austronesian prehistory in Oceania. In P. Bellwood, J. Fox and D. Tryon (eds), *The Austronesians: History and Comparative Perspective,* pp. 119–142. Canberra: The Australian National University.

Spriggs, M. 1997. *The Island Melanesians.* Oxford: Blackwell.

Spriggs, M. 2003. Post-Lapita evolutions in Island Melanesia. In C. Sand (ed), *Pacific Archaeology: Assessments and Prospects*, pp. 205–212. Nouméa: Département Archéologie.

Terrell, J. and E. Schechter 2007. Deciphering the Lapita code: The Aitape ceramic sequence and late survival of the "Lapita face". *Cambridge Archaeological Journal* 17:59–85.

Valentin, F., E. Herrscher, H, Buckley, S. Bedford M. Spriggs and K. Neal 2007. Subsistence strategies in a Lapita community: Teouma site (Vanuatu) insights from stable isotope data. Unpublished paper delivered to the Lapita Antecedents and Successors conference, Honiara, Solomon Islands.

Zubrow, E. 1985. Fractals, cultural behavior, and prehistory. *American Archaeology* 5(1):63–77.

6

Demographic expansion, despotism and the colonisation of East and South Polynesia

Douglas J. Kennett
Department of Anthropology, University of Oregon, USA
dkennett@uoregon.edu

Bruce Winterhalder
Department of Anthropology, University of California Davis, USA

Introduction

The Pacific Islands were some of the last habitable places on earth to be colonised by humans. Current archaeological evidence suggests these islands were colonised from c. 35,000 BP, and the expansion to increasingly remote islands and archipelagos was episodic rather than continuous; with bursts of migration followed by longer periods of sedentism and population growth (Anderson 2001a). The last phase of colonisation into East and South Polynesia occurred rapidly at c. 1000 BP, after a 1600-year hiatus in colonisation activity (Spriggs and Anderson 1993; Anderson 2001a, 2003).

We argued in an earlier paper (Kennett *et al.* 2006) that the episodic nature of oceanic colonisation is consistent with the predictions of Ideal Free Distribution (IFD), a population ecology model that considers the dynamic character of island suitability, along with density-dependent and density-independent variables influencing migratory behaviour. We also suggested intensive food production was one variable that contributed to decreasing suitability of island habitats, stimulating dispersal, and ultimately migrations to more distant islands in Oceania.

One of the primary assumptions of the IFD model is that all members of a group have equal competitive abilities and access to resources. Missing from our original model was an evaluation of changing despotic behavior. Despotic behaviour is an extreme bias in the control of resources by certain individuals (Summers 2005), which is documented in many Polynesian chiefdoms (Kirch 2000; Kirch and Kahn 2007). In this paper, we develop a model known as Ideal Despotic Distribution (IDD), and use it to evaluate the sociopolitical context for the colonisation of East and South Polynesia.

Ideal Free Distribution

Ideal Free Distribution (IFD) was developed in population ecology (Sutherland 1996; McClure *et al.* 2006; Shennan 2007), and it provides a starting point for predicting when individuals will disperse or migrate to a new habitat, based on density-dependent changes in the suitability of the habitats available to them (Kennett *et al.* 2006). Habitats are ranked by their quality, as assessed by the fitness of the initial occupant. Typically, fitness-related measures are used to measure quality or suitability (e.g. production of young, rate of food intake; see Winterhalder and Kennett 2006).

Quality is density-dependent and declines due to competition as populations increase. Competitors may use up resources directly – for instance, by consuming and depleting food supplies; or they may indirectly make resources harder to find or capture – for instance, by stimulating their dispersal or elevated wariness, or they may render resources less desirable due to contamination or by fighting over them. The former is known as depletion competition, the latter as interference competition (Sutherland 1996:9).

The two primary assumptions of IFD are that: (1) individuals will elect to reside in the *ideal* or best habitat available to them; and (2) they are *free* or unrestricted to make this choice. They are also assumed to be competitors with equal ability and access to resources. Under these conditions, colonising individuals will settle first in the best habitat available. The suitability of these high-ranked habitats decreases as populations increase due to immigration or in situ growth. When the habitat is diminished to the quality level of the second-ranked habitat, further population growth stimulates immigration, with populations moving to a wider range of habitats. Because each individual is ready to relocate if another habitat offers an edge in suitability, the population distribution will equalise marginal qualities across all occupied habitats. This is an equilibrium distribution, and is a consequence of the marginal equalisation of habitat suitability. In IFD, no individual has an incentive to relocate.

Despotism and Ideal Despotic Distribution

The assumption in IFD that all individuals are competitors of equal ability in the quest for resources is unrealistic, particularly in Polynesia where highly ranked chiefdoms were well established historically (Kirch 1984; Kirch and Kahn 2007). Despotism – or extreme bias in the control of resources by select individuals – is common in highly ranked societies (Summers 2005). Status competition and social inequality exist in all human groups, regardless of size or mode of production (Fried 1967; Boehm 2000; Diehl 2000). However, archaeological evidence for significant and institutionalised intra-group differences in status and wealth is confined to the past 13,000 years, well after the first evidence for anatomically modern humans in Africa (c. 150,000 years ago) and their subsequent appearance throughout much of the Old and New Worlds (Klein 2004). The preponderance of archaeological evidence suggests that for the majority of human history, groups remained small, occupied relatively large territories at low densities, and moved periodically to adapt to spatial and temporal fluctuations in resources. The archaeological record also indicates that group fissioning, environmental infilling and emigration to diverse habitats were generally favoured over localised increases in group size and density, or other forms of intensification. Under these conditions, institutionalised hereditary leadership and significant differences in status and wealth rarely emerged or persisted.

Archaeological evidence for ranked societies is often found in conjunction with clear indications of localised population aggregation, economic intensification and territorial circumscription (Carneiro 1970; Hayden 1981; Clark and Blake 1994; Blake and Clark

1999). In some instances, it co-occurs with a heightened commitment to agriculture (Price and Gebauer 1995), but similar developments also occurred among hunter-gatherers in areas where wild resources were concentrated, as with rich marine and aquatic habitats (Yesner 1980; Pálsson 1988; Erlandson 2001; Kennett 2005). In these locations, certain group members were able to acquire greater wealth and status by: (1) manipulating economic, social and political relationships to their own benefit (Earle 1987, 1997); (2) controlling the flow of exotic goods used to signal status (Flannery 1972); (3) monopolising the labour of other group members (Earle 1987; Arnold 2001); and (4) creating ideologies that justified the uneven distribution of wealth and power (Earle 1987, 1997). Increased control of resources, and, in some instances, differential reproduction (Betzig 1986) by a small number of high-status individuals accompanies the emergence of social ranking.

Ideal Despotic Distribution (IDD) is a variant of IFD that allows for individuals with different competitive abilities, highlighting competition and the possibility of differential access to resources within, and among, groups. If interference arises among competitors of unequal abilities, or if, by establishing territories, superior competitors or competing groups can protect themselves from density-dependent habitat deterioration by defending better resource opportunities, then the inferior competitors and those without territories are pushed to poorer habitats. Compared with IFD, a despotic distribution will reach equilibrium with disproportionate numbers or densities in the lower-ranked habitats. This makes intuitive sense: by garnering disproportionate resources in the best habitats, the better competitors push inferior ones more rapidly into habitats of lesser suitability. In many empirical studies, IFD serves as a null hypothesis, against which one can measure the effects of interference competition and unequal resource access (Sutherland 1996).

The decision by an individual or subgroup to leave or fission from its parent community depends on the risks of staying, the costs of moving, the likely success of relocating, and the relative advantages of alternative settlement locations. Relative advantage is dependent on the availability and suitability of adjacent habitats, and the behaviour of other groups in the area. Localised population increase, from endogenous growth or in-migration, followed by community fission, results in environmental infilling and the occupation of increasingly marginal zones (environmental packing; Binford 1968, 1983). Localised decreases in habitat suitability due to depletion or interference will stimulate group fission and emigration until most habitable areas are occupied. People may live in large groups, even under severely disadvantaged conditions, if they are circumscribed environmentally, demographically, or socially (Carneiro 1970). Circumscription includes social boundaries maintained by the threat of violence from adjacent communities, real or perceived. Socialisation for fear of others is a common form of coercion used to manipulate subordinate members of a group (Kantner 1999; Lekson 2002), and it can be used to reduce the attractiveness of settlement locations. In other words, subordination to members of one's own group may be the best alternative open to an individual. Ideological manipulation can also play an important role in the perception of the costs and benefits of staying with the group and being subjugated and exploited by others (Earle 1987).

Colonisation of Polynesia

The first appearance of people in Fiji and West Polynesia is signalled by the Lapita cultural complex, and is more broadly associated with the rapid spread of people from Island Southeast Asia (Bellwood 2001:Figure 1). Biological and linguistic data suggest the archaeological record of Lapita relates to an expansion of Austronesian-speaking people (Diamond and Bellwood 2003). Lapita-age settlements of 3300 to 2600 BP are identified by the presence of distinctive dentate-

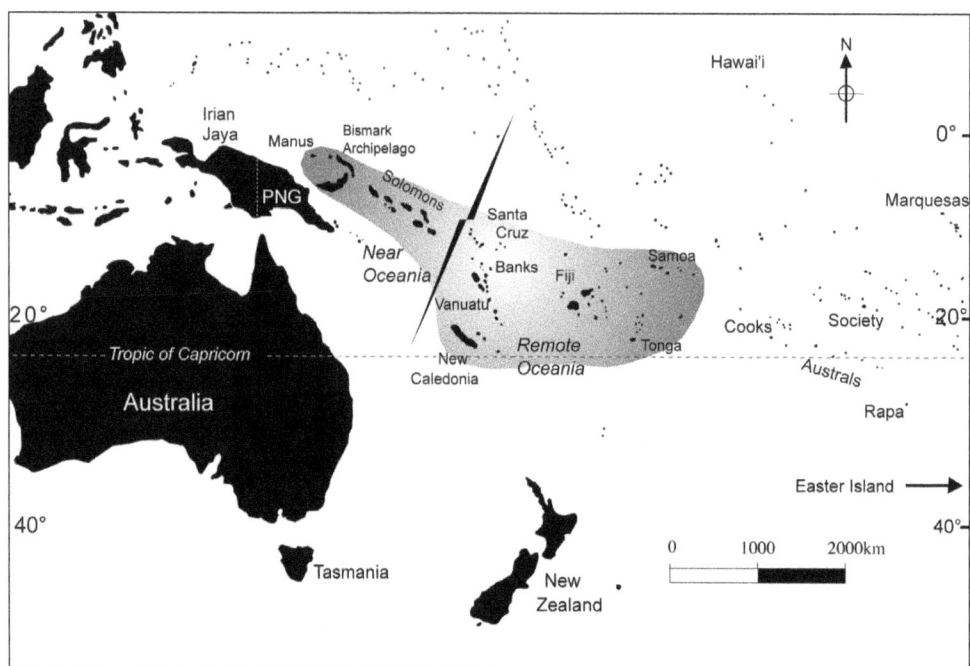

Figure 1. Map of Oceania showing the relevant islands and archipelagos. Arrow demarcates near and remote Oceania.

stamped and incised pottery (Kirch 1997; Anderson *et al.* 2001). An inventory of locations containing dentate-stamped pottery includes about 184 locations, extending 4500 km from the Bismarck Archipelago, southeast to Fiji, Tonga, Samoa and Wallis (Uvea) in the South Pacific (Anderson *et al.* 2001). The appearance of Lapita pottery east of the Solomon Islands represents the earliest known colonisation of Remote Oceania (Kirch and Hunt 1988). Sites throughout the Lapita range are most common in coastal contexts, with overall densities on larger islands being lower than smaller islands (Anderson 2001a). The earliest Lapita settlements in Fiji date to between 3000 BP and 2600 BP, with slightly later ages for the earliest Tongan and Samoan settlements, of 2950–2650 BP (Burley 1998; Anderson *et al.* 2001).

Recent archaeological studies suggest a hiatus of c. 1600 years between the expansion of Lapita peoples into Fiji and West Polynesia and the colonisation of more remote islands and archipelagos in East and South Polynesia (Anderson and Sinoto 2002; Anderson 2003). Spriggs and Anderson (1993) argued the initial colonisation of East Polynesia did not occur before 1600–1400 BP, but a series of more recent studies suggests it may have occurred closer to 1000 BP. In the Society Islands, archaeological deposits date no earlier than 1000 BP (Anderson *et al.* 1999), and current data from the Marquesas indicate settlement at 900 BP (Rolett and Conte 1995; Rolett 1998). On the remote fringes of East Polynesia, recent information suggests Easter Island (Rapa Nui) was colonised by 800 BP (Hunt and Lipo 2006), and certainly no earlier than 1000 BP (Steadman *et al.* 1994), Hawaii about 1000 BP (Athens *et al.* 1999), the Gambier Islands at 900 BP (Anderson *et al.* 2003), Rapa at 800 BP (Kennett *et al.* 2006), and New Zealand (Anderson 1991; Higham *et al.* 1999), along with several other South Polynesian islands, by 800 BP (Johnson 1995; Anderson and O'Regan 2000; Anderson and White 2001).

Colonisation of East Polynesia also includes the 25 'mystery islands' (e.g. Christmas, Norfolk and Pitcairn Islands) that were all colonised after 1000 BP, then abandoned before European contact (Anderson 2001b; Anderson *et al.* 2002). The revised archaeological ages for settlement are generally consistent with palaeoenvironmental records of anthropogenic vegetation change

(Athens *et al.* 1999; McGlone and Wilmshurst 1999; Anderson 1995, 2002; Burney 2002). The conclusion is that the colonisation of East and South Polynesia was late and rapid.

Sociopolitical context for the colonisation of East and South Polynesia

Archaeological information suggests a long period of population infilling after Lapita settlements were established in the Fijian, Tongan and Samoan archipelagos. The post-Lapita cultural sequences are remarkably similar in Fiji/West Polynesia and suggest parallel processes and continuous cultural interactions (Kirch 2000). Settlement-pattern data for these island groups indicate: (1) an increased number of settlements in coastal locations and in previously unoccupied islands in an archipelago (Spennemann 1989; Burley 1998); (2) an increase in the size of settlements (Burley 1998:363) and a reduction in settlement mobility (Clark 1999); (3) the expansion of populations into the interiors of larger islands (Hunt 1987; Burley 1998; Clark 1999; Field 2004, 2005); (4) intensified agricultural practices, inferred from inland expansion and the development of terracing and irrigation systems (Burley 1998; Kirch 1994). Burning, deforestation and resource depression parallel the increased reliance on horticulture, and eventually intensive forms of agriculture develop (Burley 1998; Anderson 2002; Steadman *et al.* 2002). All these observations are consistent with the predictions of the IFD model (Kennett *et al.* 2006).

Increasing despotism in Fiji and West Polynesia may have also played a role, particularly for the rapid colonisation of East and South Polynesia. Hierarchically organised societies with despotic chiefs were present throughout Polynesia by the time of historic contact (Kirch 1984; Kirch and Kahn 2007). Chiefs controlled agricultural production via land ownership and by manipulating labour to increase subsistence yields. Individual households increased agricultural production by making permanent modifications to the land (e.g. terraces and canals) and/or increasing labour investment (e.g. weeding and mulching). Status rivalry between competing chiefs was strongly developed and wars were waged, in part, to seize the productive agricultural land of competitors.

Kirch (2000) has argued on linguistic grounds (e.g. words for corporate groups and positions of status) that the concept of hierarchical sociopolitical structure was present in the Ancestral

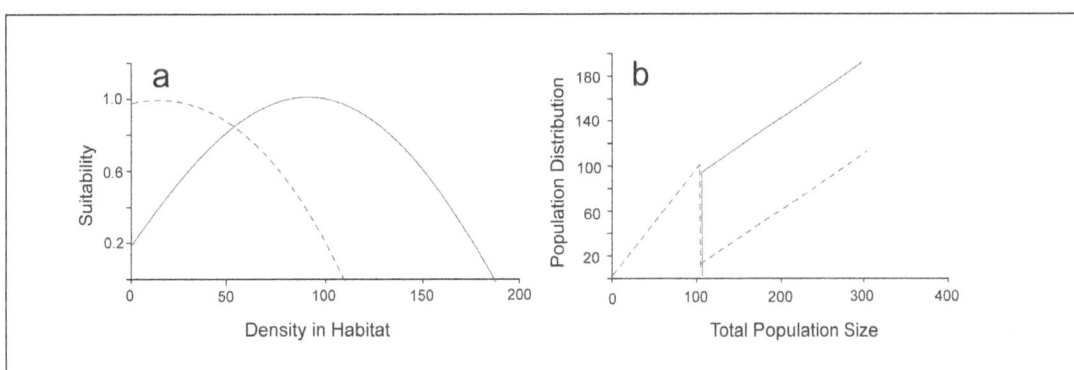

Figure 2. The Ideal Free Distribution (IFD) model determines the equilibrium distribution of populations over habitats (or spatially separable production opportunities), as a function of density and density-dependent suitability. The Ideal Despotic Distribution (IDD) model is similar, but allows for territoriality or other forms of resource defence. This example depicts the IFD and two habitats. (a) Suitability in the highest-ranked habitat declines monotonically with population growth; suitability in the second-ranked habitat first increases due to economies of scale (Allee effect), and then declines. (b) Individuals populate the highest-ranked habitat until its marginal suitability drops to the level for entry into the second-ranked habitat. There is then a rapid migration from the first to the second habitat, depopulating one and filling the other, until their marginal suitabilities again equalise and further growth is divided between them.

Polynesia groups that colonised and developed in Fiji and West Polynesia during the Lapita era. The degree of sociopolitical stratification in Polynesian societies is strongly correlated with population size and density (Kirch 1984:98–99). Population density in Fiji and West Polynesia clearly increased between initial Lapita settlement (c. 3000 BP) and the next major wave of colonisation into East Polynesia at 1000 BP. Plainware ceramics (2650–1550 BP) are spread across agricultural fields throughout the Tongan archipelago (Burley 1998:363), and occur in coastal and interior settlements (Spennemann 1989). Interior portions of the Sigatoka Valley on the island of Viti Levu (Fiji) were colonised for the first time by c. 2000 BP (Field 2005), a general trend visible in both Fiji and Samoa (Marshall *et al.* 2000). Site size and complexity also increased in comparison with the small coastal settlements common in the Lapita era (Burley 1998; Field 2004). Within this context, competition for land would have been an important factor in the emergence of social hierarchies, but direct archaeological evidence for these hierarchies is meager until about 1000 BP.

The appearance of more intensive forms of agriculture before 1000 BP is suggestive of emerging social hierarchies. Pond field irrigation systems were being built to grow *Colocasia* on the island of Futuna by c. 1300 BP (Kirch 1994). Walled dry-field agricultural systems were also expanding at this time on Futuna and the adjacent island of Alofi, and similar trends are visible in Tongan islands and in Fiji (Field 2004). Intensive agricultural systems are generally absent in Samoa, even in late prehistory when centralised polities are known to have existed. The appearance of innovative and intensive large-scale agricultural systems is partly related to the expansion of populations. However, Kirch (2000) points out that these systems were often constructed and maintained to generate agricultural surplus for despotic chiefs.

Corporate group formation and status rivalry is suggested by the increase in inter-group conflict in Fiji and West Polynesia between 1500 and 1000 BP. The fortified hilltop settlement of Tatanga-matau on the island of Tutuila (Samoa) was in use as early as 1000 BP, with most activity dating to between c. 700 and 600 BP (Leach and Witter 1990). Hilltop settlements on Futuna and Alofi are synchronous with the appearance of pond and walled field agricultural systems at 1300 BP (Kirch 2000:227). Defensive locations were employed in parts of Fiji between 1500 and 1000 BP (Field 2004, 2005), with the first large hilltop fortifications appearing at c. 1000 BP (Best 1984), and a range of other defensive sites in use by historic contact (e.g. ring ditch forts, refuges; Parry 1977, 1982, 1987). In the Sigatoka Valley of Viti Levu, many fortifications were positioned in close proximity to agricultural fields, and appear to have been strategically placed to defend these lands (Field 2005:598). The appearance of fortifications in Fiji and West Polynesia generally correlates with land improvements that would have increased their value and economic defensibility (Dyson-Hudson and Smith 1979). Warfare and territorial conquest were despotic strategies for increasing surplus production and the asymmetric distribution of wealth.

Monumental architecture is highly visible and is closely connected with political power and social hierarchies in Polynesia (Graves and Green 1993; Kirch 2000). Large-scale structures include earth and stone mounds used as platforms for high-status residences or for chiefly burials. The Pulemelei mound of Savai'i island on Samoa is a massive stepped platform that possibly served as a residence for the high chief Lilomaiave Nailevaiiliili in the 17th century (Kirch 2000; Clark and Martinsson-Wallin 2007). Monumental architecture first appears in Tonga and Samoa between about 1000 and 800 BP (Burley 1998; Green 2002), a date consistent with genealogical records for the origins of the Tongan chiefdom at 1000 BP (Gifford 1929). Clark and Martinsson-Wallin (2007) point out that the appearance of monumental architecture, and the stratified social structure that it represents, is coincident with the major colonisation pulse into East Polynesia. These data point to West Polynesia as the ultimate conceptual source of hierarchical social structures, and this provides an important socio-political mechanism for rapid population dispersal into East and South Polynesia.

Conclusions

The evidence for colonisation of East and South Polynesia starting c. 1000 BP, if accurate, suggests these migrations were initiated from West Polynesia in the context of: (1) increasing population density; (2) decreasing habitat suitability due to erosion and soil degradation, after an initial increase in habitat suitability for agriculture due to forest clearance and terracing; (3) heightened interference due to territoriality and warfare. These observations are all consistent with the IFD model as originally constructed (Kennett *et al.* 2006). However, the rapid movement of people into East and South Polynesia after c. 1000 BP is more consistent with the IDD. Agricultural intensification, warfare, the construction of large monumental structures and substantial landscape modification from c. 1500 BP to 1000 BP suggests that hierarchical subjugation and despotic control of land initially stimulated population dispersal. The replication of this sociopolitical system was a key mechanism for 'pushing' migrants to the remote fringes of East and South Polynesia.

Acknowledgements

This paper was written with fellowship support from the AHRC Centre for the Evolution of Cultural Diversity, Institute of Archaeology, University College London (DJK).

References

Anderson, A.J. 1991. The chronology of colonization in New Zealand. *Antiquity* 65:767–795.

Anderson, A.J. 1995. Current approaches in East Polynesian colonization research. *Journal of the Polynesian Society* 104:110–132.

Anderson, A. J. 2001a. Mobility models of Lapita migration. In G.R. Clark, A.J. Anderson and T. Vunidilo (eds), *The Archaeology of Lapita Dispersal in Oceania: Papers from the Fourth Lapita Conference, June 2000, Canberra*, pp. 15–23. Terra Australis 17.

Anderson, A. J. 2001b. No meat on that beautiful shore: the prehistoric abandonment of subtropical Polynesian islands. *International Journal of Osteoarchaeology* 11:14–23.

Anderson, A. J. 2002. Faunal collapse, landscape change and settlement history in Remote Oceania. *World Archaeology* 33:375–390.

Anderson, A. J. 2003. Entering uncharted waters: models of initial colonization in Polynesia. In M. Rockman and J. Steele (eds), *Colonization of Unfamiliar Landscapes*, pp. 169–189. London: Routledge.

Anderson, A.J. and G. O'Regan 2000. To the final shore: Prehistoric colonisation of the Subantarctic islands in South Polynesia. In A.J. Anderson and T. Murray (eds), *Australian Archaeologist: Collected Papers in Honour of Jim Allen*, pp. 440–454. Canberra: Coombs Academic Publishing.

Anderson, A.J. and Y.H. Sinoto 2002. New radiocarbon ages of colonization sites in East Polynesia. *Asian Perspectives* 41:242–257.

Anderson, A.J. and J.P. White (eds) 2001. *The Prehistoric Archaeology of Norfolk Island, Southwest Pacific*. Records of the Australian Museum, Supplement 27.

Anderson, A.J., E. Conte, G. Clark, Y. Sinoto and F.J. Petchey 1999. Renewed excavations at the

Motu Paeao site, Maupiti Island, French Polynesia: preliminary results. *New Zealand Journal of Archaeology* 21:47–66.

Anderson, A.J., S. Bedford, G.R. Clark, I. Lilley, C. Sand, G. Summerhayes and R. Torrence 2001. An inventory of Lapita sites containing dentate-stamped pottery. In G.R. Clark, A.J. Anderson and T. Vunidilo (eds), *The Archaeology of Lapita Dispersal in Oceania: Papers from the Fourth Lapita Conference, June 2000, Canberra*, pp. 1–13. Terra Australis 17.

Anderson, A.J., H. Martinsson-Wallin and P. Wallin 2002. The prehistory of Kiritimati (Christmas) Island, Republic of Kiribati. *The Kon-Tiki Museum*, Occasional Papers 6.

Anderson, A.J., E. Conte, P.V. Kirch, and M. Weisler 2003. Cultural chronology in Mangareva (Gambier Islands), French Polynesia: evidence from recent radiocarbon dating. *Journal of the Polynesian Society* 112:119–140.

Arnold, J.E. (ed) 2001. *The Origins of a Pacific Coast Chiefdom: The Chumash of the Channel Islands.* Salt Lake City: University of Utah Press.

Athens, J.S.; J.V. Ward, H.D. Tuggle and D.J. Welch 1999. *Environment, vegetation change and early human settlement on the 'Ewa plain: a cultural resource inventory of Naval Air Station, Barber's Point, O'ahu, Hawai'i. Part III: Paleoenvironmental investigations.* Honolulu: International Archaeological Research Institute Inc.

Best, S. 1984. Lakeba: the prehistory of a Fijian Island. Unpublished PhD thesis, Department of Anthropology, University of Auckland.

Best, S. 2002. *Lapita: A View from the East.* New Zealand Archaeological Association Monograph No. 24.

Betzig, L. 1986. *Despotism and differential reproduction.* New York: Aldine.

Bellwood, P.S. 1984. The Great Pacific Migration. In *Yearbook of Science and the Future for 1984*, pp. 80–93. Chicago: Encyclopedia Britannica.

Bellwood, P. 2001. Early agriculturalist population diasporas? Farming, languages, and genes. *Annual Review of Anthropology* 30:181–207.

Binford, L.R. 1968. Post-Pleistocene adaptations. In S.R. Binford and L.R. Binford (eds), *New Perspectives in Archaeology*, pp.313–341. Chicago: Aldine Publishing Co.

Binford, L.R. 1983. *In Pursuit of the Past: Decoding the Archaeological Record.* New York: Thames and Hudson.

Blake, M. and J.E. Clark 1999. The emergence of hereditary inequality: the case of Pacific coastal Chiapas, Mexico. In M. Blake (ed), *Pacific Latin America in Prehistory*, pp. 55–73. Pullman: Washington State University Press

Boehm, C. 2000. Forager Hierarchies, innate dispositions, and the behavioral reconstruction of prehistory. In M.W. Diehl (ed), *Hierarchies in Action: Cui Bono?*, pp. 31–58. Carbondale: Southern Illinois University.

Burley, D.V. 1998. Tongan Archaeology and the Tongan Past, 2850–150 BP. *Journal of World Prehistory* 12:337–392.

Burney, D.A. 2002. Late Quaternary chronology and stratigraphy of twelve sites on Kaua'i. *Radiocarbon* 44:13–44.

Carneiro, R.L. 1970. A theory of the origin of the state. *Science* 169:733–738.

Clark, G.R. 1999. Post-Lapita Fiji: Cultural Transformation in the Mid-Sequence. Unpublished PhD thesis, Department of Archaeology and Natural History, Research School of Pacific and Asian Studies, Australian National University.

Clark, G. and H. Martinsson-Wallin 2007. Monumental architecture in West Polynesia: Origins, chiefs, and archaeological approaches. *Archaeology in Oceania* 42:28–40.

Clark, J.E. and M. Blake 1994. Power of prestige: competitive generosity and the emergence of rank in lowland Mesoamerica. In E.M. Brumfiel and J.W. Fox (ed), *Factional Competition and Political Development in the New World*, pp.17–30. Cambridge: Cambridge University Press.

Diamond, J. and P. Bellwood 2003. Farmers and their languages: the first expansions. *Science* 300:597–603.

Diehl, M.W. 2000. Some thoughts on the study of hierarchies. In M.W. Diehl (ed), *Hierarchies in Action: Cui Bono?*, pp. 11–30. Carbondale: Southern Illinois University.

Dyson-Hudson, R. and E.A. Smith. 1978. Human territoriality: an ecological reassessment. *American Anthropologist* 80:21–41.

Earle, T. 1987. Chiefdoms in archaeological and ethnohistorical context. *Annual Review of Anthropology* 16:279–308.

Earle, T. 1997. *How chiefs come to power: The political economy in prehistory.* Stanford: Stanford University Press.

Erlandson, J.M. 2001. The Archaeology of aquatic adaptations: Paradigms for a new millennium. *Journal of Archaeological Research* 9:287–350.

Field, J.S. 2004. Environmental and climatic considerations: a hypothesis for conflict and the emergence of social complexity in Fijian prehistory. *Journal of Anthropological Archaeology* 23:79–99.

Field, J.S. 2005. Land tenure, competition and ecology in Fijian prehistory. *Antiquity* 79:586–600.

Flannery, K.V. 1972. The cultural evolution of civilizations. *Annual Review of Ecology and Systematics* 3:399–426.

Fried, M.H. 1967. *The evolution of political society: An essay in political anthropology.* New York: Random House.

Gifford, E.W. 1929. *Tongan society.* Bernice P. Bishop Museum Bulletin 61.

Graves, M.W. and R.C. Green (eds) 1993. *The evolution and organisation of prehistoric society in Polynesia.* New Zealand Monograph Association 19.

Green, R.C. 2002. A retrospective view of settlement pattern studies in Samoa. In T.N. Ladefoged and M.W. Graves (eds.), *Pacific landscapes. Archaeological approaches*, pp. 125–152. Los Osos: Easter Island Foundation:

Hayden, B. 1981. Research and development in the Stone Age: Technological transitions among hunter-gatherers. *Current Anthropology* 22:519–548.

Higham, T.G.F., A.J. Anderson, C. Jacomb 1999. Dating the first New Zealanders: The chronology of Wairau Bar. *Antiquity* 73:420–427.

Hunt, T.L. 1987. Patterns of human interaction and evolutionary divergence in the Fiji Islands. *Journal of the Polynesian Society* 96:299–334.

Hunt, T.L. and C.P. Lipo 2006. Late Colonization of Easter Island. *Science* DOI: 10.1126/science.1121879

Johnson, L. 1995. *In the midst of a prodigious ocean: Archaeological investigations of Polynesian settlement of the Kermadec Islands.* Auckland: Department of Conservation, Resource Series 11.

Kantner, J. 1999. Survival cannibalism or sociopolitical intimidation? Explaining perimortem mutilation in the American Southwest. *Human Nature: An interdisciplinary biosocial perspective* 10(1):1–50.

Kennett, D. J. 2005. *The Island Chumash: Behavioral ecology of a maritime society.* Berkeley: University of California Press.

Kennett, D.J., A. Anderson, M. Prebble, E. Conte and J. Southon, 2006. Human Impacts on Rapa, French Polynesia. *Antiquity* 80:340–354.

Kennett, D.J., A. Anderson, and B. Winterhalder 2006. The Ideal free distribution, food production, and the colonization of Oceania. In D.J. Kennett and B. Winterhalder (eds), *Behavioral Ecology and the Transition to Agriculture*, pp. 265–288. Berkeley: University of California Press.

Kirch, P.V. 1984. *The evolution of the Polynesian chiefdoms.* Cambridge: Cambridge University Press.

Kirch, P.V. 1994. *The Wet and the Dry: Irrigation and agricultural intensification in Polynesia.* Chicago: University of Chicago Press.

Kirch, P.V. 1997. *The Lapita peoples: Ancestors of the Oceanic world.* Oxford: Blackwell.

Kirch, P.V. 2000. *On the road of the winds. An archaeological history of the Pacific Islands before European contact.* California: University of California Press.

Kirch, P.V. and T.L. Hunt (eds) 1988. *Archaeology of the Lapita Cultural Complex: A critical review.*

Thomas Burke Memorial Washington State Museum Research Report No. 5. Seattle: Burke Museum.

Kirch, P. V. and J.G. Kahn 2007. Advances in Polynesian Prehistory: A review and assessment of the past decade (1993–2004). *Journal of Archaeological Research* 15:191–238.

Klein, R.G. 2004. *The human career: Human biological and cultural origins*. Chicago: University of Chicago Press.

Leach, H.M. and D.C. Witter 1987. Tataga-Matau 'rediscovered'. *New Zealand Journal of Archaeology* 9:33–54.

Lekson, S.H. 2002. War in the Southwest, War in the World. *American Antiquity* 67:607–624.

Marshall, Y., A. Crosby, S. Matararaba and S. Wood. 2000. *Sigatoka. The shifting sands of Fijian prehistory*. University of Southampton Department of Archaeology Monograph No.1.

McClure, S.B., M.A. Jochim and C.M. Barton 2006. Human behavioral ecology, domestic animals, and land use during the transition to agriculture in Valencia, eastern Spain. In D.J. Kennett and B. Winterhalder (eds), *Behavioral Ecology and the Transition to Agriculture*, pp. 197–216. Berkeley: University of California Press.

McGlone, M.S. and J.M. Wilmshurst 1999. Dating initial Maori environmental impact in New Zealand. *Quaternary International* 59:5–16.

Pálsson, G. 1988. Hunters and gatherers of the sea. In T. Ingold, D. Riches and J. Woodburn (eds), *Hunters and Gatherers 1: History, Evolution and Social Change*, pp. 189–204. New York: Berg.

Parry, J. 1977. *Ring-ditch fortifications: Ring-ditch fortifications in the Rewa Delta, Fiji: Air photo interpretation and analysis*. Bulletin of the Fiji Museum No. 3.

Parry, J. 1982. *Ring-ditch fortifications II: Ring-ditch fortifications in the Navua Delta, Fiji: Air photo interpretation and analysis*. Bulletin of the Fiji Museum No. 7.

Parry, J. 1987. *The Sigatoka Valley–Pathways into prehistory*. Fiji Museum Bulletin No. 9.

Price, T.D. and A.B. Gebauer (eds) 1995. *Last hunters-first foragers: New perspectives on the prehistoric transition to agriculture*. Santa Fe: School of American Research Press.

Rolett, B.V. 1998. *Hanamiai: prehistoric colonization and cultural change in the Marquesas Islands (East Polynesia)*. Yale University Publications in Anthropology 81.

Rolett, B.V. and E. Conte 1995. Renewed investigation of the Ha'atuatua Dune (Nuku Hiva, Marquesas Islands): A key site in Polynesian prehistory. *Journal of the Polynesian Society* 104:195–228.

Shennan, S. 2007. The spread of farming into Central Europe and its consequences: Evolutionary models. In T. Kohler and S.E. van der Leeuw (eds), *Model-based Archaeology*, pp. 143–157. Sante Fe: SAR Press.

Spennemann, D.H.R. 1989. 'Ata 'a Tonga mo 'Ata 'o Tonga: Early and later Prehistory of the Tongan Islands. Unpublished PhD thesis, Australia National University.

Spriggs, M. and A.J. Anderson. 1993. Late colonization of East Polynesia. *Antiquity* 67:200–217.

Steadman, D., P. Vargas and C. Cristino 1994. Stratigraphy, chronology and cultural context of an early faunal assemblage from Easter Island. *Asian Perspectives* 33:79–96.

Steadman, D.W., A. Plourde and D.V. Burley 2002. Prehistoric butchery and consumption of birds in the Kingdom of Tonga. *Journal of Archaeological Science* 29:571–584.

Summers, K. 2005. The evolutionary ecology of despotism. *Evolution and Human Behavior* 26:106–135.

Sutherland, W.J. 1996. *From individual behaviour to population ecology*. Oxford: Oxford University Press.

Winterhalder, B. and D. J. Kennett 2006. Behavioral ecology and the transition from hunting and gathering to agriculture. In D.J. Kennett and B. Winterhalder (eds), *Behavioral Ecology and the transition to agriculture*, pp.1–21. Berkeley: University of California Press.

Yesner, D.R. 1980. Maritime hunter-gatherers: ecology and prehistory. *Current Anthropology* 21:727–750.

7

The long pause and the last pulse: Mapping East Polynesian colonisation

Tim Thomas

Anthropology Department, University of Otago, New Zealand

tim.thomas@otago.ac.nz

Introduction

Maps are rarely neutral depictions of space. They encode, simplify and abstract human experiences of landscapes according to particular needs and histories. More often than not, they are *arguments* – about how we should perceive the world in particular contexts (Wood 1992). Accordingly, maps are socially and culturally embedded. European maps, for example, have been identified as embodying the post-Cartesian Enlightenment project – a means of inquiry, examination and control, promoting the 'rational' utilisation of space (Tilley 1994:21) and thus a tool of imperialist and colonial practice (Carter 1987). In contrast, Marshall Islands navigation charts are more personal, indexing wave swells formed around islands as experienced by an individual canoe pilot/mapper – a kinaesthetic cartography, perhaps, far from the visuality and mathematics of the Cartesian map, but politicised, too, by social restrictions of ritual and access (Winckler 1901). The map is not the territory (Bateson 1972:460), but rather a purpose-driven model.

Accepting maps as models enables us to explore them as visual representations of the human experience of movement in particular landscapes. We can be freed somewhat from the constraints of depicting pure geography by recognising that experiences of geography are never pure – they are mediated by technology, past experience, economic considerations and so on. The perception of distance, for example, is heavily mediated by modes of travel (whether one swims, takes a boat, or takes an aeroplane), the conditions of the terrain (a sheltered bay, a current-riven sea), and the attractiveness of the destination. The effect is to increase or decrease friction to movement, causing distance to be measured by effort, time and desire. What would a map look like if it could take such factors into consideration? In this paper, I explore this question by addressing debates about the pattern and pace of the prehistoric colonisation of East Polynesia through a series of analyses that model the geography of the Pacific as just such a 'friction landscape'.

My central focus is the long-standing problem of the 'long pause' in eastward migration after the Lapita-era colonisation of the Fiji–Samoa–Tonga region, before a belated last pulse of movement into East Polynesia. Recent academic debate has mostly focused on determining the duration of this pause, but this has also frequently required forays into determining cause. Here, I concentrate on the latter issue, but first, some background to the former will be necessary.

Mapping East Polynesian colonisation

Te Rangi Hiroa (Buck 1954) famously depicted the origin and culture of Polynesians as an octopus (Tangaroa) centred on the Society Islands, its tentacles snaking out over the map (Figure 1). The image reflects the importance of comparative ethnology and cosmology as evidence for early scholars and is of interest for its identification of Ra'iatea as the homeland (Havai'i) of Polynesian cultural development after migrations through Micronesia. It stands in contrast to an altogether more modernist map (Figure 2) first drawn by Emory and Sinoto (1965), but appearing in several subsequent publications (e.g. Jennings 1979). With the advent of stratigraphic excavation and radiocarbon dating, narratives of Polynesian origins increasingly stressed a stepwise progression of island-hopping migrations – leaving behind the timelessness and unity evident in Hiroa's map, and depicting instead a series of developmental pauses punctuated by sudden voyages of colonisation.

In what came to be known and critiqued as the 'authorised version' (Irwin 1981) or 'orthodox scenario' (Kirch 1986) of Polynesian dispersals, this second model postulated that the Marquesas were the first eastern archipelago settled by voyagers from West Polynesia. Successive dispersals radiated out from this 'homeland' to the Society Islands and the rest of East Polynesia. The evidence here was purely archaeological, drawing on typological comparisons of excavated artefacts and radiocarbon dates, with very little (in comparison with later research) speculation or assumptions made about *expected* patterns of colonisation. Retrospectively, this conservatism is surprising, given that archaeological coverage at the time was very sparse, and that the Marquesas are some 1800 nautical miles (3300 km) northeast of Samoa. The questionable likelihood of such a direct voyage is elided in Emory and Sinoto's map by a subtle scale and distance transformation – the Marquesas are enlarged and drawn southward and closer to Samoa than their geographic position warrants, and the Cook Islands are not shown at all. The map reifies the model. It was, however, the chronological gap between the Lapita-era settlement of West Polynesia c. 1000 BC

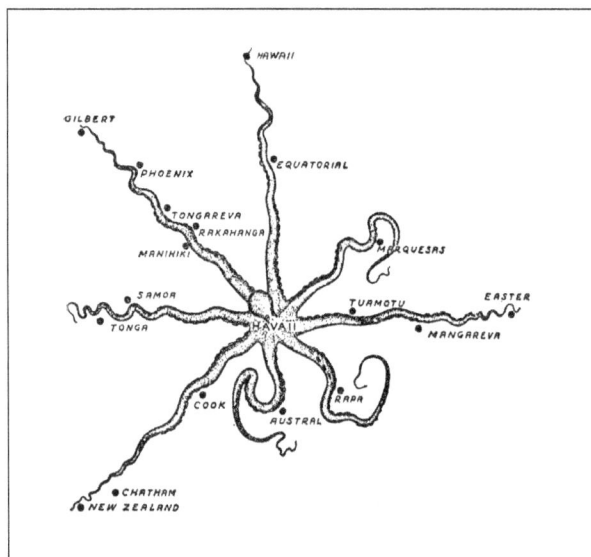

Figure 1. 'The hub of Polynesia, Havai'i, with its eight radials' (Buck 1954:88).

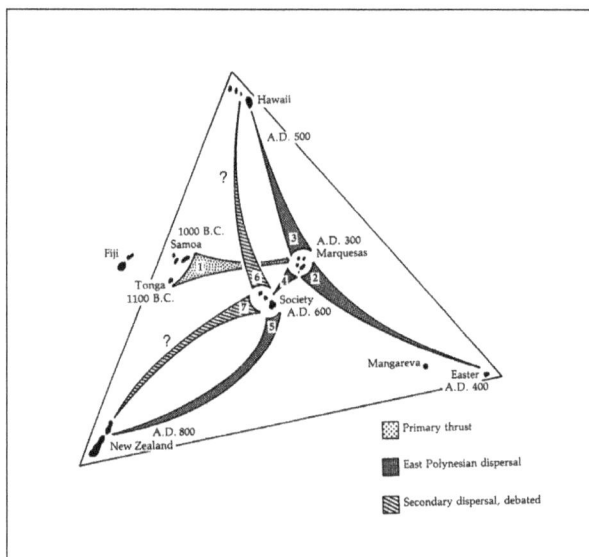

Figure 2. The 'orthodox model' of East Polynesian colonisation (Jennings 1979:3).

and the Marquesas c. 300 AD that drew most attention, coming to be seen as representing a problematically 'long pause' in the eastward trend of colonisation.

For Irwin (1981), the pause was an artefact of archaeological sampling – Lapita voyaging was argued to have continued on past Samoa through the southern Cooks, but archaeologists had not yet detected any settlements due to patchy fieldwork, low visibility of early sites, and environmental change. Kirch (1986) added to this a re-interpretation of the radiocarbon dates, suggesting earlier settlement of the Marquesas than originally accepted (Figure 3). These arguments sought to temporally compress the pause, framing East Polynesian colonisation as part of a continuous process of eastward movement. This was further reinforced by computer simulations arguing that no navigational threshold existed between western and eastern Polynesia (Irwin 1992:83). In the absence of early archaeological sites, positive confirmation of the scenario was sought in palaeo-environmental proxies for human impact on island environments (Kirch and Ellison 1994).

A clear epistemological shift is apparent here – this 'early-settlement' model is predictive, relying on a set of assumptions about voyaging technology and behaviour, and it appeals to logic, in contrast to the postdictive 'orthodox scenario' with its sole reliance on archaeological data. One problem, however, is that the early-settlement model is not falsifiable, since we can always argue early ephemeral sites have been destroyed and thus remain undiscovered. A critique was soon mounted, mobilised largely by Atholl Anderson, and grounded again in a more data-centred postdictive approach. The East Polynesian radiocarbon corpus was subjected to systematic screening (Spriggs and Anderson 1993), resulting in the rejection of some early dates and the proposal that the colonisation pause may have been as long as 1600 years – a 'late-settlement' model. Subsequent investigation of key sites in East Polynesia supported the hypothesis, with the earliest sites in the Marquesas now dated to about 900 BP (Rolett and Conte 1995; Rolett 1998; Anderson and Sinoto 2002), the Society Islands about 1000 BP (Anderson *et al.* 1999), Easter Island (Rapa Nui) and Hawaii soon after (Steadman *et al.* 1994; Athens *et al.* 1999), and New Zealand about 800 BP (Anderson 1991; Higham *et al.* 1999). In addition, the accuracy and stacked assumptions of palaeo-environmental modelling (i.e. pollen signatures as a proxy for environmental change are a proxy for human impact) have been subjected to critique (Anderson 1995, 2002; McGlone and Wilmshurst 1999), as has the use of the performance characteristics of replica Polynesian voyaging canoes made with modern

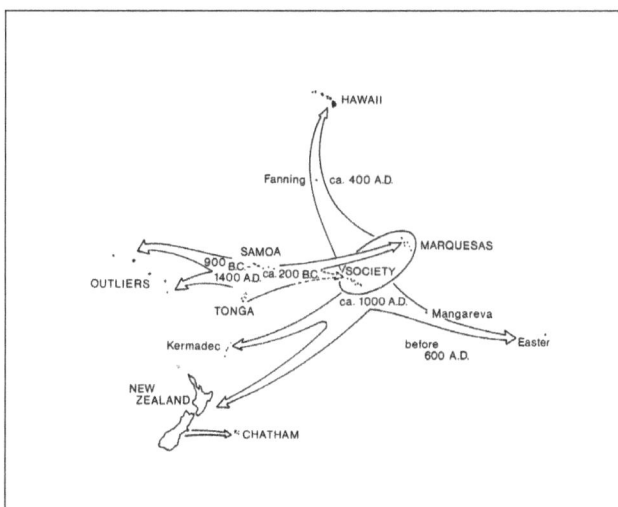

Figure 3. The early-settlement model (Kirch and Green 1987:Figure 3).

materials for assumptions about the pace and difficulty of reaching various island targets beyond West Polynesia (Anderson 2000, 2001a).

Again, there is an epistemological quandary in this late-settlement model, for while it is potentially falsifiable (by the discovery of an older-than-anticipated site), it is not easily proven, given the nature of archaeological data. Nevertheless, in the absence of unequivocal evidence for early settlement, the late-settlement model can be regarded as currently favoured. Its acceptance requires a new map of colonisation – a pulse model (Figure 4) in which eastward migrations were episodic and punctuated by long periods of spatial stasis (Anderson 2001b). This pattern begs explanation, but this is somewhat more difficult than for the early-settlement model. The assumption of the latter is that voyaging was continuous across the Pacific, with the timing of island discoveries determined largely by geographic patterning and island size – modelled as the relative accessibility of islands to voyagers (Irwin 1992) – and a strategy of preferential upwind voyaging (Irwin 1989), or at least of waiting for seasonal westerly reversals of prevailing winds (Buck 1954:64; Finney *et al.* 1989). The pulse model, on the other hand, requires explanation for each pause, and also for each renewed burst of migration. Anderson (2001b:15) argues the underlying shaping factor was probably demographic rhythms, but it is clear we do not yet know enough about the role of demography in Pacific colonisation (cf. DiPiazza and Pearthree 1999).

Other large-scale factors might include the patterning of millennial-scale variations in the El Niño–Southern Oscillation (ENSO), with periods of increased westerly wind reversals correlating tolerably well with the radiocarbon chronology of colonisation pulse periods (Anderson *et al.* 2006). This hypothesis in itself relies on there being significant difficulties in sailing against the prevailing winds using prehistoric voyaging technologies. Consequently, the influence of small-scale technological developments may also be important, with each new pulse perhaps representing the surmounting of a previous boundary. The colonisation of East Polynesia, for example, which requires more direct travel against the prevailing winds for longer periods than is the case in Melanesia, may only have been possible with the development of the double-hulled canoe (Anderson 2001a; Anderson *et al.* 2006:2).

This point bears some examination because it challenges the assumptions of earlier advocates of the continuous-voyaging model. Irwin (1992:83) argued that the most difficult voyage faced during the Lapita period was between central Vanuatu and Fiji – a distance of 500 nm and a target angle of 21° – which was considered not significantly easier than a voyage from Samoa to the southern Cooks, a distance of 630 nm and a target of 15°. This somewhat understates the difference, however, since southern Vanuatu is only 410 nm from Fiji (i.e. West Futuna to Viti Levu), and Viti Levu is relatively easy to detect, given that it is theoretically visible up to 50 nm offshore due to its height. Furthermore, during the Austral winter, such a voyage sails at some 90° to the prevailing winds, allowing near peak speed and a straight-line voyage,

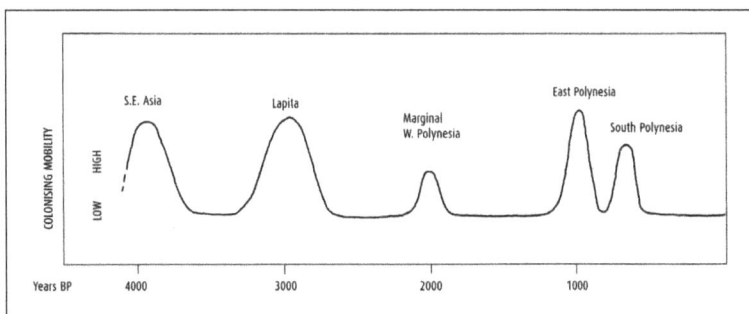

Figure 4. Anderson's (2001b) 'pulse model' or late-settlement model.

whereas the trip from Samoa to the southern Cook Islands is directly into the prevailing winds, requiring tacking (thus increasing the distance travelled fourfold), or the arrival of fortuitous wind reversals (Finney *et al.* 1989:262–264). Recent computer simulations by Di Piazza *et al.* (2007) using accurate weekly wind data and generous canoe-performance capabilities (canoes able to sail up to 75° off the wind) highlight this difference. Voyages within the region of Lapita settlement occurred over routes with arcs of success greater than 20° for much of the year, while voyages to islands east of Samoa have arcs of success rarely surpassing 10°, and then only for a few weeks each year. For the rest of the time, such voyages are impossible (Di Piazza *et al.* 2007:1223–1225). The implication is that there was a significant requirement for increased accuracy of navigation and knowledge of seasonal wind patterns beyond West Polynesia.

To some extent, however, Irwin's argument that the navigational difference was not significant enough to warrant a pause of more than 1000 years still stands. Statistically, a boundary that is barely permeable will still be crossed given enough time: even if voyages to the southern Cooks were only viable for three weeks of every year, that amounts to 92 years of continuous possibility in a 1600-year period. Stochastic events are not well accounted for in current voyaging models relying on computer simulation – Buck (1954:64) gives the example of the missionary John Williams, who, on catching a favourable wind, once sailed from Samoa to the Cook Islands on a straight course without changing tack (see Williams 1837:360). In that case, the destination and distance were known, and the likelihood of such a voyage being involved in colonisation may be very small, but exactly how small is rarely estimated. Ultimately, simulation models address the question of the long pause as a matter of probability given certain static technological parameters – thus geography is their primary determining variable. A more conservative approach might be to take the longest, most difficult voyage achieved during the Lapita era as a standing technological threshold for that period – that is, only voyages less than 410 nm, reaching targets with success arcs greater than 20° and which are accessible for most of the year should be considered feasible. This, at least, is demonstrable by actual archaeological data. We could then consider any voyage beyond this threshold as representing some technological innovation in the form of higher-performance canoes, accurate navigation, or increased endurance, however incremental. The fact that the best-performing double-hulled canoes modelled by Di Piazza *et al.* (2007) are still rarely able to reach distant eastern targets given the wind conditions is perhaps enough to suggest that further consideration of the role of technological developments in the long pause is warranted.

What these debates make evident is the true complexity of attempting to comprehend human dispersals as an archaeological phenomenon. This can be highlighted further by considering the nature of colonisation as a process encompassing various temporally ordered components. For example, we can at minimum separate the initial discovery of an island from its settlement, and from the final establishment of a long-term community (cf. Graves and Addison 1995). Thus some small, inaccessible islands may well have been reached occasionally, but were not occupied long enough to leave an archaeological trace. Niue, for example, is 255 nm from Lifuka in Tonga – within the threshold for Lapita-era voyages – but was not settled until c. 2000 BP, perhaps due to its isolation and comparatively depauperate environment (Walter and Anderson 2002). So the probability of voyages at or near the limit of extant technological bounds may be weighted according to the attractiveness of the destination: the islands of Fiji are a much more rewarding reason for a long voyage than Niue. I would argue that a truly holistic model of colonisation as a process requires an account of the interaction of socio-cultural, technological, environmental and demographic factors operating differently at different periods (Figure 5). Ultimately, our ability to produce a convincing explanation or understanding of the patterning and pace of

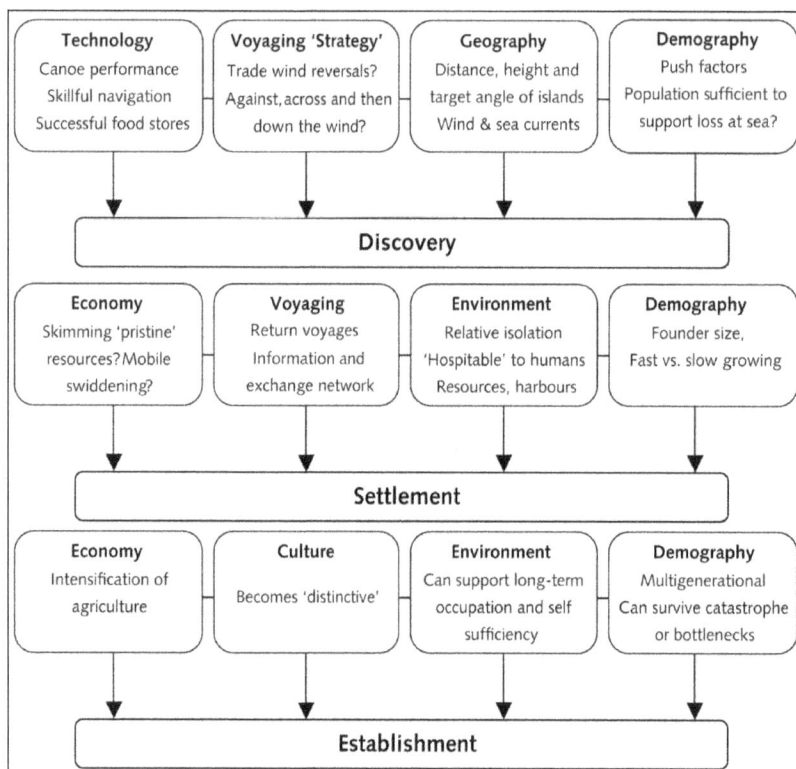

Figure 5. The colonisation process (Thomas 1997).

island settlement, as measured by radiocarbon dating, will require explicit consideration of how these factors are linked. In the remainder of this paper, I argue that one way of achieving this linking is to think about the colonisation process within the frame of the concept of 'landscape' as a cultural product (Bender 1993; Gosden and Head 1994; Tilley 1994). By way of example, I use the concept as a way of beginning to assess the role of island environments in shaping the pace of transitions between components of the colonisation process.

The landscape of colonisation

Ingold (1992:49–51) has argued that we can think of all human-experienced landscapes as an embodiment of past activity, as 'works in progress' created over generations. He stresses the role of practical action or the everyday deployment of technical skills (informed by gradients of power, ideology etc) as being the means through which we come to perceive landscapes, to know them, or to interpret parts of them within the framework of our experience. It is through such practical 'taskscapes' (Ingold 1993) that cultural landscapes are 'built' over time and subsequently inherited. This, in a nutshell, is the process of colonisation theorised. Taking the long view, the entire history of human movement into the Pacific involved just this productive encounter – a landscape, a seascape, interpreted and domesticated by experience via the socially informed technical skills of voyaging, land clearance, food gathering and production – a result of the processes plotted in Figure 5, encompassing all of its variables (see also Thomas 2001).

Given this, it might be assumed that the archaeological record of island colonisation offers a unique opportunity to study landscape encounters from their beginnings. But this is not so. Movement to a new place does not result in total change, nor complete structural transformation. Polynesian landscapes can be thought of as 'transported', not only in the usual sense of brought domesticates, but also in a conceptual sense, whereby the practical knowledge engendered in past landscapes is brought to new ones. This still allows us to think of landscapes in terms of difference. We may ask how each newly discovered island was different from those perceived through technically informed activity in the past, or what elements were previously unknown. A key part of understanding the colonisation of East Polynesia is therefore to be found in the environments and social structures of the west before 1000 BP. Experienced differences may be reflected in such things as geology, biota, climatic variation, isolation and so on – all elements of landscape. Upon discovery, differences such as these would gradually be encompassed through skilled action, perhaps in the form of experimentation or technical development. Monitored action, or what Giddens (1981:19) calls 'bounded knowledgability', forms the basis for making decisions, and it would be this kind of partial experience that influenced decisions such as whether to establish settlement in a specific locale.

The problem for us is how to model this process, or how to visualise and analyse it. We need to balance and evaluate the interaction of extant technologies, environmental characteristics, social patterns of access and control, and cultural preferences. Here, I want to focus on only one specific element – the modelling of how environmental difference was experienced and how this might have influenced the duration of the 'long pause'. To what extent did encounters with new landscape elements east of Fiji/Tonga/Samoa delay settlement or cause 'friction' to the colonisation process? Is it possible to quantify this? Irwin (1992) has modelled the role accessibility may have played after the islands of Polynesia were encountered – showing how increasing isolation and decreasing target size is correlated with later settlement or short-term occupation – but as yet, there have been no attempts to extend this to other elements of the experiential geography of the Pacific.

My first step is to compile a dataset of environmental variables that seeks to show similarities and differences between islands. This will then serve as a basis for comparative analysis. The most parsimonious and useful variables here include island area, geological formation, height, rainfall and isolation. Each of these has been demonstrated to play a role in the biogeographically determined diversity of an island environment. MacArthur and Wilson's (1967) theory of island biogeography famously used island area as a surrogate for environmental diversity, but this can be profitably extended via the other variables. For example, the effects of area on biodiversity are most relevant in the case of high volcanic islands which show more variation with area than do homogenous low-lying atolls (Stoddart 1992:283, 287). The main constraints on atoll diversity are thought to be ecological – that is, related more to the amount of rainfall and the frequency of drought than to area. The relationship is recursive, however, in that larger, higher islands may receive orographic rainfall and are more able to support a fresh-water lens – islands smaller than about nine hectares are essentially beaches. Isolation, too, has an effect on diversity, in that oceans are effective barriers to species transfer (Cox and Moore 1993:136–138), and in terms of human perception, isolation clearly has social ramifications. The complex interaction of each variable, then, is directly related to the patterning seen in vegetation, soils, topography, geology and hydrogeology throughout the Pacific. I derive my data for area, geology, height and rainfall from the *Pacific Islands Yearbook* (Carter 1984), except in cases where there are omissions, in which case data was generated from the GSHHS world shoreline dataset (Wessel and Smith 1996), and Dale (1981). Isolation can be measured using the distance of an island from its nearest neighbour and the target angle it presents, as demonstrated by Irwin (1992). But target angle is actually a function of island size (area) and distance, and distance is an effect of actual geographic position. So I have also recorded the latitude and longitude values for the centre of each island.

Differences in this dataset can be illuminated using the statistical procedure of multidimensional scaling (MDS), which is designed to analyse *dissimilarity data* – data that indicate the degree of dissimilarity (or similarity) between things. MDS analyses dissimilarity data in a way that displays their structure as a geometrical picture or 'map'. In MDS, each object (an island in this case) is represented by a point in multidimensional space, so that the (Euclidean) *distances* between pairs of *points* have the strongest possible relation to the *similarities* among pairs of *objects*. MDS thus produces a map of the locations of objects relative to each other from data that specify how different the objects are (Kruskal 1971). Goodness-of-fit is evaluated using the *stress* measure, which amounts to the sum of squared deviations of observed distances from expected distances. Thus the smaller the stress value, the better is the fit between the distances on the produced map and the original observed distances.

The datasets of environmental variables are in the form of 'raw' data of greatly varying ranges. Consequently, it is necessary to standardise the data, and to convert the raw data into dissimilarity data in order to apply the method of MDS. In this instance, standardisation was performed as follows: standard score = (raw score − mean)/standard deviation. Distance matrices were then generated using the cluster analysis module that comes with the STATISTICA software package for Windows. These matrices were used as the basis for analysis in the multidimensional scaling module of the same software.

As a test of the method, the data for latitude and longitude were standardised, converted to a distance matrix and then analysed in MDS. The result was an accurate map of the Pacific, with each island in its correct location relative to others (although not necessarily oriented according to geographical map conventions of north at the top, and east to the right). Thus, theoretically at least, the addition of any combination of the other variables would result in the spatial position of each island being transformed according to how similar or different it is from all other islands. For example, if two islands were of similar size, they would be placed closer than their true geographical position, and if of different size, they would appear further apart. The latter is demonstrated in Figure 6. Here, the islands of Viti Levu and Vanua Levu in Fiji are depicted much further away from other islands in West Polynesia due to their disproportionate size, while the majority of central Polynesian islands are compressed together, and the smaller, isolated mystery islands are scattered on the outskirts. This map is not, however, particularly informative, since the latitude and longitude variables clearly have the greater influence. If we are to understand the environmental differences encountered as voyagers moved from west to east, we need to remove these variables.

Figure 7 is an MDS analysis of all recorded environmental variables for 68 islands selected for their representativeness and access to complete data. The island of Viti Levu has been removed from the analysis because it is an outlier that compresses the scatter – on this map, it would have occupied a position far to the right of Vanua Levu (the same is true for New Zealand and Hawaii). Islands that are close together on the map are very similar in terms of the four environmental characteristics, while differences in one or more of these create separations. Area, height and geology can very generally be interpreted as being represented by dimension one – that is, as we travel from positive to negative values along dimension one, the area of islands decreases, the height of islands decreases, and the geology of islands shifts from continental origin through to islands made solely of coral – although there are some obvious exceptions here. Rainfall can be seen to be reflected in dimension two – negative values represent increasing dryness, while positive values represent increasing wetness.

A series of notable clusterings occur on the map. At the very bottom left there is a group of mystery islands, clustered because they are all small, low-lying, dry, coral-reef islands. The Phoenix group and islands of the Tuamotus occur slightly above this cluster. To the right of this group is the Marquesas archipelago, separated from the rest of central East Polynesia because of

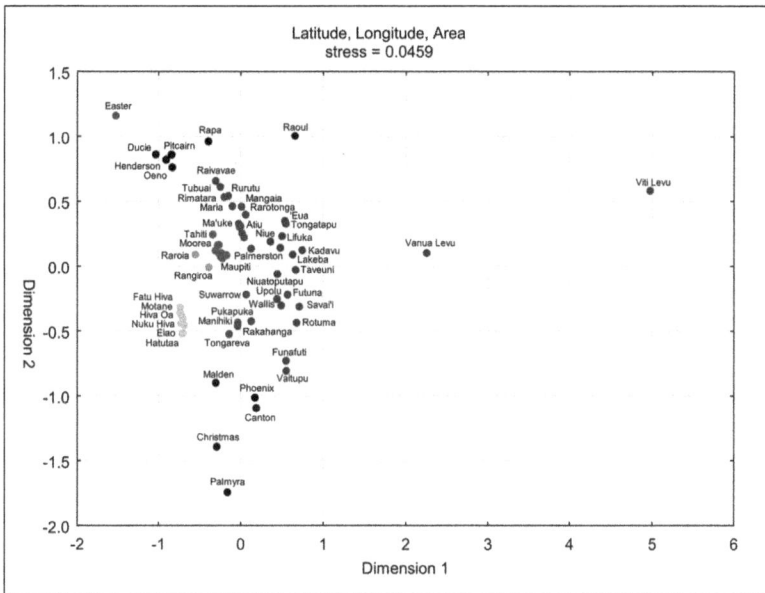

Figure 6. MDS scatterplot of 69 Polynesian islands, depicting differences in latitude, longitude and area.

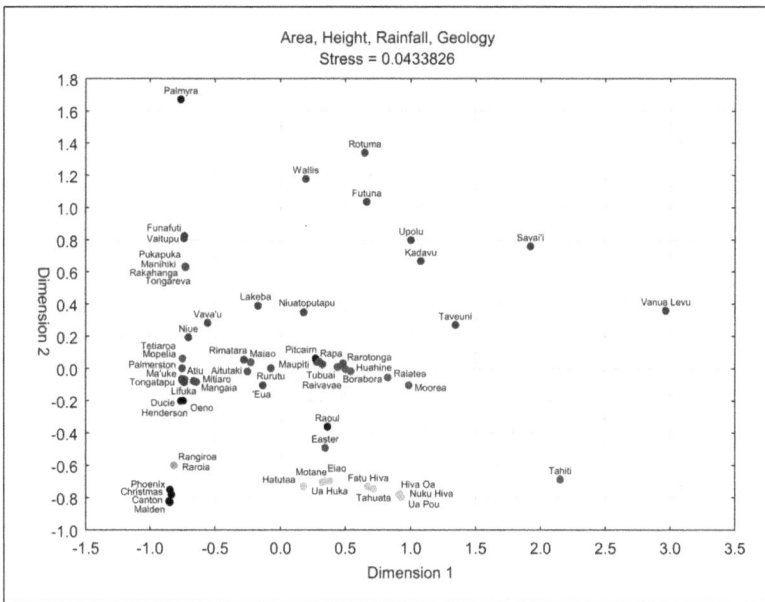

Figure 7. MDS scatterplot of 69 Polynesian islands, depicting differences in area, height, rainfall and geology.

below average rainfall. Tahiti occupies a position to the right of the Marquesas – separated from the rest of the Societies because of its size. Above these clusters is a dense band of islands with rainfall values around the mean (about 1943 mm per annum); a clear separation can be seen between the small coral islands and the larger volcanic islands. The western islands of Lifuka, Tongatapu and 'Eua fall within this central band, while Niue, Vava'u, Lakeba and Nuiatoputapu are located slightly above it. The next notable grouping occurs above the small central East Polynesian islands and consists of the northern Cooks and Tuvalu. Palmyra alone occupies the very top left of the map – it is one of the smallest islands, but is by far the wettest. The remaining islands occur in a spread throughout the upper right of the map, and comprise the major large islands of the West Polynesia/Fiji region.

Approximately half of the western islands included in the analysis are noticeably different in terms of their environments from those of the eastern Pacific. Those remaining, however, express a range that is similar to the majority of East Polynesian islands. Area is not necessarily the primary differentiating variable here, since there are many small islands in West Polynesia, as was shown in Figure 6 (and many more could not be included due to lack of data). These generally have higher rainfall, however, and more importantly, are located near large continental landmasses – thus they have been colonised by a more diverse range of biota than islands to the east. Fiji, for example, has more than 300 islands, many of which are atolls and raised coral islands, but these are all located close to Vanua Levu, Viti Levu and other large continental and volcanic islands. Consequently, their soil and biota is comparatively rich. An eastward decline in biotic diversity is well documented, leading Stoddart (1992:288) to state that the most dramatic biogeographic divide is at the Tonga Trench. Stoddart (1992:282–285) also notes, however, that the environments of atolls and raised coral makatea islands are remarkably consistent throughout the Pacific.

Consequently, we can interpret the embedding of islands such as 'Eua, Lifuka and Tongatapu among the islands of East Polynesia as indicative of their general shared similarities, but it is clear there are some important differences associated with their location in relation to potential sources of propagules. Another important point is that although we can expect that prospective colonisers had experienced environmental conditions similar to those in East Polynesia before they actually arrived, such 'similar islands' occur in western archipelagos containing many different islands – including large fertile landmasses. Human experiences of place are relational and holistic, such that locations are not evaluated in isolation, but in the context of other locales nearby – thus resource-poor islands adjacent to comparatively rich landmasses would be experienced differently than if they were isolated. Figure 7 indicates that the total range of environments in the western Pacific far exceeds that of East Polynesia – all of the East Polynesian islands cluster very tightly within a smaller range than the spread-out western islands. The problem facing the colonisers of East Polynesia, then, was perhaps not one of unfamiliar environments per se; rather, it may have been that there was in effect no relief from poorer environments in the form of nearby large, fertile islands. This issue is, however, a matter of scale. It is true the total range of environments is more limited in East Polynesia, but this does not mean to say there is an unrelenting sameness. All of the major central archipelagos contain a variety of island types, and for many, this includes larger volcanic islands. We can expect these central archipelagos posed less of a challenge to a way of life than more uniform, resource-poor islands, such as the Line Islands, the northern Cook Islands, Easter Island and the Kermadecs, among others. Figure 7 depicts these latter groups clearly separated from both central East Polynesia and the western islands. The Marquesas is an interesting case. Closer on Figure 7 to Easter and Raoul than anything else, the group is revealed to be noticeably different. Although an archipelago, the Marquesas islands are particularly dry and have rugged terrain. Additionally, their isolation, deep seas and runoff from steep valleys prevent the formation of any continuous fringing reef. These factors must have been significant differences compared with the abundant coral flats of the west.

Figure 8 compares the islands of the western Pacific with their nearest eastern neighbours – the Cook Islands. The grouping here clearly shows that the majority of the Cook Islands are either very different from the majority of western islands, or at least are to be counted among the smaller, lower and dryer of the coral islands in the west. It is worthwhile noting that Lapita sites occur on Niuatoputapu, Lakeba and Tongatapu, which are all located within the environmental range of various islands in the Cooks. Taken alone, this would seem to indicate that the larger islands of the southern Cooks may have posed few problems for immediate settlement during the Lapita era. Many Lapita sites in the western Pacific are located in coastal and lagoon-edge environments, usually on raised coral platforms and marine terraces (Green 1979:32) – all quite common in the southern Cooks. Crucially, however, the mutual accessibility between these regions is not great (see above). Taking into account colonisation from the west, the Cook Islands were unusually isolated from other islands occupied at that time. From this perspective, we could describe the Cook Islands as being, in an environmental and spatial sense, 'extremely marginal West Polynesia' – the bottom of the barrel in terms of islands expected to be settled. As noted above, the timing of settlement on Niue in the post-Lapita period is indicative of the difference that environmental marginality coupled with isolation makes.

The remaining islands of the Cooks are, for the most part, very small atolls – many of these islands are little more than raised beaches, and it is hard to see how these would have attracted early settlement. Many of them may have only recently emerged during the initial stages of human movement into the remote Pacific (Woodroffe *et al.* 1990; Kerr 2003). The poverty of their land area and resources is reflected in the fact that Palmerston and Suwarrow had been abandoned by the time of European contact.

The MDS maps demonstrate that there may have been some friction to movement into East Polynesia caused by the comparative marginality of island environments. But drawing any conclusions about how this may have affected the pace of colonisation is very difficult. We can compare, however, the dating of colonisation provided by archaeological data with the environmental data in a direct way. Consider the following contour plots. Figure 9 plots the latitude and longitude of several Pacific islands against their date of first settlement, as documented by the most conservative interpretation of the radiocarbon corpus (see above for references). The contour lines on the map consequently represent the speed of human movement into the remote Pacific. Most relevant here is the general slowing of the pace of colonisation towards West Polynesia, and the compression of contour bands before Rarotonga is reached. This is the 'long pause'. Much of East Polynesia, on the other hand, is contained within a relatively

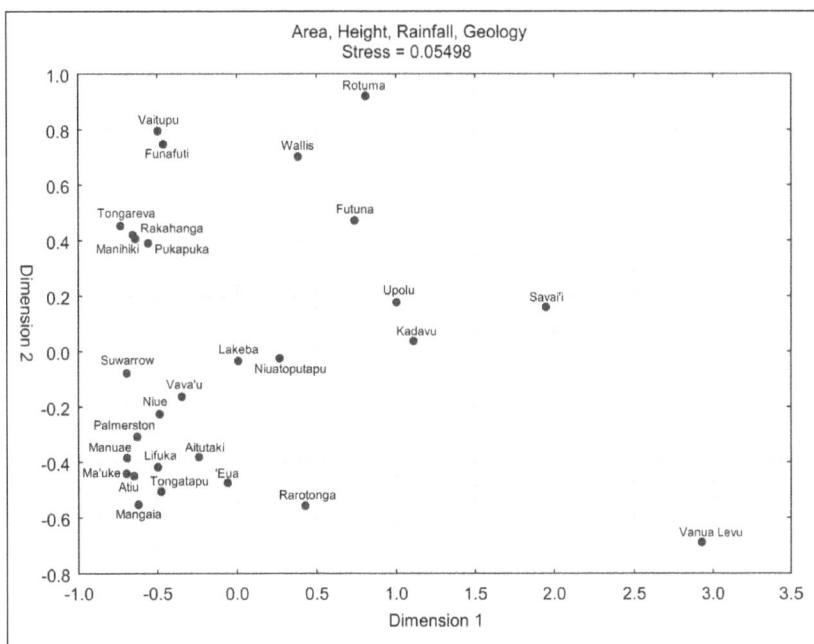

Figure 8. MDS scatterplot of West Polynesian islands compared with the Cook Islands, depicting differences in area, height, rainfall and geology.

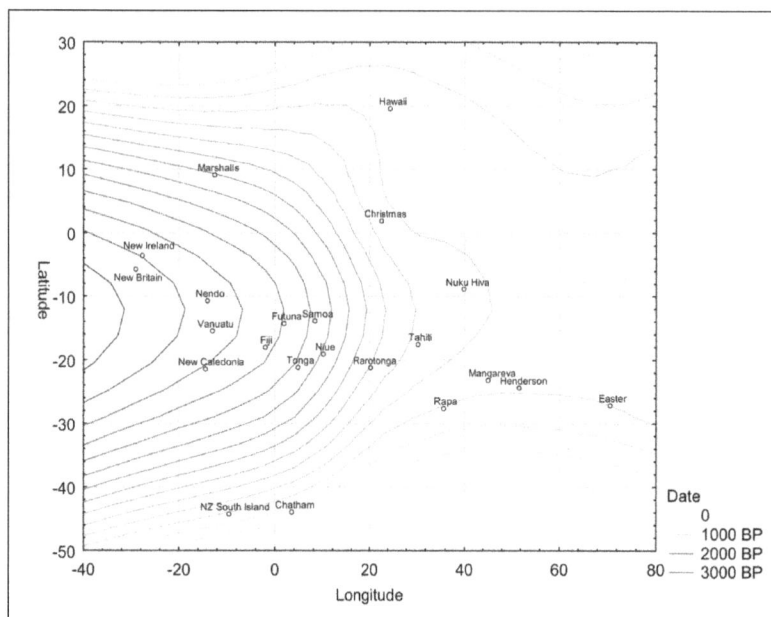

Figure 9. Contour plot showing dates of island colonisation post-Lapita. Date contours smoothed with distance weighted least squares method.

'flat' area, indicating the rapidity of settlement once the boundary was crossed – a massive area covered in a very short time. This is a sudden last pulse (though note the compression of contours beyond New Zealand towards marginal South Polynesia).

Figures 10–12 are similar contour plots depicting the gradients of change in island area, height and rainfall. Island area is seen to decrease rapidly east of West Polynesia, before flattening off throughout central East Polynesia. To a slightly lesser extent, the same pattern emerges for island height and the amount of rainfall experienced. There are clear subtle variations in the pattern, but generally these maps can be taken to demonstrate a rapid decline in biodiversity east of West Polynesia, resulting in a restriction of island environments in terms of their range. More to the point, this clearly correlates with the pattern seen in the dating of colonisation. The long pause in colonisation progress east of West Polynesia is paralleled by the decline in size, height and average rainfall experienced in the same region. The sudden rapidity of colonisation once this boundary was crossed is also paralleled by the uniformity of island environments encountered. In terms of a friction landscape, then, we might say that the boundaries of West Polynesia represent a steep increase in resistance to movement, but once this was overcome, friction was reduced to zero.

Conclusion

The island landscapes of the Pacific were gradually encompassed through time, during movements that required the development and deployment of skills sufficient to overcome unimagined conditions. The somewhat crude analyses produced here indicate that the pulse-like model documented by Anderson (2001b) is partially correlated with this process, with the pace of encompassment tied to gradients of environmental difference. As Lapita colonists reached Fiji/Samoa/Tonga, they encountered islands that were smaller, more isolated and less environmentally diverse that those further west near their proximal origins. In comparison with East Polynesia, however, the islands of Fiji/Samoa/Tonga occur in dense clusters with much diversity, with large, rich islands in close proximity to more marginal atolls and raised reefs. We might imagine that early settlers took advantage of this proximity, growing gradually accustomed (or 'adapting') to the landscapes of these marginal environments in the midst of greater 'support groups'. The colonisation of Niue nearly 1000 years after the Lapita colonisation of Tonga, and then central

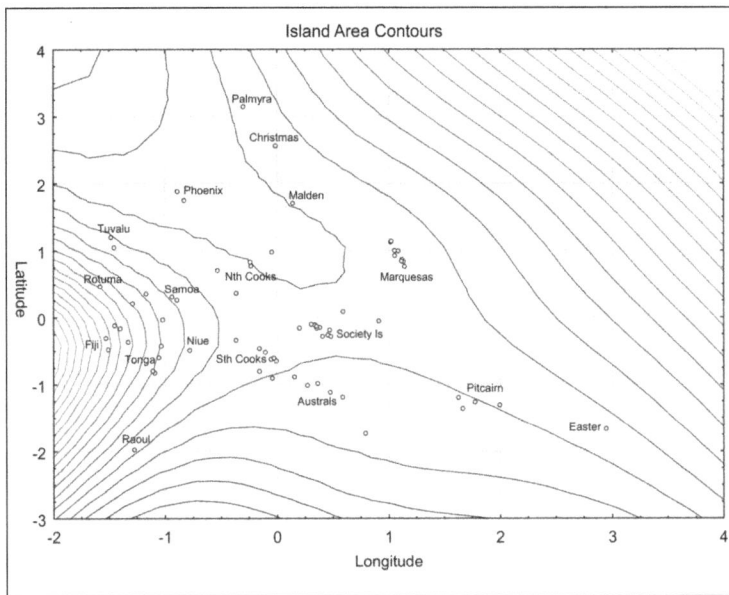

Figure 10. Contour plot showing island area. Contours smoothed with distance weighted least squares method.

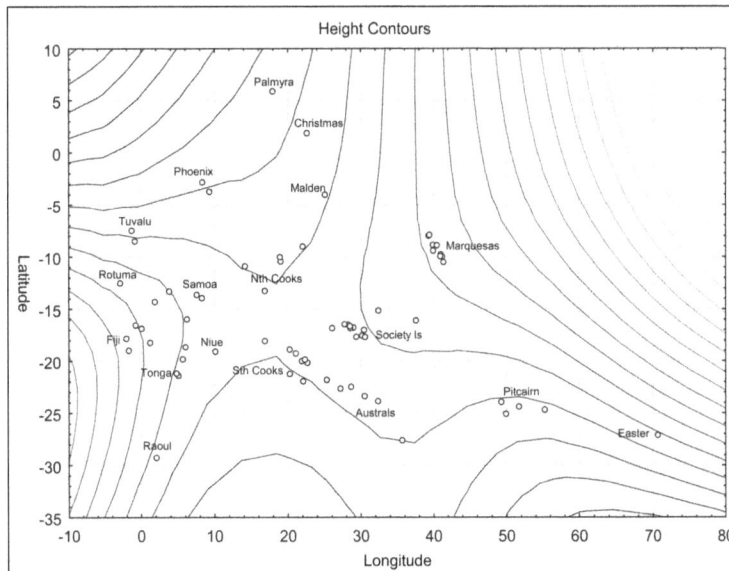

Figure 11. Contour plot showing island height. Contours smoothed with distance weighted least squares method.

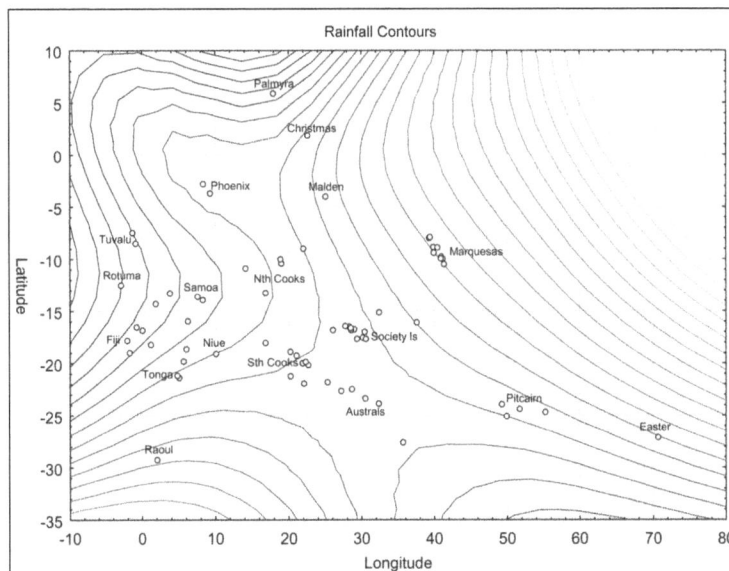

Figure 12. Contour plot showing average annual rainfall. Contours smoothed with distance weighted least squares method.

East Polynesia some time after that, is perhaps indicative of a new ability to confidently dwell in such landscapes permanently, a refinement of maritime and terrestrial skills and technology that took some time to acquire. As demonstrated in the above maps, central East Polynesia contains relatively homogenous groups of islands that are more similar to each other than to the islands of West Polynesia – as a whole, they present a narrow environmental niche. The speed with which East Polynesia was settled is probably linked to this phenomenon – their uniformity presented no friction to colonisation after human learning and knowledge encompassed the challenges of the new landscape. The great distances separating the archipelagos of the east are perhaps less relevant than the smallness of the islands within them, because the amount of land settled is but a tiny fraction of that settled during the Lapita era. To some extent, this answers Kirch's (2000:232) critique of the late-settlement model on the grounds that its rapidity would require massive fertility and population increase. Clearly, with a 1600-year-long pause in West Polynesia, source populations had plenty of time to grow large, and it would perhaps not take a great many people to populate the much smaller islands of the east. Nevertheless, the question bears more examination.

Environmental and population modelling address only a small part of the process of colonisation, as does the study of modes of travel (canoes and navigation). Ultimately, we will need to bring the many different forces in play together to fully comprehend the pattern and pace of colonisation in the Pacific. I have argued that one way of beginning to address this is to begin with a theoretical perspective whereby colonisation is understood to include a process of socially, technically, economically and demographically informed engagements with the world, resulting in a gradual process of domestication of the unknown – a production of landscape. This stresses the geographic nature of colonisation experience, but is fundamentally holistic in that it expresses the wider forces shaping human behaviour. With Polynesian colonisations, we have an opportunity to understand the processes by which humans make landscapes out of environments, the way 'nature' is appropriated and encultured, and more importantly, the reasons behind this and the meanings that the processes have for the people involved. This will most certainly require much more sophisticated analyses than I have presented here, but it is worth aiming for.

Acknowledgments

Some of the material presented here was first developed during the production of my MA thesis in the mid-1990s, at a time when debates about Polynesian colonisation were at their peak. I owe my decision to write about the topic to Atholl Anderson, Helen Leach and Richard Walter who, through undergraduate (AA) and postgraduate (HL) lectures, and during fieldwork discussions (RW) encouraged my interest. Richard Walter supervised my MA, and was the first to suggest using MDS as a method.

References

Anderson, A. 1991. The chronology of colonization in New Zealand. *Antiquity* 65:767–795.

Anderson, A. 1995. Current approaches in East Polynesian colonisation research. *Journal of the Polynesian Society* 104:110–132.

Anderson, A. 2000. Slow boats from China: issues in the prehistory of Indo-Pacific seafaring. In S. O'Connor and P. Veth (eds), *East of Wallace's Line: studies of past and present maritime cultures of the Indo-Pacific region*, pp.13–50. Amsterdam: Balkema.

Anderson, A. 2001a. Towards the sharp end: the form and performance of prehistoric Polynesian voyaging canoes. In C.M. Stevenson, G. Lee and F.J. Morin (eds), *Pacific 2000: proceedings of the fifth international conference on Easter Island and the Pacific*, pp. 29–36. Los Osos: Easter Island Foundation.

Anderson, A. 2001b. Mobility models of Lapita migration. In G. Clark, A. Anderson and T. Vunidilo (eds), *The Archaeology of Lapita dispersal in Oceania*, pp. 15–23.Terra Australis 17.

Anderson, A., E. Conte, G. Clark, Y. Sinoto, and F. Petchey 1999. Renewed excavations at Motu Paeaeo, Mapiti Island, French Polynesia: Preliminary Results. *New Zealand Journal of Archaeology* 21:47–65.

Anderson, A.J. and Y.H. Sinoto 2002. New radiocarbon ages of colonization sites in East Polynesia. *Asian Perspectives* 41:242–257.

Anderson, A.J., J. Chappell, M. Gagan, and R. Grove 2006. Prehistoric maritime migration in the Pacific islands: An hypothesis of ENSO forcing. *Holocene* 16:1–6.

Athens, J., J. Ward, H. Tuggle and D.Welch 1999. *Environment, Vegetation Change and Early Human Settlement on the 'Ewa Plain: A Cultural Resource Inventory of Naval Air Station, Barber's Point, O'ahu, Hawai'i. Part III: Palaeoenvironmental Investigations.* Honolulu: International Archaeological Research Institute Inc.

Bender, B. (ed) 1993. *Landscape: politics and perspectives.* Oxford: Berg.

Bateson, G. 1972. *Steps to an ecology of mind: collected essays in Anthropology, Psychiatry, Evolution, and Epistemology.* London: Chandler.

Buck, P. 1954. *Vikings of the Sunrise.* Christchurch: Whitcombe and Tombs.

Carter, J. (ed) 1984. *Pacific Islands Yearbook*, 15th edition. Sydney: Pacific Publications.

Carter, P. 1987. *The road to Botany Bay: an essay in spatial history.* London: Faber and Faber.

Cox, C.B. and P.D. Moore 1993. *Biogeography: an Ecological and Evolutionary Approach.* Oxford: Blackwell Scientific Publications.

Dale, W.R. (ed) 1980. *Pacific Island Water Resources.* Wellington: DSIR.

Di Piazza, A. and E. Pearthree 1999. The spread of the 'Lapita People': A demographic simulation. *Journal of Artificial Societies and Social Simulation* 2(3):1–15.

Di Piazza, A., P. Di Piazza and E. Pearthree 2007. Sailing virtual canoes across Oceania: revisiting island accessibility. *Journal of Archaeological Science* 34:1219–1225.

Emory, K.P. and Y.H. Sinoto 1965. Preliminary report on the archaeological investigations in Polynesia. Report for the National Science Foundation, Bernice P. Bishop Museum Archives.

Finney, B., P. Frost, R. Rhodes, and N. Thompson 1989. Wait for the west wind. *Journal of the Polynesian Society* 98:261–302.

Giddens, A. 1981. *A contemporary critique of historical materialism: Power, property and the State.* London: Macmillan.

Gosden, C. and L. Head 1994. Landscape – a usefully ambiguous concept. *Archaeology in Oceania* 29:113–116.

Graves, M.W. and D.J. Addison 1995. The Polynesian settlement of the Hawaiian Archipelago: Integrating models and methods in archaeological interpretation. *World Archaeology* 26:380–399.

Green, R.C. 1979. Lapita. In J.D. Jennings (ed), *The Prehistory of Polynesia*, pp. 27–60. Canberra: Australian National University Press.

Green, R.C. and P.V. Kirch 1987. History, Phylogeny and Evolution in Polynesia. *Current Anthropology* 28:431–456.

Higham, T.F.G., A. Anderson and C. Jacomb 1999. Dating the first New Zealanders: the chronology of Wairau Bar. *Antiquity* 73:420–427.

Ingold, T. 1992. Culture and the perception of the environment. In E. Croll and D. Parkin (eds), *Bush Base: Forest Farm – Culture, Environment and Development,* pp. 39–56. London: Routledge.

Ingold, T. 1993. The temporality of the landscape. *World Archaeology* 25:152–174.

Irwin, G. 1981. How Lapita lost its pots: the question of continuity in the colonisation of Polynesia. *Journal of the Polynesian Society* 90:481–494.

Irwin, G. 1992. *The prehistoric exploration and colonisation of the Pacific.* Cambridge: Cambridge University Press.

Jennings, J.D. (ed) 1979. *The Prehistory of Polynesia.* Canberra: Australian National University Press.

Kerr, R.A. 2003. Pacific migration arrested by meltdown's high waters. *Science* 302:1888–1889.

Kirch, P.V. 1986. Rethinking East Polynesian prehistory. *Journal of the Polynesian Society* 95:9–40.

Kirch, P.V. and J. Ellison 1994. Palaeoenvironmental evidence for human colonization of remote Oceanic islands. *Antiquity* 68:310–321.

Kruskal, J.B. 1971. Multidimensional scaling in archaeology: Time is not the only dimension. In F.R. Hodson, D.G. Kendall, and P. Tautu (eds), *Mathematics in the Archaeological and Historical Sciences,* pp. 119–132. Edinburgh: Edinburgh University Press.

MacArthur, R.H. and E.O. Wilson 1967. *The theory of island biogeography.* Princeton: Princeton University Press.

McGlone, M. and J. Wilmshurst 1999. Dating initial Maori environmental impact in New Zealand. *Quaternary International* 59:5–16.

Rolett, B.V. 1998. *Hanamiai: Prehistoric Colonization and Cultural Change in the Marquesas Islands (East Polynesia).* New Haven: Publications in Anthropology, Yale University.

Rolett, B.V. and E. Conte 1995. Renewed Investigation of the Ha'atuatua Dune (Nukuhiva, Marquesas Islands): A key site in Polynesian prehistory. *Journal of the Polynesian Society* 104:195–228.

Spriggs, M. and A. Anderson 1993. Late colonisation of East Polynesia. *Antiquity* 67:200–217.

Steadman, D., P.Vargas and C. Cristino 1994. Stratigraphy, chronology and cultural context of an early assemblage from Easter Island. *Asian Perspectives* 33:79–96.

Stoddart, D.R. 1992. Tropical Pacific biogeography. *Pacific Science* 46:279–293.

Thomas, T. 1997. The practice of colonization in East Polynesia. Unpublished MA thesis, Anthropology Department, University of Otago.

Thomas, T. 2001. The social practice of colonisation: Re-thinking prehistoric Polynesian migration. *People and Culture in Oceania* 17:27–46.

Tilley, C. 1994. *A phenomenology of landscape: Places, paths and monuments.* Oxford: Berg.

Walter, R. and A. Anderson 2002. *The Archaeology of Niue Island, West Polynesia.* Bishop Museum Bulletins in Anthropology 10.

Wessel, P. and W. Smith 1996. A global self-consistent, hierarchical, high-resolution shoreline database. *Journal of Geophysical Research* 101:8741–8743.

Williams, J. 1837. *A Narrative of missionary enterprises in the South Sea Islands.* London: J. Snow.

Winkler, Captain. 1901. On sea charts formerly used in the Marshall Islands, with notices on the navigation of these islanders in general. *Smithsonian Institute Report for 1899* 54:487–508.

Wood, D. 1992. *The power of maps.* New York: The Guildford Press.

Woodroffe, C.D., D.R. Stoddart, T. Spencer, T. Scoffin, and A. Tudhope 1990. Holocene emergence in the Cook Islands, South Pacific. *Coral Reefs* 9(1):31–39.

8

Be careful what you ask for: Archaeozoological evidence of mid-Holocene climate change in the Bering Sea and implications for the origins of Arctic Thule

Susan J. Crockford

Pacific Identifications Inc., 6011 Oldfield Rd., Victoria, B.C., Canada

Anthropology Department, University of Victoria B.C., Canada

sjcrock@shaw.ca

Introduction

The last great migration of people into Arctic North America involved the Thule, a highly mobile group that spread rapidly from northern Alaska to the islands of the Canadian Arctic and northwest Greenland about 1000 years ago (Schledermann and McCullough 1980; McGhee 2005). Archaeological investigations in Siberia and Alaska have so far failed to identify where and when the most basic elements of Thule culture developed. The fact that Thule used whale skeletal elements as architectural material in the construction of their semi-subterranean houses has led many researchers to characterise them as primarily subsistence whalers (e.g. Schledermann 1976, 1979; Dawson 2001; Dyke and Savelle 2001; Le Mouël and Le Mouël 2002; Savelle and McCartney 2003). As a consequence, the search for Thule origins has become virtually synonymous with finding the earliest evidence of whaling in the Bering Strait (e.g. Birket-Smith 1947; Larsen and Rainey 1948; Giddings 1960; Mason 1998; Dumond 2000).

While it has been assumed the technical skills, social structure and material culture necessary for Arctic whaling must have ancient roots on the Siberian shores of Chukotka (Figure 1), in part because it is adjacent to the route taken by virtually all whales on their spring migration through the Bering Strait, there are very few archaeological sites in that region older than 2300 years BP and none of those contain convincing evidence of subsistence whaling (e.g. Giddings 1960; Dinesman and Savinetsky 2003). In fact, whaling seems to have arisen fully developed on Chukotka about 2300 BP (Mason 1998; Mason and Barber 2003), leaving unresolved the questions of why, where and when whaling technology and culture developed.

Thule hunted bowhead (*Balaena mysticetus*) almost exclusively, while their ancestors in the Bering Strait also hunted gray whale (*Eschrichtius robustus*): although both species migrate through the Bering Strait each summer to feed in Arctic waters, gray whales tend to head west into the Chukchi Sea, while most bowhead move east into the Beaufort and beyond (Braham *et al.* 1984; Moore *et al.* 2002; Braham 2003; Dinesman and Savinetsky 2003; Savelle and McCartney 2003; Moore and Laidre 2006). In the Bering Strait, the predictable availability of migrating whales is inextricably tied to the seasonal ebb and flow of sea ice. All migrating whales (including beluga, *Delphinapterus leucas*) must wait until the receding sea ice clears the strait in late spring. The timing of this event varies from year to year, at times dramatically so (Dixon 2003; Grebmeier *et al.* 2006).

During the so-called 'Medieval Climatic Optimum', which began just before the start of the Thule 'migration' period at c. 1000 BP, sea ice is known to have retreated much further north in summer than it does today, leaving many island passes of the Canadian Arctic Archipelago ice-free (Dyke and Savelle 2001). It appears that as more and more open water became available during the Medieval period, bowhead and beluga migrated as far northeast as they could every summer. Was this extended migration of whales into the central Arctic the primary motive for the Thule exodus from Alaska (e.g. Schledermann 1976; Schledermann and McCullough 1980), or did it merely facilitate a resettlement of Thule that began for other reasons? Robert McGhee (2005), who once believed the former, now suggests that early Thule were keen traders who knew the value of metal and headed directly from northern Alaska for the northwest coast of Greenland in search of meteoric iron that had been discovered by earlier (Dorset) inhabitants. However, for the purposes of this discussion, the reason Thule decided to move into the eastern Arctic is immaterial; at issue is where they learned the skills that enabled survival in such an environment.

I contend bowhead whales were merely one aspect of a sea ice-edge ecosystem to which Bering Sea maritime hunters had adapted during the exceptionally cold conditions of the preceding Neoglacial, and when retreating sea ice moved northeastwards with climatic amelioration in the later Medieval period, those who had by that time become uniquely 'Thule' were well positioned to follow. In other words, Thule were not adapted to a specific migratory resource (i.e. bowhead whales), but to a particularly mobile habitat (the southern edge of seasonal sea ice) – a habitat where seals, as well as whales, were plentiful and first made extensive contact with prehistoric maritime hunters of the southern Bering Sea during the Neoglacial period.

The Neoglacial was a period of cold climate that began in the mid-Holocene and lasted more than 2000 years, from about 4700 to 2500 yr BP (see Crockford and Frederick 2007). Arctic regions of the Northern Hemisphere were the most significantly impacted by the Neoglacial, although some effects were certainly felt further south. I contend the Neoglacial is key to this story of developing, interacting and migrating human cultures in the North American Arctic because it precipitated a significant southward extension and persistence of the sea-ice edge that redistributed ice-obligate pinnipeds and migrating whales for more than 2000 years. Evidence of that redistribution comes from analysis of marine-mammal remains recovered from a recently excavated site in the eastern Aleutians, occupied during the last 1000 years of the Neoglacial.

Here, I summarise a comprehensive analysis of mammal remains from the Amaknak Bridge site (UNL50) on Unalaska Island (Crockford *et al.* 2004), dated to the period c. 3500–2500 BP, and include a comparison with fauna from two adjacent sites that were occupied before and after (Davis 2001; Knecht and Davis 2001, 2003; Crockford and Frederick 2007). These analyses indicate that sea ice and its associated fauna must have been present as far south as the eastern

Aleutians until at least early summer at the height of the Neoglacial, and as a consequence, sea ice must have persisted in the Bering Strait until late summer/early fall.

Such an expansion and seasonal persistence of sea ice (even if it did not occur every year to the same degree) would have effectively prevented whales from making summer migrations through the Bering Strait into the Arctic as they have done for the past 2500 years. Lack of whales passing through the Bering Strait into the Arctic for the 2000 years before 2500 BP not only explains the limited time depth for whaling cultures in the Bering Strait, but the virtual lack of coastal archaeological sites in that region before 2500 BP (the so-called 'Old Whaling' culture deposits at Cape Krusenstern, on the north shore of Kotzebue Sound (Mason and Ludwig 1990; Dumond 2000), are the notable exception). It is apparent, however, that maritime hunters in the eastern Aleutians successfully adapted techniques used to procure temperate pinnipeds and small cetaceans and applied them to the ice-obligate seals and whales that Neoglacial ice brought to their doorstep. I contend, therefore, that Arctic whaling technology developed as a component of ice-edge hunting in the southern Bering Sea during the Neoglacial and was later transmitted north into the Bering Strait and east into the Canadian Arctic and Greenland.

Bering Sea and sea ice

The Bering Sea is an immense semi-contained extension of the Pacific Ocean, bound on the south by the Aleutian Islands and on the north by the Bering Strait, the Pacific passage to the Arctic Ocean (Figure 1). The shallow Bering Strait lies just below the Arctic Circle, at about the same latitude as the northern half of Iceland.

Sea ice (also known as 'pack ice') is a defining feature of the highly productive Bering Sea

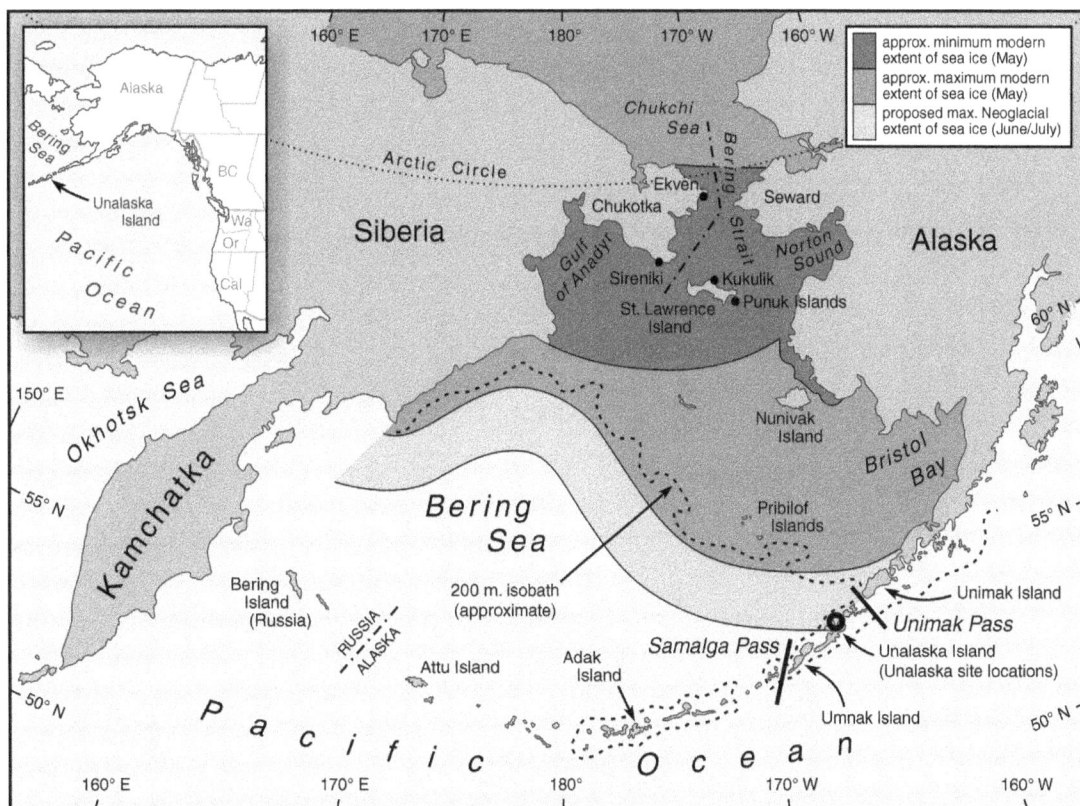

Figure 1. Modern minimum/maximum extent of spring pack ice (May) for the central and eastern Bering Sea, with proposed maximum Neoglacial pack ice extent (June/July). Archaeological sites mentioned in the text are labelled, with those on Unalaska circled (adapted from Crockford and Frederick 2007: Figure 1).

ecosystem (Grebmeier *et al.* 2006). Coverage of sea ice is governed primarily by wind, although air temperature has some bearing (Rigor and Wallace 2004). Sea ice forms over the Arctic continental shelf to the north in the early autumn (over the Chukchi and Beaufort Seas) and is pushed south by strong winds through the Bering Strait. Sea ice covers most of the shallow eastern portion of the Bering Sea by early winter, where it persists until spring and then recedes – at least, this has been the modern pattern.

Records show that historically, the leading edge of the sea ice usually reached its southernmost position by April or May, extending (on average) from the north end of Bristol Bay in the east (c. 58° N) to the Pribilof Islands at the shelf edge in the west, approximately following the 200 m contour line (Figure 1). While this line of maximum extent varies somewhat from year to year, the sea-ice edge generally recedes quickly by early summer (Grebmeier *et al.* 2006); in fact, during most of the 20th century, sea ice moved away from the Pribilofs by May and cleared the Bering Strait by June (Overland and Stabeno 2004).

The extent, persistence and movement of sea ice determines many aspects of life history for animals in the Bering Sea, especially marine mammals. While some whales, including humpback (*Megaptera movaeangliae*), North Pacific right whale (*Eubalaena japonica*), fin (*Balaenoptera physalus*) and gray whale, migrate in from the North Pacific in spring to feed in the Bering Sea over the summer and autumn, other cetaceans appear to be resident, including bowhead, beluga, Dall's porpoise (*Phocoenoides dalli*), harbour porpoise (*Phocoena phocoena*) and Baird's beaked whale (*Berardius bairdii*) (Moore *et al.* 2002; Reeves *et al.* 2002; Sheldon *et al.* 2005; Zerbini *et al.* 2006). Bowhead, gray whale and beluga move beyond the Bering Sea into the productive waters of the Beaufort and Chukchi Seas (Braham *et al.* 1984; O'Corry-Crow *et al.* 1997; Moore *et al.* 2000, 2002, 2003; Braham 2003; Dixon 2003). Arctic-adapted carnivores and pinnipeds that use sea ice as a substrate for mating, giving birth and nursing their young move with the ice as it ebbs north and south: these 'ice-obligate' or 'pagophilic' species include polar bear, *Ursus maritimus,* walrus, *Odobenus rosmarus,* bearded seal, *Erignathus barbatus,* ringed seal, *Phoca hispida,* spotted seal, *Phoca largha,* and ribbon seal, *Phoca fasciata* (Fedoseev 1975; Finley *et al.* 1983; O'Corry-Crow and Westlake 1997; Kelly 2001; Reeves *et al.* 2002; Simpkins *et al.* 2003). In contrast, 'temperate' Bering Sea pinnipeds prefer ice-free terrestrial beaches for these activities, including northern fur seal, *Callorhinus ursinus,* Steller's sea lion, *Eumatopias jubata,* and harbour seal, *Phoca vitulina* (Kenyon and Wilke 1953; Shaunghnessy and Fay 1977; Trites and Antonelis 1994; Ragen *et al.* 1995; Reeves *et al.* 2002).

Neoglacial marine mammal hunters in the Eastern Aleutians

Amaknak Bridge: Site location and archaeology

Unalaska is the second large island west of the Alaska Peninsula in the Aleutian chain (Figure 1). The region has been occupied by people for at least 9000 years (Knecht and Davis 2001). The Amaknak Bridge site (UNL50) is situated close to the major fishing port of Dutch Harbor on the Bering Sea side of the island, as shown in Figure 2. The archaeological deposits are classic shellfish middens with abundant well-preserved vertebrate fauna excavated from within and between seven recognisable house structures (Knecht and Davis 2004), dated c. 3500–2500 BP (selected ^{14}C dates: #862 – RCYBP 2590±90 BP, calibrated age BC 910–420, Beta-181341; #2909 – RCYBP 3000±70 BP, calibrated age BC 1410–1010, Beta-184634; #3152 – RCYBP 3470±70 BP, calibrated age BC 1950–1620, Beta-184633).

The semi-subterranean dwellings found at the Amaknak Bridge site are similar to those found at the nearby Margaret Bay site (dated c. 4700–4100 BP) and are basically rectangular in design, defined by rock walls about 1 m high. Uniquely styled fire-pit complexes are built into

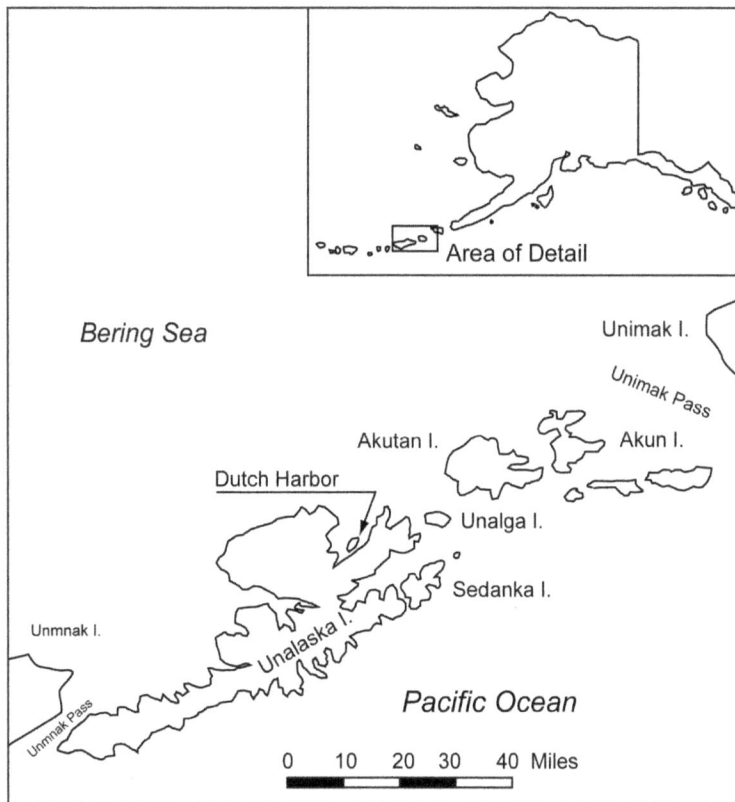

Figure 2. Location of the fishing port of Dutch Harbor on Unalaska Island, the general locale of the Amaknak Bridge site (UNL50), Margaret Bay (UNL48), and Amaknak Spit (UNL55), near the modern city of Unalaska. Note that Akutan Island (Stewart *et al.* 1987; Sheldon *et al.* 2005) hosted a shore-based whaling station in the early 20th century (processing mainly fin, humpback, sperm and blue whales but a few right whales), indicating many whales of these species were available within a short distance of the Amaknak Bridge site location (from Knecht and Davis 2004: Figure 1.02).

side walls: these fire pits have well-constructed chimneys extending above the rock wall and two rock-lined and rock-covered floor channels leading into the hearths in a converging V-shaped pattern. It now seems likely these unique floor channels were a necessary adaptation to the strong persistent north winds that must have characterised the Neoglacial, providing critical draft to the fire from below (cf. Knecht and Davis 2004). Similar draft arrangements are often prescribed today for maintaining an open fire under extremely windy conditions (Solid Fuel Association 2005).

Archaeozoological sample and analysis results

The total number of mammal specimens identified to species for the Amaknak Bridge assemblage is 5947, with 12,548 pieces identified to family level or better (Crockford *et al.* 2004). Age-at-death and sex determinations for all suitable pinniped specimens identified to species were based on comparison with modern specimens of known age and sex, as well as published references (Stora 2000). Basic quantification is by Number of Identified Specimens (NISP), the count of all specimens identified to species; however, NISP numbers designated as 'augmented' (as per Davis 2001) for comparison with other sites (Table 1) partition the undistinguished family NISP totals proportionally among the species identified.

Both resident and seasonally available temperate and pagophilic marine-mammal species are well represented at the Amaknak Bridge site: 40% northern fur seal (temperate, seasonal), 32% ringed seal (pagophilic, seasonal), 10% harbour porpoise (temperate, resident), 10% harbour and/or spotted seal (mixed temperate resident/pagophilic seasonal), 4% bearded seal (pagophilic, seasonal) and 3% Steller's sea lion (temperate, resident). All other taxa are present at a frequency of 1% or less, including Dall's porpoise, ribbon seal, walrus, polar bear, sea otter (*Enhydra lutris*), long-finned pilot whale (*Globicephala melaena*), beluga, fin whale, humpback, Baird's beaked whale, and North Pacific right whale. No dog remains were found.

Pagophilic species – ringed seal

Specimens of ringed seal, a species strongly associated with sea ice year round, comprise the second largest category of mammals recovered at Amaknak Bridge. Remains of newly weaned ringed seals (estimated at two-four months of age), which typically feed at the edge of sea ice (Wiig *et al.* 1999; Reeves *et al.* 2002), make up 90% of all ringed-seal remains for which an age could be estimated (Figure 3). Ringed seals in the Bering Sea, like bearded seals, move south with advancing sea ice in the spring, although their preferred habitat is generally towards the interior of the ice, where it is thick and unbroken (Kelly 2001; Simpkins *et al.* 2003). Ringed seals manage to continue feeding in this habitat because they maintain breathing holes in the ice. Ringed seals are born in March–May, with pups weaned at three to six weeks (Fedoseev 1975). Thus a pup born late in the season (around mid-May) might not be weaned until the end of June. Throughout the summer, newly weaned ringed seals feed close to the ice edge (Holst *et al.* 1999).

The very high proportion of young ringed seals represented at this site suggests that the sea-ice-edge habitat preferred by this age group must have been available close to the site location from early to mid-summer (May–July).

Pagophilic species – bearded seal

Analysis results reveal that although bearded-seal remains represent only 4% of the NISP, animals of all ages were harvested, including mature adults (17%) and newborns or newly weaned young less than two months of age (49%). Bearded seals haul out at the edges of consolidated sea ice or on large pieces of broken ice to give birth, nurse their young and moult (Reeves *et al.* 2002; Simpkins *et al.* 2003). Bearded seals move south in spring with advancing sea ice and north again as summer progresses. Birth of bearded seal pups occurs mid-March to early April (Reeves *et al.* 2002) and females wean their young after about 24 days. While newly weaned bearded seals feed at the ice edge, all other age classes (including adults, subadults and older juveniles) haul out on the ice for an extended moulting period that can last until August. As a consequence,

Table 1. Relative abundance and augmented NISP of pinniped species from Amaknak Bridge compared with adjacent sites in Unalaska Bay occupied before and after (pagophilic species in bold), adapted from Frederick and Crockford (2007).

Site	Ringed seal	Bearded seal	Steller's sea lion	Northern fur seal	Other seals	Site totals
Margaret Bay						
NISP	**604**	**0**	442	340	2653	5333
Percent	**11%**	**0**	8%	6%	50%	75%
Amaknak Bridge						
NISP	**4672**	**519**	389	4672	1298	12549
Percent	**36%**	**4%**	3%	36%	10%	89%
Amaknak Spit						
NISP	**0**	**0**	440	3534	314	4714
Percent	**0**	**0**	9%	75%	7%	91%

NISPs augmented as per Davis (2001), excluding whales. Age of the sites are: Margaret Bay (UNL48), c. 4700–4100 BP; Amaknak Bridge (UNL50), c. 3500–2500 BP; Amaknak Spit (UNL55), c. 600–350 BP. Taxa: Steller's sea lion, *Eumatopias jubata*; Northern fur seal, *Callorhinus ursinus*; Ringed seal, *Phoca hispida*; Bearded seal, *Erignathus barbatus*; 'Other seals' include *Phoca vitulina* and/or small amounts of *P. largha* and/or *P. fasciata*.

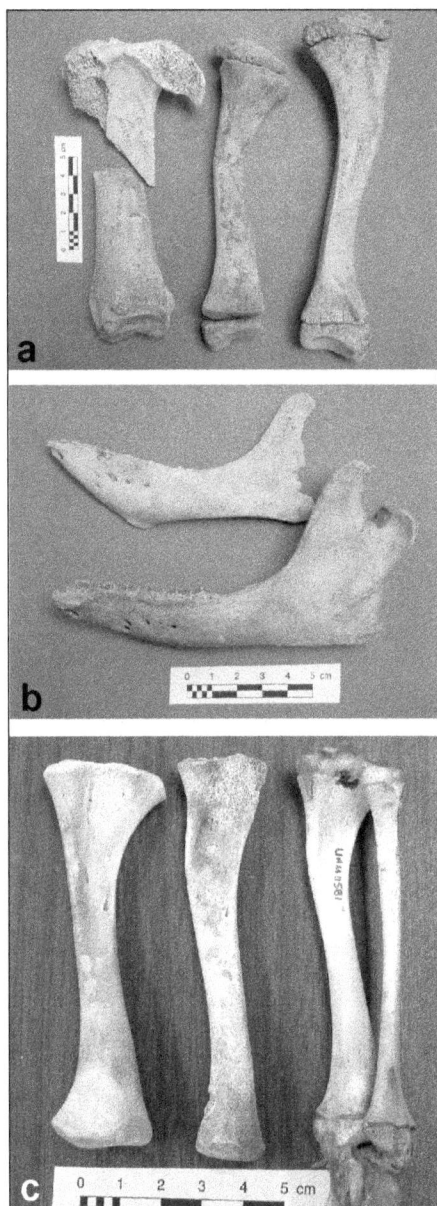

Figure 3. Juvenile ringed seal and bearded seal remains provide the strongest evidence that sea ice was present in spring/early summer adjacent to the Amaknak Bridge site, top to bottom panels. a) Amaknak Bridge bearded seal tibiae: far left, mature adult, proximal and distal ends (epiphyses completely fused, shaft missing); middle, estimated near-term foetus, complete (epiphyses poorly developed and unfused); far right, estimated 2–4 week old newborn, complete (epiphyses unfused); b) Amaknak Bridge bearded seal mandibles: top, young juvenile estimated 2–3 months old; bottom, mature adult; c) Tibiae of modern spotted seal vs. prehistoric and modern ringed seal: far left, University of Alaska Museum specimen #UA16605 spotted seal (ca. 3–4 weeks old); middle, Amaknak Bridge specimen #AB200152 ringed seal (estimated 2–4 months old); far right, University of Alaska Museum specimen #UA11581 ringed seal (ca. 6–8 weeks old).

both young pups and older animals are strongly associated with the sea-ice edge throughout the spring and summer, regardless of where the moving ice takes them.

If the timing of births for bearded seals was similar during the Neoglacial, pups two months old or less would have been available at the southern-most ice edge until the end of May. The strong representation of both adults and young pups (Figure 3) throughout the site assemblage suggests the preferred birthing and moulting haul-out habitat for bearded seals must have been very close to Unalaska Island at least through spring and early summer of most years (March–May) at the time the site was occupied.

Pagophilic species – walrus and others

Only six specimens of walrus were recovered from the area of the site covered by this report, representing at least four individuals (one adult male, one adult female, two juveniles). Walrus, being both larger and more gregarious in their hauling-out habits than bearded and ringed seals, require stronger, more consolidated pack ice. These particular ice conditions perhaps existed only rarely off the Amaknak Bridge site 3500 to 2500 years ago, since today in the northern

Bering Sea, walrus often occur in the same habitats as bearded and ringed seals (Kelly 2001; Simpkins *et al.* 2003). Alternatively, ice may have been present only over water too deep for effective walrus foraging.

The remains of other Arctic and pagophilic species, albeit recovered in low numbers, add to the picture of a cold, ice-dominated habitat at Amaknak Bridge: spotted seal (NISP=27), ribbon seal (NISP=6), beluga (NISP=1) and polar bear (NISP=8).

Cetaceans and evidence for whaling

All whale species identified to date have had the identifications confirmed by mitochondrial DNA (mtDNA) analysis (Frey *et al.* 2005). At least two individuals each of humpback, Baird's beaked whale, right whale and long-finned pilot whale have been identified so far, based on the distinct mtDNA haplotypes present; other whale species are represented by a single haplotype each. Surprisingly, each sequence recovered from the Amaknak whale remains represents a haplotype not found in modern animals tested so far.

The long-finned pilot whale remains represent a new record for this species off western North America. All previous records come from archaeological sites in Japan and as there is no evidence of an existing population, long-finned pilot whale is considered extinct in the North Pacific (Kasuya 1975; Reeves *et al.* 2002).

Interestingly, while Dall's porpoise appears to be the most common small cetacean noted in recent surveys of the southeast Bering Sea (e.g. Moore *et al.* 2002; Sinclair *et al.* 2005), harbour porpoise is not only strongly represented in the Amaknak Bridge assemblage, but comprises a surprisingly high proportion of the NISP (10%, 578/5947), with all age classes (including newborns and mature adults) represented. In contrast, although both gray whale and the smaller minke whale (*Balaenoptera acutorostrata*) are both fairly common during summer in the Bering Sea today (Moore *et al.* 2002; Sinclair *et al.* 2005; Zerbini *et al.* 2006), none have yet been positively identified from Neoglacial-age sites on Unalaska.

It is not surprising, however, that both right and fin whales are represented in the Amaknak Bridge assemblage, since the preferred summer habitat for both species in the Bering Sea is the shelf region just north of Unalaska (Stewart *et al.* 1987; Moore *et al.* 2002; Sheldon *et al.* 2005; Zerbini *et al.* 2006). Similarly, the preferred habitat for Baird's beaked whale (the largest of the beaked whale family, reaching 12.8 m) is the shelf slope (Stewart *et al.* 1987; Moore *et al.* 2002; Reeves *et al.* 2002); a portion of this habitat lies adjacent to Unalaska, suggesting this species may have been relatively common in the area prehistorically.

The assertion that Amaknak Bridge inhabitants deliberately hunted whales is supported not only by the presence of toggling harpoons and lances (Knecht and Davis 2004), but by the large number of whale elements found in the faunal midden that were not used for building purposes. While few very large pieces of architectural whale bone (including crania, mandibles and a few vertebrae) were included in the faunal assemblage presented for analysis, a sizeable number of relatively intact whale elements (including vertebrae) were nevertheless identified among the analysed faunal remains (Crockford *et al.* 2004). Of 40 pieces of whale bone from the analysed faunal subsample that could be assigned to body part (excluding rib and hyoid fragments, which were often indistinguishable), 14 (35%) were flipper elements, 15 (37.5%) were skull fragments and 11 (27.5%) were vertebrae (three of these vertebrae were near-terminal caudals); of an additional 30 whale elements identified from units not included in the analysed subsample, 15 (50%) were flipper elements, 7 (23%) were skull fragments, 7 (23%) were vertebrae (three were near-terminal caudals) and one (3%) was an intact sternum (Figure 4).

Savelle and McCartney (2003) consider whale flipper, sternum and hyoid elements found

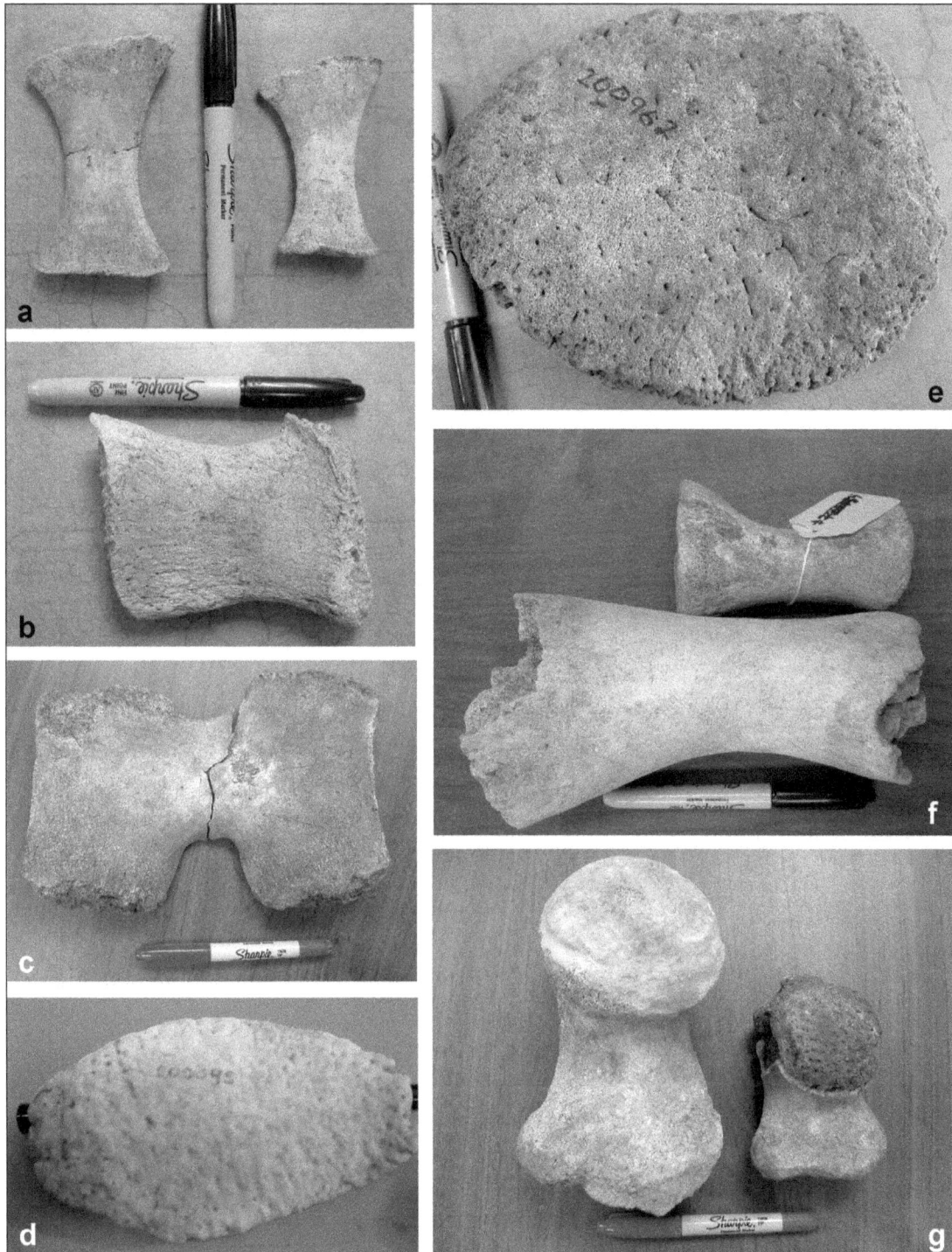

Figure 4. Much of the whale bone recovered from the Amaknak Bridge site represent body parts generally considered to represent food remains rather than architectural material and all species identifications have been confirmed by mtDNA analysis (Frey *et al.* 2005). Shown are: a) phalanges, humpback whale; b) metacarpal, fin whale; c) sternal plate, Baird's beaked whale; d) proximal epiphysis of radius, humpback whale; e) proximal epiphysis of radius, North Pacific right whale; f) phalanges, North Pacific right whale; g) humeri (adult, left; juvenile, right), long-finned pilot whale (first North American record of this species).

archaeologically to represent food items, and Jolles (2003) states that modern Bering Strait whalers distribute the flippers and tail stalk with flukes (presumably with the last few caudal vertebrae attached) to the boat captain of the whaling crew. Thus, while some whale bone was clearly used for architectural purposes, whales were evidently being consumed as food at Amaknak Bridge as well, and this implies active hunting.

Comparison with other assemblages

Two previously excavated sites with analysed faunal assemblages appropriate for comparison are located within 3 km of the Amaknak Bridge site: 1. Margaret Bay (UNL48), with fauna-bearing layers dated c. 4700–4100 BP, as well as deposits without fauna dated to c. 5500 BP (Davis 2001; Knecht and Davis 2001); 2. Amaknak Spit/Tanaxtaxak (UNL55), identified by David Yesner (University of Alaska) and dated to c. 600–350 BP (Knecht and Davis 2003). Comparison of dominant taxa at these sites (Table 1) shows that seasonally available pagophilic pinnipeds (ringed and bearded seal) are absent from post-Neoglacial-age deposits at Amaknak Spit and only weakly represented at the early Neoglacial-age site of Margaret Bay.

Archaeozoological analysis conclusions

Together, juvenile remains of the two pagophilic pinnipeds, ringed and bearded seal, provide incontrovertible evidence that at the height of the Neoglacial, spring sea ice reached a more southerly position than it does today, and persisted until summer. Increased polar winds in the Bering Sea (Rigor and Wallace 2004) must have forced sea ice, along with its associated pagophilic fauna, south to the eastern Aleutians by early April, where it persisted into June or July. Sea-ice coverage may not have reached the suggested extent every year during the Neoglacial, but much more extensive coverage than occurs at present must have been the predominant condition.

In addition, such an extent of sea ice and its persistence into summer indicates the Bering Strait must have been blocked with ice virtually year-round from c. 4700 BP to c. 2500 BP, preventing migration of whales into Arctic waters during the Neoglacial. Sea ice probably retreated north as summer advanced during the Neoglacial, as it does today, but it is unlikely that ice cleared the Bering Strait much before late summer or early autumn. With the Bering Strait ice-bound until late summer at the earliest, whales that currently use the Beaufort and Chukchi Seas for summer feeding, including bowhead, beluga and gray whales, must have either established resident populations in the Bering Sea or migrated elsewhere. The lack of subfossil (non-cultural) bowhead remains in the western Arctic and the virtual absence of archaeological sites with bowhead or gray-whale bone in the Bering Strait during this period support this conclusion (Dyke and Savelle 2001; Dixon 2003; Dyke and England 2003; Mason and Barber 2003; Savinetsky *et al.* 2004; Fisher *et al.* 2006). The oldest deposits at Cape Krusenstern on Kotzebue Sound, variously dated to c. 3200–2800 BP (e.g. Mason and Ludwig 1990) and termed 'Old Whaling,' appear to be the only real anomaly in this pattern. The Devil's Gorge site on Wrangel Island (also known as Chertov Ovrag), dated to c. 3100 BP, may be another (Dumond 2000). However, the evidence for subsistence whaling at Cape Krusenstern is not particularly strong.

Thule origins, ice-edge hunting and whaling

Due in part to a long tradition of characterising Thule as a whaling culture with a Bering Strait ancestry, determining Thule origins has become synonymous with finding the earliest northern Bering Sea sites with evidence of large-scale Arctic whaling. However, there are few archaeological sites in the Bering Strait older than 2300 BP, and none of these contain evidence of subsistence whaling (Mason and Barber 2003). Bering Strait sites with abundant bowhead remains are not at all common until after about 1300 BP, a few centuries before the emergence of Thule culture in Northern Alaska; virtually all sites in the 2300–1300 BP range are on the Siberian side of the Bering Strait (Chukotka) and contain primarily gray-whale remains (Dinesman and Savinetsky 2003; Savinetsky *et al.* 2004). Nevertheless, the oldest sites in the Bering Strait that have evidence of whaling are considered the first to show resemblance to Thule culture. Termed 'Old Bering Sea' and 'Birnirk', sites with many Thule-like material-culture elements appeared quite suddenly about 2300 BP and were widespread on both sides of the Bering Strait by c. 1500 BP (Mason 1998). A culture with even more Thule-like elements, 'Punuk', emerged about 1300 BP.

The similarities between Bering Strait cultures and Thule are quite apparent archaeologically and are summarised in Table 2. Thule, like their Bering Strait ancestors, were accomplished whalers, and this is reflected archaeologically by remains of skin boats, lances and large toggling harpoons, as well as by bowhead-whale skeletal remains left around their habitation sites; whales were not only consumed, but the bones were used for house construction. However, both Thule and their Bering Strait predecessors hunted walrus, as well as ringed and bearded seals, evidenced by the large accumulations of pinniped remains at their archaeological sites (e.g. Møhl 1979; Staab 1979; Morrison 1983; Gusev *et al.* 1999; Woollett *et al.* 2000; Savinetsky *et al.* 2004). For transport, skin boats were supplemented by Thule and some late Bering Strait predecessors (e.g. Kukulik on St Lawrence Island, Table 2) with sleds pulled by teams of dogs, reflected archaeologically by harness parts, line swivels and sled runners, as well as by the remains of dogs themselves (Morey and Aaris-Sørensen 2002). Thule took Beringian-style pottery lamps and pots with them on their initial eastward migrations, but appear to have used traditional stone lamps for heating and cooking, as their houses in the high Arctic had no hearths for open fires, in contrast to most Bering Strait dwellings. The environment in which all Arctic-adapted people lived demanded skin clothing with tightly sewn waterproof and windproof seams, reflected archaeologically by fine bone needles with very small, drilled eye holes – in rare cases in the high Arctic, the clothing itself has also been preserved. Thule prowess at carving walrus ivory, utilising small bits of iron acquired through trade, is legendary and unique, although ivory carving has a long tradition in the Bering Sea also.

Thule archaeological sites, as well as those of earlier Bering Sea people, thus contain these distinctive elements of their material culture: large toggling-type harpoons, lances, pottery, stone lamps, dog-harness components and sled parts, fine bone needles with very small eyes, elaborately carved ivory, and faunal assemblages containing the remains of dogs, bowhead whales, walrus, bearded seals and ringed seals.

In contrast, summarised as bold entries in Table 2, some Arctic Thule elements (especially small-eyed needles) are represented archaeologically in the eastern Aleutians by c. 4700 BP, at Margaret Bay. By c. 3500 BP, at Amaknak Bridge, quite a few Thule-like artefacts are found, including toggling harpoons, stone lamps, labrets, carved ivory and small-eyed needles, in addition to the remains of whales and other ice-edge marine mammals. I propose, therefore, that the most essential element of Thule culture, sea ice-edge hunting technology (including the boats and clothing required to hunt in such habitats), has its most ancient roots in the eastern Aleutians during the Neoglacial.

In contrast, a few researchers (e.g. Clark 1966, 1996; Dumond and Bland 1995; McGhee 2005) have looked to the Gulf of Alaska (particularly Kodiak Island) for the origins of Thule culture. There, by c. 3500 BP, there are stone lamps, ground slate tools and small-eyed needles. Collins (1937) and others, such as Giddings (1960), have noted especially strong similarities between Thule material culture and that of late-prehistoric inhabitants of St Lawrence Island (referred to as 'Punuk' culture, one example being the site of Kukulik, listed in Table 2). Mason and Barber (2003:72) have suggested that, ultimately, 'whaling arose during the last centuries BC on the south shore of the Chukotka Peninsula, from Ekven to Sirenki, during a cooler interval', but note that sites on Chukotka with evidence of whaling appear suddenly and fully developed about 2300 BP, without local antecedents. Dumond (2006) has revised his earlier opinion on this issue, especially in light of the finds from Margaret Bay, and now deems an eastern Aleutian origin for essential Thule cultural elements to be the most parsimonious explanation.

I suggest that ice-edge hunting technology developed in the eastern Aleutians as strong north winds during the early Neoglacial occasionally drove spring sea ice as far south as Unalaska and kept it there until early summer (see Margaret Bay items in Table 1). Well-developed maritime hunting and fishing strategies were already in place at this time. From the abundance of porpoise remains at Margaret Bay (Davis 2001), for example, we can confidently infer that boats of some kind must have been in use by at least 4700 BP. While sea-mammal hunting was directed primarily towards temperate species in the early decades of the Neoglacial (especially harbour seals and sea lions), a few pagophilic species were also taken (primarily ringed seal, but

Table 2. Eastern Aleutian and Bering Strait sites versus early Thule site comparion (see Figure 1 for locations).

Location	Eastern Aleutians		Kotzebue, AK	St. Lawrence Island		E. Greenland and Alaska
Material culture	Margaret Bay 5500–3000 BP	Amaknak Bridge 3500–2500 BP	Choris c. 2600 BP	Okvik ?2300 BP	Kukulik 1300–1100 BP	Early Thule* c. 1000 BP
Toggling harpoons and lances	no	yes	no	yes	yes	yes
Stone lamps	yes	yes	yes	yes	yes	yes
Ground slate tools	few	no	few	yes	yes	yes
Labrets	yes	yes	yes	yes?	yes	yes
Fine needles	yes	yes	yes	yes	yes?	yes
Pottery	no	no	yes	yes	yes	yes
Iron	no	no	no	no	yes	yes
Open hearth	yes	yes	yes	yes?	yes?	no
Dog harness parts	no	no	no	no	yes	yes
Ivory carvings	no	yes	?	yes	yes	yes
Fauna						
Dogs	no	no	no?	yes	yes	yes
Large whales	few	yes	yes	yes	yes	yes
Ringed seals	yes	yes	yes	yes?	yes	yes
Bearded seals	no	yes	yes	yes?	yes	yes
Walrus	few	yes	no	yes	yes	yes

Table references: Geist and Rainey 1936; Rainey 1941; Larsen and Rainey 1948; Giddings 1960; Schledermann 1976, 1979; Møhl 1979; Staab 1979; Schledermann and McCullough 1980; Mason 1998; Woollett et al. 2000; Davis 2001; Knecht et al. 2001, 2004; Crockford et al. 2004; McGhee 2005.

* these early Thule cultural components are a composite of several.

some walrus and polar bear), although these may only have been available in years of particularly severe ice cover.

At the height of the Neoglacial – with sea ice pressing down from the north virtually every spring – very large numbers of ringed seal were available for hunting at the edge of the ice, as were bearded seals and the occasional walrus (as reflected by the faunal component at Amaknak Bridge in Table 1). Extensive sea ice to the east of Unalaska (along the Bristol Bay coast of the Alaska Peninsula and Unimak Island, Figure 1) would have blocked one of the main passages into the Bering Sea used by modern cetaceans (Moore *et al.* 2002; Ladd *et al.* 2005; Sheldon *et al.* 2005; Sinclair *et al.* 2005; Zerbini *et al.* 2006), forcing them to enter the Bering Sea west of Unalaska, where an eastward migration route would take all animals directly past the site location.

Today, spring migrating whales in the northern portion of the Bering Sea travel in the narrow strip of open water that lies between the shore and wind-driven sea ice, where they are far easier to hunt than autumn whales in relatively ice-free open water: modern Bering Strait whalers still find that spring whaling is the most successful (Bogoslovskaya 2003; Braham 2003; Jolles 2003). Along this moving edge of offshore sea ice, relatively large numbers of seals are also available during the spring and early summer (Nelson 1969).

Successful hunting in seasonal sea-ice-edge habitats not only would have demanded that prehistoric hunters amass detailed knowledge of how spring ice behaves (e.g. Nelson 1969; Oozeva *et al.* 2004), but also would have required the development of strategies for dispatching and butchering enormous animals with minimal manpower. Ethnographic information suggests that small group size probably did not preclude taking very large whales: early in the 20th century, for example, small groups of Bering Strait hunters were known to secure large whales to the ice edge and butcher them in the water (cutting off manageable chunks only, which would almost certainly include flippers), rather than hauling them on to land or ice, as is usual today (Carol Jolles pers comm. 2004). Harpooning seals that are in the water, when the hunter must work from a boat or the edge of sea ice, must have required quite different tactics from those used to hunt seals and sea lions on terrestrial haul outs, or even ringed seals from breathing holes (e.g. Pelly 2001). Of course, none of the above could have taken place without the invention and diligent construction of windproof and waterproof clothing; the ability to sew tight seams demanded careful butchering of carcasses to produce the essential skin and gut segments for such clothing (e.g. Wigen and Lam 2006), as well as very small needles and fine sewing line.

I agree with Morrison (1983) and others (e.g. Staab 1979; Henshaw 2003) who have suggested that early Thule and their immediate Bering Strait ancestors practised ice-edge hunting of ringed seals, rather than breathing-hole hunting. However, I contend that whales were almost certainly hunted in this habitat also (not in 'open water', as is often asserted, which implies lack of constraint by sea ice) and that this spring ice-edge hunting strategy was developed during the Neoglacial by remote ancestors of the Thule who lived far to the south. This ice-edge habitat became available in the Eastern Aleutians only during the late spring/early summer and was not so much an 'adapt or perish' situation, but an 'adapt for success' one: it is clear that plenty of temperate resources had been available for millennia at this location, but ice-edge resources must have added considerably to overall success, if only for the extra oil from such a surplus of marine mammals.

Once Neoglacial conditions ameliorated, however, people who chose to maintain the lifestyle of ice-edge hunting would have had to move north with the receding ice – or perhaps all were forced out by competing groups re-invading from the south. Regardless, virtually the first stop on such a journey northwards would have been St Lawrence Island, which lies smack in the middle of the Bering Strait and is now surrounded by sea ice about eight months of the year (Figure 1). Therefore, the archaeological record of St Lawrence Island has great significance to this story.

St Lawrence Island and the origins of Thule

St Lawrence Island lies just south of, and perpendicular to, the Bering Strait. It is a massive barrier that catches, along its full length, the brunt of wind-driven ice, whether the wind comes from the north or the south (Figure 1). While it is only about 65 km from the Siberian coast to the western end of St Lawrence, it is more than 160 km from Alaska in the east. Cultural ties on St Lawrence, today as in the past, are with Siberia; the Alaskan coast is beyond the range of traditional skin boats, which must be taken out of the water after a few hours or they sink (Rainey 1941; Giddings 1960). Many archaeological sites line the shoreline of St Lawrence, but few have been systematically excavated and many have been destroyed by looters (Mason 1998).

One of the best-known archaeological sites on St Lawrence Island is Kukulik, on the north shore. Kukulik dates to c. 1300–1100 BP and has a material culture known as 'Punuk' (Geist and Rainey 1936). Punuk-culture sites contain evidence of dog-drawn sleds, pottery, elaborately carved ivory, small-eyed needles and the toggling harpoons characteristic of whaling (Table 2).

What appears to be the oldest site in this region (Okvik) is on one of the Punuk Islands off the eastern end of St Lawrence, from which the later culture draws its name. Although the initial occupation date of c. 2300 BP has been contested (e.g. Mason 1998), there seems little doubt that these distinctive early deposits underlay those of true Punuk type and have some typical Old Bering Sea elements (Rainey 1941; Giddings 1960). Okvik contains virtually all elements of Thule material culture, including small-eyed needles and pottery, except dog-drawn sleds (Table 2). There are dog remains, but no sled or harness parts.

Aboriginal whalers thus seem to have arrived on St Lawrence Island with a fully developed Arctic-adapted culture, although admittedly the record is far from complete or well dated. However, no sites with similar elements that predate these deposits have been found so far on the Siberian coast (Mason 1998; Dumond 2000; Mason and Barber 2003; Savinetsky *et al.* 2004). Therefore, unravelling the origin of both Thule culture and Arctic whaling may hinge on determining where the initial colonisers of St Lawrence Island called home. I contend Punuk Islanders probably came initially from the south, along with retreating spring sea ice at the end of the Neoglacial. Thule and their immediate ancestors were thus not exclusively whaling specialists, but highly skilled sea ice-edge hunters, who harvested all species within that ecological zone, including bowhead whales, beluga, ringed and bearded seals, and walrus.

Key elements that continue from Amaknak Bridge through St Lawrence Island sites include evidence of whaling (both toggling harpoons and whale remains), evidence of ice-edge hunting (walrus, bearded seal and ringed seal remains), ivory carvings, small-eyed needles and stone lamps. New elements that appear on St Lawrence Island and elsewhere in the Bering Strait region about 1300 BP are indicative of an active Siberian trade network with Korea and China (Mason 1998). These Siberian elements include: 1. dogs and the technology for dog traction, such as harness buckles and line toggles (Morey and Aaris-Sørensen 2002); 2. smelted iron for arming lances, harpoon heads, arrows and carving tools (Mason 1998; McGhee 2005); 3. clay and associated skills for making fired pottery.

This integration of Siberian culture items is part of what made Thule so unique and successful: they were not only proficient at living in their sea-ice-edge habitat, they were also uniquely mobile. From early spring through mid-summer, dog-drawn sleds could have hauled boats and gear across expanses of moving or stationary sea ice (not just snow-covered land), while boats could have transported dogs, sleds and people between ice flows – a habitat where food was plentiful and easily available. Although travel during the winter would have been virtually impossible in the High Arctic because of constant darkness, dogs and boats could have been used together in spring/early summer to travel rapidly over quite large distances, especially if the receding spring ice was used as a moving platform. In other words, the Thule migration east need not have been confined to shorelines, but almost certainly was seasonally constrained.

Conclusions

I have argued that Thule were not adapted to a specific migratory resource (i.e. bowhead whales), but to the particularly mobile habitat that was the southern edge of sea ice, and that Thule ancestors learned how to hunt the various pinniped and cetacean species of this new habitat during the Neoglacial period, c. 4700–2500 BP, when that sea-ice habitat became a regular seasonal component of life in the eastern Aleutians.

Comprehensive analysis of the marine-mammal fauna from the Amaknak Bridge site documents the presence of seasonal sea ice and its associated fauna as far south as the eastern Aleutians and its persistence until at least early summer on a regular basis during the last half of the Neoglacial. Expansion and persistence of sea ice in the south must have been associated with a persistence of sea ice in the Bering Strait until late summer/early autumn, which would have prevented whales making early summer migrations through the Bering Strait into the Arctic, as they do today. Indeed, the presence of thick, virtually omnipresent sea ice over the northern half of the shallow Bering Shelf during the Neoglacial would have made all coastlines bordering the Bering Strait and Chukchi Sea virtually uninhabitable for whales as well as people, from the Gulf of Anadyr in the west, to the mouth of the Yukon River in the east, including St Lawrence Island.

I maintain that human adaptation to the dramatic increase in sea ice in the eastern Aleutians during the Neoglacial explains the sudden appearance of Arctic whaling in the Bering Strait just afterward, and ultimately, the origins of Thule culture. The most essential element of Thule culture, ice-edge hunting technology (including the boats and clothing required to hunt in that habitat), has its most ancient roots in the eastern Aleutians during the Neoglacial. I suggest that the earliest inhabitants of St Lawrence Island, including Punuk Islanders, probably came initially from the south along with retreating spring sea ice at the end of the Neoglacial, and over time, contact with Siberian cultures to the west introduced the remaining items of Thule culture: dog traction, smelted iron and pottery. Dog-drawn sleds, in combination with skin boats, made Thule people uniquely mobile, allowing them to travel rapidly over large distances.

Acknowledgements

I thank the Museum of the Aleutians (Unalaska) and local Aleut Corporation members for permission to study their collections, a project funded through the State of Alaska Department of Transport. Ole Haggen produced the map presented here and Pacific ID colleague Gay Frederick assisted with bone identification of Amaknak Bridge marine mammals. Managers and curators of the following institutions kindly made their skeletal collections available: Department of Anthropology, University of Victoria, Canada; Smithsonian Institution, Washington, DC; University of Alaska Museum, Fairbanks; Burke Museum, Seattle, WA. Robert McGhee, Don Dumond and Owen Mason provided useful commentary during discussions at the 2008 meeting of the Alaska Anthropology Association in Anchorage.

References

Birket-Smith, K. 1947. Recent achievements in Eskimo research. *Journal of the Royal Anthopological Institute of Great Britain and Ireland* 77:145–157.

Bodenhorn, B. 2003. Fall whaling in Barrow, Alaska: A consideration of strategic decision-making In A.P. McCartney (ed), *Indigenous Ways to the Present: Native Whaling in the Western Arctic*, pp. 277–306. Edmonton: Canadian Circumpolar Institute Press.

Bogoslovskaya, L.S. 2003. The bowhead whale off Chukotka: integration of scientific and traditional knowledge, In A.P. McCartney (ed), *Indigenous Ways to the Present: Native Whaling in the Western Arctic*, pp. 209–254. Edmonton: Canadian Circumpolar Institute Press.

Braham, H. W. 2003. Ancient whaling the biogeography of bowhead and gray whales, In A.P. McCartney (ed), *Indigenous Ways to the Present: Native Whaling in the Western Arctic*, pp. 185–207. Edmonton: Canadian Circumpolar Institute Press.

Braham, H.W., B.D Krogman and G.M. Carroll 1984. *Bowhead and white whale migration, distribution, and abundance in the Bering, Chukchi, and Beaufort Seas, 1975–78*. NOAA Technical Report NMFS SSRF-778.

Clark, D.W. 1966. Perspectives in the prehistory of Kodiak Island, Alaska. *American Antiquity* 31:358–371.

Clark, D.W. 1996. The old Kiavak site, Kodiak Island, Alaska, and the early Kachemak phase. *Arctic* 49:211–227.

Collins, H.B. Jr., 1937. Cultural migrations and contacts in the Bering Sea region. *American Anthropologist* 39:375–384.

Crockford, S. and G. Frederick 2007. Sea ice expansion in the Bering Sea during the Neoglacial: evidence from archaeozoology. *The Holocene*17:699–706.

Crockford, S., G. Frederick, R. Wigen and I. McKechnie 2004. Final Report on the analysis of the vertebrate fauna from Amaknak Bridge, Unalaska, AK, UNL050. Report on file, Museum of the Aleutians, Unalaska, AK. [Supplement to *Amaknak Bridge Site Data Recovery Project Final Report*, Knecht, R. and Davis, R. 2004]

Davis, B.L. 2001. Sea mammal hunting and the neoglacial: An archaeological study of environmental change and subsistence technology at Margaret Bay, Unalaska. *University of Oregon Anthropological Papers* 58:71–85.

Dawson, P.C. 2001. Interpreting variability in Thule Inuit architecture: a case study from the Canadian High Arctic. *American Antiquity* 66:453–470.

Dinesman, L.G. and A.B. Savinetsky 2003. Secular dynamics of the prehistoric catch and population size of baleen whales off the Chukchi Peninsula, Siberia. In A.P. McCartney (ed), *Indigenous Ways to the Present: Native Whaling in the Western Arctic*, pp. 137–166. Edmonton: Canadian Circumpolar Institute Press.

Dixon, J.C. 2003. Environment and environmental change in the western Arctic and Subarctic: implications for whaling. In A.P. McCartney (ed), *Indigenous Ways to the Present: Native Whaling in the Western Arctic*, pp. 1–24. Edmonton: Canadian Circumpolar Institute Press.

Dumond, D.E. 2000. A Southern Origin for Norton Culture? *Anthropological Papers of the University of Alaska* 25:87–102.

Dumond, D.E. 2006. A Backward Glance from Alaska. In D.E. Dumond and R.L. Bland (eds), Archaeology in Northeast Asia: On the Pathway to Bering Strait. *University of Oregon Anthropological Papers* 65:207–226.

Dumond, D.E. and R.L. Bland 1995. Holocene prehistory of the northernmost North Pacific. *Journal of World Prehistory* 9:401–451.

Dyke, A.S. and J.M. Savelle 2001. Holocene history of the Bering Sea bowhead whale (*Balaena mysticetus*) in its Beaufort Sea summer grounds off southwestern Victoria Island, western Canadian Arctic. *Quaternary Research* 55:371–379.

Dyke, A.S. and J.England 2003. Canada's most northerly postglacial bowhead whales (*Balaena mysticetus*): Holocene sea-ice conditions and polynya development. *Arctic* 56:14–20.

Fedoseev, G.A. 1975. Ecotypes of the ringed seal (*Pusa hispida* Schreber, 1777) and their reproductive capabilities. In K. Ronald and A.W. Mansfield (eds), *Biology of the Seal*, pp. 156–160. Rapports et Proces-verbaux des Reunions, Conseil International Pour L'Exploration de la Mer.

Finley, K.J., G.W. Miller, R.A. Davis and W.R. Koski 1983. A distinctive large breeding population of ringed seal (*Phoca hispida*) inhabiting the Baffin Bay pack ice. *Arctic* 36:162–173.

Fisher, D., A. Dyke, R. Koerner, J. Bourgeois, C. Kinnard, C. Zdanowicz, A. de Vernal, C. Hillaire-Marcel, J. Savelle and A. Rochon 2006. Natural variability of arctic sea ice over the Holocene. *EOS (Transactions of the American Geophysical Union)* 87:273–280.

Frey, A., S.J. Crockford, M. Meyer and G. O'Corry-Crowe 2005. Genetic analysis of prehistoric marine mammal bones from an ancient Aleut village in the southeastern Bering Sea. *Abstracts of 16th Biennial Conference on the Biology of Marine Mammals,* p. 98. San Diego.

Geist, O.W. and F.G. Rainey 1936, *Archaeological excavations at Kukulik, St. Lawrence Island, Alaska.* Miscellaneous Vol. II. Washington, DC: Publications of the University of Alaska.

Giddings, J.L. 1960. The archaeology of Bering Strait. *Current Anthropology* 1:121–138.

Grebmeier, J., J.E. Overland, S.E. Moore, E.V. Farley, E.C. Carmack, L.W.Cooper, K.E. Frey, J.H. Helle, F.A.McLaughlin and S.L. McNutt 2006. A major ecosystem shift in the northern Bering Sea. *Science* 311:1461–1464.

Gusev, S. V., A.V.Zagoroulko and A.V. Porotov 1999. Sea mammal hunters of Chukotka, Bering Strait: Recent archaeological results and problems. *World Archaeology* 30:354–369.

Henshaw, A. 2003. Polynyas and ice edge habitats in cultural context: Archaeological perspectives from southeast Baffin Island. *Arctic* 56:1–13.

Holst, M., I. Stirling and W. Calvert 1999. Age structure and reproductive rates of ringed seals (*Phoca hispida*) on the northwest coast of Hudson Bay in 1991 and 1992. *Marine Mammal Science* 15:1357–1364.

Jolles, C.Z. 2003. When whaling folks celebrate: A comparison of tradition and experience in two Bering Sea whaling communities. In A.P. McCartney (ed), *Indigenous Ways to the Present: Native Whaling in the Western Arctic*, pp. 307–339. Edmonton: Canadian Circumpolar Institute Press.

Kasuya, T. 1975. Past occurrence of *Globicephala melaena* in the western North Pacific. *Scientific Reports of the Whales Research Institute* 27:95–110.

Kelly, B.P. 2001. Climate change and ice breeding pinnipeds. In G.R.Walther, A.B. Conradin and P.J. Edwards (eds.), *Fingerprints of Climate Change*, pp. 43–55. New York: Plenum.

Kenyon, K.W. and F. Wilke 1953. Migration of the Northern fur seal, *Callorhinus ursinus*. *Journal of Mammalogy* 34:86–98.

Knecht, R.A. and R.S. Davis 2001. A prehistoric sequence for the Eastern Aleutians. *University of Oregon Anthropological Papers* 58:269–288.

Knecht, R. and R. Davis 2004. *Amaknak Bridge Site Data Recovery Project Final Report* #MGS-STP-BR-0310(S)/52930. On file, Museum of the Aleutians, Unalaska and Alaska Department of Transportation, Anchorage.

Knecht, R. and R. Davis 2003. *Archaeological evaluation of Tanaxtaxak, the Amaknak Spit site (UNL-055) final report*. Unpublished report, Museum of the Aleutians, Unalaska.

Ladd, C., G.L. Hunt Jr., C.W Mordy, S.A Salo and P.J. Stabeno 2005. Marine environment of the eastern and central Aleutian Islands. *Fisheries Oceanography* 14(1):22–38.

Larsen, H. and F.G. Rainey 1948. Ipiutak and the Arctic whale hunting culture. *Anthropological Papers of the American Museum of Natural History* 42.

Le Mouël, J.F. and M. Le Mouël 2002. Aspects of early Thule culture as seen in the architecture of a site on Victoria Island, Amundsen Gulf area. *Arctic* 55:167–189.

McGhee, R. (ed) 2005. *The Last Imaginary Place: A Human History of the Arctic World.* Chicago: University of Chicago Press.

Mason, O.K. 1998. The contest between the Ipiutak, Old Bering Sea, and Birnirk polities and the origin of whaling during the first millennium A.D. along the Bering Strait. *Journal of Anthroplogical Archaeology* 17:240–325.

Mason, O.K. and V. Barber 2003. A paleo-geographic preface to the origins of whaling: cold is better. In A.P. McCartney (ed), *Indigenous Ways to the Present: Native Whaling in the Western Arctic,* pp. 69–107. Edmonton Canadian Circumpolar Institute Press.

Mason, O.K. and S.L. Ludwig 1990. Resurrecting beach ridge archaeology: parallel depositional records from St. Lawrence Island and Cape Krusenstern, western Alaska. *Geoarchaeology* 5:349–373.

Møhl, J. 1979. Description and analysis of the bone material from Nugarsuk: An Eskimo settlement representative of the Thule culture in west Greenland. In A.P. McCartney (ed), *Thule Eskimo Culture: An Anthropological Retrospective,* pp. 380–394. National Museum of Man, Mercury Series, Archaeology Survey of Canada 88.

Moore, S.E., D.P. DeMaster and P.K. Dayton 2000. Cetacean habitat selection in the Alaskan Arctic during summer and autumn. *Arctic* 53:432–447.

Moore, S.E., J.M. Grebmeier and J.R.Davies 2003. Gray whale distribution relative to forage habitat in the northern Bering Sea: current conditions and retrospective summary. *Canadian Journal of Zoology* 81:734–742.

Moore, S.E. and K.L. Laidre 2006. Trends in sea ice cover within habitats used by bowhead whales in the western arctic. *Ecological Applications* 16:932–944.

Moore, S.E., J.M. Waite, N.A. Friday and T. Honkalehto 2002. Cetacean distribution and relative abundance on the central-eastern and the southeastern Bering Sea shelf with reference to oceanographic domain. *Progress in Oceanography* 55:249–261.

Morey, D.F. and K. Aaris-Sørensen 2002. Paleoeskimo dogs of the eastern Arctic. *Arctic* 55:44–56.

Morrison, D.A. 1983. *Thule culture in western Coronation Gulf, N.W.T.* National Museum of Man, Mercury Series, Archaeological Survey of Canada (Ottawa) 116.

Nelson, R.K. 1969. *Hunters of the Northern Ice.* Chicago: University of Chicago Press.

O'Corry-Crowe, G.M., R.S. Suydam, A. Rosenberg, K.J. Frost and A.E. Dizon 1997. Phylogeography, population structure and dispersal patterns of the beluga whale *Delphinapterus leucas* in the western Nearctic revealed by mitochondrial DNA. *Molecular Ecology* 6:955–970.

O'Corry-Crow, G.M. and R.L. Westlake 1997. Molecular investigations of spotted seals (*Phoca largha*) and harbor seals (*P. vitulina*), and their relationship in areas of sympatry. In A.E. Dizon, S.J. Chivers and W. F. Perrin (eds), Molecular Genetics of Marine Mammals. Special Publication Number 3, pp. 291–304. Lawrence: The Society for Marine Mammalogy.

Oozeva, C., C. Noongwook, G. Noongwook, C. Alowa and I. Krupnik 2004. *Watching Ice and Weather Our Way.* Washington DC: Arctic Studies Center, Smithsonian Institution.

Pelly, D.F. 2001. *Sacred Hunt: A Portrait of the Relationship Between Seals and Inuit.* Seattle, University of Washington Press.

Overland, J.E. and P.J. Stabeno 2004. Is the climate of the Bering Sea warming and affecting the ecosystem? *EOS (Transactions of the American Geophysical Union)* 85:309–316.

Ragen, T.J., G.A. Antonelis and M. Kiyota 1995. Early migration of northern fur seal pups from St.Paul Island, Alaska. *Journal of Mammalogy* 76:1137–1148.

Rainey, F.G. 1941. Eskimo prehistory: the Okvik site on the Punuk Islands. *Anthropological Papers of the American Museum of Natural History* 37(IV):455–569.

Reeves, R.R, B.S. Stewart, P.J. Clapham and J.A. Powell 2002. *National Audobon Society's Guide to Marine Mammals of the World.* New York: Alfred A. Knopf.

Rigor, I.G. and J.M Wallace 2004. Variations in the age of Arctic sea ice and summer sea ice extent. *Geophysical Research Letters* 31:L09401.

Savelle, J.M. and A.P. McCartney 2003. Prehistoric bowhead whaling in the Bering Strait and Chukchi Sea regions of Alaska: A zooarchaeological assessment. In A.P. McCartney (ed), *Indigenous Ways to the Present: Native Whaling in the Western Arctic,* pp. 167–184. Edmonton: Canadian Circumpolar Institute Press.

Savinetsky, A.B., N.K. Kiseleva and B.F. Khassanov 2004. Dynamics of sea mammal and bird populations of the Bering Sea region over the last several millennia. *Palaeogeography, Palaeoclimatology, Palaeoecology* 209:335–352.

Schledermann, P. 1976. The effects of climatic/ecological changes on the style of Thule culture winter dwellings. *Arctic and Alpine Research* 8:37–47.

Schledermann, P. 1979. The "baleen period" of the Arctic whale hunting tradition. In A.P. McCartney (ed), *Thule Eskimo Culture: An Anthropological Retrospective*, pp. 134–148. National Museum of Man, Mercury Series, Archaeology Survey of Canada Paper No. 88.

Schledermann, P. and K. McCullough 1980. Western elements in the early Thule culture of the eastern high Arctic. *Arctic* 33:833–841.

Shaunghnessy, P.D. and F.H. Fay 1977. A review of the taxonomy and nomenclature of North Pacific harbour seals. *Journal of Zoology (London)* 182:385–419.

Sheldon, K.E.W., S.E. Moore, J.M. Waite, P.R. Wade and D.J. Rugh 2005. Historic and current habitat use by North Pacific right whales *Eubalaena japonica* in the Bering Sea and Gulf of Alaska. *Mammal Review* 35:129–155.

Simpkins, M.A., L.M. Hiruki-Raring, G. Sheffield, J.M Grebmeier and J.L. Bengtson 2003. Habitat selection by ice-associated pinnipeds near St. Lawrence Island, Alaska in March 2001. *Polar Biology* 26:577–586.

Sinclair, E.H., S.E. Moore, N.A. Friday, T.K. Zeppelin and J.M. Waite 2005. Do patterns of Steller sea lion (*Eumetopias jubatus*) diet, population trend and cetacean occurrence reflect oceanographic domains from the Alaska Peninsula to the central Aleutian Islands? *Fisheries Oceanography* 14(1):223–242.

Solid Fuel Association. 2005. *Curing chimney problems.* Solid Fuel Association, Derbyshire, UK, viewed 12 November 2007. http://www.solidfuel.co.uk/frame/main.html

Staab, M.L. 1979. Analysis of faunal material recovered from a Thule Eskimo site on the island of Silumiut, N.W.T., Canada. In A.P. McCartney (ed), *Thule Eskimo Culture: An Anthropological Retrospective*, pp. 349–379. National Museum of Man, Mercury Series, Archaeology Survey of Canada Paper No. 88.

Stewart, B.S., S.A. Karl, P.K. Yochem, S. Leatherwood and J.L. Laake 1987. Aerial surveys for cetaceans in the former Akutan, Alaska, whaling grounds. *Arctic:* 40:33–42.

Stora, J. 2000. Skeletal development in the grey seal *Halichoerus grypus,* the ringed seal *Phoca hispida botnica,* the harbour seal *Phoca vitulina vitulina,* and the harp seal *Phoca groenlandica:*epiphyseal fusion and life history. *Archaeozoologia,* XI:199–222.

Trites, A. W. and G.A. Antonelis 1994. The influence of climatic seasonality on the life cycle of the Pribilof Northern fur seal. *Marine Mammal Science* 10:311–324.

Wiig, O., A.E. Derocher and S.E. Belikov 1999. Ringed seal (*Phoca hispida*) breeding in the drifting pack ice of the Barents Sea. *Marine Mammal Science* 15:595–598.

Wigen, R. J. and Y. Lam 2006. Tool manufacturing and skinning marks on bird bones from the Amaknak Bridge site, Aleutian Islands, Alaska. Paper presented at the 10th meeting of the International Council for Archaeozoology, Mexico City, 23–28 August 2006.

Woollett, J. M., A.S. Henshaw and C.P. Wake 2000. Palaeoecological implications of archaeological seal bone assemblages: Case studies from Labrador and Baffin Island. *Arctic* 53:395–413.

Zerbini, A. N., J.M. Waite, J.L. Laake and P.R.Wade 2006. Abundance, trends and distribution of baleen whales off western Alaska and the central Aleutian Islands. *Deep-Sea Research Part I* 53:1772–1790.

9

Ritualised marine midden formation in western Zenadh Kes (Torres Strait)

Ian J. McNiven
School of Geography and Environmental Science, Monash University, Australia
Ian.McNiven@arts.monash.edu.au

Duncan Wright
Centre for Australian Indigenous Studies, Monash University, Australia

Introduction

Marine subsistence specialisation is a central theme in the archaeology of Oceania. Shell middens provide the main material evidence for marine specialisation through food remains (e.g. bones and shells) and technology (e.g. fishhooks). For the most part, middens are considered domestic refuse deposits and the byproduct of people living their daily lives. In contrast, sites such as houses and ritual structures are considered part of the built domain and architecture of settlements. Over the past decade or so, the role of refuse deposits as secular byproducts of society has been challenged by the concepts of 'ritual rubbish' and 'ceremonial trash' (e.g. Hill 1995; Walker 1995; Needham and Spence 1997; Chapman 2000; Cameron 2002; see also Hodder 1982:161). This reconceptualisation recognises the biographical and symbolic dimensions of 'refuse' and the embeddedness of midden materials in ritual behaviour, place-marking strategies, construction of cultural landscapes and maintenance of social identity. In Australia, appreciation is slowly emerging of the agency and symbolic value of domestic 'refuse' given monumental expression as curated mounds to inscribe landscapes with new and ongoing social meanings (e.g. Morrison 2003; Bourke 2005; Hiscock and Faulkner 2006; see also Meehan 1982). In the 1980s, Barbara Ghaleb (1990) pioneered Australian archaeological investigations into the 'ceremonial' and 'symbolic' role of mounded midden deposits with her PhD research on the 'old village' site of Goemu on the island of Mabuyag, Zenadh Kes. Since Ghaleb's research, Mabuyag has been the focus of investigations into another type of ritual site constructed of food remains – dugong bone mounds (McNiven and Feldman 2003; McNiven and Bedingfield 2008). In light of new insights into dugong bone mounds and ritual treatment of subsistence remains, this paper re-examines conceptualisation and identification of mounded midden deposits at Goemu, based on excavations at the site by Harris and Ghaleb in 1985 and by us in 2005.

Middens and mounds

In Zenadh Kes, middens are layers of occupation deposit typically comprising marine shells, bones (dugong, turtle and fish), stone artefacts, charcoal and cooking stones, dating back to at least 4000 years ago (e.g. Barham and Harris 1985; Carter *et al.* 2004; David and Weisler 2006; McNiven 2006; Crouch *et al.* 2007; Ash and David In press). Ethnographic information on middens is scant, with Haddon (1912:131) making a passing comment that '[k]itchen-middens are not formed now, nor did I come across traces of ancient refuse heaps'. Dugong bone mounds are oval-shaped and range up to 13 m long and 1 m high. Excavations at Tudu and Pulu reveal that 50–65 percent of cultural material (by weight) in these elaborately made structures is dugong bone (increasing to 96–97 percent when likely dugong bone is included), of which nearly all is ribs and rear skull bones (McNiven and Feldman 2003). Estimates of the number of dugongs (MNI) represented in individual bone mounds range from c. 140 to c. 10,000–11,000 (David and Mura Badulgal Committee 2006; McNiven and Bedingfield 2008). Radiocarbon dates suggest these sites date to the past 400–500 years (McNiven and Feldman 2003; David and Mura Badulgal Committee 2006; McNiven and Bedingfield 2008). While bone mounds are described ethnographically simply as 'ceremonial' and 'shrines' (Haddon 1901:139; 1912:131), archaeological research associates these sites more specifically with hunting magic, social cohesion and collective identity (McNiven and Feldman 2003).

Published literature on Zenadh Kes ethnography and archaeology makes a morphological and functional distinction between secular midden deposits and ritual dugong bone mounds. Yet unpublished archaeological recordings of numerous constructed midden mounds at Goemu 'old village' site on Mabuyag in western Zenadh Kes blur this distinction and call into question the secularity of middens (Barham and Harris 1987; Ghaleb 1990; see also Vanderwal 1973:183). To characterise the extent of this blurred distinction, the following sections of the paper describe the form and content of the Goemu mounded middens and examine the extent to which they differ compositionally from: (1) underlying and adjacent non-mounded midden deposits; and (2) dugong bone mounds excavated on Pulu and Tudu.

Goemu village

Ethnographic context

Goemu is one of the major 'old village' sites of Mabuyag, a small island (8.3 km^2) located in central-western Zenadh Kes (Figure 1). At the time of early European contact in the 1870s, the Goemulgal (people of Mabuyag) had a population of at least 300 (Mullins 1992). The island and adjacent seas are divided into four major clan/totemic districts and Goemu is the settlement focus of the southeast district of the kaigas (shovel-nosed shark), waru (turtle) and umai (dog) totemic clans (Haddon 1904:266; Davis and Prescott 1992; Eseli 1998). Whereas the settlements of Dabangai and Panai on the northeast coast are the centre of the dhangal (dugong) and kodal (crocodile) clans and dugong-hunting rituals, Goemu is the focus of turtle-hunting rituals (Haddon 1935:59). Apart from houses, structures at Goemu once included a skull-house (kuiku-iut), a ceremonial kod (special men's area) and the wiwai turtle-hunting shrine (Haddon 1904:3, 306, 333–36; 1935:59).

Archaeological mapping

Archaeological surveys of Mabuyag indicate that the largest and most extensive midden deposits are at Goemu. These deposits reveal that Goemu was a major settlement place on Mabuyag. A detailed map of Goemu was produced by David Harris and Barbara Ghaleb (Institute of

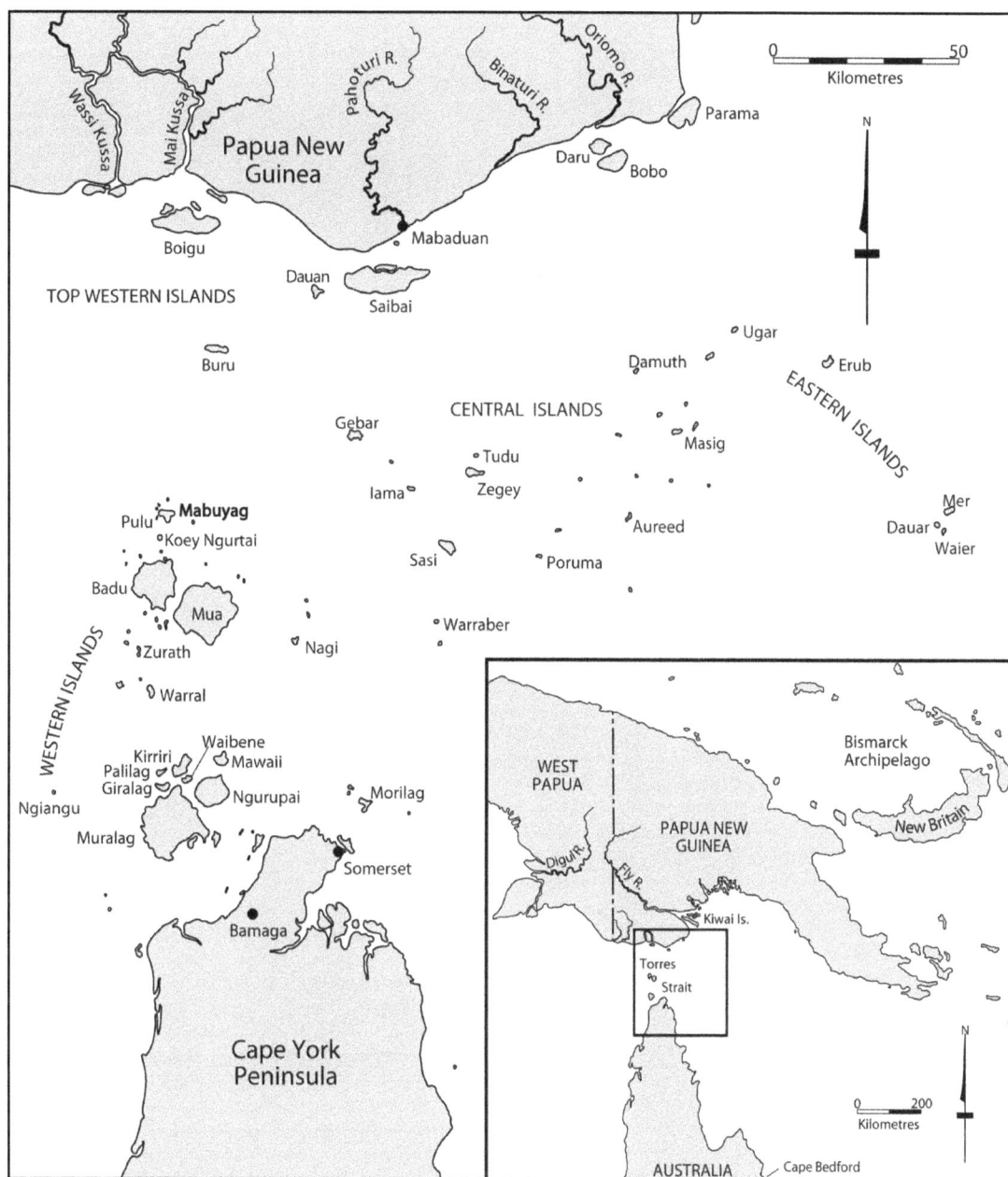

Figure 1. Map of Zenadh Kes.

Archaeology, University College London) and their team in 1985 (Barham and Harris 1987) (Figure 2). The village is located on the coast across a 320 m-long wedge-shaped flat area of prograded shelly-sand deposits, fronted by the high-water mark and backed mostly by rocky hills supporting open shrubland and woodland. The site has a maximum width of 140 m (in the south) and covers an area of c. 20,000 m² (2 ha) (Barham and Harris 1987:12). Vegetation across the village is dominated by anthropogenic grassland, with scattered coconut trees and a zone of shrubs adjacent to the high-water mark (Figure 3). Controlled burning by local community members of the thick grass cover in 1985 provided a rare opportunity to record and map the location of more than 100 surface features (e.g. mounded middens and stone arrangements). This map has added historical importance, as extensive levelling of the site by machinery in 2005 to accommodate construction of four tin sheds (domestic structures) has removed nearly 70 percent of these surface features.

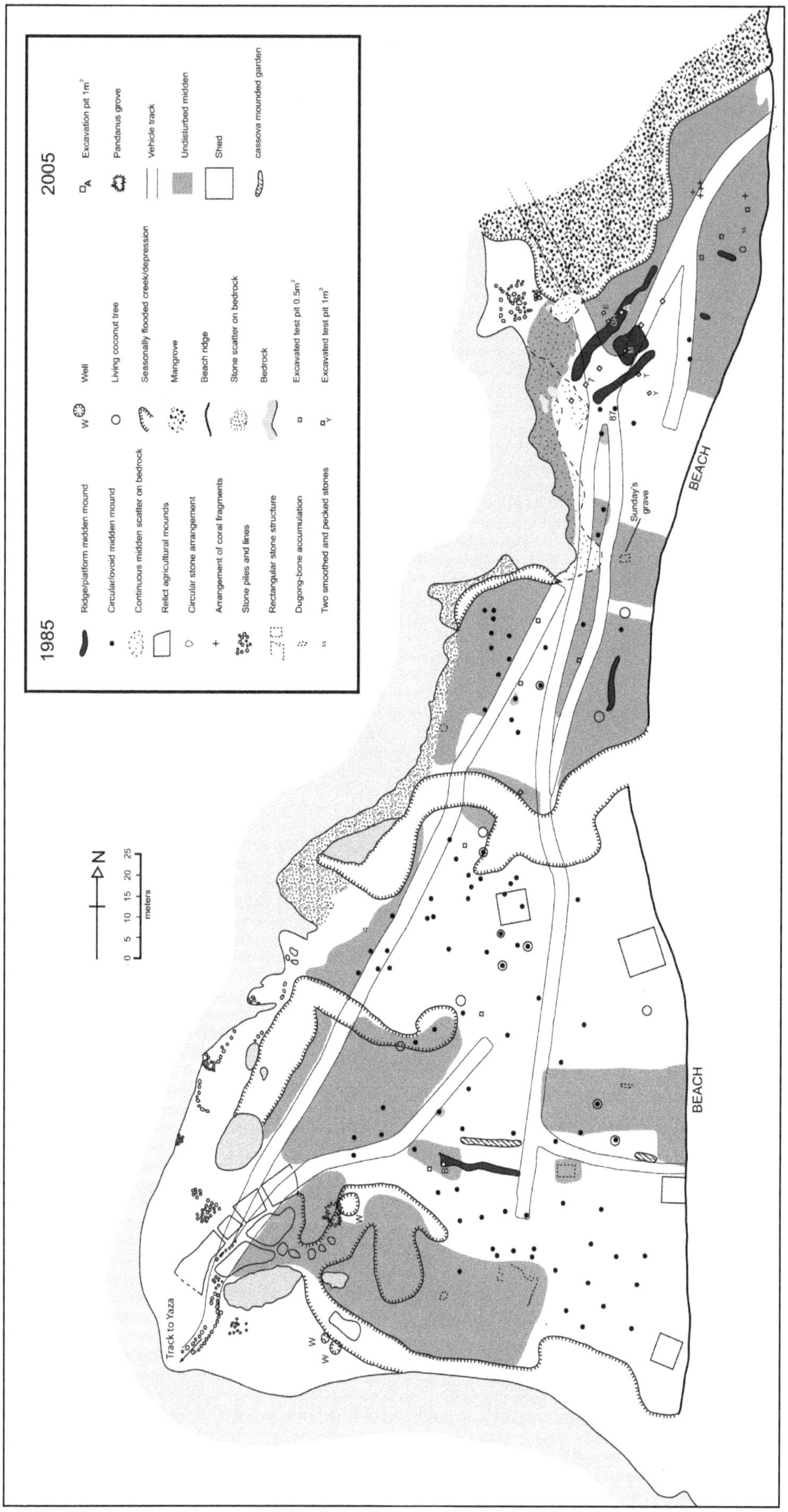

Figure 2. Map of Goemu 'old village' site, Mabuyag (after Barham and Harris 1987:Figure 4).

Three types of midden deposit which 'superficially consist of bone (primarily dugong), angular chunks of stone, and shell' were identified at Goemu (Ghaleb 1990:181–185, 212–213, 226, 267, 303; Harris *et al.* 1985:44, 48):

1. Level midden. 'Discontinuous surface scatters', forming 'level' midden deposits with considerable sub-surface components.

2. Circular midden mounds. Ninety-five 'discrete circular or ovoid mounds averaging 1.0–1.5 m in diameter and 30 cm in height, sometimes bordered by large stones or Syrinx shells' occur mostly across the southern half of the village (Figure 2). Circular mounds cover c. 180 m^2 or about 0.9 percent of the surface area of Goemu.

3. Ridge and platform midden mounds. Seven 'large linear and rectangular accumulations' occur mostly across the far northern part of the village (Figure 2). The northern complex consists of a midden 'platform' (8 x 5–7 m with a mean height of 15 cm), flanked by two 'ridges' – the west ridge measures 35 x 3 m (mean height 28 cm) and the east ridge measures 20 x 2 m (mean height 18 cm). Ridges and the platform cover c. 170 m^2 and 48 m^2 respectively, or about 1.1 percent of the surface area of Goemu.

Excavations

In 1985, Harris and colleagues excavated examples of the three types of midden at Goemu – level middens across the village, a circular midden mound (Mound 87), and the platform-ridge midden mound complex at the northern end of the village (Barham and Harris 1987; Ghaleb 1990). A key aim of these excavations was to test whether the mounded midden features differed compositionally from the level midden deposits. In 2005, we excavated the northern platform-ridge mounded midden complex (Square A) and a ridge mounded midden feature at the southern end of the village (Square B). Key aims of our excavations were to obtain more detailed stratigraphic and chronological information about the development of mounded midden features at the site. For the purposes of this paper, analysis focuses on Harris and Ghaleb's circular Mound 87 and platform midden mound excavations and our northern-ridge midden mound excavation (Square A). Our analysis includes neither the 16 small 'test pits' excavated by Harris *et al.* across level midden deposits, nor our Square B excavation, as none has been analysed compositionally.

Figure 3. Goemu looking northeast, 1996 (photo by Ian McNiven).

Circular midden mound

Mound 87 is located immediately south of the platform-ridge complex at the northern end of Goemu (Figure 2). Half of the 23.5 cm-high mound was excavated by Harris *et al.* but only one quarter was analysed (see Barham and Harris 1987 and Ghaleb 1990 for details). It was excavated in seven units to the level of the surrounding ground surface, where excavation changed to 'two small pits', which continued through sediment with 'dark matrix' and '[f]ew midden remains' for 25 cm, where 'beach sand' was encountered. The mound is dominated by dugong bones, 'an abundance' of 'chunks' of local rock, marine shells (19 species), and some turtle and fish bones, coral fragments, and a quartz flake. Units 4 and 6 contained 'fragments of glass', while Unit 7 'had very few remains'. These glass fragments are the only 'stratified material remains of European origin' excavated by Harris *et al.* at Goemu (Ghaleb 1990:234). Assuming the glass fragments are not stratigraphically intrusive, they indicate the mound 'was made sometime after Torres Strait Islanders had access to glass' (Ghaleb 1990:301). As Mabuyag Islanders had little contact with Europeans before the arrival of missionaries and pearl shellers in the 1870s, it is likely the glass in Mound 87 dates to after 1870. However, an earlier 19th century date for the glass should not be discounted, as bottle glass was a commodity of the 19th century 'passing trade era' (McNiven 2001). As such, Mound 87 most likely dates to the 19th century (Haddon makes no mention of settlement at Goemu in 1898).

In terms of total weight of dugong bone, a range of skeletal elements is represented – skull (42%), ribs (42%), vertebrae (13%) and limbs (3%) (Ghaleb 1990:251). An extrapolated MNI of eight dugongs was calculated for the entire mound (Ghaleb 1990:365). The relatively high quantity of dugong bones in Mound 87, combined with the high representation of dugong skull (including ear ossicles) and rib bones, is typical of ritual dugong bone mounds on Pulu and Tudu (Figure 4). Similarly, the low representation of stone artefacts and bones of turtle and fish are typical of dugong bone mounds. In contrast, the proportion of dugong limb bones and vertebrae in Mound 87 is higher than that recorded for the Pulu and Tudu bone mounds, while the high concentrations of rocks (cooking stones) and shells, and the low MNI of eight dugongs are also atypical of bone mounds.

Mound 87 is similar in form and content to the more than 90 circular midden mounds recorded across Goemu. Surface recordings indicate that these mounds contain marine shells, dugong bones and angular rocks (cooking stones), and half exhibit stone artefacts (Ghaleb 1990:187, 192). In terms of dugong bone elements, most midden mounds contain rib (n=93) and skull fragments (n=71), with few exhibiting vertebrae (n=22), humeri (n=13), phalanges (n=9) and scapula (n=6) (Ghaleb 1990:187). While the high representation of skull and rib

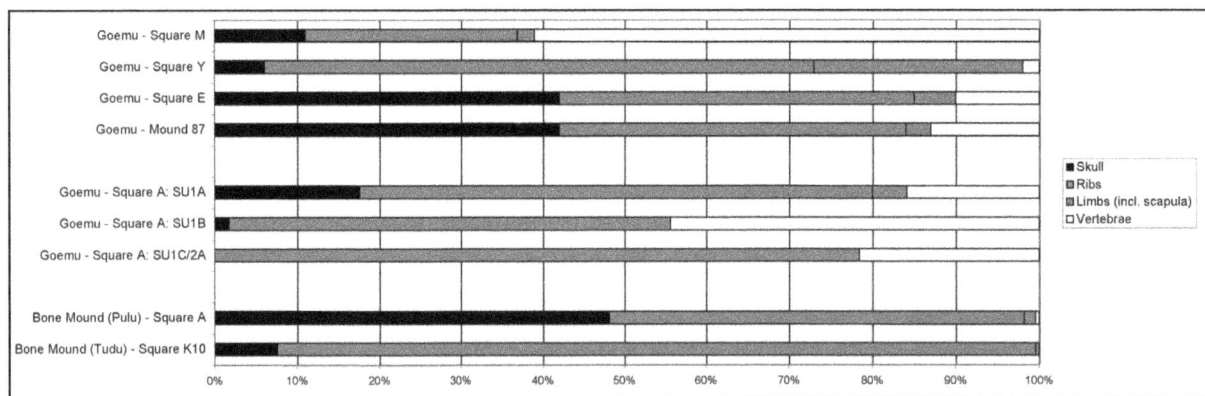

Figure 4. Relative proportion of dugong bone elements from Goemu and ritual bone mounds on Pulu and Tudu.

bones is consistent with ritual bone mounds, the representation of vertebrae and limbs is not. Furthermore, ear ossicles, which are a signature component of ritual bone mounds, were recorded in only 5 percent of the Goemu mounds (Ghaleb 1990:193; McNiven and Feldman 2003). The number and diversity of marine shells (more than 50 species in total) and the presence of cooking stones is also atypical of dugong bone mounds. The presence of glass on the surface of 25 percent of circular mounds (Barham and Harris 1987:13) indicates construction continued into the 19th century.

Platform midden mound

A series of five 1 x 1 m pits spaced along a 25 m transect was excavated by Harris *et al.* across the platform-ridge midden mound complex at the northern end of Goemu (see Barham and Harris 1987 and Ghaleb 1990, 1998 for details) (Figure 2). Two to four 50 x 50 cm quadrants in each square were excavated, but only single quadrants from Squares M, E and Y were analysed. Square M was located on the 'platform' mounded midden, with Squares E and Y located on 'level' (non-mounded) midden deposit to the side of the west and east 'ridges' respectively. Excavations used 5 cm spits and all excavated materials were sieved through 4 mm and 2 mm mesh. Excavations continued 'until sterile deposits were reached'. The depth of midden deposit in each of the three analysed squares varied, with sterile beach sands reached at depths of 50 cm (Square M), 40 cm (Square Y) and 25 cm (Square E). A date of 600±70 years BP (c. 550 years ago) was obtained from a single charcoal fragment from Square M within midden deposit at 'a depth of 35 cm', which is below the 15 cm-deep base of the mounded midden feature (Table 1). From the same stratigraphic context, an anomalous date of 'modern' was obtained on 'small charcoal fragments' collected between 30 cm and 40 cm below the surface in Square M.

For the most part, Ghaleb analysed deposits in all three squares as single units. No attempt was made to analytically isolate the upper level of Square M, representing 'platform' mounded midden, to explore compositional differences from or similarities to underlying or adjacent 'level' midden deposits. However, the densest midden deposit encountered during excavation was from the upper 15 cm of Square M, corresponding to the mounded 'platform' feature. In contrast, Squares E and Y revealed 'moderate' and 'low' density ('level') midden deposits. The abundance of dense midden deposit in the platform mounded feature is indicated by Square M, containing the majority of shell (67% by MNI), turtle bone (>80% by weight), fish bone (82% by number) and dugong bone (>90% by weight) recovered from all three squares. All three squares have a similar range of remains, dominated by shells and bones of dugong, turtle and fish. The number of marine shellfish species in each square is similar – Square M (19 species), Square E (21 species) and Square Y (19 species), while at least 88 percent of fish in each square comes from the same three families (Labridae, Scaridae and Lethrinidae).

In terms of total weight of dugong bone, a broad range of skeletal elements is represented in Square M – skull (11%), ribs (26%), vertebrae (61%) and limbs (2%) (Ghaleb 1990:251,257) (Figure 4). The considerable presence of dugong vertebrae, as with the considerable representation of dugong limb/vertebrae in Squares E and Y, are all atypical of ritual bone mounds (Figure 4). Equally atypical are the low dugong MNIs: Square M=3; Square E=1; Square Y=1 (Ghaleb 1990:258), and the considerable presence of other midden materials (e.g. shells, turtle and fish bones and rocks) in all squares.

Ridge midden mound

In 2005, we excavated a 1 x 1 m pit (Square A) on the eastern edge of the 28 cm-high western ridge of the northern platform-ridge complex (Figures 2 and 5). The pit was excavated to a

Table 1. Goemu radiocarbon dates.

Laboratory Code	Square and Excavation Unit	Depth below surface (cm)	Sample and ¹⁴C technique	Sample weight (g)	¹³C‰	¹⁴C Age (years BP)	Calibrated Age BP 2 sigma range	Years Ago (cal BP)
Beta-21385	M:?	35	Charcoal Conventional	1.8	?	600±70	498–658	550
Beta-21384	M:?	30–40	Charcoal Conventional	2.17	?	101.3±1.6% modern	—	—
Wk-21514	A:3	1.5–3.4	Charcoal AMS	0.01	-22.7±0.2	131±32	0–146* 222–263	50
Wk-21515	A:7	9.5–12.5	Charcoal AMS	0.01	-9.8±0.2	160±31	0–153* 173–177 208–277	100
Wk-21516	A:11	24.1–28.3	Charcoal AMS	0.06	-25.2±0.2	524±32	496–545	500
Wk-21517	A:15	37.5–41.1	Charcoal AMS	0.06	-26.8±0.2	893±32	683–801* 875–882 887–897	750
Wk-21518	A:18c	49.8–54.9	Charcoal AMS	0.02	-25.6±0.2	523±32	496–545	500
Wk-21519	A:23	81.6–90.1	Charcoal AMS	0.07	-25.1±0.2	6133±41	6792–7029* 7045–7069 7079–7085 7106–7156	6950
Wk-21520	A:25	98.3–104.7	Charcoal AMS	0.04	-27.8 ±0.2	878±32	681–794	750
Wk-21521	A:32	156.2–171.2	Charcoal AMS	0.02	-26.5 ±0.2	954±32	745– 909	800

Dates calibrated into calendar years using the online calibration program Calib 5.0.2 (Stuiver and Reimer 1993; Stuiver *et al.* 2005) and the Southern Hemisphere calibration datasets (McCormac *et al.* 2004). Dates expressed as 'years ago' (cal BP – i.e. before AD 1950) represent approximates based upon the midpoint of the 1 sigma highest probability.

*=highest probability of calibrated ranges.

maximum depth of 202 cm, using 34 excavation units (XUs). Spit or excavation unit (XU) thickness averaged <4 cm in midden levels and all excavated materials were sieved through 2.1 mm mesh. Two major and seven minor stratigraphic units (SUs) were identified (Figure 6). The upper 25–30 cm (SU1a) was dark grey-brown loamy sediment with dense midden deposit and considerable amounts of bone (dugong, turtle and fish), fragments of rock (most likely cooking stones), marine shells, crustacean exoskeleton, stone artefacts, charcoal and ochre. A low number of small fragments of glass and rusty metal was recovered down to depths of 12 cm and 20 cm respectively. SU1a corresponds in thickness to the mean height of the mounded ridge feature. SU1b extends down to c. 35–40 cm below the surface and is slightly lighter-coloured loamy sediment with lower-density midden deposit. SU1c is a c. 10 cm thick zone of grey loamy sediment mixed with shelly sand from SU2 and few cultural materials. The change to SU2 is marked by a change to foraminifera-rich shelly beach sands with very few cultural remains. SU2a is light grey and is mixed with darker midden matrix from SU1 above. SU2b is coarse-grained shelly sand with few cultural materials and a zone of charcoal and pumice. An ash-rich zone in the upper sections of SU2b appears to be a cooking pit. SU2c is laminated shelly sands with little cultural material, except for an alignment of six stones running across the square between the south and north walls at a depth of c. 95–100 cm below the surface. The basal 30–35 cm of the pit is fine-grained shelly sands (SU2d) with no obvious cultural materials.

Figure 5. Excavation of Square A on ridge midden mound, Goemu 'old village', November 2005 (photo by Ian McNiven). From left to right: Alice Bedingfield, Duncan Wright, Beeboy Whop, and senior site custodian Cygnet Repu.

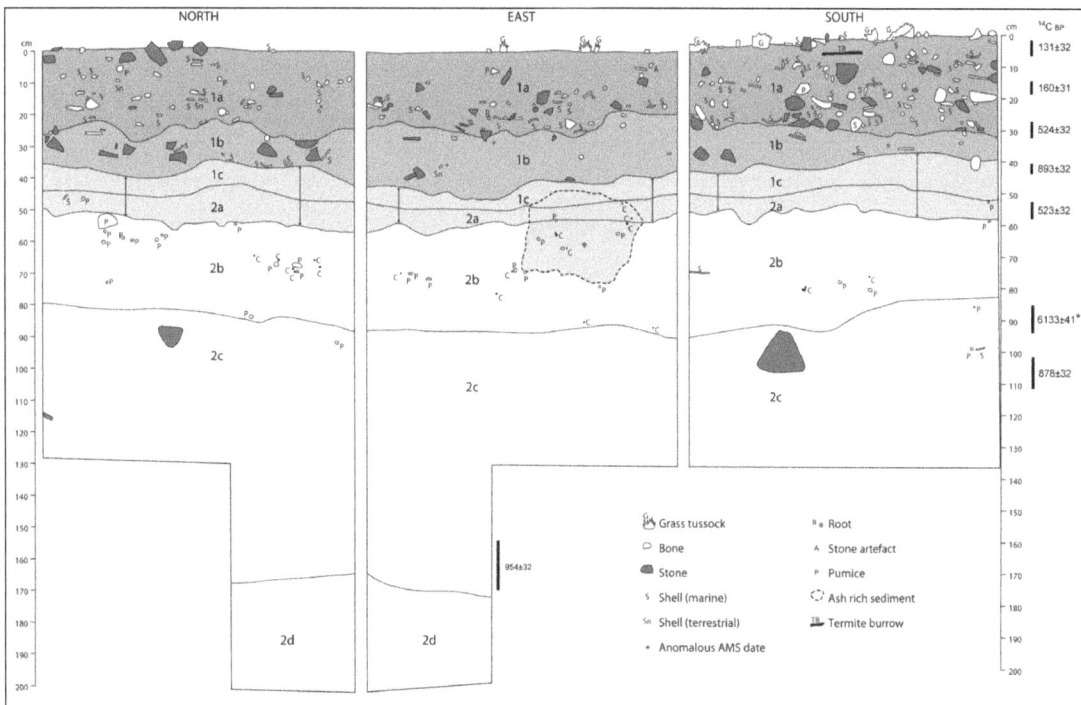

Figure 6. Stratigraphy and radiocarbon dates for Square A, Goemu.

Eight radiocarbon dates (AMS) were obtained on single charcoal fragments from Square A (Table 1). SU1a, taking in the mounded ridge feature and the main midden deposit, has three ^{14}C dates of 113±32 BP (top), 160±31 BP (middle) and 524±32 BP (base), which all calibrate to within the past c. 500 years. The older date of c. 500 years ago matches well the date of c. 550 years ago obtained by Ghaleb for the base of the main midden deposit in Square M, located 5 m to the southeast. The date of c. 100 years ago at a depth of 9.5–12.5 cm marks the maximum depth of nearly all glass and metal items and is consistent with the start of European contact with Mabuyag Islanders in the 19th century. As such, the foundations for the mounded ridge feature most likely were formed about 500 years ago, with much of the upper half of the feature added after European contact.

Underlying dates of 893±32 BP (c. 750 years ago) and 523±32 BP (c. 500 years ago) for the base of SU1b and SU2a respectively are stratigraphically inverted, a result consistent with the interface (mixed) nature of sediments represented by these levels. Dates of 878±32 BP (c. 750 years ago) and 954±32 BP (c. 800 years ago) for the upper and lower sections of SU2c indicate that SU2, taking in more than 1 m of sediment, accumulated rapidly over less than a century. A date of 6133±41 BP from the base of SU2b is anomalous and suggests the charcoal-pumice zone includes ancient charcoal from eroded sediments of unknown origin.

Cultural materials were grouped stratigraphically into the mounded ridge feature (SU1a), underlying cultural deposits (SUs 1b–2a) and shelly beach sands with few cultural materials (SU2b = Ghaleb's 'culturally sterile' layer) to investigate whether the mounded ridge feature is compositionally different from underlying cultural deposits. As seen with Ghaleb's platform excavation results, the range of cultural materials in Square A is similar for the mounded midden feature (SU1a) and underlying deposits (SUs 1b–2b) (Figure 7). Also similar is a major increase in the abundance and density of midden deposit with the formation of the mounded feature (SU1a), particularly with regards to shell, bone and ochre (Figure 7). In contrast, stone artefacts, rocks and charcoal increase only moderately with formation of the upper (mound) layer. Most of the dramatic increase in bone density in SU1a is accounted for by dugong after it enters the sequence in SU2a (Figure 8). These data indicate that compositional changes coincide with development of the mounded midden feature.

A comparison of dugong bone elements in different levels of Square A reveals the same broad representation found by Ghaleb in the platform excavations (Figure 4) – that is, a high proportion of ribs and vertebrae, with varying representations of skull and limb bones. As with Ghaleb's excavations, our excavations reveal dugong-bone assemblages that contain much higher representations of vertebrae and limb bones than ritual bone mounds on Pulu and Tudu. While dugong skull bones in the upper sections of the sequence forming the ridge mounded midden feature are consistent with ritual bone mounds, the continued presence of reasonable quantities of dugong vertebrae (and considerable quantities of other midden materials, such as shells, stone artefacts and rocks) is not. Furthermore, only 7 percent of cultural material in SU1a (by weight) is definite dugong bone, compared with 50–65 percent definite dugong bone in dugong bone mounds on Tudu and Pulu.

Discussion

Compositional analysis of the three types of mounded midden features at Goemu (circular, platform and ridge) reveal some similarities with ritual dugong bone mounds, viz. ribs and usually skull bones are the majority component (by weight) of dugong-bone assemblages. On the other hand, key features of the midden mounds that distinguish them from ritual bone mounds are the higher representation of dugong limb bones and vertebrae and considerable quantities of other midden materials (e.g. shells, fish and turtle bones, stone artefacts, cooking stones and charcoal). In terms of diversity of materials, few compositional differences exist between mounded and non-mounded middens. For the most part, our results from Square A concur with Ghaleb's (1990:303) finding that faunal differences between these midden deposits differ mainly in terms of 'the relative abundance of the types of remains found'. Despite these differences, it was concluded tentatively by Ghaleb (1990:367) that 'there is little about the

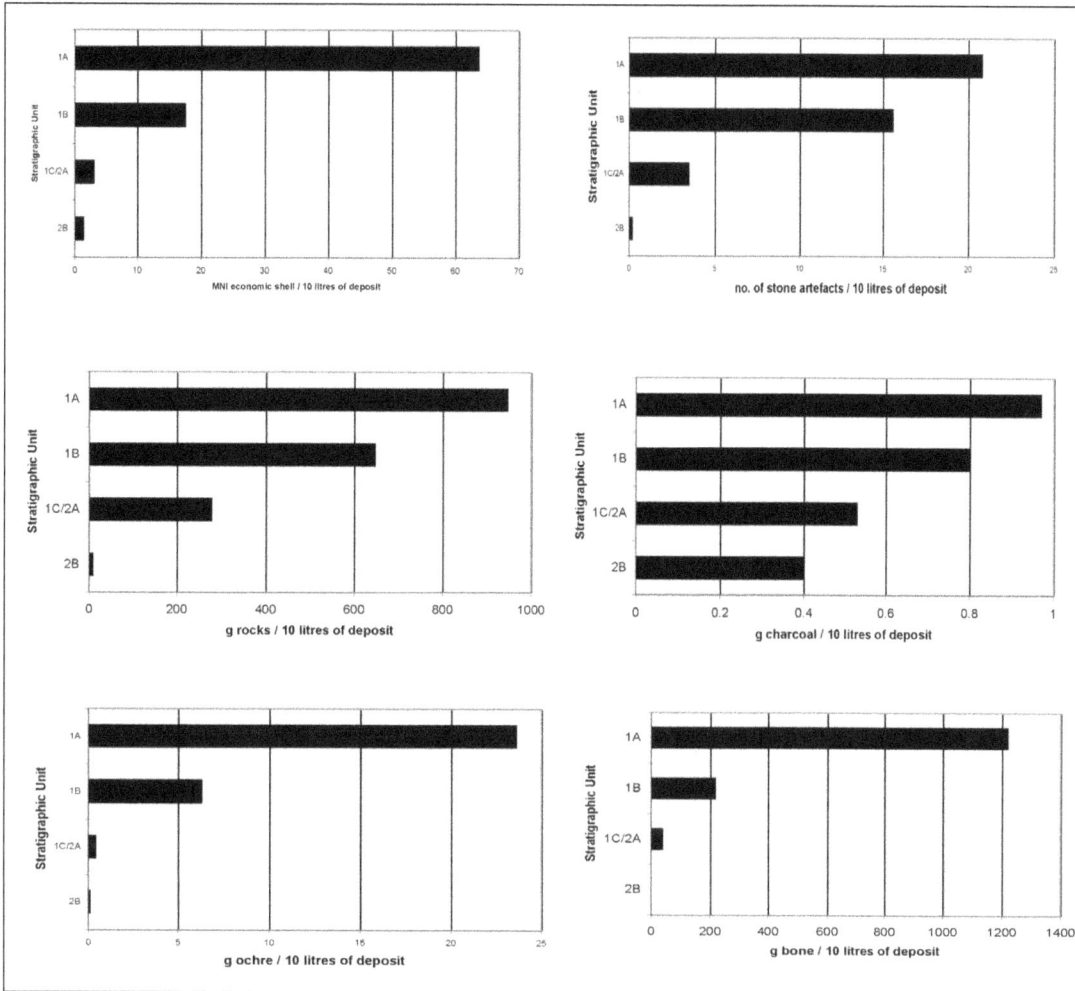

Figure 7. Vertical change in density for cultural materials in Square A, Goemu.

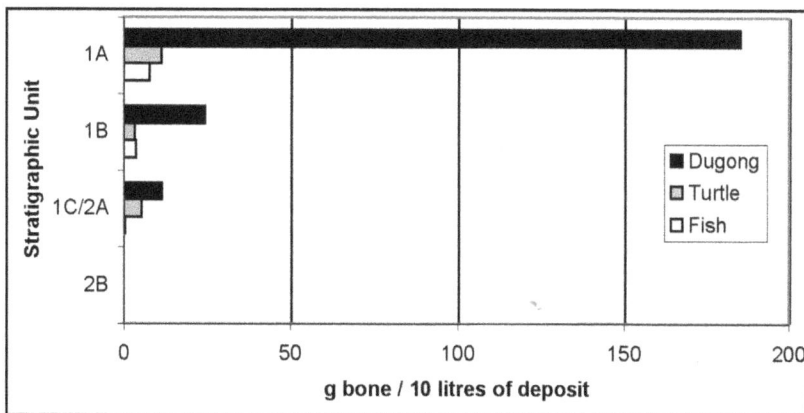

Figure 8. Vertical change in density of dugong, turtle and fish bone in Square A, Goemu.

composition of these discrete raised midden deposits to suggest anything other than their being piles of refuse from past Islander meals'.

Ghaleb (1990:367, 378) realised that the 'abundance and surface morphology' of mounded middens at Goemu was 'out of the ordinary' and beseeched further explanation. Drawing on 19th century ethnographic recordings of ceremonial mounding in the form of dugong bone mounds (Haddon 1904:4–5, 1912:131), burial earthen mounds (Haddon 1904:259–261), memorial stone cairns/earthen mounds (Haddon 1904:83, 185, 368) and turtle lookout stations with cairns of stones and turtle/dugong bones (Haddon 1912:160) from western Zenadh Kes, Ghaleb (1990:209) suggested: 'it does not seem unreasonable to view (some of) the midden features of Gumu … as representing loci of past ceremonial activity in addition to economic activities'. Furthermore, 'it seems conceivable that many of the … [95] discrete [midden] mounds may represent past 'shrines' which symbolised some sort of power or magic' (Ghaleb 1990:379). Developments in archaeological understandings of the ritual dimensions of subsistence remains, and dugong bone mounds in particular, add weight to Ghaleb's (1990) hypothesis on the ceremonial and symbolic dimensions of the mounded middens at Goemu. This hypothesis was also underpinned by Haddon's demonstration of 'how inter-related were the social organisation, ceremonial life, settlement patterns and subsistence' of the Mabuyag Islanders (Ghaleb 1990:357). Ethnographically, Goemu exemplifies this 'inter-relatedness' as a key totemic/clan settlement that included ritual places such as a turtle-hunting 'shrine', a skull-house and a men's kod site. Goemu village was a complex space where the boundary between domestic and ritual domains was negotiated, blurred and expressed materially through structured, formalised and patterned behaviours.

In many respects, Ghaleb's approach to midden deposits at Goemu was an early attempt at coming to terms with socially structured deposits that in more recent years have been conceptualised in the broader archaeological literature as 'ritual rubbish' and 'ceremonial trash'. In the context of Zenadh Kes, this paper demonstrates that the Goemu mounded middens have minor compositional similarities to ritual dugong bone mounds and major compositional similarities to non-mounded midden deposits. In this sense, the major material difference between midden mounds and dugong bone mounds is compositional, whereas the major material difference between midden mounds and non-mounded middens is morphological. These differences reveal two features that conceptually confined and defined mounded middens in the eyes of the Goemulgal: (1) composition ensured the sites remained within the broader conceptual category of midden and the myriad social behaviours they represent; (2) morphology ensured the sites could be distinguished as a separate and special class of midden, primarily through the process of mounding. In contrast, dugong bone mounds were compositionally constructed to fall outside the conceptual category of midden by a highly specialised assemblage of selected dugong bone elements.

Mounded middens at Goemu are the result of the ritualised tethered deposition of a wide range of typical domestic refuse that in some cases accumulated over hundreds of years. Thus it is likely the mounded midden features on public display at Goemu were conceptualised as works in progress, continually unfolding as material expressions of the shared routines of life (habitus) for occupants of the village. As such, it was not so much the final form of the midden mounds that was important, but the structured and formalised process of their construction. While mounded middens represent only 2 percent of the area of Goemu, the absolute area of coverage (400 m²) is substantial. The number and spread of the circular midden mounds across Goemu suggests strongly that they were fundamental to the social construction and organisation of space across the village, perhaps associated with individual households and families. The lower number of large ridge middens suggests a more restricted and perhaps more collective social context for deposition. Whether the smaller circular and larger ridge/platform midden mounds represent family and clan feasting respectively is a matter for future investigation. Whatever the case, domestic refuse in certain contexts maintained an ongoing biographical trajectory that necessitated its special formalised storage and curation in particular locations to create the mounded midden features we see today. In these situations, domestic refuse never left the 'systemic context' of society (see Schiffer 1996). Building on Ghaleb (1990), we posit that midden mounding was a performative strategy that facilitated the management, containment and remembrance of the myriad symbolic values associated with the wide array of activities and social contexts represented by the items comprising these midden deposits.

Conclusion

Goemu reveals that midden sites in Zenadh Kes can be complex social structures. Far from simply representing refuse dominated by the discarded remains of meals, midden deposits were also a key part of the formal and enduring ritualised architecture of a village. Mounded midden features were constant visual reminders to the occupants of Goemu that their everyday social activities, such as the use of cooking stones and the consumption of dugong, turtle, fish and shellfish, had historical continuities with the everyday social lives of their ancestors. As a 'structuring structure' (Bourdieu 1977), the practice of midden mounding resulted in features that provided visual anchors to the past and social beacons for normative behaviour by framing, constraining and structuring future social acts and interactions. Unlike perishable food items, bones and shells allow the long-term storage of information on subsistence-based social activities (see Jones 1980:160). The dramatic increase in density of bones (especially dugong) and shells in the ridge midden mound (Square A) is consistent with an increased focus on ritualisation of subsistence remains. In this sense, the Goemu midden mounds had an intimate and complementary relationship with ritual dugong bone mounds located across other parts of the Mabuyag landscape. Both mounded structures were constructed of what were seen as decay-transcending food remains by successive generations of Goemulgal as an affirmation of shared cultural identity, past, present and future. That these structures emerged as ritualised material expressions of integrated social developments across Mabuyag is supported by both types of sites having similar chronologies within the past 400–500 years. A key aim of our ongoing research is to establish more solid foundations to better understand the nature of this integration and developmental history through continued analysis, excavation and characterisation of mounded and non-mounded middens at Goemu and other 'old village' sites across Mabuyag.

Acknowledgements

Special thanks to the Mabuyag community for hosting our research. In particular, we thank the traditional owners of Goemu for permission to undertake research on their totemic/clan lands. For support and guidance, we thank Cygnet Repu and other members of the Goemulgau Kod cultural organisation. Fieldwork was made possible by the efforts of Beeboy Whop and Leon Elia of Mabuyag and Alice Bedingfield (Monash University). Thanks to David Harris for permission to redraw and use his 1985 map of Goemu. Gary Swinton and Kara Rasmanis (School of Geography and Environmental Science, Monash University) created the figures. This research was supported by ARC Discovery-Projects Grant DP0344070. Helpful comments on earlier drafts of this paper were kindly provided by Joe Crouch and Bruno David.

References

Ash, J. and B. David In press. Mua 22: Archaeology at the old village site of Totalai. In B. David, D. Tomsana and M. Quinnell (eds), *Gelam's Homeland: Cultural and Natural History on the Island of Mua, Torres Strait*. Memoirs of the Queensland Museum, Cultural Heritage Series.

Barham, A.J. and D.R. Harris. 1985. Relict field systems in the Torres Strait region. In I.S. Farrington (ed), *Prehistoric Intensive Agriculture in the Tropics*, pp. 247–283. BAR International Series 232.

Barham, A.J. and D.R. Harris 1987. Archaeological and Palaeoenvironmental Investigations in Western Torres Strait, Northern Australia. Final report to the Research and Exploration Committee of the National Geographic Society on 'The Torres Strait Research Project'.

Bourdieu, P. 1977. *Outline of a Theory of Practice*. Cambridge: Cambridge University Press.

Bourke, P. 2005. Archaeology of shell mounds of the Darwin coast: totems of an ancestral landscape. In P. Bourke, S. Brockwell and C. Fredericksen (eds), *Darwin Archaeology: Aboriginal, Asian and European Heritage of Australia's Top End*, pp. 29–48. Darwin: Charles Darwin University Press.

Cameron, C.M. 2002. Sacred earthen architecture in the northern southwest: The Bluff Great House berm. *American Antiquity* 67(4):677–695.

Carter, M., A.J. Barham, P.D. Veth, D.W. Bird, S. O'Connor and R.B. Bird 2004. The Murray Islands Archaeological Project: preliminary results of excavations on Mer and Dauar eastern Torres Strait. In I.J. McNiven and M. Quinnell (eds), *Torres Strait Archaeology and Material Culture*. Memoirs of the Queensland Museum, Cultural Heritage Series 3(1):163–182.

Chapman, J. 2000. 'Rubbish-dumps' or 'places of deposition'?: Neolithic and Copper Age settlements in central and eastern Europe. In A. Ritchie (ed), *Neolithic Orkney in its European Context*, pp. 347–62. Cambridge: MacDonald Institute.

Crouch, J., I.J. McNiven, B. David, C. Rowe, and M. Weisler 2007. Berberass: marine resource specialisation and environmental change in Torres Strait over the past 4000 years. *Archaeology in Oceania* 42:49–64.

David, B. and M.I. Weisler 2006. Kurturniaiwak (Badu) and archaeological evidence of villages in Torres Strait. *Australian Archaeology* 63:21–34.

David, B. and Mura Badulgal Committee 2006. What happened in Torres Strait 400 years ago? Ritual transformation in an island seascape. *Journal of Island and Coastal Archaeology* 1:123–143.

Davis, S.L. and J.R.V. Prescott 1992. *Aboriginal Frontiers and Boundaries in Australia*. Carlton: Melbourne University Press.

Eseli, P. 1998. Eseli's Notebook. A. Shnukal, R. Mitchell, Y. Nagata (eds), *Aboriginal and Torres Strait Islander Studies Unit Research Report Series*, Vol. 3, University of Queensland, St. Lucia.

Ghaleb, B. 1990. An Ethnoarchaeological Study of Mabuiag Island, Torres Strait, Northern Australia. Unpublished PhD thesis, Institute of Archaeology, University College London.

Ghaleb, B. 1998. Fish and fishing on a Western Torres Strait Island, Northern Australia. In A.K.G. Jones and R. Nicholson (eds), *Fish remains and humankind: part two*. Internet Archaeology 4 (http://intarch.a c. uk/journal/issue4/ghaleb/to c. html).

Haddon, A.C. 1901. *Head-Hunters: Black, White and Brown*. London: Methuen.

Haddon, A.C. (ed) 1904. *Reports of the Cambridge Anthropological Expedition to Torres Straits. Vol. V. Sociology, Magic and Religion of the Western Islanders*. Cambridge: Cambridge University Press.

Haddon, A.C. (ed) 1912. *Reports of the Cambridge Anthropological Expedition to Torres Straits. Vol. IV. Arts and Crafts*. Cambridge: Cambridge University Press.

Haddon, A.C. 1935. *Reports of the Cambridge Anthropological Expedition to Torres Straits. Vol. I: General Ethnography*. Cambridge: Cambridge University Press.

Harris, D.R., A.J. Barham and B. Ghaleb 1985. Archaeology and Recent Palaeoenvironmental History of Torres Strait, Northern Australia. Preliminary report to the Research and Exploration Committee of the National Geographic Society on Part IIA of The Torres Strait Research Project July–October 1984.

Hill, J.D. 1995. *Rituals and Rubbish in Iron Age Wessex*. BAR 242. Oxford: British Archaeological Reports.

Hiscock, P. and P. Faulkner 2006. Dating the dreaming? Creation of myths and rituals for mounds along the northern Australian coastline. *Cambridge Archaeological Journal* 16(2):209–22.

Hodder, I. 1982. *Symbols in Action: Ethnoarchaeological Studies of Material Culture*. Cambridge: Cambridge University Press.

Jones, R. 1980. Different strokes for different folks: sites, scale and strategy. In I. Johnson (ed), *Holier Than Thou*, pp. 151–71. Canberra: Department of Prehistory, Research School of Pacific Studies, The Australian National University.

McCormac, F.G., A.G. Hogg, P.G. Blackwell, C. E.Buck, T.F.G. Higham, and P.J. Reimer 2004. SHCAL04 southern hemisphere calibration, 0–11.0 cal kyr BP. *Radiocarbon* 46:1087–1092.

McNiven, I.J. 2001. Torres Strait and the maritime frontier in early colonial Australia. In L. Russell (ed), *Colonial Frontiers: Indigenous-European Encounters in Settler Societies*, pp. 175–197. Manchester: Manchester University Press.

McNiven, I.J. 2006. Dauan 4 and the emergence of ethnographically-known social arrangements across Torres Strait during the last 600–800 years. *Australian Archaeology* 62:1–12.

McNiven, I.J. and A. C. Bedingfield 2008. Past and present marine mammal hunting rates and abundances: dugong *(Dugong dugon)* evidence from Dabangai Bone Mound, Torres Strait. *Journal of Archaeological Science* 35:505–515

McNiven, I.J. and R. Feldman 2003. Ritually orchestrated seascapes: bone mounds and dugong hunting magic in Torres Strait, NE Australia. *Cambridge Archaeological Journal* 13(2):169–194.

Meehan, B. 1982. *Shell Bed to Shell Midden*. Canberra: Australian Institute of Aboriginal Studies.

Morrison, M. 2003. Old boundaries and new horizons: the Weipa shell mounds reconsidered. *Archaeology in Oceania* 38(1):1–8.

Mullins, S. 1992. Torres Strait pre-colonial population: the historical evidence reconsidered. *Queensland Archaeological Research* 9:38–42.

Needham, S. and T. Spence 1997. Refuse and the formation of middens. *Antiquity* 71:77–90.

Schiffer, B.B. 1996. *Formation Processes of the Archaeological Record*. Salt Lake City: University of Utah Press.

Stuiver, M. and P.J. Reimer 1993. Extended 14C database and revised CALIB radiocarbon calibration program. *Radiocarbon* 35:215–230.

Stuiver, M., P.J. Reimer and R.W. Reimer 2005. CALIB 5.0. [WWW program and documentation].

Vanderwal, R. 1973. The Torres Strait: Protohistory and beyond. *The University of Queensland, Anthropology Museum*, Occasional Papers in Anthropology 2:157–194.

Walker, H.W. 1995. Ceremonial trash? In J.M. Skibo, W.H. Walker and A.E. Nielsen (eds), *Expanding Archaeology*, pp. 67–79. Salt Lake City: University of Utah Press.

10

Sailing between worlds: The symbolism of death in northwest Borneo

Katherine Szabó

Anthropology Program, University of Guam, Guam

kszabo@uguam.uog.edu

Philip J. Piper

Archaeological Studies Program, University of the Philippines, Diliman, Philippines

Graeme Barker

McDonald Institute for Archaeological Research, University of Cambridge, United Kingdom

Introduction

The Niah Caves complex in northwest Borneo is best known for its early *Homo sapiens* remains, but the various Niah entrances and nearby caves also contain a wealth of archaeological deposits from later time periods. The rich metal-age record (from c. 2000 years ago) of Niah is nearly exclusively represented by burials, and while some attention has been directed to understanding the West Mouth cemetery zone (e.g. B. Harrisson 1967; Zuraina 1982), other deposits have received less attention. Kain Hitam was one of the last sites in the Niah area to be excavated by Tom and Barbara Harrisson, and only received brief or popular treatment in the published literature (e.g. T. Harrisson 1958, 1960, 1964). Nevertheless, it has been regarded as a remarkable expression of metal-age mortuary ritual and the Kain Hitam rock art has been mentioned numerous times in press (e.g. Ballard *et al.* 2004; Lape *et al.* 2007). Based on a study of the field archive and curated materials, we present here details of the Kain Hitam mortuary site. We further assess claims about cultural affinities for the site (e.g. Chêng 1969) and situate Kain Hitam within the larger realm of commentary on Southeast Asian 'ship-of-the-dead' rites.

Background

Kain Hitam was discovered by Barbara Harrisson in 1958, when excavations in the various mouths of the Niah Caves were well underway (see Figure 1). On the cave floor, a group of dugout canoes lay 'beached' (Figure 2), and closer inspection revealed associated scatters of human bone, shell, earthenware and trade ware. A profusion of red pictographs was also noted,

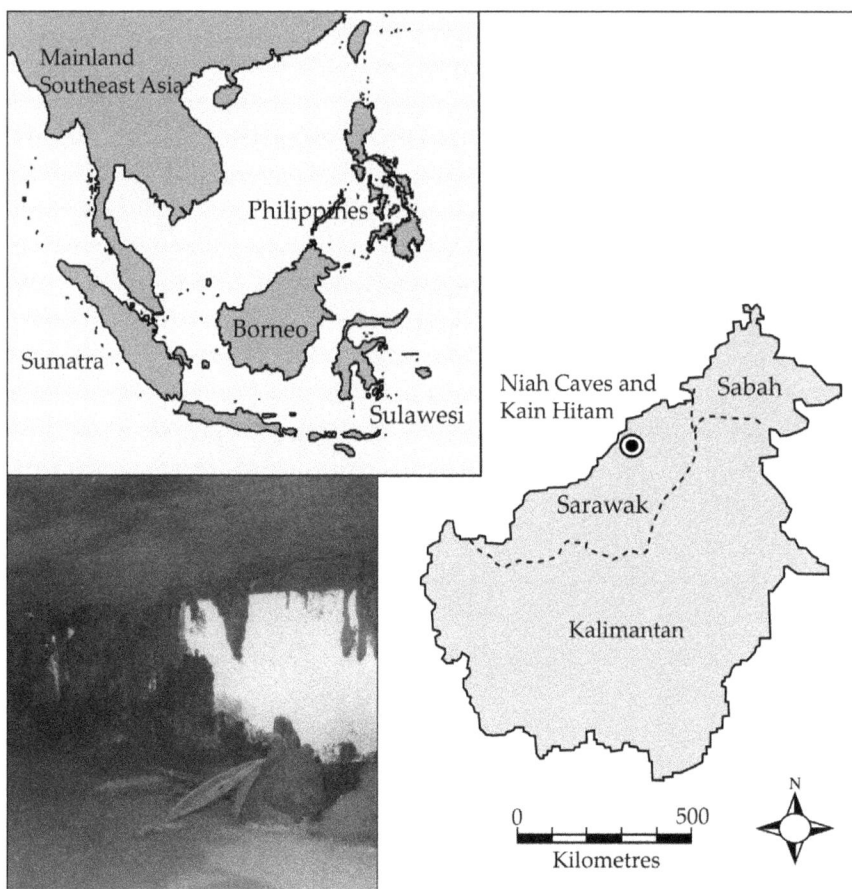

Figure 1. Map to show the location of Kain Hitam within Southeast Asia and Borneo. The picture on the lower left is of the Upper Cave at discovery, looking out from the rock art towards the entrance.

forming a 46 m panel along the west wall and acting as a back-drop 'mural' to the boats. The cave has opposing north and south openings on different levels, with a steep slope connecting the two. The rock-art mural is in the Upper Cave, which is the area largely considered in this paper. The Lower Cave had a smaller number of boat burials, and, as revealed by the photographic and artefact archive, was also excavated by Harrisson.

It appears from the photographic archive that much of the excavation was done by brush, with provenance of artefacts recorded by grid-square and depth. All material was accessioned on site. Deposits were shallow, with rarely more than 15 cm of deposit removed before reaching a layer of flowstone. Tom Harrisson published very little on Kain Hitam – or the 'Painted Cave' as it is otherwise known.[1] All excavated material is held in the Sarawak Museum Kuching or Niah National Park branches, and includes unworked and worked shell, human bone, bone artefacts, bronze, earthenware and trade ware ceramics, and glass artefacts, while the paper archive contains some of Tom Harrisson's original field notes, on-site renderings of the spatial distribution of artefacts, and unpublished correspondence and manuscripts on aspects of the archaeological assemblage.

The material record

In April 2006, parts of the Kain Hitam assemblage were studied by Szabó and Piper, and the photographic and paper archives were digitised. Material physically analysed during this period included unworked and worked shell, and bone, bronze and glass artefacts.

Figure 2. View of part of the Kain Hitam showing death ships in situ before the area is gridded for excavation.

The 'death ships'

A number of dugout wooden canoes were identified in the Upper Cave with an unknown smaller number located in the Lower Cave. Harrisson puts the Upper Cave number at 16, however each 'death ship' (following the terminology of T. Harrisson) consisted of two parts: an upper and lower 'boat' which slotted together, and it is unclear whether his numerical value related to whole coffins or individual halves. Most of the canoes were instantly associated by Harrisson with standard Dyak river perahu, although slightly smaller and shallower (T. Harrisson 1958:200). One of the death ships was significantly smaller in size, and labelled as a 'child coffin'. The spatial arrangement of the death ships was recorded on-site by Harrisson, before any movement of archaeological materials[2] (see Figure 3). The boats were largely oriented along an east-west axis, and were 'pulled up' on a gently sloping surface, which was separated from the rock-art panel by a 7 m long flat expanse. This area between the death ships and the rock art is notably lacking in material culture, which is found in profusion around the death ships themselves and on a travertine platform adjacent to the rock-art panel. The discovery of a wooden post with a v-shaped end still propping up the stern of death ship A1 indicates that at least some of the boats were literally 'facing' the rock art. Harrisson (1958:200) states that it was likely both ends of the boats were elevated using such posts, perhaps by analogy with his Sabah data (e.g. Harrisson and Harrisson 1971:48–49).

While the death ships resembled standard river craft, the bowsprits of the Kain Hitam death ships were elongate and carved with representations of various stylised animal heads. Easily recognisable are those of crocodiles, in particular (see Figure 4), however clouded leopards (*Pardofelis nebulosa*) and a 'sabre-toothed dragon' (Harrisson 1958:200, 203) were also present. It would appear from the Harrisson archive that human remains were not found *inside* the death

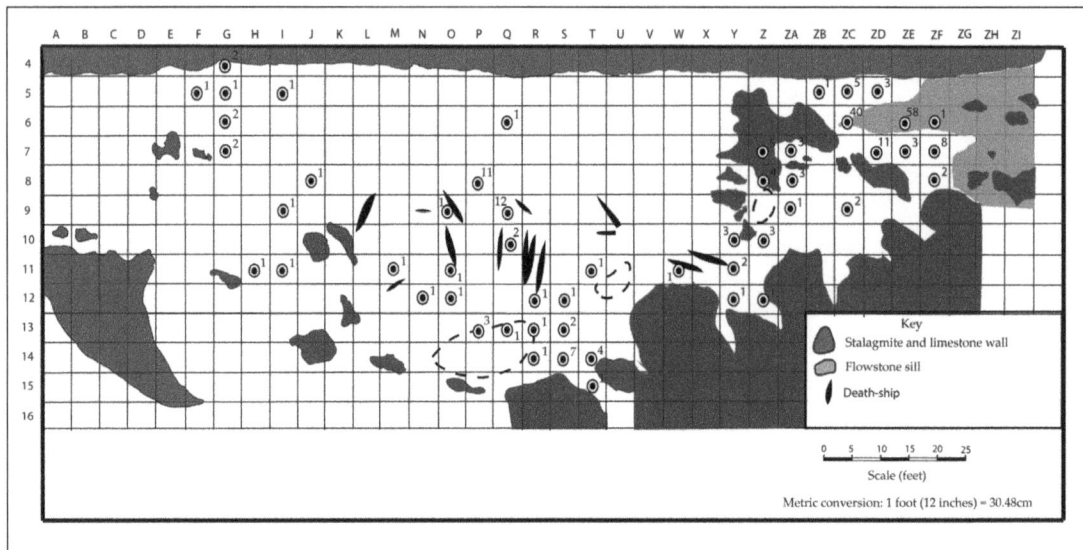

Figure 3. Schematic plan view of Kain Hitam, with the locations of all shell, bone, glass and metal artefacts in relation to the death ships. The numbers represent individual artefacts present. Areas in broken lines represent the extent of scattered pieces of a single death ship (redrawn from Tom Harrisson's site plans).

ships themselves, but rather were scattered around the boats. Their poor condition is at odds with the excellent state of preservation of most other material recovered from the Kain Hitam deposits and suggests the remains, once emptied from the coffins, received no further special treatment. While such an elaborate death staging would seem to conflict with such apparently casual treatment of the skeletal remains themselves, there are certainly precedents; generally based on beliefs in which the soul is seen to leave the body after decomposition, leaving simply 'matter' in the form of bodily remains (see Huntington and Metcalf 1979:Chapter III *passim*).

Other locales in Southeast Asia and the Pacific have furnished evidence of boat burials, where the body is interred within a boat or boat-like coffin (e.g. Spriggs *et al.* 2005:81 for Aru, Bellwood *et al.* 2007 for Vietnam, and Tenazas 1986 for the Philippines). While a comparative analysis of boat-associated mortuary practices is not the goal of this paper, it is worth pointing out that we do not believe the Kain Hitam death ships acted as coffins associated with single bodies, nor that the scattering of the human remains is a result of site disturbance. The remarkable preservation of the often-fragile death ships and the elevated position of death ship A1 (mentioned above) suggest that taphonomic agents such as medium-large carnivores and/or scavengers have not seriously interfered with the mortuary setting. Furthermore, the 1000-year span of the death ships themselves (see below), coupled with the many bags of fragmented human remains, suggest the same death ships were used repeatedly. A more parsimonious explanation is that the death ships were receptacles for bodies, to facilitate the transition to the afterlife. After the successful passage of the soul, the earthly remains were of little import, and simply 'cleared away'. For ethnographic parallels within Southeast Asia, see Huntington and Metcalf (1979:86–91).

Bone artefacts

In total, 75 complete or fragmentary bone artefacts were recorded from the Sarawak Museum archive (see Table 1). These include 24 finished and unfinished cylindrical beads, one barrel bead, one bead curated to make a toggle, 10 'ear cuffs' (Figure 5a), one rectangular plaque made from a male pig canine with holes bored in each corner, three teeth with holes bored through the root, two carved fragments of soft-shell turtle carapace/plastron (Figure 5c), two bead spacers (Figure 5b), one expedient bone point and one formal bone point. Where identifiable, different skeletal elements from various taxa had been utilised, including the radius, ulna, humerus, femur and metapodials of monkeys, squirrels, civet cats and small deer, the carapace or plastron of soft-shell turtles and bird bone (see Table 1). Further observations of techniques associated with bone-ornament production will be presented elsewhere. Holes drilled through the teeth of clouded leopard, civet cat and dog (cf. *Canis familiaris*), as well as those seen in the bead spacers, are absolutely straight, with no evidence of bevelling or counter-sinking. Such perforation morphology is generally indicative of the use of metal-tipped drills (Szabó 2005:264; Basilia *et al.* 2006). Also worthy of note are four shark vertebrae, one of which has a large, worn, central perforation and an abraded perimeter.

Shell artefacts

Artefacts produced for shell are less common than those in bone within the Kain Hitam assemblage, but nevertheless show a range of forms and raw materials. There are 24 shell artefacts, including a perforated *Conus* sp. spire, two disc beads hewn from *Melo* sp. shell (Figure 5d), two *Cypraea annulus* shells with the dorsum removed, one *Nassarius pullus* with the dorsum removed and ground, and two *Oliva* sp. shells with worn holes at the apex. A collection of three *Anadara granosa* and 11 *Polymesoda erosa* valves has hewn holes at the umbo, and technological analysis supports an interpretation of them as shell sinkers from casting nets (Szabó and Yang In preparation). The final 'artefact' is an unmodified *Vexillum* cf. *citrinus* which, as an occupant of clean coral sand, is clearly an import from some distance away.

Earthenware and ceramic trade wares

The trade-ware ceramics from Kain Hitam were not viewed by the authors, but the paper archive revealed that a number of sherds were sent to the Ashmolean Museum, Oxford, in 1963 for comment. According to correspondence between Ms Eine Moore (Sarawak Museum) and Ashmolean staff, the Kain Hitam ceramic trade wares can generally be characterised as 'Yueh-ware' (following Gompertz 1958) and ascribed to the T'ang Dynasty (618–906 AD), with a handful of examples possibly more closely associated with early Northern Sung wares (from 960 AD).[3] The assemblage consists mainly of smaller vessels, including jars, vases, bowls and ewers. Some bear lotus-leaf-pattern decoration. While seemingly early in a regional context (e.g. see Bellwood 1997:275), a number of sites in Sarawak contain volumes of trade wares contemporaneous with those at Kain Hitam – such as Bukit Saripah and various of the Santubong Delta sites (Harrisson 1958:200; Moore nd).

There is little information in Harrisson's notes about the earthenware pottery, but a number of details can be discerned from his on-site plans and keys. Firstly, earthenware pottery appears to be at least as abundant as ceramic trade wares within the site. The range of vessel forms includes double-spouted vessels, impressed and incised earthenware,

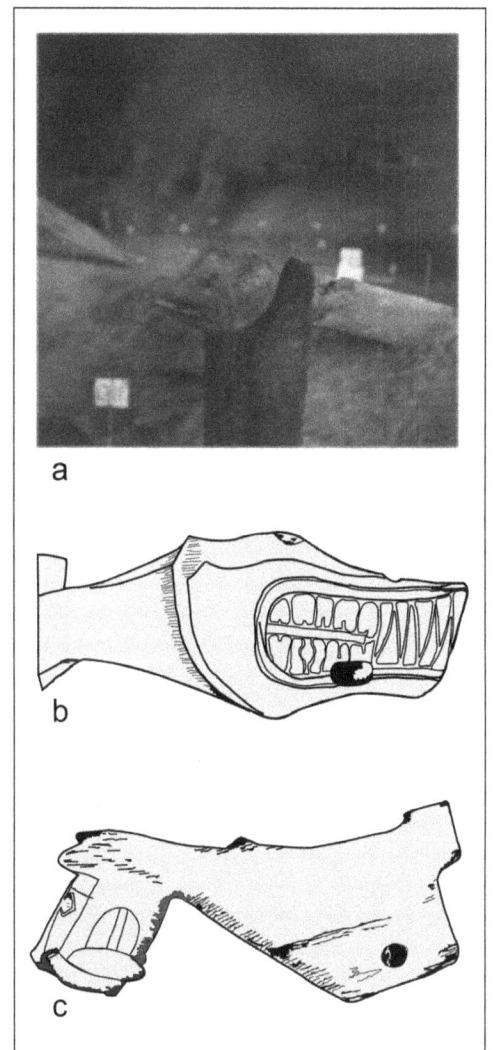

Figure 4. Details of bowsprits of death ships: (a) site photograph of death ship A13 with a crocodile bowsprit; (b) 'sabre-toothed dragon' bowsprit after Harrisson (1958:figure 5); (c) clouded leopard bowsprit after Harrisson (1958:Figure 4).

Table 1. Bone artefacts recovered from Kain Hitam recorded by Szabó and Piper in 2006.

Grid	Material	Common Name	Element	Artefact Type
I/9	cf. *Amyda cartiliagena*	Asian soft-shell turtle	Carapace/plastron.	Carved sub-cutineous bone
R/13	Aves sp.	Bird	Tibiotarsus	Expedient point
R/13	Aves sp.	Bird	Humerus	Finished bead
R/14	Indeterminate	Indeterminate	Unknown	Finished 'ear cuff' fragment
R/19	Aves sp.	Bird	Longbone shaft fragment	Finished artefact fragment
S/14	Indeterminate	Indeterminate	Unknown	Finished 'ear cuff' fragment
S/14	Aves sp.	Bird	Humerus	Finished bead fragment
S/14	Aves sp.	Bird	Longbone shaft fragment	Finished artefact fragment
S/14	Aves sp.	Bird	Longbone shaft fragment	Finished artefact fragment
S/14	Aves sp.	Bird	Longbone shaft fragment	Finished artefact fragment
S/14	Aves sp.	Bird	Longbone shafl fragment	Finished artefact fragment
S/14	Aves sp.	Bird	Longbone shaft fragment	Finished artefact fragment
S/14	Indeterminate	Indeterminate	Caudal vertebra	Vertebra with bored hole
T/14	Indeterminate	Indeterminate	Longbone shaft fragment	Finished artefact fragment
T/14	Aves sp.	Bird	Longbone shaft fragment	Finished artefact fragment
T/14	Aves sp.	Bird	Longbone shaft fragment	Finished artefact fragment
Y/10	Indeterminate	Indeterminate	Unknown	Curated bead - toggle?
Y/11	Cercopithecidae	Leaf monkey/Macaque	Femur	Unfinished bead fragment
Z/7	Indeterminate	Indeterminate	Unknown	Fragment of bead separator
Z/7	Cercopithecidae	Leaf monkey/Macaque	Radius	Finished bead
Z/7	Petauristinae sp.	Flying squirrel	Femur	Unfinished artefact fragment
Z/7	Cercopithecidae	Leaf monkey/Macaque	Ulna	Unfinished bead
Z/8	Indeterminate	Indeterminate	Radius?	Finished bead fragment
Z/8	Aves sp.	Bird	Tibiotarsus	Finished head fragment
Z/8	Sus sp.	Pig	Male lower canine	Artefact fragment
Z/10	Aves sp.	Bird	Longbone shaft fragment	Finished bead fragment
Z/10	Aves sp.	Bird	Longbone shaft fragment	Finished artefact fragment
Z/l0	Sus sp.	Pig	Male lower canine	Artefact fragment
Z/A7	Aves sp.	Bird	Longbone shaft fragment	Finished bead
Z/A7	Indeterminate	Indeterminate	Longbone shaft fragment	Finished bead fragment
Z/A7	Cercopithecidae	Leaf monkey/Macaque	Radius	Finished bead fragment
Z/B7	Indeterminate	Indeterminate	Fibula?	Shaft of a point
Z/C5	Viverridae	Civet Cat	Tibia	Finished bead fragment
2/C5	Cercopithecidae	Leaf monkey/Macaque	Radius	Finished bead
Z/C5	Indeterminate	Indeterminate	Unknown	Unfinished artefact fragment
Z/C5	cf. Sciuridae	Squirrel?	Femur	Unfinished artefact fragment
Z/C5	Cercopithecidae	Leaf monkey/Macaque	Femur	Finished bead fragment

continued on facing page

Grid	Material	Common Name	Element	Artefact Type
Z/C5	Sus sp.	Pig	Male lower canine	Small plaque
Z/C5	Indeterminate	Indeterminate	Unknown	Piece of carved bone
Z/C5	cf. *Amyda cartiliagena*	Asian soft-shell turtle	Rib fragment	Point
Z/C6	Elasmobranch sp.	Shark/ray	Vertebra	Modified neural canal
Z/C6	Aves sp.	Bird	Longbone shaft fragment	Finished bead fragment
Z/D5	Indeterminate	Indeterminate	Longbone shaft fragment	Finished artefact fragment
Z/D7	cf. *Tragalus* sp.	Mouse deer	Femur	Complete 'ear cuff'
Z/D7	Indeterminate	Indeterminate	Longbone shaft fragment	Finished artefact fragment
Z/D7	Indeterminate	Indeterminate	Longbone shaft fragment	Finished 'ear cuff' fragment
Z/D7	Indeterminate	Indeterminate	Femur	Finished 'ear cuff' fragment
Z/D7	Cercopithecidae	Leaf monkey/Macaque	Ulna	Finished bead fragment
Z/D7	Petauristinae sp.	Flying squirrel	Humerus	Finished bead
Z/D7	Indeterminate	Indeterminate	Longbone shaft fragment	Finished 'ear cuff' fragment
Z/D7	Indeterminate	Indeterminate	Longbone shaft fragment	Finished artefact fragment
Z/D7	Indeterminate	Indeterminate	Longbone shaft fragment	Finished artefact fragment
Z/D7	Indeterminate	Indeterminate	Longbone shaft fragment	Barrel 'bead' fragment
Z/D7	Cercopithecidae	Leaf monkey/Macaque	Humerus	Complete 'ear cuff'
Z/E6	Cercopithecidae	Leaf monkey/Macaque	Radius	Finished bead
Z/E6	Cercopithecidae/*Hylobates*	Leaf monkey/Macaque/Gibbon	Metatarsal	Finished bead
Z/E6	Phasianidae	Pheasant/wild fowl/ domestic chicken	Tibiotarsus	Unfinished artefact fragment
Z/E6	Indeterminate	Indeterminate	Longbone shaft fragment	Complete 'ear cuff'
Z/E6	Aves sp.	Bird - fowl-sized	Tibiotarsus	Finished bead
Z/E6	Cercopithecidae	Leaf monkey/macaque	Ulna	Finished bead
Z/E6	Viverridae	Civet Cat	Canine	Bored hole pendant
Z/E6	*Pardofelis nebuiosa*	Clouded leopard	Canine	Bored pendant
Z/E6	Indeterminate	Indeterminate	Unknown	Fragment of bead separator
Z/E7	Indeterminate	Indeterminate	Longbone shaft fragment	Unfinished artefact fragment
Z/E7	Cercopithecidae	Leaf monkey/macaque	Femur	Finished 'ear cuff' fragment
Z/E7	*Muntiacus* sp.	Muntjac	Metatarsal	Finished artefact fragment
Z/F6	Cercopithecidae	Leaf monkey/macaque	Femur	Complete 'ear cuff'
Z/F7	Cercopithecidae	Leaf monkey/macaque	Femur	Unfinished artefact fragment
Z/F7	cf. Petauristinae sp.	Flying squirrel?	Radius	Finished bead (in two fragments)
Z/F7	Indeterminate	Indeterminate	Unknown	Finished bead
Z/F7	Indeterminate	Indeterminate	Unknown	Finished bead
Z/F7	Aves sp.	Bird	Longbone shaft fragment	Unfinished bead fragment
Z/F7	*Canis familiaris*	Dog	Canine	Bored pendant
Z/F8	Indeterminate	Indeterminate	Unknown	Finished artefact fragment

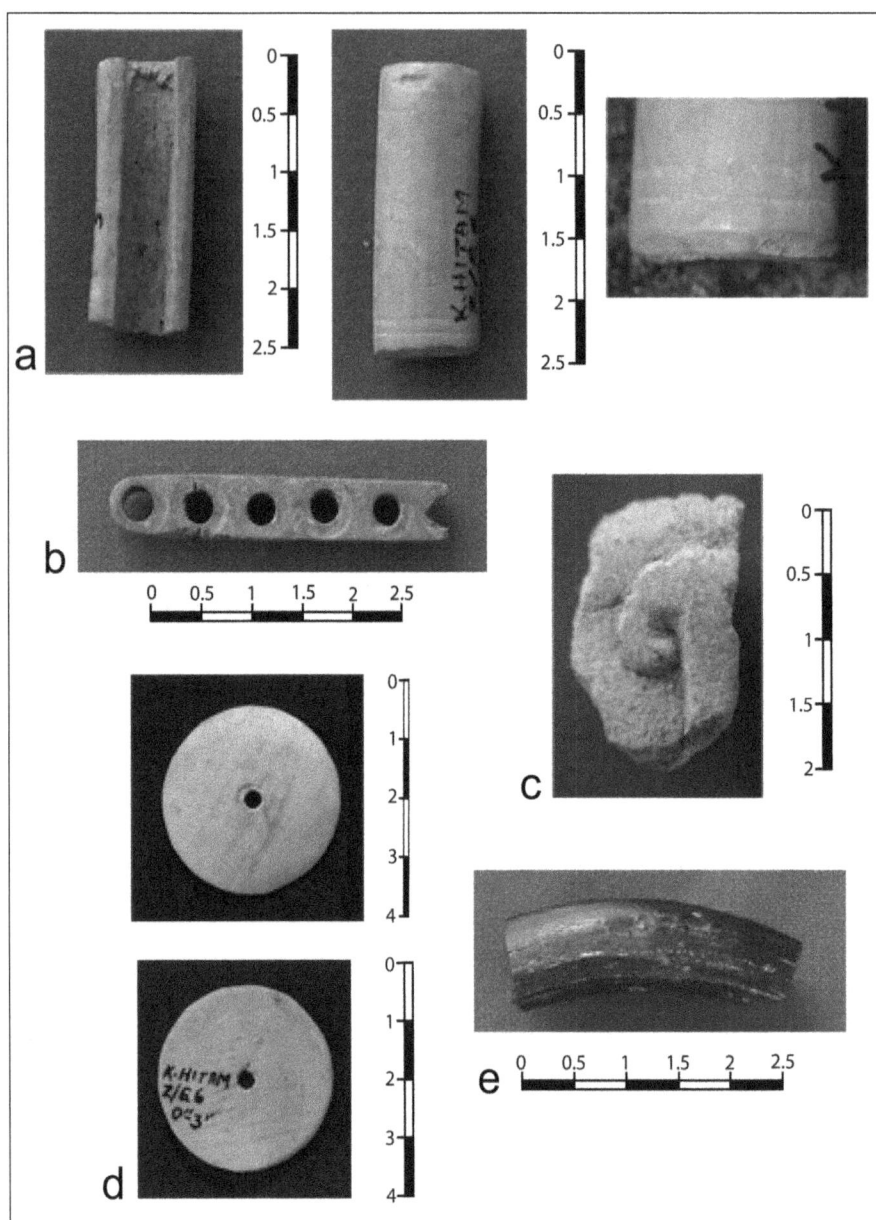

Figure 5. Artefacts from Kain Hitam: (a) three views of a bone cuff (Z/E6:0–3"). The cutting of the ends in stages following by grinding can be clearly seen, as well as the typical concentric incisions seen on most bone beads and cuffs. The image in the top right corner is at 10x magnification; (b) bone bead spacer (Z/7:0–3"), with the impressions of beads visible; (c) soft-shell turtle carapace or plastron carved in low relief (I/9:0"). Two further pieces from Lobang Tulang suggest the motif may be that of a tree of life; (d) inner and outer views of a *Melo* sp. disc bead (Z/E6:0–3"); (e) fragment of reworked blue glass bracelet (N/12:0"). Scale bars are in centimetres.

'corrugated' (paddle-impressed?) earthenware, box vessels with lids, and a further category called 'nose pots' by T. Harrisson. The distribution of earthenware vessels in Kain Hitam also matches the spatial patterning observed in the trade wares and other artefacts (see below for further discussion of spatial patterning).

Beads and ornaments in glass and semi-precious stone

A total of 185 beads and one fragment of a glass bracelet were recovered from the Kain Hitam upper and lower caves, and a number of 'grottos' within Kain Hitam investigated by the Harrissons. The majority (82 percent) are glass 'Indo-Pacific' beads (terminology following Francis 2002), in an assortment of colours, including red, yellow, orange, green, black, white and blue. None of the beads was chemically analysed in this recent study, but details of technology were recorded, including whether beads were generated through 'drawing' or 'coiling' techniques. The coiling of molten glass around the central mandrel to produce beads is distinctive of Chinese glass-making technologies, whereas pulling molten glass lengthwise along the mandrel has its roots in Indian technologies (Francis 2002:Chapter 8; Munan 2005:27). Out of 153 Indo-Pacific beads, 100 were drawn and 68 were coiled, clearly indicating that the Kain Hitam bead assemblage is composed of trade items of mixed origin.[4] This is reinforced by chemical analysis of a sample of glass beads from Kain Hitam and other Sarawak locales sent by T. Harrisson to the Corning Glass Museum in New York. The variation in lead values within the Sarawak samples indicates that while some beads correspond to 'high-lead' Chinese glass, others do not (Brill 1999:171, XV E).

The single bracelet fragment is of dark blue translucent glass, with an internal diameter of c. 7 cm and a triangular cross-section (see Figure 5e). Closer inspection under a low-power microscope indicated that the surface of the bracelet had been extensively ground, with the two corners intersecting with the interior of the bracelet having been ground flat on single facets. This is not the first time that the grinding of glass bracelets has been noted for Borneo, with a transparent green glass bracelet fragment sent to the Corning Glass Museum being published as having 'some ground surfaces' (Brill 1999:171). Interestingly, the morphology after grinding matches precisely the cross-section common in metal-age bracelets produced in *Tridacna* sp. shell, with one such example being recovered from the upper/metal age deposits of the Gan Kira entrance of the Niah Caves. A further eight beads in varying morphologies were produced from semi-precious stone, including carnelian, crystal, onyx and unidentified dark grey stone. A barrel bead produced in baked clay is clearly an imitation of the opaque red glass barrel beads also present in the Kain Hitam assemblage.

Bronze and precious metal artefacts

There are only three bronze artefacts within the Kain Hitam assemblage and none in iron. Two of the bronze pieces are identical Chinese coins, and a note in T. Harrisson's hand links it to the reign of Emperor Kao Tsu (618–625 AD) in the Early T'ang dynastic period. The third bronze artefact is a fragment of a small vessel with a rim diameter of c. 7 cm. The only other evidence of metal at Kain Hitam is a human incisor with three gold plugs. The insertion of gold plugs into human incisors is also seen in proto-historic-period sites in the Philippines, such as Calatagan (see Barretto 2002), and in the Bolinao skull, as well as the First Millennium AD deposits in Burma (Hudson 2003), however these plugs have a 'fish-scale' appearance not seen in the Kain Hitam tooth.

Unworked shell

Eleven large boxes of unworked fresh-water shell from Kain Hitam are present at the Niah National Park branch of the Sarawak Museum. Hundreds of individuals of the stagnant/slow-moving water species *Cipangopaludina* sp. and *Pila ampullacea* occur, along with valves of the brackish water bivalve *Polymesoda erosa* and lesser numbers of *Melanoides tuberculata* and *Ellobium aurismidae*. These species have been recovered throughout the Niah Caves archaeological sites, associated with later deposits, in most cases clearly representing shell midden (Szabó In preparation).

The occurrence of discrete fresh-water shell deposits within the Niah burial cave Lobang Tulang led Barbara Harrisson to comment that these, together with lumps of iron slag, represented the only evidence of 'casual incidents not linked to the burial rites' (B. Harrisson 1959–60:171). While this is certainly a viable interpretation, we feel the fresh-water shell may well be linked to burial rights. This interpretation is reinforced by the spatial distributions of the fresh-water shell remains, which map on to the highly patterned distributions of other artefact types. Fox (1970:72) has also noted the association between shellfish, sometimes covered in red pigment, and burials in the Tabon Caves sites of Palawan, just north of Borneo in the southwestern Philippines.

Rock art

The rock art was systematically photographed and sketched by a local artist, Paul Kerek, during excavations. While we have been able to scan the photograph proof sheets, we could not locate the sketches and paintings done by Kerek. The rock-art panel is so extensive, and the photographic archive so fragmented, that we will not endeavour to reproduce the panel in its entirety, nor statistically analyse motif occurrences here. Rather, we will discuss prominent motifs and the main themes. While the site has been visited on multiple occasions by the authors, present-day observations do little to supplement information from the Harrisson archive, as since 2006, much (if not most) of the rock art has been obscured by the growth of green micro-algae over the rock surface. All of the rock art has been executed in red pigment, and it has recently been demonstrated that this is not a hematite-based compound, but rather derives from an organic source, probably a tree resin (Pyatt *et al.* 2005). There is minimal evidence of superimposition of pictographs, and all of the mural components fall comfortably within the 'curvilinear red tradition' identified by Wilson for the western Pacific and the eastern reaches of Southeast Asia (2003). Thus, there is an overall cohesiveness to the rock art that, while not suggesting synchronicity, implies a totality in design and motivation. Dominant motifs include boats, isolated human figures and animals, interspersed with abstract curvilinear designs. The boats are the most strikingly dominant (Figures 6 and 7), with more than 20 examples still visible.

Figure 6. Section of the rock-art panel from Kain Hitam, including ships of the dead, anthropomorphs and animals. Note the trees of life emerging from some of the vessels and the double-crescentic motifs at the prow (drawn from a colour photograph taken in 2005 by Szabó and Piper).

While the Kain Hitam boat representations have been compared with those from Timor (e.g. Glover 1972:42; Lape *et al.* 2007:4), it is unclear whether the two are in any way related. While it is argued that the Timorese boats contain visual traces indicating past maritime technologies, the Kain Hitam boat representations are stylised to such an extent that they contain no such information, but rather a wealth of symbolic imagery. At least eight boats have 'trees of life' sprouting from the deck and a recurrent double-crescent motif associated with the bows and/ or sterns (see also Adams 1977:97). Most of the boats contain rows of highly stylised figures, some with additional anthropomorphs in a row with hands joined (refer to Figure 6). Individual anthropomorphs outside boats are typically in active poses, though we hesitate to ascribe such postures to dancing (e.g. T. Harrisson 1958:202).

Recognisable animals include a crocodile (Figure 7), snails, turtles, quadruped mammals, and figures with both bird and human features. It could be argued that a number of the human-like figures wear head dresses or costumes, however the common representation of a tail on such figures shrouds in ambiguity their human, or true, nature. As originally pointed out by T. Harrisson (1958), and elaborated on below, recognisable features of the Kain Hitam rock art clearly link with death symbolism, and thus the archaeological site at the panel's base.

Notes on chronology and spatial patterning

T. Harrisson obtained a number of radiocarbon dates on wood from the death ships in the 1960s. He was fully cognisant of the 'old-wood' problem regarding long-lived trees, and thus he employed a local Penan worker to construct a boat out of Belian *(Eusideroxylon zwageri)* wood and dated samples of this, along with the archaeological specimens, to check inbuilt age. The modern death ship returned a date of 276±80 BP, indicating a general inbuilt age of c. 250–300 years. The radiocarbon dates (Table 2 and Figure 8) indicate a c. 1000-year spread for the death ships, beginning around the early metal age – or even late Neolithic – (c. 2300 BP) and continuing until around the 10th century AD. The latter part of this age range coincides well with the chronological reckonings based on ceramic trade-ware types and Chinese coins, but also affirms a significant pre-trade-ware period for the Kain Hitam site. It should be mentioned that two radiocarbon dates on charcoal from the Harrisson archive were recently obtained, both returning Pleistocene dates (see Table 2). These samples seem to derive from deposits surrounding broken flowstone underlying the visible deposits. Thus, while not shedding light on the material discussed here, these dates demonstrate an older history for Kain Hitam.

While it is clear from the radiocarbon dates that the Kain Hitam sites span the introduction of mainland Asian ceramic trade wares to the region, it is of particular significance that the high-fired ceramic, glass and bronze distributions map precisely on to intra-site spatial patterning observed in the local earthenwares, bone and shell artefacts (see Figures 3, 9 and 10). Indeed, apart from the gross distributions around the death ships and

Figure 7. Two further pictographs from the Kain Hitam rock-art panel, showing a ship of the dead with emergent tree of life, and a crocodile (drawn from a black and white photograph from the Harrisson archive).

Table 2. Radiocarbon determinations for Kain Hitam and the Samti death-ship site. All dates are Harrisson's, except for the two charcoal dates obtained by Szabó, Piper and Barker in 2006 on material collected by T. Harrisson.

Sample code	Sample	Radiocarbon age (BP)	Calibrated dates (1 sigma)
GX0212	Death Ship X - Upper Cave	1780±150	(77 AD:413 AD) - 1
GX0213	Fragment of dense wood	2115±125	(356 BC:286 BC) - 0.215675
			(252 BC:251 BC) - 0.00257
			(234 BC:1 AD) - 0.781756
GX0214	Wood lower cave (Death Ship A20?)	1450±125	(433 AD:498 AD) - 0.217013
			(501 AD:675 AD) -0.782987
GX0307	Child Death Ship A4	2300±80	(485 BC:464 BC) - 0.056146
			(448 BC:444 BC) - 0.009874
			(416 BC:342BC) -0.404504
			(326 BC:204 BC) - 0.529476
GX0308	Modern Death Ship	276±80	(1486 AD:1669 AD) - 0.898092
			(1780 AD:1798AD) - 0.080257
			(1944 AD:1950 AD) - 0.021651
GX0309	Death Ship AI 8 - Lower Cave	1045±80	(891 AD:1042 AD) - 0.958061
			(1107 AD:1117 AD) -0.041939
GX0310	Mixed bone sample - Upper Cave	4135± 330	(3264 BC:3242 BC) - 0.017356
			(3103 BC:2205 BC) - 0.982644
OxA 16694	Charcoal from grid square Z/C5: 6-9	16515±60	Uncalibrated
OxA16695	Charcoal from grid square R/13: 3-6	26510±120	Uncalibrated

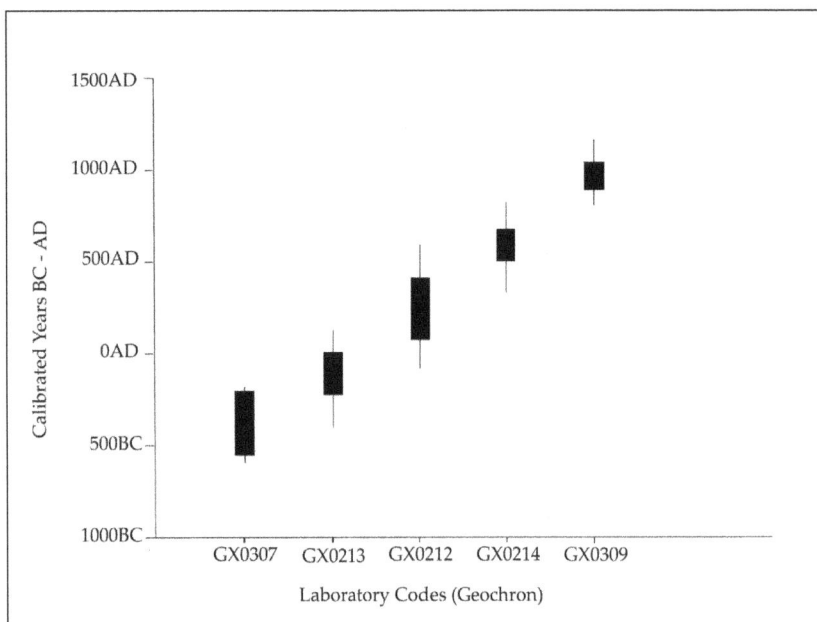

Figure 8. Box and whisker plot showing the calibrated radiocarbon dates for Kain Hitam at 1 and 2 sigma. Sample GX0213 is from the Samti death-ship site in the Niah Cave system. Full details of radiocarbon dates are presented in Table 2. Harrisson's modern death ship and the aggregate bone date have been excluded from this graph.

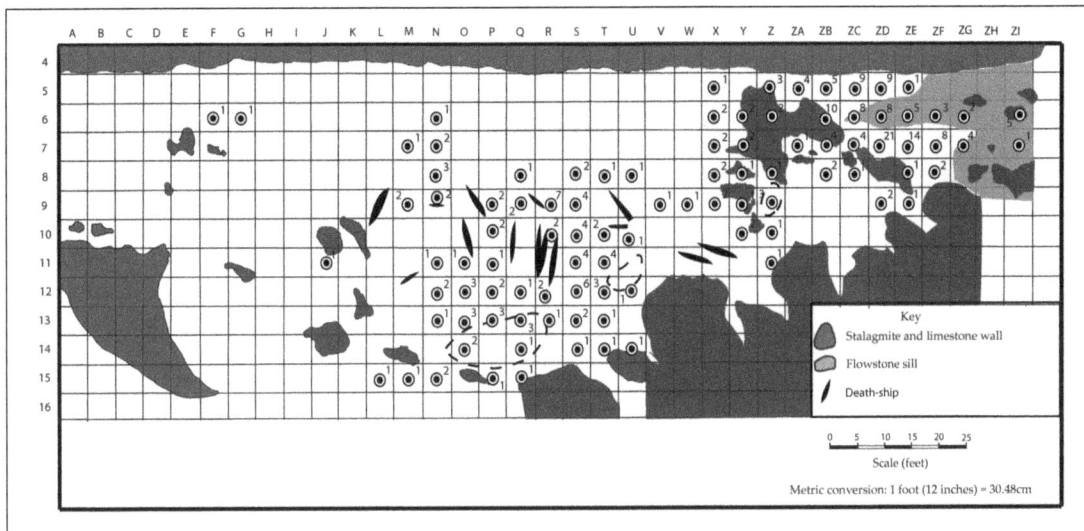

Figure 9. Distribution plan of occurrence of double-spouted vessel sherds at Kain Hitam. Numbers represent vessel fragments. Areas within dotted lines represent the scattered remains of individual death ships (redrawn from Tom Harrisson's original plans).

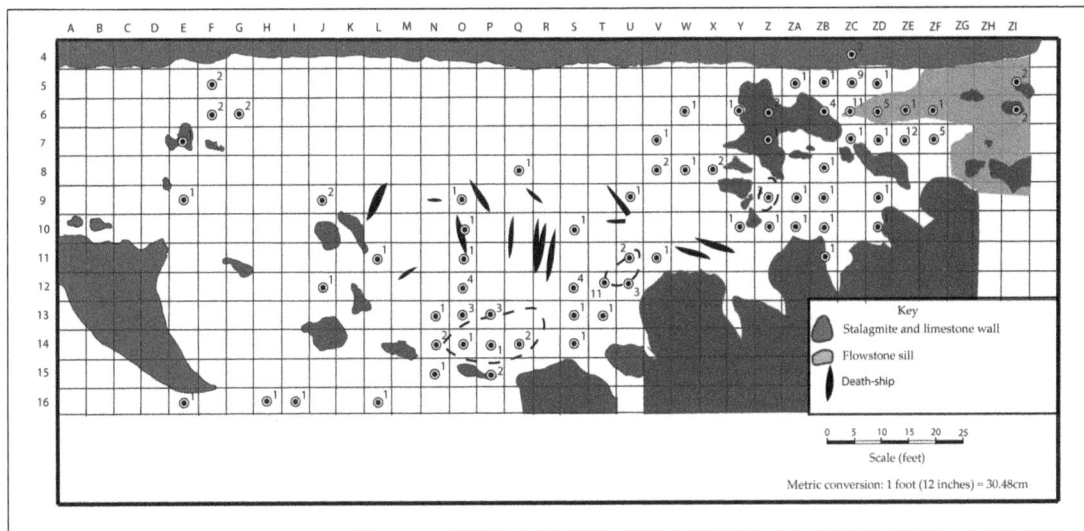

Figure 10. Distribution plan of occurrence of ceramic trade wares at Kain Hitam. Values represent individual vessels. Areas within dotted lines represent the scattered remains of individual death-ships (redrawn from Tom Harrisson's original plans).

travertine shelf, no differential patterning of different types of artefacts can be discerned. This observation contradicts any argument that the importation of these goods revolutionised local cultures in either a structural or symbolic sense. Furthermore, it also argues strongly against the influx of new peoples synchronous with the extension of trade routes, replacing and/or transforming local cultures (e.g. Chêng 1969). It is also worthy of note that although artefacts in bone and shell are often, implicitly or explicitly, associated with Neolithic deposits in Southeast Asia (e.g. Francis 2002:151), the radiocarbon chronology points to a metal-age association at Kain Hitam.

Archaeological representations of death: An Island Southeast Asian context for Kain Hitam

While the use of death ships has parallels with only two other known sites in Sarawak (see below), the diverse types of material culture represented at Kain Hitam link it strongly to various locales within the Niah Caves complex. Pieces of bone carved with relief-scroll designs identical to the distinctive fragment recovered from Kain Hitam (Figure 5c), have also been excavated from the Lobang Tulang mouth of the Niah Caves (T. Harrisson and Medway 1962:Plate 2), where tubular bone beads were also recovered in some numbers (B. Harrisson 1958). Bone cuffs were recovered from the upper levels of Gan Kira, and bone bead separators were recovered from both Lobang Tulang and Gan Kira (Harrisson and Medway:Table 7). Lobang Tulang is a metal-age jar-burial site, while Gan Kira has two stratigraphic layers, of which the lower is Neolithic and the upper strata, with primary extended burials, is associated with the metal age (Piper and Szabó Unpublished data). The inter-site linkages observable in the bone artefacts can also be seen in artefacts produced from shell. We know of no analogues for the hewn disc beads in *Melo* sp. in Island Southeast Asia, but those recovered from Kain Hitam have exact parallels in examples from Gan Kira. A less restrictive spatio-temporal distribution is seen in the ground and perforated *Conus* sp. spires which occur widely across the Neolithic and metal ages of the Philippines and other locales in Borneo (Szabó 2005; Szabó Unpublished data). The same can be said of beads in *Cypraea annulus*, *Oliva* spp., *Pyrene* spp. and *Nassarius* spp. (see Szabó 2005).

The Kain Hitam rock art has not been dated,[5] but the relative dates ascribed by Wilson (2003) for the curvilinear red tradition of the western Pacific fit seamlessly with the radiocarbon sequence for the site. Wilson (2003:277–278) goes on to make the important point that the curvilinear red tradition appears to be an outgrowth of the early Red1/Red2 painting styles, with an infusion of new motifs generated, most likely, by the expanding contacts and networks of the Southeast Asian metal age. The Kain Hitam site, as a cohesive whole, reinforces this interpretation, with metal-age trade goods clearly being drawn into extant cultural practices. It seems clear to us that the rock art is not chronologically disjunct from the archaeological material. The same themes and motifs bind the two together, and when this point is combined with the highly ordered structuring of space within the site, it argues for a direct association.

The symbolism of death: Kain Hitam and beyond

Ballard *et al.* (2004) summarise the ethnohistorical and archaeological evidence for the interwoven nature of boat symbolism and death ritual in Southeast Asia (see also Manguin 1986). While there is no need to reiterate their discussion here, there are particular aspects which we would like to develop, related to (1) the intertwined dichotomy between the sacred/profane or ritual/prosaic nature of boat and maritime themes in many Southeast Asian societies; and (2) the nature of the spatio-temporal patterning in boat/death symbolism, with the Kain Hitam evidence allowing us to tie together connections between mortuary expressions which have hitherto been overlooked. It is clear the Kain Hitam site is a very structured 'deathscape'. With a period of utilisation apparently in excess of 1000 years, the placement of items of material culture, including the death ships themselves, in relation to the rock art and the cave mouth remains constant. While this constancy clearly reflects replicative practice related to mortuary ritual and (at least outward) expressions of social relations, it also binds all the items of material culture together within such practice. This is significant in that many such items are traditionally interpreted as 'prosaic' items of material culture (see discussion of B. Harrisson's interpretation of Lobang Tulang above). In the context of Kain Hitam, spatial distributions and material associations make it plain that fresh-water shellfish remains, casting nets for fishing, and earthenware pottery are invested with meaning *as a part of* the deathscape. As suggested by Ballard *et al.* (2004:398), such blurring between the margins of the 'prosaic' and 'sacred' reflects the fundamental basis of the sacred in everyday patterns of life. At Kain Hitam, such everyday patterns clearly revolve around boats, and the movement of material goods, people and ideas.

The fact that boats and boat transport are structuring ideas within many and varied

Southeast Asian societies is nothing new (e.g. Manguin 1986), and to leave the interpretation of the Kain Hitam site at such a point would be rather trite. Boat symbolism is clearly part of a wider conceptual structure that is expressed in a variety of different ways throughout insular Southeast Asia. The diversity in expression is, we feel, as important as the threads of connection. While the internal features of the Kain Hitam deposit are clearly highly structured, a wider gaze demonstrates that the location of Kain Hitam on the landscape itself is also structured. Located 91 m up a difficult cliff face, the cave of Kain Hitam is located over a point where the Sungai (River) Tangap[6] disappears underground.

On noting this feature of geography, the Harrissons investigated other locales where tributaries in the vicinity of the Niah Caves disappeared underground, and found two more cave sites replete with death ships.[7] Tom and Barbara Harrisson were quick to recognise the importance of such a location (T. Harrisson 1958, 1964), but did not fully explicate in print the importance of the river as a conduit between the worlds of the living and the dead.

While the location of the sites in relation to the river could be seen as fortuitous, there are a number of good reasons to think it is indeed important. Huntington and Metcalf (1979) elaborate a number of death rites from different ethnic groups in Borneo, and despite differences, strong themes are present. The Berawan of Long Jegan consider that souls travel upriver to the ancestral homeland, and in doing so, simultaneously move back in time, and from the everyday mundane world back past mythical ancestors to the realm of the sacred (Huntington and Metcalf 1979:72). Ngaju belief holds that the soul is transported on two different boats to the city of souls (Antoni 1982). Furthermore, the lance of the leader of souls takes the form of the mast of the boat, as well as a Garangin tree symbolising the tree of life at journey's end (Steinmann 1939:40; Schärer in Antoni 1982:150). The Maloh place the dead in dedicated structures set on high poles (kulambu), but transport the body to the kulambu in a boat-shaped coffin. Prohibitions were also placed on movement across the river during the period of mourning (King 1985:90, 191). Maloh cosmology holds that upstream regions of the river were associated with goodness, health, life and ancestral and aristocratic spirits, whilst downstream regions led directly to the land of the dead in the form of the underworld, populated by serpents and fish (King 1985:93). In the Philippines, the Sulod of Panay believe souls use rivers to travel between the lands of the living and the dead (Jocano 1970:187). One could continue listing examples, but as noted by van Gennep (1960 in Huntington and Metcalf 1979:12), 'water journeys and island-like afterworlds appear over and over again' as motifs in death rites and symbolism across very many cultures. The close association between boats, rivers, the afterworld and the ship-of-the-dead motif seen in Borneo are replicated across Island Southeast Asia (Ballard et al. 2004).

Two mechanisms have traditionally been proposed for explaining these connections between cultural groups: (1) the influence of the Dongson culture of northern Vietnam with the expanding trade networks of the Southeast Asian metal age; and (2) demic diffusion of trading populations, resulting in a generally Sinicized cultural expression. We find both these explanations unsatisfactory, and believe a closer analysis of the nature and variability of mortuary expression across the region will illuminate why. Various ideas surrounding mortuary practices can be seen across the Island Southeast Asian region, often as far east as Remote Oceania. These include the ship of the dead, 'tree of life', animal associations including crocodiles, hornbills, sea serpents and turtles, and the curvilinear red art style (though not simply restricted to rock art) identified by Wilson (2003) for the western Pacific. While all of these elements have a wide geographical distribution, expression and recombination of elements differs. Here, we investigate mortuary expressions in Palawan, Philippines, as well as a new 'bronze ship' from Flores, Indonesia, to investigate both persistence and variability in the expression of major themes.

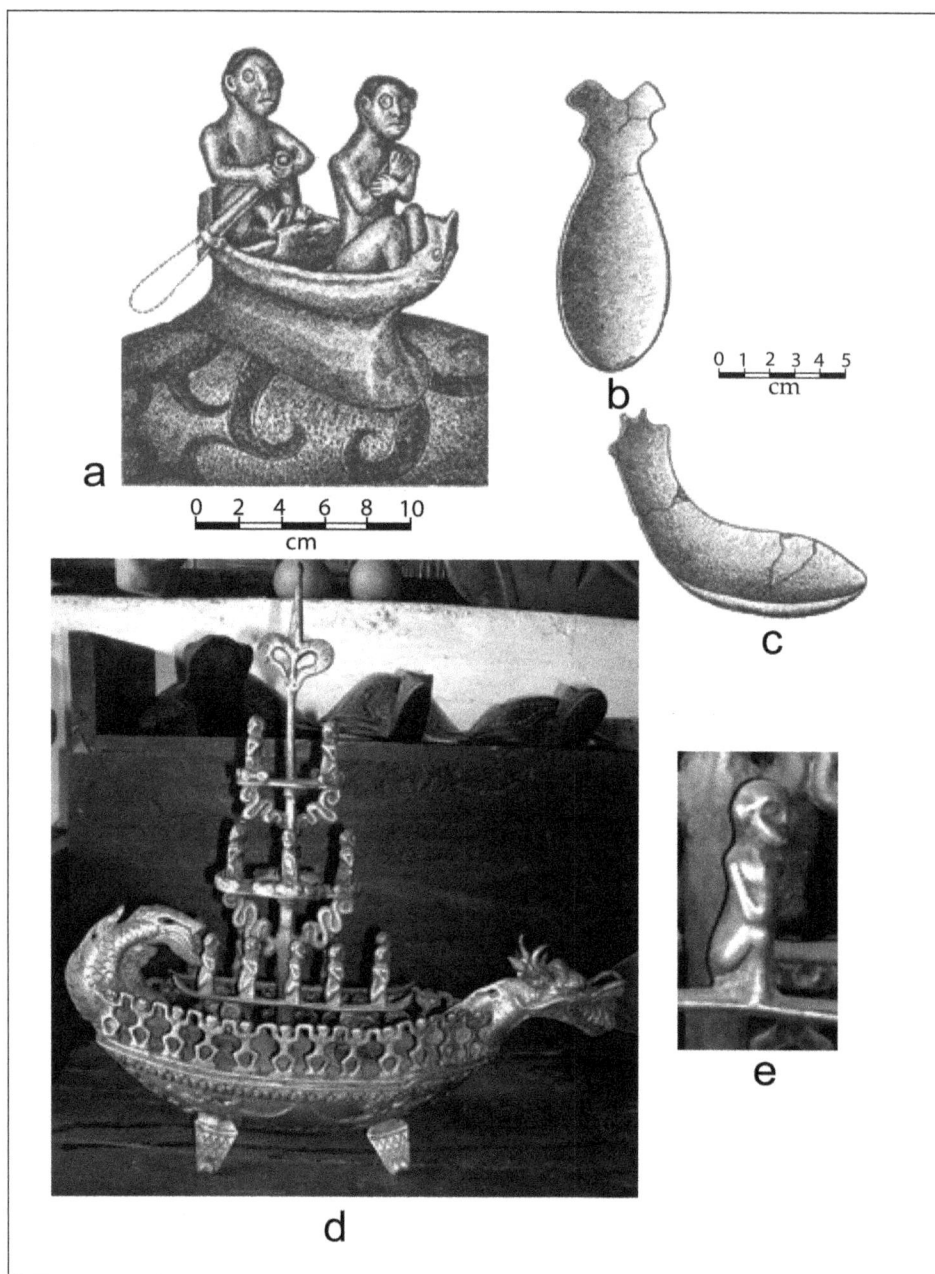

Figure 11. Ship-of-the-dead expressions from Palawan and Flores: (a) detail of the moulded lid of the Manunggul jar, Manunggul Chamber A, Palawan, Philippines (from Fox 1970); (b) and (c) *Turbo marmoratus* 'spoons' from the Tabon Caves complex (from Fox 1970); (d) cast bronze ship of the dead from Flores, Indonesia. Photographed by Szabó and Piper 2006 in Labuanbaju; (e) detail of seated figure from the Flores ship of the dead. Compare with (a). Figures a, b and c reproduced with the permission of the National Museum of the Philippines.

The Manunggul Chamber A mortuary site within the Tabon Caves complex in Palawan, Philippines (Fox 1970), has yielded perhaps the most famous piece of Philippine earthenware: the Manunggul burial jar (Figure 11a). This large vessel is topped with a cover bearing a molded 'ship of the dead', where two figures sit in a vessel with a distinctively shaped figurative prow. Both figures gaze forward, with the rear figure steering and the front figure sitting with arms folded across his/her chest. The boat is assumed to have originally had a central mast/cosmic tree (Tenazas 1986:17). While the sculpture on the Manunggul jar has been repeatedly linked to ship-of-the-dead ideology since its discovery (Fox 1970:112–113), the association with red-painted curvilinear designs on the vessel itself is also worthy of note. Such designs are further replicated on various burial vessels from Ayub Cave, Mindanao (Dizon and Santiago 1996). The shape of the death ship is distinctive, and this precise design is replicated in artefacts produced in the large *Turbo marmoratus* shell,[8] and generally referred to as 'spoons' (Figure 11b and 11c). Such artefacts have been repeatedly found in metal-age burial contexts in Palawan, sometimes associated with jar burials (Szabó 2005:Chapter 6 for Batu Puti; Fox 1970:54, 118, 140 for Duyong Cave and Manunggul Chamber B), and sometimes with extended inhumations (Szabó 2005 for Leta Leta; T. Vitales pers comm. for Ille Cave).

While most of the spoons are in a clear metal-age association, a *Turbo marmoratus* ship-of-the-dead artefact is associated with a firm Neolithic context in Leta Leta Cave, northern Palawan (Fox 1970; Szabó 2005), confirming the pre-metal presence of ship-of-the-dead beliefs in this region. Such 'spoons' have also been excavated from other Philippine locales (Bautista 1996), as well as from the Ryukyu Islands, southern Japan (e.g. Takemoto and Asato 1993), and from southern Taiwan (Li 1983), but have not been recovered from Borneo or Indonesia.

An arresting example of death-ship imagery comes from Flores Island in eastern Indonesia in the form of a cast bronze sculpture recorded by Szabó and Piper in Labuanbaju, Flores, in 2006 (Figure 11d and Figure 11e) (see Adams 1977 for a different example). Many elements of death imagery combine in this piece, including the crocodiles around the hull of the boat (see Tenazas 1986 for more examples of crocodile imagery and death in the Philippines and Borneo), the central tree-of-life mast, and the sea-serpent form of the bow and stern. The similarity between the seated figures (Figure 11e) and those represented on the Manunggul jar can hardly be missed, and the frieze of stylised figures around the edge of the deck mirror those represented in the Kain Hitam rock art.

While the Kain Hitam deathscape, mortuary sites in Palawan, and the Flores bronze ship are strongly connected in terms of imagery, the differences in expression and context must not be forgotten. There are no clear, recurrent linkages between the types of burial (i.e. jar burial, death ship, primary extended inhumation) and associated imagery. Thus, while ship-of-the-dead imagery is apparently confined to death-ship contexts in Sarawak, it is associated with both jar and primary extended burials in Palawan. Media and modes of expression are likewise different, with a complete absence of prehistoric rock art in Palawan, and differing associated artefacts, with bone ornaments near absent in Palawan and expressions in shell being rather understated in Sarawak.

Tantalising lines of evidence further suggest in Sarawak and Palawan that ship-of-the-dead beliefs pre-date the metal age. Variability in mortuary expression has implicitly or explicitly been assumed to represent chronological patterning (e.g. Bellwood 1997:296), but the evidence from Niah, coupled with that from Palawan, demonstrate that these various articulations are, at least to some degree, synchronous (see also Tenazas 1986:15). Thus, while Kain Hitam is characterised by boat burials, Lobang Tulang is a jar-burial site, and Gan Kira has extended burials including Tom Harrisson's 'murder' type.[9]

Associated artefacts of both local and foreign manufacture, however, overlap between all three sites, stalling any interpretation that would seek to attribute the differences to distinct cultural groups. There are those who have attributed later prehistoric burial practices at Niah and elsewhere in Sarawak to Chinese immigrants (e.g. Chêng 1969), and there are some obvious Chinese parallels in beliefs surrounding death, including watery journeys, crocodiles, sea serpents and trees of life (see Antoni 1982 for a discussion of Wang Ch'ung's *Lun-heng* 27–97 AD). According to Rawson's (1998) analysis of changing mortuary expressions in China, many of these distinctive beliefs in animal spirits and 'imaginary' beings are found in the southern Chinese record contemporaneous with very different Shang (c. 1200–1050 BC) and Western Zhou (c. 1050–771 BC) expressions in the north (Rawson 1998:122). She also points to a growing incorporation of these southern belief systems detectable from the Eastern Zhou (771–221 BC) into the Han Dynasty (BC 206–220 AD) as China was unified (Rawson 1998:112–113, 122).

The links between the Southeast Asian evidence and that of southern China – perhaps associated with the 'Hundred Yueh' – hint that such belief systems may not originate in 'China', but were already extant among local indigenous peoples with connections to Southeast Asia. The continuity witnessed in the Southeast Asian archaeological record across the Neolithic/ metal-age boundary further serves to confound an attempt at unsubtle Sinicization.

Rather than simply attributing any (perceived) change to immigrant populations, the more popular mechanism invoked for explaining the wide spatial distribution of cultural expressions of the Southeast Asian metal age is the influence of the Dongson culture of northern Vietnam (e.g. Harrisson 1958; Spriggs in Wilson 2003:277; Ballard *et al.* 2004:393). Tangibly, this influence is seen in the wide distribution of bronze kettle drums of Dongson manufacture,[10] but it has been the boat motifs incised on the drums which have perhaps been credited with widespread influence. Such motifs have encouraged an interpretation in which the Dongson culture is seen as the progenitor of ideas such as the 'ship-of-the-dead cult', with an influence (e.g. economic, stylistic) that spread to encompass insular Southeast Asia and as far as Near Oceania (e.g. Goloubew 1929; van Heekeren 1958:96; Badner 1974). While the clear presence of 'ship-of-the-dead' philosophies in Neolithic Island Southeast Asia could alone act to undermine the directionality of such connections, we feel that such interpretations mask, rather than elucidate, the interactions developed and sustained by maritime contact.

Thomas (1991:27) points out that socio-economic evolutionary thinking turns on and recapitulates the divisions between 'modern' and 'traditional' societies. The assumed impact of metal and prestige trade goods from the Asian mainland into Island Southeast Asia can be seen in this light. Thomas (1991:27) suggests it should not be the [pre-]historian's aim to shift such divisions back in time, 'but rather to displace such exercises through an analysis of process and grounded regional distinctions which actually relate to peoples rather than rhetorical types'. Recognising this, any analysis of 'influence' and 'trade' must consider *how* new goods and ideas were integrated into local economies and psyches. It is this appropriation and reinterpretation of foreign goods and ideas that patterns the archaeological record, rather than any simple presence of strangers or trading vessels. In the words of Thomas (1991:88):

> Indigenous interests in trade are not presumed to be straightforward or predictable but must instead be contextualized in prevailing ideas of what foreign visitors and their goods represented. This cultural context is not easy to apprehend, especially since interpretation must be based mainly upon what can be discerned of indigenous reactions at the time … But the analytical problems must not prevent us from attempting to give an account of the local way of recognizing new strangers: these perceptions conditioned what was at stake in contact and exchange.

With reference to Kain Hitam, the spatial/structural replication of burial practices over a 1000-year period, with the simple insertion of overseas trade goods into this structure when they entered local economies, testifies to the local continuity through this economic 'transition'. It is clear that boats, water, maritime contacts and connections between worlds over water were already configuring features of indigenous consciousness, as represented by death ships, casting nets, shark vertebrae beads, the rock art and the (votive?) deposits of fresh-water shell. Such expressions can also be clearly seen in Palawan and elsewhere throughout the Island Southeast

Asian region, but they manifest in different ways. These entangled connections projected through local response serve to remind us that trade goods and (seemingly) extra-local ideas should always be 'interpreted in the context of the place into which they are introduced, and not taken as essences that have merely been moved physically from places of origin' (Thomas 1991:186).

Endnotes

1. The name Kain Hitam literally translates as 'Black Cloth' in Bahasa Melayu.
2. It is worthy of note that published photographs of the Kain Hitam death ships (e.g. Harrisson 1958, 1960) were 'staged' by Harrisson, and do not represent the original positions of the boats.
3. Solheim (1983) states that the Kain Hitam ceramics more likely date to the 14th–15th century AD, however it appears that this upward revision was not based on an analysis of the material. Given the disjuncture between other features of the site and a Ming-period age for the trade wares, we continue with Tom Harrisson's chronology, although further analysis of the Kain Hitam trade wares would be valuable.
4. Francis (2002:77) comments on the Kain Hitam glass beads, relying on the commentary by Solheim (1983), and thus duplicates the erroneous conclusions that there were no Chinese ceramics in Sarawak before the 10th century AD, and no coil beads at other Sarawak sites until the 12th century AD.
5. Dating of the rock art from Kain Hitam has been attempted, but was unsuccessful due to the low organic levels.
6. Erroneously referred to by Tom Harrisson as the 'Subis River' (T. Harrisson 1958:202).
7. One of these sites is the 'Samti' site, while the other is unnamed. Both are apparently located in the Great Cave within the Niah system (see Harrisson 1958).
8. Such artefacts were originally thought by Fox (1970) to have been produced in the Chambered Nautilus (*Nautilus pompilius*), however further study (Bautista 1996; Szabó 2005) has confirmed *Turbo marmoratus* as the raw material.
9. Tom Harrisson's 'murder' burials are primary extended burials demonstrating violent deaths. One example from Gan Kira has the shaft of a spear still protruding from the body.
10. Although, notably, no bronze drums have been recorded for the Philippine archipelago, and few from Borneo.

Acknowledgements

The analysis of the Kain Hitam material was made possible through a British Academy Small Research Grant to the authors. The British Academy also funded the new radiocarbon determinations for Kain Hitam. Katherine Szabó was assisted in the shell analysis by Hsiu-Ying 'Shawna' Yang and Christopher Wong. We thank the Sarawak Museum for their ongoing support, and in particular Haji Sanib bin Said, Ipoi Datan and Noel Laman of the Niah Museum. At Niah Caves National Park, we wish to thank Abang Mutalib, Madame Rose and Lyn; and in Kuching, Helen bin Kurui. We thank Corazon Alvina and Eusebio Dizon of the National Museum of the Philippines for permission to reproduce the drawing of the Manunggul jar from Fox (1970). For discussion of particular points and assistance with references, thank you to Meredith Wilson, Chris Ballard, Douglas Farrer, Christopher Stimpson, Lindsay Lloyd-Smith, the Earl of Cranbrook and Judith Cameron.

We also thank the Corning Glass Museum for locating and sending the results of analysis of glass samples originally sent by Tom Harrisson. For further information on mortuary deposits in the Philippines, we thank Jack Medrana and Grace Barretto-Tesoro, and for assistance with references, Janine Ochoa and Isa Campos.

References

Adams, M.J. 1977. A "Forgotten" Bronze Ship and a Recently Discovered Bronze Weaver from Eastern Indonesia: A Problem Paper. *Asian Perspectives* 20:87–109.

Antoni, K. 1982. Death and Transformation: The Presentation of Death in East and Southeast Asia. *Asian Folklore Studies* 41:147–162.

Badner, M. 1974. Some evidences of Dong-Son-derived influence in the art of the Admiralty Islands In N. Barnard (ed.), *Early Chinese Art and its Possible Influence in the Pacific Basin*, pp. 597–629. New York: Columbia University.

Ballard, C., R. Bradley, L. Nordenborg M. and M. Wilson 2004. The ship as symbol in the prehistory of Scandinavia and Southeast Asia. *World Archaeology* 35:385–403.

Barretto, M.G.L.D 2002. Evaluating status in Philippine Prehistory through grave goods. Unpublished MA, University of the Philippines, Diliman.

Basilia, P., A. Bautista and K. Szabó 2006. Post-Neolithic Shell Beads from Ille Cave, El Nido, Palawan: A Case of Specialisation?, Paper presented at the 18th Indo-Pacific Prehistory Association Congress, Manila 2006.

Bautista, A. 1996. Shell Spoon from Chamber B of Manunggul Cave, Palawan and Mataas Site Albay: Nautilus or Turbinate Shell? *National Museum Papers* 6:59–63. (National Museum of the Philippines).

Bellwood, P. 1997. *Prehistory of the Indo-Malaysian Archipelago*, Revised edition. Honolulu: University of Hawaii Press.

Bellwood, P., J. Cameron, N. Van Viet and B. Van Liem 2006. Ancient Boats, Boat Timbers, and Locked Mortise-and-Tenon Joints from Bronze/Iron-Age Northern Vietnam. *International Journal of Nautical Archaeology* 36(1):2–20.

Brill, R.H. 1999. Chemical Analyses of Early Glasses, Volume 1, Catalogue of Samples. New York: The Corning Museum of Glass.

Chêng, T. 1969. *Archaeology in Sarawak*. Cambridge: W. Heffer and Sons and the University of Toronto Press.

Dizon, E.Z. and R. Santiago 1996. *Faces From Maitum: The Archaeological Excavation of Ayub Cave*. Manila: National Museum of the Philippines.

Fox, R.B. 1970. *The Tabon Caves*. Manila: National Museum of the Philippines.

Francis, P. Jr. 2002. Asia's Maritime Bead Trade: 300 B.C. to the Present. Honolulu: University of Hawaii Press.

Glover, I. 1972. Excavations in Timor. Unpublished PhD thesis. Department of Prehistory, Research School of Pacific Studies, Australian National University.

Goloubew, V. 1929. L'age du bronze au Tonkin. *Bulletin de l'École Française d'Extrême-Orient*, 29:1–46.

Gompertz, G. St. G.M. 1958. *Chinese Celadon Wares*. London: Faber and Faber.

Harrisson, B. 1958. Niah's Lobang Tulang: ("Cave of Bones"). *Sarawak Museum Journal* 8:596–619.

Harrisson, B. 1959–60. Cave of Bones – New Finds, 1959. *Sarawak Museum Journal* 9:164–178.

Harrisson, B. 1967. A classification of Stone Age burials from Niah Great Cave, Sarawak. *Sarawak Museum Journal* 15:126–200.

Harrisson, T. 1958. The Great Cave Sarawak: A Ship-Of-The-Dead Cult and Related Rock Paintings, *The Archaeological News Letter*. 6:199–204.

Harrisson, T. 1960. Stone Age Ships of Death: World's oldest boat coffins found in Sarawak caverns reveal ancient culture. *Life*, January 11 1960, pp. 49–51.

Harrisson, T. 1964. 100,000 Years of Stone Age Culture in Borneo. *Journal of the Royal Society of Arts* (1964):174–191.

Harrisson, T. and B. Harrisson 1971. The Prehistory of Sabah. *Sabah Society Journal*, Monograph 4.

Harrisson, T. and Lord Medway 1962. A first classification of prehistoric bone and tooth artifacts (based on material from Niah Great Cave). *Sarawak Museum Journal* 11:335–362.

Hudson, B. 2003. Dental Wealth. *Archaeology News*, July/August 2003, p. 10.

Huntington, R. and P. Metcalf 1979. *Celebrations of Death: The Anthropology of Mortuary Ritual.* Cambridge: Cambridge University Press.

Jocano, F.L. 1970. Death, Bone Washing, and Jar Burial among the Sulod of Central Panay, Philippines. In R. Fox (ed), *The Tabon Caves*, pp. 181–188. Manila: National Museum of the Philippines.

Lape, P., S. O'Connor and N. Burningham 2007. Rock Art: A Potential Source of Information about Past Maritime Technology in South-East Asia-Pacific Region. *International Journal of Nautical Archaeology* 36:238–253.

Li, K. 1983. Report of Archaeological Investigations in the O-luan-pi Park at Southern Tip of Taiwan. Taipei: Kenting Scenic Area Administration, Ministry of Communication; Department of Anthropology, National Taiwan University; Council for Cultural Planning and Development, Executive Yuan.

Manguin, P.Y. 1986. Shipshape societies: boat symbolism and political systems in insular Southeast Asia. In D.G. Marr and A.C. Milner (eds), *Southeast Asia in the 9th to 14th Centuries*, pp. 187–213. Canberra: Institute of Southeast Asian Studies and Research School of Pacific Studies, Australian National University.

Moore, E. n.d. Bukit Saripah Cave. Kuching: Unpublished typescript, Sarawak Museum.

Munan, H. 2005. *Beads of Borneo.* Singapore: Editions Didier Millet.

Pyatt, F.B., B. Wilson and G.W. Barker 2005. The chemistry of tree resins and ancient rock paintings in the Niah Caves, Sarawak (Borneo): Some evidence of rain forest management by early human populations. *Journal of Archaeological Science* 32:897–901.

Rawson, J. 1998. Chinese Burial Patterns: Sources of Information on Thought and Belief. In C. Renfrew and C. Scarre (eds), *Cognition and Material Culture: the Archaeology of Symbolic Storage*, pp. 107–133. Cambridge: McDonald Institute for Archaeological Research.

Solheim, W.G. II. 1983. Archaeological Research in Sarawak, Past and Present. *Sarawak Museum Journal* 32:35–58.

Spriggs, M., P. Veth, S. O'Connor, H. Mohammad, A. Jatmiko, W. Nayati, A. Diniasti and D. Witjaksono 2005. Three seasons of archaeological survey in the Aru Islands, 1995 – 1997. In S. O'Connor, M. Spriggs and P. Veth (eds), *The Archaeology of the Aru Islands, Eastern Indonesia*, pp. 63–83. Terra Australis 23, Canberra: Pandanus Press.

Szabó, K. 2005. Technique and Practice: Shell-working in the western Pacific and Island Southeast Asia. Unpublished PhD thesis, Australian National University.

Szabó, K. and H-Y Yang In preparation. Shell net-sinkers from casting nets: an exercise in identification.

Szabó, K. In preparation. The Molluscan Remains from the Niah Caves. In G. Barker, D. Gilbertson and T. Reynolds (eds), *The Archaeology of the Niah Caves, Sarawak: Excavations 1954 – 2004.* vol. 2. Cambridge: McDonald Institute for Archaeological Research.

Takemoto, M. and S. Asato 1993. Nihon no Kodai Iseki: 47 Okinawa: Hoikusha.

Tenazas, R. 1986. The Boat-Coffin Burial Complex in the Philippines and its Relation to Practices in Southeast Asia. *SPAFA Digest* 4:11–18.

Thomas, N. 1991. *Entangled Objects: Exchange, Material Culture, and Colonialism in the Pacific.* London: Harvard University Press, Cambridge MA.

Van Heekeren, H.R. 1958 The Bronze-Iron Age of Indonesia. Gravenhage: Martinus Nijhoff.

Wilson, M. 2003 Rock-art transformations in the western Pacific. In C. Sand (ed), *Pacific Archaeology: assessments and prospects*, pp. 265–284. Noumea: Service des Musées et du Patrimoine.

Zuraina M. 1982. The West Mouth, Niah in the prehistory of Southeast Asia. *Sarawak Museum Journal* 31(3):1–200.

11

Land and sea animal remains from Middle Neolithic Pitted Ware sites on Gotland Island in the Baltic Sea, Sweden

Helene Martinsson-Wallin
Department of Archaeology and Osteology, Gotland University, Sweden
Helene.Martinsson-Wallin@hgo.se

Introduction

Prehistoric bone material from Gotland Island situated in the centre of the Baltic Sea (Figure 1) is remarkably well preserved due to the island's limestone substrate. Archaeological research and excavation has been ongoing on the island since the beginning of last century (Wennersten 1907; Nihlén 1927; Stenberger *et al.* 1943), and the use of traditional farming methods has spared many prehistoric sites from destruction. The numerous archaeological excavations have resulted in a large and well-documented sample of human and animal bone material from Mesolithic and Neolithic sites. The bones occur both as food residue in occupation areas and as human remains in graves, which are sometimes associated with grave goods in the form of worked and unworked animal bone. In this paper, I investigate differences in the faunal assemblages recovered from five Pitted Ware sites dating to the Middle-Late Neolithic using a statistical comparison, and then examine whether the inter-site variation was caused by site chronology and environmental variability, or whether the difference might be due to cultural practices, such as the use of particular animals as symbols of group identity by Pitted Ware communities.

Background

Gotland Island formed in a tropical sea some 425 million years ago during the Silurian Era, after which the island was pushed down by the expansion of ice sheets during the Pleistocene. During the Holocene, parts of Gotland had risen above sea level by around 9000–10,000 years ago, and the island is still uplifting at a rate of 1 mm/year. The northern part of the island was the first to emerge above sea level from the evidence of sites such as Strå, Svalings and Gisslause (Figure 2). However, the earliest human occupation has been found in the cave Stora Förvar on the islet Stora Karlsö, just to the west of Gotland (Figure 2) (Österholm 1989; Lindqvist and

Figure 1. Map of the Baltic Sea.

Possnert 1999), which is dated to 9500–9300 BP. The early Mesolithic sites are interpreted as hunting sites from the numerous bones of seals, fish and aquatic birds (Lindqvist and Possnert 1999:81). Finds of human remains and bones of several types of seasonally available animals suggest the presence of permanent or semi-permanent camps. Seal bones are mostly of grey seal (*Halichoerus grypus*) and ringed seal (*Phoca hispida botnica*) in the Early Mesolithic phase, and of harp seal (*Phoca groenlandica*) and porpoise (*Phocoena phocoena*) in the Late Mesolithic phase (Lindqvist and Possnert 1997:29).

Before early settlement on Gotland, the Baltic Sea was cut off from the Atlantic Sea because of the uplift of areas around Denmark and North Germany – a process which turned the Baltic Sea into an inland fresh-water sea, known as the Ancylus Lake (named for the fresh-water shell *Ancylus fluviatilis*). The maximum transgression of the Ancylus Lake is dated to c. 10,300 BP (Svensson 1989), but by about 9200–9000 BP, it began to become more brackish, when it is termed the Mastogloia Sea after brackish water diatoms of the *Mastogloia* species (Lindqvist and Possnert 1997:52). The environment gradually became less brackish, and it became known as the Litorina Sea (named after the saltwater gastropod *Litorina litorea*), which reached its maximum by c. 7000 BP and experienced a series of transgressions.

During the end of the milder Atlantic climate which prevailed during the Mesolithic, farming and the domestication of animals became widespread. Ideas about house building and megalith

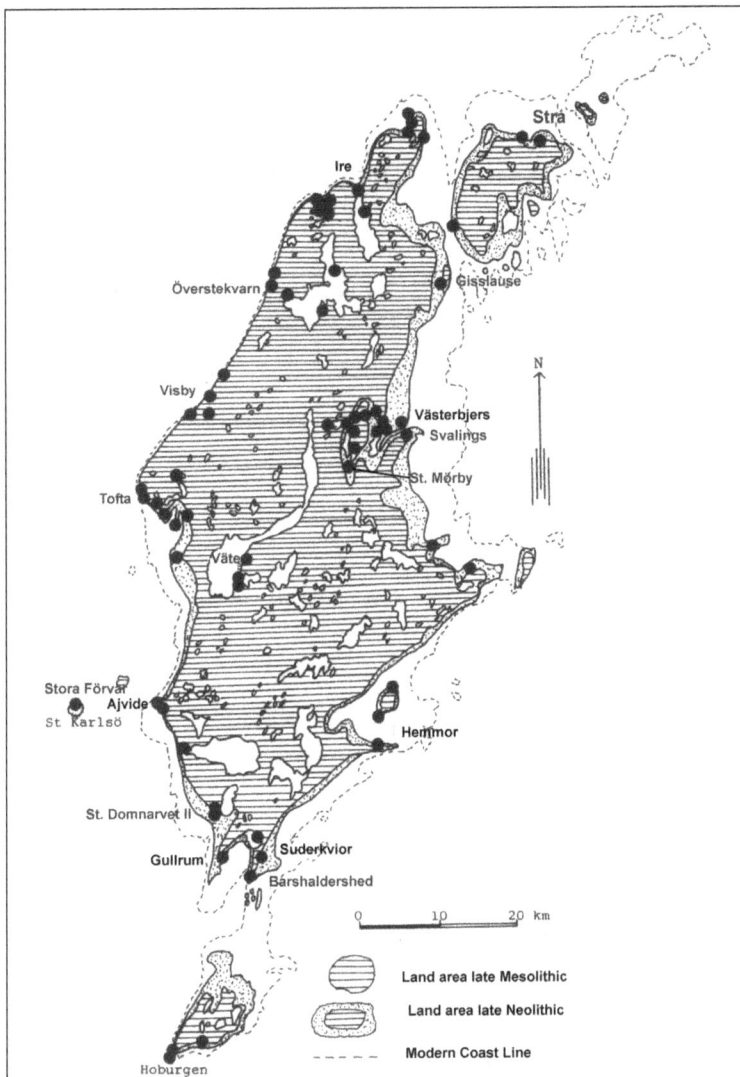

Figure 2. Map of Gotland with all known Mesolithic and Neolithic sites and site names mentioned in the text. Based on research by Österholm (1989).

graves from other parts of Europe were incorporated by pottery-using farmers in south Scandinavia (Hodder 1990). Farming and husbandry, in particular, were transmitted to Scandinavia from the continent by tribes using banded-ware ceramics, while the megalith culture had its roots in coastal Western Europe. It is postulated that the reduced saline content in the Baltic Sea during the Ancyulus and Mastogloian phases caused a decline in marine resources and the climate became colder and wetter. These conditions facilitated the uptake of farming and husbandry in south Scandinavia, a lifestyle which had long prevailed in continental Europe (Rowley-Conway 1983; Zvelebil and Rowley-Conway 1984). The shift towards a farming lifestyle is suggested by the increased use of adzes, and pollen diagrams show the clearance of inland areas suitable for farming. On Gotland, the introduction of farming activities, husbandry, and construction of megaliths occurred c. 6000–5000 years ago (Wallin and Martinsson-Wallin 1997; Österholm 1999:340). In occupation areas near to the coast, such as the Tofta area (Figure 2), a multitude of stone adzes have been found and pollen cores show large-scale land clearance (Österholm 1999:340). The construction of a megalith grave (a rectangular dolmen) has been dated to 5300–5000 BP (Lindqvist and Possnert 1997:48; Wallin and Martinsson-Wallin 1997). Finds of funnel-beaker pottery associated with megalith-building farmers have been found inland at the Mölner-Gullarve settlement (Österholm 1989:75), and at other sites including Stora Mörby, the cave site Stora Förvar, Överstekvarn I, Stora DomerarveII, Barshalderhed and Suderkvior

(Figure 2) (Lindqvist and Possnert 1997:48). ^{13}C results from human skeletal remains from a megalith grave suggest a terrestrial or mixed terrestrial/marine diet, which contrasts with the high marine intake identified in human remains from the Mesolithic (Lindqvist and Possnert 1997:29).

During the Late Mesolithic and Early Neolithic phases the climate changed and the Baltic again became a saline sea. The return to saline conditions is likely to have had a positive effect on the productivity of the marine environment. On Gotland, this seems to have led to marine resources once again becoming the dominant source of subsistence. The emergence of substantial Pitted Ware sites in coastal locations occurred during the Middle-Late Neolithic phase, oriented toward marine subsistence, although domesticated animals such as the pig, cattle, sheep/goat and dog were utilised. Marine foods such as seals and cod were important to the diet, but domesticated or semi-domesticated pig were probably of greater social value (Rowley-Conway 1983). The Pitted Ware pots differ from the funnel-beaker ceramics in shape and decoration, and a connection between the Pitted Wares and the comb-decorated ceramics in the southeast of Scandinavia has been suggested (Wyszomirska 1984; Martinsson 1986:10; Papmehl-Dyfay 2006:37). The dominant decoration on Pitted Ware ceramics are small pits located on the shoulder and rim of the vessel (Figure 3). These pots, along with a similar marine subsistence orientation, site coastal location and tool kit, characterise sites found in east, west and south Sweden, east Denmark, south Norway and the islands in the Baltic Sea (Papmehl-Dufay 2006:32–45).

Methodology

Archaeologists study prehistoric material by grouping, separating and simplifying different types of data. The interpretation of past material culture is often based on analogy, and it is important to examine how analogies are employed in each case. One way of analysing archaeological data is by the use of statistical methods. In this study, a descriptive statistical method, the chi-squared test was applied to faunal assemblages from Pitted Ware sites, along with qualitative observations of their association with human skeletal remains. A discussion about the age of the sites follows, but all of the analysed samples are from Pitted Ware sites on Gotland, which are considered to comprise a single cultural entity, and which experienced similar environmental conditions during the Middle Neolithic.

Figure 3. Typical Pitted Ware pot (drawing by Sven Österholm).

When studying prehistoric bone remains from occupation sites there is a tendency to regard differences in assemblage composition as the result of chronological and environmental factors. It is suggested, for instance, that during the Late Mesolithic and Early Neolithic, people went from a marine diet to a terrestrial diet because of an environmental change. The analysis of skeletal remains in megalith graves on Gotland and Öland supports this shift in particular instances (Lindqvist and Possnert 1997:48). Taking several cases of skeletal remains into account, however, the isotope evidence for prehistoric diet shows substantial variation (Papmehl-Dufay 2006:133). The same variation is also seen in a comparison of the animal bones from four Pitted Ware sites on Gotland, where the ratio of marine animals to terrestrial mammals and the contribution of both to the prehistoric diet has been examined (Storå 2001:Table 2). These differences might result from the cultural views about the use of animals by different Pitted Ware groups. Analogies drawn from traditional societies show that animals are important sources of food, yet they frequently have a significant role in a belief system (Lévi-Strauss 1969, 1971). It is suggested, then, that the variability in the bone remains from Pitted Ware sites might reflect the different ideologies and belief systems of Pitted Ware groups, and the remains are worthy, therefore, of a comparative analysis.

Comparative studies of faunal bone remains from Pitted Ware sites on Gotland

During the Middle and Late Neolithic phase (c. 5300–4250 BP), several large coastal settlements emerged on Gotland. Human skeletal remains from such sites have been dated to c. 4200–3700 BP, and seal bone from the sites has been dated to 4800–4350 BP. Additional dates from these sites include a pig bone dated to 4100 BP, while two dates on hedgehog bone have a span of c. 4400–4000 BP (Possnert 2002:171). The recovered bone material suggests that marine subsistence, especially the hunting of seals, was of great importance, but there was also husbandry of semi-domesticated pig (*Sus scrofa*), cattle (*Bos taurus*) and sheep/goat (*Ovis aries/Capra hircus*) (Lindqvist and Possnert 1997:29). The need for pasture to feed cattle and sheep/goats might have been accommodated by vegetation clearing and the expansion of pastoral areas near settlements. Sedentary occupation in Pitted Ware settlements is suggested from the presence of domestic structures and extensive cemeteries (Österholm 1989).

During the Middle Neolithic on Gotland, Österholm (1989) suggests there were 13 coastal settlements. One inland site is suggested to have been utilised during earlier settlement, but during the Pitted Ware phase it was used as a resource procurement area, rather than as a permanent residential site. The coastal sites were also likely to have been utilised previously, since many of them have some funnel-beaker pottery in the earliest layers (Österholm 1989).

Several of the largest Pitted Ware sites have been subject to archaeological investigation. The grave field at Västerbjers on the east side of Gotland (Figure 2) was excavated because it was being destroyed by gravel and sand quarrying (Stenberger *et al.* 1943). The cemetery remains were analysed (Stenberger *et al.* 1943; Janzon 1974; Eriksson 2004), but the settlement itself was not systematically excavated nor reported in detail. The most extensively excavated Pitted Ware site is Ajvide on the southwest of Gotland (Figure 2) (Österholm 1989; Burenhult 1997, 2002). Material from this site has not been incorporated in the statistical analysis, although the Ajvide bone remains are discussed below (Lindqvist and Possnert 1997).

Faunal remains from Pitted Ware sites

The bone database consisted of identified faunal bone remains recovered from five Pitted Ware sites: Hemmor (Hedell 1921), Visby (Wallin and Eriksson 1985), Ire (Landin 1981; Hegert 1982), Västerbjärs and Gullrum (Ekman 1974). The bone remains were recovered from different-sized excavation units, using different recovery techniques, but they represent the full range of Pitted Ware sites on Gotland. The statistical analysis of the faunal remains with the chi-squared method was carried out in two parts. The first comparison examined the percentile share of the remains from four animal groups in each site: (1) pig; (2) other domesticated animals (sheep/goat, cattle and dog); (3) seals; (4) other wild animals. The second analysis compared the percentile share of domesticated (groups 1 and 2) and wild (groups 3 and 4) animal remains (Wallin and Martinsson-Wallin 1992:9–16).

The results of the analysis are shown in Figure 4 and Table 1. The composition of the analysed samples from Hemmor and Västerbjers sites on the east side of Gotland is similar, with both high in pig and domesticated-animal remains (groups 1 and 2). The bone samples from Visby and Gullrum on the west side of the island are also similar, and they have a higher proportion of wild animals. The fifth bone sample from the site of Ire in the north of Gotland is significantly different from the other four sites (Wallin and Martinsson-Wallin 1992:10–16), as it has a very high proportion of remains from wild animals (mainly seals), compared with domestic animals (Wallin and Martinsson-Wallin 1992:16).

There are also substantial differences between the composition of fauna at the Ajvide site and several Pitted Ware sites suggested by Lindqvist and Possnert (1997:49–50) to be contemporaneous. Over the course of settlement at Ajvide, there was a change from the utilisation of wild animals early on, to an increasing reliance on domesticated animals. However, compared with other Gotland sites (Table 1) considered contemporaraneous, there are still significant inter-site differences in the archaeofauna.

Since the faunal samples differed between sites in the type and the quality of recovery techniques, it was important to determine whether other sorts of archaeological data also displayed significant differences. A craniometric study of discrete traits was carried out on human remains from six Pitted Ware sites on Gotland by Sjøvold (1974). The analysis demonstrated a rather homogeneous 'Pitted Ware' population, but there was a statistically significant difference between the groups from Visby in the west and Västerbjers in the east (Sjøvold 1974:201). Another inter-group difference was that females from the Ire site had a significantly higher stature than females from other sites. The males from Ire also differed in size from males at the other sites, but this difference was not statistically significant.

Animal burials and animal parts in Pitted Ware graves have also been studied. It is clear that parts of pigs (mainly tusks and mandibles) were a frequent grave good that accompanied human burials at Ire (Table 1) (Janzon 1974:262–290), but these elements were uncommon in the bone remains from the habitation site. Seal teeth, used as ornaments, were a common grave good, and animals such as the hedgehog, especially hedgehog mandibles, and parts of exotic animals, such as beaver teeth and elk antler, were also regular grave goods (Janzon 1974). Parts of long bones from various sea birds were common in some graves, and have been interpreted as

Table 1. Statistical analysis of animal-bone samples from five Pitted Ware sites on Gotland. The compared sites and their chi-squared values are listed, along with the significance value for each inter-site association.

Site comparison	chi-squared	significance	similarity/difference
1 Hemmor/Gullrum	16.45	0.000	significant difference
2 Hemmor/Visby	12.26	0.000	significant difference
3 Hemmor/Ire	118.68	0.000	significant difference
4 Hemmor/Västerbjers	0.046	0.831	significant similarity
5 Visby/Ire	61.28	0.000	significant difference
6 Visby/Västerbjers	12.26	0.000	significant difference
7 Visby/Gullrum	0.34	0.556	significant similarity
8 Ire/Västerbjers	112.51	0.000	significant difference
9 Ire/Gullrum	58.68	0.000	significant difference
10 Västerbjers/Gullrum	16.45	0.000	significant difference

whistles. A comparative analysis of all of the animal remains found in graves from Pitted Ware sites would be useful, but at the Hemmor and Gullrum sites, only a few skeletal remains and grave goods have been recovered (Janzon 1974:257–260).

Discussion

Site chronology and environmental variation

A clear difference can be seen between the faunal remains from sites on the east of Gotland and those from the two west-coast sites, but the main difference is between the Ire site in the north and the sites of Gullrum and Hemmor in the south (Figure 2). What is the reason for the inter-site variability in the faunal remains? The variation might be interpreted, for instance, as a difference in archaeological sampling methods, environmental variation, chronological difference in site age, or the result of different cultural views about animals among Pitted Ware groups.

Lindqvist and Possnert (1997:34) criticised the bone samples discussed above – which were first examined by Wallin and Martinsson-Wallin (1992) – and argued that the Pitted Ware sites were not contemporary with one another and that different recovery procedures had caused the inter-site differences in the fauna. They suggest the Middle Neolithic should be divided into two phases: Middle Neolithic A (MNA) from c. 5250 to 4750 BP, and Middle Neolithic B (MNB) from 4750 to 4250 BP. Lindqvist and Possnert (1997) base this chronology on differences in pottery style, with MNA characterised by the Säter/Fagervik style III pottery, which equates

with the Hemmor/Gullrum phase on Gotland, and the MNB characterised by Säter/Fagervik IV pottery, which equates with the Visby/Ire/Västerbjärs stage pottery (Lindqvist and Possnert 1997:33). However, radiocarbon dates from Pitted Ware sites on Gotland (Papmehl-Dufay 2006:114) demonstrate that graves from the Västerbjers stage, interpreted as MNB by Lindquist and Possnert (1997), are actually contemporary with the Hemmor/Gullrum stage, interpreted by them as from MNA.

Further, several studies of Pitted Ware ceramics support the view that variability in Säter/Fagervik pottery styles may be related to vessel function (i.e. utilitarian, special function) and are not as chronologically defined as Lindqvist and Possnert (1997) suggest (e.g. Löfstrand 1974; Segerberg et al. 1991; Glørstad 1996; Kjellberg and Ytterberg 1996). In the future, the detailed intra-site analysis of fauna and ceramic remains should help to clarify this issue. Such a study was started at the Hemmor site in 1991, but heavy disruption of the site by ploughing meant that fine-grained faunal data could not be recovered (Hedemark et al. 2000).

At the intensively examined site of Ajvide (Lindqvist 1997; Lindqvist and Possnert 1997; Storå 2001; Burenhult 2002), significant variation in the distribution of faunal remains has been recorded, and is unlikely to be due solely to chronological factors,

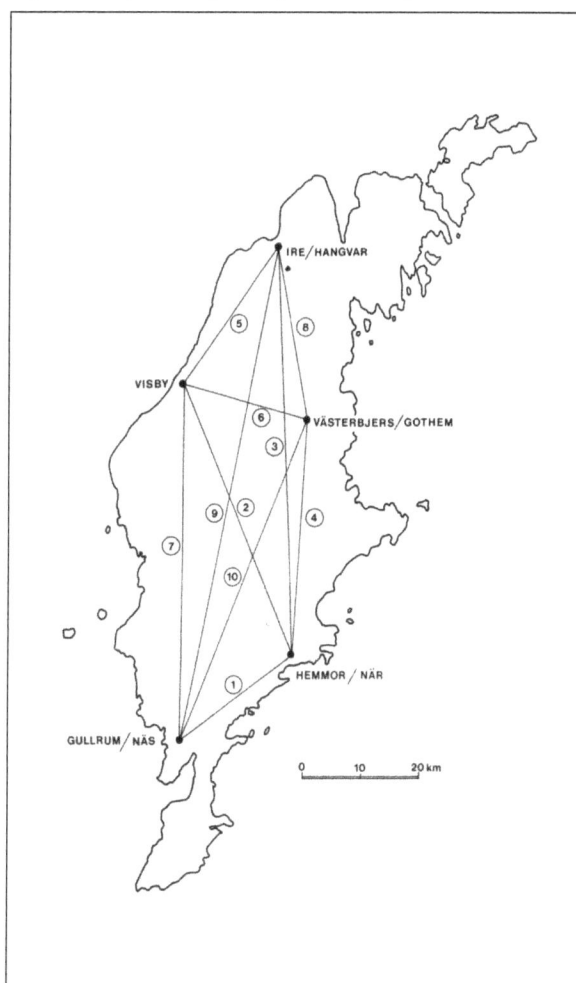

Figure 4. Analysis of the association between fauna from five Pitted Ware sites.

although some change in animal use over time is apparent. As mentioned previously, Ajvide shows a shift from seal and sea-mammal hunting early on, to an increasing reliance on domesticated animals. A similar trend is also apparent at Hemmor, which has large amounts of fish bone in the basal levels of the site compared with the upper levels. As there is no stratigraphic evidence for a Litorina (brackish) transgression at Hemmor that would impact the range and abundance of marine species, it has been argued that there was a subsistence shift during occupation of the site (Wallin and Martinsson-Wallin 1992, 1993; Hedemark *et al*. 2000).

From an environmental perspective, some locations on Gotland were clearly more attractive for seals and fish, and Pitted Ware sites in such places might be expected to contain a greater proportion of marine foods (Storå 2001:7). Studies of seal and pig remains from Ajvide suggest resource scheduling, with pigs slaughtered from early autumn to mid-winter and seals (especially harp seals) hunted in late autumn and early winter (Rowley-Conway and Storå 1997). Gotland Island comprises a relatively small land area within the same climate zone, and Pitted Ware sites were all situated on the sea shore. Ethnohistorical accounts of Gotland suggest that seal hunting could be carried out all around the Gotland coast and on the nearby smaller islands (Säve 1867; Lithberg 1914:118; Linnaeus 1977; Wallin and Sten 2007). However, there is a marked environmental difference on Gotland, which has a high coast on the west and northwest, which may have reduced the amount of marine resources able to be taken in these areas.

The possibility that environmental variation is the cause of faunal variation needs to be investigated further, but the suggestion of Lindqvist and Possnert (1997:34) that winters would have been more severe in the north of Gotland, and that pigs could not cope with the cold conditions does not appear to be likely. Lindqvist and Possnert (1997) also remark that pig bones do not occur in Neolithic sites on Åland Islands further to the north in the Baltic Sea (Figure 1). Recent excavations at the Pitted Ware site of Jettböle on Åland and the analysis of archaeofauna from other Pitted Ware sites in the region demonstrate the presence of pig and other domesticated animals (Storå 2000). Analysis of diet from the study of human remains from Västerbjers and Öland indicates significant variation in subsistence during the Middle Neolithic, consistent with a mixed marine-hunting-farming subsistence economy (Eriksson 2004; Papmehl-Dufay 2006). Overall, while Pitted Ware groups emphasised marine foods, it is clear that domestic animals and vegetable foods were also being utilised.

Animals with special meaning

In modern and traditional societies the death and burial of an individual is a significant event for a community (Van Gennep 1981). The occurrence of entire-animal burials and parts of animals in Pitted Ware graves suggests these animals had special meaning to the people who carried out the burial ceremony. Using information from traditional cultures, Van Gennep (1981) and Turner (1969) describe death as a dangerous liminal stage where different rituals are used to secure the spirit of the dead and to make sure that it travels to the right place. Animal remains are often associated with death activity, sacrificed to guide/accompany the spirit of the dead, used for feasting, and because particular animals are significant in a community belief system, and symbolise clan/group affiliation. They are also associated with magic and the transformation from human to animal and animal to human, as well as creatures that are part-human and part-animal. These beliefs might be represented in a clay figurine found at the Pitted Ware site of Jettböle on Åland that appears to depict a human with a bird's head (Figure 5). The most common animal remains found in Pitted Ware graves are the remains of pigs (particularly tusks, mandibles and trotters), beaver (incisors), hedgehog (mandibles and spines), seals (teeth), sea bird (long bones), deer (antler), and teeth from cattle and other domestic mammals (Janzon

1974). A common association is to have teeth and mandibles from the locally available seal and pig, and teeth and antler from animals foreign to Gotland, such as the beaver and elk. Many of the artefacts found in the graves, like harpoons and awls, are commonly made from pig bone.

It is worth considering that the type and age of animals associated with Pitted Ware burials might be related to the status of an individual, but the faunal remains could also signify the group/clan affiliation of an individual (Wallin and Eriksson 1985:16). Thus, differences in the bone remains from five Pitted Ware sites might reflect the community belief system, particularly the use of animals as group identifiers and symbols. In traditional societies it is common for animals to be seen as spiritual beings and ancestors of clan groups (Lévi-Strauss 1971). The relationship uniting the clan members and their totemic symbol is usually genealogically based, and is defined by complicated taboo regulations, including the use of particular animals in ritual and subsistence activity (Lauriston Sharp 1943:66–71; Lévi-Strauss 1969:56).

Group identity and invisible borders

Within any community, there exists unifying and dividing symbols that create borders and define social groups (Cohen 1992:12). Such borders are for the most part 'invisible' to archaeology, but by recognising that even quite similar groups were often distinguished from one another by their association with particular animals or plants, we can interrogate the faunal record for evidence of symbolic identity. Borders and divisions among groups or individuals are linked to symbols that express an individual's religion, status, gender and overall cultural identity (Cohen 1992:14).

Cohen (1992:19) described these cultural 'badges' thus: 'symbols of community are mental constructs: they provide people with the means to make meaning.' Using analogies from traditional societies, it is suggested that Neolithic societies were probably organised as tribes. The smallest unit within the tribe was probably the household, arranged as an extended family based on kinship. Several such groups probably formed a lineage group, which coalesced from a connection to a common ancestor. Several such lineage groups would comprise a clan, and while different lineages could claim they all were related, the relationship was not always clear because genealogical connections could be manipulated to strengthen ties to popular and strong clans.

The common ancestor might well have taken a mythological form, or been linked to a totem animal or plant. A number of clans probably made up a tribe that held a common territory (Sahlins 1968; Keesing 1981:227). Based on differences in the archaeofauna and consideration of the human

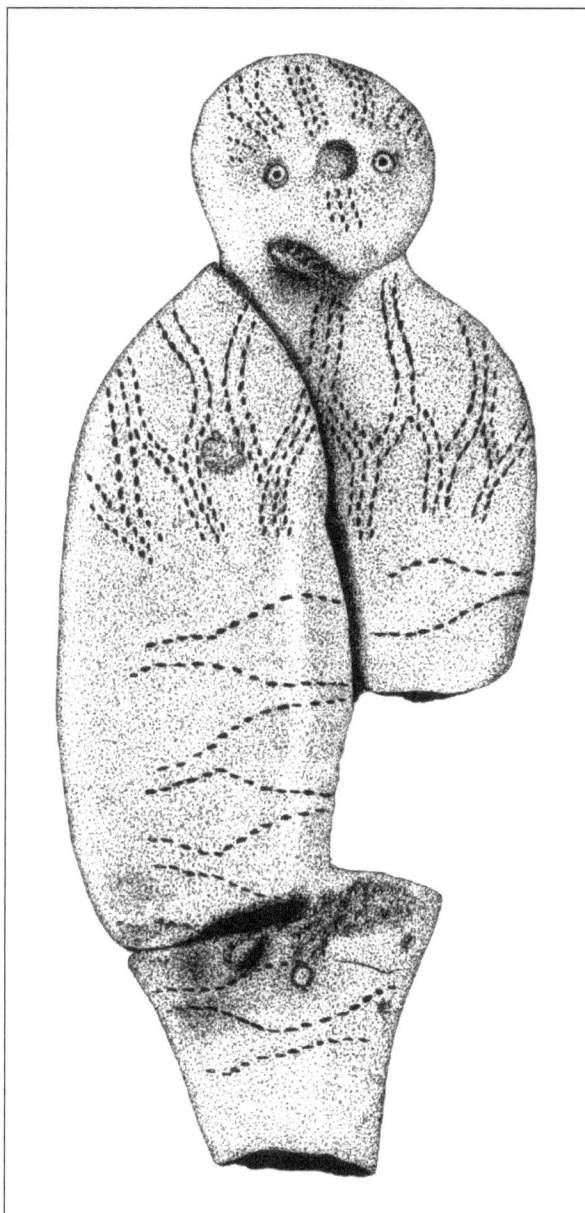

Figure 5. The Jettböle idol (drawing by Sven Österholm).

skeletal remains and grave goods, an interpretation suggested here is that Gotland was divided into three major clan groups making up a Pitted Ware 'Gotland tribe'. There are notable differences in the composition of the faunal remains between Pitted Ware sites on the east and the west of Gotland, and there are also substantial differences between the faunal assemblage from Ire in the north and those of all other sites.

The difference between Hemmor/Västerbjers on the east of Gotland and Ire in the north might be explained by the hunting and consumption of seals and the avoidance of pigs at Ire. This contrasts with Hemmor/Västerbjers, where the consumption of pigs was favoured and seal consumption was avoided or restricted. At Visby and Gullrum on the west of Gotland, pigs and seals do not seem to have been viewed in a particular way, and other animals or plants might have been of greater ritual importance. The size and borders of clan areas were probably established using natural borders such as lakes and streams, and the location of neighbouring sites was probably also taken into consideration. A hypothetical division of clans and lineage groups based on faunal differences and the natural environment is given in Figure 6. The hypothesis outlined above from the differences identified in assemblages of faunal remains can be tested by additional isotope study of human bone from Pitted Ware sites, along with further chronological examination of Pitted Ware sites and a detailed intra-site analysis of faunal remains.

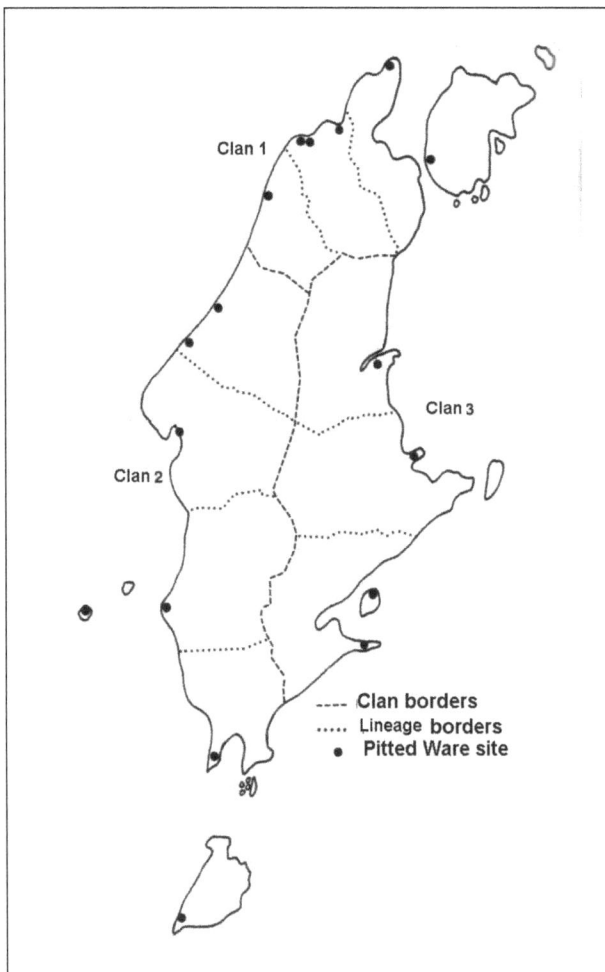

Figure 6. Hypothetical division of territorial units on Gotland during Middle Neolithic times based on differences in the faunal assemblages and natural landscape divisions.

Conclusion

This paper identified significant differences among faunal remains from five Pitted Ware sites on Gotland. Differences in the fauna occur between sites on the east and west of the island as well as with the north of Gotland. These differences have also been noted in the study of human skeletal remains and are manifest in the grave goods found at some sites. Chronological and environmental variations have been reviewed, but such factors do not appear to account for all of the inter-site variability. How various Pitted Ware groups on Gotland might have viewed and incorporated different animals as symbols of community identity was also explored.

Various animals or parts of animals were intentionally buried with Pitted Ware dead. Since the inclusion of animal or animal parts in graves results from community activity, it shows that different animals had a particular status and role within a community group. An analysis of discrete skeletal traits and evidence for diet variability found in isotope studies of human remains is also consistent with inter-site variability. Taken together with natural landscape divisions, the evidence suggests the possibility of a Gotland Pitted Ware tribe consisting of three clan groups: one in the east, one in the west and one in the north. Each clan group is suggested to have been tied to a specific totem animal, which for the north clan may have been the pig, and for the east clan, the seal (the harp seal?). As mentioned previously, archaeology is often ill-equipped to identify how prehistoric social boundaries were constructed and maintained by symbols and behavioural restrictions. One common method of doing this among traditional societies is the use of animals in death rituals, feasting and subsistence. In the future, studies of archaeofauna might profit from a broader perspective that considers the social relationships between animals and people in the past.

Acknowledgements

This paper is based on analyses carried out in collaboration with Dr Paul Wallin in the early 1990s. I am most grateful to Paul that he has allowed me to use the data and for his support and discussions on Pitted Ware issues over the years. I also express my great appreciation for the support given to me by my good friend and colleague the late Dr. Inger Österholm and her husband Fil.Lic Sven Österholm, who both have been dedicated to the research on the Gotland Neolithic, and have at the same time introduced international perspectives and views gained from experimental archaeology.

References

Burenhult, G. (ed) 1997. Remote Sensing, vol. I. *Theses and Papers in North-European Archaeology* 13:a. Stockholm: Stockholm University.
Burenhult, G. (ed) 2002. Remote Sensing, vol. II. *Theses and Papers in North-European Archaeology* 13:a. Stockholm: Stockholm University.
Cohen, A. 1992. *The Symbolic Construction of Community*. London: Routledge.
Ekman J. 1974. Djurbensmaterialet från Stenålderslokalen Ire, Hangvar Sn. Gotland. In G. Janzon (ed.), *Gotlands Mellanneolitiska Gravar*, pp. 212–246. Studies in North-European Archaeology 6. Stockholm, Almqvist and Wiksell Stockholm.
Eriksson, G. 2003b. Part time farmers or hard-core sealers? Västerbjers studied by stable isotope analysis. *Journal of Anthropological Archaeology* 23:135–162.

Glørstad H. 1996. *Neolitiske Smuler. Små teoretiske og praktiske bidrag til debatten om neolitisk keramik og kronologi i Sør-Norge.* Varia 33. Oslo: Universitetets Oldsaksamling

Hedell, L. 1921. *Osteologisk analys från Hemmor, När Sn,* Gotland. Unpublished report, Stockholm,Vitterhetsakademin.

Hegert, A. 1982. *Osteologisk analys av djurbensmaterial från stenåldersboplatsen Ire på Gotland.* Unpublished thesis, Osteologi II. Osteologiska forskningslaboratoriet. Stockholms universitet, Solna.

Hedemark, Å., C. Samuelsson and N. Ytterberg 2000. Stenåldersboplatsen vid Hemmor i ny belysning. *Gotländskt arkiv* (2000):7–28.

Hodder, I. 1990. *The Domestication of Europe.* Cambridge: Blackwell.

Janzon, G. 1974. *Gotlands mellanneolitiska gravar.* Studies in North-European Archaeology 6.

Keesing, R.M. 1981. *Cultural Anthropology. A Contemporary Perspective.* New York: Rinehart and Winstone.

Kjellberg A. and N. Ytterberg 1996. *Analys av Gropkeramik.* Unpublished report, Department of Archaeology, Uppsala University.

Landin, M. 1981. *Osteologiska bestämningar av materialet från stenåldersboplatsen Ire på Gotland.* Unpublished thesis in Osteologi II. Osteologiska forskningslaboratioriet, Stockholms universitet, Solna.

Lauriston S.R. 1943. Notes on Northeast Australian Totemism. *Studies in the Anthropology of Oceania and Asia 1943.* Papers of the Peabody Museum of American Archaeology and Ethnology, Volume XX.

Lévi-Strauss, C. 1962. *La Pensée sauvage.* Paris: Plon.

Lévi-Strauss, C. 1963. *Totemism.* Boston: Beacon Press.

Lindqvist, C. 1997a. About the importance of fine-mesh sieving, stratigraphical and spatial studies for interpretation of faunal remains at Ajvide, Eksta parish, and other Neolithic dwelling sites on Gotland. In G. Burenhult (ed), Remote Sensing, vol. 1. *Theses and Papers in North-European Archaeology* 13:a:91–111. Stockholm, Stockholm University.

Lindqvist, C. and G. Possnert. 1997b. The subsistence economy and diet at Jakobs/Akvide, Eksta parish and other prehistoric dwellings and burial sites on Gotland in a long-term perspective. In G. Burenhult (ed), Remote Sensing, vol. 1. *Theses and Papers in North-European Archaeology* 13:a:29–90. Stockholm University.

Lindqvist, C. and G. Possnert. 1999. The First Seal hunter Families on Gotland, on the Mesolitich Occupation in the Stora Förvar Cave. *Current Swedish Archaeology* 7:65–87.

Linnaeus, C. 1977. *Öländska och gotländska resa förrättad år 1741.* London: Wahlström and Widstrand.

Lithberg, N. 1914. *Gotlands stenålder.* Stockholm: Jacob Bagges Söners AB.

Löfstrand, L. 1974. *Yngre stenålders kustboplatser. Undersökningar vid Äs och studier i den gropkeramiska kulturens kronologi ich ekologi.* AUN 1. Uppsala.

Martinsson, H. 1986. Ålands stenålder. kronologi, komparativa studier samt försök till en bosättningsmodell. Unpublished BA thesis, Stockholm University.

Nihlén J. 1927. Gotlands stenåldersboplatser. *Kungl. Vitterhets Historie och Antikvitetsakademiens Handlingar* 36:3.

Österholm, I. 1989. *Bosättningsmönster på Gotland under stenåldern.* En analys av fysisk miljö, ekonomi och social struktur. Theses and Papers in Archaeology 3. Visby: Gotland University.

Österholm, I. 1999. Stenåldern på Gotland. In G. Burenhult (ed), *Arkeologi i Norden* 1, pp. 340–341. Stockholm: Natur och kultur.

Papmehl-Dufay. L. 2006. *Shaping an identity. Pitted Ware pottery and potters in southeast Sweden.* Theses and papers in Scientific Archaeology. Stockholm: Stockholm Univeristy.

Possnert, G. 2002. Stable and radiometric carbon results from Ajvide. In G. Burenhult (ed), Remote Sensing, vol. 1. *Theses and Papers in North-European Archaeology* 13:a:169–172. Stockholm: Stockholm University.

Rowley-Conway, P. 1983. Sedentary hunters: the Ertebølle example. In G. Bailey (ed), *Hunter gatherers in prehistory. A European perspective,* pp. 111.126. New York: Cambridge University.

Rowley-Conway, P. and J. Storå 1997. Pitted Ware seals and pigs from Ajvide, Gotland: Methods of study and first results. In G. Burenhult (ed), Remote Sensing, vol. 1. *Theses and Papers in North-European Archaeology* 13:a:113–125. Stockholm: Stockholm University.

Sahlins, M. 1968. *Tribesmen*. New Jersey: Engelwood Cliffs, Prentice-Hall, Inc.

Segerberg, A., G. Possnert, B. Arrenius and K. Lidén 1991. Ceramic chronology in view of 14C datings. *Laborativ arkeologi* 5:83–91.

Sjøvold, T. 1974. Some Aspects of Physical Anthropology on Gotland During Middle Neolithic Times. In G. Janzon (ed), *Gotlands mellanneolitiska gravar*. Stockholm, Studies in North-European Archaeology 6.

Stenberger, M., E. Dahr und H. Munthe 1943. *Das Grabfeld von Västerbjers auf Gotland*. Stockholm: Kungl. Vitterh. Hist. och Anitkv. Akademien.

Storå, J. 2000. Sealing and animal husbandry in the Ålandic Middle and late Neolithic. *Fennoscandia archaeology* XVII:57–81.

Storå, J. 2001. Seal Hunting on Ajvide. A Taphonomic Study of Seal Remains from a Pitted Ware culture Site on Gotland. Reading Bones. Stone Age Hunters and Seals in the Baltic. *Stockholm Studies in Archaeology* 21.

Svensson, N.O. 1989. Late Weichselian and Early Holocene shore displacement in Central Baltic, based on stratigraphical and morphological records from Eastern Småland and Gotland, Sweden. *Lundqua Thesis* 25, Department of Quarternary Geology, Lund.

Turner, V. 1969. *The ritual process. Structure and Anti-structure*. Chicago: Aldine Publishing Company.

Van Gennep, A. 1981. *Les rites de passage. Etude systématique des rites*. Paris: Picard.

Wallin, P. and T. Eriksson 1985. *Osteologisk analys av djur- och människoben från stenåldersboplatsen i Visby på Gotland*. Uppsats för Osteologi II. Osteologiska forskningslaboratoriet, Stockholms universitet, Solna.

Wallin, P. and H. Martinsson-Wallin 1992. Studier kring gropkeramisk identitet på Gotland. *Gotländskt arkiv* (1992):7–26.

Wallin, P. and H. Martinsson-Wallin 1993. Lokalkorologiska studier eller mönster med mening. Provundersökning av den gropkeramiska boplatsen Hemmor, När sn., Gotland del 2. Unpublished report, Länstyrelsen på Gotland.

Wallin, P. and H. Martinsson-Wallin 1997. Osteological analysis of skeletal remains from a megalith grave at Ansarve, Tofta parish, Gotland. In G. Burenhult (ed), Remote Sensing, vol. 1. *Theses and Papers in North-European Archaeology* 13:a:23–28. Stockholm: Stockholm University.

Wallin, P and S. Sten 2007. Säljakten på Gotland. *Gotländskt arkiv* (2007):23–40.

Wyszomirska, B. 1984. Figurplastic och gravskick hos Nord och Nordösteuropas neolitiska fångstkultur. *Acta archeologica Lundensia* 18.

Zvelebil, M. and P. Rowley-Conway 1984. Transition to farming in northern Europe: a hunter-gatherer perspective. *Norwegian Archaeological Review* 17:104–128.

12

A cache of one-piece fishhooks from Pohara, Takaka, New Zealand

Janet Davidson

Honorary Research Associate, Museum of New Zealand Te Papa Tongarewa, New Zealand
Janet.Davidson@University-of-Ngakuta.ac.nz

Foss Leach

Honorary Research Associate, Museum of New Zealand Te Papa Tongarewa, New Zealand

Introduction

More than 40 years ago, Atholl Anderson carried out his first major archaeological fieldwork in Tasman Bay, in the northwest of the South Island (Anderson 1966). This paper describes an important cache of fishhooks found recently near Takaka in Mohua (Golden Bay), immediately to the west of Tasman Bay. We offer the paper to Atholl in recognition of his pioneering archaeological work in Te Tau Ihu (the top of the South Island) and his life-long commitment to the study and practice of fishing. In his MA thesis in geography, Atholl acknowledged the help of Don Millar, who provided him with unpublished information. We also acknowledge the generous assistance of Don Millar during our present study.

In July 2002, W. Butler, a resident of Takaka, discovered the fishhooks while he was preparing a new climbing route on a limestone cliff at Pohara (Figure 1). The limestone scarp is in coastal scrub about 15 m back from the inner edge of the roadway (Figure 2). The formation is part of the late Oligocene-early Miocene Takaka Limestone, which is usually less than 100 m thick and regarded as 'platform facies'; in other words, it formed on a stable platform and includes shallow-water bioclastic limestone with a muddy micaceous component (Rattenbury *et al.* 1998). The limestone is relatively pure. An average analysis has 90 percent $CaCO_3$, 2.5 percent SiO_2, 0.42 percent Al_2O_3, and 1.68 percent Fe_2O_3 (K. Miller pers comm.). Although this rocky headland extends down to sea level, the marine environment in the vicinity and elsewhere in Golden Bay is dominated by sandy shorelines and the marine faunas associated with these.

The fishhooks were on a ledge about 400 mm long and 200 mm deep, and were covered by about 25 mm of lime dust. The limestone in this vicinity is horizontally bedded with numerous crevices, ledges and blocks, and the ledge where the hooks were found was only 2.5 m above the ground. Above the ledge is a high overhang, representing a suitable challenge for rock climbers.

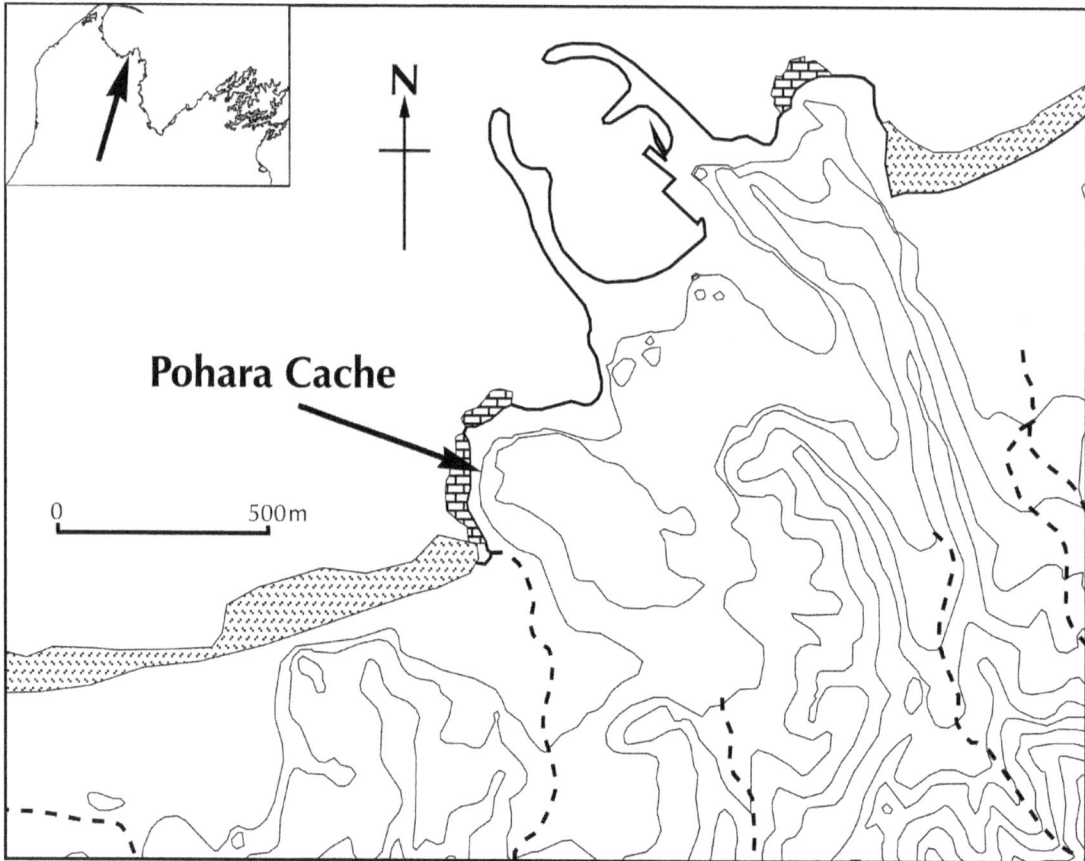

Figure 1. The Pohara fishhook cache was found on the eastern side of Mohua (Golden Bay) near Takaka.

Figure 2. The limestone bluff where the fishhook cache was found (courtesy of Steve Bagley).

There is no obvious evidence of midden or cooking debris at the base of the limestone cliff, but there is a substantial surface deposit of limestone that has eroded from the face, and there could be archaeological layers buried deeply below present ground level. The site number is N25/119.

Fifteen hooks were recovered and taken to the Nelson Provincial Museum. The Maori community at Takaka, Manawhenua ki Mohua, has taken an active interest in these hooks and a meeting was held at the museum to discuss their conservation and study. In April 2003, another meeting was held at the Onetahua marae at Pohara so more members of Manawhenua ki Mohua could see the hooks and decide what studies were appropriate. It was agreed a small fragment of the fibre should be taken for identification and radiocarbon dating.

Description of the hooks

The 15 hooks are beautifully finished and all are in an excellent state of preservation. Several have fragments of their original snood lashing.[1] The fibre is very fragile and powders easily. The fact that these fibres are still present is no doubt due to the extremely dry limestone dust covering them on the ledge. The fragments of cordage are shown in Figure 3. Hook 8 has parts of the original lashing close by in unravelled form. Hook 13 has a considerable quantity of the original lashing still present at the top of the shank, but again partly unravelled. Hook 14 also has unravelled cordage at the top of the shank. Finally, Hook 15 has loose loops of the original lashing around the top of the shank. In addition to these pieces of cordage that were still loosely attached to the hooks, there are several separate pieces, which can also be seen in Figure 3. One piece is above Hook 12, another is below Hook 5, and the largest piece is a small coil of line to the right of Hook 5.

The most notable feature of these fragments of cordage is that almost all are rectangular-sectioned pieces of unscutched strips of plant. The species has not been definitely identified yet. Rod Wallace, who examined the fibre under plain microscopy, is certain that it is not New Zealand flax (*Phormium tenax*). He suggests either pohuehue (*Muehlenbeckia* cf. *complexia*) or nikau (*Rhopalostylis sapida*). Scanning electron microscopy and micro-computed tomography by Catherine Smith and Debra Carr failed to identify the species. Goulding (1971) found very few references to fibre plants used for fishing gear. Strips of unscutched flax were commonly used by pre-European Maori for making fishing nets (Leach 2006:104ff.); a few accounts suggest that actual fishing lines were made of dressed flax fibres (Colenso 1875:265; Hiroa 1950:216; Best 1977:45). On most museum specimens of Maori bone and wooden fishhooks from the early European period, the snood lashing uses very fine fibre cordage, at least on the exterior. It is possible that in at least some cases, coarser lengths of unscutched strips are hidden inside this outer lashing. The snood lashing of the Pohara hooks appears rather crude, but this may not be so. These strips of untreated plant may have been deliberately chosen for use around the shank of the hook for extra strength, woven into the main two or three-ply cordage, and then covered with finer fibres.

Hook shape

The shape of the hooks is illustrated in Figure 4. All are close to U-shaped, with the point leg almost as long as the shank. The points of the hooks all curve downwards, in a form that appears similar to the barb on a European metal hook. Directly opposite the point in most cases there is a projection from the shank reminiscent of a shank barb on a European metal hook. When viewed together, these two projections, on the point leg and the shank, enclose a near symmetrical heart shape in the interior open space (see for example Figure 4 item 8). Entrance to this open space is smooth, rather like the entrance to an eel trap (hinaki), but once through the gap, there is little chance of escape. Of the four hooks without shank barbs, Hook 2 has a slight bulge and Hook 12 a slight protrusion on the inner side of the shank head, while in Hooks 3 and 6 the shank is smooth.

At the head or top of the shank leg there are projections that assist the binding of cord to the hook. These are rather variable in form.

Seven hooks have a small feature at the base of the U-shape. In Hooks 1, 2, 8 and 9, this takes the form of a simple notch. In Hooks 5, 12 and 14, there is a slight projection, rather than a notch. Some ethnographic specimens of Maori bone fishhooks with notches have fine lines attached. They are generally thought to have been used to tie bait on to the hook to prevent it coming off when fish bite it. The features on Hooks, 5, 12 and 14 could also have secured a bait string, as Hiroa (1957:327) suggested for a similar feature on some Hawaiian hooks. In one case (Hook 5), there are several notches towards the bottom of the point leg that might have served the same function. However, they might simply have been decorative features.

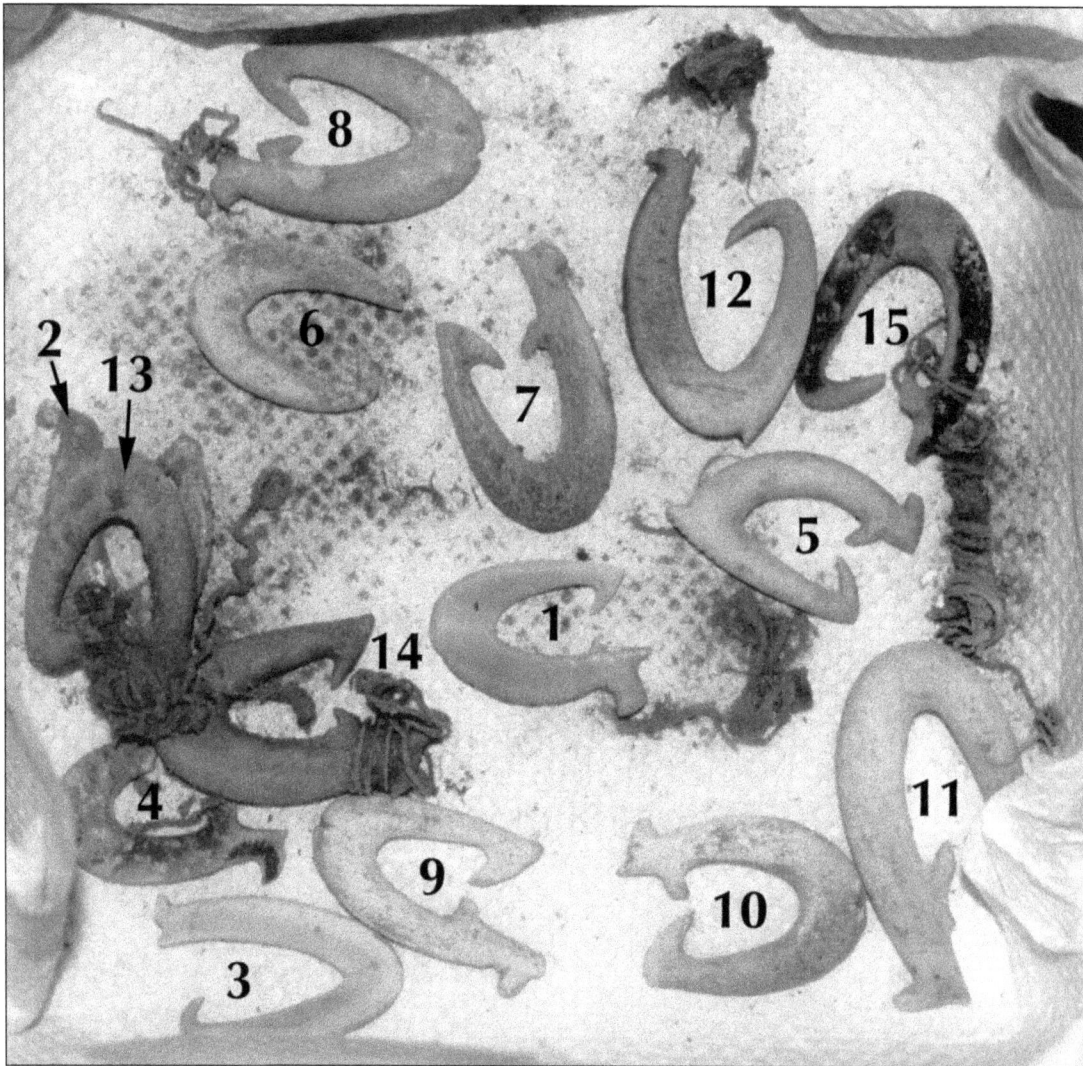

Figure 3. The hooks shortly after removal from the cleft, showing the remains of cordage (courtesy of Nelson Provincial Museum).

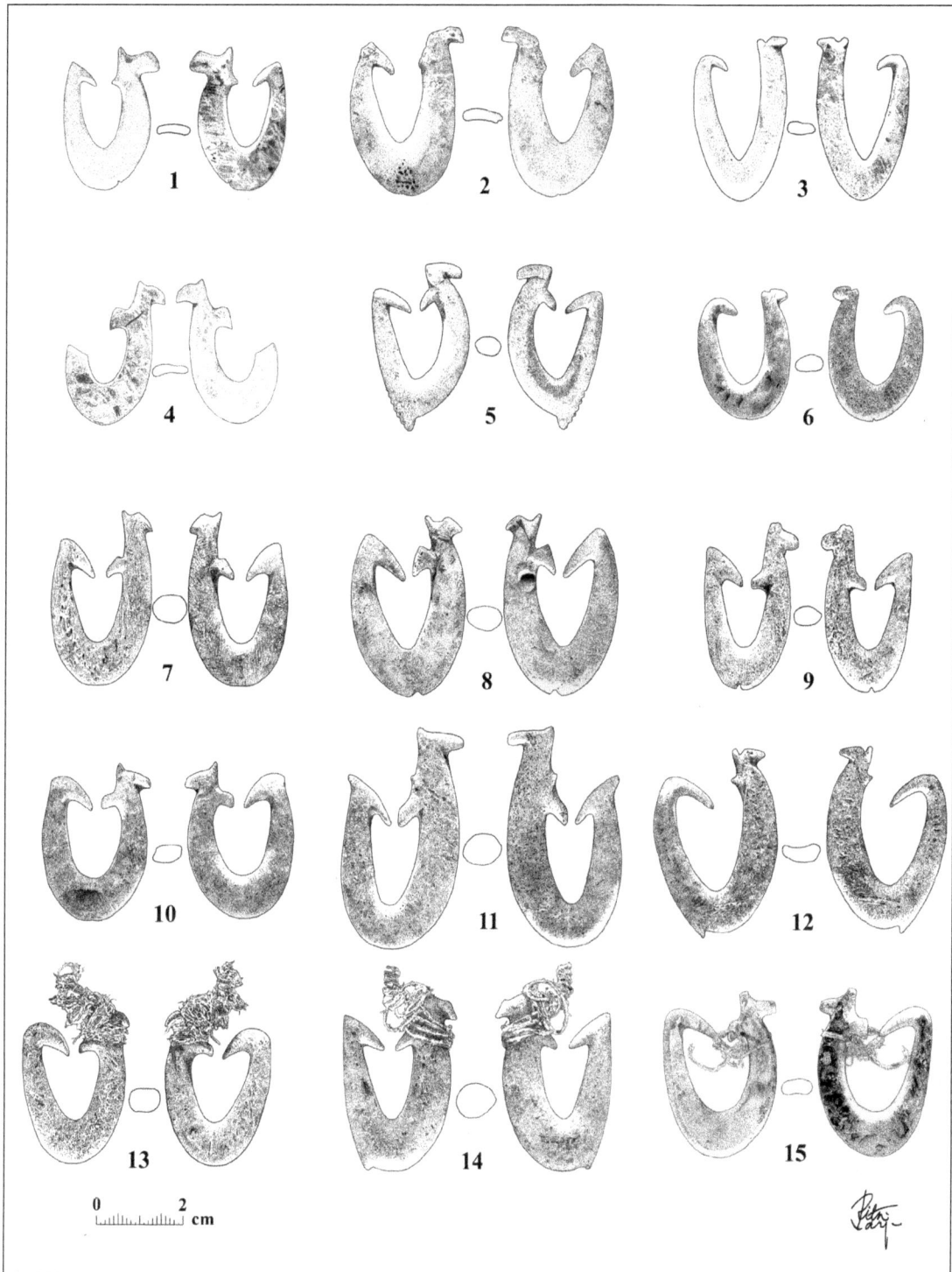

Figure 4. Details of the Pohara fishhooks (drawing by Rita Larje).

The point gap

A striking feature of many of these hooks is the small gap between the point and the shank. This is documented below (Table 1). Hook 4 has a broken point, so the gap could not be measured. The height measurement is the overall height in mm at right angles to the base of each specimen, and the gap is the distance in mm between the point and the shank.

Materials

Identifying the species of plants or animals used for making artefacts is always very difficult. Unfortunately, very little research has been done in New Zealand to characterise the most common organic materials that may have been used by pre-European Maori. This can involve the use of scanning electron microscope for minute detail, and/or elemental characterisation with X-ray fluorescence analysis, and/or molecular characterisation with techniques such as infra-red or Raman spectroscopy. In the absence of such background research, hand specimen identifications are little better than guesswork.

With considerable reservations, therefore, some possible identifications are made here of the materials used for these hooks (Table 2). These are based on observations with low power binocular microscope and comparison with identified specimens of materials. Sea mammal bone, for example, has quite diagnostic features, such as a porous trabecular framework, compared with human lamellar bone, which is very dense.

Table 1. Pohara fishhook measurements. Overall hook height (mm) and point gap (mm).

Hooks with no shank barb		
Hook #	Height	Gap
2	38.0	5.5
3	36.0	8.0
6	30.5	6.7
12	41.0	7.0

Hooks with shank barb		
Hook #	Height	Gap
1	32.0	3.0
4	34.0	—
5	36.0	2.0
7	40.0	2.9
8	40.0	2.0
9	38.0	2.0
10	36.0	2.3
11	50.0	1.9
13	34.7	2.5
14	40.0	2.7
15	37.1	2.6

Radiocarbon dating

A few of the loose threads were submitted for radiocarbon dating. These were teased apart and cleaned by washing in warm water, followed by consecutive treatments in hot solutions of acid, alkali, and acid. This ensured any limestone dust would be removed. The clean threads were then burnt in a sealed quartz tube at 900C, which converted all organic material to carbon dioxide gas. The gas was then purified and converted to graphite for measurement in an accelerator mass spectrometer. A small sample was used for determination of ^{13}C, which proved to be -27.2 percent, consistent with terrestrial plants. The conventional radiocarbon age NZA-19380 was calculated as 389±35 BP. This conventional radiocarbon age was converted to calendrical years using the IntCal04 atmospheric curve (Reimer *et al.* 2004) and OxCal software (v4.0.3 Bronk Ramsey (2007); r:5). This gave the following result (Figure 5).

68.2% probability
55.7%   AD 1447 to 1514
12.5%   AD 1600 to 1617
95.4% probability
63.9%   AD 1440 to 1525
31.5%   AD 1557 to 1632

It is unfortunate that there was a significant change in the level of ^{14}C in the atmosphere between AD 1450 and 1650, which is readily seen in the calibration graph in Figure

Table 2. Pohara fishhook material from low-power microscopic observation.

Hook #	Possible identification
1	Shell. This could be *Alcithoe* sp. or *Cookia* sp.
2	Shell. ?sp.
3	Shell. ?sp.
4	Shell. The specimen has nacreous layers interspersed with conchiolin, suggesting a shell such as *Hyridella* sp.
5	Bone. Very dense, ?sp., possibly *Homo sapiens*.
6	Bone. Probably either whale or seal.
7	Bone. Probably either whale or seal.
8	Bone. Very dense, ?sp., possibly *Homo sapiens*. Snooding fibres present.
9	Bone. Probably either whale or seal.
10	Bone. Probably either whale or seal.
11	Bone. Probably either whale or seal.
12	Bone. Very dense, ?sp., possibly *Homo sapiens* calvarium.
13	Bone. Probably either whale or seal. Snooding fibres present.
14	Bone. Very dense, ?sp., possibly *Homo sapiens*. Snooding fibres present.
15	Shell. With thick periostracum, ?sp. Snooding fibres present.

5. This is the cause of ambiguity in converting the radiocarbon years BP to calendrical years AD. There are two peaks, centred on AD 1465 and AD 1610. Even with the excellent standard error of ± 35 years for the CRA, this ambiguity is unable to be resolved and reveals a fundamental weakness in using radiocarbon dating for an important portion of the pre-European period of Maori history. It is hoped that in the future alternative methods, such as electron spin resonance dating, which do not have this inherent problem will find greater application in New Zealand. ESR spectra from minute samples of human bone and teeth have been successfully used to date events within the past 1000 years (Dennison *et al.* 1985, 1993; Whitehead *et al.* 1986; Dennison and Peake 1992).

Comparison with hooks elsewhere

Two forms of hook were recognised above: four hooks with in-turned points but no shank barb, and the remaining eleven hooks with shank barbs (all the complete ones also have in-turned points). Hook 1, which we have grouped with the shank-barbed hooks, has a less pronounced protrusion from the shank than the other hooks and might not be classed as shank-barbed by some archaeologists.

Plain unbarbed U-shaped hooks with in-turned points are an old Polynesian form, found in early archaeological sites in the Society and Marquesas Islands and throughout New Zealand, although they seem to have been particularly popular in Northland and Coromandel (Davidson 1984:66–68). There is considerable variation in the exact shape and in the way the head of the shank is modified to facilitate line attachment, but forms not unlike Hooks 3, 6 and 12 at Pohara can be seen among fishhooks in early sites from Northland to Otago (e.g. Hjarno 1967:59, 61; Furey 2002:59). Hook 2, with its rather clumsy-looking in-turned point, is less easily matched elsewhere. However, it is noteworthy that in all four of these Pohara hooks, the point turns

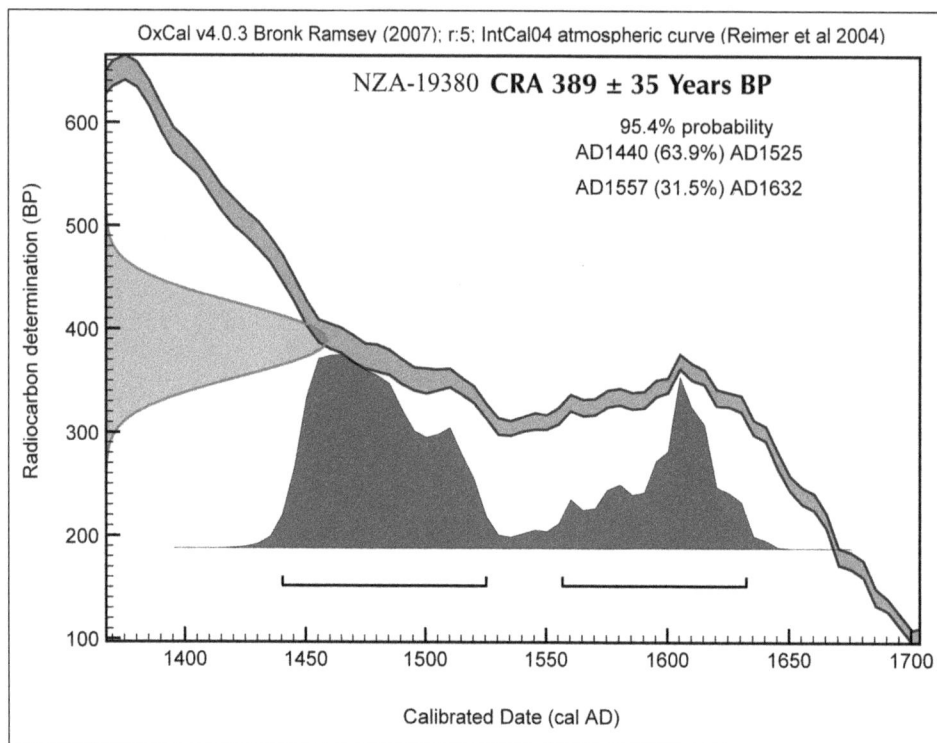

Figure 5. Calibration of the radiocarbon date for the Pohara fishhooks.

downwards far more markedly than in most examples from New Zealand. Downward-turned points do not seem to be present in early archaeological sites, but are occasionally found in later sites as far afield as Kaikoura and the Bay of Plenty (Davidson 1984:Fig. 49n, 50l). Such sharply down-turned points are also seen in some tropical Pacific examples.

Shank-barbed hooks have long been recognised as a distinct form in New Zealand. Skinner pointed to comparable examples from Hawai'i and Easter Island and suggested that shank-barbed hooks were an 'old Polynesian feature' (Skinner 1942:218). He made a distinction between hooks with a projection on the inner bend of the shank leg immediately below the snood lashing knob (similar to that seen in Pohara hooks 1 and 12), which he thought might have been intended to protect the snood lashing from friction, and 'small one-piece hooks made from human bone and common on the east coast of the North Island', in which this projection did seem designed 'to assist in hooking the fish' (ibid).

Trotter discussed shank-barbed hooks as a 'well marked variety of one-piece hooks' (Trotter 1956:245), describing examples from mainland New Zealand and comparing them with hooks from the Chatham Islands, Hawai'i, Easter Island and Japan. Crosby (1966:200, 221, Fig. 66) classified shank-barbed hooks as a 'Portland Type', which she described as mostly small, well-known ethnographically, and characterised by a gap of only 2 to 3 mm between barbs. Trotter and Crosby both reported occasional examples from Northland, Coromandel, Otago and Southland, but found that the main distribution was between Mahia Peninsula and Wellington, down the lower east coast of the North Island. Trotter (1956:251) correlated this distribution with Skinner's (1921) East Coast culture area.

The importance of shank-barbed hooks on the east coast of the North Island has been reinforced in several studies by Millar (nd, 1992, 1999) of well-localised private collections. Twenty-three complete examples from Portland Island (Millar 1992) are small (ranging from 24 mm to 30.5 mm long) and have gaps of no more than 2.75 mm between the barbs. Seventy-eight percent have bait notches, and 41 percent of a larger sample, including broken hooks, have serrations on the outer edge. This is the form of shank-barbed hook that is sometimes found in museum collections with snoods and lines still attached (Te Papa 2004:1, 300#10).

Shank-barbed hooks similar to those from Portland Island, described by Trotter, Crosby and Millar, were collected during James Cook's visits to New Zealand between 1769 and 1777. Several attributed to Cook's voyages are in Te Papa. Two shank-barbed hooks (Figure 6) are among 17 hooks now in the Georg August University of Göttingen (Hauser-Schäublin and Krüger 1998:300–302); they are serrated like many protohistoric hooks from New Zealand. The other 15 Göttingen hooks include an unbarbed one-piece shell hook with in-turned point, an unbarbed serrated bone hook with a small barb-like protrusion at the base of both point and shank, two different forms of trolling lure, and a variety of composite bait hooks with wooden shanks and bone points. These hooks were purchased from a London dealer, George Humphrey, in 1782 and derive from Cook's second and third voyages. The main locality for collecting Maori objects on these two voyages was Queen Charlotte Sound. Hooks were certainly collected there on June 1 and November 22 1773 (Forster 2000:125, 276) and probably on other occasions as well. Hooks were also acquired off the entrance to Wellington Harbour on November 2 (Forster 2000:268), near an area where elaborately notched shank-barbed hooks have been found (Beckett 1953). There were also opportunities for hooks to be acquired during trading just south of Cape Kidnappers on October 22 1773 (Forster 2000:265) and at Tolaga Bay in November (Beaglehole 1969:742).

The two shank-barbed hooks in Göttingen are 30 mm long and have narrow gaps of 1.5 mm and 2.3 mm. Both are serrated. Both the snoods and the lines are noticeably thick for such small hooks. The thin line near the top of the snood lashing in Figure 6A might at first glance be mistaken for a bait line coming from the snood lashing, but it is actually the terminal strands of the main line, twisted downwards. A similar example of untwisted loose strands is more clearly seen in the second hook (Figure 6B). A shank-barbed hook illustrated by Beasley (1928:Fig. XIIA) and Trotter (1956:Fig. 5) has a thin twisted cord attached to the snood lashing

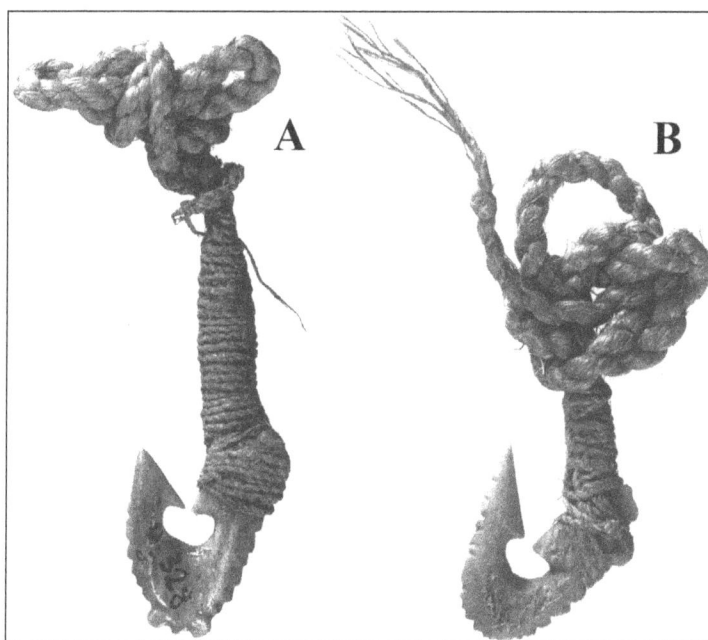

Figure 6. Two shank-barbed fishhooks collected during the visits of James Cook to New Zealand in AD 1773–1777, and now in the Institute of Cultural and Social Anthropology, Georg August University of Göttingen, catalogue numbers A: Oz 328, and B: Oz 329 (courtesy of Gundolf Krüger).

in addition to the main line. This appears to be a bait line. This arrangement is puzzling since the hook also has a bait notch in the bend. We know of no other ethnographic example with a similar ancillary line.

The Pohara shank-barbed hooks are somewhat larger than and differ in an important respect from the Göttingen and Te Papa examples and most of those illustrated by Trotter and Crosby. In all of the latter, the feature on the point leg is more like an inner barb, while in the Pohara hooks it is a distinctive down-turned point. The space in the centre of the hook is heart-shaped in the Pohara hooks, but not in the others. However, the Pohara hooks find a striking parallel in a recently described collection from Ocean Beach, just south of Hawkes Bay. The Hamish Gordon collection now in Lindisfarne College (Millar 1999) includes bone and shell shank-barbed hooks remarkably similar to those from Pohara, differing only in the presence of serrations on most of the bone ones (Figure 7). The collection also includes unbarbed hooks with in-turned points, although these are not as sharply down-turned as the Pohara ones. In this Ocean Beach collection, the feature on the point leg of the shank-barbed hooks is an in-turned point, not an inner barb. The Ocean Beach hooks are smaller than most of the Pohara hooks, ranging in length from about 28 mm to 34 mm.

Shank-barbed fishhooks from reliable archaeological contexts are extremely rare and none are well dated. There are single broken examples from Hot Water Beach and Opito on the Coromandel Peninsula, Pariwhakatau in Marlborough (Davidson 1984:fig. 50e–g) and Panau on Banks Peninsula (Jacomb 2000:67–68). Complete examples are reported from Oruarangi in the Hauraki Plains (Furey 1996:figs 339–340), Paremata near Wellington, and Murdering Beach in Otago (Davidson 1984:fig. 50h–j). The last two are thought to be of early 19th century age. The broken examples are plain; the others have serrations on the outer edges. Together, they probably date from middle pre-European to early post-contact times.

In summary, our review suggests the Pohara hooks represent a relatively early form of the shank-barbed hook in New Zealand, with down-turned point rather than inner-barbed point, lacking the serrations more common on later hooks, and being somewhat larger than the known

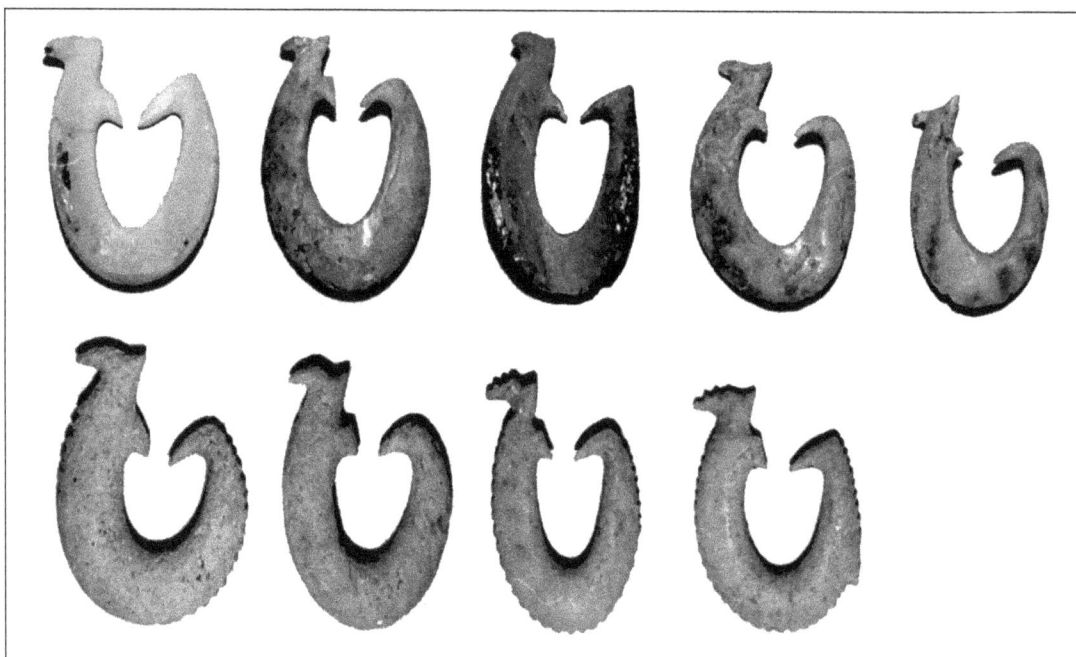

Figure 7. A selection of fishhooks from the Hamish Gordon Memorial Collection at Lindisfarne College (courtesy of Don Millar). Top row shell, bottom row bone.

Portland Island hooks and ethnographic examples. The similarities to some hooks from Ocean Beach are very striking and raise questions about connections between the two areas.

Form and function

Classifications of fishhooks in New Zealand and the Pacific have tended to focus on form, with less attention to function. Discussions of hanging baited hooks often distinguish between jabbing hooks and rotating hooks, which are thought to function differently. Nordhoff (1930:156) first described the action of rotating hooks used in still-fishing (rather than trolling) for albacore in the Society Islands. Reinman (1970:56) suggested particular types of hooks were intended to exploit particular environments and the fish that inhabit them. He emphasised the inter-relationship between structural variables (primarily the effect of material on form), functional variables (particularly how the hook is presented to the fish to maximise penetration and prevent escape) and ecological variables (such as fish size, behaviour and habitat). More recently, Allen (1996) endeavoured to distinguish stylistic and functional variables in East Polynesian hooks, and found that functional aspects of hook morphology are still poorly understood. Most studies, however, have concentrated on form without considering what kinds of fish were targeted and how the hooks actually captured and held them. The Pohara hooks, with their tiny gaps between point and shank, highlight these issues.

Previous writers have commented on the narrow gap between point and shank in Maori fishhooks in general, and in the shank-barbed hooks in particular (Trotter 1956:245; Crosby 1966:221). Anell (1955:107–108), in a wide-ranging review of fishing in Oceania, suggested Maori hooks with double inner barb (his term for shank-barbed hooks) might have been ornamental rather than functional, whereas Trotter (1956:246) considered they were mostly functional. It is possible the single known example in pounamu or greenstone (Oldman 2004:Plate 20 no. 97) was ornamental or ceremonial, because of the value of the raw material and its frequent use in ornaments, although in form it is identical to the many small bone examples attributed to the Portland Island area. Unfortunately, it is part of the Oldman Collection, repatriated to New Zealand in 1948, and its original provenance is unknown.

There is no reason to doubt that the Pohara hooks were functional. One of us (Leach 2006: 117–130) has considered the question of the function of Maori one-piece hooks in detail, drawing on studies of hook function in relation to fish behaviour in other parts of the world. It has been proposed that Maori hooks with narrow gaps were rotating hooks, which functioned in the following way (Figure 8):

> According to this theory the fish does the catching, not the fisherman. ... at A, the fish approaches the hook (bait not shown). Many fish are accustomed to eating extraneous matter, such as fragments of shell, with their food and a hook with no projection could easily be swallowed without discomfort (shown at B). If the line is tugged at this point, the hook would come out of the fish's mouth, but if left alone, the fish will swim away, carrying the line along its side (shown at C). The line will eventually become taut, and begin to pull the hook out of the fish's mouth. At first, the force on the hook is towards the front of the fish, but the instant the shank becomes clear of the mouth the direction of the force changes towards the rear of the fish, causing it to rotate rapidly. It will come to rest with the shank of the hook lying outside the jaw, and the point lying inside the jaw (shown at D). From this stage on the fish cannot escape. If the line is now tugged or the fish tries to change direction, the hook will rotate in the mouth, acting as a lever, and the point will penetrate behind the jawbone. In theory, to a certain extent, the narrower the gap between the shank and the point, the better. In addition, the hook rotates more effectively if the shank is the same length as the leg on which the point occurs. (Leach 2006:118–119)

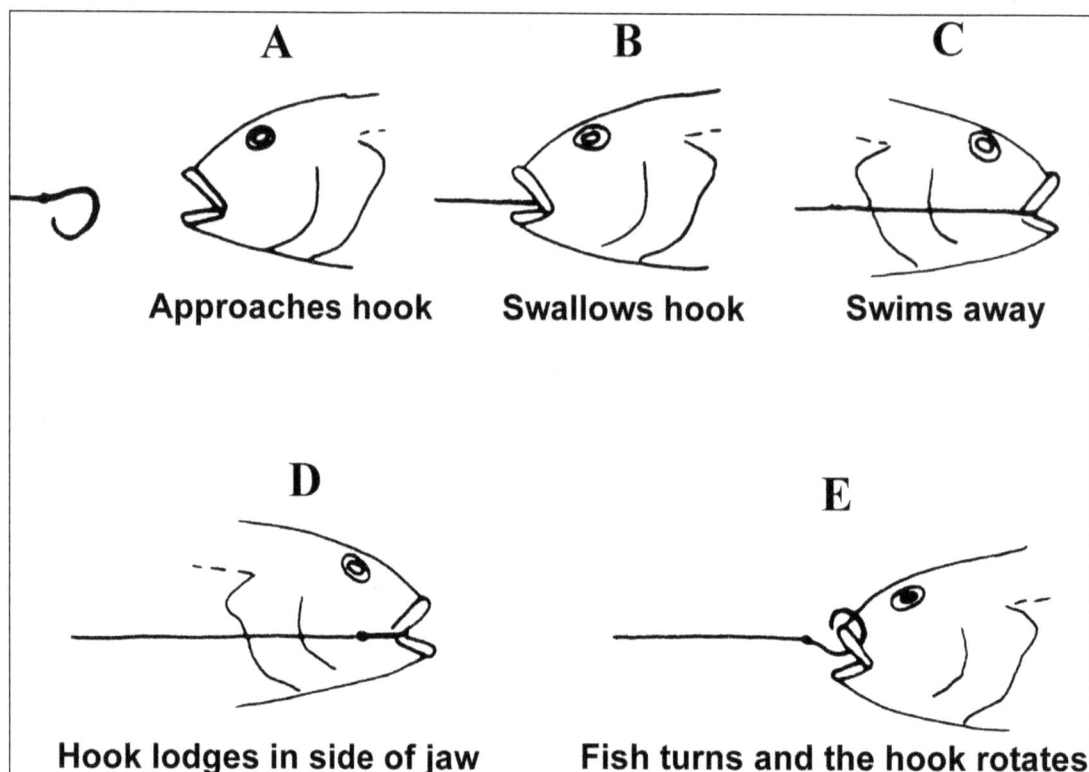

Figure 8. A theory of how the rotating hook might work (from Leach 2006:118).

It was stressed that this is a theory, which needs to be tested by observations of real fish, using replica hooks. But would this theory apply to shank-barbed hooks with tiny gaps, such as the Pohara hooks? Elsewhere in Polynesia, shank-barbed fishhooks are best documented from Hawai'i. Emory *et al.* (1959:42) found shank-barbed hooks in both early and late contexts in archaeological sites at South Point on the island of Hawai'i and classified them (without discussing the issue) as jabbing hooks. In Sinoto's revised classification of Hawaiian hooks, shank-barbed hooks are variously considered to be jabbing or rotating hooks, depending on whether or not the point is in-turned (Sinoto 1991:100). Although this is a functional classification, it is not based on any experimental or ethnographic evidence. In this respect, it is worth quoting comments on this subject by Elsdon Best as follows:

> The shape of native-made fish-hooks often surprises observers, in that the point is so close to the shank, but old natives have assured me that such hooks were the most effective, and decidedly superior to the wide-mouthed ones for taking certain fish (Best 1977:43). ... The somewhat slender hooks employed in taking albatross were much more open than most fish-hooks, and the shanks thereof were often adorned with finely executed carved designs (ibid:45).

Clearly, the size of the point gap was of considerable functional importance. The point gaps of the two hooks illustrated in Figure 6 are especially small, at only 1.5 mm and 2.3 mm, and the 10 Pohara specimens with shank-barb average a mere 2.39 mm, causing one to wonder what part of the fish anatomy could possibly pass through such a tiny entrance? One possibility is one of the bones in the gill arch of fish. The bones that make up the branchial arch, while flexible, are strongly held together and thin enough to pass through a narrow gap in a fishhook, such as those illustrated in Figures 4, 6 and 7. When fish identify non-food debris during feeding, they can spit this out either through the mouth or through the gill arch. Ejection of debris through the gill arch has been observed with snapper (*Pagrus auratus*) in aquaria (Larry Paul pers comm.

2007), and this species is one of the most common in Golden Bay. The particular elements in the branchial arch most likely to have been caught by such a hook passing out through the gill arch would be one of the long thin bones known as the epibranchial and ceratobranchial elements. European fishermen are used to baiting their hooks with the bait attached to the point leg. However, bait could be attached to the bait line at some distance below the hook, so that when the fish swallowed the bait, the small hook would remain unswallowed in the back of the throat. If the main line was slack, the hook could be ejected through the gill arch, and if the fish pulled against the line, the epibranchial or ceratobranchial could easily pass through the tiny gap in the hook and be inextricably captured. An interesting feature of a hook functioning in the manner described is that a very small hook could catch a very large fish, and in fact it would be an advantage for such a hook to be as small as possible. We might now look at the two hooks illustrated in Figure 6 with a somewhat different perspective. It will be observed that the snood lashing is very large and strong and seems out of character with the small size of the hook itself. The line attached to the hook is also very thick and strong, when we might have expected a delicate line for these small hooks. On the other hand, if these small hooks were really designed for capturing large, strong fish, these features would make a lot more sense.

The idea that these Pohaha shank-barbed hooks with such a narrow gap were designed for capturing large fish in the bones of the gill arch is only a hypothesis at the moment, but it certainly deserves testing. This would require making replicas, baiting them in various ways, and observing the behaviour of different species of fish using scuba equipment or in an aquarium.

One final point – all of these hooks with such a narrow gap, forged by the in-curved point and the shank barb and displaying this heart-shaped interior mentioned earlier, display a feature reminiscent of the 'non-return' principle present in numerous types of fishing equipment (Brandt 1984:166ff.). This occurs when there is a barrier with an in-curved entrance that permits fish to enter a trap but not exit. The principle is well known in many forms of Maori and Polynesian fishing technology, from eel traps (hinaki) to fish weirs. Thus characterised, the pre-European Maori fisherman might see these hooks as symbolically similar to other forms of fish trap.

Whatever the reality, the owner of the Pohara cache obviously believed that his fishhooks, made of various materials and with subtle variations in form, would catch fish.

The question of what species of fish these hooks might have been designed to catch, or been most effective in catching, is not easy to answer. At best, only very broad guidelines can be given. For example, one-piece baited hooks are quite effective in catching pelagic predators, such as kahawai (*Arripus trutta*) and barracouta (*Thyrsites atun*), which are instantly attracted to lures, although flashing red-coloured lures are more effective. Conversely, lure hooks are known to catch groper (*Polyprion oxygeneios*) and even stargazers (*Kathetostoma giganteum*) hugging the bottom. One possible clue to species caught by these hooks might be the common species in the vicinity of Pohara, such as snapper (*Pagrus auratus*) and seasonally abundant kahawai. However, this is a weak interpretation because the owner of the hooks may have used them primarily at a more distant rocky-shore location where blue cod (*Parapercis colias*) are abundant. Finally, the composition of nearby midden might be used to help interpret the species caught with such hooks. Unfortunately, this is also highly questionable, as detailed research on this matter with middens and large collections of hooks on small Pacific islands has shown (Leach and Davidson 1988; Davidson and Leach 1996). All these forms of indirect argument, from cause to effect and then back again, to help identify species from form are prone to such difficulties. It is more sensible simply to accept this problem and pay greater attention to interpretations that are on safer ground.

Discussion

A find such as the Pohara cache offers a unique glimpse into the past. It is almost certainly the collection of a single fisherman, who hid his hooks in a safe place, expecting to return and reclaim them, but failed to do so, for reasons we can never know.

The cache represents fishing gear last used by one person at one time and place. Wherever the fisherman lived, he probably last used his hooks in the eastern part of Mohua and expected to do so again. This goes some way towards meeting Reinman's ecological variable. We have already discussed the possible way these hooks functioned. Experiments with replicas may in future confirm how they functioned, and assist in understanding the fish targeted. In this case, the influence of material on form appears to be slight. Very similar forms could be rendered in more than one kind of shell and at least two different kinds of bone. This use of different materials may reflect the fisherman's beliefs about what was appropriate for different kinds of fish or different fishing conditions, or even the need to conform to ritual observance.

Archaeologists try to describe and classify fishhooks using assemblages consisting mostly of broken fragments of hooks that had probably been used by a variety of different fishermen over a period of uncertain duration. In the very large collection of 1016 hooks from Houhora in Northland, only 31 were intact (Furey 2002:56). Ethnographic collections are more likely to include complete hooks belonging to one person, or deriving from one time or place, but the contextual information is seldom good enough to be sure of this.

The Pohara hooks encompass variations in detail which could be mistaken by archaeologists for regional or chronological markers. There is a range in shape, from an almost V (Hook 3) to several perfect U-shapes. Most hooks are symmetrical, but Hook 5 is not. There are several different head types. The head is a favourite feature in archaeological classifications because it is variable (Sinoto 1962; Hjarno 1967; Allen 1996; Furey 2002). Allen (1996:113) suggests these variations are stylistic rather than functional and some variants, at least, may reflect ancestral relationships and patterns of interaction. The Pohara hooks provide a warning about attempting to interpret variations in head form. Any suggestion that such variations may be functional or stylistic features with regional or chronological meaning is fraught with problems.

Some of the Pohara hooks have 'bait notches' and others do not; on several, the bait notch is like a tiny non-functional barb. Only one has a small series of notches that could be a precursor to the more extensive notching seen on many shank-barbed hooks elsewhere. The single most defining feature of these hooks is the sharply down-turned point, which is present on all of them, although it is least pronounced on Hooks and 3 and 6. Unfortunately, points are very often missing from the hooks archaeologists usually have to deal with.

Nothing is known ethnographically about the making of fishhooks. Were there specialist makers or did most fishermen make their own? Are the Pohara hooks the work of one maker (either their owner, or a specialist from whom he obtained them), or are they the work of several different makers? In the latter case, the makers obviously would have shared a conviction that sharply down-turned points were effective.

The Pohara cache can be compared with another fisherman's kit found at Jackson Bay in Westland (Leach 2007). This consists of 38 bone points from composite hooks – 26 lure points and 12 points for composite bait hooks that would have had wooden shanks. These items are completely different in form from the Pohara hooks, and most of them are parts of trolling hooks, rather than hanging baited hooks. The Jackson Bay cache is also surprising in that it contains nine points of a form unknown in the South Island, and previously described from the site of Oruarangi in the Hauraki Plains of the North Island. Both of these caches, found on or towards the South Island west coast, seem to point to North Island connections. Maori oral histories give some insights into the web of interconnections between the islands.

The complex sequence of tribal occupation in Te Tau Ihu (the top of the South Island), including Mohua, has been reviewed in detail by Mitchell and Mitchell (2004:43–98), who describe movements into the area from both the east and west coasts of the North Island. At the time of Tasman's brief and unhappy visit to Mohua in AD 1642, Mohua was part of the region occupied by Ngati Tumatakokiri, a tribe said to have moved there from the central North Island via Whanganui (Mitchell and Mitchell 2004:74). Ngati Tumatakokiri was, however, a Kurahaupo tribe, a tribal ancestor Tumatakokiri being a son of Whatonga (Mitchell and Mitchell 2004:59). Kurahaupo tribes occupied much of the southern North Island, including Skinner's (1921) East Coast culture area, as well as moving progressively into the South Island. Connections and movements between the east coast of the North Island and the top of the South Island are well documented (e.g. O'Regan 1987). The similarity in fishhooks as far as apart as Mohua and Ocean Beach may not, therefore, be so surprising.

Conclusions

The Pohara cache is a unique collection of fishhooks, representing one man's kit at one point in time, and used at one particular place. Although the hooks show some variability in form, they are characterised by the sharply down-turned point of all examples and the narrow gap between point and shank, which is most marked in the 11 shank-barbed examples. How these hooks actually functioned remains unknown. Hypotheses on this issue can only be tested by direct observations using replicas.

The radiocarbon date places the hooks in the early to middle part of the pre-European sequence in New Zealand, earlier than the extensively serrated examples of shank-barbed hooks from Portland Island and other places, some of which are known to date to the 18th and early 19th centuries. There are striking similarities to one undated collection of hooks from Ocean Beach, just south of Hawkes Bay, although many of these carry the serrations which are present on the later examples from Portland Island and elsewhere, but not on the Pohara hooks.

The Pohara cache has probably doubled the number of known examples of shank-barbed hooks from secure contexts outside the previously known main distribution from Mahia to Wellington. This suggests how much remains to be learned about pre-European Maori fishhooks.

Endnote

1. The term 'snood' refers to the short line connecting the hook to the main line; 'snood lashing' refers to the attachment of the snood to the hook. Snood lashings on some Polynesian hooks were very complex (Hiroa 1957:339–341).

Acknowledgements

We are most grateful to Chris Hill and Manawhenua ki Mohua for the opportunity to study this important collection and for their interest and encouragement. We would also like to thank the Nelson Provincial Museum for access to the collection. Steve Bagley (Department of Conservation, Nelson) took the photographs of the site, and Rita Larje drew the hooks. Hamish Campbell (GNS Science) and Keith Miller (Holcim [New Zealand] Ltd) provided information on the limestone, and Larry Paul (formerly of NIWA) provided useful comments on fish behaviour in aquaria. The radiocarbon date was run free of charge for Mana Whenua ki Mohua by the Rafter Laboratory, GNS, through the good offices of Rodger Sparks. Rod Wallace (Auckland University) and Catherine Smith and Debra Carr (Otago University) examined the fibres. Gundolf Krüger (Georg August University of Göttingen) sent us measurements and photographs of the hooks in Göttingen. Last but not least, Don Millar (Honorary Curator of New Zealand Archaeology, Hawke's Bay Cultural Trust) shared his knowledge of Hawke's Bay collections of fishhooks, and was as helpful to us now as he was to Atholl Anderson more than 40 years ago.

References

Allen, M.S. 1996. Style and function in East Polynesian fish-hooks. *Antiquity* 70:97–116.

Anderson, A.J. 1966. Maori Occupation Sites in Back Beach Deposits around Tasman Bay. Unpublished MA thesis (Geography), University of Canterbury.

Anell, B. 1955. *Contribution to the History of Fishing in the Southern Seas*. Studia Ethnographica Upsaliensia IX.

Beaglehole, J.C. (ed) 1969. *The Voyage of the Resolution and Adventure 1772-1775*. Cambridge: Cambridge University Press for the Hakluyt Society.

Beasley, H.G. 1928. *Pacific Island Records: Fishhooks*. London: Seeley and Service.

Beckett, P. 1953. Two fish hook parts from a midden in Wellington. *Journal of the Polynesian Society* 62(2):196.

Best, E. 1977. *Fishing Methods and Devices of the Maori*. Dominion Museum Bulletin 12. Wellington: Government Printer [Repaginated reprint of 1929 edition].

Brandt, A. von. 1984. *Fish catching methods of the world*. Farnham: Fishing News Books.

Bronk Ramsey, C. 2007. Deposition models for chronological records. *Quaternary Science Reviews* (INTIMATE special issue). In press.

Colenso, W. 1875. On the geographic and economic botany of the North Island of New Zealand. *Transactions and Proceedings of the New Zealand Institute, 1868,* Vol. 1:233–283.

Crosby. E.B.V. 1966. Maori Fishing Gear: A study of the development of Maori fishing gear, particularly in the North Island. Unpublished MA thesis, Anthropology, University of Auckland.

Davidson, J.M. 1984 *The Prehistory of New Zealand*. Auckland: Longman Paul.

Davidson, J.M. and B.F. Leach 1996. Fishing on Nukuoro Atoll: Ethnographic and archaeological viewpoints. In M. Julien, M. Orliac, and C. Orliac (eds), *Mémoire de Pierre, Mémoire D'Homme: Tradition et Archéologie en Océanie. Hommage à José Garanger*, pp.184–202. Paris: Publication de la Sorbonne.

Dennison, K.J. and B.M. Peake 1992. ESR bone dating in New Zealand. Proceedings of the 6th International Specialist Seminar on Thermoluminescence and Electron Spin Resonance Dating. Clermond-Ferrand, France. 2–6 July, 1990. *Quaternary Science Reviews* 11:251–255.

Dennison, K.J., P. Houghton, B.F. Leach and B.M. Peake 1985. Sample preparation and instrumental aspects of EPR dating of New Zealand human bone. In M. Ikeya and T. Miki (eds), *ESR dating and dosimetry*, pp. 341–352. Tokyo: Ionics.

Dennison, K.J., A.D. Oduwole and K.D. Sales 1993. Some ESR observations on bone, tooth enamel and eggshell. Proceedings of the 3rd International Symposium on ESR Dosimetry and Applications. Gaithersburg, Maryland, 14–18 October, 1991. *Applied Radiation and Isotopes* 44:261–266.

Emory, K.P., W.J. Bonk, and Y.H. Sinoto 1959. *Hawaiian Archaeology: Fishhooks*. Bernice P. Bishop Museum Special Publication 1959, Honolulu, Bishop Museum Press.

Forster, G. 2004. *A Voyage Round the World*. 2 Vols. Edited by N. Thomas and O. Berghof. Honolulu: University of Hawai'i Press.

Furey, L. 1996. *Oruarangi: The Archaeology and Material Culture of a Hauraki Pa*. Auckland Institute and Museum Bulletin 17.

Furey, L. 2002. *Houhora: A Fourteenth Century Maori Village in Northland*. Auckland Museum Bulletin 19.

Goulding, J.H. 1971. Identification of archaeological and ethnological specimens of fibre-plant material used by the Maori. *Records of the Auckland Institute and Museum* 8:57–101.

Hauser-Schäublin, B. and G. Krüger (eds) 1998. *James Cook: Gifts and Treasures from the South Seas*. Munich and New York: Prestel.

Hiroa, Te Rangi (P.H. Buck) 1950. *The Coming of the Maori*. Wellington: Maori Purposes Fund Board.

Hiroa, Te Rangi (P.H. Buck) 1957. *Arts and Crafts of Hawaii*. Bernice P. Bishop Museum Special Publication 45. Honolulu: Bishop Museum Press.

Hjarno, J. 1967. Maori fish-hooks in southern New Zealand. *Records of the Otago Museum Anthropology* 3:1–63.

Jacomb, C. 2000. *Panau: The Archaeology of a Banks Peninsula Maori Village*. Canterbury Museum Bulletin 9.

Leach, F. 2006. *Fishing in Pre-European New Zealand*. New Zealand Journal of Archaeology Special Publication, Wellington.

Leach, F. 2007. A cache of fishhooks from Serendipity Cave, Jackson Bay, New Zealand. In A. Anderson, K. Green and F. Leach (eds), *Vastly Ingenious: The Archaeology of Pacific Material Culture*, pp. 79–95. Dunedin: Otago University Press.

Leach, B.F. and J.M. Davidson 1988. The quest for the rainbow runner: prehistoric fishing on Kapingamarangi and Nukuoro atolls, Micronesia. *Micronesica* 21 (1, 2):1–22.

Millar, D. 1992. Maori Artifacts from Waikawa Hawke's Bay. Unpublished report to the Hawke's Bay Museum.

Millar, D. 1999. Hamish Gordon Memorial Collection of Maori Artefacts – Lindisfarne College. Unpublished report, Hawke's Bay Cultural Trust.

Millar, D. nd. Taonga Waipuka. A Collection of Artefacts Mainly from Ocean Beach, Hawke's Bay. Unpublished report to Hawke's Bay Museum.

Mitchell, H. and Mitchell, J. 2004. *Te Tau Ihu o Te Waka. A History of Maori of Nelson and Marlborough. Volume 1. Te Tangata me Te Whenua - The People and the Land*. Wellington : Huia in association with Wakatu Incorporation.

Nordhoff, C. 1930. Notes on the off-shore fishing of the Society Islands. *Journal of the Polynesian Society* 39:137–173, 221–262, 380.

Oldman, W.O. 2004. *The Oldman Collection of Maori Artifacts*. Polynesian Society Memoir 14, Auckland.

O'Regan, S. 1987. Queen Charlotte Sound: Aspects of Maori traditional history. In G. Barrett (ed), *Queen Charlotte Sound, New Zealand: the Traditional and European Records, 1820*, pp. 139–158. Ottawa: Carleton University Press.

Rattenbury, M.S., R.A. Cooper and M.R. Johnston 1998. *Geology of the Nelson area*. Institute of Geological and Nuclear Sciences 1:250,000 Geological Map 9.

Reimer, P.J., *et al*. 2004. IntCal04 terrestrial radiocarbon age calibration, 0–26 cal kyr BP. *Radiocarbon* 46(3):1029–1058.

Reinman, F.M. 1970. Fishhook variability: Implications for the history and distribution of fishing gear in Oceania. In R.C. Green and M. Kelly (eds), *Studies in Oceanic Culture History Volume 1*, pp. 47–59. Pacific Anthropological Records 11. Department of Anthropology, Bernice P. Bishop Museum.

Sinoto, Y.H. 1962. Chronology of Hawaiian fishhooks. *Journal of the Polynesian Society* 71(2):162–166.

Sinoto, Y.H. 1991. A revised system for the classification and coding of Hawaiian fishhooks. *Bishop Museum Occasional Papers* 31:85–105.

Skinner, H.D. 1921. Culture areas in New Zealand. *Journal of the Polynesian Society* 30:70–78.

Skinner, H.D. 1942. A classification of the fish-hooks of Murihiku with notes on allied forms from other parts of Polynesia. *Journal of the Polynesian Society* 51(3):208–221, (4):256–286.

Te Papa 2004. *Icons Nga Taonga from the Museum of New Zealand Te Papa Tongarewa*. Wellington: Te Papa Press.

Trotter, M.M. 1956. Maori shank barbed fish-hooks. *Journal of the Polynesian Society* 65(3):245–252.

Whitehead, N.E., S.D. Devine and B.F. Leach 1986. Electron spin resonance dating of human teeth from the Namu burial ground, Taumako, Solomon Islands. *New Zealand Journal of Geology and Geophysics* 29:359–361.

13

Trans-oceanic transfer of bark-cloth technology from South China–Southeast Asia to Mesoamerica?

Judith Cameron

Department of Archaeology and Natural History, Australian National University, Australia

judith.cameron@anu.edu.au

Introduction

Scholars have long recognised the important role bark cloth plays in articulating status in Polynesian societies. In life (and death), Polynesian chiefs were traditionally presented (or shrouded) with copious quantities of bark cloth, the precise number of strips contingent on status. The considerable economic expenditure required to produce such large quantities reflects the significance of this item of material culture in its cultural context, as well as the importance of hierarchy in traditional Polynesian societies. Kleinschmidt's unforgettable drawing (Figure 1) of a Fijian chief wearing more than 180 m of tapa during a ceremony to mark the conclusion of 100 days of mourning for a paramount chief captures this symbolism dramatically.

It is therefore fitting that on his retirement, we honour our Polynesian colleague (archaeologist and chief) by symbolically presenting him with paper through this festschrift. From a technological perspective, bark cloth and paper are not markedly different, but they represent different stages of production. Both are produced by beating plant fibres; paper simply requires additional pounding and softening to completely macerate the fibres. Chinese historical documents indicate that bark-cloth production was abandoned in the early dynastic period when paper was invented; greater returns could be obtained from the processing of paper and clothing made from woven bast fibres (Shih Sheng-Han 1961). Elsewhere, I have demonstrated firm parallels between prehistoric bark-cloth beaters from Neolithic sites in southeast China and prehistoric bark-cloth beaters from mainland and Island Southeast Asian contexts (Cameron 2006). This chapter extends this typological reconstruction to Mesoamerica, which suggests the possibility of pre-Columbian contact long before bark-cloth technology diffused into the Pacific.

South China

The earliest archaeological evidence for bark-cloth production is from coastal Neolithic sites in the Pearl River delta region of southeast China (Figure 2). During the 1985 excavations,

Figure 1. Kleinschmidt's depiction of bark cloth worn by a chief of Viti Levu at a ceremony (from Kooijman 1972:436).

archaeologists from the Shenzhen Museum (1990, 1991) recovered 14 stone beaters in the basal layers of the site of Xiantouling. The first reports dated the site between c. 4500 and 3700 BC, but recent radiocarbon dates from the fifth season of excavations push the date back to 5000 BC (Shenzhen Museum 2007). The beaters were not isolated finds; the same tool types were recovered from an additional 10 archaeological sites in the region, including the site of Dahuangsha, which has a calibrated radiocarbon age of 4680–3870 BC (Chan Hing-Wah in Shenzhen Museum 1993:Table 1). Not only are the Xiantouling finds the earliest bark-cloth beaters in the archaeological record, they also form the largest assemblage of prehistoric beaters found at a single site. The concentration of early forms in this region is significant from an 'origin' perspective, since the coastal Neolithic of South China has long been linked to early population movements into Island Southeast Asia (Chang 1964, 1977; Bellwood 1979; Higham 2003).

All of the Neolithic stone beaters from the Pearl River sites are distinguished by longitudinal grooves (1–2 cm in depth) carved on their surfaces. Some have parallel rows of grooves, while others have grooves intersecting at right angles and a few feature intersecting diagonal grooves.

Southeast Asia

Stone bark-cloth beaters have been recovered from many Neolithic sites in mainland and Island Southeast Asia. Figure 3 provides a typology of the basic types. All but one of the eight different types have been identified in Island Southeast Asia. Because of geographic proximity, the parallels between the beaters from South China and those from Southeast Asia have previously been interpreted as evidence for diffusion from South China, rather than independent invention (Cameron 2006).

Type 1

Despite their obvious ambiguity, ungrooved beaters with smooth surfaces are classified as Type I beaters in the typology. Such basic forms have been recovered from Neolithic sites in South China (Ling 1962), Taiwan (Ling 1962) and Cambodia (Levy 1943). In Taiwan, they were immediately identified as bark-cloth beaters because of their ethnographic parallels, and it is very likely that this basic type was used more widely than generally recognised, and perhaps it was a multi-functional tool.

Type II

Regional differences are clearly discernible in Type II forms. Distinguished by horned protuberances, Type II beaters are confined to archaeological contexts in a small group of adjoining islands in Southeast Asia, such as Taiwan (Ling 1961), the Philippines (Beyer 1948) and Sulawesi (Stein Callenfels 1951), with surface finds from Borneo (Harrisson 1964). Most are devoid of surface grooves, although a horned version with deep longitudinal grooves on its upper face was excavated from Ampah in Borneo (van Heekeren 1972:125).

Type III

Modifications of the basic pounder form include Type III beaters, which are elongated oval pebbles with grooves carved on the upper surface. Type III beaters first appear in South China in the middle layers of Xiantouling, which is dated c. 2900–2200 BC. They occur slightly later at Yuanshan sites in Taiwan (Chang 1989), the Batanes Islands (Bellwood and Dizon 2005) and Sabah (Chia 1979), with a similar form found in Thailand (Evans 1930).

Type IV

Type IV beaters are distinguished by rows of parallel grooves extending over the entire surface of the tool face, and this form has a different distribution pattern. Not only does this type occur at Neolithic sites in the Pearl River region, it is also found on Hong Kong islands (Chiu and Ward 1979; Meacham 1994), Vietnam (Ha Van Tan 1980) and Sulawesi (Stein Callenfels 1951; van Heekeren 1972) as early as 3000 BC.

Type V

Type V beaters differ from other forms in one important respect; while their surfaces have the same grooves that distinguish other types, the stone is hafted so the handle is incorporated into the implement itself. These beaters have a different distribution. The earliest handled Type V beaters are from Vietnam (Colani 1933; Ha van Tan 1979), where they are known as *ban dap*; they also occur as surface finds in Sabah (Harrisson 1964:Plate XIII), the Philippines (Cameron In press) and Taiwan (Lien 1991). These appear to be prototypes for the handled wooden beaters widely used throughout Polynesia.

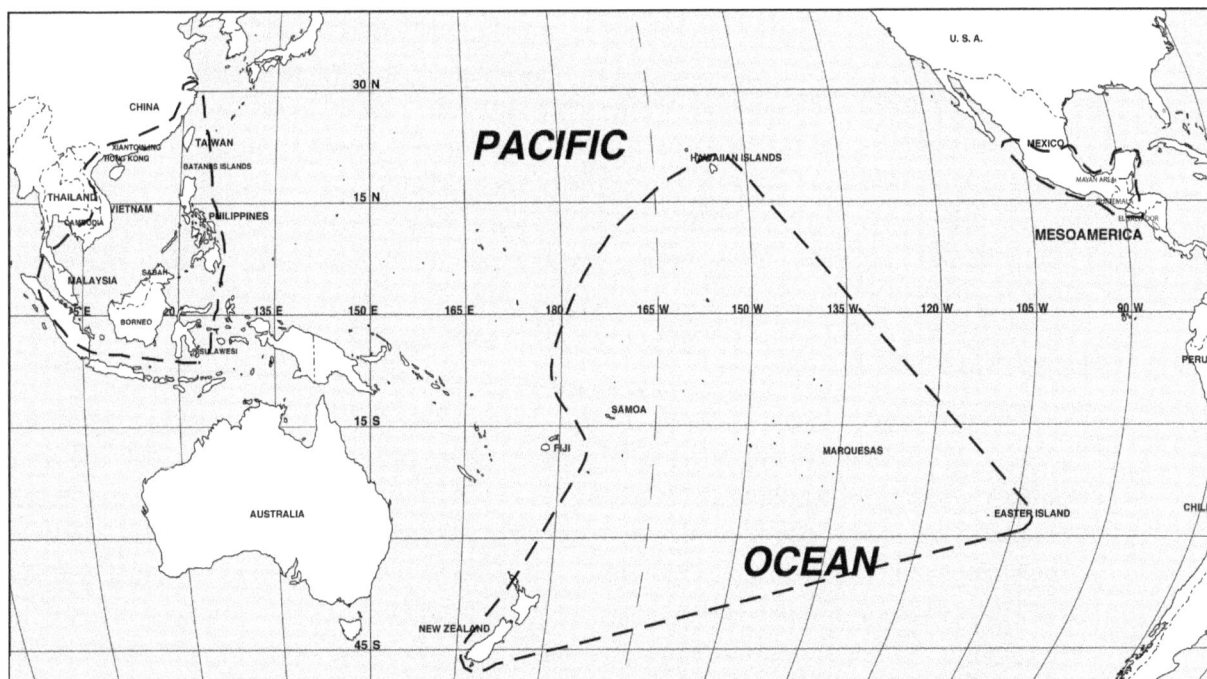

Figure 2. Location of Xiantouling and other early bark-cloth beater sites in Southeast China. Distribution of bark-cloth beaters in South China and Southeast Asia (left dotted line), Mesoamerica (right dotted line), and the Polynesian triangle (middle dotted line).

Type VI

A very different distribution pattern is discernible for the Type VI beaters, which differ from other forms in that they have three worked faces. This type first occurs at Neolithic sites in Vietnam, where they have been described as 'small blocks of parallel elliptic schist with parallel lines on two opposed lateral faces while a big line goes through other faces' (Ha Van Tan 1979:80). The Type VI beater would have been attached to a basketry handle; the hafted lateral surfaces ensure that the handle can be firmly fixed. Examples of the type have also been unearthed in Taiwan (Kano 1952:Plate 14) and the Philippines (Beyer 1948).

Type VII

Type VII beaters differ morphologically and functionally from other types. These beaters are effectively stone choppers with grooves on a rounded base. Known as the 'Malay type', they have been found in Thailand (Chiraporn Aranyanak 1991), Malaysia (Sieveking 1956) and the island of Borneo (Harrisson 1964).

Mesoamerica

More than 100 years ago, the German anthropologist Max Uhle (1889–90) recognised parallels between prehistoric Mexican and Mayan bark-cloth beaters and bark-cloth beaters used by contemporary groups in Sulawesi. As well as using the same types of beater, the Maya used similar fibres and production techniques for making tunics, ceremonial clothing, banners and codices. The earliest bark-cloth beaters in Mesoamerica come from sites in the Maya area and its periphery, particularly along the coasts of Guatemala and El Salvador, where they first appear about 2500 years ago (Tolstoy 1961, 1991). The technology then moved westwards and eastwards from the Maya homeland. Tolstoy has long maintained that the above-mentioned parallels are the result of pre-Columbian contact with Southeast Asia, but Tolstoy's proposition (and others based on different data sets) has been met with scepticism by archaeologists.

Tolstoy was not aware of the Chinese finds and we do not really know whether Tolstoy's proposition can be extended to the Southern Chinese Neolithic. Two of the beater types in the typology (Figure 3) are represented at Mesoamerican sites. The modifications of basic pounders (Type III beaters) first appear c. 2500 BC at Xiantouling (South China), then in Taiwan, the Philippines and Sabah. The elongated oval pebbles with grooves carved on the upper surface (Type IV) first appear in South China in the middle layers of Xiantouling that are dated 2900–2200 BC, then later in the Hong Kong islands, Fu Tei Wan (Meacham 1994:40) and Man Kok Tsui (Chui and Ward 1979:89), the Yuanshan layers in Taiwan (Chang 1989), Sabah (Chia 1997) and Sulawesi (Stein Callenfels 1951; van Heekeren 1972) as early as 3000 BC.

Discussion and conclusion

Typological reconstructions are based on the premise that similarities in artefact form are the result of a shared mental template. My earlier typological study demonstrated this with Southern Chinese and Southeast Asian bark-cloth beaters (Cameron 2006). For this reason, the unequivocal parallels between prehistoric bark-cloth beaters from China, Southeast Asia and Mesoamerica outlined in this paper could also be interpreted as evidence for shared origins. However, there are problems with such an interpretation. If bark-cloth technology diffused to Mesoamerica during the prehistoric period, where is the intermediate evidence? How do we explain the absence of stone bark-cloth beaters in archaeological (and ethnographic contexts) in Polynesia? Fragments of bark cloth have been excavated from archaeological sites in Tonga (Davidson 1969) and French Polynesia (Suggs 1961), but stone bark-cloth beaters have not

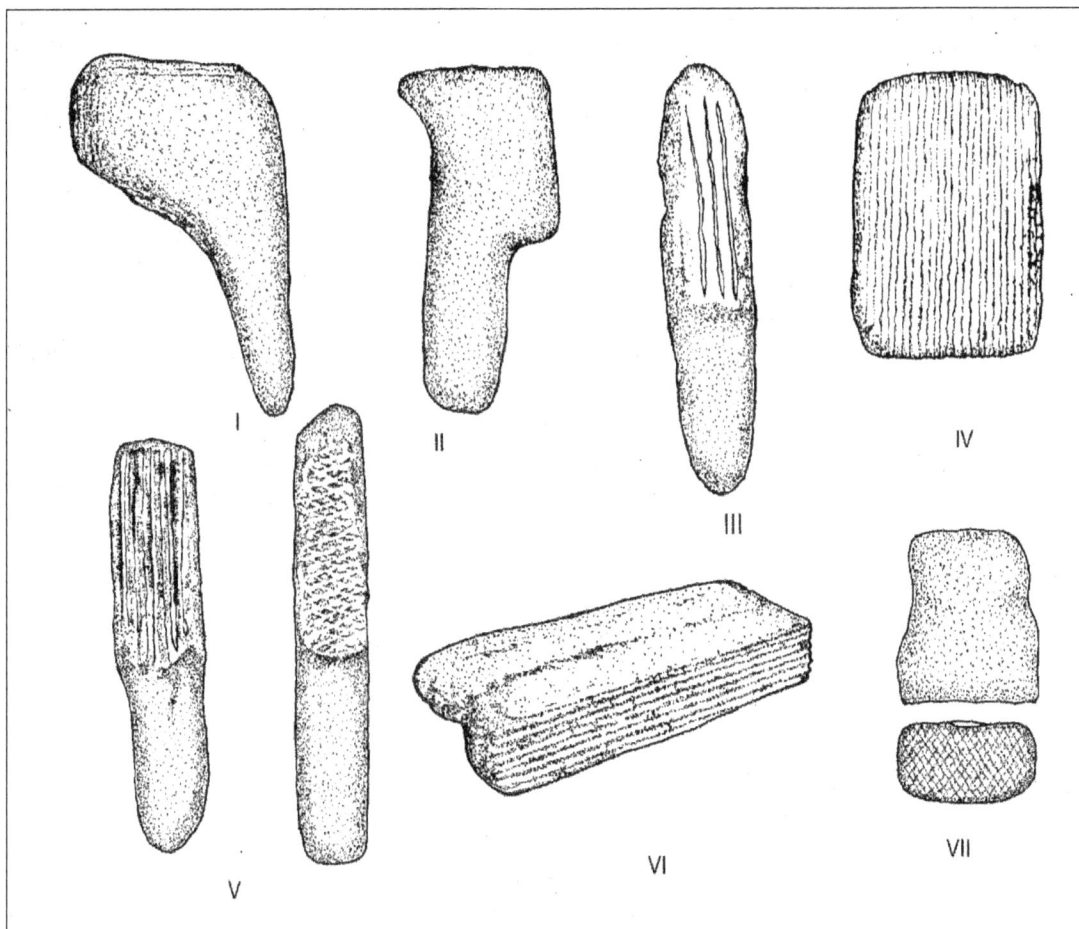

Figure 3. Typology of prehistoric bark-cloth beaters from South China and Southeast Asia (from Cameron 2006).

been reported. One plausible explanation for this absence comes from the anthropologist Tolstoy (1963, 1991), who rejects any notion that the tapa of Polynesia provides a credible link between Southeast Asia and Mesoamerica, and he argues instead that bark-cloth technology was introduced into Mesoamerica, not island to island, but in a single voyage sailing north of Hawaii along an island-less route to Mesoamerica.

Notwithstanding the above-mentioned parallels, there is also the possibility that the Meso-american archaeological bark-cloth beaters belong to an independent cultural tradition that has no links with Southeast China or Southeast Asia. Although the Southern Chinese and Southeast Asian beaters suggest interaction, parallels are neither necessarily nor exclusively resultant from interaction. An alternative explanation is that prehistoric groups in Mesoamerica independently developed stone bark-cloth beaters. In manufacturing material culture, there is a limited range of raw materials and there could be geological reasons, such as an abundance of river-smoothed pebbles of appropriate size and weight in both regions. The diagnostic features of the beaters in the typology might also be purely functional, rather than stylistic. Grooves on the faces of beaters enhance the maceration of bark fibres and prehistoric groups in Mesoamerica could have realised this quite independently. In the same way, prehistoric groups with hafted beaters on the two continents could have invented hafting independently, as groups in other parts of the world have done.

Some of the questions raised in this paper warrant further investigation, not the least being the absence of stone bark-cloth beaters in the Polynesian archaeological record. Although stone beaters have never been identified, it is significant that the ungrooved beaters classified as Type 1 beaters in my typology are widely distributed at Polynesian sites, where they are identified as pounders. Certainly, these are ambiguous artefacts, and their function might be determined through residue analysis.

Further research into the factors influencing the material composition of contemporary Polynesian beaters is needed. There is evidence to indicate that choice was not environmentally determined. For example, in Tonga, where bark cloth is made daily, women use wooden beaters despite having access to volcanic stone (Geoff Clark pers comm.).

A technological explanation for the use of wooden beaters in Polynesia seems plausible. By the time the Pacific was colonised, bark-cloth production had been practised for millennia. While Neolithic groups would certainly have used plants such as *Broussonetia* sp. for their bark cloth, domestication was only in its initial stages during the Neolithic, and it is reasonable to assume that food-producing plants would have been domesticated first. By the time the Polynesians colonised the Pacific, knowledge of agronomy was more advanced and cultivation practices better developed. Young cultivated plants harvested annually do not require as much maceration as tougher, older fibre-producing plants, and wooden beaters would suffice. Craft production is also inextricably linked to social changes in prehistoric societies. As societies become more complex, elites use prestige goods to display status. When the Polynesians moved into the remote Pacific, the role of bark cloth as a semiotic system would almost certainly have been established, and control over the production, distribution and consumption of high-quality bark cloth would have enabled chiefs to attract, maintain and increase followers.

Finally, diffusionist paradigms linking China with Mesoamerica are not new and the list of material-culture parallels, best documented by Joseph Needham and Gwei-Djen Lu (1984), is extraordinary. Nevertheless, there is no compelling evidence that the parallels between Mesoamerican, Southeast Asian and Chinese bark-cloth beaters outlined in this paper are the result of Neolithic trans-oceanic movement. The available evidence suggests Neolithic groups from the two regions simply came up with the same solution to a technological problem. While Needham's other material-culture parallels are unequivocal, there are such temporal differences between them and the beaters that it seems far more likely they relate to a later period when trade and exchange would have been well established.

Endnote

The term bark cloth is generally used for felted bark fibres, produced through the application of moisture, heat and pressure, and does not include unbeaten bark sewn into clothing. Bark cloth is produced by beating the inner bark of certain trees and shrubs after the fibres have been softened through soaking or boiling. Fibres from the *Moraceae* family (*Antiaris* spp., *Artocarpus* spp., *Ficus* spp.) are best suited to the process because of the natural interlacing of their internal structures, while *Broussonetia papyrifera* (paper mulberry) produces the softest and finest cloth. Strips of bark are pounded with beaters to bond them together and increase the area and thickness of the material. This combined soaking and beating causes the superimposed strips to adhere to each other in a process called felting.

Acknowledgments

This research is funded by the Australian Research Council and supported by the Australian National University. The typology (Figure 3) draws from a classification produced by Ling Shun-Sheng (1962), but differs from it in several important respects. In terms of classification, Ling showed a propensity to clump, whereas the writer would be described as a 'splitter'. This typology also differs markedly in scope, including the Shenzhen Museum data (not known in the 1960s) and Vietnamese data. I am indebted to the anonymous reviewers whose comments greatly improved the paper.

References

Aranyanak Chiraporn 1991. *Archaeological Textiles in Thailand*. Bangkok: Fine Arts Department.

Bellwood, P. 1979. *Man's Conquest of the Pacific*. New York: Oxford University Press.

Bellwood, P. and E. Dizon 2005. The Batanes Archaeological Project and the "Out of Taiwan" Hypothesis for Austronesian Dispersal. *Journal of Austronesian Studies* 1(1):1–35.

Beyer, H.O. 1948. *Philippine and East Asian Archaeology, and its relation to the origin of the Pacific Islands Population*. National Research Council of the Philippines: Quzon City.

Cameron, J. 2006. The Origins of bark cloth production in Southeast Asia. In M. Howard (ed), *Bark Cloth in Southeast Asia*, pp. 65–74. Bangkok: White Lotus Press.

Cameron, J. In press. Report on the bark cloth beater from the Linaminan Site, Palawan. In K. Szabo, the Linaminan Site, Palawan. *Hukay*.

Chau Hing-wah 1994. Periodization of Prehistoric Culture of Pearl River delta. In Shenzhen Museum (ed), *Archaeological Discoveries and Research in Shenzhen*, pp. 54–62. Beijing: Cultural Relics Publishing House (in Chinese).

Chang, K-C. 1964. Prehistoric and early historic horizons and tradition in South China. *Current Anthropology* 5:335, 368–75, 399–400.

Chang, K-C. 1989. Taiwan Archaeology in Pacific Perspective. In Kuang-chou Li, Kwang-chih Chang, A. Wolf and Chien-chung Yin (eds), *Anthropological Studies of the Taiwan Area: Accomplishments and Prospects*, pp. 87–97. Taipei: The National Taiwan University.

Chia, S. 1997. *The Prehistory of Bukit Tengkorak as a major pottery making site in Southeast Asia*. Unpublished PhD thesis, Universiti Sains Malaysia, Penang.

Chiu, T.N. and V. Ward 1979. A Bark-cloth Beater? *Journal of the Hong Kong Archaeological Society* 7:98.

Colani, M. 1933. Céramique, procédés anciens de decoration:Racquettes de potiers en schiste. *Bulletin de l'Ecole Francaise d'Extrême-Orient* 33 (1933):349–354.

Davidson, J. 1969. Archaeological excavations in two burial mounds at 'Atele', Tongatapu. *Records of the Auckland Institute and Museum* 6:251–286.

Evans, H. 1930. Stone objects from Surat, Peninsular Siam. *Man* 30:157–160.

Ha Van Tan 1980. *Ve nhung cai goi la ban dap trong cac di chi van hoa Phung Nguyen*. In *Nhung Phat Hien Moi Ve Khao Co Hoc Nam*, pp. 52–54. Hanoi: Vien Khao Co Hoc (in Vietnamese).

Harrisson, T. 1964. Bark-cloth beaters from Sabah, Sarawak and Kalimantan. *Sarawak Museum Journal* 11:597–602.

Heekeren, H. R. van 1972. *The Stone Age of Indonesia*, Second edition. The Hague: Martinus Nijhoff.

Higham, C. 2003. Southern China and Southeast Asia during the Neolithic. In *Prehistoric Archaeology of South China and Southeast Asia. Proceedings of the International Conference to celebrate the 30th anniversary of the excavation of Zengpiyan*, pp. 23–39. Beijing: Cultural Relics Publishing House.

Holbé T.V. 1915. Quelques mots sur les préhistorique Indochinois à propos des objects receuillis par M. de Pray. *Bulletin des Amis du Vert Hué*, 2 ème année 43 (in French).

Kooijman, S. 1972. *Tapa in Polynesia.* Bishop Museum Press, Honolulu, Hawaii.

Levy, P. 1943. *Recherches prehistoriques dans la region de Mlu Prei (Cambodge). Hanoi: Imprimerie d'Extreme-Orient* (in French).

Lien, C. 1991. *Excavations of the Peinan site. Vol.3.* Taipei: University of Taipei.

Ling Shun-sheng 1962. Bark cloth culture and the invention of paper-making in Ancient China. *Bulletin of the Institute of Ethnology, Academia Sinica* 11(1961):29–50.

Meacham, W. 1994. *Fu Tei Wan: Archaeological Investigations of Chep Lap Kok Island.* Hong Kong: Hong Kong Archaeological Society.

Needham, J. and Gwei-Djen Lu 1984. *Trans-Pacific echoes and resonances: listening once again.* Singapore: World Scientific.

Shenzhen Museum 1990. The Preliminary report of the excavation at Xiantouling. *Wenwu* 2:1–11 (in Chinese).

Shenzhen Museum 1991. *Archaeological Finds from the Pearl River delta inGuangdong, China.* Hong Kong: Chinese University of Hong Kong (in Chinese).

Shenzhen Museum 1994. *Archaeological Discoveries and Research in Shenzhen.* Beijing: Cultural Relics Publishing House (in Chinese).

Shenzhen Museum 2007. Neolithic site at Xiantouling in Shenzhen City, Guangdong. *Kaogu* 7:9–16.

Shih Sheng-Han 1961. *Chhi-Min Yao-Shu Hsuan Tu-Pen (Selections from the Chhi Min Yao Shu).* Shanghai (in Chinese).

Sieveking, G. de G. 1954. Excavations of Gua Cha, Kelantan. *Federation Museums Journal* 1–2:75–143.

Stein Callenfels, P. V. van 1951. Prehistoric sites on the Karama River. *Journal of East Asiatic Studies* 1(1957):77–97.

Suggs, R.C. 1961. *The Archaeology of Nuka Hiva, Marquesas Islands, French Polynesia.* Anthropological Papers of the American Museum of Natural History 49(1).

Tolstoy, P. 1963. Cultural parallels between Southeast Asia and Mesoamerica in the Manufacture of Bark-cloth. *Transactions of the New York Academy of Sciences* 25:646–662.

Tolstoy, P. 1991. Paper Route. *Natural History* 100:6.

Uhle, M. 1889–90. *Kultur und industrie Sudamerickanischler Volker Leipzig Museum fur Volkerkunde.* Berlin: A. Ascher.

14

Are islands islands? Some thoughts on the history of chalk and cheese

Matthew Spriggs

School of Archaeology and Anthropology, Australian National University, Australia
Matthew.Spriggs@anu.edu.au

The islands of the great Southern Sea comprising those which are in the neighbourhood of the Indian Continent, and the clusters which extend into more distant spaces in the ocean, present a field of enquiry extremely interesting to the natural historian of mankind. These insular countries are distributed through almost every variety of climate, and contain abundant diversity of local situation; therefore they afford us an opportunity of observing whatever influence physical causes may be supposed to exert over our species. James Cowles Prichard (1813:248–249)[1]

From continental to island life the change for the worse is very great with respect to opportunities and incitements to progress … every nation upon a continent had one or more contiguous nations between whom and itself there was more or less of intercourse. Amongst contiguous nations there would be a free propagation of arts and inventions, which would tend to the general advancement of society throughout the entire area in which these influences are felt. Nations are apt to share in the more important elements of each other's progress.

On the other hand, the islands of the Pacific, except those adjacent to the main land, may be likened to so many cages in which their insulated occupants were shut in from external influences, as well as denied a knowledge of the uses of flocks and herds and of the principal cereals. Intercourse, at most, was limited to the inhabitants of particular groups of islands, who were thus compelled to sustain their national growth upon the development of their own intelligence exclusively, and without the great instruments of progress afforded by continental areas. Lewis Henry Morgan (1868:448–449)[2]

Introduction

I append these two quotations to show that, in island archaeology at least, there is nothing new under the sun. They provide a rich source of tropes that remain with us as theoretical postulates of island singularity: the contrast with more complex continental situations, climatic and ecological variability, isolation through distance and navigational limitations that prevent 'external influences', evidence of cultural conservatism and/or loss, small populations and clear variations in social structure – all within a context of historical relatedness.

The first quotation, dating from 1813, shows that we can go back long before Darwin's account of his visit to the Galapagos Islands to find a Pacific foundational text – and in this case an explicitly anthropological one – that implies 'islands as laboratories' (possibly contra Kuklick's (1996) otherwise excellent discussion of the island model in British anthropology). In the extended quotation (Endnote 1), Prichard refers to 'informed voyagers' and in his book he makes much use of the literature generated by the voyages of Captain Cook and others. One could, therefore, trace back these ideas even further if required. I have seen neither of these quotations referred to so far in the underdeveloped literature on the history of island archaeology and the milieu from which it developed.

Island archaeology as a comparative topic has remained popular in conference titles and publications in archaeology for 50 years since some of the classic formulations of the 'islands-as-laboratories' trope were published in *Journal of the Polynesian Society* in 1957. Introduced by Margaret Mead, papers by Irving Goldman, Ward Goodenough and Marshall Sahlins set the scene for much subsequent discussion of cultural evolution in the Pacific and the wider world, particularly the better-known paper of Vayda and Rappaport on 'Island Cultures', first published in 1963. American and Southern Hemisphere scholars have tended to trace the ancestry of island archaeology explicitly to these works, and to the publication of *The Theory of Island Biogeography*, by MacArthur and Wilson (1967). Ten years ago, a special issue of *Human Ecology* (1997), edited by Ben Fitzhugh and Terry Hunt, considered the continued relevance of the laboratory trope (see particularly the papers by the editors, Burney, Dewar, and Terrell).

An explicitly archaeological treatment of island cultures by John Evans in 1973 in the *Explanation in Culture Change* volume, and his later contribution to *World Archaeology* (see Evans 1973, 1977) were decisive publications in introducing British scholars to the issues involved, and led on to much of the important comparative effort concerning Mediterranean islands found in the works of John Cherry (1981, 1990), Mark Patton (1996), Cyprian Broodbank (2000) and others.[3] The series of papers on island archaeology published in the June 1977 issue of *World Archaeology*, edited by Ian Glover, followed immediately after the February 1977 issue of the same journal on human biogeography, originating from a 1974 conference organised by John Terrell and William Fitzhugh (as discussed in Terrell 1997:419–420). This represented an approach heavily informed by MacArthur and Wilson (1967).[4] The island-archaeology volume represented a significant cross-fertilisation of the American and British traditions, with various papers there also referring to MacArthur and Wilson, as well as Vayda and Rappaport (1963), Goodenough (1957) and Sahlins (1958). The sole paper from New Zealand characteristically referenced papers from both the British and US traditions (Davidson 1977).

More recent general publications on island archaeology have tended to muddy the waters somewhat on what the comparative basis of the study is really all about, particularly by raising trenchant criticisms of the 'islands as laboratories' concept – Fitzpatrick (2004) and Rainbird (1999, 2007) are examples. But as they get further away in time from the foundational literature, I feel these treatments have forgotten some of the original ideas and contexts. It is worth questioning whether, to misuse maritime metaphors, island archaeology is being drawn ever onward by strong winds or currents in full sail, as might be hoped, or whether it is entering the ever-decreasing circles of a whirlpool, spinning faster – measured by increasing publication rates – but more terminally towards the hole in the middle!

It seems important therefore to return to the foundational papers of the 1950s and early 1960s – while bearing in mind the farther horizons from which they in turn derived – and recall what these early publications actually said about islands, and about what sort of islands. The 'ambivalence' about islands identified by Atholl Anderson (2004) in the Fitzpatrick volume can be seen as having been there since the beginning. One might suggest that confusion in the minds of the early authors has simply been reproduced, rather than having been examined explicitly, creating a dangerous shoal in island-archaeology theorising.

The foundational texts of the 1950s

Mead 1957

Mead's 1957 introductory paper, precisely one paragraph long, was titled 'Introduction to Polynesia as a Laboratory for the Development of Models in the Study of Cultural Evolution' (Mead 1957). The three papers it introduced came out of a session on evolution and the comparative method at the December 1956 meetings of the American Association for the Advancement of Science. The theoretical context was the resurgence in evolutionary anthropology during the late 1940s and early 1950s associated with names such as Leslie White (1949) and Julian Steward (1955), but informed too by the writings of Vere Gordon Childe (for instance Childe 1951). The 'multilinear' evolution of Steward was particularly favoured by American anthropologists of the time (see for instance Mead 1958), not least because of the McCarthy-era witch-hunt of suspected communists, a brush with which both White and Childe were directly tarred (cf. Harris 1969:637–639).

What were needed to bring forward the evolutionary agenda were 'very detailed comparative studies of particular societies in a given culture area' (Mead 1957). Mead also tipped the hat to the 'related sciences' of archaeology and 'modern genetic theory', the former because of the recent development of radiocarbon dating and its application to Pacific sites, and the latter because of processes of adaptive radiation and genetic drift that might be seen as analogous to processes in cultural evolution. Works on genetics by Simpson (1949), Boyd (1950) and Muller (1956) are referred in Goodenough's article that follows on from Mead's. She believed that archaeology and genetics would provide a new perspective into which the more traditional analyses of genealogies and navigation patterns might be fitted. Mead was certainly prescient in that regard! Goodenough's own work on star navigation was probably among those she had in mind (Goodenough 1953), and in his own paper he further references Heyerdahl (1955), Whitney (1955), Gladwin (1956) and Sharp (1956). Goodenough (1957) also notes how Emory's synthesis of earlier genealogical dating by Fornander and Cartwright for the settlement of Hawaii fitted in with the first radiocarbon date to be obtained from that archipelago, from the Kuli'ou'ou rock shelter on O'ahu (as cited in Elbert 1953:168).

Goodenough 1957

Goodenough's paper was called 'Oceania and the Problem of Controls in the Study of Cultural and Human Evolution' (1957). He notes that such laboratory-like conditions are not found over much of the earth, where it is impossible to sort cultures into phylogenetic units because 'even as they change, elements blend and reblend in the course of migrations, conquests and trade' (1957:146). Under these 'normal conditions', it is hard to examine cultural change 'within the framework of what biological evolutionists have called 'radiation'; that is to examine critically the processes by which phylogenetically related cultures become progressively different from each other' (ibid). He continues: 'Only when a culture X splits and moves into two previously unoccupied regions can we be certain that subsequent differences are due either to environmental adaptation or to something akin to what the geneticists call 'drift'. Only under these conditions can we get some idea of the capacity of the parent culture for modification without the addition of new cultural strains from new contact and borrowing.'

He recommends parts of the Pacific as being just such suitable laboratory-like locations for phylogenetic study. In establishing this, he uses the nascent study of historical linguistics as a framework for discussion of the settlement of the Pacific Islands, particularly the notional sequence (and dating) of settlement provided by glottochronology (Elbert 1953). This he links to Sharp's (1956) views on the limitations of Polynesian navigational abilities and the prevalence of accidental drift voyages to suggest that 'once settled, eastern Polynesia as a whole remained isolated from the rest of the Pacific; and its remoter island groups remained isolated from each other' (1957:150). He concludes that 'Cultural differences in Polynesia, especially in eastern Polynesia, must be due to the adaptation of a common heritage to local ecological conditions or to random loss of portions of the common heritage in very small populations, as in the presumably frequent instances in which an island's inhabitants were derived from a canoe-load or two of initial settlers' (ibid).

Noting progressive genetic isolation from west to east in the Pacific and the correspondingly homogeneous physical appearance of Polynesians towards the eastern end of their distribution, Goodenough seeks analogous processes in culture: 'Thus in eastern Polynesia we should expect to find a more intense utilization of a narrower cultural heritage so as to lead to distinctive "flowerings" or "specializations" of ideas which in the west remain relatively unelaborated and more "generalized". Cultural differences relating to *mana* and *tabu* are a possible example. The greater elaboration of social stratification in some eastern islands may also reflect this process' (1957:151). He points to a tendency to cultural and linguistic loss, again citing Elbert (1953), who mentions loss of domestic plants and animals as one moves east in the Pacific. Again, continental situations are contrasted in which cultural loss is compensated for by borrowed elements from contact with other groups and the causes of loss are harder to discern.

Cultural adaptation to distinctive environments is brought into play here, with both Polynesian and Micronesian atoll cultures seen as independent developments, but both stemming from ultimately common high island cultures. Contrasting eastern Polynesian high island and atoll cultures would bring out environmentally specific adaptations of the original society, and comparison of Micronesian with Polynesian atolls 'would show how two closely related branches of a single cultural tradition were independently adapted to similar environmental pressures' (1957:153).

Isolation is clearly the key here, as it is to Goodenough's final reason for comparison: the reconstruction of the ancestral form before migration. He writes: 'Because the island societies were free from contact with unrelated cultures, all of the modifications and adaptations which have taken place, and all of the new elaborations, are expressions of the potential for change and development inherent in the ancestral culture' (ibid). As well as Micronesia and Polynesia being suitable for such comparisons, the Massim area of Island Melanesia is singled out for potential comparison among 'a number of small societies with a common linguistic and cultural heritage, every one of which has diverged from that heritage in a slightly different way from every other. Here again, the radiation process seems to have been operative, and once again in relative isolation' (1957:154).

Sahlins 1957

As noted by Mead (1957), Marshall Sahlins takes a different explanatory tack in his paper 'Differentiation by Adaptation in Polynesian Societies'. He states: 'My thesis is that Polynesian cultural differentiation was produced by processes of adaptation under varying technological and environmental conditions. A single culture has filled in and adapted to a variety of ecological niches' (1957:291). He contrasts two forms of descent system – ramages and truncated descent lines – and asserts that the first form is 'well constituted for exploitation of different, scattered resources' (1957:294), such as the pattern found of coastal fishing and inland taro or yam gardening where a number of different production zones are found across the landscape, requiring redistribution of produce organised through genealogical seniority. Truncated descent lines 'are associated with an ecology wherein resource zones are not widely separated, but are clustered such that all domestic groups can engage in the entire range of production activities' (ibid), such as where narrow concentric production zones concentrate near the coast and small groups are capable of self-sufficiency.

This classification applies to high islands and is further contrasted with atoll organisation. Sahlins summarises the latter systems as deriving 'from the high islands and typically show divergence through adaptation to the unfavourable atoll opportunities. This divergence becomes more marked in proportion to the length of time in occupation, and is occasionally facilitated by small population effect. The direction of extreme modification of low island organization is toward an intricate system of interlocking social groups, each tending to be exclusively associated with control of different resources and specific forms of production and distribution' (1957:299).

Apart from noting the small size, poor resource base and vulnerability to natural disaster of atolls, the paper does not seek to explain differential degrees of social stratification in Polynesia, but merely to contrast ideal types. The paper is, however, in part a summary of some of the conclusions of his book then in press, *Social Stratification in Polynesia* (Sahlins 1958), completed in November 1955 and itself based on his 1954 PhD dissertation. There, it is quite explicit that resource productivity is at the root of differences in social stratification in Polynesia, allowing him to rank 14 Polynesian societies. Sahlins had been a student of Leslie White, which might explain the somewhat different emphasis than in Goodenough's paper, which is more in the Mead-Steward camp.

In the monograph, Sahlins states that 'the choice of Polynesia as a laboratory for the study of cultural adaptation is a judicious one, for all Polynesian cultures have a great part of their history in common – tradition is almost a constant. Nevertheless, cognisance will be taken of the possibility that diffusion or some other historical process, perhaps nonadaptive, may have been operating differentially on features of social stratification in particular cases' (1958:x). This certainly suggests that Sahlins was less sanguine about the isolation of Polynesian societies than Goodenough appeared to be, but he still used the same genetic metaphors, such as 'adaptive radiation' of the Polynesians as a 'single cultural genus that has undergone adaptive differentiation' (1958:248). It should be remembered, however, that beyond this, his model is not necessarily about islands per se: it could theoretically apply to any set of situations where both nucleated and dispersed resources can be found among related cultures.

Goldman 1957a

Irving Goldman's paper, the third and final paper of the series, is called 'Variations in Polynesian Social Organization' and thus covers some of the same concerns about social structure as that of Sahlins, but from a somewhat different perspective. To Goodenough's justification for studying cultural evolution within a culture area, Goldman adds 'the central problem of evolution, namely variation' with an aim to 'reconstruct evolutionary processes, directions and stages' (1957a:374). In this case, he is interested in examining how kinship-based societies become transformed into 'social systems governed primarily by political and territorial principles' (ibid). Echoing Goodenough, he notes that: 'As a result of their relative cultural isolation, islands are more sheltered from the overwhelming effects of diffusion, and variant forms are more clearly observable. In this respect, the Polynesian Islands, the most removed from continental masses, are most favourably situated for our purposes' (1957a:374–375). In a footnote, he references Sharp's (1956) book as 'corroboration of the thesis that Polynesian culture is to be explained primarily from internal developments rather than from diffusion' (ibid).

The engine of evolution is not in this case adaptation to environmental variation in any direct sense but is status rivalry: 'A constant in every Polynesian society, status rivalry seems to have provoked stresses to which the status system, along with other components of the social structure, adapted. These adaptations rearranged the total social structure producing new structural types' (1957a:375).

Based on this principle, Goldman arranged 18 Polynesian societies for which he had data into a hypothetical sequence of social stratification, a gradient or continuum he divided into three successive evolutionary types: traditional (the most conservative and close to a proto-Polynesian form of organisation), open and stratified. He admitted that economic, political, military and other factors were relevant as well to social change (1957a:377), but simply ignored them, or saw their effects as again a result of more generalised status rivalry. His major monograph, *Ancient Polynesian Society* (1970), substantially written before 1966, did not pay any greater attention to factors other than status rivalry. Despite the very different emphases as to the driving force of cultural evolution between Goldman and Sahlins, their two ranking systems produce roughly the same sequence of stratification, with no very significant shifts in position (Goldman 1957a:376; Sahlins 1958:249–250).

A slightly earlier paper of Goldman's reproduces his sequences of culture change, but notes that they 'take their character and direction in part from the momentum of status rivalry itself and in part from the particular physical and cultural setting of each island. Thus the differing ecologies of atolls and high islands, variations in population density, varieties of subsistence techniques, levels of economic productivity, systems of property relations, the role of migrations and military conquests, diffusion, and, finally the specific historical 'accidents' that occur in wars, migrations and contests for power – all influence and are in turn influenced by the dominant motive of status rivalry' (1955:680). The 1955 paper, which is a much more coherent statement of his views than the 1957 one, also has an enlightening discussion of parallel cultural trends that Goldman identifies as being present as societies moved from traditional to open to stratified forms in Polynesia (1955:689–694). Of the trio of papers that followed Mead's (1957) introduction, Goldman's is clearly the weakest, and is the least referred to today.[5]

Islands as laboratories and the culture area concept

We can thus see how the 'islands as laboratories' idea came of age with a heady mix of new developments in genetics, archaeology, cultural evolutionary anthropology, and historical linguistics during the early- to mid-1950s. However, it was not really the fact of being islands per se that created the 'controls', the laboratory-like conditions in the Pacific Islands that would reflect back on more complex continental situations. These 'controls' were grounded in the culture area concept, going only slightly beyond the old geographical and assumed cultural divisions of Polynesia, Micronesia and Melanesia in Goodenough's paper to the extent that they were united by the presence of Austronesian languages, descendent from a common linguistic and assumed cultural ancestor to the northwest in Asia. In Sahlins' and Goldman's contributions, it was explicitly the Polynesian culture area that was the unit of analysis.

As Rainbird has noted (2007:29), there is a straight line back through Mead's teacher, Ruth Benedict, to her teacher, Franz Boas, who came out of a geographic background to 'found' American anthropology around 'a close study of limited geographic areas', as Goldman, another Boas student, put it (1970:xi). This led on to the concept of 'culture area', suggested by Boas

(1896) as an alternative to a failing 19th century evolutionist viewpoint, much developed by his students, such as Kroeber and Wissler (see Harris 1969 for a detailed discussion of this historical sequence). As Goldman (1955:680) summarises the concept: 'A culture area comprises historically related societies each showing significant variations from a common area pattern.' The concept of Polynesia as a culture area was already well known within Polynesian studies before the 1950s, based particularly on the work of American anthropologist Edwin Burrows (1938, 1939, 1940), who cited some of Wissler's works (1926, 1938) on Native American culture areas as a direct inspiration. The New Zealand scholar H.D. Skinner had published a paper on 'Culture areas in New Zealand' as far back as 1921. Skinner drew directly on the work of otherwise-unidentified 'American ethnologists' (1921:71), noting that 'some fourteen cultural areas' in the Americas were constructed on the basis of subsistence practices, whereas in the Pacific they would be better based on the origins of the cultures. From the context it is clear his immediate source is Wissler (1917). If Pacific parallels are to be used by island archaeology colleagues working in the Caribbean and the Mediterranean areas or elsewhere, the underpinnings of the culture area concept need to be understood. It could be argued to be more important in the original formulations discussed above than the fact of islands in a big ocean.

Vayda and Rappaport 1963

The end of the formative period of anthropological contributions to island archaeology is marked by the paper of Andrew Vayda and Roy Rappaport, 'Island Cultures', published in 1963 in the proceedings of the 1961 *Man's Place in the Island Symposium* of the 10th Pacific Science Congress held in Honolulu.[6] Vayda and Rappaport didn't claim originality for many of the points they made; indeed, some of them are referenced back to the Sahlins and Goodenough papers already discussed. But they expressed them in a clear, almost dot-point, fashion and that is why their paper is still regularly cited more than 40 years on in the island-archaeology literature. Again, what they actually said is less ably reported in subsequent citations. Their starting question was a simple one: 'What influence do relative isolation and limited territory have upon the evolution and differentiation of cultures?' (1963:133). Although islands are used to illustrate their answers to this, there is nothing island-specific in the question. Indeed, they straight away exclude from consideration large islands such as New Guinea and New Zealand which are continent-like, and even small ones regularly in touch with larger continental areas such as Zanzibar or the Maldives. They note there are other kinds of 'natural barriers' than the sea, and include remote valleys and mountaintops in continental situations as equivalent to the small islands they do consider, as well as communities such as ghettoes cut off by 'man-made barriers'.

Vayda and Rappaport introduce another concept borrowed from genetics, the 'founder principle' or 'founder effect' so important to discussions of island biogeography: 'For the operation of the founder principle, isolation rather than limited territory seems to be critical. If the migration to an isolated place, whether a small island or a large continent, is by a relatively small group of people who are unable to reproduce in full the culture of the population from which they derived, then the culture in the new place will be immediately different from the culture in the homeland.' (1963:134–135) One of the first archaeologists to take up this biogeographical idea was Richard Pearson (1969) in his monograph on the Ryukyu Islands, between Japan and Taiwan, where Vayda and Rappaport's paper was extensively cited.

Vayda and Rappaport discuss next the idea of cultural 'drift', following Goodenough (1957), but put their own – not island-specific – spin on it by asking: 'whether appreciable cultural differences can develop among people only if they are kept from one another by geographical or other barriers ... We badly need further investigations, not simply to determine whether isolation is a precondition of cultural differentiation but to determine just what kinds and degrees of cultural differentiation may presuppose just what kinds and degrees of isolation' (1963:135–136). This question underlies any archaeology of frontiers and boundaries, such as later developed in the 1970s with the work of Ian Hodder and others (Hodder 1978, 1982; Green and Perlman 1985).

They turn next to the role of limited territory and 'the development of cultural traits affecting the dispersion and size of island populations' (1963:136–137). They consider population limitation practices such as infanticide or voyages of exile, subsistence intensification and adaptations in social structure to match population distribution to resources across the landscape (cf. Sahlins 1957).

The final issue they discuss goes all the way back to the Prichard (1813) quotation with which this paper starts, the rate of change in isolated island cultures and its corollary, the openness or not of such cultures to outside influences when their isolation is broken by colonial or other forces: 'Are innovations in the ways of doing things less frequent in more or less isolated and small populations because there are not many people interacting with one another and making new combinations of acts and ideas? Or do such innovations as occur tend to spread among the members of a population more quickly and to become established in the culture more readily when the population is small and isolated? Might cultural change, therefore, be rapid in such a population despite a low incidence of innovations?' (1963:139–140)

Discussion

Questions of scale and connectivity

One of the commentators on the paper as given orally in 1961, David Schneider, raised the core issue, noting that 'it may very well be that there is nothing peculiar about water around a piece of land insofar as the cultural problems are concerned' (Fosberg (ed) 1963:143). Vayda and Rappaport had let themselves in for this criticism by making a distinction between what they called 'island cultures' and other kinds of cultures found on islands that were large or interconnected. Far from being the synthesis of the idea of island cultures that it is often cited to be, the paper, perhaps inadvertently, points to some fatal flaws in the idea. For instance, there are important issues of scale revealed: when is an island so large that it operates like something else? There might be little sense, for instance, in talking about New Guinea as an island in the same breath as Easter Island. And what about substantial inland island populations which have no direct links to the sea? Do these represent 'island cultures' in any meaningful sense (cf. Roe 2000)?

There are also issues of connectivity. Even small islands in regular communication with others present a different kind of phenomenon from more isolated ones. They are perhaps best conceived of as archipelagic cultures, rather than island ones, or examined in terms of their links to neighbouring coasts and mainlands. Their interrelations can be modelled by various kinds of network and peer polity interaction models that might be equally applicable to continental situations (see Bedford and Spriggs 2008 for an Island Melanesian example). There are also suggestive parallels between island colonisation and patterns of mainland coastal colonisation by sea travel in both the Mediterranean and the western Pacific that still await detailed examination (cf. Zilhao 1993).

How isolated do you have to be?

Talk of 'relative isolation' always begs the question of how isolated is that, exactly? Work by Atholl Anderson and others on some of the 'mystery islands' of Polynesia, those that show evidence of Polynesian settlement but that were abandoned by European contact, is documenting this precisely: see, for instance, Anderson's early work on the Kermadec Islands, and his subsequent work on Norfolk Island (Anderson and White 2001), the Subantarctic Islands south of New Zealand (Anderson and O'Regan 2000) and Christmas Island in Kiribati (Anderson *et al.* 2002), as well as the work of Weisler (1994, 2004) on Pitcairn, Henderson and Ducie.

Another major contribution has been Irwin's (1992) work on island size and accessibility in the Pacific that can now be compared directly in most cases with detailed settlement histories. Irwin (1992:175) plotted the islands of Polynesia and Fiji according to their distance and target angle of expanded sighting radius from their nearest occupied neighbours. Greater isolation occurs with greater distance and smaller angle of target. The table shows (relatively) large and isolated islands away in one corner – the 'stranded margins' of Easter Island, Hawaii and New Zealand, and the empty and abandoned mystery islands in the top left corner – at varying distances but with very low target angles. In the middle ranges we find islands that remained occupied but where inter-island voyaging had declined or ceased by European contact, and in the bottom left are the islands that maintained active voyaging spheres up to European contact, such as the Societies and the Tuamotus, Tonga, Fiji and Samoa. The table might even be read as predicting what islands were most likely to have become abandoned next: Manihiki, Pukapuka, Chatham, Penryn, Niue and Rotuma!

A further analysis factors in island size, as well as accessibility, with this time, the mystery islands appearing as the apex of a triangle and small and inaccessible (Irwin 1992:192). Intermittently occupied or utilised islands are seen to be those that are small but more accessible, and all other islands are occupied permanently. Rather unhelpfully, Irwin doesn't include quite the same set of islands in this diagram as in the previous table, covering only central and 'eastern' Polynesia. But again, we can identify potentially vulnerable islands: Manihiki, Pukapuka, Tongareva, Rakahanga and Rapa. Tongareva and Rakahanga hadn't been considered in the earlier table, and Chatham, Penryn, Niue and Rotuma did not appear in this one. Irwin's conclusion is that the pattern of abandonment and isolation is systematic and can be measured, dependent as it is on accessibility from other islands (Irwin 1992:195). An archaeology of isolation, as a special topic within island archaeology, might be most productive.

All factors are time-dependent

One other important issue to consider when talking of factors such as isolation and connectivity, and even island size, is that all of them are time-dependent. This factor was not at all evident to the 1950s anthropologists who inspired island archaeology. Radiocarbon dating was only in its infancy and modern archaeology had barely begun in much of the Pacific outside of New Zealand during the 1950s, pioneered by scholars such as Avias, Emory, Golson, Green, Shutler, Sinoto and Suggs (Kirch 2000:27–32). Recall too that the first modern archaeological excavations in New Guinea took place only in 1959 (Bulmer and Bulmer 1964) and in Vanuatu only in 1963 (Shutler and Shutler 1966); even today, there are inhabited Pacific islands yet to experience the loving tickle of the archaeologist's trowel.

The discovery of a Pleistocene prehistory for the Bismarcks and Solomons only began at the turn of the 1980s with Jim Specht's excavation of Misisil Cave on New Britain (Specht *et al.* 1981). Only then did it become obvious that archaeologists working on Pacific islands outside of New Guinea would have to deal with the prospect of the changing size and location of islands, and even whether they were islands when humans first reached them, owing to the effects of glacial and post-glacial sea-level fluctuations. Many atolls in the Pacific may have only become habitable after about 2000 BP as land-forming processes caught up with a stabilised sea level. The age of the island terrain itself can be seen as important to human habitability, as Rolett and Diamond (2004) recently reminded us in a paper examining environmental predictors of pre-European deforestation on Pacific islands.

There have been major changes too in climatic conditions that we are only now becoming able to map on to possible cultural responses. Not least among these are changes in the strength of El Nino conditions, as again Anderson, among others, has pointed out in key papers (Anderson 2002; Anderson *et al.* 2006).

The ability to reach most islands is dependent on boat technology, and as Anderson has strongly argued over the past few years, there have been major thresholds reached in this during the time people have lived on Pacific islands, not least the invention of the sail and, within the past 1000 years or so, several further major developments in central and eastern Pacific boat technology in particular (Anderson 2000, 2001, 2004).

Any discussion of time-dependent processes also has to address those historical contingencies of what Vayda and Rappaport (1963:133) called 'man-made barriers', citing a Neolithic village surrounded by hostile (hunter gatherer?) neighbours or ethnic communities living in ghettoes. The isolation of particular communities can increase or decrease through time, often in a cyclical pattern, depending on a range of socio-economic factors, both external and internal. For the Pacific, where there is a rapid decrease of long-range communication between islands after a couple of generations of the Lapita expansion around 3000 BP, a variety of reasons have been adduced. These include exchange system contraction, or specialisation, sociopolitical transformation (including 'system collapse'), absorption and/or secondary migration by other cultural groups, and local adaptation (Spriggs 1997:152–162).

This last theme has been developed most elegantly not by an archaeologist but by the linguist Andrew Pawley in his theory of the 'cycle of linguistic diversification' (Pawley 1981). A similar contraction of the inter-island exchange system is envisaged as in other models, but in this case not because the system was too socially costly to maintain but because it was no longer functionally necessary for the economic and biological survival of individual communities in Island Melanesia. Any effective links to the Lapita 'homeland' therefore became attenuated and finally broken. New factors must have spurred on the renewed contacts between western Pacific Island groups seen within the past 1000 years, a phase associated with, but not restricted to, the 'Polynesian Outlier' phenomenon (Bedford and Spriggs 2008:107–110; Spriggs 1997: Chapter 7).

Although the apparent cessation of widespread canoe travel in eastern Polynesia after about 1450 AD is often attributed to changing climatic conditions discouraging long sea voyages, a more social explanation along the same lines could potentially be equally applicable there. One recalls that for Micronesia, 'the late survival of voyaging here has been partly explained by the fact that almost all the eastern Micronesian islands are atolls, which are among the most precarious human habitats on earth' (Irwin 1992:194). Continued inter-island exchange there was thus certainly linked to the economic and biological survival of communities to an extent not found in the generally larger and/or more accessible eastern Polynesian islands that remained inhabited.

Conclusion and postscript

All research and theory-building is of its time. By providing a wider context for a series of key theoretical texts significant in the development of island archaeology and reminding us of their actual content, I have sought to expose the limitations of their concerns and ideas for practitioners today. The same tropes, the same issues and questions from that era remain fundamental to the constitution of island archaeology 50 years later. As Kuklick (1996) has shown, sociocultural anthropology has now very largely worked through these issues in a decisive break. They are now perhaps preventing the field from either reinventing itself as something else, or at the very least overcoming some important limitations and escaping the whirlpool of an under-theorised subject, into – if not calmer waters – at least those freshening conditions that an experienced sailor like Atholl can confidently handle.

This paper was complete and the final onerous task of reference checking was underway when I came upon the latest set of exchanges involving the usefulness of a concept of island archaeology (Boomert and Bright 2007; Fitzpatrick *et al.* 2007). Not surprisingly, Atholl was right in amongst it as one of the authors of the response to Boomert and Bright's call for the replacement of 'island archaeology' by 'an archaeology of maritime identity' (2007:18). Between them, the two papers provide a very up-to-date set of references in the field and Boomert and Bright provide a detailed overview of its recent history. As is often the case when finishing a paper, you wonder whether what you have written is of any use; don't people already know all this stuff? I am heartened to see that in this case, they don't. Boomert and Bright believe the concept of islands as laboratories for the study of cultural evolution 'was introduced to anthropology by Vayda and Rappaport' (2007:6). They state that: 'Evans (1973; 1977) was the first to apply biogeographical principles to insular archaeology' (ibid). Finally, they also contend that the insight of dramatic ancient human impacts upon island environments and biota in places such as the Pacific 'has only been reached over the last twenty years or so' (2007:12). Clearly, there is still a need to rehearse the earlier history and 'prehistory' of the island archaeology field!

Endnotes

1. The passage continues: 'In this point of view we also derive advantage from the remote distances which separate the islands, and from the imperfect knowledge of navigation which the natives possess: for these circumstances prevent intercourse among the different tribes, and preclude those frequent changes or intermixtures of population, which perplex our inquiries into the history of continental nations. An equal diversity characterizes the moral condition of these people. Some tribes are the rudest and most destitute savages found on the face of the globe, while others have gained a considerable advantage in the arts of society ... The regions above mentioned are inhabited by races of people who bear strong indications of a near connexion in history, if indeed their affinity be not so clear as to justify the opinion of the best informed voyagers, that they are all propagated from one original.'

2. The passage continues: 'They were also denied the advantages of numbers which is a most important element in the progress of human society. Under such circumstances it would be expected that isolated populations would remain in a stationary condition through longer periods of time than the inhabitants of continents. Immigrants, presumptively, from original continental homes, their posterity would be expected to reflect the condition of their ancestors at the epoch of their migration, since the probabilities of retrograding in knowledge would be at least equal to those of progress under the physical limitations with which they were subsequently surrounded. These hindrances would tend to preserve their domestic institutions within narrow limits of change.'

3. Evans' two publications, particularly the 1973 one, are deserving of a paper on their own for their foundational influence on British island-archaeology studies. Indeed, there is now some evidence that they are pushing out any memory of the 1950s background to these discussions: in

Fitzpatrick's edited volume (2004) there is only a single reference to Vayda and Rappaport (1963) and that in the editor's introduction, whereas Evans (1973) is referenced in no fewer than five other papers and Evans (1977) in three papers other than the introduction. In Rainbird's two works on island-archaeological theory (1999, 2007) both of these Evans papers are cited but none of the key American foundational texts discussed in this paper get a mention. Colin Renfrew has recently gone so far as to declare that Evans 'introduced the idea of islands as laboratories for the study of culture process' (2004:283)! Even if only the archaeological field is being referred to, this is scarcely fair to Pacific scholars who have been aware of this trope at least since the 1950s texts discussed here – and indeed before. In 1961, for instance, Robert Suggs in his monograph on the archaeology of the Marquesas Islands stated: 'The simpler environmental situation of Polynesian cultures makes the area an ideal laboratory for study of cultural ecology, as has already been demonstrated' (1961:194; cf. Kirch 1982). Golson (1958, cf. 1959) was equally aware of this literature, referencing Goldman, Goodenough, Hawthorn and Belshaw, Mead and Sahlins from the relevant *Journal of the Polynesian Society* issues. The lack of references in Evans (1973) is perhaps partly to blame for obscuring this genealogy, one he makes clear in his later paper (Evans 1977), where Vayda and Rappaport (1963) occurs among the citations. It is clear from his earlier remark that the particular qualities of islands are 'more fully recognized by natural scientists and anthropologists' (1973:517) that earlier literature informed his views, confirmed in personal communications from Professor Evans to me in October 2007 and January 2008. In the second of these, he recalled the influence of MacArthur and Wilson (1967), particularly the final chapter 'Prospect', on his original 1973 paper.

Golson (1958:27) also reminds us that New Zealand archaeologist Roger Duff had explicitly used the 'islands as laboratories' concept before its popularisation by Mead (1957). He cites Duff (1956:1), but the same wording occurs in Duff (1950:1), a book completed in 1947–1948: 'The student of the ethnography of Polynesia has at hand a remarkable human laboratory in which to study whatever laws determine the evolution of human culture in time and space.' The statement is unreferenced, suggesting it was a commonly used idea at the time. Duff also provides an elegant discussion of the concept of 'cultural drift' without, however, naming it as such (1950:2–3). His contributions on these topics appear to have been generally ignored by scholars apart from Golson.

4. Terrell is certainly among the earliest archaeologists to engage with MacArthur and Wilson's (1967) ideas. He refers to having come across a copy of their book in 1971 (Terrell 1974:ii), and its influence was plain in publications by Terrell and his associates that reference it not long afterwards (for instance, Kaplan 1973; Terrell 1972).

5. Goldman was kept busy during 1957 in the pages of *Journal of the Polynesian Society* answering his critics. Hawthorn and Belshaw (1957) published a critique of Goldman (1955) in the first issue of the *Journal* for the year, to which Goldman (1957b) replied in the second issue immediately after Goodenough's paper. The 1957 paper that has already been discussed appeared in the fourth issue for the year, the issue after that in which Sahlins' paper appeared, but was evidently written before Goldman had seen Hawthorn and Belshaw's critique, which is not referred to.

6. The symposium volume (Fosberg (ed) 1963) was enormously influential in several areas, not least as being the first sustained discussion of human impacts, negative and positive, on island ecosystems in the pre-European contact period. Major programs of archaeological research on human-induced environmental impacts on Pacific islands in particular over the succeeding decades were directly or indirectly inspired by this publication (Kirch 2000:57–62), not least by a companion paper originally delivered by Vayda and Rappaport at the symposium and revised for publication by Rappaport, entitled 'Aspects of Man's Influence upon Island Ecosystems: Alteration and Control' (Rappaport 1963).

Acknowledgements

A now-unrecognisable version of some of these ideas was presented as a keynote address to the *Global Perspectives on the Archaeology of Islands* conference, held at the University of Auckland, December 8–11 2004. I would like to thank the conference organisers James Connolly and Matthew Campbell for inviting me and defraying my airfare to New Zealand. The Department of Archaeology and Natural History, RSPAS, ANU provided further financial support. Helpful comments on my presentation were given by David Addison, Roger Green, Geoff Irwin and Peter White. Most recently, my thoughts were further crystallized by attending the *Global Origins and the Development of Seafaring* conference, held at the McDonald Institute for Archaeological Research, University of Cambridge, September 19–21 2007, organised by Atholl Anderson and Graeme Barker. I am grateful to Prof. John Evans for information about the intellectual influences on his 1973 paper, and to Albert Ammerman and Pamela Smith for recent discussions on some of the issues in this paper.

References

Anderson, A. 1980. The archaeology of Raoul Island (Kermadecs) and its place in the settlement history of Polynesia. *Archaeology and Physical Anthropology in Oceania* 15:131–141.

Anderson, A. 2000. Slow boats from China: Issues in the prehistory of Indo-Pacific seafaring. In S. O'Connor and P. Veth (eds), *East of Wallace's Line: Studies of Past and Present Maritime Cultures of the Indo-Pacific Region, Modern Quaternary Studies in Southeast Asia* 16, pp. 13–50. Rotterdam: Balkema.

Anderson, A. 2001. Towards the sharp end: The form and performance of prehistoric Polynesian voyaging canoes. In C.M. Stevenson, G. Lee and F.J. Morin (eds), *Pacific 2000: Proceedings of the Fifth International Conference on Easter Island and the Pacific*, pp. 29–36. Los Osos: Easter Island Foundation.

Anderson, A. 2002. Taking to the boats: The prehistory of Indo-Pacific colonization, National Institute for Asia and the Pacific Public Lecture, December 18, Canberra.

Anderson, A. 2004. Islands of Ambivalence. In S.M. Fitzpatrick (ed), *Voyages of Discovery: The Archaeology of Islands*, pp. 251–273. Praeger: Westport.

Anderson, A. and G. O'Regan 2000. To the final shore: Prehistoric Colonisation of the Subantarctic Islands in South Polynesia. In A. Anderson and T. Murray (eds), *Australian Archaeologist: Collected Papers in Honour of Jim Allen*, pp. 440–454. Canberra: Coombs Academic Publishing.

Anderson, A. and J.P. White (eds) 2002. *The Prehistory of Norfolk Island, Southwest Pacific*. Records of the Australian Museum Supplement 27.

Anderson A., H. Martinsson-Wallin and P. Wallin 2002. *The Prehistory of Kiritimati (Christmas) Island, Republic of Kiribati: Excavations and Analysis, Occasional Papers of the Kon-Tiki Museum* 6, Oslo.

Anderson A., J. Chappell, M. Gagan and R. Grove 2006. Prehistoric maritime migration in the Pacific islands: An hypothesis of ENSO forcing. *The Holocene* 16(1):1–6.

Bedford, S. and M. Spriggs 2008. Northern Vanuatu as a Pacific crossroads: The archaeology of discovery, interaction and the emergence of the "ethnographic present". *Asian Perspectives* 47(1):95–120.

Boomert, A. and A.J. Bright 2007. Bright Island archaeology: In search of a new horizon. *Island Studies Journal* 2(1):3–26.

Broodbank, C. 2000. *An Island Archaeology of the Early Cyclades*. Cambridge: Cambridge University Press.

Boas, F. 1896. The limitations of the comparative method in anthropology. In F. Boas Race, *Language and Culture*, pp. 270–280. New York: MacMillan.

Boyd, W.C. 1950. *Genetics and the Races of Man*. Boston: Little Brown.

Bulmer, S. and R. Bulmer 1964. The prehistory of the Australian New Guinea Highlands. *American Anthropologist* 66:29–76.

Burney, D.A. 1997. Tropical islands as paleoecological laboratories: Gauging the consequences of human arrival. *Human Ecology* 25(3):437–457.

Burrows, E.G. 1938. Western Polynesia: A study in cultural differentiation. *Ethnological Studies* 7.

Burrows, E.G. 1939.Breed and border in Polynesia. *American Anthropologist* 41:1–21.

Burrows, E.G. 1940. Culture areas in Polynesia. *Journal of the Polynesian Society* 49:349–363.

Cherry, J.F. 1981. Pattern and process in the earliest colonization of the Mediterranean islands. *Proceedings of the Prehistoric Society* 47:41–68.

Cherry, J.F. 1990.The first colonization of the Mediterranean islands: A review of recent research *Journal of Mediterranean Archaeology* 3(2):145–221.

Childe, V.G. 1951. *Social Evolution*. Henry Schuman: London and New York.

Davidson, J.M. 1977. Western Polynesia and Fiji: Prehistoric contact, diffusion and differentiation in adjacent archipelagos. *World Archaeology* 9:82–94.

Dewar, R.E. 1997. Does it matter that Madagascar is an Island? *Human Ecology* 25(3):481–489.

Duff, R. 1950. *The Moa-Hunter Period of Maori Culture*. R.E. Owen, Government Printer: Wellington.

Duff, R. 1956. *The Moa-Hunter Period of Maori Culture*. Department of Internal Affairs: Wellington.

Elbert, S.H. 1953. Internal relationships of Polynesian languages and dialects. *Southwestern Journal of Anthropology* 9:147–173.

Evans, J.D. 1973. Islands as laboratories for the study of culture process. In C. Renfrew (ed), *The Explanation of Culture Change: Models in Prehistory*, pp. 517–520. London: Duckworth.

Evans, J.D. 1977. Island archaeology in the Mediterranean: Problems and opportunities. *World Archaeology* 9(1):12–26.

Fitzhugh, B. and T.L. Hunt 1997. Introduction: Islands as laboratories: Archaeological research in comparative perspective. *Human Ecology* 25(3):379–383.

Fitzpatrick, S.M. (ed) 2004. *Voyages of Discovery: The Archaeology of Islands*. Praeger: Westport.

Fitzpatrick, S.M., J.M. Erlandson, A. Anderson and P.V. Kirch 2007. Straw boats and the proverbial sea: A response to Island archaeology: In search of a new horizon. *Island Studies Journal* 2(2):229–238.

Fosberg, F.R. (ed) 1963. *Man's Place in the Island Ecosystem*. Honolulu: Bishop Museum Press.

Gladwin, T. 1956. Canoe travel in the Truk area: Technology and its psychological correlates, Paper read at the 55th Annual Meeting of the American Anthropological Association.

Goldman, I. 1955. Status rivalry and cultural evolution in Polynesia. *American Anthropologist* 57:680–697.

Goldman, I. 1957a. Variations in Polynesian social organization. *Journal of the Polynesian Society* 66:374–390.

Goldman, I. 1957b. Cultural evolution in Polynesia: A reply to criticism. *Journal of the Polynesian Society* 66:156–164.

Goldman, I. 1970. *Ancient Polynesian Society*. Chicago: University of Chicago Press.

Golson, J. 1958. The peopling of the South Pacific. In *Western Pacific: Studies of Man and Environment in the Western Pacific*, pp. 26–40. Department of Geography, Victoria University of Wellington: Wellington.

Golson, J. 1959. Archéologie du Pacifique Sud: résultats et perspectives. *Journal de la Société des Océanistes* 15:5–54.

Goodenough, W.H. 1953. *Native Astronomy in the Central Carolines*. Philadelphia: University Museum.

Goodenough, W.H. 1957. Oceania and the problem of controls in the study of cultural and human evolution. *Journal of the Polynesian Society* 66:146–155.

Green, S.W. and S.M. Perlman (eds) 1985. *The Archaeology of Frontiers and Boundaries*. Orlando: Academic Press.

Harris, M. 1969. *The Rise of Anthropological Theory: A History of Theories of Cultures*. London: Routledge and Kegan Paul.

Hawthorn, H.B. and C.S. Belshaw 1957. Cultural evolution or cultural change? The case of Polynesia. *Journal of the Polynesian Society* 66:18–35.

Heyerdahl, T. 1955. The balsa raft in aboriginal navigation off Peru and Ecuador. *Southwestern Journal of Anthropology* 11:251–264.

Hodder, I. 1978. The maintenance of group identities in the Baringo District, W. Kenya. In D. Green, C. Haselgrove and M. Spriggs (eds), *Social Organisation and Settlement: Contributions from Anthropology, Archaeology and Geography, Part I*, pp. 47–73. Oxford: BAR International Series (Supplementary) 47(i).

Hodder, I. 1982. *Symbols in Action*. Cambridge: Cambridge University Press.

Irwin, G. 1992. *The Prehistoric Exploration and Colonisation of the Pacific*. Cambridge: Cambridge University Press.

Kaplan, S. 1973. *A Style Analysis of Pottery Sherds from Nissan Island. Solomon Island Studies in Human Biogeography 2*. Chicago: Field Museum of Natural History.

Kirch, P.V. 1982. Advances in Polynesian prehistory: Three decades in review. *Advances in World Archaeology* 1:51–97.

Kirch, P.V. 2000. *On the Road of the Winds: An Archaeological History of the Pacific Islands before European Contact*. Berkeley: University of California Press.

Kuklick, H. 1996. Islands in the Pacific: Darwinian biogeography and British anthropology. *American Ethnologist* 23(3):611–638.

MacArthur, R.H. and E.O. Wilson 1967. *The Theory of Island Biogeography*. Princeton: Princeton University Press.

Mead, M. 1957. Introduction to Polynesia as laboratory for the development of models in the study of cultural evolution. *Journal of the Polynesian Society* 66:145.

Mead, M. 1958. Cultural determinants of behavior. In G. Simpson and A. Roe (eds), *Behaviour and Evolution*, pp. 480–503. New Haven: Yale University Press.

Morgan, L.H. 1868. *Systems of Consanguinity and Affinity of the Human Family*. Smithsonian Contributions to Knowledge 218.

Muller, H.J. 1956. Genetic principles in human populations. *The Scientific Monthly* 83:277–286.

Patton, M. 1996. *Islands in Time: Island Sociogeography and Mediterranean Prehistory*. London: Routledge.

Pawley, A. 1981. Melanesian diversity and Polynesian homogeneity: A unified explanation for language. In J. Hollyman and A. Pawley (eds), *Studies in Pacific Languages and Cultures in Honour of Bruce Biggs*, pp. 269–309. Auckland: Linguistic Society of New Zealand.

Pearson, R.J. 1969. *Archaeology of the Ryukyu Islands: A Regional Chronology from 3000 B.C. to the Historic Period*. Honolulu: University of Hawaii Press.

Prichard, J.C. 1813. *Researches into the Physical History of Man*. London: Sherwood, Gilbert and Piper.

Rainbird, P. 1999. Islands out of time: Towards a critique of Island Archaeology. *Journal of Mediterranean Archaeology* 12(2):216–234.

Rainbird, P. 2007. *The Archaeology of Islands*. Cambridge: Cambridge University Press.

Rappaport, R.A. 1963. Aspects of man's influence upon island ecosystems: Alteration and control. In F.R. Fosberg (ed), *Man's Place in the Island Ecosystem*, pp. 155–174. Honolulu: Bishop Museum Press.

Renfrew, C. 2004. Islands out of time? Toward an analytical framework. In S.M. Fitzpatrick (ed), *Voyages of Discovery: The Archaeology of Islands*, pp. 275–294. Westport: Praeger.

Roe, D. 2000. Maritime, coastal and inland societies in Island Melanesia: The bush-saltwater divide in Solomon Islands and Vanuatu. In S. O'Connor and P. Veth (eds), *East of Wallace's Line: Studies of*

Past and Present Maritime Cultures of the Indo-Pacific Region, pp. 197–222. Modern Quaternary Studies in Southeast Asia 16. Rotterdam: Balkema.

Rolett, B. and J. Diamond 2004. Environmental predictors of pre-European deforestation on Pacific islands. *Nature* 431:443–446.

Sahlins, M.D. 1957 Differentiation by adaptation in Polynesian societies. *Journal of the Polynesian Society* 66:291–300.

Sahlins, M.D. 1958. *Social Stratification in Polynesia*. American Ethnological Society Monograph 29.

Sharp, A.1956. *Ancient Voyagers in the Pacific*. Polynesian Society Memoir 32.

Shutler, M.E. and R.J. Shutler Jr 1966. A preliminary report of archaeological exploration in the southern New Hebrides. *Asian Perspectives* 9:57–166.

Simpson, G.G. 1949. *The Meaning of Evolution*. New Haven: Yale University Press.

Skinner, H.D. 1921. Culture areas in New Zealand. *Journal of the Polynesian Society* 30:71–78.

Specht, J., I. Lilley and J. Normu 1981. Radiocarbon dates from West New Britain, Papua New Guinea. *Australian Archaeology* 12:13–15.

Spriggs, M. 1997 *The Island Melanesians*. Oxford: Blackwell,

Steward, J.H. 1955. *Theory of Culture Change: The Methodology of Multilinear Evolution*. Urbana: University of Illinois Press.

Suggs, R.C. 1961. *The Archeology of Nuku Hiva, Marquesas Islands, French Polynesia, Anthropological Papers of the American Museum of Natural History* 49(1).

Terrell, J.E. 1972. *Geographic Systems and Human Diversity in the Northern Solomons. Reports of the Bougainville Archaeological Survey* 5. Chicago: Field Museum of Natural History.

Terrell, J.E. 1974. *Comparative Study of Human and Lower Animal Biogeography in the Solomon Islands. Solomon Island Studies in Human Biogeography* 3. Chicago: Field Museum of Natural History.

Terrell, J.E. 1997. The postponed agenda: Archaeology and human biogeography in the twenty-first century. *Human Ecology* 25(3):419–436.

Vayda, A.P. and R.A. Rappaport 1963. Island cultures. In F.R. Fosberg (ed), *Man's Place in the Island Ecosystem*, pp. 133–142. Honolulu: Bishop Museum Press.

Weisler, M.I. 1994. The settlement of Marginal Polynesia: New evidence from Henderson Island. *Journal of Field Archaeology* 21(1):83–102.

Weisler, M.I. 2004. Contraction of the Southeast Polynesian interaction sphere and resource depletion on Temoe Atoll, *New Zealand Journal of Archaeology* 25: 57–88.

White, L.A. 1949. T*he Science of Culture*. New York: Farrar and Strauss.

Whitney, H. 1955. An analysis of the design of the major sea-going craft of Oceania, Unpublished MA thesis, University of Pennsylvania.

Wissler, C. 1917. The American Indian: An Introduction to the Anthropology of the New World. New York: D.C. McMurtrie.

Wissler, C. 1926. *The Relation of Nature to Man in Aboriginal America*. London: Oxford University Press.

Wissler, C. 1938. *The American Indian*, third edition. New York: Oxford University Press.

Zilhao, J. 1993. The spread of agro-pastoral economies across Mediterranean Europe: A view from the far west. *Journal of Mediterranean Archaeology* 6(1):5–63.

15

No fruit on that beautiful shore: What plants were introduced to the subtropical Polynesian islands prior to European contact?

Matthew Prebble
Department of Archaeology and Natural History, Australian National University, Australia
matiu@coombs.anu.edu.au

Introduction

The introduction of plants to Remote Oceania has been a subject alluded to throughout the development of Pacific botany (e.g. Seemann 1865–73; Guppy 1906; Ridley 1930; Brown 1935; Merrill 1946) and is important given the potential overlapping roles of natural dispersal (e.g. Carquist 1996) and human introduction in shaping island floras. In recent ethnobotanical treatments of Remote Oceania (e.g. Kirch and Yen 1982; Whistler 1991) and in a number of floral compendiums of island archipelagos (e.g. Wagner *et al.* 1990; Florence 1997, 2004), there has been a tendency for the introduced botanical status of plant species to be given on the basis of their human introduction potential. This potential may include, for any plant, its ethnographic, historical or current status of human utility as wild (natural), domesticated or feral. In this paper, I address a number of additional sources of botanical information, including palaeobotanical and archaeobotanical data, as a means of better defining the human introduction potential of a range of plant taxa. This human introduction potential of many species is discussed with particular reference to New Zealand, where relatively few Polynesian plant introductions have been described with any certainty.

Of the 11 subtropical islands, both >4 km^2 in area and situated south of the Tropic of Capricorn (23°26'22"S), there is no evidence that Lord Howe, Alejandro Selkirk, Robinson Crusoe and San Ambosio were ever colonised before European arrival (Anderson 2001). Four islands, including Henderson, Pitcairn, Norfolk and Raoul, were colonised and then abandoned before European arrival (Anderson 1980, 1996; Weisler 1995). Three small islands, including Raivavae, Rapa, Rapanui and the largest Polynesian island, New Zealand, were apparently occupied continuously after initial colonisation. Based on recently constructed archaeological chronologies, Polynesian colonisation took place between 800 and 700 cal. BP (Higham *et al.* 1999; Hogg *et al.* 2003; Kennett *et al.* 2006; Hunt and Lipo 2006). In this study of the introduced floras of the subtropical islands of Remote Oceania, I focus on all the Polynesian islands including Raivavae, Henderson, Pitcairn, Rapanui, Rapa, Norfolk and Raoul (Figure 1, Table 1 and Table 2).

The floras of Raivavae, Henderson and Pitcairn are derived largely from the western Pacific, species having mainly dispersed via island archipelagos stretching from the Indo-Malaysian basin. Rapa has a strong floral affinity with Norfolk and New Zealand, but also retains many Indo-Malaysian elements. Raoul has a predominant New Zealand flora, but shares a number of elements with Norfolk Island, which has a floral affinity with both New Caledonia and New Zealand. By contrast, Rapanui retains a predominantly American flora, with some Indo-Malaysian elements.

The defining characteristic of the indigenous subtropical island floras is the attenuated representation of Indo-Malaysian elements. Coastal strand taxa like *Scaevola taccada* (Goodeniaceae) and *Calophyllum inophyllum* (Clusiaceae) common to most tropical Pacific Islands are absent in the subtropical islands. Many species-rich Indo-Malaysian genera are reduced to few or no species in the subtropics. A number of plant cultigens, including breadfruit (*Artocarpus altilis*, Moraceae), are currently absent on many of the subtropical islands, but may have been present in the past. This attenuation probably follows a reduction in geological diversity, as all islands are volcanic and, with the exception of northern New Zealand, are entirely oceanic in origin. The climates of the subtropical Polynesian islands are influenced by the 23C summer isotherm (Figure 1), marking the approximate southern limit of surface coral growth, and the decreasing sea surface winter isotherms (Figure 1) that incline from the west to the east

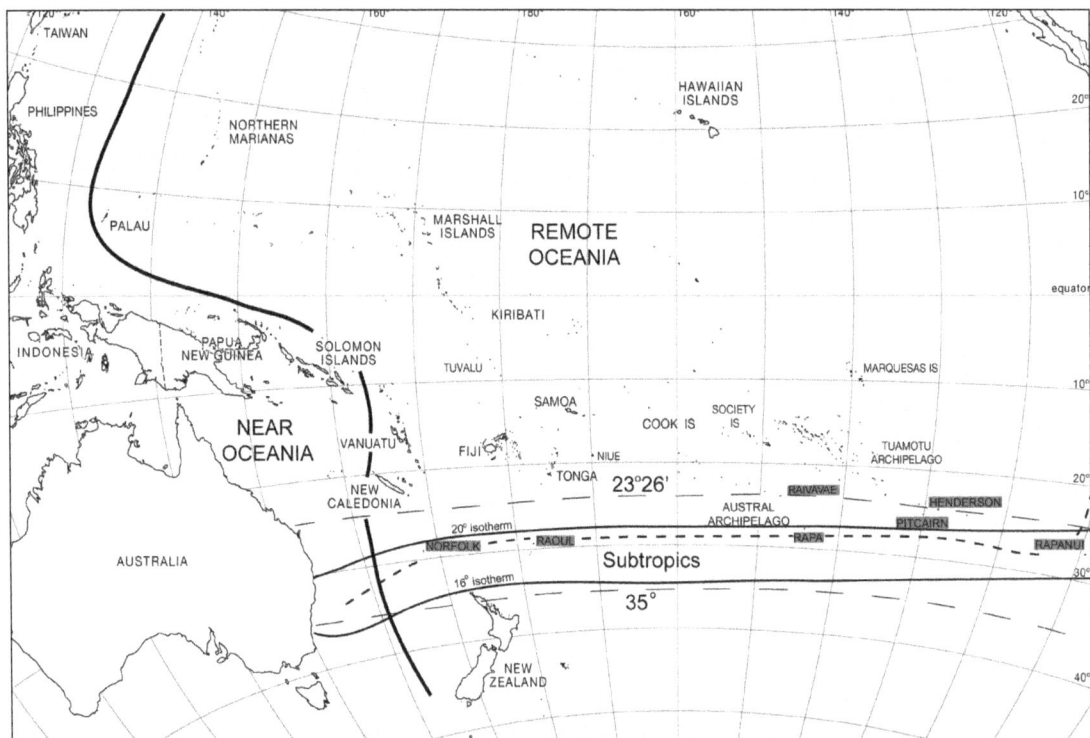

Figure 1. Map of the Pacific: the division between Near and Remote Oceania, the subtropics between 23°26′22″S and 35°S, showing the main archipelagos and the subtropical Polynesian islands (shaded labels). Sea-surface winter isotherms (20 and 16C; thick black lines) and the summer isotherm (23C, dashed black line), marking the approximate southern margin of surface coral growth.

Table 1. The subtropical islands of Remote Oceania colonised by Polynesians before European contact. Listed are the main geographic and climatic characteristics of each island.

Island (Sovereign)	Latitude / Longitude	Area (km²)	Highest elevation (m)	Temperature range (°C)/ min and max recorded temp (°C)	Mean annual rainfall (mm)	No. vascular plants (no. endemics)	Reference
Raivavae (French Polynesia)	23°52'S/ 147°39'W	20.3	437	?	?	147(43)	Meyer (unpublished)
Henderson* (United Kingdom)	24°22'S/ 128°18'W	37.2	33	16–24 (Winter) 22–30 (Summer)	1623	54 (9)	Florence et al. (1995)
Pitcairn* (United Kingdom)	25°04'S/ 130°06'W	4.6	347	13–23 (Winter) 17–28 (Summer)	1716	57 (9)	Florence et al. (1995)
Rapanui (Chile)	27°09'S/ 109°6'W	166	511	14–22 (Winter) 15–28 (Summer)	1365	43 (4)	Zizka (1991)
Rapa (French Polynesia)	27°36'S/ 144°20'W	38	631	16–21 (Winter) 22–26 (Summer)	2664	212 (79)	Rapa Meteo (unpublished data); Meyer (2002), Motley (unpublished)
Norfolk* (Australia)	29°02'S/ 167°56'E	34.6	316	13–19 (Winter) 18–25 (Summer)	1312	345 (149)	www.bom.gov.au; Green (1994)
Raoul* (New Zealand)	29°15'S/ 177°55'W	29.38	516	16–22	1554	104 (6?)	Sykes (1977)

* Islands abandoned by Polynesians before European contact. Rapanui and Rapa continuously occupied. Islands abandoned by Polynesians prior to European contact. It is assumed that Raivavae, Rapanui, Rapa and subtropical northern New Zealand have been continuously occupied since initial colonisation.

Table 2. First-European-contact accounts for the subtropical Polynesian islands and the main floral compendium for each island.

Island	Polynesian colonisation chronology	First European contact	First comprehensive floral compendium	Most recent floral compendium	References
Raivavae	700 BP	1775 Aguila, Jupiter	1921–1934	2002	Corney (1913-1919); St. John and Fosberg (1934); Meyer (unpublished)
Henderson	600 BP	1606 San Pedro y San Pablo, San Pedro and Los Tres Reyes	1962	1995	Weisler (1995); St. John and Philipson (1962); Fosberg et al. (1983); Florence et al. (1995).
Pitcairn	600 BP	1767 HMS Swallow	1987	1995	St. John (1978); Florence et al. (1995); Weisler (1996)
Rapanui	700 BP	1721 Arend, Tienhoven and De Afrikaansche Galey	1917	1991	Corney (1913-1919); Skottsberg (1920-1956); Zizka (1991); Hunt and Lipo (2006)
Rapa	700 BP	1791 HMS Discovery	1921–1934	2002–2004	Vancouver (1803); St. John and Fosberg (1934); Shineberg (1986); Meyer et al. 2004); Kennett et al. (2006)
Norfolk	500 BP	1774 HMS Resolution	1804–1805	1963–1985	Endlicher (1833); Hoare (1987); Anderson et al. (2001); Green (1994)
Raoul	700 BP	1793 La Recherche and d'Hesmity-d'Auribeau	1854	1977	Hooker (1856); Sykes (1977); Anderson (1980); Higham and Johnson (1996)

Pacific. Such climatic gradients are likely to influence plant dispersal, the distribution of animal dispersers and plant establishment and recruitment on subtropical Pacific Islands.

The introduced floras of the subtropical Polynesian islands

Of the subtropical Polynesian islands, pre-contact introduced plants are best known for Rapanui, Rapa and New Zealand, largely because first European contact records of these islands are available and these islands were inhabited at contact, unlike Henderson, Pitcairn, Norfolk and Raoul. The availability of rich late-Holocene palaeobotanical deposits from these islands is important for defining pre-contact introductions, especially weeds, but these data thus far are only available for Rapa (e.g. Kennett *et al.* 2006), Norfolk (MacPhail 2001) and Rapanui (e.g. Flenley *et al.* 1991). Archaeobotanical records provide useful sources of information data on economic plants and are now available for most of the subtropical Polynesian islands. Much is known about the distribution and introduction of several crops to these islands, including *Colocasia esculenta* (Matthews 2004), *Cordyline fruticosa* (Hinkle 2004), *Ipomoea batatas* (Green 2005) and *Lagenaria siceraria* (Clark *et al.* 2006). In this paper, I examine a number of plants introduced to the islands of subtropical Remote Oceania, focusing on those poorly known plants, but which have been discussed more broadly for Remote Oceania by a number of authors, including Guppy (1906), Ridley (1930), Merrill (1946), Barrau (1965), Yen (1973, 1974a) and Whistler (1991). Some of these taxa have an uncertain introduction status and the reasons for this uncertainty are explored. I focus on taxa represented in subtropical Polynesian island floras and described in the main floral compendiums for each island (Brown 1931, 1935; Sykes 1977; Green 1994; Florence *et al.* 1995; Florence 1997, 2004). Taxa are grouped in separate tables for trees and shrubs (Table 3a and 3b), herbs (Table 4) and inadvertent introductions (Table 5). Each table is divided into the following categories of presence/absence data: pre-human palaeobotanical records; archaeobotanical records; anthropogenic palaeobotanical records; and botanical survey records.

As the availability of botanical information for each taxon varies considerably, with no one taxon having a complete record (i.e. some taxa have no palaeobotanical record and have only been recorded in modern botanical surveys), I focus on taxa that reflect the variation of available palaeobotanical, archaeobotanical and botanical survey data.

Probable intentional tree and shrub introductions

A number of tree and shrub taxa sometimes regarded as indigenous to subtropical Polynesian islands appear to survive only in cultivation (e.g. *Cocos nucifera* and *Thespesia populnea*). Others appear to have become naturalised from cultivated populations (e.g. *Cordyline fruticosa*). For some taxa, the introduced and cultivation status is clear, given the lack of sexual reproductive traits whereby plants are reliant on human propagation of vegetative clones. For example, in *Broussonetia papyrifera*, the cumulative effects of increasing mutations evident in wild and cultivated populations eventually led to vegetative propagation dependence (Matthews 1996). For other taxa, the status of indigenous plants, given the pre-human extent of their sub-fossil records, is difficult to define, given the possibility that people may have introduced additional populations or varieties (e.g. *Pandanus tectorius*). For many taxa, the botanical status cannot be securely given because of the lack of botanical source evidence.

Pandanus tectorius Parkinson (Pandanaceae)

Whistler (1991) earlier questioned the status of *Pandanus tectorius* as an introduced species to Remote Oceania. He suggested that *P. tectorius* of both Tonga and Samoa is represented by both

Table 3a. (Anacardiaceae to Malvaceae) Botanical source list of pre-contact introduced or indigenous trees and shrubs (including known arboricultural species) for the subtropical Polynesian islands (arranged by family), recognised in the references and by Whistler (1991).

Botanical species	Pre-human palaeo-botanical records	Archaeobotanical records	Anthropogenic palaeobotanical records	First contact accounts 1606–1793	Botanical survey data	
					Earliest flora compendium	Recent flora compendium
Alyxia stellata (J.R. Forst. and G. Forst.) Roem. and Schult. (Apocynaceae)[2]	—	—	—	—	Raivavae, Henderson (?), Rapa	Raivavae, Henderson (?)
Cocos nucifera L. (Arecaeceae: Cocoeae)[1]	—	—	—	Rapa (introduced)?	Raivavae, Henderson, Rapanui, Rapa	Raivavae, Henderson, Rapanui, Rapa, Raoul[12]
Barringtonia asiatica L. Kurz (Barringtoniaceae)[5]	—	—	—	—	Raivavae, Pitcairn	Raivavae, Pitcairn
Cordia subcordata Lam. (Boraginaceae)[9]	—	—	—	—	—	Henderson
Casuarina equisetifolia L. (Casuarinaceae)[4]	Rapanui, (pollen)[10], Rapa (pollen)[6]	—	Rapanui, (pollen), Rapa (pollen)[6]	—	Raivavae	Raivavae, Rapa
Calophyllum inophyllum L. (Clusiaceae)[4]	—	—	—	—	Raivavae, Pitcairn	Raivavae, Pitcairn
Corynocarpus laevigatus	—	—	Raoul, Northern New Zealand		Raoul, northern New Zealand	Raoul, northern New Zealand
Terminalia catappa L. (Combretaceae)[2]	—	—	—	—	Raivavae	Raivavae
Aleurites moluccana L. Willd. (Euphorbiaceae)[3]	—	Rapa (endocarp)[5] Raoul (endocarp)[8]	Rapa (pollen)[6]	Rapanui ?	Raivavae, Henderson, Pitcairn, Rapa, Raoul	Raivavae, Henderson, Raoul, Rapa
Erythrina variegata L. (Fabaceae)[2]	—	—	Rapa (pollen)[6]	—	Raivavae, Pitcairn, Rapa	Raivavae, Pitcairn, Rapa
Cordyline fruticosa L. Chev. (Laxmanniaceae)[1]	Norfolk (pollen record may be of an endemic species)[9]	Rapanui (charcoal)[11], Rapa? (charred tuber)[5]	Rapa (pollen)[6] Norfolk (pollen?)[9]	Rapanui (?), Rapa	Raivavae, Rapanui, Rapa	Raivavae, Henderson, Pitcairn, Rapanui, Rapa, Norfolk, Raoul
Hibiscus tiliaceus L. (Malvaceae)[4]	Rapa (pollen)[6], Norfolk (pollen)[9]	Rapa (fibre)[5]	Norfolk (pollen?)[9]	Rapanui (?), Rapa (?)	Raivavae, Rapa, Raoul	Raivavae, Rapa, Norfolk, Raoul
Thespesia populnea L. Sol. Ex Correa (Malvaceae)[4]	—	Rapanui (charcoal)[11]	—	Rapa	Raivavae, Henderson, Rapa	Raivavae, Rapa

[1]Brown (1931); [2]Brown (1935); [3]Florence (1997); [4]Florence (2004); [5]Prebble and Anderson (In press); [6]Prebble *et al,* (submitted); [7]Macphail *et al.* (2001); [8]Anderson (unpublished); [9]Macphail *et al.* (2001); [10]Flenley (1991); [11]Orliac (1998); [12]Sykes and West (1996).

Table 3b. (Moraceae to Urticaceae) Botanical source list of pre-contact introduced or indigenous trees and shrubs (including known arboricultural species) for the subtropical Polynesian islands (arranged by family), recognised in the references and by Whistler (1991).

Botanical species	Prehuman palaeo-botanical records	Archaeobotanical records	Anthropogenic palaeobotanical records	First European contact accounts 1606–1793	Botanical survey data	
					Earliest compendium	Latest compendium
Artocarpus altilis Parkinson (Fosberg) (Moraceae)[3]	—	—	—	—	Raivavae, Rapa	Raivavae
Broussonetia papyrifera L. Vent. (Moraceae)[3]	—	Rapanui (charcoal)	—	Rapanui (?), New Zealand	Raivavae, Rapa, New Zealand	Raivavae, Rapa, New Zealand
Ficus tinctoria Forst. subsp. *tinctoria* (Moraceae)[3]	—	—	Rapa (pollen)?	Rapanui (?)	Raivavae, Rapa	Raivavae, Rapa
Musa spp. (AAB group) [syn. *M. x paradaisica, M. sapientum*] (Musaceae: section Eumusa)[1]	—	—	—	Rapanui, Rapa, Norfolk[6]	Raivavae (?), Rapa, Rapanui	Raivavae, Rapa, Rapanui
Musa spp. [syn. *M. fehi, M. troglodytarum, M. balbisiana*] (Musaceae: section Australimusa and Callimusa)[1, 3]	—	—	—	Rapa (introduced?)	Raivavae, Rapa	Raivavae, Rapa
Musa spp. (AAA group) [*M. acuminata, M. nana, M. sinensis*] (Musaceae: section Eumusa)[1]	—	—	—	—	Raivavae (?), Rapa	Raivavae, Rapa[4], Raoul
Syzygium malaccense L. Merrill and Perry (Myrtaceae)[2]	—	Rapanui (charcoal)	Rapa (pollen)?	—	Raivavae, Rapa	Raivavae, Rapa
Pandanus tectorius Parkinson (Pandanaceae)[6]	Rapa (pollen)	Rapa (pollen, syncarp)	Henderson (pollen), Pitcairn (pollen), Rapa (pollen)	Rapa	Raivavae, Henderson, Pitcairn, Rapa	Raivavae, Henderson, Pitcairn, Rapa
Sapindus saponaria L. (Sapindaceae)[4]	—	—	—	Rapanui	Rapanui	Pitcairn, Rapanui
Solanum viride Forst. f. ex Spring (Solanaceae)[5]	—	—	—	—	?	Rapa

[1]Brown (1931a); [2]Brown (1935); [3]Florence (1997); [4]Zizka (1991); [5]Hoare (1987:12–14); [6]Not all information available.

Table 4. Botanical sources of probable herb introductions (including tuber, corn and rhizome cultigens) (arranged by family) to the subtropical Polynesian islands, recognised in the references and by Whistler (1991). None of these species have been located in any pre-human palaeobotanical record.

Botanical species	Archaeobotanical records	Anthropogenic palaeobotanical records	First-contact accounts 1606–1793	Botanical survey data for Rapa	
				Earliest compendium	Latest compendium
Alocasia macrorrhiza L. (Araceae)	Pitcairn (pollen)[7]	—	Rapa?	Raivavae, Rapa	Raivavae, Rapa
Colocasia esculenta L. Schott. (Araceae)[1]	Rapa? (tuber peelings)[4]	Rapa (pollen)[5]	Raivavae, Rapa, northern New Zealand	Raivavae, Rapanui, Rapa, northern New Zealand	Raivavae, Rapanui, Rapa, Raoul, northern New Zealand
Cyrtosperma merkusii (Haask.) Schott. (syn. *C. chamissonis*) (Araceae)	Henderson (leaf)[6]	—	—	—	—
Ipomoea batatas L. (Convovulaceae)[2]	Rapanui (charcoal, starch)[8], New Zealand (starch)[8]	—	Rapanui, New Zealand	Raivavae, Rapanui, Rapa, New Zealand	Raivavae, Rapa, Raoul, New Zealand
Lagenaria siceraria (Molina) Standl. (Cucurbitaceae)[2]	Rapa (pericarp, phytoliths)[4], New Zealand (phytoliths)[8]	—	Rapa, northern New Zealand	Rapa, northern New Zealand	northern New Zealand
Dioscorea spp. [*D. alata, D. bulbifera, D. pentaphylla, D. sativa*] (Dioscoreaceae)[1]	—	—	Rapa	Raivavae (*D. sativa*), Rapa (*D. alata, D. bulbifera, D. pentaphylla, D. sativa*)	Rapa (*D. alata, D. bulbifera, D. pentaphylla, D. sativa*)
Manihot esculenta Crantz (Euphorbiaceae)[3]	—	—	—	Raivavae, Rapa	Raivavae, Rapa
Tephrosia pupurea L. Pers. (Fabaceae)	—	—	—	—	Raivavae, Rapa
Erianthus maximus Brongn. (Poaceae)	—	—	—	Rapa	Rapa
Saccharum officinarum L. (Poaceae)[1]	Rapanui (charred leaf)[8]	—	Rapa	Raivavae, Rapa	Raivavae, Rapa
Tacca leontopetaloides L. Kuntze (Taccaceae) 1	—	—	—	Rapa	Rapa
Curcuma longa L. (Zingiberaceae)[1]	—	—	—	Raivavae, Rapa	—
Zingiber zerumbet L. Smith (Zingiberaceae)[1]	—	—	—	Raivavae, Rapa	Raivavae, Rapa

[1]Brown (1931); [2]Brown (1935); [3]Florence (1997); [4]Prebble and Anderson (In press), [5]Prebble *et al.* (submitted), [6]Hather and Weisler (2000), [7]Horrocks and Weisler (2006), [8]tentative records from a number of sources (for *Ipomoea batatas* in New Zealand see Yen and Head 1993).

Table 5. Botanical sources of probable inadvertent plant introductions (arranged by family) to the subtropical Polynesian islands, recognised in the references and by Whistler (1991). None of these species have been located in any prehuman palaeobotanical or first-contact record.

Botanical species	Anthropogenic palaeobotanical records	Botanical survey data	
		Earliest compendium	**Latest compendium**
Achyranthes aspera var. *aspera* L. (Amaranthaceae)[3,6]	Probable prehuman *Achyranthes* record on Norfolk, but may represent an endemic species[9]	Raivavae	Raivavae, Pitcairn, Rapa, Norfolk, Raoul
Amaranthus viridis L. (Amaranthaceae)[3]	Rapa (pollen?)[7] Raoul (pollen?)[8]	Raivavae, Rapa	Raivavae, Pitcairn, Rapa
Bidens pilosa L. (Asteraceae)[6]	Rapa (pollen?)[7]	Raivavae, Rapa	Raivavae, Pitcairn, Rapa, Norfolk, Raoul, northern New Zealand
Sigesbeckia orientalis L. (Asteraceae)[6]	Raoul (pollen?)[7]	Raivavae, Rapa, Raoul, northern New Zealand	Raivavae, Pitcairn, Rapa, Norfolk, northern New Zealand
Sonchus oleraceus L. (Asteraceae)[2]	Rapa (pollen)[7], Raoul (pollen?)[8]	Raivavae, Rapa	Raivavae, Pitcairn, Rapanui, Rapa, Norfolk
Canna indica L. (Cannaceae)[2]	—	Raivavae, Rapa	Raivavae, Pitcairn, Rapa, Norfolk, Raoul
Commelina diffusa Burm. f. (Commelinaceae)[2]	Rapa (pollen)[7]	Raivavae, Rapa	Raivavae, Pitcairn, Rapanui, Rapa
Sida rhombifolia L. (Malvaceae)[3,5]	—	Raivavae, Rapa	Raivavae, Rapanui, Rapa, Norfolk, Raoul
Ludwigia octovalvis (Jacq.) Raven (Onagraceae)[2,4]	Rapa (pollen, seeds)[7]	Raivavae, Rapa	Raivavae, Rapa
Oxalis corniculata L. (Oxalidaceae)[4,6]	(Rapa, seeds?)[7]	Raivavae, Rapa, Raoul, northern New Zealand	Raivavae, Norfolk, Raoul, northern New Zealand
Eleusine indica (L.) J. Gaertner (Poaceae)[1–6]	—	Raivavae, Rapanui, Rapa, Raoul	Raivavae, Pitcairn, Rapanui, Rapa, Norfolk, Raoul
Oplismenus compositus, O. hirtellus (Poaceae)[11]	—	Raivavae, Rapanui, Rapa	Raivavae, Pitcairn, Rapanui, Rapa
Paspalum conjugatum, P. orbiculare (Poaceae)[11]	—	Raivavae, Rapanui, Rapa	Raivavae, Pitcairn, Rapanui, Rapa
Thuarea involuta (G. Forst.) R. brown ex J. Roemer and J.A. Schultes (Poaceae)[10]	—	—	Henderson (?)
Sapindus saponaria L. (Sapindaceae)[4]	—	Rapanui	Rapanui, Pitcairn
Rorippa sarmentosa (G.Forst. ex DC.) J.F. Macbr. (Solanaceae)[4,6]	—	Rapanui	Rapa
Solanum americanum P. Mill (Solanaceae)[5,6]	Rapa (pollen ?, seeds)[7], Raoul (pollen?)[8]	Raivavae, Rapa, northern New Zealand	Raivavae, Henderson, Pitcairn, Rapa, Norfolk, Raoul, northern New Zealand

[1]Brown (1931a); [2]Brown (1935); [3]Florence (2004); [4]Zizka (1991); [5]listed in St. John (1978) from Daniel Nelson's records of possible inadvertent pre-contact introductions to the Hawaiian Islands made in 1779; [6]listed in Whistler (1988) as a possible inadvertent pre-contact introductions to Western Samoa. [7]Prebble *et al.* (submitted); [8]Prebble and Wilmshurst (nd); [9]MacPhail *et al.* (2001); [10]Florence *et al.* (1995); [11]Not all information available, probable European introductions.

indigenous and introduced populations, but queried the indigenous status of *Pandanus* on the Cook, Society, Marquesas, and Hawaiian Islands. High concentrations of *Pandanus* pollen from Holocene-aged sediments on Rapa (macrofossils also present) establish its indigenous status there, and presumably across the Austral Archipelago (Prebble 2006; Prebble *et al.* submitted). With the unequivocal subfossil evidence, it is interesting that no reference was made to the palm-like *Pandanus tectorius* trees at first European contact. *Pandanus* was often noted as 'screw palm' or 'palm apple', as described by Morrison (1935:61) on Tubuai, to the north of Rapa, in the botanical vernacular of early European explorers. While immediately offshore from Rapa on the HMS *Discovery* in 1791, Menzies (in Shineberg 1986:67) mentioned *Dracena* leaves, which probably refers to *Pandanus*, in reference to a girdle should be suspened around the waist of one of the islanders, but this determination remains unclear.

Both leaf material and fruit keys from *Pandanus* have been identified from the Tangarutu rock-shelter sequence on Rapa, with an earliest inferred radiocarbon age of about 500 cal. BP (Prebble 2006; Prebble and Anderson In press). Horrocks and Weisler (2006) identified *Pandanus* pollen from archaeological sediments from both Pitcairn and Henderson, dated to c. 600 cal. BP and 800 cal. BP respectively. The archaeobotanical and palaeobotanical evidence, however, does not rule out the possibility, suggested by Whistler (1991), that additional varieties of *Pandanus tectorius* were introduced pre-contact. *Pandanus* is a dioecious genus with extreme morphological diversity that can be considerably influenced by cultivation practices. This has resulted in a number of inconsistent taxonomic determinations of members of this genus (see Stone 1976, 1988; St. John 1976, 1979). St. John (in Fosberg and St. John 1934) identified 13 endemic species of *Pandanus* on Rapa alone. Most of these species have subsequently been grouped into *Pandanus tectorius* and one other species has yet to be described (Tim Motley and Jaques Florence pers comm. 2004).

As yet, no phylogenetic studies have been undertaken for *Pandanus tectorius*. Such studies might yet distinguish different intraspecific populations. The morphological diversity in *Pandanus* that St. John identified on Rapa may be a result of genetic or environmental processes, but may also reflect the introduction of cultivated varieties by islanders both pre and post contact. The ethnobotanical importance of *Pandanus* on Rapa (e.g. Stokes ms), attested by the archaeobotanical record, but also from first-contact and ethnographic sources, highlights the potential for additional introductions. The indigenous status of *Pandanus* is only unequivocal from Rapa, but it is probably also indigenous to Henderson and Pitcairn. The human introduction of particular cultivars cannot be discounted as a factor in the current population distribution of this tree.

Casuarina equisetifolia L. (*Casuarinaceae*)

Florence (2004) determined *C. equisetifolia* subsp. *equisetifolia* from modern populations on Rapa. He suggests its distribution is problematic because of its wind-dispersed seeds and possible extension by human introduction to many islands of the Pacific. It was likely to have been introduced to Rapa in the historic period or earlier, but is probably indigenous to the northern islands of the Austral Archipelago. Whistler (1991) suggests that the distribution of *C. equisetifolia* in the east-Polynesian Pacific is a result of human introduction. This tree is represented in large stands across the Austral Archipelago, including on the atoll of Maria. On Rapa, its distribution is limited to small littoral stands on many of the least exposed bays or persistence in remnant cultivations (e.g. Anarua Bay).

The palynological record is important when discussing the status of this tree on Rapa and Rapanui. *Casuarina* pollen is represented throughout a Holocene swamp record on Rapa

(Tukou) where it is only ever represented in trace counts. This is more likely to represent either contamination from modern airborne *Casuarina pollen*, or long-distance wind transport from the western Pacific (Close *et al*. 1978). At Maunutu on Rimatara, palynological records of *Casuarina* show a marked increase in representation within the past 1000 cal. BP (Prebble and Wilmshurst In press). This rise in pollen abundance is indicative of local pollen production and dispersal and is unequivocally associated with increases in a range of human-impact indicators (e.g. *Colocasia esculenta* pollen and charcoal particle concentrations).

It is difficult to determine the indigenous status of *Casuarina* for the subtropical Polynesian islands, given its vagility and affinity within secondary habitats (Florence 2004). From the palynological records from Rapa (Prebble 2006; Prebble *et al*. submitted) and Rapanui (Flenley *et al*. 1991) it is possible that *Casuarina* was originally present and then subsequently proliferated on Rapa and was extirpated on Rapanui with the advent of human settlement and environmental disturbance. Florence (2004) has tentatively given *C. equisetifolia* subsp. *equisetifolia* the status of naturalised or indigenous for all of the islands of the Austral Archipelgo except Rapa. *Casuarina* was not recorded by Fosberg and St. John (1934) on Rapa and since their 1934 survey, this tree has become naturalised after human introduction or from beach drift.

Aleurites moluccana (L.) Willdenow (Euphorbiaceae)

The tough endocarps of *Aleurites moluccana* have been excavated from numerous Polynesian archaeological sites dating from early to late settlement. There is an abundance of preserved endocarps in the archaeobotanical record from Rapa (Prebble 2006; Prebble and Anderson In press) and Henderson (Weisler 1997), but this tree was not listed in any first-contact accounts of Rapa and was not recorded until the pearl trader and amateur naturalist Jacques Moerenhout (1837:64) visited there in 1834. On Henderson, *A. moluccana* was not recorded until 1912 and then again in 1922 (St. John and Philipson 1962; Paulay and Spencer 1989), and is currently absent (Florence *et al*. 1995). *A. moluccana* has been recorded from four localities on Raoul, and a number of authors have suggested it was indigenous to Raoul (e.g. Cheeseman 1888), although this was doubted by Oliver (1910) and later Sykes (1977), who suggest it may have been introduced by Polynesians. Johnson (1995) noted a distinct 10–30 cm band of 'melanized soil' and artefacts which may represent historic settlement. Higham and Johnson (1996) radiocarbon-dated a fragment of *A. moluccana* excavated from this melanized palaeosol, yielding a modern age. Although it was located alongside artefacts characteristic of Polynesian settlement, the site may be disturbed, and thus it may represent either an early or historic introduction.

On Rapa, Stokes (ms) noted the use of *A. moluccana* wood for the construction of canoes, and the nuts for lighting. From visits to Rapa in the 1920s and 1930s, both Stokes (ms) and Fosberg (Mueller-Dombois and Fosberg 1998:403) considered *A. moluccana* a major component of moist forests on Rapa. Robinson (1957) noted the use of *A. moluccana* candlenuts as the major source of night lighting on his visit to the island in 1952. Despite its importance only 50 years ago, few trees currently exist on the island. Some trees are located precariously on the margins of coastal plains or in a few localities around the major settlements of Ha'urei and Area, where the nuts provide fodder for pigs.

It is likely that until recently, *A. moluccana* formed a major component of lowland forests across most of the Austral Archipelago and the Gambiers. Tomás Gayangos (in Corney 1913–1919:126) recorded the presence of *A. moluccana* on Ra'ivavae in 1775, describing it as 'Tutuy'. With the exception of the larger high islands of the Fijian archipelago and the Hawaiian Islands, where *A. moluccana* forms a conspicuous component of mesic vegetation from low to mid elevations (Smith 1981; Wagner *et al.* 1999), the tree may require human maintenance and protection from browsing animals. On some islands, such as Henderson Island, the tree has been recorded in the past but is noted more recently as absent (Paulay and Spencer 1989).

Aleurites pollen has been located in anthropogenic stratified sedimentary deposits from Tukou, Rapa, dated to about 500–600 BP (Prebble *et al.* submitted). Other records of this kind have been located elsewhere in Remote Oceania, including Maunutu on Rimatara (Prebble and Wilmshurst In press), O'ahu in the Hawaiian Islands (e.g. Athens and Ward 1997) and Lahakai on Manus Island in Papua New Guinea (Southern 1988). In each case, *Aleurites* pollen is associated with *Colocasia* pollen and other agricultural indicators. In addition to this list are records from Hawai'i in Athens *et al.* (1997) and Moloka'i in Denham *et al.* (1999), in which *A. moluccana* is one of the primary agricultural indicators. Clark and Cole (1997) also identified *A. moluccana* pollen in sediments from Totoya Island in Fiji, but not in contexts associated with other potential cultigens. Athens and Ward (1997) located *A. moluccana* endocarp and wood from a sediment core at Maunawili, O'ahu, associated with *Colocasia* pollen and other agricultural indicators. Such records suggest *A. moluccana* is in some way associated with cultivation activity. I would suggest that, on the basis of this cultivation site association, *A. moluccana* has been dispersed beyond its indigenous range and either maintained in cultivation or become naturalised on the island.

Cocos nucifera L. (Arecaceae)

Cocos nucifera has been found throughout the humid tropical Pacific in both wild and cultivated populations on atolls, high islands and the coastlines of the peripheral continents, from sea level to elevations of c. 1000 m (Harries *et al.* 2004). The extent of natural dispersal of *C. nucifera* over long distances by floating coconuts has been widely debated and is largely unresolved (Ward and Brookfield 1992). Harries *et al.* (2004) suggest the wild type *C. nucifera* evolved by floating between areas that fringe larger landmasses and islands.

The status of *C. nucifera* has been debated for Remote Oceania at least since the Enlightenment voyages. Merrill (1946:34) suggested coconut 'normally occurs only where it has been planted by man' and said it is likely to have an Indo-Pacific origin. Fosberg (1960) regarded *C. nucifera* as a cultivated species, domesticated in some tropical region where its wild relatives are presumably extinct. Sauer (1971) favoured the view that coconut populations may be wild and a product of natural dispersal. Harries (1990) distinguished the morphological differences (fruit component analysis) between wild and domesticated *C. nucifera* and proposed the Indo-Malayan region as the centre of domestication. The use of molecular markers such as RFLP (e.g. Lebrun *et al.* 1999) and AFLP (e.g. Teulat *et al.* 2000) generally support the conclusions of Harries' morphological analysis.

Arguments for the natural dispersal of *C. nucifera* in Remote Oceania (e.g. Ward and Brookfield 1992) were to some degree confirmed by excavation of *C. nucifera* endocarp from Anawau Swamp on Aneityum in Vanuatu (Spriggs 1984), dated to 6410–5950 cal. BP. This provided the first radiocarbon age outside the expected age range for human occupation of a site in Remote Oceania. Palynological records from Atiu (Parkes 1997) and Mangaia (e.g. Kirch *et al.* 1992; Ellison 1994) in the Cook Islands indicate a prehuman presence of *C. nucifera* in this part of Remote Oceania. A number of palynological records from the Hawaiian Islands (e.g. Athens and Ward 1997; Denham *et al.* 1999) suggest *C. nucifera* may have been introduced, given the presence of pollen only in anthropogenic sediment horizons.

The presence of coconut trees on Rapa presents an interesting case in the debate on the natural vagility and human translocation. No palaeobotanical evidence for indigenous *C. nucifera* in subtropical Polynesian islands has been forthcoming. The *C. nucifera* pollen record from Rimatara indicates this tree may have been recently introduced to the island, given its representation in sediments dating to the post-European contact period. *C. nucifera* was noted in the early European contact accounts for Ra'ivavae, Tubuai and Rurutu, but not for Rapa and Rimatara. On the HMS *Discovery* sighting of Rapa in 1791, both George Vancouver and his ship's botanist, Archibald Menzies, 'observed no Cocoa Nut Trees anywhere on the Island' (Shineberg 1986:67–68). Vancouver chose not to circumnavigate the island, nor venture much closer than a league (c. 4.5 km). No landfall was made and the ship was only anchored for one day along the west coast of the island. In all the European contact accounts recorded to 1834 on Ra'ivavae, only Tomás Gayangos recorded *C. nucifera* (in Corney 1916–1919:126), in 1775. Like the HMS *Discovery* visit to Rapa, no landfall was made with the *Aguila* and the *Jupiter* only moored for one night. No coconut husks were observed, without which botanical determinations of early explorers tended to be misinformed. There is a possibility that the trees Gayangos observed were, in fact, another species of palm.

In 1829, the LMS missionaries, Reverends Pritchard and Simpson (1830 in Stokes ms), visited Rapa, noting that 'One coconut palm was reported as present from a drift and was not recognised by the local natives'. After his visit to Rapa in 1865, John Vine Hall ascertained from one informant that 'there were cocoa-nuts formerly on the Island, but blight destroyed them all some years ago' (Hall 1869:135). In his unpublished ethnography of Rapa, compiled between 1921 and 1922, Stokes (ms) noted that:

> Many coconut palms are now scattered through the island. Though vigorous and growing to a fair height, according to report – they drop their fruit before it matures. Other introductions at Tupuaki, on the northern coast, are said to have borne fruit that was 'killed by thunder'.

He also noted that a 'white man who tried to grow coconuts for commerce at the northern end of the harbor apparently abandoned the venture as a failure' (Stokes ms).

Coconut has been introduced within the past 60 years to Rapa, where it is located around Ha'urei village and as isolated trees in some sheltered embayments on the island. On Rapa, these palms currently produce small fruits that do not develop to full maturity, probably as a result of the more sub-tropical climate of the island. On most of the Austral Archipelago, *C. nucifera* fruits do reach full maturity, and the established plantations are used primarily for local consumption and as pig fodder.

Cocos nucifera was probably introduced historically to Pitcairn, where trees produce mature fruits. On Rapanui, however, there has been debate about whether *C. nucifera* was introduced before European contact (Brown 1935). Zizka (1991) suggests the first plants were probably brought to the island in 1877. There are currently some small plantations and isolated populations of coconut on Rapanui, but few trees produce mature fruits. Coconut trees have also been growing since being planted on Raoul in the 1970s in two coastal locations (Sykes and West 1996). Coconuts regularly wash up on the island shores of the Kermadecs, but none examined have germinated. Sykes and West (1996) suggest coconuts may have washed up after having been dropped off ships in the vicinity of the island.

With the exception of Henderson, *C. nucifera* has probably been introduced to the subtropical Polynesian islands (Pitcairn, Rapa, Rapanui and Raoul) from cultivated progenitors after European contact, but naturally dispersed populations may have existed before human colonisation.

Broussonetia papyrifera (L.) Ventenat (Moraceae)

Matthews (1996) has provided a summary of the biogeography and ethnobotany of *Broussonetia papyrifera* in Oceania. *B. papyrifera* is dioecious, having a natural range, with both male and female populations extending from East Asia to mainland Southeast Asia. Limited information is available on its fertile status outside this range, with no flowering specimens known from herbarium records from Remote Oceania. Populations in Remote Oceania may also be derived entirely from clones from an entirely male population. Within Remote Oceania, climate appears not to be a major limiting factor in its distribution, as it is known from early ethnographic and botanical surveys to have been grown in high-latitude situations as far south as the North Island of New Zealand. As yet, no molecular phylogenetic research has been undertaken on *B. papyrifera* populations in Oceania. Matthews (1996) suggests populations of *B. papyrifera* in Remote Oceania are derived from cultivated progenitors and have been dependent on human dispersal and cultivation for survival.

No archaeobotanical or palaeobotanical material has been identified from Rapa. Orliac (1998) has identified *B. papyrifera* wood from archaeological charcoal assemblages from Rapanui (dating to 690–500 cal. BP), suggesting the same may be possible from sources on the Austral Archipelago. These trees are small and are unlikely to constitute significant proportions of charcoal unless the oven feature was directly associated with a processing site where heartwood was directly discarded in large quantities. This is likely to be the case at the Akahanga rock-shelter site on Rapanui, where *B. papyrifera* made up 32 percent of the total identified oven charcoal (Orliac 1998:139).

As *B. papyrifera* does not generally flower or set seed (Whistler 1991:55) within Remote Oceania, it is unlikely pollen or seed will be located in archaeological or sedimentary settings (Matthews 1996). Identifying *B. papyrifera* pollen is problematic because of the morphological similarity with pollen from other members of the Moraceae and also the Urticaceae family. In the Austral Archipelago, a number of species within the Moraceae are common, including *Ficus prolixa* var. *prolixa* and the introduced arboricultural crop, *Artocarpus altilis*. On Rapa, this problem is conflated by the two species in the indigenous tree genus *Streblus* (*S. anthropophagorum* and *S. pendulinus*). Horrocks *et al.* (2004a) identified *B. papyrifera* pollen and hair-type phytoliths from a swamp core from Rangihoua Bay, Northland, New Zealand. Mid-Holocene dates for a section of peat with *B. papyrifera*-type phytoliths, coupled with the likelihood that these plants may not have flowered in Maori cultivations, reduces the validity of this claim.

Stokes (ms) documented bark-cloth production on Rapa, where a 'tapa' beater was located as a surface archaeological find (Kooijman 1972). No first-contact records of bark-cloth production have been noted for any of the islands of the Austral Archipelago, although all of the main ethnographic treatments of the islands suggest its antiquity pre-dates contact.

Ethnographic accounts (e.g. Stokes ms) and botanical records (e.g. Fosberg and St. John 1934) of the Austral Archipelago from as early as the 1920s all indicate *B. papyrifera* was cultivated within extensive groves, including on Rapa. It is likely that on most Polynesian islands, cultivation became increasingly limited after the introduction of domestic animals, including pigs, cattle and goats. William Colenso (1880:18, in Matthews 1996) suggested the plant was extirpated in New Zealand soon after 1844, due primarily to browsing by cattle. This may well have been the case on the other subtropical Polynesian islands, namely Rapa and Rapanui. Bark-cloth production is now minimal on the islands, with plants generally cultivated within or adjacent to household gardens. Some small groves are still maintained, but only in areas protected from domestic and feral livestock.

Cordia subcordata Lam. (Boraginaceae)

Fruit remains of *Cordia subcordata* from Maha'ulepu cave excavations on Kaua'i Island have been dated to 5945–5300 cal. BP (Burney *et al.* 2001). Apparently, Sinclair (1885 in Burney *et al.* 2001) earlier considered *C. subcordata* to be indigenous to the Hawaiian Islands, but this tree was formerly regarded by many authors as introduced (e.g. Whistler 1991). No macrofossil remains of *C. subcordata* have been located on any of the subtropical Polynesian islands. The tree has been recorded in recent botanical surveys on Henderson, although it is thought to have been introduced. *C. subcordata* was located in the northern Austral Archipelago, including on Tubuai, during the 1921–1934 surveys, and on Rimatara during the most recent botanical surveys, in the vicinity of local villages.

Probable intentional herbaceous introductions

There are several herbaceous taxa that may have been intentionally or inadvertently introduced to the Pacific Islands by people. Of the list of herbs probably intentionally introduced into the subtropical Polynesian islands (Table 5), most have been proposed in a number of botanical compendiums by several authors (e.g. Whistler 1991), but none have been recorded in the palaeobotanical record from any of the islands in sediments that exceed the age for human colonisation established by the archaeological record. Many taxa are well known and have been widely discussed in the Polynesian ethnobotanical literature.

Relatively little information is available for many of the herb taxa listed in Table 4. *Manihot esculenta* Crantz, in the Euphorbiaceae, appears to have been a recent introduction to all of the Austral Islands, where it is now one of the staple foods. *Tephrosia pupurea* (L.) Pers. appears to have been a recent introduction to the Austral Archipelago, but a pre-contact introduced species to most of Remote Oceania, including the Hawaiian Islands (Whistler 1991). Both species' pollen types are distinctive, but neither have been found in any pollen records from subtropical Polynesian islands.

Three cane-grass species (*Erianthus maximus* Brongn., *Saccharum officinarum* L. and *Schizostachyum glaucifolium* (Rupr.) Munro) are listed by Whistler (1991) as possible pre-contact introductions to most of Remote Oceania. The status of *E. maximums* and *S. glaucifolium* is unclear for the Austral Archipelago, as they have only been recorded since 1934 and have been rarely noted in the most recent botanical surveys. Sugarcane (*Saccharum officinarum*) was noted by Stutchbury (Branagan 1996) on Rurutu in 1826 and by Cuming (St. John 1940) on Rapa in 1832, but these records are not early enough to determine its pre-contact introduction. *S. officinarum* is still cultivated on most of the Austral Islands, with some formerly large stands either poorly maintained or abandoned. Sugarcane phytoliths have been identified on some archaeological sites in the Pacific, but none have been located in the few samples examined for phytoliths from sites on Rapa.

Arrowroot (*Tacca leontopetaloides* (L.) Kuntze) was identified by both Stutchbury (Branagan 1996) and Paulding (1970) on Tubuai in 1826. These late-first-contact records are not early enough to determine whether or not it was grown before European contact. Cranwell (1964) identified *Taccaceae*-type pollen from the Arahu lignite deposit on Rapa, but this is unlikely to represent this species. The plant is now rarely grown on the Austral Archipelago.

Two ginger species, the tumeric *Curcuma longa* (L.) and *Zingiber zerumbet* (L.) Smith, are also listed in Table 4. *C. longa* was recorded on Rapa during St. John and Fosberg's 1934 botanical survey, but has not been recorded in recent surveys. The ginger *Z. zerumbet* was only recorded in the Austral Archipelago, including Rapa, by 1934, and has become naturalised on most of the islands.

Inadvertent herbaceous introductions (weeds)

The problem of characterising the phytogeography of weeds in the Pacific was illustrated by Guppy (1906:416) in his analysis of the long-distance dispersal mechanisms of Pacific plants:

> Weeds follow the cultivators in all climates ... [and the cultivator's] share in weed dispersal is often as not merely restricted to producing the conditions favourable to the growth of weeds, and that the seeds are often brought by birds and other agencies.

Guppy lists *Waltheria americana* (syn. *W.* indica), *Oxalis corniculata* (Oxalidaceae), *Urena lobata* (Malvaceae), *Sida* spp. (Malvaceae) and *Bidens pilosa* (Asteraceae) among a list of 37 possible 'aboriginal weeds' that may have reached the islands through a range of dispersal mechanisms, including purposeful transport by people (Guppy 1906:604–605). He defines aboriginal weeds on the basis of vagility, as well as historically documented locations cited by James Cook's botanists during the 1769–1779 voyages to the Pacific. The involvement of humans in weed dispersal, as Guppy admits, is complicated not only by the range of other possible dispersal mechanisms, but also by the plants' uncertain geographical origins, given their capacity to naturalise in many different habitats. Contrary to Guppy, Ridley (1930:634) to some extent downplays the role of alternative dispersal mechanisms, suggesting some of these plants (e.g. *Oxalis corniculata*) were more likely to be inadvertent introductions brought directly by people. The status of weeds as aboriginal introductions to islands in Remote Oceania has been addressed specifically by Whistler (1988) and Leach (2005), and is referred to in the most recent compendiums of island floras (e.g. Wagner *et al.* 1990; Webb *et al.* 1998; Florence 1997, 2004).

Table 5 lists a number of weed species that may have been inadvertently introduced to the subtropical Polynesian islands before European contact. Determinations of pre-contact presence are based primarily on the records of the botanists on Cook's voyages to other islands in Remote Oceania (e.g. Forster 1786; Nelson in St. John 1978; Drake de Castillo 1893; Merrill 1954; Solander in Leach 2005), but also on relevant palynological records from these same islands. For the Austral Archipelago, determinations of the pre-contact presence of a number of weed species have been inferred by Florence (1997, 2004) in the latest compendium of the *Flore de la Polynésie française*, following Drake de Castillo (1893) and Brown (1935). First-contact accounts are concentrated on economic species (e.g. *Colocasia esculenta*), and no records of weed species, apart from cultivated vegetables, were recorded between 1606 and any of the earliest botanical compendiums for the subtropical Polynesian islands.

The palaeobotanical record for the Amaranthaceae, Malvaceae, Poaceae, Polygonaceae and Solanaceae, in which several inadvertent weed species (Table 5) are represented, is complicated by the presence of indigenous representatives of these families on the islands. The pollen morphology of these families is often indistinguishable to genus or species, and thus the presence of pollen cannot be used to determine the presence of these weed species.

Ludwigia octovalvis (Kunth) Raven (Onagraceae): syn. Jussiaea villosa, J. suffruticosa

Ludwigia octovalvis appears to have originated as a pan-tropical species like most of its close relatives (e.g. *L. peoploides*), but its current distribution extends also into sub-tropical and temperate areas, where it is commonly found invading wetland environments. *L. octovalvis* is noted as a persistent weed in irrigated *Colocasia esculenta* pondfields throughout the Pacific, where in abandoned fields it can form dense monotypic stands. Kirch (1994) noted that *L. octovalvis* is a common weed on field systems in the western Pacific island of Futuna. Riley (1926) first collected this plant from Rapa in 1924, the earliest known record for the Austral Archipelago.

Fosberg and St. John (1934) later recorded *L. octovalvis* from most of the Austral Islands.

Guppy (1906:533) has indicated that the seeds of *Ludwigia* (Jussiaea) demonstrate a degree of buoyancy ('a few days'), and may be capable of long-distance dispersal, although this has not been successfully demonstrated. It seems more likely that this plant was transported as an inadvertent introduction embedded in soil attached to plants traded between or introduced to islands.

L. octovalvis pollen has been recorded in the upper human-impact horizons of palynological records from the Hawaiian Islands (e.g. Athens and Ward 1991, 1997) but also Yap in Micronesia (Dodson and Intoh 1999) and in post-European contact-period sediments on Moorea in French Polynesia (Parkes and Flenley 1997; Parkes 1997). Athens (1997:269) maintains that *Ludwigia* pollen can be constrained to Polynesian-phase levels as early as about A.D. 1250. Athens and Ward (1997) located Ludwigia pollen from two samples associated with *Colocasia esculenta*, *Aleurites moluccana* and *Cordyline fruticosa* pollen from a sedimentary core from the Maunawili Valley, O'ahu, of an age younger than 655 cal. BP.

The Hawaiian records contrast with the Austral Archipelago pollen record in which *L. octovalvis* appears late in the human-impact horizons from both Rapa and Rimatara. *Ludwigia* pollen, as on the Hawaiian Islands, is likely to represent a population of weeds growing on or adjacent to active or fallow *Colocasia* pondfield cultivations, but the lack of pollen from these weeds in the early agricultural horizons, defined by the presence of *Colocasia* pollen, attests to its late introduction.

The lateness of the *Ludwigia* record in the Austral Archipelago and Mo'orea may be explained by two historical factors. The increased trade of produce between more distant archipelagos during the early-European-contact period (e.g. as recorded for Alocasia from the Cook Islands) might explain the late arrival *L. octovalvis* and other agricultural weeds. Alternatively, if *L. octovalvis* was present on the island during the early Polynesian-colonisation period, it is possible agriculturalists prevented the weed from establishing. During the European-colonisation period, the wide-scale abandonment of agricultural systems that followed population decline may have allowed already present *L. octovalvis* to encroach into fallow or abandoned fields.

Despite the historical and palaeobotanical indications, it is still plausible that *L. octovalvis* is indigenous to islands northwest of Rapa, but not to any of the subtropical Polynesian islands.

Commelina diffusa Burm. f. (Commelinaceae): syn. C. nudiflora, C. pacifica

Commelina diffusa is regarded as a pan-tropical species, but its precise origin is unclear. On Cook's second voyage to the Pacific in 1773, Georg Forster collected *C. pacifica* (syn. *C. diffusa*) from Tonga (Forster 1786:358) and New Caledonia. The plant was also known from the Hawaiian Islands at the time of Cook's arrival (Hillebrand 1888).

Like *L. octovalvis*, *C. diffusa* is noted as a persistent weed in irrigated *Colocasia esculenta* pondfields throughout the Pacific, where in abandoned fields it can form dense monotypic stands. According to Meyer (2004) and Florence (1997), this plant is regarded as an invasive weed, where on Mangareva (Gambier Islands, French Polynesia) it threatens a small population of the rare endemic plant *Pilea sancti-johannis* (Urticaceae), along with a number of other indigenous species. Located on Rapa in the earliest botanical surveys and on Pitcarin and Rapanui in recent surveys, it appears to be equally invasive, especially in lowland swamp and marsh environments and abandoned *Colocasia* agricultural fields.

C. diffusa pollen has also been recorded in the upper human-impact horizons of palynological records from the Hawaiian Islands (e.g. Beggerley 1990; Athens and Ward 1997) and in probable post-European-contact sediments on Mo'orea (Parkes and Flenley 1990; Parkes 1997), but less so from other sites in the Pacific. Like *L. octovalvis*, *C. diffusa* appears to be a pre-European-contact introduction to the Hawaiian Islands. Again, the Hawaiian records contrast with Austral Archipelago pollen records in which *C. diffusa* appears late in the human-impact horizons from both Rapa and Rimatara (Prebble *et al.* submitted; Prebble and Wilmshurst In press).

Sonchus oleraceus L. (Asteraceae)

Leach (2005:278) suggests edible foliage of *Sonchus* (specifically referring to *S. aspera*) may have been an intentional introduction into the Pacific, distributed as far south as New Zealand. She also suggests its ecological preference for disturbed soils 'would also have given its seeds a good chance of accidental inclusion with dirt-encrusted root crops'. Solander, on James Cook's first voyage to New Zealand in 1769, identified *Sonchus oleraceus* (possibly *S. aspera*) from a range of cultivation sites (Solander in Leach 2005). On Cook's second voyage in 1773–1774, Georg Forster collected *S. oleraceus* from Tonga (Forster 1786) and from Norfolk Island (Hoare 1988; Hicks 1988), although some of these determinations are debatable (Leach 2005).

Cheeseman (1903), in compiling his early flora of Rarotonga, suggested the plant is indigenous to the Pacific region. Such an interpretation may have come in recognition of its very widespread representation across most islands in the Pacific. Fosberg and St. John (1934) recorded *S. oleraceus* from Rapa and the other populated Austral Islands in 1934.

Palynological records of *S. oleraceus* have not been forthcoming from Remote Oceania. Trace counts of *S. oleraceus* pollen were identified in four records from Rapa (Prebble *et al.* submitted). The majority of these records suggest this plant was introduced post-European contact, as it is most frequently in strata associated with *Commelina diffusa* and *Ludwigia octovalvis* in the uppermost human-impact sequences.

Canna indica L. (Cannaceae)

The origin of this pan-tropical plant is uncertain, as it is naturalised throughout its range. Also uncertain is the timing of its introduction or naturalisation in Remote Oceania. The earliest botanical record of the presence of *C. indica* in the subtropical Polynesian islands comes from Fosberg and St. John's 1934 survey of Rapa. The pollen record from Rapa suggests the arrival of *C. indica* was late, and perhaps after European contact (Prebble *et al.* submitted), as was the case on Raoul (Sykes and West 1996).

Cyclosorus interruptus (Willd.) H. Ito (Thelypteridaceae)

Along with *Ludwigia octovalvis*, Nelson also collected *Cyclosorus interruptus* from the Hawaiian Islands in 1779 (St. John 1978). Leach (2005) suggests that despite not being recorded by Daniel Solander in New Zealand, its presence in far-northern New Zealand suggests an inadvertent relationship with *Colocasia* introduction and production, given this was the prime area for introduction of a tropical cultigen (Matthews 1985). Leach (2005 after Sykes) suggests that for most of the Cook Islands, this fern is dominant only in areas around *Colocasia* fields. For this reason, Leach suggests *Cyclosorus interruptus* may be one of many good candidates for Polynesian introduction to New Zealand.

Cyclosorus interruptus was not identified in any of the palynological records obtained from Rapa, but on Rimatara, two records from the Maunutu moat swamp provide good evidence that this shield fern may have been introduced to the island before European contact. In both cores, *Cyclosorus interruptus* was present in the earliest anthropogenic sediments, in some cases in high proportions (Prebble and Wilmshurst In press).

Table 6. Known and probable Polynesian plant introductions to the subtropical Polynesian islands and northern New Zealand.

Island	Inadvertent introductions	Intentional introductions	References
Raivavae	*Achyranthes aspera* var. *aspera*, *Bidens pilosa, Sigesbeckia orientalis, Solanum americanum*	*Aleurites moluccana, Cocos nucifera, Broussonetia papyrifera, Colocasia esculenta, Cordyline fruticosa, Ipomoea batatas, Lagenaria siceraria, Musa* sp., *Thespesia populnea*	Meyer (unpublished)
Henderson	*Solanum americanum*	*Aleurites moluccana, Colocasia esculenta, Cordyline fruticosa, Cyrtosperma merkusii, Musa* sp., *Thespesia populnea*	Florence *et al.* (1995)
Pitcairn	*Achyranthes aspera* var. *aspera*, *Bidens pilosa*	*Aleurites moluccana, Cocos nucifera, Colocasia esculenta, Cordyline fruticosa, Thespesia populnea*	Florence *et al.* (1995)
Rapanui	*Rorippa sarmentosa*	*Broussonetia papyrifera, Colocasia esculenta, Cordyline fruticosa, Ipomoea batatas*	Zizka (1991)
Rapa	*Achyranthes aspera* var. *aspera*, *Bidens pilosa, Sigesbeckia orientalis, Solanum americanum*	*Aleurites moluccana, Hibiscus tiliaceus, Broussonetia papyrifera, Colocasia esculenta, Cordyline fruticosa, Ipomoea batatas, Lagenaria siceraria, Musa* sp., *Thespesia populnea*	Meyer *et al.* (2004)
Norfolk	*Achyranthes aspera* var. *aspera*, *Bidens pilosa, Sigesbeckia orientalis, Solanum americanum*	*Cordyline fruticosa, Musa* sp.	Green (1994)
Raoul	*Achyranthes aspera* var. *aspera*, *Bidens pilosa, Sigesbeckia orientalis, Solanum americanum*	*Aleurites moluccana, Cordyline fruticosa*	Sykes (1977)
Subtropical northern New Zealand	*Bidens pilosa, Sigesbeckia orientalis, Solanum americanum*	*Broussonetia papyrifera, Colocasia esculenta, Cordyline fruticosa, Ipomoea batatas, Lagenaria siceraria*	Best (1925); Leach (1984); Webb *et al.* (1988)

Table 7. Possible Polynesian plant introductions to the subtropical northern New Zealand.

Inadvertent introductions	Justification
Achyranthes aspera var. *aspera*	Naturalised on all of the subtropical Polynesian islands including northern New Zealand.
Eleusine indica	Naturalised on all of the subtropical Polynesian islands except Henderson.

Intentional introductions	Justification
Aleurites moluccana	Grows successfully without cultivation on Raoul. An important fuel source for torches/candles.
Cocos nucifera	Poor fruiting populations have been established on all of the subtropical Polynesian islands, some from beach drift propagules. Plants may have been planted then trees subsequently died.
Hibiscus tiliaceus	Naturalised on Raoul, a common strand taxa across much of Remote Oceania and likely to have been introduced on many islands. An important substitute fibre plant.
Musa sp (AAB group syn. *M. x paradaisica, M. Sapientum*; Musaceae: section Eumusa)	Grows successfully in cultivation on Raoul and in parts of New Zealand.
Thespesia populnea	A common strand taxa across much of Remote Oceania. Grows successfully in cultivation on Rapa and Rapanui. An important substitute fibre plant.

Polynesian introductions to subtropical New Zealand

In Table 6, a summary list of probable candidates for plant introduction to the subtropical islands and northern subtropical New Zealand is provided. Given the general geographical limitations posed to successful establishment of tropical and subtropical plant taxa in subtropical New Zealand, I also present a list of justifications for regarding these taxa as Polynesian introductions (Table 7). Of the inadvertent weed introductions, plants with hooked seeds, namely *Bidens pilosa*, are represented on most islands. The distribution of *Bidens pilosa*, however, is complicated by alternative long-distance dispersal by birds. Other species such as *Achyranthes aspera* and a number of grasses may also have been dispersed by migratory birds, lodged in soil or trapped in feathers. The patchy distribution of some of the non-hooked seed species across the subtropical islands suggests some limitation on long-distance dispersal.

Of the intentional introductions presented in Table 6, *Cordyline fruitcosa* is represented on all islands, including northern New Zealand. *Cordyline* can reproduce vegetatively, and produces abundant seeds readily dispersed by birds, thus naturalising on most subtropical environments. Other taxa, particularly the staple food plants, have not survived on the abandoned subtropical islands. This strongly implies that agricultural maintenance was required for the ongoing survival of these taxa. Other cultural factors may explain the decline or survival of these taxa, but these are not discussed here.

Conclusions

I have presented a partial analysis of known, probable and potential candidates for human-mediated introduction to the subtropical Polynesian islands of Remote Oceania. The distribution of these plants is difficult to compare, given the lack of archaeobotanical data for the abandoned islands and the bias towards those islands occupied at European contact. But some broad conclusions can be drawn. As Anderson (2001) suggests, the subtropical islands of Remote Oceania were difficult to colonise prehistorically, given they were relatively resource poor – too warm to support the rich coastal biomass of mammals, birds and fish which characterise more temperate islands. He also suggests the subtropics can generally be viewed as being too cool for the translocation of tropical agricultural production, which meant that for many islands, long-term survivability of colonising populations depended on subtle differences between islands. Despite these differences, Anderson (2001:21) suggests settlement on the abandoned subtropical Polynesian islands may not have been due to the lack of agricultural potential. Indeed, agricultural production on Norfolk and Pitcairn appears not to be constrained by lack of suitable soil and rainfall.

Regarding the subject of taxa introduced to subtropical New Zealand by Polynesians, the diversity and abundance of faunal resources may have meant that the diversity of agricultural crops seen in the tropical Pacific became redundant in sustaining long-term settlement. Nevertheless, the ephemeral occupation records for Norfolk (Anderson *et al.* 2001; MacPhail *et al.* 2001), Henderson and Pitcairn (Weisler 1997; Horrocks and Weisler 2006) present a diverse array of plant introductions, and on that basis, I suggest a similar situation may have existed on New Zealand. The size and temperate climate of New Zealand limits the preservation of botanical remains of tropical/subtropical plants, already limited by generally lower temperatures and frosts.

Finally, there are two problems in assessing the botanical status of plants that have a distribution or historical presence that may have been influenced by people. Firstly, assessing the status of introduced taxa that may have become naturalised on islands once released is complex, and may be represented in the different lines of botanical evidence in different ways. Secondly, the status of some taxa that may have become naturalised or declined on their own accord, particularly in response to other environmental factors independent of human activity, is equally difficult to assess. The following would enable a better understanding of Polynesian plant introductions in Remote Oceania:

- Development of phylogeographic data based on fine-resolution molecular phylogenies.

- Greater emphasis on the taxonomic resolution of the palaeobotanical and archaeological record, focusing on key taxa with well-defined phytogeographic distributions.

- Spatial sampling approaches to anthropogenic palaeoenvironmental sequences at a greater number of sites and on more islands.

Acknowledgments

In 2001, Atholl Anderson published a paper titled 'No Meat on that Beautiful Shore' in the *International Journal of Osteoarchaeology*. In the paper, he explored the role of impoverished faunas of the subtropical Polynesian islands, in the context of the prehistoric abandonment of the 'Mystery islands'. Drawing on the same title, this contribution was put together on Atholl's insistence that we need to know more about Polynesian weeds and introduced floras. I thank Jean-Yves Meyer for botanical data pertaining to the Austral Archipelago. I also thank Jean Kennedy and Geoff Hope (both of the ANU) for comments on earlier editions of this paper.

References

Anderson, A. 1980. The archaeology of Raoul Island (Kermadecs) and its place in the settlement history of Polynesia. *Archaeology and Physical Anthropology in Oceania* 15:131–141.

Anderson, A. 1996. Discovery of a prehistoric habitation site on Norfolk Island. *Journal of the Polynesian Society* 105:479–486.

Anderson, A. 2001. No meat on that beautiful shore: The prehistoric abandonment of subtropical Polynesian islands. *International Journal of Osteoarchaeology* 11:14–23.

Anderson, A., I. Smith and P. White 2001. Archaeological fieldwork on Norfolk Island. In A. Anderson and P. White (eds), *The prehistoric archaeology of Norfolk Island, southwest Pacific*, pp. 11–32. Sydney: Records of the Australian Museum Supplement.

Athens, J.S. and J.V. Ward 1996. A sediment coring record at Kapunahala Marsh, Kane'ohe, O'ahu, Hawaii. Honolulu: International Archaeological Research Institute.

Athens, J.S. and J.V. Ward 1997. The Maunawili core: Prehistoric inland expansion of settlement and agriculture, O'ahu, Hawai'i. *Hawaiian Archaeology* 6:37–51.

Athens, J.S., J.V. Ward and H.D. Tuggle 1997. Environment, vegetation change, and early human settlement on the 'Ewa Plain: Paleoenvironmental investigations. Honolulu: International Archaeological Research Institute.

Barrau, J. 1965. Histoire et prehistoire horticoles de l'Oceanie tropical. *Journal de la Société des Océanistes* 21:55–78.

Best, E. 1925. *Maori agriculture*. New Zealand, Board of Maori Ethnological Research for the Dominion Museum, Wellington.

Branagan, D.F. 1996. *Science in a sea of commerce: Seas trading adventure (1825–1827), by Samuel Stutchbury*. Rosebery: Hippo Books.

Brown, F.B.H. 1931. *Flora of Southeastern Polynesia I. Monocotyledons*. Bishop P. Bishop Museum Bulletin 84.

Brown, F.B.H. 1935. *Flora of Southeastern Polynesia III. Dicotyledons*. Bishop P. Bishop Museum Bulletin 130.

Burtenshaw, M.K. 1999. Maori gourds: An American connection? *Journal of the Polynesian Society* 108:427–433.

Carlquist, S. 1996. Plant dispersal and the origin of the Pacific island floras. In A. Keast and S.E. Miller (eds), *The origin and evolution of Pacific Island biotas, New Guinea to Eastern Polynesia: Patterns and processes*, pp. 153–164. Amsterdam: SPB Academic Publishing.

Cheeseman, T.F. 1888. On the flora of the Kermadec Islands; with notes on the fauna, *Transactions and Proceedings of the New Zealand Institute* 20:151–181.

Clark, J.T. and A.O. Cole 1997. Environmental change and human prehistory in the central Pacific: Archaeological and palynological investigations on Totoya Island. Suva: The Fiji Museum.

Clarke, A.C., M.K. Burtenshaw, P.A. Mclenachan, D.L. Erickson and D. Penny 2006. Reconstructing the origins and dispersal of the Polynesian bottle gourd (*Lagenaria siceraria*). *Molecular Biology and Evolution* 23:893–900.

Close, R.C., N.T. Moar, A.I. Tomlinson and A.D. Lowe 1978. Aerial dispersal of biological material from Australia to New Zealand. *International Journal of Biometeorology* 22:1–9.

Colenso, W. 1880. On the vegetable food of the ancient New Zealanders before Cook's visit. *Transactions of the New Zealand Institute* 13:3–38.

Corney, B.G. 1913–1919. *The quest and occupation of Tahiti by emissaries of Spain* 32. London: Hakluyt Society.

Cranwell, L.M. 1964. Rapa Island coal and its microfossils: A preliminary report. In L.M. Cranwell (ed), *Ancient Pacific Floras*, pp. 43–47. Honolulu: University of Hawaii Press.

Davies, J. 1851. *A Tahitian and English dictionary*. London: London Missionary Society Press.

Decker-Walters, D., J. Staub, A. Lopez-Sese and E. Nakata 2001. Diversity in landraces and cultivars of bottle gourd (*Lagenaria siceraria; Cucurbitaceae*) as assessed by random amplified polymorphic DNA. *Genetic Resources and Crop Evolution* 48:369–380.

Denham, T., F.J. Eble, B. Winsborough and J.V. Ward 1999. Palaeoenvironmental and Archaeological Investigations at 'Ohi'apilo Pond, Leeward Coast of Moloka'i, Hawai'i. *Hawaiian Archaeology* 7:35–59.

Drake De Castillo, E. 1893. *Flore de la Polynésie française*. Paris: G. Masson.

Ellison, J. 1994. Palaeo-lake and swamp stratigraphic records of Holocene vegetation and sea-level changes, Mangaia, Cook Islands. *Pacific Science* 48:1–15.

Endlicher, S.F.L. 1833. *Prodromus Florae Norfolkicae*. Vienna: F. Beck.

Flenley, J.R. S.M. King, J. Jackson and C. Chew 1991. The Late Quaternary vegetational and climatic history of Easter Island. *Journal of Quaternary Science* 6:85–115.

Florence, J. 1997. *Flore de la Polynésie française*. Collection Faune et Flore tropicales, vol 1. Paris: Éditions de l'Orstom.

Florence, J. 2004. *Flore de la Polynésie française*. Collection Faune et Flore tropicales, vol. 2. Paris: Éditions de IRD, Publications Scientifiques, Museum National D'Histoire Naturelle.

Florence, J., S. Waldren and A.J Chepstow-Lusty 1995. The flora of the Pitcairn Islands: A review. *Biological Journal of the Linnean Society* 56:79–119.

Fosberg, F.R. 1960. A theory on the origin of the coconut. In *Symposium on the impact of man on humid tropics vegetation*, pp. 73–75. Goroka, Territory of Papua and New Guinea. Canberra: Commonwealth Government Printers.

Fosberg, F.R., M.H. Sachet and D.R. Stoddart 1983. Henderson Island (South eastern Polynesia): summary of current knowledge *Atoll Research Bulletin* 272:1–47.

Fosberg, F.R. and H. St. John 1934. Check list and field notebook of the plants of Southeastern Polynesia: Society Islands, Tuamotus, Austral Islands, Rapa. Honolulu, B.P. Bishop Museum Herbarium Archive.

Green, P.S. 1994. *Flora of Australia Volume 49, Oceanic Islands 1*, Canberra: Government Publishing Service.

Green, R.C. 2005. Sweet potato transfers in Polynesian prehistory In C. Ballard, P Brown, R.M. Bourke and T. Harwood (eds), *The sweet potato in Oceania: A reappraisal*, pp. 43–62. Canberra: Oceania Monograph.

Guppy, H.B. 1906. *Observations of a naturalist in the Pacific between 1896 and 1899*. London: Macmillan.

Hall, J.V. 1869. On the island of Rapa. *Transactions and Proceedings of the New Zealand Institute* 1:128–134.

Harries, H., L. Baudouin and R. Cardeña 2004. Floating, boating and introgression: Molecular techniques and the ancestry of the Coconut palm populations on Pacific Islands, *Ethnobotany Research and Applications* 2:37–53.

Harries, H.C. 1990. Malesian origin for a domestic Cocos nucifera. In P. Baas, K. Kalkman and R. Geesink (eds), *The plant diversity of Malesia Proceedings of the Flora Malesiana Symposium commemorating Prof CGGJ van Steenis. Kluwer*, pp. 351–357. Dordrecht: Academic Publishers.

Hather, J. and M.I. Weisler 2000. Prehistoric giant swamp taro (Cyrtosperma chamissonis) from Henderson Island, Southeast Polynesia. *Pacific Science* 54:149–156.

Hather, J.G. 1994. The identification of charred root and tuber crops from archaeological sites in the Pacific. In J.G. Hather (ed), *Tropical archaeobotany: Applications and new developments*, pp. 51–64. London: Routledge.

Heiser, C.B.J. 1973. Variation in the bottle gourd. In B. Meggers, E. Ayensu, and W. Duckworth (eds), *Tropical forest ecosystems in Africa and South America: A comparative review*, pp. 121–128. Washington: Smithsonian Institution Press.

Heiser, C.B.J. 1979. *The gourd book*. University of Oklahoma: Oklahoma.

Henry, T. 1928. *Ancient Tahiti*. Bernice P. Bishop Museum Bulletin 48.

Heyerdahl, T. 1952. *American Indians in the Pacific*. London: Allen and Unwin.

Heyerdahl, T. 1963. Prehistoric voyages as agencies for Melanesian and South American plant and animal dispersal to Polynesia. In J. Barrau (ed), *Plants and the migrations of the Pacific peoples*, pp. 23–35. Honolulu: Bishop Museum Press.

Heyerdahl, T. and E.N. Ferdon (eds) 1961. *Reports of the Norwegian Archaeological Expedition to Easter Island and the East Pacific, 1955–1956*. Monographs of the School of American Research and the Kon Tiki Museum 1(24). London: Allen and Unwin.

Higham, T.F.G., A. Anderson and C. Jacomb 1999. Dating the first New Zealanders: The chronology of Wairau Bar. *Antiquity* 73:420–427.

Higham, T.F.G. and L. Johnson 1996. The prehistoric chronology of Raoul Island, the Kermadec. *Group Archaeology in Oceania* 31:207–213.

Hinkle, A. 2004. The distribution of a male sterile form of Ti (Cordyline fruticosa) in Polynesia: A case of human selection? *Journal of the Polynesian Society* 113:263–290.

Hoare, M. 1987. *Norfolk Island: An outline of its history 1774–1987*. Brisbane: University of Queensland Press.

Hogg, A.G. T.F.G. Higham, D.J. Lowe, J.G. Palmer, P.J. Reimer and R.M. Newnham 2003. A wiggle-match date for Polynesian settlement of New Zealand. *Antiquity* 77:116–125.

Hooker, J.D. 1856. On the botany of Raoul Island, one of the Kermadec Group in the South Pacific Ocean, *Proceedings of the Linnean Society of London* 1:125–129.

Horrocks, M., P.A. Shane, I.G. Barber, D.M. D'costa and S.L. Nichol 2004a. Microbotanical remains reveal Polynesian agriculture and mixed cropping in early New Zealand. *Review of Palaeobotany and Palynology* 131:147–157.

Horrocks, M. and L. Lawlor 2006. Plant microfossil analysis of soils from Polynesian stonefields in South Auckland, New Zealand. *Journal of Archaeological Science* 33:200–217.

Horrocks, M. and M.I. Weisler 2006. Analysis of plant microfossils in archaeological deposits from two-remote archipelagos: The Marshall Islands, Eastern Micronesia, and the Pitcairn Group, Southeast Polynesia. *Pacific Science* 60:261–280.

Hotta, M. 2002. The Origins and Spread of Tuber Crops (Imo). In S. Yoshida, and P.J. Matthews (eds), *Vegeculture in Eastern Asia and Oceania. Japan Center for Area Studies*, pp.17–30. Osaka: National Museum for Ethnology.

Hunt, T.L. and C.P. Lipo 2006. Late colonization of Easter Island. *Science* 311:1603–1606.

Johnson, L. 1995. *In the midst of a prodigious ocean*. Auckland Conservancy Historic Resources Series 11.

Kennett, D., A. Anderson, M. Prebble, E. Conte and J. Southon 2006. Prehistoric human impacts on Rapa, French Polynesia. *Antiquity* 80:340–354.

Kirch, P.V. 1994. *The wet and the dry: Irrigation and agricultural intensification in Polynesia*. Chicago: University of Chicago Press.

Kirch, P.V., J.R. Flenley, D.W. Steadman, F. Lamont and S. Dawson 1992. Ancient environmental degradation: Prehistoric human impacts to an island ecosystem: Mangaia, Central Polynesia. *National Geographic Research and Exploration* 8:166–179.

Kirch, P.V. and D.E. Yen 1982. *Tikopia: The prehistory and ecology of a Polynesian outlier*. Honolulu: Bishop Museum Press.

Kooijman, S. 1972. *Tapa in Polynesia*. Bernice P. Bishop Museum Bulletin No. 234. Honolulu: Bishop Museum Press.

Leach, H. 1984. *1,000 years of gardening in New Zealand*. Wellington: A. H. and A. W. Reed.

Leach, H. 2005. Gardens without weeds? Pre-European Maori gardens and inadvertent introductions. *New Zealand Journal of Botany* 43:271–284.

Lebot, V. 1999. Biomolecular evidence for plant domestication in Sahul. *Genetic Resources and Crop Evolution* 46:619–628.

Lebrun, P., L. Grivet and L. Baudouin 1999. Use of RFLP markers to study the diversity of the coconut palm. In C. Oropeza, J.L. Verdeil, G.R. Ashburner, R. Cardeña, R. and J.M. Santamarja (eds), *Current advances in coconut biotechnology*, pp. 73–87. Dordrecht: Kluwer Academic Publishers.

Macphail, M.K., G.S. Hope and A. Anderson 2001. Polynesian plant introductions in the Southwest Pacific: Initial pollen evidence from Norfolk Island In A. Anderson and P. White (eds), *The prehistoric archaeology of Norfolk Island, southwest Pacific*, pp.123–134. Sydney, Records of the Australian Museum Supplement,

Matthews, P.J. 1985. Nga taro o Aotearoa, *Journal of the Polynesian Society* 94:253–272.

Matthews, P.J. 1996. Ethnobotany, and origins of Broussonetia papyrifera in Polynesia: An essay on tapa prehistory In J.M. Davidson, G. Irwin, B.F. Leach, A. Pawley, and D. Brown (eds), *Oceanic culture history: Essays in honour of Roger Green*. Auckland: New Zealand Journal of Archaeology Special Publication.

Matthews, P.J. 2004. Genetic diversity in Taro, and the preservation of culinary knowledge. *Ethnobotany Research and Applications* 2:57–71.

Merrill, E.D. 1946. Man's influence on the vegetation of Polynesia, with special reference to introduced species, *Chronica Botanica* 10:334–345.

Merrill, E.D. 1954. The botany of Cook's voyages, *Chronica Botanica* 14:164–383.

Meyer, J.-Y. 2004. Threat of invasive alien plants to native flora and forest vegetation of Eastern Polynesia. *Pacific Science* 58:357–375.

Morrison, J. 1935. *The journal of James Morrison, boatswain's mate of the Bounty describing the mutiny and subsequent misfortunes of the mutineers together with an account of the island of Tahiti, with an introduction by O.Rutter*. London: Golden Cockerel Press.

Mueller-Dombois, D. and F.R. Fosberg, 1998. *Vegetation of the tropical Pacific islands*. New York: Springer.

Oliver, W.R.B. 1910. The vegetation of the Kermadec Islands. *Transactions and Proceedings of the New Zealand Institute* 42:118–175.

Orliac, C. 1998. Données nouvelles sur la composition de la flore de l'île de Pâques, *Journal de la Société des Océanistes* 107:135–143.

Parkes, A. 1997. Environmental change and the impact of Polynesian colonization: Sedimentary records from Central Polynesia In P.V. Kirch and T.L. Hunt (eds), *Historical ecology in the Pacific Islands*, pp. 166–199. New Haven: Yale University Press.

Parkinson, S. 1973. *A journal of a voyage to the South Seas in his Majesty's ship, the Endeavour*, Adelaide: Library Board of South Australia.

Paulay, G. and T. Spencer 1989. Vegetation of Henderson Island. *Atoll Research Bulletin* 328.

Paulding, H. 1970. *Journal of a cruise of the U.S. Schooner Dolphin*. Honolulu: University of Hawaii Press.

Prebble, M. 2006. Islands, floras and history: An environmental history of plant introduction and extinction on the Austral Islands, French Polynesia. Unpublished PhD thesis, Australian National University, Canberra.

Prebble, M. and A. Anderson In press. The archaeobotanical record from rockshelter deposits from Rapa. In A. Anderson and D. Kennett (eds), *The prehistory of Rapa: An isolated high island in French Polynesia*. New Zealand Archaeological Association Monographs.

Prebble, M., D. Kennett, J. Southon, N. Porch and A. Anderson Submitted. Tracing human impact on islands in Remote Oceania: Holocene coastal swamp forest profiles from Rapa, Austral Islands, French Polynesia. *Quaternary Science Reviews*.

Prebble, M. and J. Wilmshurst In press. Palaeoecological detection of initial human impacts on island environments in Remote Oceania using introduced plant cultigen pollen and rat-gnawed seeds. *Biological Invasions*.

Pritchard, W.T. and J.F. Simpson 1830. Extracts from the journal of Messrs. Pritchard and Simpson, during their voyage to the islands of Tubuai, Raivavai, Rapa. London: Missionary Society Transactions.

Ridley, H.N. 1930. *The dispersal of plants throughout the world*. London: Lovell Reeve and Co.

Robinson, W.A. 1957. *To the great southern sea*. London: Book Club Associates.

Rosendahl, P.H. and D.E. Yen 1971. Fossil sweet potato remains from Hawaii, *Journal of the Polynesian Society* 80:379–385.

Sauer, J.D. 1971. A re-evaluation of the coconut as an indicator of human dispersal In C.L. Riley, C.W. Kelley, C.W. Pennington and R.L. Rands (eds), *Man across the sea*, pp. 309–319. Austin: University of Texas.

Seemann, B. 1865–73. *Flora Vitiensis: A description of the plants of the Viti or Fiji Islands with an account of their histories, uses, and properties*. London, L. Reeve and Company.

Shineberg, D.E. 1986. Archibald Menzies account of the visit of the Discovery to Rapa and Tahiti, 22 December 1791–25 January 1792. *Pacific Studies* 9:59–102.

Skottsberg, C. 1956 *The natural history of Juan Fernandez and Easter Island*. Uppsala: Almqvist and Wiksells.

Smith, A.C. 1981. *Flora Vitiensis Nova*, vol. 1. Hawaii: Pacific Tropical Botanic Garden.

Spriggs, M. 1984. Early coconut remains from the South Pacific. *Journal of the Polynesian Society* 93:71–76.

St. John, H. 1940. Itinerary of Hugh Cuming in Polynesia. *B.P. Bishop Museum Occasional Paper* 16:81–90.

St. John, H. 1976. Revision of the Genus *Pandanus* Stickman. Part 40. The Fijian species of the section Pandanus. *Pacific Science* 30:249–315.

St. John, H. 1978 The first collection of Hawaiian plants by David Nelson in 1779. Hawaiian Plant Studies 55. *Pacific Science* 32:315–324.

St. John, H. 1979. Revision of the Genus *Pandanus* Stickman. Part 42 *Pandanus tectorius* Parkins. ex Z and *Pandanus odoratissimus* L.f. *Pacific Science* 33:395–401.

St. John, H. and F.R. Fosberg 1921–1934. Unpublished botanical survey data of the Mangareva Expedition. Bernice P. Bishop Museum, Honolulu, Hawaii.

St. John, H. and W.R. Philipson 1962. An account of the flora of Henderson Island, South Pacific Ocean. *Transactions of the Royal Society of New Zealand* 1:175–194.

Stokes, J.F.G. ms. Ethnology of Rapa. Unpublished manuscrupt in the Bernice P. Bishop Museum Archives, Honolulu, Hawaii.

Stone, B.C. 1976. The Pandanaceae of the New Hebrides, with an essay in intraspecific variation in *Pandanus tectorius*. *Kew Bulletin* 31:47–70.

Stone, B.C. 1988. Notes on the genus *Pandanus* (Pandanaceae) in Tahiti. *Botanical Journal of the Linnean Society* 97:33–48.

Sykes, W.R. 1977. Kermadec Island Flora: An annotated checklist. *New Zealand Department of Scientific and Industrial Research Bulletin* 219.

Sykes, W.R. and C.J. West 1996. New records and other information on the vascular flora of the Kermadec Islands. *New Zealand Journal of Botany* 34:447–462.

Teulat, B., C. Aldam, R. Trehin, P. Lebrun, J.H. Barker, G.M. Arnold, A. Karp, L. Baudouin and F. Rognon 2000. Analysis of genetic diversity in coconut (*Cocos nucifera* L.) populations from across the geographic range using sequence tagged microsatellites (SSRs) and AFLPs. *Theoretical and Applied Genetics* 100:764–771.

Vancouver, G. 1803. *A voyage of discovery round the world*. Cambridge: Hakluyt Society.

Wagner, W.L., D.R. Herbst and S.H. Sohmer 1990. *Manual of the flowering plants of Hawai'i*. Bernice P. Bishop Museum Special Publication 83.

Ward, R.G. and M. Brookfield 1992. The dispersal of the coconut: Did it float or was it carried to Panama? *Journal of Biogeography* 19:467–480.

Webb, C.J., W.R. Sykes and P.J. Garnock-Jones 1988. *Flora of New Zealand Volume IV*. Christchurch: Botany Division, D.S.I.R.

Weisler, M.I. 1995. Henderson Island prehistory: Colonization and extinction on a remote Polynesian island. *Biological Journal of the Linnean Society* 56:377–404.

Weisler, M.I. 1997. Prehistoric long-distance interaction at the margins of Oceania. In M.I. Weisler (ed), *Prehistoric long-distance interaction in Oceania*, pp. 149–172. New Zealand Archaeological Association Monograph.

Whistler, W.A. 1990. The other Polynesian gourd. *Pacific Science* 44:115–122.

Whistler, W.A. 1991. Polynesian plant introductions. In P.A. Cox and S.A. Banack (eds), *Islands, plants, and Polynesians*, pp. 41–66. Portland: Dioscorides Press.

Yen, D.E. 1973. The origins of oceanic agriculture, *Archaeology and Physical Anthropology in Oceania* 8:68–85.

Yen, D.E. 1974. *The sweet potato and Oceania: An essay in ethnobotany*. Honolulu: Bishop Museum Press.

Yen, D.E. and J. Head 1993. Kumara remains in pit O at P5/288. In D.G. Sutton (ed), *The archaeology of the peripheral Pa at Pouerua, Northland, New Zealand*, pp. 56–64. Auckland: Auckland University Press.

Zerega, N.J., D. Ragone and T.J. Motley 2004. Complex origins of breadfruit: Implications for human migrations in Oceania. *American Journal of Botany* 91:760–766.

Zizka, G. 1991. Flora of Easter Island. *Palmarum Hortus Francofurtensis* 3:1–108.

16

One thousand years of human environmental transformation in the Gambier Islands (French Polynesia)

Eric Conte
Centre International de Recherche Archéologique sur la Polynésie,
Université de la Polynésie Française, French Polynesia
eric.conte@upf.pf

Patrick V. Kirch
Departments of Anthropology and Integrative Biology,
University of California, Berkeley, USA

Introduction

Landscapes and their biodiversity result, to be sure, from natural processes (geological, biological), but also from the actions – direct and indirect – exercised by humans on their habitat over time. It is important, therefore, to take into account this historical dimension of the interactions between humans and their habitat, to better understand contemporary situations, and hopefully, to gain information which might aid in the better management of resources.

The islands of the eastern Pacific, distant from continental influence and settled very late by humans (during the past 3000 years or fewer), offer 'model systems' (Kirch 2007a, 2007b) where it is possible to study, in large part thanks to archaeological excavations, ecological conditions before the arrival of humans and following human influence. These islands provide less complex histories than continents that have been overrun and modified by our species over hundreds of thousands of years. We can also assess the impact of human arrival on these fragile environments which were formerly isolated, and follow over the longue durée the dynamic relationships between the colonising human populations and their island ecosystems. Since 2001, an international program has been carried out in the Gambier Islands (Figure 1), with our colleague Atholl Anderson participating in the first season of field research. One of the main objectives of this program has been the reconstruction of landscapes and the relationships between humans and their habitat over time (Conte and Kirch 2004).

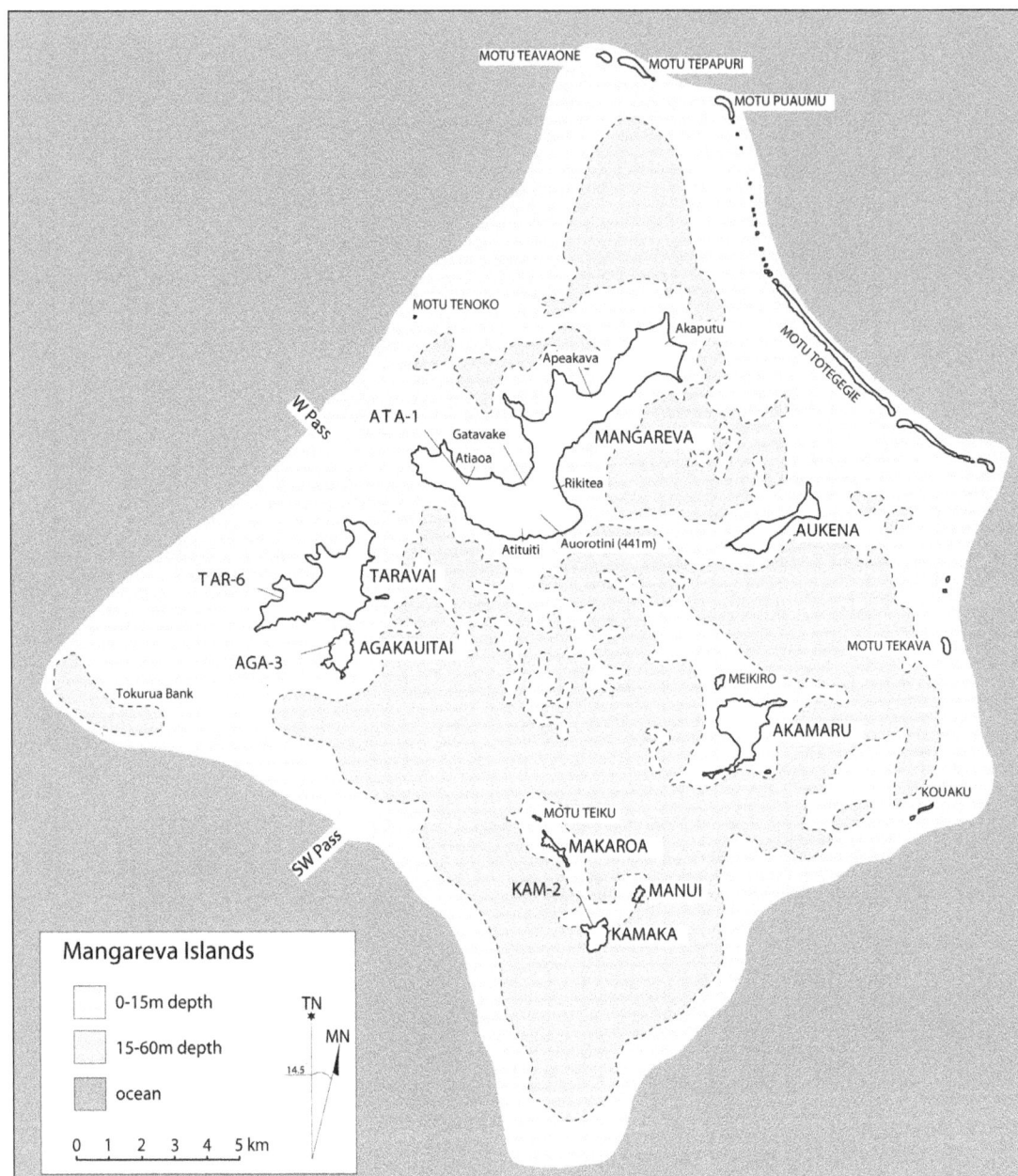

Figure 1. Map of the Mangareva Islands, showing the location of excavated sites.

The Gambier Islands: An unusual environment

At the eastern extremity of French Polynesia, this archipelago presents unusual characteristics which make this case study especially interesting. Enclosed by the same barrier reef, 10 small high islands (Figure 2) are the vestiges of the collapsed crater of a large volcano, of which the former caldera constitutes the present lagoon. While the land area is limited and the terrestrial habitat impoverished, the immense lagoon and reefs present a rich marine fauna. Historically, the steep slopes and ridges are destitute of primary forest, and are covered in pyrophytic *Miscanthus* cane and *Dicranopteris* ferns, while the vegetation of the small valleys and coastal plains is dominated by economic plants, largely introduced by the Polynesians (e.g. coconut, breadfruit, *Hibiscus tiliaceus*, *Pandanus*). This degradation of the vegetation on the hills is not a recent phenomenon, having been observed by Captain Wilson, the first European to arrive at the island, in May 1797. More generally, in 1934, the botanist of the Bishop Museum's Mangarevan Expedition bemoaned the total destruction of the indigenous flora (St. John 1935). Nonetheless, the islands are noteworthy for having at one time possessed a rich endemic fauna of terrestrial gastropods (including at least 38 endemic species in the families Achatinellidae, Endodontidae, Punctidae, Euconulidae, and Assimineidae). These endemic taxa are known only from sub-fossil specimens in recent sedimentary contexts, suggesting a major phase of extinction (Bouchet and Abdou 2003:169).

We have attempted to establish a chronology for this drastic environmental transformation, and have addressed ourselves to the matter of the factors both natural (such as climate change) and cultural responsible for these changes. Another question concerns the domestic dog and pig. Widely introduced throughout the Pacific Islands by people, these animals were not observed in the Gambiers by the first European visitors. Were these important domestic animals formerly present in the Gambiers, and if so, when and why did they disappear?

In contrast to the impoverished terrestrial habitat, the richness and diversity of the marine resources are notable, with, for example, 246 species of fish and 20 species of molluscs (Fourmanoir *et al.* 1974; Salvat 1974; Richard 1974). This does not stop us from asking whether human predation had significant consequences for these marine resources, a topic we also address below.

Ethnographic sources and archaeological evidence

After descriptions of the first explorers and missionaries, notably those of Père Laval (1938), very little ethnographic or archaeological work was carried out in the Gambier Archipelago during the first half of the 20th century. The primary work was conducted by Hiroa (1938) and Emory (1939) in 1934, during the Mangarevan Expedition of the Bishop Museum. But Emory was only interested in surface architecture (such as the remains of marae), and in searching for artefacts through his rather crude excavations in rock shelters. His work thus provides little information useful for our project. Not until 1959, with the research of Roger Green, did stratigraphic excavations using rigorous methods commence, yielding relevant evidence. Green excavated in five rock shelters on three islands: two on Kamaka, two on Aukena, and one on

Figure 2. Island landscape: View of Agakauitai Island from the north.

Mangareva. Green's work remained largely unpublished until recently, although he has now issued a series of reports and articles on the results of his 1959 excavations (Green and Weisler 2000, 2002, 2004).

In April–May 2001, M. Orliac made a research trip with the stated objective of studying the 'composition and evolution of the flora' of the Gambier Islands (Orliac 2002, 2003). Focusing his work on the coast and littoral zone of Mangareva Island (the largest island), especially in the Gatavake and Rikitea (and Atirikigaro) areas, he discovered a buried cultural deposit, dating between AD 1030 and AD 1290. This deposit included artefacts (e.g. fishhooks, pearl-shell graters) and plant remains characteristic of coastal trees. Since launching our research program in the Gambiers in 2001, three seasons of fieldwork have been carried out. All of the principal islands have been reconnoitered, more or less thoroughly. Among the different sites investigated, several have provided information relevant to the questions posed above; we briefly review the key sites below, followed by a discussion of general trends in the evolution of the Mangarevan environment.

Onemea: A colonisation-phase site

The site of Onemea consists of cultural deposits in an aeolian dune at the mouth of a small valley on the southwest coast of Taravai, the second largest island. As shown in Figure 3, recent shoreline erosion had exposed cultural materials, and we excavated two test pits, of 1 m² each, in 2003, and an additional 10 test units in 2005. However, our analysis of the 2005 materials is still in progress, hence we restrict our discussion to the materials obtained in 2003, especially those from TP-2, which yielded the most important information relative to the early phase of human ecology in Mangareva. The stratigraphy of TP-2, visible in Figure 4, comprised three layers, as follows:

Layer I: A brown, organically enriched layer about 15 cm thick.

Layer II: The main cultural deposit, consisting of greyish sand with considerable charcoal and oven stones, about 40 cm thick.

Layer III: Yellowish-orange aeolian sand, containing a high density of bird bones, particularly in the 15 cm immediately underlying Layer II, although bird bones extended down to about 115 cm below surface. Layer III was tested to a depth of 175 cm.

Three radiocarbon dates were obtained from TP-2 (Conte and Kirch 2004:Tables 4.1 and 4.2). A sample from the interface of Layers I and II, and thus probably dating the latest phase of occupation, returned a calibrated age of AD 1250–1280 (Beta-190119). A lens of fine charcoal at the base of Layer II, just above the contact with Layer III, was dated to cal AD 1000–1030 (Beta-190118). Finally, a sea-bird bone (Procellariidae) from 103 cm below surface within Layer III was dated to cal AD 1000–1050 (using the marine calibration curve with a DeltaR of 0). These ages suggest the Onemea site was occupied between about AD 1000 and AD 1200, which fits quite well with other recent radiocarbon dating of colonisation-phase sites in southeastern Polynesia (Anderson *et al.* 1999; Anderson and Sinoto 2002; Conte and Anderson 2003).

Nenega-Iti and Atiaoa: Two intermediate-period sites

Two sites correspond to an 'intermediate' period in the archipelago's history, between initial human colonisation and the late period immediately preceding European contact. Both of these are small rock shelters, on the islands of Agakauitai and Mangareva.

In the Nenega-Iti rock shelter on the western side of Agakauitai, we excavated a single test pit of 1 m². Despite some perturbation of the surface of the rock-shelter floor by pigs, the underlying cultural deposit is intact and well stratified, with four distinct cultural layers, and

Figure 3. View of the Onemea dune site (TAR–6) from the shore.

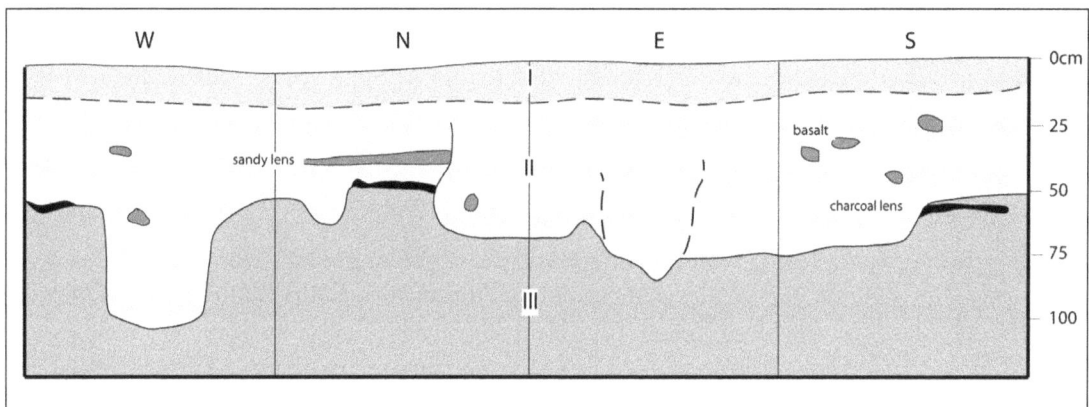

Figure 4. Stratigraphy of Test Unit 2 in the Onemea site.

multiple lenses of charcoal and ash, indicating considerable hearth and/or earth-oven activity in the shelter. The main cultural layers (Figure 5) are as follows:

Layer I (0–4 cm): Very dark-grey, fine-grained sandy loam, containing midden material, but somewhat disturbed by pig rooting.

Layer II (4–10 cm): Dark-grey clay loam, mixed with a considerable amount of calcareous sand, the latter evidently having been brought into the shelter from the nearby beach, probably to provide a clean living floor.

Layer IIIA (10–50 cm): Very dark-grey to black midden deposit, with distinct lenses of compact light-gray ash interspersed. The latter are interpreted as rake-out deposits from nearby combustion features.

Layer IIIB (50–72 cm): Dark reddish-grey cultural deposit lacking ash lenses, mixed with some calcareous sand.

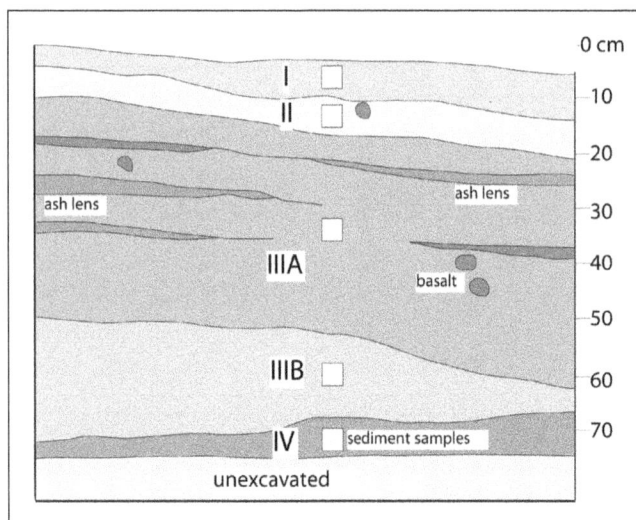

Figure 5. Stratigraphic section of Test Unit 1 in the Nenega-Iti rock-shelter site (AGA-1).

Layer IV (72+ cm): Dark reddish-brown clay with numerous natural cobbles. This layer represents the natural rock-shelter surface before human occupation.

Two radiocarbon dates were obtained from samples excavated from TP-1 at the Nenega-Iti rock shelter. The uppermost sample (Beta-190116) consisted of *Pandanus* wood from the interface of Layers I and II, and yielded a calibrated age of AD 1430–1460. The lower sample (Beta-190117), of *Hibiscus tiliaceous* wood, came from the base of cultural Layer III, and yielded an age of AD 1260–1290. Both of these samples are of relatively short-lived taxa, and should not therefore have any significant in-built age factor. They suggest the cultural deposits in the Nenega-Iti rock shelter were accumulated over about two centuries, from roughly AD 1250 to AD 1450.

On the main island of Mangareva, a rock shelter at Atiaoa on the northwest coast is part of a small valley settlement complex (Conte and Kirch 2004:Figure 3.23). The shelter has a protected surface area of about 4 m x 8 m, and we excavated a single 1 m² test unit near the rear wall (Figure 6). The stratigraphy of that unit consisted of the following layers:

Layer I: A black, compact, silty clay loam, somewhat disturbed by pig rooting.

Layer II: Very dark-grey silty clay with some calcareous sand admixture, with an earth-oven feature in one part of the unit. This is the primary cultural deposit.

Layer III: Dark reddish-brown clay, with dispersed charcoal particles probably derived from anthropogenic burning in the rock-shelter vicinity.

A single radiocarbon date was obtained from the Atiaoa site, on charcoal from within the earth-oven feature in Layer II (Beta-174777). This yielded a calibrated age of AD 1280–1300, indicating that this deposit is roughly contemporaneous with that of the Nenega-Iti rock shelter on Agakauitai Island.

Other sites excavated by Green in 1959 on the islands of Kamaka and Aukena, as well as the Gatavake site studied by Orliac on Mangareva Island, relate to the same period as the Nenega-Iti and Atiaoa sites, and provide additional information.

Recent-period sites

The final phase of Mangareva prehistory, before the arrival of Europeans, is represented in our field data by two stratigraphic sections on the main island of Mangareva, at Gaeata and Gatavake, respectively. Both sections reveal a phase of significant erosion of upland slopes and deposition of terrigenous sediment on to the coastal plains. The Gaeata deposits also contain subfossil endemic land snails. One radiocarbon sample from Gaeata and two from Gatavake indicate that these depositional events occurred during the 17th and 18th centuries.

Drawing on the data recovered from the several sites described above, it is possible to outline in very general terms a sequence of the evolution of the Mangarevan environment over the period of human occupation, beginning about AD 1000 and continuing to the period of European arrival.

Transformation of the terrestrial environment

Terrestrial gastropods and vegetation cover

Ideally, the best direct evidence for changes to the vegetation of the Mangareva Islands would come from micro- and/or macro-botanical remains, including pollen and charcoal. However, the islands lack good sites for pollen analysis, although there may be some potential in swampy deposits such as lie behind the dune ridge at Rikitea. Charcoal is abundant in cultural deposits such as Onemea and the rock shelters, and in the future, we hope to exploit this source of data on vegetation change. Another proxy indicator of generalised vegetation conditions, however, may be found in the endemic and indigenous terrestrial gastropods for which the Mangareva group is well known to malacologists. As noted earlier, at least 38 endemic species of land snails are known from sub-fossil specimens in sedimentary contexts; all of these species are extinct today. The specimens were collected in the course of several scientific expeditions, beginning with the 1934 Mangarevan Expedition and continuing with recent work by the Paris Natural History Museum (Cooke 1935; Kondo 1962; Solem 1976; Abdou and Bouchet 2000; Bouchet and Abdou 2001, 2003). To date, however, this malacological work has focused exclusively on the taxonomy of the snails, with virtually no attention to the geomorphological or sedimentary contexts from which the specimens were collected.

In our work, we paid particular attention to the presence of terrestrial gastropods in our archaeological deposits, and thus for the first time, have obtained a sequence of endemic land-snail specimens in dated contexts. The early TAR-6 site at Onemea contains abundant small endodontid snails (large samples obtained from the 2004 excavations will be described and

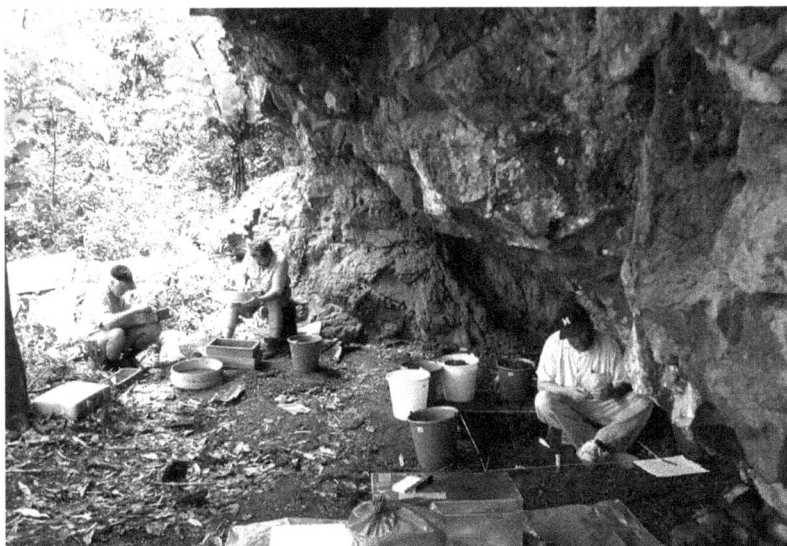

Figure 6. View of the Atiaoa rock shelter (ATA–1) during test excavation in 2001 (A. Anderson, P. Kirch, M. Weisler).

published elsewhere), as well as significant quantities of the assimineid snail *Omphalotropis margarita*. The presence of these abundant endemics suggests relatively little disturbance to the local vegetation conditions surrounding the site. The Nenega-Iti and Aitaoa rock shelters, dating to the intermediate phase, both contained representatives of the large endemic genus *Gambiodonta* (either *G. grandis*, or a closely related extinct species or subspecies), as well as large quantities of *O. margarita*. Again, the existence of these taxa suggests the continued presence of native forest in the vicinities of these sites. At the late Gaeata site, however, the only endemic present in low frequency was *O. margarita*, which is today extinct as well. Although tentative, these distributions of endemic land snails can be taken as a rough proxy indicator of the persistence of native vegetation through the intermediate phase, with increased deforestation and extinction of gastropods in the late period.

Our sites also contain two species of land snails that were introduced to the islands by Polynesian colonists: *Allopeas gracile* (Subulinidae) and *Lamellidea oblonga* (Tornatellinidae). Both of these taxa have been shown by previous studies to have been widely dispersed by Polynesians and other Pacific peoples, presumably adhering to plant materials and/or soil with plants during inter-island voyages (Christensen and Kirch 1981; Kirch 1984:136–37). *Allopeas gracile* appears in significant quantities in the basal deposits (upper Layer III) of the Onemea site. It and *Lamellidea oblonga* have both been identified from the late-period deposits at Gaeata; these anthropophilic taxa which inhabit gardens were thus able to survive the deforestation events that led to the extinction of the endemic snails.

Birds

Even more significant than the temporal patterns of changing frequency of land snails is the evidence from our sites for severe reductions over time in the presence of land and sea birds. Historically, the Mangareva avifauna is highly depauperate in native land birds (other than the introduced chicken and common rock dove, being limited to a kingfisher species also found in the Tuamotus [*Halcyon gambieri*] and a reed-warbler [*Conopoderas caffra*]; Lacan and Mougin 1974). Most of the bird taxa known to Mangareva thus consist of sea birds, but as Lacan and Mougin (1974) observe, these are largely confined to the three small, unoccupied, high islands in the southern part of the lagoon (Makaroa, Manui and Motu Teiku). The larger, inhabited islands are notable for the general absence of bird fauna.

Clearly, the situation at the time of initial Polynesian settlement of Mangareva was quite different. Steadman and Justice (1998) previously identified 15 species of sea birds, three species of resident land birds, a migrant shore bird, and the Polynesian-introduced chicken (*Gallus gallus*) from archaeological samples excavated by Roger Green in 1959. Our excavations add considerably to this inventory, especially thanks to the sample of 153 bird bones (Figure 7) recovered from the early Onemea site (Worthy and Tennyson 2004). The high density of sea-bird bones in Layer III and to some extent at the base of Layer II in this site suggest that Taravai Island was a significant rookery or nesting site for several species of Procellaridae, especially a species in the genus *Pseudobulweria*, which today does not exist in Mangareva and indeed has a very restricted distribution in the Pacific. Also present in the early Onemea desposits are three species of *Puffinus* (shearwaters), one or two species of *Pterodroma* (petrels), the red-tailed tropic bird (*Phaethon rubricauda*), and the white tern (*Gygis alba*). In addition, there are several bones from a species of *Ducula* (Columbidae), a genus of fruit pigeons with numerous endemic taxa known from archaeological contexts from other Pacific Island groups (Steadman 2006). This hints at the likely presence of an endemic land-bird fauna on the main Mangareva Islands, which further excavations and enlarged sample sizes will hopefully reveal.

The vertebrate sample from the 'intermediate' phase Nenega-Iti site contrasts markedly with that from the earlier Onemea deposits. (Unfortunately, the vertebrate remains from Atiaoa were lost in transit to the University of Florida and hence are not available for comparison.) From this rock shelter, there were only 13 bird bones, mostly confined to the base of Layer III. Only three taxa were represented: the *Pseudobulweria*, which dominated the sample with 10 bones, a species of *Pterodroma*, and a single bone of the brown Noddy (*Anous stolidus*).

While these patterns need to be augmented by additional samples, one may nonetheless suggest there was a significant decline in the taxonomic richness and frequency of birds over time on the Mangareva Islands. Such patterns of extirpation and extinction of island avifaunas have been well documented for a number of oceanic islands (Steadman 2006), and Mangareva appears to add yet another case of this phenomenon. If the formerly extensive bird populations constituted a significant food resource for the first Polynesian colonists, they also are likely to have played a non-trivial role in the enrichment of soil nutrients through the regular deposition of guano, essential for the maintenance of the terrestrial ecosystem. Thus one may hypothesise that the decimation of these bird colonies, whether directly through human hunting, or indirectly, for example through the introduction of the Pacific rat (*Rattus exulans*), interrupted this cycle of nutrient enrichment. Combined with forest clearance for horticulture, and possibly climatic factors (Allen 2006), the elimination of a major input source for soil nutrients on old, weathered volcanics may have hastened the deforestation which was so evident at the time of European contact.

Mammals

The only mammals described ethnographically for Mangareva were pigs and the Pacific rat (*R. exulans*). Pigs, however, were known only from oral traditions, and were not present on the islands at the time of initial European contact (Hiroa 1938:194–195). Green and Weisler (2004), who analysed the vertebrate remains from Green's 1959 excavations, reported abundant rat bones at all sites, but only 11 bones of pig and five bones of dog; clearly, however, pigs and dogs had both been introduced to the islands by Polynesians. Our excavated vertebrate assemblages reinforce this picture of limited quantities of pig and/or dog, with only a single identified premolar of *Sus scrofa* from the Nenega-Iti site, and a few other fragmentary post-cranial remains of medium mammal which represent either pigs or dogs. The rarity of pig remains in all sites studied to date suggests these animals were never abundant in pre-European times. As Kirch (2000) has suggested, pigs were eliminated in some islands due to their trophic competition with humans for limited horticultural productions, and this appears also to have been the case for Mangareva. The fact that the majority of pig bones recovered by Green on Kamaka Island came from a marae context, or religious site, demonstrates that pigs were a food item reserved for the elite and offered during their rituals.

The bones of the Pacific rat (*Rattus exulans*) are present in small quantities in Onemea, but are quite abundant in the Nenega-Iti deposits, suggestive of an increase in their populations from the early to intermediate periods. In contrast to the situation in the Tangatatau rock shelter (Site MAN-44)

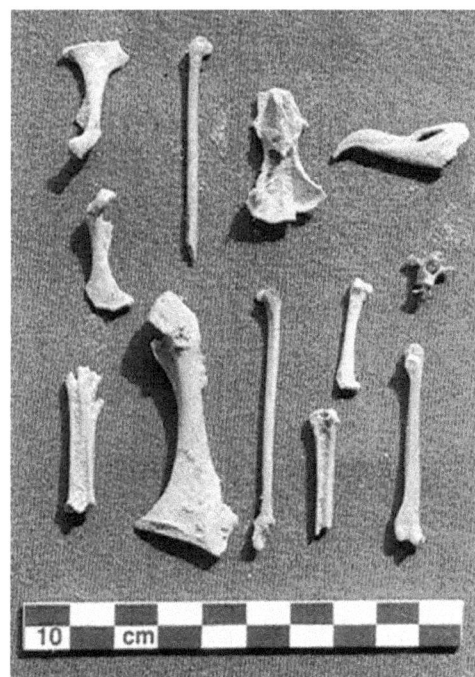

Figure 7. Bird bones from the Onemea site.

on Mangaia Island (Kirch 1996; Kirch *et al.* 1995), there are no taphonomic traces (burning or chewing marks) on the Mangareva rat bones, which would seem to confirm Hiroa's statement that rats were not consumed by the Mangarevans (Hiroa 1938). Whereas Mangaia also has a sequence in which pigs were eliminated and there was severe terrestrial resource limitation, in Mangareva one may suppose that the extensive marine resources were sufficient to provide for the protein needs of the human population.

Human impact on marine resources?

In all of the excavated sites, marine food remains (fish bones and shellfish) constitute the majority of the faunal assemblages. For example, 94 percent of the vertebrate remains at Nenega-Iti, and 64 percent of those at Onemea, consist of fish bones. The most commonly taken fish are the major inshore reef and lagoon species (in the families Scaridae, Balistidae and Serranidae), with very few pelagic fish represented. For both fish and marine molluscs, we have no evidence for significant changes between the different sites, nor between levels of the same site, which might indicate anthropogenic impact on marine resources (e.g. size diminution, or decreasing representation of particular high-value taxa). This is again a significant contrast to the situation in Mangaia, where Butler (2001; and see Kirch *et al.* 1995) has demonstrated considerable resource depression over time. The relative vastness of the Mangarevan marine and lagoon ecosystem, in comparison with the diminutive land area, may thus have provided a sufficiently rich and resilient resource base such that the small human population never had a significant impact on it. Of course, we again stress that this is a hypothesis to be confirmed by further excavations and enlarged faunal samples.

Conclusion

Before the arrival of humans (about 900–1000 AD), the Gambier Islands possessed a diverse bird fauna, with at least 19 species, as evidenced by the zooarchaeological assemblage of the Onemea site. As in many other Pacific islands, these bird populations were decimated within several centuries after the arrival of Polynesians, who hunted them, and who presumably also hastened their demise indirectly through the introduction of predatory rats and through the habitat destruction resulting from forest clearance for gardens. Two of these species are extinct today, and others are no longer present in the Gambier archipelago. Among the secondary effects of this major episode of bird extinction and extirpation may have been the curtailing of a critical cycle of nutrient inputs to the terrestrial ecosystem, through the regular deposition of the guano of large sea-bird populations.

As elsewhere in Polynesia, the colonising population introduced a variety of other organisms, not only the Pacific rat and at least two species of land snail that inhabit plants and garden soils, but chickens, pigs and dogs. Naturally, it also introduced the key tree and root crops essential for Polynesian horticulture. The gradual reduction in native-forest cover, presumably correlating with an expansion of human horticultural activity, is mirrored in the gradual reduction in the presence of various taxa of endemic land snails, now entirely extinct, such as the large *Gambiodonta cf. grandis* which last appears in the upper levels of our intermediate-phase sites. While forest clearance for horticulture was presumably one factor influencing the decline in native-vegetation cover, this is not necessarily the sole cause of the extreme deforestation witnessed in Mangareva in the historic period. We have already alluded to the possible negative effects of the elimination of sea-bird nutrients on islands with five to six million-year-old soils, already limited in such key nutrients as phosphorus. The final phase of near total deforestation of the upper slopes and ridges of the main high islands appears to correlate with a major phase of erosion and deposition of terrestrial sediments, evidenced at the recent (17th–18th century) sites of Gaeata and Gatavake. A similar chronology of deforestation has been noted by Orliac and Orliac (2006) for Easter Island, and the timing may not be entirely coincidental.

We would not rule out possible climatic effects, such as those that brought on the Little Ice Age (Allen 2006), although we question whether climate change without the combined effects of human actions would have resulted in the sequence in evidence for either island. Finally, in contrast to the major changes in the terrestrial environment discussed above, thus far we have no evidence for any significant impact on marine resources. The marine resource base may simply have been so extensive and rich in Mangareva that it was resilient to the anthropogenic effects of the limited human population which was capable of being supported on the small and increasingly fragile high islets. In the end, the ethnographic sources indicate that this marine resource base was fundamental to the late-period Mangarevan economy. Where else in Polynesia could the simple act of a fisherman withholding the gift of his catch bring down the ruling chief (Hiroa 1938:76)?

References

Abdou, A. and P. Bouchet 2000. Nouveaux gastéropodes Endodontidae et Punctidae (Mollusca, Pulmonata) récemment éteints de l'archipel des Gambier (Polynésie). *Zoosystema* 22:689–707.

Allen, M. 2006. New ideas about Late Holocene Climate Variability in the Central Pacific. *Curent Anthropology* 47:521–535.

Anderson A. and Y. Sinoto 2002. New Radiocarbon Ages of Colonization Sites in East Polynesia. *Asian Perspectives* 41:242–257

Anderson A., E. Conte, G. Clark, Y. Sinoto and F.Petchey 1999. Renewed Excavations at Motu Paeao, Maupiti, French Polynesia: Preliminary Results. *New Zealand Journal of Archaeology* 21:47–65.

Bouchet, P. and A. Abdou 2001. Recent extinct land snails (Euconulidae) from the Gambier Islands with remarkable apertural barriers. *Pacific Science* 55:121–127.

Bouchet, P. and A. Abdou 2003. Endemic land snails from the Pacific Islands and the museum record: Documenting and dating the extinction of the terrestrial Assimineidae of the Gambier Islands. *Journal of Molluscan Studies* 69:165–170.

Butler, V.L. 2001. Changing fish use on Mangaia, southern Cook Islands: Resource depression and the prey choice model. *International Journal of Osteoarchaeology* 11:88–100.

Christensen, C.C., and P.V. Kirch 1981. Nonmarine mollusks from archaeological sites on Tikopia, Southeastern Solomon Islands. *Pacific Science* 35:75–88.

Conte E. and A. Anderson 2003. Radiocarbon Ages for two sites on Ua Huka, Marquesas. *Asian Perspectives* 42:155–160.

Conte, E. and P.V. Kirch (eds) 2004. *Archaeological Investigations in the Mangareva Islands (Gambier Archipelago), French Polynesia.* Contribution No. 62, Archaeological Research Facility. Berkeley: University of California.

Cooke, C.M., Jr. 1935. Report of C. Montague Cooke, Jr., Malacologist and Leader [of the 1934 Mangarevan Expedition]. In H.E. Gregory, *Report of the Director* for 1934. Honolulu: Bernice P. Bishop Museum Bulletin 133.

Emory, K.P. 1939. *Archaeology of Mangareva and Neighboring Atolls.* Honolulu: Bernice P. Bishop Museum Bulletin 163.

Fourmanoir, P., J.M. Griessinger and Y. Plessis 1974. Faune ichtyologique des Gambier. *Cahiers du Pacifique* 18:543–559. Paris: Fondation Singer-Polignac.

Green, R.C. and M.I. Weisler 2000. *Mangarevan Archaeology: Interpretations Using New Data and 40*

Year Old Excavations to Establish a Sequence from 1200 to 1900 AD. University of Otago Studies in Prehistoric Archaeology No. 19. Dunedin.

Green, R.C. and M.I. Weisler 2002. The Mangarevan sequence and the dating of geographic expansion into southeast Polynesia. *Asian Perspectives* 41:213–241.

Green, R.C. and M.I. Weisler 2004. Prehistoric introduction and extinction of animals in Mangareva, Southeast Pacific. *Archaeology in Oceania* 39:34–41.

Hiroa, Te Rangi (P.H. Buck) 1938. *Ethnology of Mangareva*. Honolulu: Bernice P. Bishop Museum Bulletin 157.

Kirch, P.V. 1984. *The Evolution of the Polynesian Chiefdoms*. Cambridge: Cambridge University Press.

Kirch, P.V. 1996. Late Holocene human-induced modifications to a central Polynesian island ecosystem. *Proceedings of the National Academy of Sciences, USA*, 93:5296–5300.

Kirch, P.V. 2000. Pigs, humans, and trophic competition on small Oceanic islands. In A. Anderson and T. Murray (eds), *Australian Archaeologist : Collected Papers in Honour of Jim Allen*, pp. 427–439. Canberra: Australian National University.

Kirch, P.V. 2007a. Hawaii as a model system for human ecodynamics. *American Anthropologist* 109:8–26.

Kirch, P.V. 2007b. Three islands and an archipelago: Reciprocal interactions between humans and island ecosystems in Polynesia. *Earth and Environmental Science Transactions of the Royal Society of Edinburgh* 98:1–15.

Kirch, P.V., D.W. Steadman, V.L. Butler, J. Hather, and M.I. Weisler 1995. Prehistory and human ecology in Eastern Polynesia: Excavations at Tangatatau rockshelter, Mangaia, Cook Islands. *Archaeology in Oceania* 30:47–65.

Lacan, F. and J.-L. Mougin 1974. Les oiseaux de l'archipel des Gambier. *Cahiers du Pacifique* 18:533–542.

Laval, Père H. 1938. *Mangareva: l'Histoire Ancienne d'un Peuple Polynésien*. Paris: Librairie

Orliac C. and M. Orliac 2006. La flore disparue de l'île de Pâques. *les Nouvelles de l'Archéologie* 102: 29–33.

Orliac, M. 2002. *Composition et Évolution de la Flore de l'Archipel Gambier du 12è au 19è Siecle*. Rapport sur les Travaux de la Mission Archéologique, Avril–Mai 2001. Paris: C.N.R.S.

Orliac, M. 2003. Un aspect de la flore de Mangareva au XIIème siècle (archipel Gambier, Polynésie française. In C. Orliac (ed), *Archéologie en Océanie insulaire. Peuplement, sociétés et paysages*, pp. 150–171. Editions Artcom.

Richard, G. 1974 Bionomie des mollusques littoraux des baies envasées de l'île de Mangareva. *Cahiers du Pacifique* No. 18(II):605–614. Paris: Fondation Singer-Polignac.

Salvat, B. 1974. Mollusques des "récifs d'îlots" du récif barrière des îles Gambier. *Cahiers du Pacifique* No. 18(II):601–603. Paris: Fondation Singer-Polignac.

St. John, H. 1935. Report of Harold St. John, Botanist. In H. E. Gregory, *Report of the Director for 1934*. Honolulu: Bernice P. Bishop Museum Bulletin 133.

Solem, A. 1976. *Endodontoid Land Snails from Pacific Islands (Mollusca: Pulmonata: Sigmurethra)*. Part I. *Family Endodontidae*. Chicago: Field Museum of Natural History.

Solem, A. 1983. *Endodontoid Land Snails from Pacific Islands (Mollusca: Pulmonata: Sigmurethra)*. Part 2. *Families Punctidae and Charopidae*. Chicago: Field Museum of Natural History.

Steadman, D. 2006. *Extinction and Biogeography of Tropical Pacific Birds*. Chicago: University of Chicago Press.

Steadman, D.W. and L.J. Justice 1998. Prehistoric exploitation of birds on Mangareva, Gambier Islands, French Polynesia. *Man and Culture in Oceania* 14:81–98.

17

Stora Karlsö – a tiny Baltic island with a puzzling past

Rita Larje
Swedish Museum of Natural History, Stockholm, Sweden
larita00@hotmail.com

Introduction

In the middle of the Baltic Sea, about 75 km from the Swedish mainland, lies the Swedish island Gotland. On its west coast are three small islands, the two Karlsö islands and the Västergarn islet. The largest island, Stora Karlsö, is 6.5 km from the west coast of Gotland, and is a nature reservation owned by a non-profit shareholders' association, the Karlsö Hunting and Animal Protection Association, founded in 1880 on the initiative of Willy Wöhler, a farmer from Gotland. The island is about 2.5 km² in size and about 1 km wide (north-south) and 2 km long (east-west), with the highest point 51.6 m above sea level. For such a small island, prehistoric remains are exceedingly abundant. From an elevated point in the centre of the island, you can visually travel in time over the landscape from Middle Neolithic, to later prehistoric, to historic sites (Figure 1).

The making of an island

Understanding the formation of Stora Karlsö is important for understanding the distribution and location of prehistoric sites, particularly those associated with early human occupation. The bedrock is coral reef that was transformed into limestone. There are steep cliffs towards the sea on all sides of the island, except to the south, where the limestone strata has a downward slope. Between the cliffs in the north is a good harbour. The landscape configuration is a result of erosion. The general outline was created by the erosive force of a thick ice cap that covered the Baltic basin during the last glaciation. After the ice melted some 12,000 years ago, Stora Karlsö was submerged, but with the pressure of the heavy ice gone, the land began to rise quickly. Once the island emerged, it was exposed to the force of sea waves. Fresh-water lakes and saltwater seas alternated in the Baltic basin and during this time, the water level varied greatly. The sea waves created the intricate coastal outline of the island, flushed away loose soil, scraped out caves and built up beach ridges. These processes left a plateau island divided by a broad valley with a north-south extension that was crossed by two large beach ridges. The oldest, the Ancylus ridge,

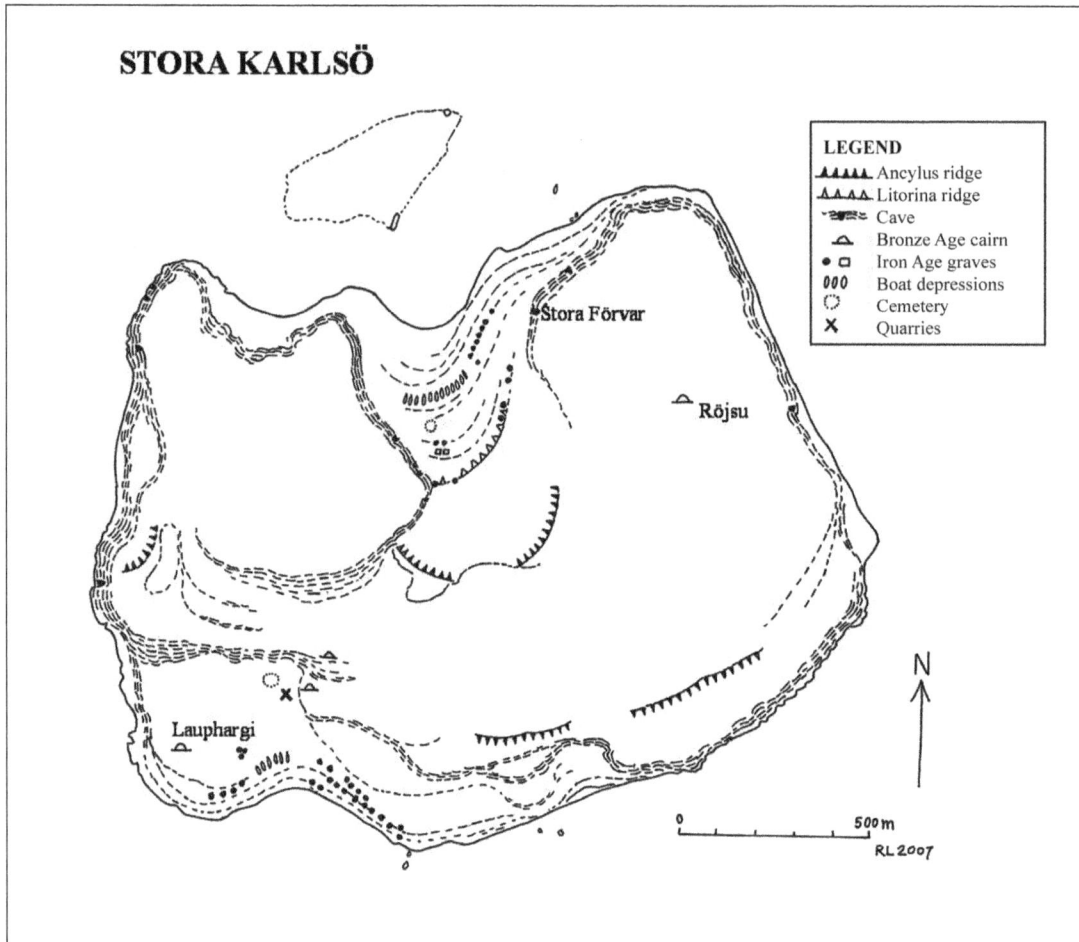

Figure 1. Map of Stora Karlsö showing the location of prehistoric monuments.

formed in a fresh-water lake 10,700–10,000 years ago and is now 28 m above sea level (Munthe *et al.* 1927). The melting ice cap led to a rise in the sea level that exceeded at times the rate of land emergence, with sea levels rising as much as 5–10 cm a year.

Finally, the Ancylus Lake was forced to find a new outlet in the south. Within only 200 years, the water level sank to the ocean level and saltwater filled the Baltic basin. The Ancylus Lake was replaced with a saltwater body, the Litorina Sea, which lasted for about 7000 years. This sea had six transgressions, the last and highest about 6000 BP. The Litorina maximum formed another beach ridge on Stora Karlsö that is now 18–20 m above sea level. The formation of beach ridges is still in progress in the Limnea Sea, the 'modern' Baltic Sea.

In the past, the Karlsö islands were named Foulleholmene (the Bird Islands), a name easily understood given the presence of thousands of guillemots (*Aria aalge*) and razorbills (*Alca torda*) which nest on the cliff walls and rocky shores on both islands. All the islands are rich in sea birds, and land birds also nest there. In prehistory, hunters and fishermen made the most of island resources such as seals, birds, eggs and fish. Stora Karlsö was never thickly forested and there was good grazing without the need for forest clearing.

Stora Förvar cave: The start of human impact

Humans first set foot on the island about 9500 years ago, according to evidence found in the Stora Förvar (large storage) cave in the cliff wall of the eastern plate. Numerous bone remains and artefacts were uncovered in 1887, and the discovery led to a five-year excavation campaign under the direction of Lars Kolmodin and Hjalmar Stolpe between 1888 and 1893. The cave was created by the Ancylus Lake and is about 25 m deep. The entrance is some 21 m above sea level and is 9.5 m wide and 6.5 m high. The cave narrows from the entrance and the floor has an upward slope to the interior (Figure 2).

The excavation of Stora Förvar in the late 19th century uncovered a cultural layer more than 4 m deep, producing six tons of animal bone, some human remains, bone and stone artefacts and a multitude of potsherds. The deposit spanned the Mesolithic to Iron Age. Excavation was carried out in 30 cm layers over defined horizontal areas, labelled Area A to Area I. No consideration was taken of the stratigraphy of the sloping floor, which reduces the possibility of accurately dating particular layers. This means that cultural finds from a particular area and depth are not necessarily contemporary with those excavated from the same depth in another area.

The excavation produced a huge quantity of material to analyse, but both Kolmodin and Stolpe died in 1905 without finishing the work. The task was then entrusted to Bror Schnittger, who, in 1913, published the description of the cave and the excavations, but who did not publish on the cultural material.

Some animal bones from Stora Förvar were analysed by A. Pira and C.O. Roth, and C. Fürst examined the human remains from the cave. Unfortunately, all three died before finishing their studies. Pira's work on the pig remains from the cave was published in 1909 and another general study of the bone remains was published posthumously in 1926. When Schnittger died in 1924, the responsibility for the excavated material was given to Schnittger's widow, Hanna

Figure 2. Stora Förvar, the cave entrance (photo by R. Larje).

Rydh. In 1931, she published an outline of the prehistory of Stora Karlsö, which also gave a survey of the archaeological studies, and included Roth's list of bird species identified from the cave. Rydh decided to publish an analysis of the cave artefacts together with a revised version of Schnittger's 1913 publication. The analysis of bones had to be postponed. The publication was finished in 1940 (Schnittger and Rydh 1940), and included an extensive catalogue of the cave finds.

Subsequently, several archaeozoologists could not resist the temptation offered by the six tons of bone remains collected from Stora Förvar material. Erikson and Knape (1991) used bones from Area F in the middle of the cave to study occupation seasonality. Lindqvist and Possnert (1997) included Stora Förvar in an accelerator mass spectrometry (AMS) ^{14}C dating project to date the original occupation of Gotland, as extensive ^{14}C dating could overcome the chronological problem created by the poor recording of excavation stratigraphy. Johansson and Larje (1993) analysed a soil sample from the cave and verified that the 19th century excavation by 'spade and knife' had missed many of the smaller cultural remains.

In 1889, human skulls and associated splintered long bones found deep in Area D were interpreted to be the result of cannibalism or a ritual ancestor cult (Retzius 1890; Rydh 1931). The cannibalism theory was not proven, and is still under investigation. The human bones were unfortunately lost, but more human remains were found by Lindqvist (1996) in the analysis of bone from excavation Area G. The Area G remains comprised some 50 bones from more than five individuals: a baby two to four months old, a young teenager, an older teenage boy, an adult woman and probably two adult men. The bones came from the oldest, pre-ceramic layers, and AMS dating (Lindqvist and Possnert 1997) places the baby and the boy in the Late Mesolithic (Boreal) period (c. 9500 to 8200 cal. BP). This makes these remains the oldest humans found on Gotland to date (Lindqvist 1996). A burnt fragmentary human frontal skull bone with numerous cut marks raised again the question of ritual behaviour. The way the human bones were scattered and mixed with animal-bone refuse, artefacts and ashes was taken as an indication of cult activity. The question of 'cult' behaviour can be examined further in the study of human bone from the unanalysed excavation areas. The catalogue published in Schnittger and Rydh (1940) mentions human remains in various areas and from various layers, but does not mention the presence of intact human burials.

Mesolithic subsistence strategy

The Mesolithic economy was based largely on grey-seal and ringed-seal hunting. An occasional mountain hare was on the menu, as indicated by sparse hare bones, together with birds and fish. The Baltic Basin was a fresh-water lake that only gradually became more brackish from about 9200–9000 cal. BP (Lindqvist and Possnert 1997). Bones of Whooper swan (*Cygnus cygnus*) and a number of ducks were found, but no auks. It is likely the cliffs of Stora Karlsö swarmed with birds in the past, as today (Storå 2006). The most common fish caught was salmon. The climate at this time was mild, with a mean temperature higher than today, and the island was covered with open woodland of pine and hazel (Eriksson 1988, 1992).

Ericson and Knape (1991) found that grey-seal bones in the pre-ceramic layers in Area H were from young animals, nearly six months old, as indicated by mandible length. These researchers are of the opinion that Stora Karlsö was a seasonal seal-hunting station and the Stora Förvar cave was used as a refuse dump for seal-cub carcasses. The seal hunting, mainly done with nets, was primarily for skins, based on the scarcity of metacarpals and metatarsals, and the way some mandibles were chopped, consistent with skinning. Lindqvist (1991) assessed the age range of the seals, from the length of the molar row, as from one to four months in the early layers of Area G. Assuming the cubs were born on ice in early March, as is the case in the Baltic today (Roos 2000), six-month-old cubs could be caught at the earliest in August–September. Seal cubs born in March and killed aged from one to four months would have been hunted between April and May. This suggests a non-winter season for hunting in both cases.

Lindqvist and Possnert (1997) discuss the introduction of grey seals in the Baltic Basin and note the adaptability of the animals' reproduction strategy. AMS ^{14}C dating of grey seals in the bottom layers of Area G to the early Mesolithic probably implies entry from the south during the Yoldia Sea stage before 9600 BP. The adaptable grey seal could have endured the fresh-water Ancylus Lake stage of the Baltic and changed its reproduction strategy from autumn birth on shores in the west Atlantic, to spring birth on ice in the Baltic.

Whereas Ericson and Knape (1990) argue in favour of a seasonal hunting station, Lindqvist (1996) suggested a more permanent occupation. He based this on the estimated age of the human remains, which included nursing babies, and the evidence of intense fire use in the cave. Lindqvist also studied the human, seal, pig and fish remains from the Mesolithic layers to consider seasonal versus sedentary occupation, but died in April 2006, before the work was completed.

During the Mesolithic, people were clearly on the island, having arrived by boat. If Stora Karlsö was not a permanent base, where did they spend the rest of the year? Most likely in a camp on the coast of Gotland close to the islands, and there is archaeological evidence of a Mesolithic site close to the 'Pitted Ware' site at Ajvide in Eksta parish (Österholm 1989). Future investigations of Mesolithic sites on Gotland should cast light on the matter of permanent settlement on Stora Karlsö.

Mesolithic–Early Neolithic transition

There is a discontinuity in the cultural deposits of Stora Förvar between the Mesolithic (9500–8000 cal. BP) and Neolithic layers. AMS dating of bone from younger layers dated to c. 6200–5800 cal. BP indicates an occupation hiatus of about 2000 years. It was observed at the Mesolithic site at Ajvide that the bottom layers had been repeatedly covered by beach deposits (Österholm 1989). This happened at an early stage of the Litorina transgression about 6000 BP, when people lived close enough to the sea so that heavy storms could reach the settlement. Stora Karlsö must have been affected by the transgression, too, and waves probably came very close to the Stora Förvar cave entrance. Small-scale investigations of cultural deposits outside the cave entrance in 1973 uncovered a layer of eel grass (*Zostera marina*) 22.3 m above current sea level (a height which corresponds to sea level during the Mesolithic–Neolithic transition) in the northeastern area (Almgren 2007). Eel grass is a common water plant at 2–4 m depth in the bay outside the cave today (Fredriksson 1976), and it was probably also common in the Litorina Sea. Heavy storms during a transgression could easily have swept masses of eel grass into the cave. The cave is open to northwesterly winds and any wave-swept material would accumulate against the northeastern cave wall. Finds of eel grass from the Mesolithic–Neolithic transition levels at Stora Förvar have been reported previously (Schnittger and Rydh 1940), but were interpreted as the debris from sleeping mattresses.

Thus, during the Litorina transgressions, Stora Förvar could have been an uncomfortable, or even inaccessible, place for habitation. During this time, did people go to mainland Gotland, or did they simply move to parts of Stora Karlsö out of reach of the sea? There is very little evidence for other early settlement areas, although there are reports of early flint artefacts from various locations. Extensive and detailed phosphate mapping might be used to reveal the location of old occupational areas in the future.

Early Neolithic

This period is dated from 6000 BP to 5550 BP (Lindqvist and Possnert 1997) and the animal species represented differ from those in underlying layers. Seal bones still dominate, but ringed seal is more abundant than grey seal. Harp seal was also present in small amounts. Different seal species require specialised hunting techniques. The increasing number of ringed seals indicates there was more sea ice in the area as a result of lower winter temperatures. The seals hunted in this period were adult animals rich in blubber as well as meat.

Seal hunting and fishing were undoubtedly the base of the economy, but finds of cattle bone, among the oldest in Sweden, show that domestic cattle was introduced early on Gotland and on Stora Karlsö. Might this also imply permanent settlement? An important issue is the supply of forage in winter. In historic times, sheep have foraged on Stora Karlsö year round, although very cold and snowy winters take their toll. The vegetation in the Neolithic was lush deciduous woodland and grasses, so there was probably sufficient food and firewood for year-round settlement. Did people live in the cave? Charcoal, ash and fireplaces occur in the Stora Förvar deposits in all areas and layers, but they do not necessarily imply year-round living. A common view among archaeologists is that caves are used for temporary shelter, rather than permanent living. It is unclear whether a tent of seal skins on a well-drained terrace was preferable to a damp lodging in a cave with the risk of falling rocks.

Middle Neolithic

This phase contains characteristic pottery of Pitted Ware culture and dates from 5200 BP to 4000 BP. The Stora Förvar excavations recovered a great number of 'pitted pot sherds'. Österholm (1989) places Stora Karlsö within the resource area of the large Pitted Ware settlement of Jakobs/Ajvide on the Gotland coast facing the Karlsö islands. As in other Middle Neolithic sites, there is a shift in the animal species represented. Harp seal and ringed seal now outnumber grey seal. The hunting strategy also changed from netting and clubbing to hunting with harpoons. Most of the harpoons found in the cave are from this phase (Clark 1976).

The salinity of the Litorina Sea was higher than in the Baltic today, possibly twice as high (Munthe *et al.* 1927). The Middle and late-Middle Neolithic coincide with a transgression that had a considerable influence on the Baltic as a whole by producing favourable conditions for marine life (Gräslund 1978). The marine fauna at this time was rich in both species range and population abundance. Species exotic in the Baltic today identified in Stora Förvar include harp seal, killer whale, tuna, gannet and even great auk (Ericson 1989). The gannet is an excellent indicator of the presence of herring shoals. Herring probably occurred in great numbers during this period. The presence of herring in the cave is attested by finds of herring bone in a cave soil sample (Johansson and Larje 1993). The introduction to the Litorina Sea of the other species could be the result of the growth of vast herring populations. Bird life on the island at this time included guillemots, razorbills, gannets and probably the great auk. Tuna, cod and harp seal probably came to feed on the abundance of herring, and killer whales followed to catch the seals.

Again, the question of seasonal or year-round occupation is important. The dominance of sheep is reduced, in favour of pigs, with cattle present in low numbers. Seal hunting and fishing is still important, and bird trapping and egg collecting are other significant sources of protein. But was all this food consumed on the island, or was it 'exported' to a home camp, such as the Ajvide settlement? What about the domestic stock? Could cows, pigs and sheep be left over winter on the island, or were they shipped to and fro? Then there is the question of housing – did people live in caves or build houses? Sea transport was a minor problem, with outrigger or double canoes probably used. In tests of replica boats built on Gotland (Österholm 1988), it took two men two hours in a 4.5 m long outrigger log boat to reach Stora Karlsö from the coast of Gotland. This suggests the people at Ajvide could easily have made short trips to Stora Karlsö.

There is one interesting peculiarity concerning seal hunting and fishing in the Middle Neolithic. In most coastal settlements on Gotland, harp seal is the most common catch, but on Stora Karlsö, the ringed seal is dominant. In addition, the cod from Karlsö were larger than the ones from Ajvide. Lindqvist and Possnert (1997) present various scenarios to explain this, but there were clearly environmental differences between Stora Karlsö and Gotland.

The Bronze Age

This period in the prehistory of Stora Karlsö is still poorly known. Bone in the upper layers in Stora Förvar is dominated by remains of domestic cattle, mostly sheep and goat with a few remains of domestic fowl. The number of seals and pigs decreases. The function and importance of the cave appears to change, coinciding with the appearance of stone cairns built around the island.

Röjsu

On the highest point of the eastern part of the island, 51.6 m above sea level, is a large cairn. Fineman identified it on his 1725 map and mentioned that a tree was growing inside that could be seen from far away (Jacobson 2005). Linnaeus (1745) also noticed the mound and the single tree on his visit to Stora Karlsö in 1741. The tree and the cairn provided an excellent navigation mark for seafarers. The cairn was called 'röjsu', which simply means 'cairn'. The tree associated with the cairn (an ash) survives today.

Röjsu was examined but not fully excavated in 1889 when Fredrik Nordin (1889) excavated most of the prehistoric cairns and monuments on the island during a summer season. His report recorded 51 monuments. Röjsu has a diameter of 28 m, a height of 2.5 m and was built from limestone slabs and boulders, with smaller stones used in the filling. Nordin noticed that an irregular hollow was already dug out around the tree and found inside the cairn a fairly evenly built wall, parallel to the diameter of the cairn and 1.6 m high. A trench was opened from the southwest into the cairn centre, at the bottom of which he found the frontal part of a human skull and some other human bones. The only artefact found was a small pointed object made of slate. Rydh (1931) dates the cairn to the Early Bronze Age (3750–3050 BP), based on the presence of non-burnt human bones. In the Late Bronze Age, cremation became the preferred burial custom.

Lauphargi

In a less-elevated, but nevertheless conspicuous, location in the southwest is another large Bronze Age cairn, called Lauphargi (Figure 3), which was probably also used as a navigation mark. The cairn has a diameter of about 25 m and the intact southwestern part stands about 4 m above the ground. The description by Nordin (1889) records a 1 m high wall built of limestone slabs in better condition than the one in Röjsu. Nordin thought the cairn had been plundered and the interior disturbed, as he found displaced large slabs that might have belonged to a stone cist. A stone cist indicates a date in the Early Bronze Age, as for Röjsu, but no human remains were found, only large numbers of pot sherds and a few burnt bone fragments spread over a 5 m wide area. With no datable finds, there is a dating problem. But if the large slabs were not from a stone cist, the finding of a cremation suggested by the unidentified burnt bone would place the cairn in the Late Bronze Age.

Figure 3. Lauphargi, the undamaged west wall (photo by R. Larje).

Smaller cairns

Northeast of Lauphargi on the hillside there are two more smaller cairns, believed to be from the Bronze Age. The largest has a diameter of 8 m and contained some bones (not burnt), and the smaller one, with a diameter 4 m, contained a ceramic vessel with some burnt bone fragments. The elevated location of the cairns is consistent with the Bronze Age, but the structures have not been absolutely dated. The ceramic vessel in the smaller cairn is of an uncommon type and probably dates to the Late Bronze Age.

Only a few of the c. 400 large Bronze Age cairns on Gotland have been scientifically investigated, but it is clear the large cairns are more than just heaps of stones. Interesting details include the presence of a tower-like construction in the interior, built from horizontally placed limestone slabs, and inside this tower a cist with a compact lining of stone slabs, found in cairns at Hau in Fleringe and at Kauparve in Lärbro, both in the northern part of Gotland (Lindquist 1979). Nordin (1889) noticed well-constructed walls in Röjsu and Lauphargi, but judged the interior had been disturbed in both cases. In the autumn of 2007, all of the vegetation in and around Lauphargi was removed. Traces of the interior wall were visible around most of the cairn. There is also a slab-wall construction, which could be taken for a cist. The larger slabs thrown about might have been a roof covering. Obviously, we have two kinds of Bronze Age graves on the island; larger with inner walls, and smaller without inner walls.

Four Bronze Age cairns on the tiny island suggest it was an important place strategically or culturally. The construction of the large cairns was not an easy enterprise; they required social and economic investment in labour.

It should be noted that the Bronze Age cairns were excavated during a hectic summer season in 1889 which also included the excavation of all the other stone mounds on the island. Unfortunately, no details were published by Fredrik Nordin, the archaeologist in charge, except for a short field report. In 1931, Hanna Rydh examined Nordin's report and the artefacts in a chapter on the Bronze Age on Stora Karlsö. She included items such as an Early Bronze Age knife from Stora Förvar and a well-preserved Late Bronze Age spear head found by Willy Wöhler reportedly wedged into a cliff wall. No identification of the bone was done and the material is now almost certainly lost.

The Iron Age

Graves

On a beach ridge at the northern harbour there are seven white, shiny mounds of limestone (Figure 4) marking the graves of Iron Age people. There are about 60 Iron Age stone sites on Stora Karlsö. Nordin's earlier report included information about the size and internal construction of the tombs, the orientation of burials, and grave goods. Information about the Iron Age of the island was compiled by Rydh (1931). Some graves could be dated from accompanying artefacts to the Early Roman–Migration Period (200–400 AD). No osteological identification was done, and today, much of the bone material has been lost or mixed so that individual bones cannot be linked with a particular grave.

Human remains

An attempt was made by Sundeen (2005) to establish the status of the human bone recovered by Nordin, but it soon became clear that not all of the remains were from Iron Age burials. A ^{14}C dating on three thigh bones gave ages of 95±40 BP, 525±40 BP and 160± 40 BP. None of these individuals were from the Iron Age. There are at least two recent inhumations in the Nordin material and the individual dated to 525±40 BP might have been a worker from the 17th

Figure 4. Iron Age graves on a beach ridge in the north (photo by R. Larje).

century stone quarry. One skeleton was found high up in a small cairn, with a stone sinker with initials in Latin letters. Finding relatively recent graves on Stora Karlsö is not uncommon. One skeleton believed to be from a body swept ashore on the island can be seen in a hollow covered with slabs on the eastern rocky shore, and parts of another probably recent skeleton were found in a rock shelter by the author in September 2007 (Jacobsen and Larje 2008).

Despite the complicated situation regarding the age of the remains, an analysis was done on the human bones that, from the Museum of National Antiquities inventory number, were judged as deriving from the 1889 investigations.

Nordin believed most of the individuals found in the burials were males. Sundeen (2005) found that in general, male characteristics were predominant in all skeletal elements examined. A calculation based on the maximum length of eight right femora gives a mean stature of 173.6 cm ± 3.94 cm, which corresponds well to Nordin's field observations that the buried individuals were tall, around 170 cm. Sundeen (2005) also tried to assess the age distribution of the remains, based on dental attrition and tooth eruption, judging most individuals to have been quite young, nine aged from 17 to 25, and 10 aged from 25 to 35, with only one older than 35. The osteological investigation recorded healed injuries and patterns of bone wear consistent with hard physical activity.

Graves re-used

Some graves contained two bodies, either laid out beside each other, or with one burial on top of the other – the grave having been re-used on a later occasion. There is evidence of successive use in two graves. Both were round stone settings with a diameter of about 10 m and a height of 80–90 cm. About 20 cm down, a secondary burial was found in a stone cist, aligned northeast–southwest, with the head to the southwest. Underneath the grave was a primary burial, not in a cist, and in an opposite orientation, with the head to the north. The primary inhumation at the bottom of the grave was dated to the Migration Period (AD 400 to AD 800), while the secondary inhumation was thought to be from the Viking Age.

Square stone settings

Twelve graves were considered to be cremation graves, from the number of burnt bone fragments and abundant wood ash, and in some cremations there had been a secondary inhumation. Two cremation graves are particularly impressive. On the slope of the Litorina ridge in the north are two square stone settings beside each other, both with compact stone layers (Figure 5). Nordin noticed a thick layer of ashes and charcoal, with some fragments of burnt bone in the western setting, which measured 9 m x 9 m. The eastern setting, measuring 7 m x 7.7 m, contained an unusual deposit. Close to the centre and under a limestone slab was a miniature stone cist with a pot inside. The pot contained cremated bones and a scabbard chape of iron. Covering the pot was a shield buckler and a deliberately bent and broken spear head (Rydh 1931). The two quadrate stone settings were dated to about AD 0, and are the earliest Iron Age graves on the island. The grave type is well known in Sweden, but not on Gotland.

Search for the living population

Although only a few graves could be dated with certainty, most of the 50 or so stone settings are believed to span the Early Roman–Migration Period. The number of graves represents a sizable population. Where are the traces of the living people? In 1973, a test investigation was made of the remaining cultural layer outside the Stora Förvar cave, to check the stratigraphy and to map the thickness of the soil that had been cleaned out from the cave during excavations. Some surprising finds were made in the dumped soil, most spectacularly a number of Viking Age

Figure 5. The two square stone settings on the northern plain (photo by R. Jacobson).

moulds for making brooches, of types also made on Gotland and on the Swedish mainland. A pilot investigation of areas with high phosphate values was made in 1974. Between 1975 and 1981, three trenches were excavated in an area with high phosphate values. Excavations revealed traces of small-scale metallurgic production. Among the finds were a Roman silver coin, two Roman Iron Age bronze weights, and a piece of payment gold in the form of a spiral ring (Almgren-Aiken 1976, 1979, 1980). From the excavated finds, Almgren-Aiken suggested Stora Karlsö might have been a convenient resting place on the sea journey to the Swedish mainland, Öland or other places on Gotland, or some kind of free-trade port. The idea has merit. The northern bay is a sheltered landing and is also a good harbour.

Boat graves?

The free-trade-port idea brings us to unusual monuments in the northern and southern harbour area. On a beach ridge in the north are 12 depressions, about 20 m long and oriented vertically to the beach (Figure 6). Inspired by the excavation of boat-grave sites in Uppland in Sweden in 1928, Rydh suspected the depressions to be similar grave types, and not landing places for boats. Nordin had opened a trial trench in one wall, but had found nothing. Rydh made a complete excavation of one depression and found her suspicion was correct – the boat graves of the 'Valsgärde' type were a new type of grave for Karlsö. Rydh found traces of an area that had been dug out for a wide but shallow boat, 9 m long, 4 m broad and about 75 cm from 'keel to rail'. The stem was 7 m above sea level and the stern was 6 m above sea level. Only a few boat rivets were found, along with a heavily corroded iron knife, a blue glass pearl and a great variety of bones. The few and fragmentary human remains were from two individuals and the large quantity of animal bones represented several cattle, sheep or goat, horse, pig, seal and one bone from a dog. The cattle and pig bones had cut marks, but the bones and artefacts were spread out in no particular order in the boat, except for a concentration towards the stern.

A trench through another depression gave a similar result. Human bone from two

Figure 6. 'Boat-shaped' depressions in the northern plain. The arrow indicates a trench opened during the 1975-1981 excavations (photo by R. Jacobson).

individuals was found, along with the disturbed remains of cattle, sheep, horse and seal. The artefacts included a rivet plate, a yellow ceramic pearl and amber dice. A hole excavated in a third depression had similar types of animal bones and an iron nail. The six depressions and banks of stone rubble on the south plain were not investigated, but a spade hole in one uncovered a horse tooth, interpreted to be prehistoric.

Rydh (1931) dated what she believed were certainly boat graves to the Viking Age. But was she right? The current interpretation of the depressions is that they are boat landing constructions, but the human remains definitely indicate burial use. Two stone settings on the same beach ridge contain secondary graves probably from the Viking Age, so there is reason to believe in a succession of Viking inhumations to the west. This means the boat-landing constructions might be considerably younger, and were therefore further away from the shoreline, and so not comfortably accessible. The interpretation of the depressions is still open, requiring further fieldwork (Figure 7).

The Middle Ages

Graves

On the northern plain is a 'cemetery' surrounded by an oval stone setting. In it, Nordin found six burials and a few artefacts, all with medieval features. Another, even larger, irregular oval stone setting, popularly described as a Christian cemetery, is under the hill slope in the south. There, Nordin (1889) found a skeleton under a 'pile of stones', but Rydh, although she opened several trenches, only found sheep bones, which gave her reason to assume the construction was a sheep pen containing human remains from someone who was buried in secrecy. There is also a small cairn in the southern plain, with medieval features and a primary burial.

Stone quarries

The 13th century boom in church-building on Gotland created a demand for the decorative red, fossil-rich limestone from Stora Karlsö, the 'Karlsö marble'. The layered rock could be quarried into pillars and lintels and other decorative elements. The quarrying technique in the

Middle Ages made use of the properties of the rock. A row of palm-sized holes was chopped into the cliff. Dry oak wedges were driven into the holes and then soaked with water, swelling them and causing the limestone to split (Ohlsson 1960) (Figure 8). The raw material was loaded on to boats, probably from the southern shore, and shipped to Gotland for working and finishing. The Middle Age quarries were used for about 100 years. They were reopened in the 17th century, when drill holes and gunpowder were used to extract blocks. There is a written record from September 24 1605, that 'Karlsö marble' was exported to Denmark in an order for 37 stone elements from the island, to be collected by a royal ship (Jacobson 2005). The 17th century quarrying was probably not very extensive, and we can assume the quarries today look the same as when they were abandoned.

Figure 7. Ink drawing by H. Faith-Ell (1930) of the Iron Age graves and 'boat-shaped' depressions. At top right is the single ash-tree at Röjsu, the Bronze Age cairn (from Rydh 1931).

Figure 8. Remains from the stone quarry used in the Middle Ages (photo by R. Jacobson).

In the event of a fatal accident to a stone worker, the corpse was almost certainly brought back to Gotland for burial in the local churchyard. But the quarry on Stora Karlsö could have attracted people from more distant areas of the Baltic, too far away to send a body to. A grave on Karlsö would have been a natural alternative.

Conclusion

Some important pieces are missing from Stora Karlsö's prehistoric jigsaw puzzle. In the Mesolithic and Neolithic, people were on the island and used many of its wild food resources. But was the occupation permanent or seasonal? Either way, I favour the well-drained and sheltered terraces away from Stora Förvar cave as the main dwelling site during the early period. In the Bronze Age, Stora Karlsö was obviously significant, given the construction of four cairns. Where do we find evidence of the community which had an interest in the island and the economic means to build such impressive symbols of ownership? Who built the square stone-setting graves, so rare on Gotland but more common on the Swedish mainland? The great number of Roman Iron Age–Migration Period graves suggests a reasonably large population on the island. It is possible that at this time, Stora Karlsö was a trade port and had a permanent community. The graves might also have functioned as land-ownership markers. Might there have been another port on the southern shore, where there are also graves?

What role did the island play in the Viking Age? Can new excavations unmask the true nature of the 'boat graves'? The Vikings in the Baltic were traders and Stora Karlsö was on the route from Gotland to southern Scandinavia. We only have glimpses from this period, glimpses of a connection with the Swedish mainland and even Norway (Zachrisson 2006).

The 'Karlsö marble' quarries, untouched since the 17th century, are waiting to be documented, including the location of stone-worker lodgings. A study of the quarry should also include an analysis of the churches on Gotland containing red marble to establish whether the construction material was restricted to churches in particular areas, or whether it was used more widely.

References

Almgren-Aiken, E. 1979. Stora Karlsö – rastplats eller frihamn? *Arkeologi på Gotland* (1979):169–172.

Almgren, E. 1976. Utgrävningen i Norderhamn. In Stora Karls en presentation, Karls Jagt- och Djurskyddsförenings AB, pp. 13–15, Visby, Gotland.

Almgren, E. 1980. Utgrävningar på Stora Karls. *Gotländskt Arkiv* (1980):121–122.

Almgren-Aiken, E. 2007. Rapport rörande provundersökning av kulturlager utanför grottan Stora Förvar, Stora Karlsö I:3 Eksta sn. Gotland.

Clark, J.G.D. 1976. A Baltic Cave sequence: A further study in bioarchaeology. In H. Mitscha-Märheim, H. Friesinger and H. Kerchler (eds), Festschrift für Richard Pittioni zum siebzigsten Geburtstag. *Archaeologia Austriaca* 13:113–123.

Ericson, P. 1989. Faunahistoriskt intressanta stenålderfynd från Stora Karlsö. *Fauna och flora* 84:192–198.

Ericson, P.G.P. and A. Knape 1990. Stora Karlsö – en jaktstation under neolitisk tid. *Gunneria* 64:197–205.

Eriksson, J.A. 1988. Stora Karlsös vegetationshistoria. *Gotländskt arkiv* (1988):19–30.

Eriksson, J.A. 1992. *Natural History of Xerotherm Vegetation and Landscapes on Stora Karlsö, an Island in the Western Baltic Basin, Sweden*. Striae 35, Uppsala.

Fredriksson, G. 1976. Alger och vattenförhållanden kring Stora Karlsö, In *Stora Karlsö, en presentation*, pp. 35–47. Visby: Karlsö Jagt-och Djurskyddsförenings AB.

Gräslund, B. 1978. Sill och sillfiske i Östersjön under stenåldern. *Tor* 17:57–64.

Jacobson, R. 2005. Om ett par gamla Karlsökartor och lite till. In R. Jacobson and R. Larje (eds), *Stora Karlsö – människor, verksamheter och händelser kring en ö*, pp. 162–171. Visby: Ödins förlag AB.

Jacobson, R. and R. Larje. 2008. Slumpfunna skelettfynd på tidernas ö. *Karlsöbladet* 1:4–8.

Jacobson, R. and R. Larje nd. Neighbours in Vinglu. New skeletons on Stora Karlsö. Unpublished report in possession of the author.

Johansson, B.M. and R. Larje 1993. A 100 year old soil sample from Stora Förvar. Refuse or Potential Resource? *Pact* 38-III(3):297–301.

Knape, A. and P. Ericson 1988. Stora Förvar – kontinuitet och förändring i ett resursutnyttjande. *Gotländskt Arkiv* (1988):31–38.

Lindquist, M. 1979. *Storrösen In Arkeologi på Gotland* (1979):33–42.

Lindqvist, C. 1996. Gotländska stenåldersstudier I, De äldsta säljägarna på Gotland. *Benbiten* 9(3):7–13.

Lindqvist, C. and G. Possnert. 1997. The subsistence economy and diet at Jakobs/Akvide, Eksta parish and other prehistoric dwellings and burial sites on Gotland in a long-term perspective. In G. Burenhult (ed), Remote Sensing, vol. 1. *Theses and Papers in North-European Archaeology* 13:a:29–90.

Linnaeus, C. 1745. *Öländska och Gothländska Resa-förrättad år 1741*. Stockholm och Uppsala (Senare upplagor finns).

Munthe, H., J.E. Hede and L. von Post 1927. *Beskrivning till kartbladet Hemse*. Geologiska Undersökning, Ser. Aa Nr 164.

Ohlsson, E.W. 1960. *Några anteckningar om Stora Karlsö under medeltiden och nya tiden fram till år 1880*. Gotland: Visby.

Österholm, I. 1989. *Bosättningsmönstret på Gotland under stenåldern. En analys av fysisk miljö, ekonomi och social struktur*. Theses and papers in archaeology 3. Stockholm: Stockholm University.

Österholm, S. 1988. I utriggarkanot över Östersjön'. *Populär Arkeologi. Årgång* 6(2):26–30.

Pira, A. 1909. Studien zur Geschichte der Schweinerassen, insbesondere derjenigen Schwedens. *Zoologische Jahrbuecher Supplement* X:1–192.

Pira, A. 1926. On bone deposits in the cave 'Stora Förvar' on the Isle of Stora Karlsö, Sweden. *Acta Zoologica* 7:123–217.

Retzius, G. 1890. Om de i grottan Stora Förvar funna menniskokranierna. *Ymer* 10:286–287.

Roos, A. 2000. *Sälliv*. Stockholm: BonnierCarlsen.

Rydh, H. 1931. *Stora Karlsö under forntiden*. Stockholm: Karlsö Jagt-och Djurskyddsförenings Aktiebolag.

Schnittger, B. and H. Rydh 1940. *Grottan Stora Förvar på Stora Karlsö undersökt av Lars Kolmodin and Hjalmar Stolpe*. Stockholm: KVHAA.

Storå, J. 2006. Om den förhistoriska bosättningen på Stora Karlsö i skelettfyndens ljus. *Karlsöbladet* 2:5–8.

Sundeen, H. 2005. Benen från Stora Karlsö. En analys av skelettmaterialet från Fredrik Nordins utgrävning 1889. CD-uppsats, Högskolan på Gotland.

Zachrisson, T. 2006. Hägringen och fornborgen, Stora Karlsö under järnåldern. *Karlsöbladet* 2:9–12.

18

East of Easter: Traces of human impact in the far-eastern Pacific

Iona Flett
Department of Archaeology and Natural History, Australian National University, Australia
iona.flett@anu.edu.au

Simon Haberle
Department of Archaeology and Natural History, Australian National University, Australia

Introduction

Building on the work of Atholl Anderson and other Pacific archaeologists, this paper describes the methodologies employed and some preliminary results in an ongoing investigation of pre-European human impact on far-eastern Pacific Islands. Which islands in the far-eastern Pacific would Polynesian sailors have encountered if they ventured east of Easter Island? And if pre-Columbian South American explorers travelled west into the Pacific, would they have managed to reach the same islands? How would signals of human impact on these islands differ from signs of natural environmental variability? These questions form the basis of an investigation of the role played by the far-eastern Pacific Islands in the prehistoric trans-Pacific movement of people.

The islands considered in this investigation, and discussed below (Figure 1), include Isla Santa Maria, Isla Mocha, Chiloe, the Desventuradas group and the Juan Fernandez Islands, all annexed by Chile, the Galapagos Islands (Ecuador), and Cocos Island (Costa Rica). In contrast to other Pacific archipelagos, archaeologists have investigated the islands 'east of Easter' infrequently. These islands are much closer to the coast of mainland South America than they are to any of the known inhabited Polynesian islands, and some of them have American Indian archaeological sites. Historical occupation of these islands has been varied. The Chilean islands close to the coast were discovered by Europeans during exploration in the 15th century. The Juan Fernandez group was discovered in 1575, Cocos in 1541, and the Galapagos Islands in 1535. The Juan Fernandez and the Galapagos groups were both used as shelters by whalers and buccaneers, and then were permanently settled by fishermen and pastoralists by the late 19th century.

Plausible circumstantial evidence, much of it related to the distribution of various cultivars,

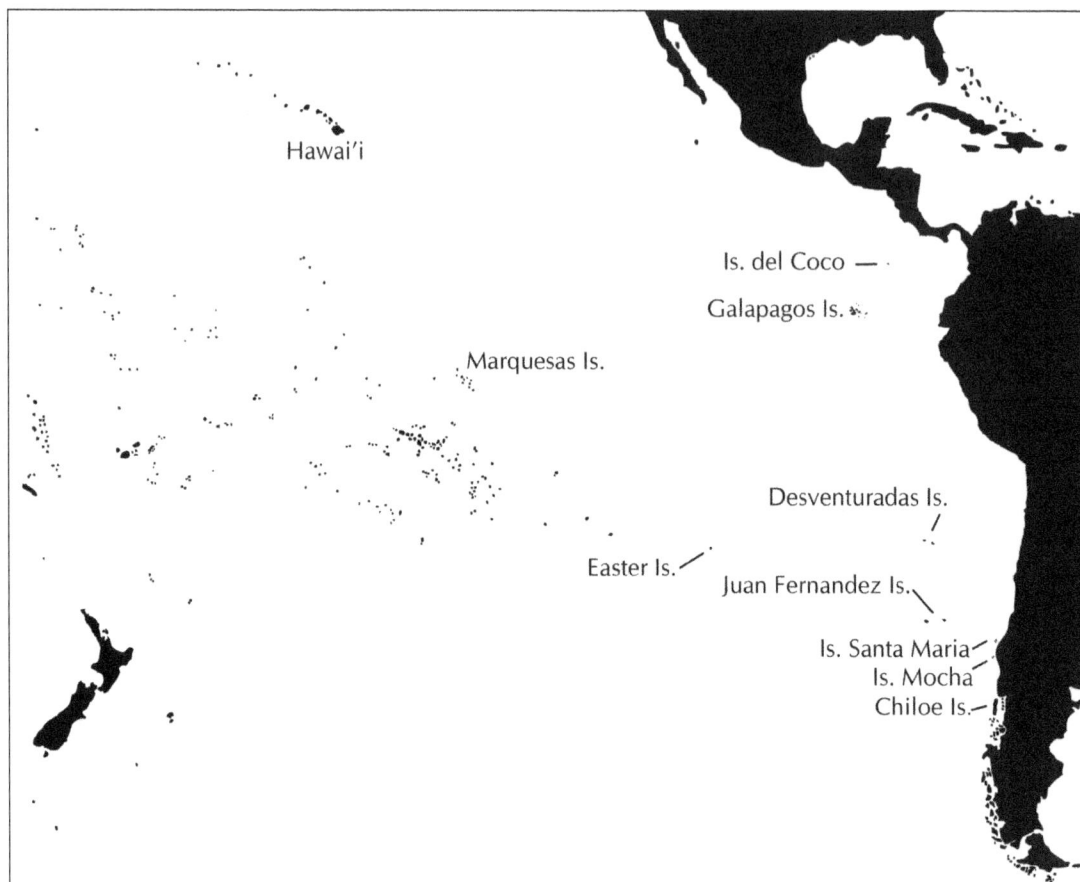

Figure 1. Map of the eastern Pacific with island groups referred to in the text.

has led to speculation that there was some contact in prehistory between Polynesians and West Coast South American Indians (Ballard 2005; Green 2005). The most widely cited evidence for the contact is the presence of the sweet potato (*Ipomoea batatas*) in Polynesia before European arrival. Regarded as a South American native, the sweet potato has been found in archaeological sites in the Pacific dating from before 1200 AD (Yen 1974; Hather and Kirch 1991; Green 2005). Since then, much cultural, linguistic, historical and archaeological evidence has been discussed in an attempt by scholars to determine how and when the sweet potato first arrived in the region. Green (2005) summarises the remaining questions: Did Polynesian sailors go to the Americas and retrieve it? Did South Americans take it to Easter Island, which became the dispersal origin? And do we still believe there had to have been human dispersal?

Westward migration

Montenegro *et al.* (2007) have recently conducted computer-simulation experiments modelling drifting of vessels and seeds west from South and Central America. This work updates previously published experiments by Levinson *et al.* (1973) and Irwin *et al.* (1990), by using more realistic oceanic and atmospheric current data, which are numerically modelled, rather than being probabilistically defined by localised observations (Montenegro *et al.* 2007). These recent simulations assume no input from human occupants of the rafts/floating debris (whereas the earlier models were designed to test likely *voyaging* routes), and allow many more points of exit from the American coasts than previously, thus simulating likely vegetation-dispersal scenarios independent of human coastal settlements. The authors conclude that with regard to the sweet potato, the central ellipse area proposed by Green (2005) and Yen (1974) is the most likely area for the plant's initial arrival into Polynesia, and an accidental drift voyage could have been responsible for the introduction (Montenegro *et al.* 2007). Interestingly, the results also indicate that hits to the Galapagos Islands both by floating vessels (influenced by wind and ocean currents) and other floating material (e.g. seed pods, influenced by ocean currents only) leaving from South and Central America have higher probabilities and faster voyaging times than hits on almost any other island.

Another Polynesian cultivar with an American origin is the bottle gourd (*Lagenaria siceraria*). Although there is an Asian variety, which was present in archaeological sites in Southeast Asia c. 5000 BP (Bellwood 1997), there is new phylogenetic evidence to support the hypothesis that the bottle gourd, like the sweet potato, was one of the cultivars obtained from the Americas (Clarke *et al.* 2006), where it was an early domesticate (Piperno *et al.* 2000). However, it should be noted that the American origins of some varieties of Polynesian bottle gourds do not necessarily imply human dispersal, since the authors note that seeds in the gourd may still be viable after up to seven months at sea (Clarke *et al.* 2006), and we know from the simulation experiments discussed above that floating material could feasibly arrive in Polynesia after leaving the American mainland in much less time (Montenegro *et al.* 2007).

Possible parallels have been observed between the Mapuche culture (of c. 1000 BC to present) in south-central Chile and Polynesia, in the form of some words, hand clubs similar to Maori clubs (patu), obsidian artefacts similar to those found in Polynesia, and sewn-plank canoes, although more information about the context and age of these finds is still required (Ramirez 1990/91; reference to Spanish text by Ramirez-Aliaga *et al.* 1992 in Anderson 2006). Earlier observations about a possible Asian influence on ancient Ecuadorian material culture (e.g. Gartelmann 1986:22–29) have been rejected by other authors, primarily because of the unlikelihood of successful Asia-to-Ecuador voyaging, rather than a lack of similarity between pottery styles or motifs (Bruhns 1994:361).

Heyerdahl's now debunked theory about South American colonisation of the Pacific Islands was based on South American indigenous oral histories, telling of a battle with a race of white Peruvians which was banished to the sea (Heyerdahl 1952; Terrell 1998; Holton 2004). His theory depended on the supposition that ocean-going sailing technology existed in South America before Europeans arrived, an issue which has been debated, for example by Suggs (1960:218), who writes, 'Although the Peruvians did use rafts to voyage off their coast long before the white men ever came, such rafts did not use sails, but were propelled by paddles.' Later, other authors have concluded that a South American vessel capable of reaching East Polynesia could have existed (e.g. Anderson 2006), and that prehistoric voyaging in *any* direction in the Pacific was probably relying on fair winds, some paddling and some drifting (Anderson *et al.* 2006). However, there is now cautious agreement among Pacific scholars that of the two groups, it was Polynesians who had the better navigation skills, and they could well have had the capability for deliberate voyaging to the coast of South America and back (Martinsson-Wallin and Crockford 2001; Anderson 2005; Anderson 2006), albeit mostly relying on downwind sailing (Anderson 2003).

Eastward migration

The best estimate for the time the colonising Lapita people moved into the west Pacific is currently c. 3300–2800 cal. BP (Anderson 2003; Hunt and Lipo 2006). After this, there seems to have been a pause before further expansion into central Micronesia and the marginal West Polynesian islands at about 2200–2000 cal. BP (Anderson *et al.* 2006:Figure 1). The initial colonisation of the Polynesian triangle, including Hawaii, the Marquesas, the Society Islands and the Cook Islands, was probably about 1250–1000 cal. BP (Anderson 2003; Anderson *et al.* 2006). New Zealand, Rapa, South Polynesia and the sub-polar region have no known signs of habitation until after 800 cal. BP (Anderson 1991; Anderson 2005; Kennett *et al.* 2006).

A question remains, however, about Easter Island. A 2001 review of the previously published radiocarbon chronologies rejected many of the early dates for the colonisation of Easter Island, and concluded colonisation occurred around the same time as the rest of East Polynesia, c. 1200–800 cal. BP (Martinsson-Wallin and Crockford 2001). Since then, Hunt and Lipo (2006) have argued that 1200 AD (i.e. 800 BP) is the earliest acceptable date, and that the human population rapidly rose, with immediate impacts on the environment, identified from the palynological record. A later colonisation of Easter Island creates an interesting picture of the expansion to the outer edges of the Polynesian realm. It suggests that all the outermost southeastern islands, the Auckland Islands, New Zealand, Rapa, Mangareva and Easter Island, were colonised at virtually the same time. Given the massive distances being traversed in this region, it seems Polynesian exploration of the eastern Pacific was close to continuous between 1200 and 800 BP and exploration for new land and resources continued even during the expansion and settlement phase immediately after arrival at each new landfall.

A recent discovery on the coast of Chile provided evidence that this phase of oceanic exploration by Polynesians also resulted in contact with the South American mainland. Bones of the domestic chicken (*Gallus gallus*) were recovered in a prehistoric site called El Arenal-1, which TL dates on ceramics indicate was occupied between AD 700 and 1390 (Storey *et al.* 2007). One of the bones was dated to AD 1304–1424, and DNA sequencing from the same piece hinted that the chicken may have had a Polynesian genetic signature (Storey *et al.* 2007), although more recent analysis has exposed doubts about the DNA sequencing and further research is required (Gongora *et al.* 2008).

What, then, are the local climatic conditions which could have been affecting migration, ease of settlement and resource availability at this time? The idea at the centre of a paper by Anderson *et al.* (2006) is that the episodic nature of eastward dispersal in the Pacific might be related to the changing frequency of El Nino events. During a period of frequent El Nino activity there are likely to be more chances for eastward drifting or sailing, since the trade winds, which characteristically blow from east to west, weaken or fail during many ENSO events (Anderson *et al.* 2006). This viewpoint implies people were trying to voyage further and opportunistically used prevailing weather systems to do so; it does not consider the cultural or environmental reasons why they might have been voyaging. Patrick Nunn, in a variety of publications since 1998, has promoted the idea that increased precipitation and sea-level fall (due to atmospheric cooling) about AD 1300 had dramatic environmental effects, leading to changes in human settlement patterns, resource use and voyaging strategies, as well as increased conflict (Nunn and Britton 2001; Nunn 2003a,b).

While not all authors agree that the AD 1300 event was as catastrophic or as widespread as Nunn (2000) describes, there are a number of localised records in which there does appear to be some sort of perturbation about this time (Allen 2006). In addition, there are several central Pacific sites where there is evidence that the Medieval Warm Period (c. AD 900–1200) and the Little Ice Age (AD 1550–1900) had distinctive climatic signatures (Allen 2006). In the central Pacific, conditions during the Medieval Warm Period were apparently cool and dry, while the Little Ice Age seems to have been characterised by warm, wet and perhaps stormy conditions. Allen (2006) concludes her extensive review of the relevant research on this topic by noting that climate across the Pacific is, and has been, heterogeneous, and that the complex ocean-atmosphere linkages lead to local-scale variability. For example, although much of the eastern

Pacific is affected by increased sea-surface temperatures and rainfall during ENSO events, Easter Island is relatively unaffected (Genz and Hunt 2003). Given that exploration was apparently proceeding in the far-eastern Pacific during this period of climatic transition (and possibly upheaval) between 800 and 500 years ago, high-resolution palaeoclimate records over this time at a local scale are crucial. The Galapagos Islands, in their strategic position between the lands of eastern and western prehistoric navigators, are an ideal place to look for a window into the regional climate of the past 1000 years.

Galapagos archaeology and palaeoecology to date

The Galapagos Islands comprise 19 major islands and many smaller rocks and islets. They are orientated in a northwest-southeast direction, lying across the equator, about 1000 km west of Ecuador (Figure 1). The Galapagos Islands were formed between 0.3 million (westernmost islands) and 6 million (easternmost islands) years ago by volcanic activity at the Galapagos Hot Spot (Geist 1996). There are currently more than 20,000 permanent inhabitants (Gumbel 2005), living on five of the islands. The largest town, Peurto Ayora (Figure 2), is the hub of the islands' main industries, tourism and fishing. Their location between Easter Island and the South American mainland, along with the fact that the islands are the largest in the eastern Pacific and are known to have been a bountiful source of meat, fish and fresh water during the 18th and 19th centuries, has led to speculation that ancient seafarers might also have stopped in the Galapagos.

The Galapagos were devoid of obvious human habitation at the time of European arrival.

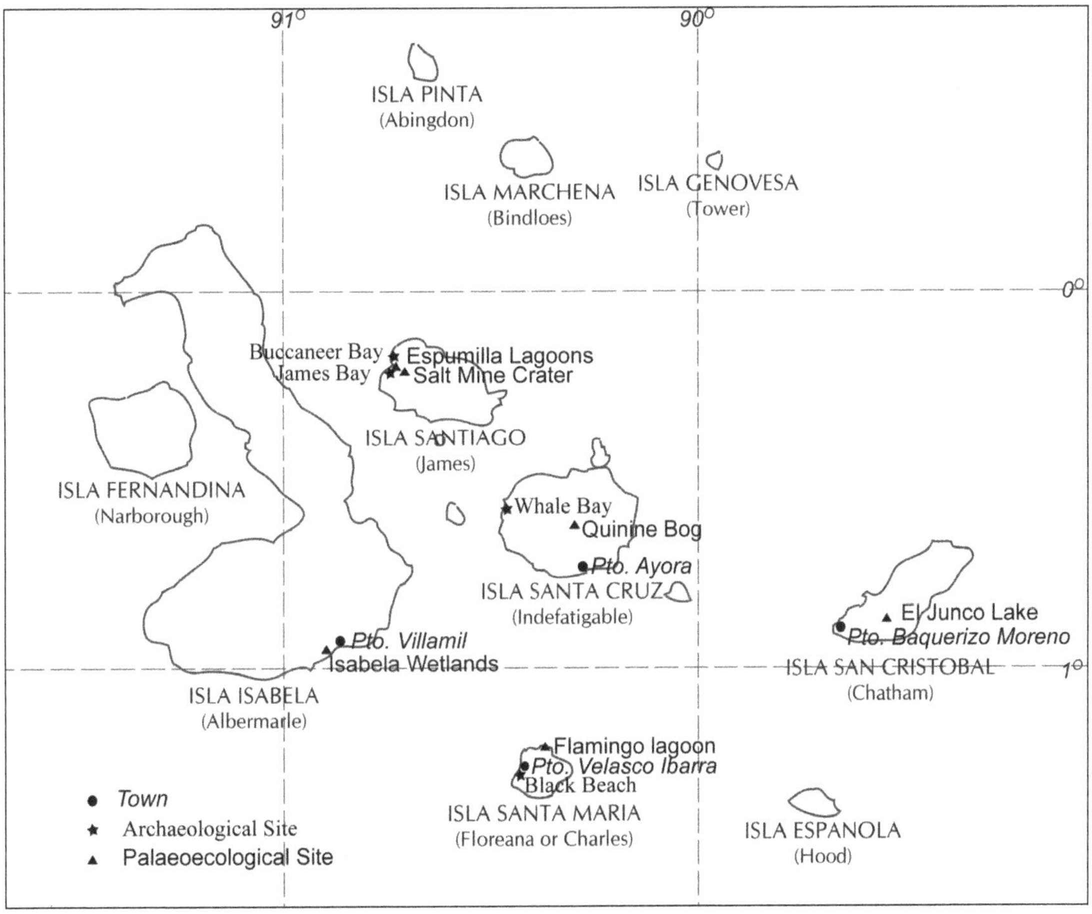

Figure 2. Map of the Galapagos Islands showing main towns, and the ANU archaeological and palaeoecological sites. Island names in brackets are the original 'English' names, not commonly used now except for 'Floreana Island' for Isla Santa Maria.

No structures, monuments, middens, ancient agricultural features nor domestic-animal intro-ductions were reported at the time, nor have any been found since. Archaeological evidence, then, comes in the form of surface and subsurface scatters of pottery and other artefacts, as well as palaeoecological information about how vegetation, insect populations and water quality have changed over time.

The ANU-led expedition to the Galapagos in 2005 was only the fourth international party to visit the Galapagos for archaeological excavations. The previous reported visits were the Norwegian Archaeological Expedition led by Thor Heyerdahl in 1953, the Walt Disney Galapagos Expedition led by J.C. Couffer and C. Hall in 1954 (Heyerdahl and Skjølsvold 1990), and a geology/archaeology field school organised by the Escuela Superior Politecnica del Litoral (ESPOL, Guayaquil) and led by Raul Maruri in 1963. Over the years, other scientists and interested non-archaeologists have deposited various finds in the small museum housed in the Charles Darwin Research Station, (Peurto Ayora, Isla Santa Cruz, Galapagos), and this material was available for analysis by our group.

Heyerdahl and Skjølsvold originally published their analysis of Galapagos archaeology in *American Antiquity* in 1956. A reprint with minor changes followed in 1990. Their primary conclusion was that some of the ceramics they discovered were of coastal Ecuadorian and Peruvian origin, and pre-dated European influence in the region. This conclusion was based on typological similarities between the Galapagos collection and pottery from mainland Ecuador and Peru, which was thought, in the 1950s, to be pre-Columbian (some has since been reclassified). At the time, there were mixed reviews of the work, with some authors finding the archaeological conclusions plausible (Bushnell 1957; Evans 1958), and others arguing that some of the identifications of Galapagos pottery were 'daring', and did not provide 'direct confirmation' of pre-Spanish visits to Galapagos (Ryden 1958). In 1967, Robert Suggs published a 'statistical re-analysis' of the Galapagos data (Suggs 1967), critiquing Heyerdahl's archaeological methods and conclusions, and summarising that 'the hypothesis of aboriginal visits to the Galapagos must be rejected', and 'historical, botanical and archaeological evidence strongly indicate that the aboriginal pottery was introduced by Europeans' (Suggs 1967).

A critical but supportive view was provided by Edward Lanning (1969), who did not agree with Heyerdahl's typological assessment, but rather identified the pottery as Ecuadorian, and dated from AD 1200 to AD 1400. Since then, several authors have been critical of Heyerdahl's Pacific colonisation theories and, in passing, his Galapagos work, but no other publications have dealt specifically with the Galapagos ceramics, and no-one has attempted to re-excavate there.

Several palaeoecological research projects have been conducted in and around the Galapagos Islands, although none with the explicit aim of searching for signs of human activity. Dunbar *et al.* (1994) used stable isotope ratios in uplifted corals from the west coast of Isabela to reconstruct annual sea surface temperature variability from AD 1587 to 1982. The authors then analysed variance in the ENSO frequency band, which was usually about 4.6 years, but shifted to higher frequencies in the early to middle 1700s and the middle 1800s (Dunbar *et al.* 1994). Riedinger *et al.* (2002) also focused on El Nino activity, using the mineralogy and geochemistry of laminations preserved in a saline lake to identify different El Nino events and their approximate intensities. They conclude that over the past 1000 years, there have been 36 strong events and five moderate events, while in the 1000 years before that, there were only 14 strong events and 152 moderate events. Mid-Holocene El Nino frequencies were estimated to have been lower than those in the late Holocene. The low lake levels inferred for El Junco lake, San Cristobal, in the mid-Holocene support this finding, as well as the idea that before 5000 BP, wetter conditions prevailed (Colinvaux 1972; Riedinger *et al.* 2002).

Palynological analysis of sediments from El Junco lake revealed remarkable stability in the taxa represented in the pollen and spore records over the Holocene (Colinvaux and Schofield 1976a; Colinvaux and Schofield 1976b), but no special attention was paid to the period of human impact. Colinvaux and Schofield attribute changes in the amounts of some taxa in the past 400 radiocarbon years to cattle disturbance and forest clearance, but higher resolution records (both temporally and taxonomically) would probably be required to confirm human environmental impacts in the San Cristobal highlands.

Fieldwork for the ANU project, led by Atholl Anderson and Simon Haberle, took place in 2005. Coring and sampling for later palaeoecological analysis was carried out over two seasons, 2005 and 2006, with some sampling equipment left in place for the intervening year. Localities investigated and referred to below are marked on Figure 2. Whale Bay, James Bay, Black Beach and Buccaneer Bay archaeological sites were re-investigated following earlier maps and descriptions (Heyerdahl and Skjølsvold 1990). Other sites, including many suitable landing sites on Santa Cruz, Santiago, San Cristobal and Isabela Islands were surveyed for the first time. Interviews were conducted with farmers, scientists and long-term residents of the archipelago about their knowledge of archaeological artefacts and clay and water sources.

About 1600 artefacts were found in excavations. About one third were ceramic fragments and the rest were pieces of metal, glass, charcoal, shell and bone. While the analysis of these materials is incomplete, the initial conjecture by Pacific and Ecuadorian archaeologists participating in this research was that the assemblages recovered date to the historical era (Anderson pers comm. 2007; Stothert 2007). The following research methodology was used to further examine this conclusion. A detailed description of our results will be published elsewhere.

Archaeology

a) Re-analysis of the sites. Heyerdahl and Skjølsvold's (1990) document has been criticised and almost certainly contains errors, some of which were the result of advice given by archaeologists from Peru and the United States, working to the best of their knowledge at the time (see Evans 1958; Heyerdahl and Skjølsvold 1990:32). Other errors may be methodological, analytical or logical (Suggs 1967). One of the suggestions is that analysis of the collections (and possibly the collecting procedures themselves) was biased towards material which was not obviously modern (i.e. glass, plastics, metal), and that therefore the resulting comparisons with mainland assemblages were flawed (Suggs 1967). The re-analysis conducted in 2005 has rectified some of these problems; both sampling and assemblage comparisons have included all artefacts, regardless of likely origin.

Heyerdahl reports no stratigraphic separation between European and Amerindian sherds at any of the sites, and it is difficult to tell whether this is a result of the sherds being 'mixed naturally as they were deposited' (Suggs 1967), or whether a combination of thin soils and post-depositional disturbance by people, animals and rainfall events would be enough to remove the stratigraphy, as Heyerdahl suggests. The ANU re-analysis has also found no clear stratigraphic delineation between modern material and ceramics that are potentially pre-European, even at the new sites. Mixing of different-aged artefacts is a common situation in archaeological sites, especially where natural or cultural post-depositional processes have been involved (Feathers 2003). This seems particularly likely in areas with periodic heavy rainfall, such as the Galapagos. A first-hand account by Heyerdahl and Skolsvold (1990) mentions that after heavy rain, pottery was being washed out of the soil at Black Beach (Heyerdahl and Skjølsvold 1990:31), and in several other locations they believed sherds had been relocated by the movement of water, in some cases into the sea (e.g. Heyerdahl and Skjølsvold 1990:26, 25).

b)   Re-analysis of the types of pottery in all the available collections. Some of the pottery classifications used by Heyerdahl are no longer used by South American archaeologists (Stothert 2007), and the periods of production of some types have been redefined to include the early colonial period. In the light of this new understanding of South American indigenous ceramics, the 2005 collections, as well as material collected by Heyerdahl and Skjølsvold (1990) and the later Galapagos archaeological expeditions, are being re-analysed. Modern statistical techniques for comparing assemblages will allow a more accurate evaluation of the similarities between Galapagos and mainland assemblages.

c)   Chemical characterisation of pottery. Ceramics can be chemically characterised to allow analysts to determine whether two pottery assemblages could be sourced from similar clay. Variability in pottery designs (morphology and decoration) is compared with chemical data, and an extra set of relationships may emerge (Summerhayes 2000). This allows assessment of the similarity of pottery over space and time. The clay matrices and the mineral inclusions (known as 'non-plastics') of selected Galapagos samples have been compared with typical coastal Ecuadorian pottery sherds, and groups of pottery have been classified based on chemical similarities.

d)   Direct dating of archaeological materials. Radiocarbon dating of pieces of charcoal discovered in hearths at four of the archaeological sites has been used to determine the likely age of the fireplaces. These could be ancient hearths used by pre-European voyagers, remnants of the whaling and sealing era, or more recent features. Charcoal fragments were identified to species where possible and dated at the Oxford radiocarbon laboratory.

Pottery fragments can also be directly dated using Optically Stimulated Luminescence (OSL). OSL is a technique that measures the amount of luminescence emitted by a sample after it has been stimulated with light. The amount of luminescence emitted is proportional to the amount of time passed since the sample was last exposed to light (or heat of about 400C). Calculations for working out the age (or time since last exposure) must take into account the natural radioactivity of the sample and its surroundings, since the luminescence signal is building up as a result of exposure to ionising radiation (Aitken 1998). Fragments of pottery from Galapagos and mainland Ecuador have been analysed using this technique at the Australian National University.

Each of the techniques for analysing the pottery is potentially able to answer part of the question of the origin (place and time) of the Galapagos ceramics. However, there is likely to be some continuing element of ambiguity, since it was apparently quite common practice in colonial times for Europeans visiting mainland South America to use locally produced pottery for storage of foods during transit, and also to souvenir (via theft or purchase) desirable ceramics and artefacts (Suggs 1967, and reference to a German work therein). Visits to the Galapagos were commonly made by ships leaving South America en route to Europe to obtain water, tortoise meat, salt and shelter, so some pre-1535 pottery could have been transported from the mainland, then abandoned in Galapagos. For this reason, multiple lines of evidence will be necessary to construct an argument about the origins of the Galapagos pottery assemblages. An argument will be more convincing if it is corroborated by radiocarbon dates from fireplaces, and palaeoecological information about anthropogenic environmental changes pre-dating European arrival.

Palaeoecology

A combination of palaeoecology and archaeology in the Juan Fernandez Islands showed it was unlikely there had been human activity in the islands before Europeans arrived (Anderson *et al.* 2002; Haberle 2003). In the Galapagos Islands, a similar approach is being used, with palaeoecological techniques selected to:

- Look for the pollen and macrofossils of a variety of plant taxa which may (or may not) have been introduced by people;

- Look for other evidence of ecological change perpetuated by humans (e.g. soil erosion, charcoal from anthropogenic burning, alteration of the native vegetation composition, insect introductions);

- Accurately determine the timing of the above changes, if present;
- Consider the impacts the regional effects of climate variability may have had on the travel strategies of the original human occupants of the Pacific.

The sites chosen for the ANU project were first recognised as potential palaeoecological archives by Paul Colinvaux during exploratory fieldwork in the Galapagos in the 1960s. He briefly described the limnology and geomorphology of many of the crater lakes, coastal lagoons and bogs (Colinvaux 1968; Colinvaux 1969). As discussed earlier, relatively little palaeoecological research has been conducted in the Galapagos, and so almost all the sites chosen had never been cored before. The sites were selected on the basis of their proximity to the archaeological locations. Sediment cores were collected from five sites in 2005: Quinine Bog, Flamingo Lagoon, Isabela Wetlands, Salt Mine Crater and Espumilla Lagoon 1 (Figure 2).

Each site will be subject to a range of sedimentological and biotic proxy analysis, with particular focus on the past 1000 years. These sedimentological methods include: (i) Grey-scale analysis (Petterson *et al.* 1999) which records frequency of colour changes related to sediment type through the cores; (ii) Magnetic susceptibility which determines the concentration and composition of magnetic minerals in a sample (Nowaczyk 2001; Zolitschka *et al.* 2001) and can be associated with climatic variability and/or anthropogenic disturbance, including fires and forest clearance (Dearing *et al.* 1981; Dearing and Flower 1982; Nowaczyk 2001; Whitlock and Larsen 2001); (iii) Loss on ignition (LOI, Dean 1974) to estimate the organic and carbonate contents of sediment; (iv) X-ray fluorescence to quantify variations in 30 elements at 0.2 mm intervals (Croudace *et al.* 2006).

A range of biotic proxies are also being used, including: (i) Palynology and micro-charcoal analysis to reconstruct vegetation succession over the late Holocene and yield specific information about human activities in relation to the flora; (ii) Testate amoebae preserved in *Sphagnum* bogs, which are sensitive to changes in hydrology, as palaeo-precipitation indicators; (iii) Diatom analysis to reconstruct water quality and depth changes through time.

Of these three biotic indicators, palynology is most likely to yield significant information on human activity, due to the potential presence of cultivars associated with the Polynesian expansion into the east Pacific, such as sweet potato (*Ipomea batatas*), banana (*Musa* sp.), coconut (*Cocos nucifera*), taro (*Colocasia esculenta*), flax (*Phormium tenax*), Pacific Island cabbage tree (*Cordyline fruticosa*) and Hibiscus (Macphail *et al.* 2001; Horrocks and Lawlor 2006). Evidence of common South American cultivars, such as maize (*Zea mays*), chilli (*Capsicum* sp.), potato (*Solanum* sp.) and cotton (*Gossypium* sp.), at any of the sites before AD 1535 could also be strong evidence for Amerindians reaching Galapagos shores (Stephens 1963; Perry *et al.* 2007).

Table 1. Origins of Galapagos taxa listed as 'Questionable Natives' that have a non-American origin.

Family	Genus	Species	Origins and Distribution after the PIER database (US Forest Service website)
Convolvulaceae	*Stictocardia*	*tiliifolia*	'Now circumtropical, apparently originally from Africa or Asia, cultivated widely and introduced into the New World' (Smith 1991).
Cyperaceae	*Eleocharis*	*geniculata*	'Widespread in tropical and subtropical regions of both hemispheres' (Smith 1979).
Fabaceae	*Galactia*	*tennuiflora*	Africa, tropical Asia, China, Taiwan, Australia (GRIN).
Poaceae	*Digitaria*	*ciliaris*	Tropical Asia
Poaceae	*Eragrostis*	*cilianensis*	'Tropical and warm temperate regions of the Old World, now naturalised in the New World' (Wagner *et al*. 1999).
Poaceae	*Oplismenus*	*compositus*	'Tropical regions of the old and new worlds.' (Smith 1979). Native or an early introduction to many Pacific islands. Considered an early introduction to Fiji (Smith 1979) and Niue. Fosberg et al. (1987) list it as native to Micronesia.
Poaceae	*Oplismenus*	*setarius*	Pantropical. Fosberg *et al.* (1987) lists as native in Micronesia. (Under O. hirtellus)
Portulacaceae	*Portulaca*	*oleracea*	'Nearly cosmopolitan, although presumably native to the Old World' (Wagner et al. 1999). 'Probably an early European introduction to Polynesia' (Whistler 1988).
Solanaceae	*Solanum*	*americanum*	Most probably an early introduction throughout the Pacific area. 'Common in disturbed areas from southern Georgia to Florida, west to California, and south through Mexico to Central and South America (Schilling 1981); additionally it now occurs as an abundant weed throughout much of the Paleotropics.' (Smith 1991). 'Aboriginally introduced, or possibly native, to Polynesia' (Whistler 1988).
Zygophyllaceae	*Tribulus*	*terrestris*	Mediterranean region, now widely naturalised in warm temperate and tropical regions (Holm *et al.* 1977)

Of the plants listed above, only coconut, hibiscus and cotton are naturalised, but most of the others are now cultivated in the Galapagos. This should allow palynologists to readily identify (and in some cases confirm) the timing of the introductions, but unfortunately, many cultivars are rarely found in the pollen record, due to poor preservation, uncertain identification, cultivation methods which prevent flowering, or the absence of wind pollination (Haberle 1994; Maloney 1994). Another category of plants to be investigated is the 62 species growing in the Galapagos today listed by local botanists as 'questionable natives'. Palaeoecology can potentially provide important information about the timing of the introductions of these plants, allowing ecologists to design appropriate management strategies (Willis *et al*. 2007). In fact, van Leeuwen *et al*. (2007) have shown that about 20 of the Galapagos' 'questionable natives' can be differentiated from similar 'native' taxa on the basis of their pollen. Of these, they have already reclassified the status of six taxa (van Leeuwen *et al*. 2007) by analysing bog deposits dating from before European discovery of the archipelago. Questionable natives listed in Table 1 have an Asia-Pacific origin, unlike much of the Galapagos flora, which originates in South America. Work continues to determine whether their introduction pre-dated AD 1535. Evidence that these taxa were growing in the Galapagos before European influence would constitute a strong line of evidence for accidental or deliberate landfall in the Galapagos by a Polynesian vessel.

The case study below demonstrates the use of these simple but important methods on a core from one of the Espumilla coastal lagoons on the island of Santiago.

Espumilla Lagoon case study

Site description and methods

Espumilla Lagoon 1 is a dry lake bed just north of the James Bay archaeological site on the northwest coast of Santiago Island (Figure 2; GPS coordinates: 0.20182°S, 90.82677°W, 2 m asl). It is the largest of three coastal lagoons separated from the ocean by a 3 m high mangrove-covered sand-dune barrier. Espumilla Lagoon was cored with a hand-operated piston corer (5 cm diameter) in July 2005. Duplicate cores (SAE1 and SAE2) with overlapping core sections were collected, wrapped in plastic, stored in PVC tubes and transported to the ANU. Each section was subsequently split lengthways, with half stored for archival purposes, and the other half logged, photographed and used for analyses.

Photographs of SAE1 and SAE2 were analysed with Scion Image, a program which can provide line plots of the grey-scale variation in images of the core. Magnetic susceptibility was measured using a 2 cm wide Bartington Magnetic Susceptibility Loop (Dearing 1999) with contiguous 1 cm sample spacing, and results were corrected for machine drift. The LOI analysis was conducted by adhering to the recommendations made by Heiri *et al.* (2001). Standardised sample sizes (1 cc) of dry material were weighed into ceramic 'boats' and oxidised in a furnace at 550C for four hours. Organic material was combusted at this stage, and after samples were cooled, and reweighed, the amount of lost organic material was calculated. Samples were then returned to the furnace, this time at 950C for two hours, and then reweighed to determine the amount of carbonate lost. Results are shown as percentages of original dry weight (Figure 3).

Twenty-two radiocarbon dates from SAE1 and SAE2 were submitted to the Australian Nuclear Science and Technology Organisation (ANSTO). 'Bulk' sediment was used for all but three samples, which were pollen extractions paired with bulk samples designed to test whether pollen extractions returned superior results. Given the similarity in the calibrated ranges between pollen extractions and bulk sediments, the rest of the AMS dates were obtained on small samples of bulk sediment. All samples were pre-treated using the acid-alkali-acid method following standard procedures (ANSTO 2008). Radiocarbon ages were calibrated with Calib (Stuiver and Reimer 1993), using the 2004 southern hemisphere calibration curve (McCormac *et al.* 2004).

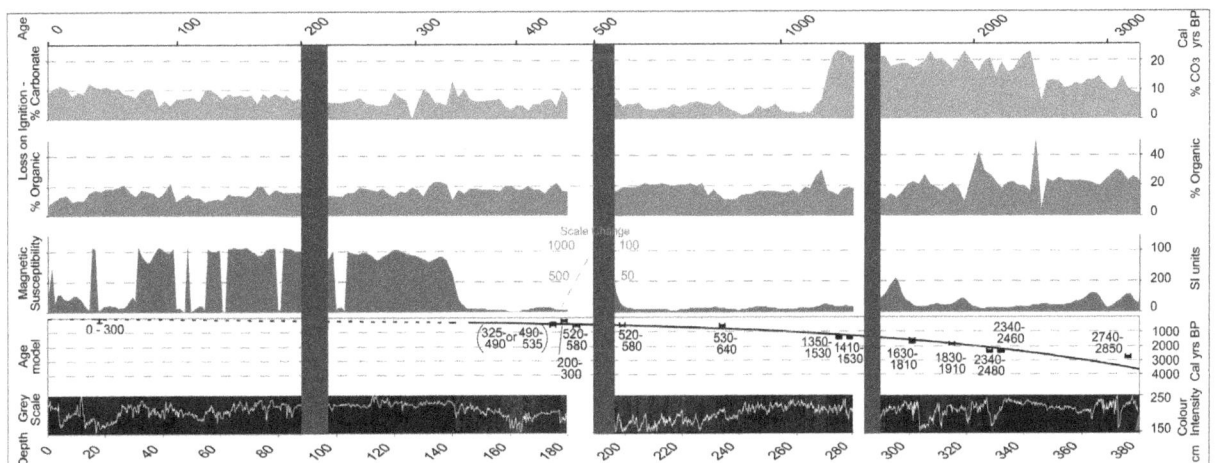

Figure 3. Results for Espumilla Lagoon 1 cores 1 and 2. From bottom to top, results shown are: Depth (cm); Grey-scale measure of colour intensity overlain on photographs of the core; Radiocarbon dates in cal. BP and age model; Magnetic susceptibility (SI units; note scale change at 2 m); and Loss On Ignition (%Organic and %CO₃). Blacked-out sections conceal areas of contamination, which occurred as a result of coring.

The overlapping sections of SAE1 and SAE2 were correlated using sedimentological parameters such as colour, texture and magnetic susceptibility. SAE1 is pictured in Figure 3 and will be described here. Grey-scale overlay plots in Figure 3 help to highlight bands of pale and dark colour intensity. The top 140 cm of the core is composed of dark red-brown silt with bands of silty clay, silty sand, firm pale-brown clay and course sandy or gravelly layers throughout. Some sections fine upwards. Between 175 cm and 140 cm, two distinct sediment types alternate. Two bands of distinctive pale-grey clay containing sand and gravel-sized clear gypsum crystals alternate smoothly with layers of the same dark reddish sediment as above. A sharp boundary marks the transition at 175 cm. From 235 cm to 175 cm, there is pale-grey crystalline sand with occasional dark coarse grain bands, or pale clay-rich bands (<1 cm). The sediment from 272 cm to 235 cm consists of much larger gypsum crystals in the same grey silty or clay matrix. The gypsum crystals do not appear to be aligned, although they were clearly disturbed during the coring process due to the large size of the crystals (some up to 5 cm, but commonly 2–3 cm long). A fairly smooth transition between 277 cm and 272 cm delineates the lowest core section. Dominated by light green-grey to dark-grey, slightly sandy silt, this section has five layers which appear on the grey-scale graph as paler bands, and are actually very fine (1–3 mm) pink, green, black and white (calcareous) laminations. Especially in the laminated sections, but elsewhere as well, hard white (probably calcareous) sand grains are distributed throughout the silt.

Statistical analysis of geochemical data from this core (Flett *et al.* 2007) confirms there are four distinct stratigraphic layers: Unit 1 from the base to about 280 cm; Unit 2 from 280 cm to 175 cm; Unit 3, a transitional layer, from 175 cm to 140 cm; and Unit 1 above 140 cm.

Distinctive sediment properties characterise the four units. Unit 1 has mostly low magnetic susceptibility, with some slightly elevated readings corresponding to non-laminated sections with slightly lower organic percentages than the rest of the unit. X-ray analysis reveals also that these elevated magnetic susceptibility readings correspond to denser material (Flett *et al.* 2007). Carbonate percentages in Unit 1 are higher than in the rest of the core, mostly between 10 percent and 20 percent. The organic component of the sediment is mostly above 20 percent for Unit 1. Unit 2 has consistently low magnetic susceptibility, a fairly low organic content, of about 18–20 percent, and a low percentage of carbonate, at about five percent. Unit 3 is very similar to Unit 2, except for the section between 175 cm and 165 cm, which is more similar to Unit 4. The sediment appearance and texture is the same as much of Unit 4, and the magnetic susceptibility is higher than in the older sediment, at about 100 units. Unit 4 is characterised by an extremely unusual magnetic susceptibility profile. Very high readings of up to 1000 units are reached, but between these high-susceptibility sediment blocks are layers with much lower magnetic susceptibility. Organic content varies between 10 percent and 20 percent over this unit, with carbonate content mostly around eight percent, but increasing towards the top of the core. A rough correlation between paler-coloured sediments and lower values of magnetic susceptibility can be noticed, and there are also several layers in which coarser-grained material tends to be related to the high-susceptibility layers.

The age model for the lower part of SAEL1 and SAE2 is based on a log curve trend line, fitted through 12 of the AMS radiocarbon dates (Figure 3). Although 22 samples were submitted for dating (Table 2), six samples were modern, and three were paired samples from the same depths as those used in the age model. The paired samples were left out of the diagram to reduce confusion, and the six modern samples were not used in this particular age model, although they are being calibrated with the 'bomb spike' calibration curve and will be discussed in a separate publication. Lead-210 analysis was attempted using the Po-Ra method and alpha spectrometry (Appleby and Oldfield 1992), but counts of the Ra and Po isotopes were too low and inconsistent to be used.

Table 2. Conventional radiocarbon ages for 22 Espumilla Lagoon samples submitted to ANSTO.

ANSTO code	Sample type	Submitter ID	¹³C	% Modern	CRA
OZI495	Lake sediment	SAE-2-20-B	-23.1	97.82	180±70
OZI481	Pollen extraction	SAE-2-20-P	-28	110.02	Modern
OZJ651	Lake sediment	SAE-1-49	-26.1	103.24	Modern
OZI494	Lake sediment	SAE-2-90	-24.8	110.69	Modern
OZJ652	Lake sediment	SAE-2-105		101.04	Modern
OZJ653	Lake sediment	SAE-1-141	-25.5	104.17	Modern
OZJ654	Lake sediment	SAE-1-144	-23.0	148.7	Modern
OZI496	Lake sediment	SAE-2-178-B	-25.4	94	495±40
OZI482	Pollen extraction	SAE-2-178-P	-25.6	95.35	385±45
OZJ663	Lake sediment	SAE-2-181	-16.9	96.74	265±50
OZJ655	Lake sediment	SAE-2-186	-19.2	92.92	590±50
OZJ656	Lake sediment	SAE-2-190	-17.5	93.03	580±45
OZJ657	Lake sediment	SAE-2-225	-16.3	93.11	570±60
OZJ659	Lake sediment	SAE-2-266	-17.0	82.1	1580±60
OZI483	Pollen extraction	SAE-2-281-P	-14.7	79.88	1800±60
OZI472	Lake sediment	SAE-2-281-B	-18.9	80.84	1710±50
OZI804	Lake sediment	SAE-2-295	-19.9	78.67	1930±40
OZJ660	Lake sediment	SAE-2-305	-16.5	74.42	2370±60
OZJ661	Lake sediment	SAE-1-332	-14.6	74.58	2355±50
OZJ662	Lake sediment	SAE-2-363	-18.5	71.69	2670±70
OZI473	Lake sediment	SAE-2-382	-15.9	64.93	3470±50

The radiocarbon results below the uppermost 175 cm fit reasonably well (R^2=0.96) to a log trend line, with equation $y=95.458Ln(x)-403.45$. For the uppermost samples, five out of the six results are modern, and most of these samples were taken from the dark red-brown sediment of the upper 140 cm. About 180 cm of sediment in the top part of the core accumulated in ~500 years, which is a dramatic change in sedimentation rate compared with the lower part of the core. The reasons for the lack of meaningful radiocarbon dates in the top half of the core warrant careful consideration.

Discussion

A basic sedimentological assessment can provide information about the changing palaeoenvironmental setting of the Espumilla basin. Although we cannot date when sediment started accumulating in lagoons behind Espumilla beach, many similar back-barrier lagoons formed during the late Holocene as a result of relative sea-level stability after post-glacial sea-level rise. In Unit 1, the lagoon sediments indicate relatively deep water, probably brackish or marine-influenced. In Bainbridge crater, Galapagos, periods of stratification in a generally deep water column, caused by an influx of fresh water during an El Nino event are suggested to be the cause of laminations (Riedinger *et al.* 2002). If the same situation caused the laminations in Unit 1 of the Espumilla core, then there were five periods of stratified conditions indicating extreme climatic events between c. 1450 cal. BP and 2800 cal. BP. Unit 2 is an evaporite sequence indicating a period in which the water was a shallow concentrated brine, with relatively stable chemistry. This allowed gypsum precipitation after the lake's previous calcareous phase, leading to the reduced carbonate content of the sediment. Low magnetic susceptibility values are often attributed to organic or autochthonous sediment, with high values signifying terrestrial erosion and run-off (Dearing 1999; Nowaczyk 2001). About 500 years ago, a transitional period began. The striking rise in magnetic susceptibility, along with other geochemical factors, are discussed in Flett *et al.* (2007), and indicate that terrestrial material began to dominate. The sedimentation rate also dramatically increased, with around the same amount of sediment accumulating in the past 500 years as in the previous 2500 years. It is unclear whether these changes were due to geomorphologic, climatic or anthropogenic factors.

The lake basin itself could have filled with sediment during the evaporite phase, resulting in a natural end to the standing-lake phase. This does not fully explain the change in sediment type, however, as the red-brown silt with high magnetic susceptibility is not evident in the earlier sediments. The magnetic susceptibility signal in Unit 4 is particularly interesting, since it allows us to speculate that the terrestrial material is not arriving in the lake constantly (e.g. via a permanent turbid stream), but in bursts. This is consistent with rainfall patterns in the Galapagos lowlands, where it is generally very dry, except during extreme rainfall events associated with El Nino periods (Snell and Rea 1999). Unfortunately, the lack of chronological certainty for the past c. 500 years frustrates efforts to attribute each influx of sediment to a particular El Nino event. It should be noted, however, that there are eight high magnetic susceptibility levels in the past 500 years, and eight extreme events reported in Bainbridge crater (Riedinger *et al.* 2002).

Instead of intensification of the frequency and/or severity of El Nino events, there are two alternative explanations for the change in sediment type. One concerns the recent volcanism in James Bay, which is the large bay on the northwest coast of Santiago encompassing the Espumilla lagoons and the James Bay and Buccaneer Bay archaeological sites. In 1835, when Charles Darwin explored the region, he noticed pieces of pottery stuck in a recent lava flow in James Bay, one of which had the date of 1684 stamped on it (Darwin 2001). The region has been volcanically active, then, during the past 400 years, and it is possible that the shape of the catchment was changed by this activity, or that the recent sediment is different from earlier material because it is, in fact, freshly eroded lava. More geochemical analysis is required to test this hypothesis.

The third possible explanation for the change in sediment type is that this is roughly the time Europeans arrived. Burning of vegetation and the introduction of goats and pigs are known to have dramatically destabilised sediment in other island environments, and this could also have occurred here. Estimates for when goats and pigs were introduced are in the early 1800s (Cruz *et al.* 2005; Woram 2005), which is slightly inconsistent with the current (preliminary) age model, but could certainly be explained by considering the significance of the inconsistent dates in Unit 3, which could make the transition as late as 300 years ago. Charcoal and pollen analysis, as well as further attempts to improve the chronology of Units 3 and 4, are underway.

Future directions

One of the most significant results of the initial archaeological and palaeoecological research underway in the Galapagos Islands is the clear indication that there have been massive changes in sediment mobilisation within the past 1000 years, with a major increase in catchment erosion in the coastal areas most likely dating to between 500 and 300 years ago. While we have outlined a number of interpretations relating this event to anthropogenic and natural processes, the final identification of the cause must depend on multi-proxy data from archaeological and palaeoecological archives. Both these lines of evidence are pointing towards anthropogenic impacts being restricted to the post-European discovery period (post AD 1535).

This still leaves one of the outstanding uncertainties of Pacific prehistory, which is the extent to which it has an Amerindian component. There is no doubt there has been some such influence, as outlined above, though the question remains as to whether this represents a single event of Amerindian or Polynesian voyaging, perhaps accidental, or is indicative of more frequent, possibly systematic seafaring behaviour in the far-eastern Pacific. While our investigations in the far-eastern Pacific Islands, at the moment, do not favour any of the hypotheses, there is a growing body of evidence to suggest the far-eastern islands did not play a 'stepping stone' role in the interaction between Amerindians or Polynesians in prehistory.

Our focus on issues of island colonisation in the remote eastern Pacific Ocean has provided the opportunity to substantially advance the knowledge base of the discipline in several areas. Firstly, the tension that exists between archaeological and palaeoecological evidence for island colonisation stems from our lack of understanding about the nature of human interaction with small island landscapes, and the difficulty of separating natural processes from human-induced environmental change. In the far-eastern Pacific Islands we have been able to overcome this problem in interpreting records of environmental change by: (1) deriving proxy data from multiple sites across a region of contrasting human occupation history in order to distinguish the regional climate trends from local human activity; and (2) deriving proxy data from areas with no, or a very short and well-defined, history of human occupation.

Finally, the islands of the far-eastern Pacific Ocean have long been considered pristine and unspoilt landscapes, and as such, have represented a unique opportunity to study the evolution and dynamics of biota in the absence of human interference (Larson 2002). However, the islands are also extremely sensitive to anthropogenic impact due to their generally small size, isolation, vulnerability to pest and weed invasion, and low biodiversity relative to continental landmasses. By applying palaeoecological and archaeological analysis at fine spatial and temporal resolutions, we will have the opportunity to define the period of human impact and assess the rate and extent of anthropogenic changes.

Acknowledgments

The research discussed in this paper is funded by the Australian Research Council (under the Stepping Stones or Barriers ARC Discovery project) and an APA to Iona Flett. Additional funding has also been provided by the Australian Institute for Nuclear Science and Engineering, which has supported research conducted at ANSTO under its Post-Graduate Research Award Scheme. The authors are grateful to Dr Henk Heijnis and Dr Geraldine Jacobsen who have provided advice on chronological techniques mentioned in this paper. We would also like to thank staff at the Charles Darwin Research Station in the Galapagos who assisted with fieldwork and permit requirements. Most importantly, we need to acknowledge the contribution of Atholl Anderson to this project, in which he is an active leader. His influence in all stages of the research, from developing the application to publishing the results, has been invaluable, and we look forward to much fruitful collaboration in the future.

References

Aitken, M.J. 1998. *An Introduction to Optical Dating*. Oxford: Oxford University Press.

Allen, M.S. 2006. New Ideas about Late Holocene Climate Variability in the Central Pacific. *Current Anthropology* 47(3):521–535.

Anderson, A. 1991. The chronology of colonization in New Zealand. *Antiquity* 65:767–795.

Anderson, A. 2003. Initial human dispersal in remote Oceania: pattern and explanation. In C. Sand (ed), *Pacific archaeology: assessments and prospects*, pp. 71–84. Noumea: Service des Musees et du Patrimoine.

Anderson, A. 2005. Subpolar settlement in South Polynesia. *Antiquity* 79:791–800.

Anderson, A. 2006. Polynesian seafaring and American horizons: A response to Jones and Klar. *American Antiquity* 71(4):759–763

Anderson, A., J. Chappell, M. Gagan and R. Grove 2006. Prehistoric maritime migration in the Pacific islands: an hypothesis of ENSO forcing. *The Holocene* 16(1):1–6.

Anderson, A., S. Haberle, G. Rojas, A. Seelenfreund, I. Smith and T. Worthy 2002. An archaeological exploration of Robinson Crusoe Island, Juan Fernandez Archipelago, Chile. In S. Bedford, C. Sand and D. Burley (eds.), *Fifty years in the field, essays in honour and celebration of Richard Shutler Jr's archaeological career*, pp. 239–249. Auckland: New Zealand Archaeological Association.

ANSTO, 2008. *Pretreatment of Organic Samples from Sediment*, pp.1–8. Australian Nuclear Science and Technology Organisation, NSW.

Appleby, P.G. and F. Oldfield 1992. Application of Lead-210 to Sedimentation Studies, In M. Ivanovich and R.S. Harmon (eds), *Uranium-series Disequilibrum: Applications to Earth, Marine and Environmental Studies*, pp. 731–778. New York: Oxford University Press.

Ballard, C. 2005. Still good to think with: the sweet potato in Oceania. In C. Ballard, P. Brown, R.M. Bourke and T. Harwood (eds), *The Sweet Potato in Oceania: A reappraisal*, pp. 1–13. Sydney: The University of Sydney and University of Pittsburgh.

Bellwood, P.S. 1997. *Prehistory of the Indo-Malaysian Archipelago*. Honolulu, Hawaii: University of Hawai'i Press.

Bruhns, K.O. 1994. *Ancient South America*. Cambridge: Cambridge University Press.

Bushnell, G.H.S. 1957. Review: 200. Reviewed Work: *Archaeological Evidence of Pre-Spanish Visits to the Galapagos Islands* by Thor Heyerdahl; Arne Skjolsvold. Man 57:156–157.

Clarke, A.C., M.K. Burtenshaw, P.A. McLenachan, D.L. Erickson and D. Penny 2006. Reconstructing the Origins and Dispersal of the Polynesian Bottle Gourd (*Lagenaria siceraria*). *Molecular Biology and Evolution* 23(5):893–900.

Colinvaux, P.A. 1968. Reconnaissance and Chemistry of the Lakes and Bogs of the Galapagos Islands. *Nature* 219:590–594.

Colinvaux, P.A. 1969. Paleolimnological Investigations in the Galapagos Archipelago. Mitt. Internat. Verein. *Limnology* 17:126–130.

Colinvaux, P.A. 1972. Climate and the Galapagos Islands. *Nature* 240:17–20.

Colinvaux, P.A. and E.K. Schofield 1976a. Historical Ecology in the Galapagos Islands I. A Holocene Pollen Record from El Junco Lake, Isla San Cristobal. *Journal of Ecology* 64:989–1012.

Colinvaux, P.A. and E.K. Schofield 1976b. Historical Ecology in the Galapagos Islands II. A Holocene Spore Record from El Junco Lake, Isla San Cristobal. *Journal of Ecology* 64:1013–1030.

Croudace, I., A. Rigby and R.G. Rothwell 2006. ITRAX: description and evaluation of a new multi-function X-ray core scanner. *Geological Society, London, Special Publications* 267:51–63.

Cruz, F., C. Josh Donlan, K. Campbell and V. Carrion 2005. Conservation action in the Galapagos: feral pig (Sus scrofa) eradication from Santiago Island. *Biological Conservation* 121(3):473–478.

Darwin, C. 2001. *Charles Darwin's Beagle Diary*. Cambridge: Cambridge University Press.

Dean, W.E. 1974. Determination of carbonate and organic matter in calcareous sediments and sedimentary rocks by loss on ignition: comparison with other methods. *Journal of Sedimentary Petrology* 44:242–248.

Dearing, J. 1999. *Environmental Magnetic Susceptibility. Using the Bartington MS2 system*. Kenilworth, England: Chi Publishing.

Dearing, J.A., J.K. Elner and C.M. Happey-Wood 1981. Recent sediment flux and erosional processes in a Welsh upland lake-catchment based on magnetic susceptibility measurements. *Quaternary Research* 16(3):356–372.

Dearing, J.A. and R.J. Flower 1982. The Magnetic Susceptibility of Sedimenting Material Trapped in Lough Neagh, Northern Ireland, and its Erosional Significance. *Limnology and Oceanography* 27(5):969–975.

Dunbar, R.B., G.M. Wellington, M.W. Colgan and P.W. Glynn 1994. Eastern Pacific sea surface temperature since 1600 A.D. The D18O record of climate variability in Galapagos corals. *Paleoceanography* 9(2):291–315.

Evans, C. 1958. Comments on Ryden's Review of Heyerdahl and Skjolsvold. *American Antiquity* 24(2):189.

Feathers, J.K. 2003. Use of luminescence dating in archaeology. *Measurement Science and Technology* 14:1493–509.

Flett, I., S. Haberle and H. Lamb 2007. High resolution geochemical analysis of laminated coastal lagoon sediments from the Galapagos Islands, Ecuador (Poster), In N.R. Catto (ed.), *XVII INQUA Congress*, p. 151. Cairns: Quaternary International.

Fosberg, F.R. and Sachet, M.H. 1987. Flora of Maupiti, Society Islands. The Smithsonian Institution. *Atoll Research Bulletin* 294:1–70.

Gartelmann, K.D. 1986. *Digging up Prehistory. The archaeology of Ecuador*. Quito: Libri Mundi.

Geist, D. 1996. On the emergence and submergence of the Galapagos Islands. *Noticias de Galapagos* 56:5–8.

Genz, J. and T.L. Hunt 2003. El Nino/Southern Oscillations and Rapa Nui Prehistory. *Rap Nui Journal* 17:7–14.

Gongora, J, N. J. Rawlence, V. A. Mobegi, H. Jianlin, J. A. Alcalde, J. T. Matus, O. Hanotte, C. Moran, G. Larson, A. Cooper 2008. Abstract: Does the genetic analysis of Chilean archaeological chicken bones support Polynesian contact? In A.J. Barham (ed), *Archaeological Science Conference, 4–6 Feb, 2008,* p. 13. Canberra: ANU.

Green, R.C. 2005. Sweet potato transfers in Polynesian prehistory, In C. Ballard, P. Brown, R.M. Bourke and T. Harwood. (eds), *The Sweet Potato in Oceania: A reappraisal*, pp. 43–62. Sydney: The University of Sydney, University of Pittsburgh.

Gumbel, A. 2005. Paradise lost in Galapagos crisis *The Canberra Times*, Monday May 2, pp. 2–3. Canberra.

Haberle, S. 1994. Anthropogenic indicators in pollen diagrams: problems and prospects for late Quaternary palynology in New Guinea. In J.G. Hather (ed), *Tropical Archaeobotany*, pp.172–201. London: Routledge.

Haberle, S.G. 2003. Late quaternary vegetation dynamic and human impact on Alexander Selkirk Island, Chile. *Journal of Biogeography* 30:239–255.

Hather, J. and P.V. Kirch 1991. Prehistoric seet potato *(Ipomoea batatas)* from Mangaia Island, Central Polynesia. *Antiquity* 65:887–893.

Heiri, O., A.F. Lotter and G. Lemcke 2001. Loss on ignition as a method for estimating organic and carbonate content in sediments: reproducibility and comparibilty of results. *Journal of Paleolimnology* 25:101–110.

Heyerdahl, T. 1952. *American Indians in the Pacific: The Theory behind the Kon-Tike Expedition*. London: Allen and Unwin.

Heyerdahl, T. and A. Skjølsvold 1990. *Archaeological Evidence of Pre-Spanish Visits to the Galapagos Islands*. Oslo: Norwegian University Press.

Holton, G.E.L. 2004. Heyerdahl's Kon Tiki Theory and the Denial of the Indigenous Past. *Anthropological Forum* 14(2):163–181.

Holm, L.G., Plucknett, D.L., Pancho, J.V. and Herberger, J.P. 1977. *The world's worst weeds: distribution and biology.* East-West Center: University Press of Hawaii.

Horrocks, M. and I. Lawlor 2006. Plant microfossil analysis of soils from Polynesian stonefields in South Auckland, New Zealand. *Journal of Archaeological Science* 33:200–217.

Hunt, T.L. and C.P. Lipo 2006. Late Colonization of Easter Island. *Science* 311:1603–1606.

Irwin, G., S. Bickler and P. Quirke 1990. Voyaging by canoe and computer: experiments in the settlement of the Pacific Ocean. *Antiquity* 64:34–50.

Kennet, D., T. Anderson, M. Prebble, E. Conte and J. Southon 2006. Prehistoric human impacts on Rapa, French Polynesia. *Antiquity* 80:340–354.

Lanning, E. P. 1969. South America As Source For Aspects of Polynesian Cultures. In R.C. Green and M. Kelly (eds), *Studies on Oceanic Culture History*, pp. 175–185. Honolulu, Hawaii: Bernice P. Bishop Museum.

Larson, E.J. 2002. *Evolution's Workshop: God and Science on the Galapagos Islands.* London: The Penguin Press.

Levinson, M., R. Ward and J. Webb 1973. *The Settlement of Polynesia: A Computer Simulation.* Minneapolis: University of Minnesota Press.

Macphail, M.K., F.S. Hope and A. Anderson 2001. Polynesian Plant Introductions in the Southwest Pacific: Initial Pollen Evidence from Norfolk Island, In A. Anderson and P. White (eds), *The Prehistoric Archaeology of Norfolk Island, Southwest Pacific*, pp. 123–134. Sydney: Australian Museum.

Maloney, B.K. 1994. The prospects and problems of using palynology to trace the origins of tropical agriculture: the case of Southeast Asia, In J.G. Hather (ed), *Tropical Archaeobotany*, pp. 139–171. London: Routledge.

Martinsson-Wallin, H. and S.J. Crockford 2001. Early Settlement of Rapa Nui (Easter Island). *Asian Perspectives* 40(2):244–278.

McCormac, F., A. Hogg, P. Blackwell, C. Buck, T. Higham and P. Reimer 2004. SHCal04 Southern Hemisphere Calibration 0–11.0 cal kyr BP. *Radiocarbon* 46:1087–1092.

Montenegro, A., C. Avis and A. Weaver 2007. Modelling the prehistoric arrival of the sweet potato in Polynesia. *Journal of Archaeological Science*, In Press, pp.1–13.

Nowaczyk, N.R. 2001. Logging of Magnetic Susceptibility, In W.M. Last and J.P. Smol Dordrecht (eds), *Tracking Environmental Change Using Lake Sediments. Volume 1: Basin Analysis, Coring and Chronological Techniques*, pp. 155–170. The Netherlands: Kluwer Academic Publishers.

Nunn, P.D. 2000. Environmental Catastrophe in the Pacific Islands around A.D. 1300. *Geoarchaeology* 15(7):715–740.

Nunn, P.D. 2003a. Nature-Society Interactions in the Pacific Islands. *Geografiska Annaler* 85 B(4):219–229.

Nunn, P.D. 2003b. Revising ideas about environmental determinism: Human-environment relations in the Pacific Islands. *Asia Pacific Viewpoint* 44(1):63–72.

Nunn, P.D. and J.M.R. Britton 2001. Human-Environment Relationships in the Pacific Islands around A.D. 1300. *Environment and History* 7:3–22.

Perry, L., R. Dickau, S. Zarillo, I. Holst, D.M. Peasall, D.R. Piperno, M.J. Berman, R.G. Cooke, K. Rademaker, A.J. Ranere, J.S. Raymond, D.H. Sandweiss, F. Scaramelli, K. Tarble and J.A. Zeidler 2007. Starch Fossils and the Domestication and Dispersal of Chili Peppers (*Capsicum* spp. L.) *Americas Science* 315:986–988.

Petterson, G., B.V. Odgaard and I. Renberg 1999. Image analysis as a method to quantify sediment components. *Journal of Paleolimnology* 22:443–455.

Piperno, D., C. Amdres and K. Stothert 2000. Phytoliths in *Cucurbita* and other neotropical Cucurbitaceae and their occurrence in early archaeological sites from the lowland American tropics. *Journal of Archaeological Science* 27:193–208.

Ramirez, J.M. 1990/91. Transpacific Contact: The Mapuche Connection. *Rapa Nui Journal* 4(4):53–55.

Riedinger, M.A., M. Steinitz-Kannan, W.M. Last and M. Brenner 2002. A ~6100 14C yr record of El Nino activity from the Galapagos Islands. *Journal of Paleolimnology* 27:1–7.

Ryden, S. 1958. Review of Arcaheological Evidence of Pre-Spanish Visits to the Galapagos Islands by Thor Hyerdahl; Arne Skjolsvold. *American Antiquity* 24(1):88–89.

Smith, Albert C. 1979. *Flora Vitiensis nova: a new flora of Fiji.* National Tropical Botanical Garden, Lawai, Kauai, Hawaii. Volume 1.

Smith, Albert C. 1991. *Flora Vitiensis nova: a new flora of Fiji.* National Tropical Botanical Garden, Lawai, Kauai, Hawaii. Volume 5.

Snell, H. and S. Rea 1999. The 1997–98 El Nino in Galapagos: Can 34 years of data estimate 120 years of pattern? *Noticias de Galapagos* p.60.

Stephens, S.G. 1963. Polynesian Cottons. *Annals of the Missouri Botanical Garden* 50(1/4):1–22.

Storey, A.A., J. M. Ramirez, D. Quiroz, D.V. Burley, D.J. Addison, R. Walter, A.J. Anderson, T.L. Hunt, J.S. Athens, L. Huynen and E. A. Matisoo-Smith 2007. Radiocarbon and DNA evidence for a pre-Columbian introduction of Polynesian chickens to Chile. *Proceedings of the National Academy of Sciences* 104(25):10335–10339.

Stothert, K.E. 2007. Report on Pottery from Galapagos (including artifacts from the ANU 2005 field season and other collections). San Antonio: The University of Texas.

Stuiver, M. and P. Reimer 1993. Calib.

Suggs, R. 1960. *The Island Civilizations of Polynesia.* New York: The New American Library.

Suggs, R. C. 1967. A Reanalysis of Galapagos Ceramics Data. *Zeitschrift fur Ethnologie* 92:239–247.

Summerhayes, G. 2000. *Lapita Interaction.* Canberra: ANH Publications and the Centre for Archaeological Research.

Terrell, J. E. 1998. The prehistoric Pacific. *Archaeology* Nov/Dec 1998:56–63.

US Forest Service, Pacific Island Ecosystems at Risk (PIER). Online resource at http://www.hear.org/pier/ accessed 10/12/07.

van Leeuwen, J., W. van der Knaap and B. Ammann 2007. The native or introduced status of plant species determined by fossil pollen in Galapagos and the Azores In N.R. Catto (ed), *XVII INQUA Congress. The tropics: Heat engine of the Quaternary*, pp. 430–431. Cairns: Quaternary International.

Wagner, W. L., Herbst, D. R. and Sohmer, S. H. 1999. *Manual of the flowering plants of Hawaii. Revised edition. Bernice P. Bishop Museum special publication.* Honolulu: University of Hawai'i Press and Bishop Museum Press.

Whistler, W. A. 1988. *Checklist of the weed flora of western Polynesia. Technical Paper No. 194*, Noumea: South Pacific Commission.

Whitlock, C. and C. Larsen 2001. Charcoal as a fire proxy, In J.P. Smol, H.J.B. Birks and W.M. Last Dordrecht (eds), *Tracking Environmental Change Using Lake Sediments. Volume 3: Terrestrial, Algal, and Siliceous Indicators*, pp. 75–97. The Netherlands: Kluwer Academic Publishing.

Willis, K.J., M.B. Araujo, K.D. Bennett, B. Figueroa-Rangel, C.A. Froyd and N. Myers 2007. How can a knowledge of the past help to conserve the future? Biodiversity conservation and the relevance of long-term ecological studies. *Philosophical Transactions of the Royal Society* 362:175–186.

Woram, J. 2005. *Charles Darwin Slept Here.* Rockville, USA: Rockville Press.

Yen, D. 1974. *The Sweet Potato in Oceania: An Essay in Ethnobotany.* Honolulu: Bishop Museum Press.

Zolitschka, B., J. Mingram, S.V.D. Gaast, J.H.F. Jansen and R. Naumann 2001. Sediment logging techniques, In W.M. Last and J.P. Smol Dordrecht (eds), *Tracking Environmental Change Using Lake Sediments. Volume 1: Basin Analysis, Coring and Chronological Techniques*, pp. 137–153. The Netherlands: Kluwer Academic Publishers

19

Subsistence and island landscape transformations: Investigating monumental earthworks in Ngaraard State, Republic of Palau, Micronesia

Sarah Phear

Historic Environment and Archaeology Service, Worcestershire County Council, Worcestershire, UK
sphear@worcestershire.gov.uk

Introduction

Monumental earthworks in Pacific islands have always attracted attention, from ethnographers visiting the islands in the 19th and 20th centuries (e.g. Krämer 1917), through to archaeologists in the modern day (e.g. Osborne 1966; Parry 1984; Liston 1999). The earthworks of the Republic of Palau, Micronesia, have not escaped attention. When asked by Andrew Cheyne (1864) in the 19th century, local Palauan people attributed the terraces to work of the gods, or the actions of the sea during the great flood (Parmentier 1987:30). These landscape features have been the focus of several archaeological investigations over the past five decades (Osborne 1966, 1979; Lucking 1984; Masse *et al.* 1984; Liston 1999; Liston and Tuggle 2001). As such, they have undergone scrutiny by application of a range of theoretical and methodological approaches, each generally a product of its time, and resulting in often similar, although at times conflicting, interpretations. A critical analysis of these approaches can be found elsewhere (Phear 2007), and a brief summary suffices here.

A popular explanation for earthwork/terrace construction focuses on subsistence-related activities, but no direct evidence has been recovered to support this. When Osborne (1966, 1979) undertook his investigation, the first for the archipelago, his conclusion was that the terraces were both agricultural and defensive, and they were abandoned when they reached a point of 'diminishing returns', with the soils being exhausted and left fallow (Osborne 1966:151, 155). Lucking (1984) looked for more direct evidence for agriculture in her study, but conceded no direct evidence was recovered, with little support in botanical surveys and Palauan land-use terminology. Yet she continued to support the agricultural argument, with the morphology of two types of terraces – back-sloping and sloping – declared 'ideally suited' for cultivating crops, due to their water-holding capabilities (Lucking 1984:164). The top terraces – crowns and brims – were seen as defensive, which coincides with Osborne's argument. A team from Southern Illinois University at Carbondale made further interpretations of Palauan prehistory following a small excavation programme (Masse *et al.* 1984). Here, terraces were said to have been constructed at the beginning of a 'three phase' settlement chronology, about AD 800–1000, in a time of agricultural intensification, a response to population growth outstripping the productivity of wetland pond-fields (Masse *et al.* 1984). This intensified system was part of the defensive element of a regional system 'imbued with competition and political strife' (Masse *et al.* 1984). Thus, crowns and terraces were also seen as defensive.

More recently, Cultural Resource Management (CRM) based projects have used new investigative techniques to understand the earthworks, and Palau's settlement history as a whole. The main wealth of new data stems from work by the International Archaeological Research Institute Incorporated (IARII) on the Compact Road Project (CRP). During Phase I, a range of excavation methods led to a general interpretation appearing 'to support the proposed shift from agricultural to defensive to residential use of terraces over time, although when and how this happened is still unclear' (Liston 1999:24). Phase II analyses were more intensive, and aimed to provide answers on chronology and mechanisms precipitating the transformation in settlement pattern (Liston 1999:226). The earthworks were re-analysed typologically and split into two groups: 'modified terrain' and 'modified ridges and slopes' (see Liston 1999 for further details). In summary, modified hilltops, including crowns and brims, were considered defensive, but formed during initial landscape modification, not later additions (contra Osborne 1966; Masse *et al.* 1984). These 'fortified polities' (Liston and Tuggle 2001:8) incorporated terraces which were considered to have had multiple functions: agriculture and habitation, but also ritual and burial (based on new evidence). Liston (1999:369) placed the earthworks within a regional settlement system: 'the long duration of terrace use (c. 1500 yrs) suggests the strong possibility of functional roles evolving to suit the needs of changing communities over time'.

Wickler's (2002) research followed on from this. Using the results from IARII investigations, Wickler introduced a 'cultural landscape study'. Incorporating new palaeoenvironmental evidence from the study of Athens and Ward (1999, 2001), Wickler looked at landscape transformation from the first signs of land use, to patterns in 'surge and decline' savanna indicators to address aspects of terrace construction (Wickler 2002:69). The focus moved from looking for agricultural indicators, to viewing the earthworks as examples of chiefly power, brought about in a period of terrace expansion at a time of conflict characterised by the struggle for socio-political hegemony and power between competing polities (Wickler 2002:82). Wickler claimed that in Ngatpang State, his local-scale study indicated transformation of terraces into systems of stone work villages. Given the evidence of this local-scale study, Wickler didn't support the suggestion the terraces were ever abandoned.

Despite the strong argument for agricultural use of the terraces based largely within defensive polities, analysis of pollen and phytoliths has been limited to just a few small additional archaeological investigations in Palau (CRM projects). The results, though, are largely restricted to more recent periods in Palauan prehistory. This low number of analyses stands in contrast to the extensive use of pollen and phytolith techniques in other Pacific archaeological projects in the past 10 years. Therefore, pollen and phytolith analyses were undertaken here to locate and assess indirect and direct evidence for subsistence practices, and identify and interpret anthropogenic and natural changes in vegetation on, and within, the vicinity of the earthworks. The latter concern is particularly relevant to addressing questions related to the formation of savanna (ked) vegetation in the islands of Micronesia, where researchers have questioned the formation of savanna as a result of slash/burn agricultural purposes.

The results discussed in this paper derive from an archaeological investigation in Ngaraard State, Babeldaob, which focused on three dominant earthwork sites: B:NA-4:11 Ngemeduu, B:NA-4:12 Toi Meduu, and B:NA-4:6 Rois. The earthworks in Ngaraard were selected for many reasons. However, of significance is that Ngaraard was investigated by a team (including the author) led by Atholl Anderson in 2000, looking at colonisation issues in the archipelago. Analyses of radiocarbon dates from the colonisation project (Phear *et al.* 2003; Anderson *et al.* 2005) were important in helping define the construction sequence of the earthworks, as well as resulting in a revised settlement chronology for Palau (also Clark 2005).

The earthwork investigation looking at Ngemeduu, Toi Meduu and Rois was set within a landscape perspective that addresses both conceptual and physical elements of monumental earthworks (see Phear 2007:18–19). Thus, the research strategy incorporated an excavation programme, with the three sites sampled in 2001. The project aimed ultimately to provide a landscape history for this area of Ngaraard, and as such, incorporated other analytical techniques (such as clay and ceramic analyses), along with the analytical techniques discussed here. Full interpretive results can be found elsewhere (Phear 2007). The aim of this paper is to specifically assesses and discuss evidence for prehistoric landscape vegetative transformations on the ridgeline of Ngaraard, including evidence for subsistence activities, from early settlement to earthwork construction.

Physical background: Palau Islands

The Republic of Palau is a group of islands in Micronesia, an area which contains more than 2000 islands. Yap and the Republic of Palau, Beluu er a Belau, form the Western Caroline Islands (Figure 1). The Palau archipelago contains more than 300 islands, extending along a 150 km arc (Figure 2). Situated about 7° north of the equator, Palau is 900 km east of Mindanao in the Philippines, and 650 km from Papua New Guinea in the south.

Most Palauan islands are of uplifted coralline limestone. They're known locally as the 'rock islands', and are located in the centre of the archipelago. Some reasonably large rock islands have high points over 200 m above sea level, but poorly developed soils with no surface drainage

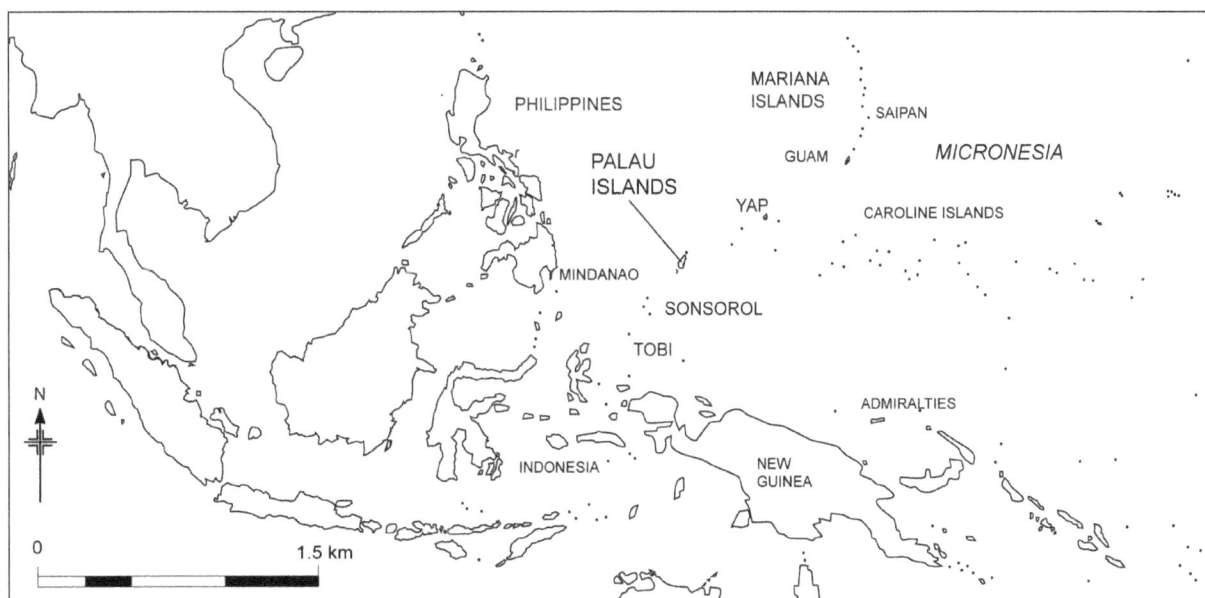

Figure 1. Map of Micronesia.

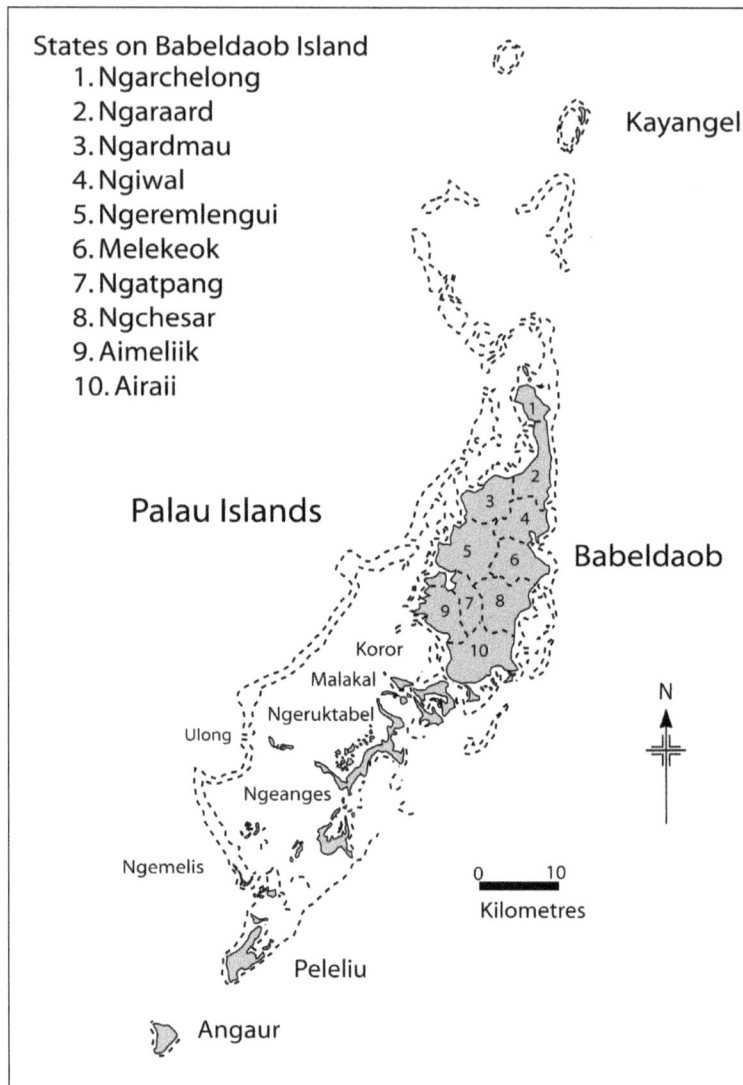

Figure 2. Map of the Republic of Palau.

systems. The islands have distinctive undercuts caused by wave action, and these cuts eventually trigger smaller islands to collapse.

Babeldaob, the largest volcanic island, at 363 km², represents the majority of Palau's land mass (Figure 2). It has a series of ridge systems that extend north–south, characterised by small, narrow valley systems and coastal plains, with tidal flats and dense mangrove forests. The highest peak on Babeldaob, Rois Ngerekelehuus, is 240 m asl. The volcanic soils are heavily weathered and form loose, and somewhat unstable, hill slopes.

An extensive blanket of limestone originally covered the volcanic strata of Babeldaob, and only a few remnants can be found (e.g. Oikull). These overlap the volcanic and volcaniclastic strata of the ancient volcanic edifice. The other volcanic islands, Ngerkebesang, Koror, Malakal and the rock islands, are less uplifted remnants of the formerly extensive blanket of Palau limestone. This uplift occurred in the Miocene, and younger limestone forms the chain of islands extending south to Anguar.

Barrier, fringing and patch reefs, comprised of inner and outer reef flats, encircle the islands (except Anguar). The barrier reef, 1–3 km wide, stretches northeast to southwest off the west coast, and is 120 km long. A 15 km wide lagoon separates the islands from the reef, and it is here that many of the patch reefs are found. The reef systems of Palau are considered the richest in the Pacific, with the highest species diversity.

Climate and vegetation

The tropical climate of Palau undergoes minor changes throughout the year, and has an average annual rainfall of 3730 mm. Temperatures average 27C, with a mean fluctuation of no more than 7C, and a relative humidity of 90 percent at night and 75–80 percent during the day. Although not in the typhoon belt, Palau endures storms and high winds associated with severe tropical disturbances.

Mueller-Dombois and Fosberg (1998) describe the volcanic half of Palau as possessing a floristically and physiognomically rich array of vegetation compared with the rest of Micronesia, although Yap possesses a similar level of diversity. These two island groups form a 'distinct phytogeographic unit, with many endemic species and the easternmost extensions of several others from the rich Indo-Melanesian flora'. The deeply weathered ancient volcanic islands, which are highly leached, and whose original structure is mostly lost, reflect differing topographical vegetation patterns to limestone islands.

Forest covers 75 percent, and grassland or savanna grassland covers 18 percent of Babeldaob. The volcanic islands also have mangrove and freshwater-swamp forests, strand and lowland vegetation, interior upland forest, and ravine and Riparian forest. The limestone islands are characterised by closed and diverse evergreen forests. These various vegetation zones are home to numerous fauna.

The project

Site location

Sites located in Ngaraard State, within the Ngebuked Village area, were sampled: B:NA-4:6 Rois Terrace Complex, B:NA-4:11 Ngemeduu Crown and Terrace complex, and B:NA-4:12 Toi Meduu Crown and Terrace Complex (Figure 3). The construction of the Compact Road has had a significant impact on earthworks in Ngaraard and surrounding traditional villages. Through archaeological investigations within the CRP, IARII has provided a large amount of information on many impacted sites, along with other small investigations (Osborne 1966; Masse and Snyder 1982; Olsudong *et al.* 2000).

B:NA-4:11 Ngemeduu Crown and Terrace Complex

Ngemeduu, 181 m asl, is a prominent modified hillside on the central ridge system in Ngaraard (Figure 4). It has a rectangular crown, with a knoll or 'peak', surrounded by a large terrace, with a steep scarp on its southern extent. Four smaller terraces extend down its northwest (NW) slope, one with a stone alignment. The north side of the site is very steep, with a northeast-facing scarp that extends to the forested lowlands. The west face extends along a secondary ridge, which is intersected by two roads. There are two rectangular depressions on the crown surface: the 'west depression' is 8.5 m wide (NS) by 10 m, and the 'east depression' is 8 m by 8 m.

Ten trenches (TR1-TR1i) and one test unit were excavated, encompassing the two depressions, the knoll, the south side of the crown and the surrounding terrace (see Phear 2007:Chapter 5 for excavation details).

B:NA-4:12 Toi Meduu Crown and Terrace Complex

Toi Meduu is a visually dominant crown and terrace complex immediately south of Ngemeduu (Figure 5). It overlooks the ridge to the south, as well as spurs which extend off the main trunk. The site itself has three crowns, separated by large ditches, one in the northern end of the site, and two to the southwest, which form a slight semi-circle. To their south, a steep slope culminates in a large back-sloping terrace, stretching into the valley below. A large flat terrace

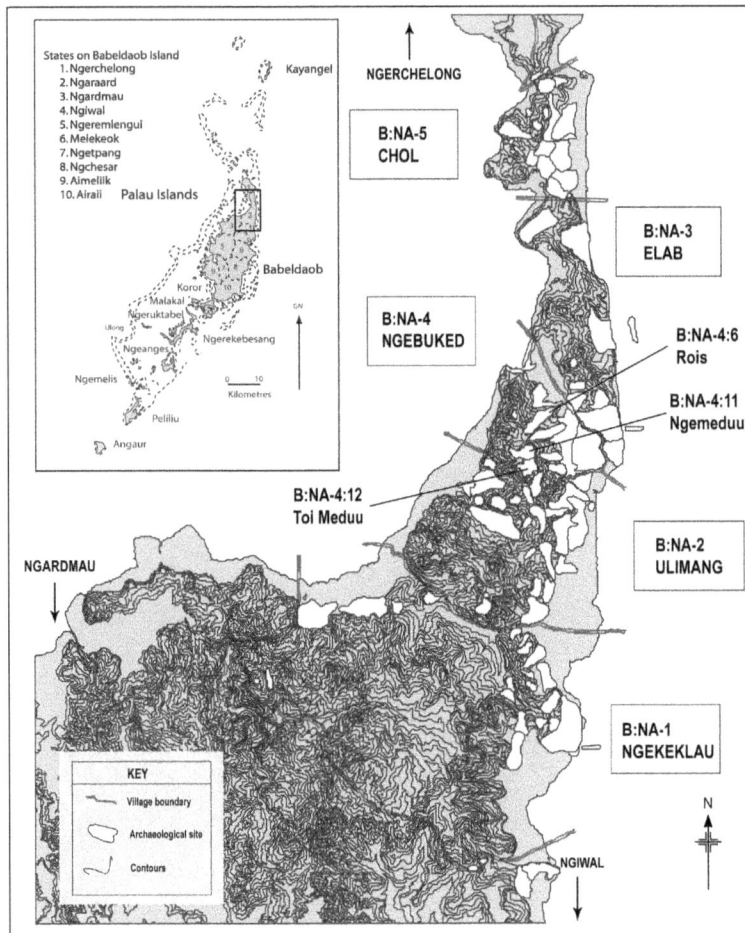

Figure 3. Map of Ngaraard illustrating the three sites investigated (the map has been modified from the BAC GIS database).

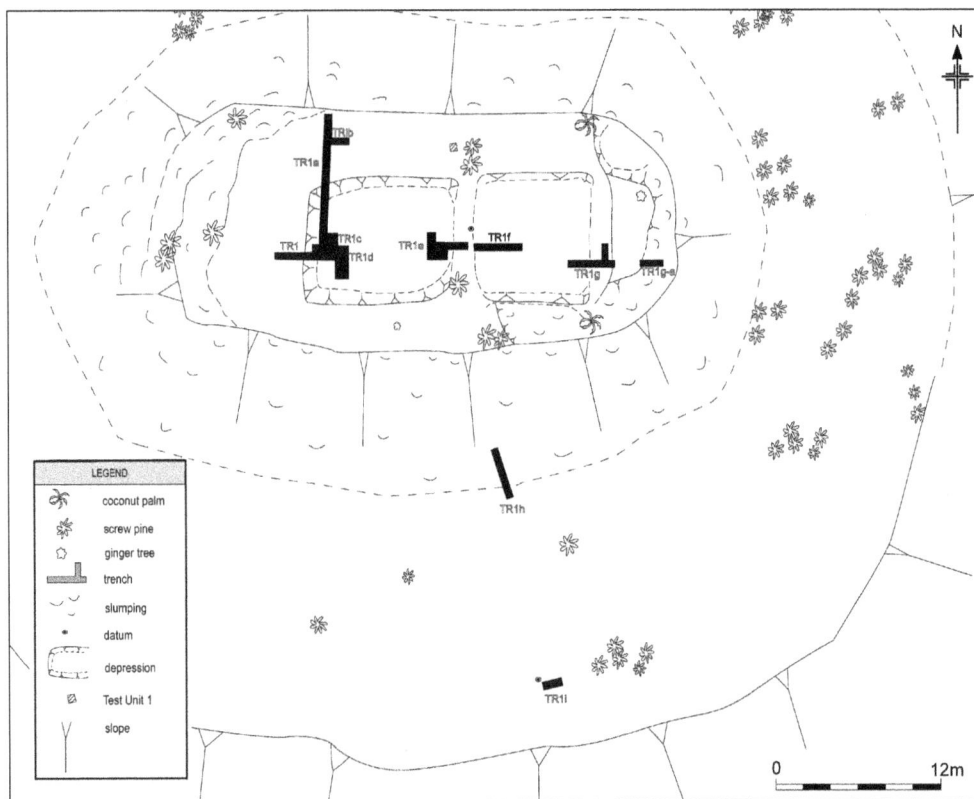

Figure 4. Plan of Ngemeduu with the 10 trenches excavated.

extends to the north of the westernmost crown, and has some basalt boulders that may have supported a platform.

The west crown, which was sampled, is 9 m higher than the terrace below. Stonework on the crown surface appears to be of an earlier pre-earthwork type, although it is heavily eroded and its original form is not clear. It most likely represents a past structure. The crown surface has eroded into the ditch, and pottery fragments were present on the surface of the crown, close to the ditch edge. Another stone platform is located on the central crown on a levelled area, with pottery lodged among the stones and eroding from the surface.

Three trenches were excavated – one on the northwest terrace (TR2), one in the ditch separating two crowns (TR5) and one on the back-sloping terrace to the south (TR3).

B:NA-4:6 Rois Terrace Complex

The Rois terraces are located on a spur between Ngetcherong and Ngebuked traditional villages, extending from the central ridgeline to the northeast of Ngemeduu. The terraces were constructed on a slope, and are considered small or 'slight', with broad surfaces and short risers (Figure 6). The lowest terraces are currently cultivated with taro and cassava. The terrace immediately above these was selected for sampling, as it complemented previous investigations which tested the upper terraces only (see Liston 1999). One trench was placed here (TR4). Slumping is evident at the rear of the terrace, like most of the terraces in the complex. The western extent is currently artificially mounded, due to the dirt road, and the terrace extends a further 4–5 m beyond the road, to the west. Large amounts of pot sherds were exposed in the road surface next to the terrace.

Pollen and phytolith analysis

Methodology

Pollen and phytolith analyses were done to identify indicators of anthropogenic and natural vegetation. Specifically, the aim in this project was to identify vegetation from various soil strata within the earthworks, to give insight into questions of land clearance before earthwork construction (i.e. whether there was savanna present or forest, and when it was cleared). Another aim was to identify direct and indirect evidence of agriculture, although obtaining direct evidence (e.g. *Colocasia* spp.) is problematic, due to factors influencing dispersal and long-term preservation of *Colocasia* pollen in soils.

Phytolith analysis provides an indication of plants growing in the immediate area of sampling, because phytoliths are returned to the soil through decay-in-place deposition of parent-plant material. With this in mind, the technique was used to attempt to identify evidence of cul-

Figure 5. Plan of Toi Meduu with Trenches 2 and 5.

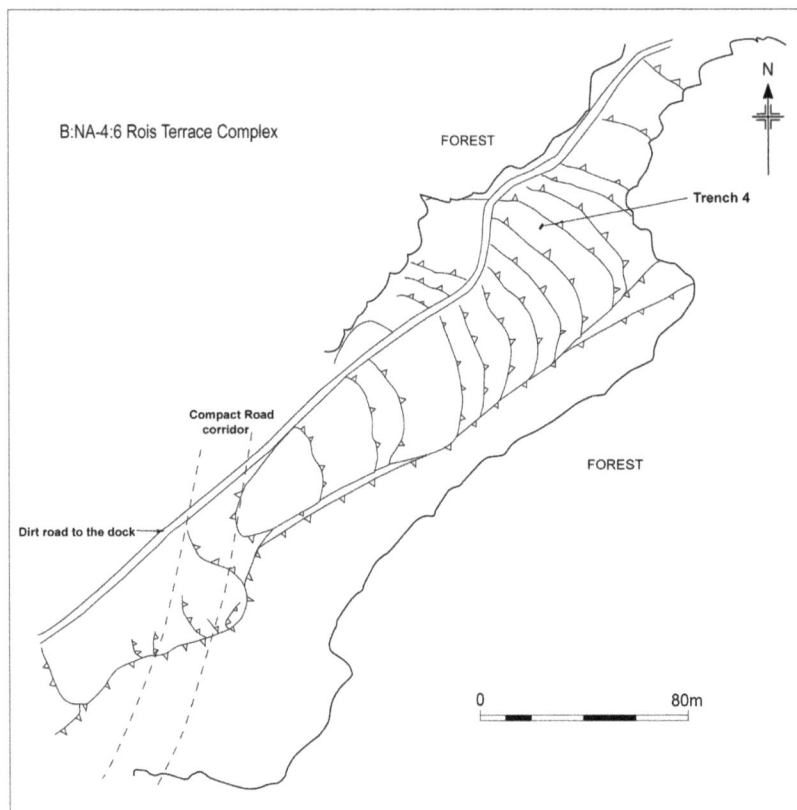

Figure 6. Plan of Rois terraces with Trench 4.

tivated crops in earthwork stratigraphy. Additionally, this method was used to provide information on other indicators of human interaction with the environment, such as the incidence of secondary growth related to clearance.

Phytolith analysis

Twelve soil samples were sent to J. Parr at the Centre for Geoarchaeology and Palaeoenvironmental Research, School of Environmental Science and Management, Southern Cross University, Australia. Parr used the Perkin-Elmer Multiwave Sample Preparation system for phytolith and starch-grain extraction from each sample. Phytoliths extracted from each were weighed, mounted on to microscope slides and scanned at 400x magnification on an Olympus BH2 microscope. All phytoliths encountered during three transects of a microscope slide were counted, although only one transect was counted for charcoal.

Fossil phytolith types were compared with those stored in a modern phytolith digital-image database of about 200 species from regionally applicable flora of Papua New Guinea and Australia. Other databases included the CD-ROM and Kealhofer and Piperno. Phytolith sizes were gauged using an ocular micrometer and the individual scale bars on each digital image.

Pollen analysis

Twenty-one pollen samples were analysed in the Department of Archaeology and Natural History at the Australian National University. All samples followed standard laboratory processing procedures, and *Lycopodium* pollen was added as a 'foreign' control measure. Once processed, the samples were mounted on to microscope slides and analysed.

Pollen was measured by moving down along a transect, and then repeated in reverse, until all transects were completed. A total slide pollen count was completed due to the relatively unknown flora of the area, although a pollen database from Papua New Guinea was consulted. Charcoal counts were made following the methodology of Clark (1982). The results were entered into a Tilia database (version 2.04b) and pollen diagrams were produced using Tiliagraph (version 2.04b). Charcoal counts were also analysed.

Results: B:NA-4:11 Ngemeduu Crown and Terrace Complex

A complex stratigraphic history was uncovered for the Ngemeduu earthworks. Only the most important stratigraphic results are discussed here.

Crown surface

The crown surface, immediately outside the west depression, is the youngest chronological surface of the feature. Therefore, Layer II (Figure 7, Table 1) was tested for both pollen and phytoliths (Table 2). The pollen identified represents 'classic' savanna grassland vegetation – e.g. *Pandanus* sp., fern spores, Polypodiaceae, and Poaceae. The charcoal concentration is low for this layer, although the phytolith charcoal level of abundance is moderate. While the phytolith data indicate a range of plants, their low number does not allow quantification beyond presence/absence. Grasses (Poaceae) are recorded, and also banana (Musaceae), a tree (Marantaceae), and a starch grain.

West depression

The layers in the central part of the depression were focused on here (Figure 7), except for LVI. This latter layer was formed through numerous temporal-fill episodes, and had a highly disturbed structure (See Phear 2007:Chapter 6), and was consequently not considered for sampling. From LVIII up to LI, there is a general fluctuation between classic savanna grasslands dominated by *Pandanus* sp. and grasses (Poaceae), and savanna dominated by the ferns and fern allies, which are disturbance indicators (Table 2). The pollen counts tend to increase vertically in the profile, with LI and LIV illustrating the highest numbers. A few secondary vegetation taxa are recorded in LV-LIV, but they are poorly represented in general. There is a clear variation in charcoal concentrations, with the basal layer (LVIII) and the top layer in the depression (LI) displaying the highest intensities.

The phytolith analysis provides comparable results. No phytoliths were recorded for the lowest two layers, however the grasses and *Pandanus* sp. observed in LV-LIV support the pollen results. Layer IV displays the most varied range of taxa, with classic savanna, secondary vegetation and disturbance plants present. The fig (Moraceae) and Liliaceae phytoliths are of note, though only one of each was found. The presence of Arecaceae in LV and LIV may indicate betel-palm growth on site. Little charcoal was recorded, although the presence of charred phytoliths suggests local fire activity (discussed later in the paper). The high concentration of charcoal recorded in the pollen record for LVIII is replicated in the phytolith charcoal results.

Encircling terrace

Pollen analysis was undertaken on samples from LIV and LIII in Trench 1i (Figure 8, Table 3). These layers were brought to the site as terrace fill, and thus formed terrace surfaces. The results reflect savanna grassland (Table 1), although LIV is dominated more by ferns/fern allies and LIII by Poaceae and *Pandanus* sp., the more classic grassland taxa. The pollen count is significantly higher for LIV, and so, too, the charcoal concentration.

Table 1. Stratigraphic descriptions for Trench 1a, Ngemeduu.

Ngemeduu (B:NA-4:11) Trench 1a (TR1a)

Layer	Description
I	7.5YR 4/4 Brown clay loam, average thickness 10 cm, friable, many roots all sizes, begins just outside of depression edge, discontinuous.
Ia	Organic A horizon, top 2 cm, located only in the depression, many roots.
II	5YR 4/4 Reddish brown clay, average thickness 30 cm, subangular blocky, roots common fine to coarse, quite friable, discontinuous.
III	10YR 4/4 Dark yellowish brown silty clay, average thickness 12 cm, firm, roots common medium sized, >1 mm sized charcoal flecks, discontinuous.
IIIa	7.5YR 5/8 Strong brown with grey flecks silty clay, average thickness 10 cm, subangular blocky, firm, few roots micro sized, discontinuous.
IV	10YR 4/3 Brown clay silt, average thickness 12 cm, subangular blocky, firm, abundant >1mm sized charcoal flecks, discontinuous.
IVb	10YR 6/6 Brownish yellow silty clay, average thickness 10 cm, subangular blocky, quite firm, roots common fine to medium sized, many >1 mm charcoal flecks.
V	7.5YR 5/8 Strong brown clay, average thickness 25 cm, firm though structureless, few roots micro sized, few charcoal flecks, lower boundary defined by iron pan, some sherds.
VI	2.5YR 3/3 Dark reddish brown clay with white and pink mottles of saprolite, average thickness 2 m, many sherds and charcoal, mixed with degrading more friable saprolite present in clasts and brown rather structureless clay, micro sized roots, upper boundary defined by iron pan in depression only.
VII	5YR 4/4 Reddish brown clay, average thickness 30 cm, plastic but firm, abundant charcoal flecking with some larger charcoal samples present, subangular blocky, consistent boundary, highly eroded bauxite nodules, some micro sized roots, small basalt pebbles, abundant sherds.
VIII	5YR 4/3 Reddish brown clay, average thickness 1.5 m, subangular blocky, charcoal flecking frequent with larger samples present, small saprolite clasts and some slight mixing with basal saprolite at boundary, many sherds though frequency decreases with depth, a few bauxite pebbles.
IX	C Horizon, Saprolite.

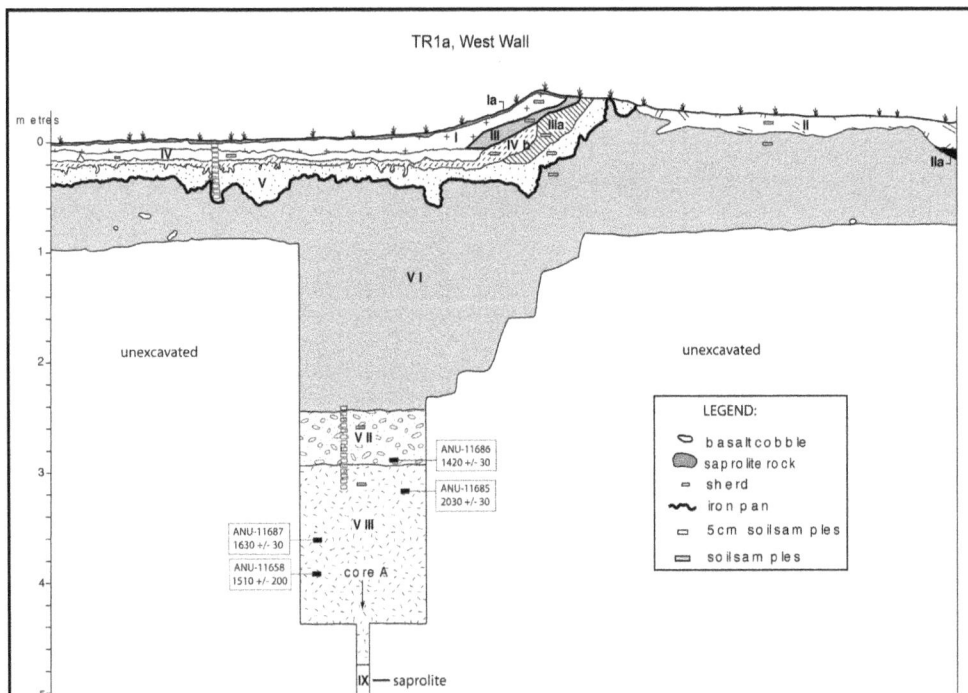

Figure 7. Main stratigraphic diagram for the crown and west depression of Ngemeduu.

Table 2. Illustrates the pollen percentages and charcoal concentrations (top), and phytolith and charcoal abundance (bottom) for Ngemeduu (B:NA-4:11).

Microfossil	TR1/LI	TR1/LII	TR1/LIV	TR1/LIVb	TR1/LV	TR1a/LVII	TR1a/LVIII	TR1i/LIII	TR1i/LIV
Pollen identified:									
Pandanus sp.	23.8	17.0	27.5	26.2	37.4	0.0	2.1	10.4	0.0
Trilete spores	12.6	7.5	17.4	35.4	33.0	15.3	31.9	8.3	3.3
Monolete spores	3.8	35.8	3.6	1.2	18.7	81.4	48.9	43.8	94.4
Poaceae	46.4	5.7	38.1	17.7	3.3	0.0	2.1	10.4	2.2
Polypodiaceae	2.5	22.6	0.4	1.2	1.1	0.0	1.1	2.1	0.0
Asteraceae	1.3	0.0	1.6	11.6	1.1	0.0	2.1	2.1	0.0
Macaranga sp.	0.4	0.0	0.8	0.0	2.2	0.0	0.0	0.0	0.0
Casuarina	1.3	0.0	0.0	0.0	0.0	0.0	1.1	0.0	0.0
Polygonum	2.1	0.0	0.0	4.3	0.0	0.0	0.0	8.3	0.0
Total pollen sum #	239.0	53.0	247.0	164.0	91.0	59.0	94.0	48.0	90.0
Charcoal concentrations on pollen slides ##	12.03	0.30	2.89	4.8	1.51	0.63	10.30	0.41	3.32
Phytoliths identified:									
Andaintaceae			X						
Arecaceae			X		X				
Areistolachaeae			X						
Compositae			X						
Cyperaceae			X						
Liliaceae			X						
Magnoliaceae									
Marantaceae		X							
Moraceae			X						
Musaceae		X							
Pandanaceae					X				
Poaceae		X	X	X					
Urticaeae			X						
Diatoms									
Starch		X							
Charcoal on phytolith slides ###		**	*	*	*	*	***		
Charred Phytoliths		X	X	X	X				

includes sum of all pollen and spores counted in sample.

point count method.

abundance of charcoal to phytolith counts.

Shaded=not analysed.

X=present.

*=relative abundance scale.

Table 3. Stratigraphic descriptions for Trench 1i, Ngemeduu.

Ngemeduu (B:NA-4:11) Trench 1i (TR1i)

Layer	Description
I	7.5YR 4/4 Brown clay, A horizon, average thickness 5 cm, many roots of all sizes, firm, humic layer.
II	5YR 4/4 Reddish brown silty clay, average thickness 40 cm, friable, some > 1 mm sized charcoal samples, many roots all sizes, saprolite clasts mixed throughout, same erosional layer as TR1h.
IV	5YR 4/4 Reddish brown clay with some pink saprolite flecking, average thickness 50 cm, compact, subangular blocky, roots of small sizes, many small saprolite clasts and 2-5 cm sized saprolite rocks, some sherds and charcoal flecks, many manganese nodules, leveling layer.
IVa	7.5YR 4/4 Brown clay mixed with saprolite breccia, average thickness 6 cm, likely formation of B horizon in progress.
V	C Horizon, Saprolite.

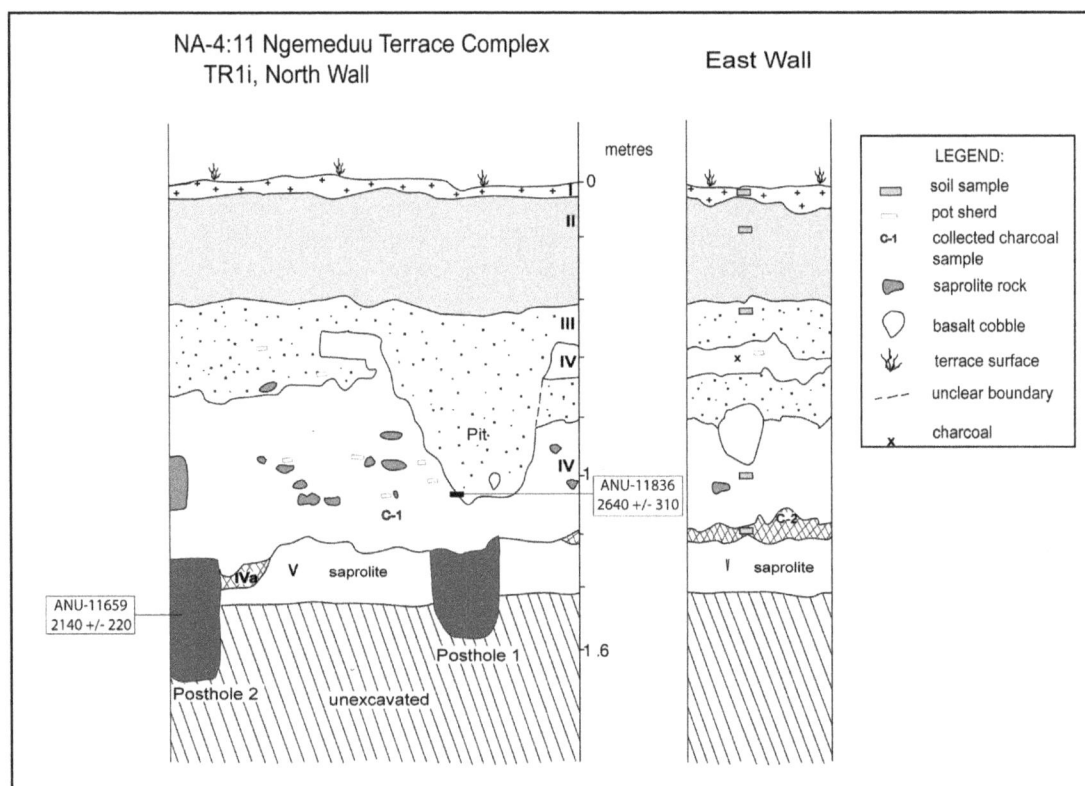

Figure 8. Main stratigraphic diagram for Trench 1i.

Results: B:NA-4:12 Toi Meduu Crown and Terrace Complex

Northwest terrace

Soil samples from LIII and LII were analysed (Figure 9, Table 4, Table 5). Both the layers are fills, forming the terrace surface at differing stages. A similar pattern to the terrace at Ngemeduu is observed, with LIII (forming the initial terrace) exhibiting a higher percentage of ferns/fern allies, and LII higher in *Pandanus* sp. and Poaceae percentages, the classic savanna taxa. However, the reverse picture is seen in the pollen sum and charcoal concentrations, with LII exhibiting higher levels of both charcoal and pollen compared with LIII. No phytoliths were recorded from LIII. The charcoal count for the phytolith analysis is exceptionally low, although a *Synedra ulna* fresh-water diatom was identified. Diatoms are microscopic forms of aquatic and sub-aquatic algae, inhabiting wetlands, lakes, estuaries and oceans. When they are present in archaeological contexts, they indicate water sources in the vicinity. *Synedra ulna*, an epilithic and pennate diatom, grows best in the presence of nitrates, and prefers to live in habitats with a pH above 7 (an alkalibionte form). They are most commonly found in puddles or pooled water in variable locations. The implications of diatoms in these samples is examined below.

Back-sloping terrace

The pollen record for Layer III of TR3 (Table 5), the main layer identified, reflects the dominance of the ferns/fern allies, with virtually no grasses represented and only a small percentage of *Pandanus* sp. pollen. The total pollen count is low, and the pollen charcoal levels moderate. In contrast, no charred material was observed in the phytolith sample, nor identifiable phytoliths. Three *Synedra ulna* fresh-water diatoms were also recorded in this terrace.

West ditch

The two main secondary fill layers (LVI and LVII) were tested for pollen (Figure 10, Table 5, Table 6). Both layers have low overall pollen counts. The ferns/fern allies dominate each layer, and there is a clear absence of grasses and an extremely low percentage of *Pandanus* sp. pollen. Charcoal counts are also minimal, with a slightly higher count recorded for LVII than LVI. This charcoal pattern is replicated in the phytolith charcoal abundance levels.

Table 4. Stratigraphic descriptions for Trench 2, Toi Meduu.

Toi Meduu (B:NA-4:12) Trench 2 (TR2)	
Layer	**Description**
I	5YR 4/3 Reddish brown silty loam, organic A horizon, average thickness 5 cm, clear lower boundary, smooth, moderate subangular blocky medium sized peds, some charcoal flecking, friable, many roots, all diameters.
II	5YR 4/4 Reddish brown clay, average thickness 5 cm, clear lower boundary, smooth, medium blocky peds, common roots, fine to medium sized, loose, two sherds.
III	5YR 5/6 Yellowish red clay with some pink, white and yellow mottling (saprolite), average thickness 40 cm, clear smooth boundary, weak subangular-blocky medium sized peds, some charcoal flecks, common fine roots, firm .
IV	C Horizon, Saprolite.

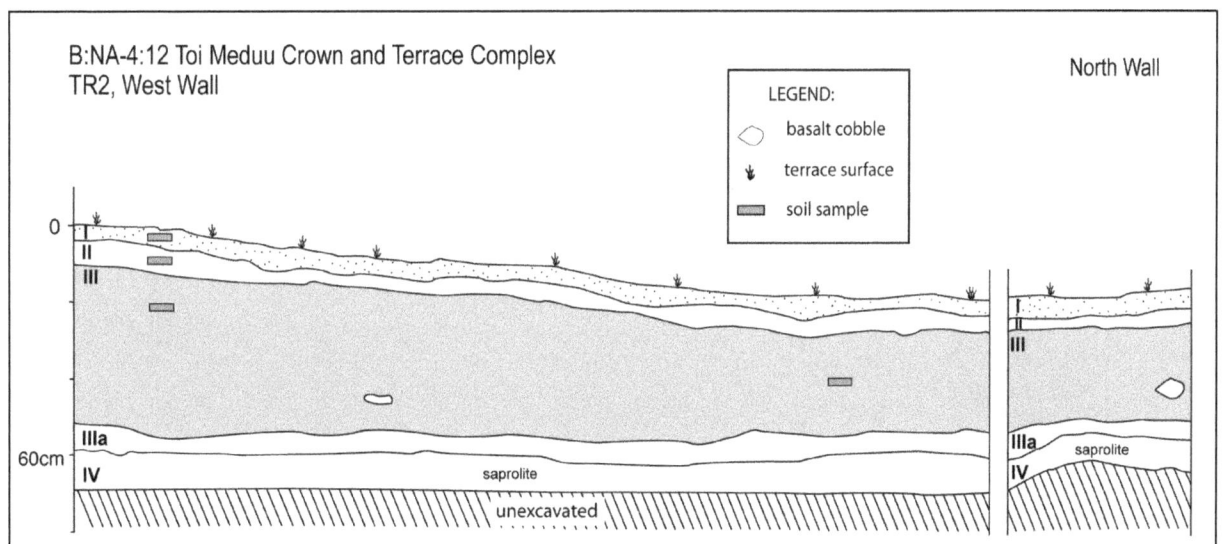

Figure 9. Stratigraphic diagram for Trench 2.

Table 5. Illustrates the pollen percentages and charcoal concentrations (top), and phytolith and charcoal abundance (bottom) for Toi Meduu (B:NA-4:12).

Microfossil	TR2/LII	TR2/LIII	TR3/LIII	TR5/LVI	TR5/LVII
Pollen identified:					
Pandanus sp.	51.5	17.5	6.2	0.0	1.8
Trilete spores	11.8	52.5	13.2	10.9	8.9
Monolete spores	5.1	6.3	66.0	81.8	89.3
Poaceae	14.7	5.0	0.7	0.0	0.0
Polypodiaceae	0.0	0.0	0.0	3.6	0.0
Asteraceae	0.0	0.0	0.0	0.0	0.0
Macaranga sp.	1.5	0.0	0.0	1.8	0.0
Casuarina	0.0	0.0	0.0	0.0	0.0
Polygonum	7.4	15.0	12.5	1.8	0.0
Total pollen Sum#	136.0	80.0	144.0	55.0	56.0
Charcoal concentrations on pollen slides ##	6.46	1.48	3.55	0.60	1.32
Phytoliths identified:					
Andaintaceae					
Arecaceae					
Areistolachaeae					
Compositae					
Cyperaceae					
Liliaceae					
Magnoliaceae					
Marantaceae					
Moraceae					
Musaceae					
Pandanaceae					
Poaceae					
Urticaeae					
Diatoms		X	X		
Starch				*	**
Charcoal on phytolith slides ###		*			
Charred Phytoliths					

includes sum of all pollen and spores counted in sample.
point count method.
abundance of charcoal to phytolith counts.
Shaded=not analysed.
X=present.
*=relative abundance scale.

Table 6. Stratigraphic descriptions for Trench 5, Toi Meduu.

Toi Meduu (B:NA-4:11) Trench 5 (TR5)

Layer	Description
I	10YR 3/2 Very dark greyish brown silty loam, organic A horizon, average thickness 8 cm, clear lower boundary, friable, many tiny rootlets.
II	10YR 4/2 Dark greyish brown silty loam, average thickness 20 cm, friable, many rootlets, flecked throughout with red, orange black and white saprolite specks.
IIa	7.5YR 3/4 Dark brown silty clay, average thickness 15 cm, east and west boundary clear, most likely a lense caused by water concentration.
III	7.5YR 4/4 Brown silty clay, average thickness 40 cm, firm subangular blocky, a few less than 1mm roots, sparse charcoal, a few small to medium cobbles, abundant saprolite flecks with a loamy texture.
IIIa	7.5YR 4/6 Strong brown clay, average thickness 21 cm, very similar to LIII with less saprolite flecks and a darker colour, some less than 1 mm roots, similar formation as Layer IIa.
IV	7.5YR 4/4 Brown silty clay, average thickness 50 cm, similar to Layer III, but with more cobbles and charcoal flecks, some sherds also, less than 1mm roots, some saprolite flecks and loamy texture.
V	7.5YR 4/6 Strong brown silty clay, average thickness 25 cm, firm, less saprolite flecking and a higher clay content, faintly mottled with orange/yellowish matrix indicative of B horizon formation, scattered subangular medium sized cobbles, scattered sherds, less than 1 mm roots, occasional charcoal chunks.
VI	7.5YR 4/6 and 5/6 Strong brown silty clay, average thickness 20 cm, heavily mottled with the orange/yellow clay indicative of B horizon formation, very sparse tiny rootlets, one large cobble.
VII	7.5YR 4/4 Brown silty clay, average thickness 20 cm, firm, occasional 2-3 cm saprolite clasts, scattered sherds and charcoal, occasional medium cobbles.
VIII	10YR 3/4 Dark yellowish brown with heavy black and yellow mottles, clay, dominated by saprolite mottling.
IX	7.5YR 4/4 and 5/6 Brown and strong brown mixed silty clay, very moist.
X	C Horizon, Saprolite.

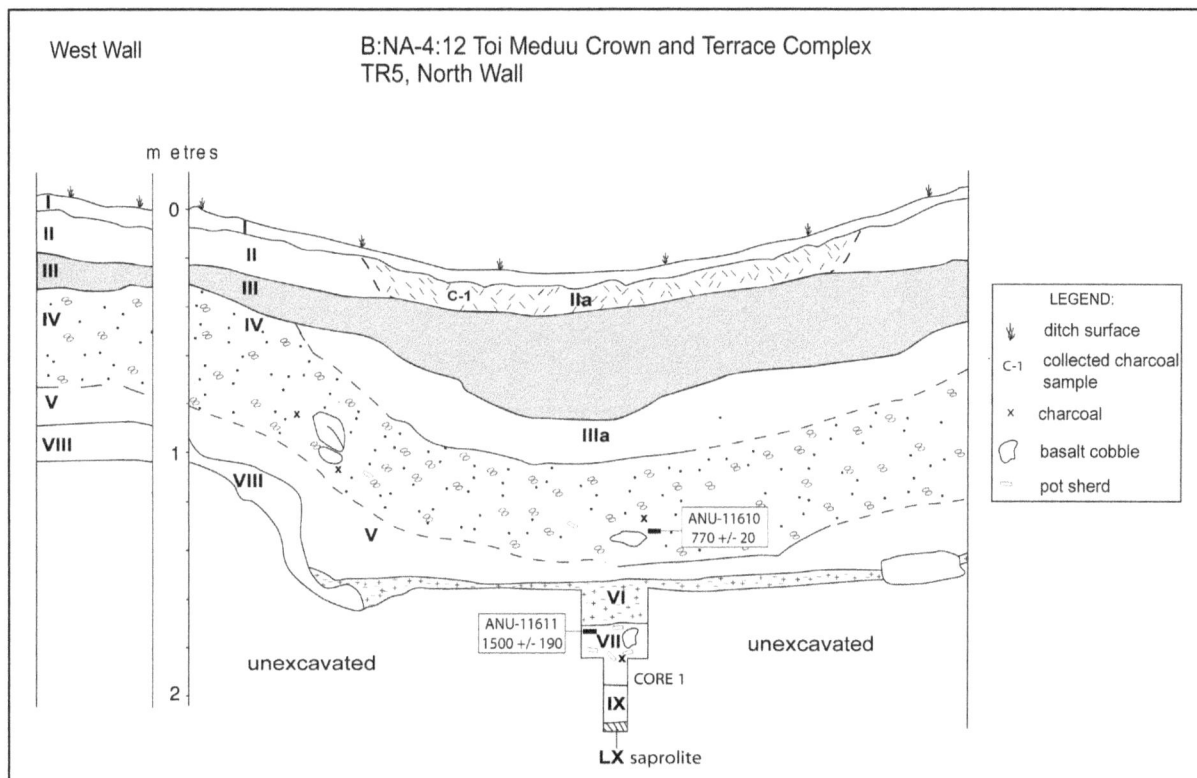

Figure 10. Stratigraphic diagram for Trench 5.

Table 7. Illustrates the pollen percentages and charcoal concentrations (top), and phytolith and charcoal abundance (bottom) for Rois (B:NA-4:6).

Microfossil	TR4/LI	TR4/LII	TR4/LIII	TR4/LIIIa	TR4/LIV	TR4/LV	TR4/LVI
Pollen identified:							
Pandanus sp.	15.2	11.5	13.9	7.1	8.8	4.9	13.6
Trilete spores	35.4	38.9	47.4	38.7	40.4	12.3	16.9
Monolete spores	8.3	11.8	10.2	35.7	42.1	67.9	50.8
Poaceae	32.3	18.2	13.9	8.3	7.0	6.2	13.6
Polypodiaceae	0.2	0.3	0.0	0.0	0.0	0.0	0.8
Asteraceae	0.0	0.0	0.0	0.0	0.0	0.0	0.0
Macaranga sp.	0.8	0.0	0.0	0.0	0.0	0.0	0.0
Casuarina	0.0	0.0	0.0	0.6	0.0	0.0	0.8
Polygonum	6.3	16.9	12.4	168.0	0.0	6.2	0.0
Total pollen Sum #	480.0	296.0	137.0	4.08	57.0	81.0	118.0
Charcoal concentrations on pollen slides ##	13.02	6.74	3.87	7.1	1.05	4.72	1.49
Phytoliths identified:							
Andaintaceae							
Arecaceae							
Areistolachaeae							
Compositae							
Cyperaceae							
Liliaceae							
Magnoliaceae			X				
Marantaceae							
Moraceae							
Musaceae							
Pandanaceae							
Poaceae			X				
Urticaeae							
Diatoms							
Starch							
Charcoal on phytolith slides ###			*			*	
Charred Phytoliths			X				

includes sum of all pollen and spores counted in sample.
point count method.
abundance of charcoal to phytolith counts.
Shaded=not analysed.
X=present.
*=relative abundance scale.

Results: B:NA-4:6 Rois Terrace Complex

Lower terrace

The savanna vegetation pattern is also apparent in the Rois pollen record (Figure 11, Table 7, Table 8). Of note is the classic savanna growth seen in LVI (a 'B' horizon remnant), which changes to a more disturbed savanna in LV. Layers IV and IIIa border on grassy-to-fern, and the classic indicators return in LIII to LI with a higher percentage of Poaceae and *Pandanus* sp. pollen. The phytolith record accounts for grasses for LIII and one tree phytolith, although

Table 8. Stratigraphic descriptions for Trench 4, Rois.

Rois Terrace Complex (B:NA-4:6) Trench 4 (TR4)	
Layer	**Description**
I	7.5YR 4/4 Brown clay, average thickness 6 cm, clear lower boundary, wavy, angular blocky, many roots, all sizes.
II	5YR 4/4 Reddish brown silty clay, average thickness 7 cm, clear smooth boundary, weak subangular blocky, quite friable, many roots, medium to coarse, some charcoal flecking.
III	5YR 5/6 Yellowish red silty clay, average thickness 10 cm, clear wavy boundary, weak subangular blocky, common fine roots, firm, a few sherds.
IIIa	5YR 5/4 Reddish brown with white and pink saprolite mottled silty clay, average thickness 12 cm, wavy boundary, weak subangular blocky, firm, few fine roots, a few sherds.
IV	Pink and yellow flecked saprolite dominates with a little 5YR 5/4 Reddish brown clay, average thickness 14 cm, abrupt lower boundary, a few roots. The saprolite is denser at northern end of the trench and less dense at southern end.
V	5YR 4/4 Reddish brown silty clay, average thickness 40 cm, clear smooth boundary, weak subangular blocky, firm, very few fine roots, many sherds, concentrated at southern end of trench.
VI	5YR 5/6 Yellowish red silty clay, average thickness 12 cm, broken boundary, angular blocky, no roots or charcoal, some sherds, firm.
VII	7.4YR 5/4 Brown silty clay, average thickness 14 cm, clear smooth boundary, subangular blocky, some micro roots, firm, no charcoal or pottery.
VIII	C Horizon, Saprolite.

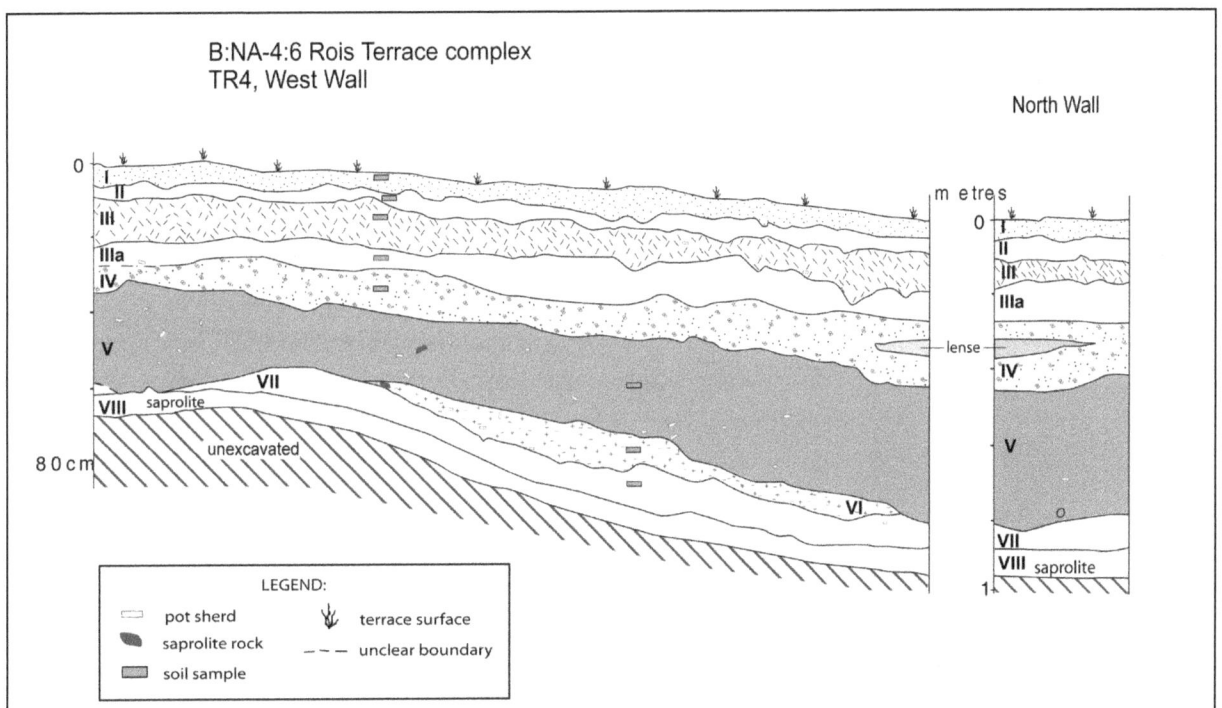

Figure 11. Stratigraphic diagram for Rois.

LV was phytolith-deficient. In general, charcoal counts on the pollen slides oscillate, with the highest concentrations present in the upper three layers, in parallel with the total pollen sums. Phytolith charcoal was minimal, although a charred phytolith observed in LIII may indicate fire activity on site.

Vegetation pattern

A detailed discussion of taphonomic and preservation factors can be found elsewhere (Phear 2007:99–100). In general, all samples were phytolith-deficient, and this may be due to factors both cultural and physical. The low number may be due to soil taphonomy (e.g. weathering), or possibly a direct result of vegetation dominated by fern/fern allies, which is not conducive to the growth of phytolith-producing plants (Phear 2007:100). Alternatively, it might be due to the fact that insufficient time elapsed between terrace layer depositions for plant growth to re-establish. Further analysis of this kind is required to fully understand the taphonomic and preservation factors for pollen and phytoliths in the Palauan landscape.

That said, the results are generally indicative of an anthropogenically disturbed landscape during the initial stages of earthwork construction, characterised by a ferns/fern allies-dominated savanna. Once the earthworks were completed/near completion, stable classic grassland was established in both the local environment and on the sites themselves, as none of the plants (from which the pollen and phytoliths derived) contributes significantly to regional pollen rain. Thus, they are likely to have been growing in the immediate vicinity (within 50 m) or on each site (Simon Haberle pers comm.). Only Rois displayed a differing pattern, whereby classic savanna was evident in the locale before construction of the lower terrace tested in this project.

With Ngemeduu, the lowest crown layers were formed through initial hilltop earthmoving activities, sometime after 1420±30 BP (ANU-11686, (1350(1310)1290 cal. BP), and there is evidence for cultural activities on the hilltop before construction at 2140±220 BP (ANU-11659, 2740(2140, 2140, 2120)1570 cal. BP). Here we see a disturbed savanna vegetation pattern. High levels of charcoal in LVIII (both pollen and phytolith) suggest land-clearance activities consistent with the initial earthmoving activities. By the time LV was deposited, the landscape had changed to classic savanna. While there is evidence in LIVb for fire activities on site, this may indicate localised burning events. The same pattern is observed in the encircling terrace, whereby the charcoal concentrations coincide with pollen indicative of disturbance, and therefore vegetation clearance through burning appears to have played a role in early terrace formation.

High fractions of Poaceae and *Pandanus* in the upper layers of the crown indicate a more stable grassland environment, and the phytolith results also support this result, with classic savanna indicators, and also others (e.g. Liliaceae – *Cordyline* sp., usually grown in coastal plains and around gardens). The Compostiteae may be related to plant growth incorporated with mulching materials. However, it is obvious that no root-crop phytoliths (nor pollen) were present in the samples. Furthermore, as only one phytolith per 'possible' food plant was noted, any conclusion focused on subsistence activities would be rather nebulous at this stage.

Toi Meduu is the older site, with a radiocarbon determination of 1500±190 BP (ANU-11611, 1820(1390, 1360, 1350)990 cal. BP), documenting cultural activity on the west crown which has eroded into the ditch. The vegetation pattern is similar to Ngemeduu, although the charcoal concentrations are remarkably low, except for two layers in the terrace. Both the terraces reflect a dominance of ferns/fern allies in their most disturbed layers, and the charcoal counts indicate regional fire activity. This is also reflected in the Secondary phase layers (LVI and LVII) in the ditch. A unique component of the Toi Meduu record are the diatoms. The immediate explanation is that both terraces must have had pooled water at some point in order for *Synedra ulna* to have grown. If so, one would have expected diatoms to have been found in the depression profiles of Ngemeduu, and they were not. Alternatively, the diatoms might have been deposited in the original soil matrix of the terrace layers, or through direct animal defecation. Further investigation of diatoms in archaeological contexts is required to clarify such depositional issues.

In sum, the general consistency in the growth of the fern/fern allies is indicative of a disturbed environment throughout the initial construction of each feature of Toi Meduu. With cultural remains recovered from the immediate landscape before Toi Meduu's construction, dating from 1860 to 2150 BP (Welch 2001), it appears people were living in the immediate vicinity and altering the landscape. Stability is reflected only later in Toi Meduu's history, when the soils had regained some nutrients through organic activities and sedimentation, and human clearance activities decreased and/or stopped.

Rois differs slightly from the ridge-top sites, with two different depositional episodes. There is potential indirect evidence for cultivation activities in LIII to LI. Firstly, the wavy layer boundaries are similar to a pattern associated with cultivation surfaces (see Beardsley 1996). Also, LIIIa appears to have been undergoing pedogenic alteration with LIV, though it also exhibits vegetative components of LIV – the dominance of ferns, and LIII – the higher charcoal concentrations, pollen sums, and Polygonum. As such, a tentative conclusion is that mixing through gardening activities eventually created LIIIa. The 'classic' savanna vegetation pattern that dominates LIII to LI may be a later development, as these layers most likely formed by the wash of sediments through erosional activities. If cultivation did occur, it is still not clear whether it was immediately after terrace construction, or later.

As the upper layers all possess higher pollen sums and higher charcoal counts, it is possible this is time-related. The implication here is that the age of the soil surfaces (in this context) correlates with pollen preservation (the younger the surface, the higher the amount of pollen (and charcoal) preserved). This certainly appears to be the case when one reviews the pollen sums (Tables 2, 5, 7) in the uppermost layers at the three sites tested in this project. Therefore, it is proposed that the upper layers of the TR4 were deposited in the late traditional or historic periods. Whether the possible 'cultivation' activity is from the later period or earlier is still uncertain.

The lower layers of the Rois terrace are certainly the result of older terrace-forming and cultural activities. The results imply that the landscape before deposition of the fill layer (LV) was quite stable, with 'classic' savanna vegetation reflected in LVI, supported by a low concentration of charcoal. A transformation occurred once LV was placed to form the terrace, as ferns and allies overshadow the record, and the charcoal concentration increases. This disturbed vegetation pattern continues into LIV.

As no samples were recovered for radiocarbon dating, a 'top-down' construction sequence is posited, whereby the lowest terraces were constructed after the upper terraces. With burials on the top terraces dated to c. 2000 BP (Liston 1999), and assuming the burials were placed in the top terrace not long after it was built, it appears the Rois terraces are potentially older than both Toi Meduu and Ngemeduu.

All told, the vegetation pattern at all three sites reflects a transformed 'physical' landscape through earth-building activities, but also through the record of both disturbed and classic savanna grasslands, supported by charcoal concentrations. It is clear that primary forest and/or forest re-growth was not part of the ridgeline landscape immediately before or after the earthworks had been formed. An absence of root-crop taxa also questions the agricultural argument posited to explain earthwork construction.

The pre-earthwork ridgeline vegetation: A 'humanised landscape'?

In arguments concerning the impact of humans on island ecosystems, we are seeing a focus now on the 'humanisation of forests' and indeed a consideration of the intense humanisation of many Pacific Island landscapes as a whole. The results of the vegetation analyses in this project, in combination with the palaeoenvironmental investigation by Athens and Ward (1999), allow investigation of just how 'humanised' the ridgeline vegetative landscape was before earthwork construction.

In their analysis of the Ngerchau core (which was located at the rear of Ulimang Village at the base of the ridgeline sampled here), Athens and Ward (2001:169–170) identified three 'pollen zones'. It is in the earliest – Zone A – that they point to the first evidence of landscape disturbance (and in their interpretation, human settlement) based on 'significant numerical changes' in disturbance pollen indicators (grass pollen, *Pandanus* pollen, fern spores) and charcoal concentrations in the core record. This activity is dated to 4291 cal. BP (Athens and Ward 2001:171). However, it is not until later, at 2750–2650 cal. BP, that we see the most consistent (and convincing) evidence for land-clearance activities. In Zone C, *Pandanus*, sedge and grass pollen peak, consistent with a very high concentration in charcoal particles. The Athens and Ward argument suggests methods of agroforestry, with 'landscape [forest] clearance, transformation to savanna formation and fire maintenance for vegetation control' (Athens and Ward 2001:170).

Wickler (2002:69–70) discusses the agricultural argument (Athens and Ward 1999), in which the first sign of disturbance indicators is proposed to mark swidden agriculture activities (i.e. burning). The decline in indicators from 3000 to 2700 cal. BP is seen to represent a shift from extensive to intensive agriculture, the intensification seen through terrace construction. The later 'surge' in indicators (2750–2650 cal. BP) is speculated to represent general expansion of agriculture spurred by population growth. So how does this compare to the archaeological remains here?

Firstly, the earliest dates for earthwork construction in the ridgeline are from Rois, at c. 2000 BP. Thus, there is no evidence at this point to suggest earthwork construction around 3000 BP, as proposed by IARII. However, there is evidence in the Uplands for occupation from 2500 BP (Liston 1999; Liston and Tuggle 2001), and structural remains were identified during excavation of Ngemeduu dating to c. 2200 BP (Phear 2007). Therefore, the savanna transformation argued by Athens and Ward from 2750–2650 cal. BP has some consistency with cultural activities in the Uplands, and may mark initial movement of people into this topographic zone. The claim that population pressure drove an 'expansion' of agriculture must remain conjectural at this stage, as there is an absence of supporting archaeological evidence. It certainly seems people were using fire to burn vegetation at this time, and it seems a reasonable proposition that they were doing this to clear the land. But why were they clearing the land?

Vegetation clearance in Pacific Island landscapes is generally argued to represent swidden agriculture, or what Zan and Hunter-Anderson (1987:19) call the 'hortigenetic hypothesis'. However, the creation of savanna grasslands is also related to other purposes, such as the creation of paths for movement through the landscape (Zan and Hunter-Anderson 1987), and the clearance of forest to create settlement locales, which are not related to agricultural pursuits. Furthermore, in this study, non-economic motivations are apparent for Upland settlement through interpretations of the cultural remains recovered (Phear 2007), and, as previously stated, no evidence for agricultural crops was recovered in this project. Thus, I argue here that there is no clear correlation between land clearance and cultivation activities in the ridgeline.

While the vegetation pattern from Rois intimates stable 'classic' savanna before terrace construction, the hilltop sites of Ngemeduu and Toi Meduu reflect a more disturbed grassland environment. My interpretation is that the vegetation in the ridge-top sites was less stable than in the Rois terraces, because the latter vegetation pattern is older. Whether the savanna was created by much earlier clearance activities, or was a natural component of the landscape, is still a matter of debate. Although Zan and Hunter-Anderson (1987) have argued for the presence of 'natural' savannas in Micronesia, recent palaeoenvironmental investigations in Guam provide evidence to the contrary. Athens and Ward declare '[t]he finding that humans are responsible for the creation of the savannas that presently extend over broad areas of the interior uplands of southern Guam appears indisputable', therefore dismissing any claims for 'natural' savanna growth. However, further work addressing the Palauan palaeoenvironment is required before the possibility of naturally occurring savannas is dismissed. For Toi Meduu and Ngemeduu, at least, it appears the landscape was cleared during, or just before, upland occupation, and thus the savanna here is anthropogenically created.

To conclude, this small project endeavoured to assess evidence for agriculture in the earthworks, and to look for direct and indirect evidence of landscape vegetative transformations. The excavation and analytical analyses have shown firstly that there is no evidence to suggest the earthworks were constructed for agricultural production. While there is some evidence of cultivation on the Rois terrace, this may have taken place long after the terrace was completed. There are problems concerning the survival of certain types of pollen and phytoliths (that would clearly indicate cultivation) in the archaeological record, and these problems have been discussed elsewhere. While such issues in preservation are acknowledged, when the evidence and results (environmental and archaeological) for this project are considered together, an argument for terrace construction within an intensified agricultural system is not supported. The results expounded here are but one facet of an investigation into the monumental earthworks of Ngaraard. When considered in concert with additional analytical evidence derived from clay and pottery analyses, along with previous earthwork studies, a detailed picture of landscape transformation is formed, one that does not support a subsistence-based argument for monumental earthwork construction (see Phear 2007). The results of this study are by no means exhaustive, and further investigations of earthworks are necessary throughout Babeldaob, looking at pollen and phytolith remains, to form a more detailed picture of landscape transformation for this volcanic island.

Acknowledgements

The earthwork project was undertaken as PhD research, with Atholl Anderson as my supervisor. It developed out of the Palau 2000 Project where I first saw the earthworks, and to which Atholl provided support for my initial project plan. I am forever grateful for Atholl's support and wisdom, and his sense of humour in the field and office, which made the PhD process more bearable! The project would not have happened without funding from the Department of Archaeology and Natural History, ANU, along with funding from the Centre for Archaeological Research, ANU. I am grateful to Vicki Kanai (Director, Bureau of Arts and Culture) and Rita Olsudong (Head of Archaeology, Ministry of Community and Cultural Affairs) for approving my project, and providing me access to the BAC GIS database. I also thank the Governor of Ngaraard for his willingness for my project to go ahead. I thank the field team in Ngaraard: Meked, Jenny, Mathius, Rocky and John, and also Vince Blaiyok for his guidance. I express thanks to IARII, which helped the project come to fruition, particularly Jolie Liston for her endless support and discussions concerning the terraces. Support and guidance also came from staff and students in the Department of Archaeology and Natural History, ANU, to whom I am grateful. I also thank Geoff Hope, Mike Macphail, Simon Haberle and Janelle Stevenson for their help and discussions concerning the analytical methods used in this project as well as vegetation interpretations, and also Domique O'Dea and Gillian Atkin for sample processing, and Jeff Parr for the phytolith analysis. My thanks also go to Paul Rainbird and Hal Dalwood for commenting on an earlier draft.

References

Anderson, A., J. Chappell, G. Clark and S. Phear 2005. Comparative radiocarbon dating of lignite, pottery and charcoal samples from Babeldaob Island, Republic of Palau. *Radiocarbon* 47:1–9.

Athens, J.S. and J.V. Ward 1999. Archaeological Data Recovery for the Compact Road, Babeldaob Island, Republic of Palau: Historic Preservation Investigations Phase II, Volume IV: The Holocene Palaeoenvironment of Palau. International Archaeological Research Institute Inc. (Draft).

Athens, J.S. and J.V. Ward. 2001. Palaeoenvironmental evidence for early human settlement in Palau: The Ngerchau core. In C.M. Stevenson, G. Lee, and F.J. Morin (eds), *Pacific 2000. Proceedings of the Fifth International Conference on Easter Island and the Pacific*, pp. 164–177. Los Osos: Bearsville Press.

Athens, J.S. and J.V. Ward 2004. Holocene vegetation, savanna origins and human settlement of Guam. *Records of the Australian Museum, Supplement* 29:15–30.

Bryant, V.M.J. and J.P. Dering 1996. *A guide to paleoethnobotany.* Texas: Texas A and M University.

Cheyne, A. 1864. *Log of the Acis.* Held by Sir Joseph Cheyne, Rome.

Clark, R.L. 1982. Point Count Estimation of Charcoal in Pollen Preparations and Thin Sections of Sediments. *Pollen et Spores* 24:523–535.

Clark, G. 2005. A 3000-Year Cultural Sequence from Palau, Western Micronesia. *Asian Perspectives* 44(2):349–380.

Clarke, W.C. and R.R. Thaman (eds) 1993. *Agroforestry in the Pacific Islands: Systems for Sustainability.* Tokyo: The United Nations University Press.

Corwin, C.G., C.L. Rogers and P.O. Elmquist. 1956. *Military Geology of the Palau Islands.* Intelligence Division, Office of the Engineer, Headquarters US Army Far East.

Easton, W.H. and T.L. Ku. 1980. Holocene sea level changes in Palau, west Caroline Islands. *Quaternary Research* 14:199–209.

Fitzpatrick, S.M., W.R. Dickinson and G. Clark. 2003. Ceramic petrography and cultural interaction in Palau, Micronesia. *Journal of Archaeological Science* 30:1175–1184.

Green, R. 1991. Near and Remote Oceania: disestablishing 'Melanesia' in culture history. In J. Davidson, G. Irwin, B.F. Leach, A. Pawley and D. Brown (eds), *Oceanic Culture History Essays in Honour of Roger C. Green,* pp. 491–502. *New Zealand Journal of Archaeology Special Publication.* Dunedin: New Zealand Journal of Archaeology.

Haberle, S.G. 1995. Identification of cultivated *Pandanus* and *Colocasia* pollen records and the implications for the study of early agriculture in New Guinea. *Vegetation History and Archaeobotany* 4:195–210.

Henry, J.D., A.E. Haun and M.A. Kirkendall 1996. Archaeological mitigation program: Palau Rural Water System Projects in Chol and Ngkeklau Villages. Paul H. Rosendahl, PhD., Inc.

Horrocks, M., M.D. Jones, J.A. Carter and D.G. Sutton 2000. Pollen and phytoliths in stone mounds at Pouerua, Northland, New Zealand: implications for the study of Polynesian farming. *Antiquity* 74:863–872.

Kayanne, H., H. Yamano and R.H. Randall 2002. Holocene Sea-level Changes and Barrier Reef Formation on an Oceanic Island, Palau Islands, Western Pacific. *Sedimentary Geology* 150:47–60.

Kealhofer, L. and D.R. Piperno 1998. Opal Phytoliths in Southeast Asian Flora. *Smithsonian Contributions to Botany* 88:1–39.

Kennedy, J. and B. Clarke 2004. Cultivated Landscape of the Southwest Pacific. *Resource Management in Asia-Pacific Working Paper* 50:1–47.

Krämer, A. 1917. Palau I. In G. Thilenius (ed), *Ergebnisse der Südsee-Expedition 1908-10. II B III*. Hamburg: Friederichsen and Co.

Liston, J. 1999. Archaeological Data Recovery for the Compact Road, Babeldaob Island, Republic of Palau: Historic Preservation Investigations Phase II, Volume V: Lab Analyses, Synthesis, and Recommendations. International Archaeological Research Institute Inc., Draft.

Liston, J and D. Tuggle 2001. Warfare in Palau. Paper presented to the Society for American Archaeology 2001 Annual Meeting: The Archaeology of Pre-State and Early State Warfare, New Orleans, Louisiana.

Lucking, L.J. 1984. An Archaeological investigation of prehistoric Palauan terraces. Unpublished PhD thesis, University of Minnesota.

Masse, W.B., D. Snyder and G. Gumerman 1984. Prehistoric and historic settlement in the Palau Islands, Micronesia. *New Zealand Journal of Archaeology* 6:107–127.

Masse, W.B. and D. Snyder 1982. The Final Report of the 1981 Field Season of the Southern Illinois University Palau Archaeological Project. Historic Preservation Office On file.

Merlin, M. and T. Keene 1990. *Dellomel er a Belau: Plants of the Palauan Islands*. Honolulu: Environment and Policy Institute, East-West Center.

Morrison, K.D. 1994. The intensification of production: Archaeological approaches. *Journal of Archaeological Method and Theory* 1:111–159.

Mueller-Dombois, D. and F.R. Fosberg 1998. *Vegetation of the tropical Pacific Islands*. Ecological Studies: Analysis and Synthesis 132. New York: Springer-Verlag.

Olsudong, R., C.T. Emesiochel and R.T. Kloulechad 2000. *Inventory of Cultural and Historical Site and Oral History in Ngaraard State. Volume I: Inventory of Cultural Historical Sites*. Division of Cultural Affairs, Historic Preservation Office, Ministry of Community and Cultural Affairs.

Osborne, D. 1966. *The Archaeology of the Palau Islands: An intensive survey*. Honolulu: Bishop Museum Press.

Osborne, D. 1979. Archaeological test excavations. Palau Islands 1968–69. *Micronesica Supplement, 1*.

Parmentier, R.J. 1987. *The Sacred Remains: Myth, history and polity in Belau*. Chicago: University of Chicago Press.

Pearsall, D.M. 1990. Application of phytolith analysis to reconstruction of past environments and subsistence: Recent research in the Pacific. *Micronesica Supplement* 1:65–74.

Pearsall, D.M. and M.K. Trimble 1984. Identifying past agricultural activity through soil phytolith analysis: A case study from the Hawaiian Islands. *Journal of Archaeological Science* 11:119–133.

Phear, S., G. Clark and A. Anderson 2003. A 14C Chronology for Palau. In C. Sand (eds), *Pacific Archaeology: Assessments and Prospects. Proceedings of the International Conference for the 50th Anniversary of the first Lapita Excavation, Koné-Nouméa*, pp. 255–263. Les Cahiers de l'Archeologie en Nouvelle-Caledonie 15, Noumea: Museum of New Caledonia.

Phear, S. 2007. The Monumental Earthworks of Palau, Micronesia: A landscape perspective. *BAR International Series* 1626.

Parry, J. 1984. Air Photo Interpretation of Fortified Sites: Ring-Ditch Fortifications in Southern Viti Levu, Fiji. *New Zealand Journal of Archaeology* 6:71–93.

Rainbird, P. 1994. Prehistory in the Northwest Tropical Pacific: The Caroline, Mariana, and Marshall Islands. *Journal of World Prehistory* 8:293–349.

Rainbird, P. 2004. *The Archaeology of Micronesia*. Cambridge World Archaeology. Cambridge: Cambridge University Press.

Runge, F. 1996. Leaf phytoliths and silica skeletons from east African plants. CD-Rom Database. Germany, Department of Physical Geography, University of Paderborn.

Snyder, D. and B.M. Butler. 1997. *Palau Archaeology: Archaeology and Historic Preservation in Palau.* Micronesian Resources Study, Anthropology Research Series 2. San Francisco: Micronesian Endowment for Historic Preservation Republic of Palau, U.S. National Park Service.

Stroermer, E.F. and J.P. Smol (eds) 1999. *The Diatoms: Applications for the Environmental and Earth Sciences.* Cambridge: Cambridge University Press.

UNEP/IUCN. 1988. *Coral Reefs of the World. Central and Western Pacific.* UNEP Regional Seas Directories and Bibliographies.

Welch, D.J. 2001. Early Upland Expansion of Palauan Settlement. In C.M. Stevenson, G. Lee, and F. J. Morin (eds), *Pacific 2000. Proceedings of the Fifth International Conference on Easter Island and the Pacific*, pp. 179–184. Los Osos: Bearsville Press.

Werner, D. (ed) 1977. *The Biology of Diatoms.* Oxford: Blackwell Scientific.

Wickler, S. 2001. The colonization of western Micronesia and early settlement of Palau. In C.M. Stevenson, G. Lee, and F. J. Morin (eds), *Pacific 2000. Proceedings of the Fifth International Conference on Easter Island and the Pacific*, pp. 85–196. Los Osos: Bearsville Press.

Zan, Y. and R.L. Hunter-Anderson 1987. On the Origins of the Micronesian 'Savannahs': An Anthropological Perspective. Paper presented to the 3rd International Soil Management Workshop on the Management and Utilization of Acid Soils of Oceania, Belau, 2–6 February.

20

Historical significance of the Southwest Islands of Palau

Michiko Intoh

National Museum of Ethnology, Osaka, Japan

intoh@idc.minpaku.ac.jp

Introduction

Micronesia occupies the northwestern corner of Oceania. Most of the islands are scattered in the northern hemisphere, except for Kiribati. The Southwest Islands of Palau are located at the southwestern corner of Micronesia. The area is adjacent to the islands in Melanesia, Indonesia and the Philippines and forms a significant locale to identify human movements around, and particularly into, Micronesia.

While the Southwest Islands of Palau are relatively isolated compared with other island groups in Micronesia, there are a number of coral islands scattered throughout Micronesia whose inhabitants developed various living strategies to enable them to survive in a resource-limited environment. The most recognised strategy was continuing cultural contacts with other islands to acquire goods and human resources (Intoh 2008). One such example in Micronesia is the sawei exchange system that was developed between Yap and the coral islands in the Central Caroline Islands. Another example is the two large trading networks developed within the archipelago of the Marshall Islands (Alkire 1978).

Reconstructing the way of life of these island groups, particularly the external relations built between coral islands and other islands, should provide new insights to enable us to better understand the adaptation strategies required to survive in a resource-limited environment.

Geography: Linking Micronesia and Island Southeast Asia

The Palau archipelago consists of four island groups, Kayangel Atoll, Babeldaob, Peleliu and Angaur, and the Southwest Islands (Figure 1). The cluster of Babeldaob, Peleliu and Angaur forms the main island group. Sonsorol, the northernmost island of the Southwest Islands, lies about 300 km southwest from Babeldaob.

The Southwest Islands consist of five coral islands and one small islet: Sonsorol and an associated small islet Fana, Pulo Anna, Merir, Tobi and Helen Reef. The southernmost island, Tobi, and Helen Reef are about 550 km away from Babeldaob. The distance from Tobi to

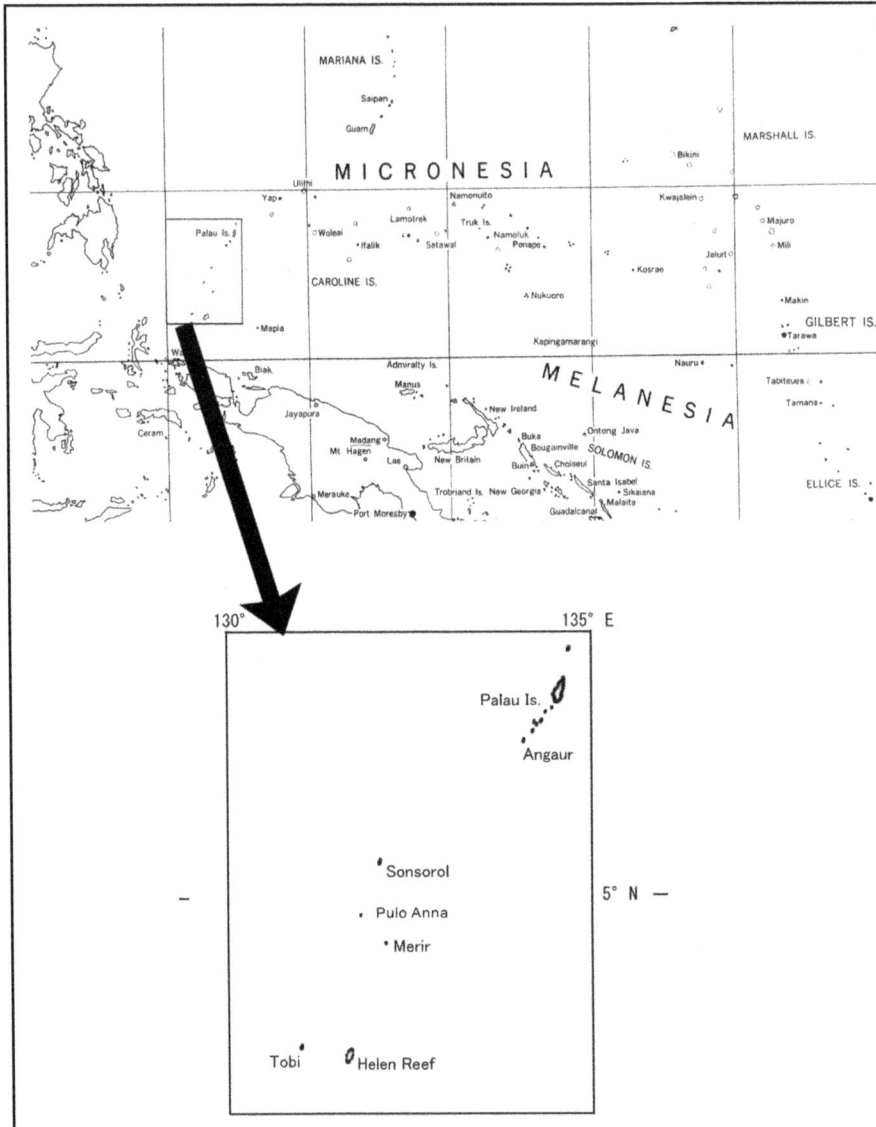

Figure 1. Map of the Southwest Islands of Palau.

Island Southeast Asia or to New Guinea is considerably less. Tobi is only about 280 km away from Morotai or Halmahera in Indonesia and about 370 km from the western coast of New Guinea.

Except for Helen Reef, all the Southwest Islands are raised coral islands and the land height varies from 3 m to 6 m above sea level. The islands are surrounded by narrow reefs and deep ocean. It is not easy to bring a large boat alongside the islands because of the strong currents outside the reef.

Helen Reef is a large atoll, about 25 km long and 10 km wide. Most of the low islets of the atoll are washed by waves at high tide. The total permanent land area is very small, only about 0.03 km². At European contact in the 18th century, this atoll was uninhabited. Three government guards, however, are now sent regularly to the atoll in order to watch out for illegal fishing activities.

The land areas of the inhabited Southwest Islands are small – the largest, Sonsorol, is only 1.36 km², while the smallest, Pulo Anna, is about 0.5 km² (Table 1). Raised coral islands lack mineral resources. The soil is not rich and plants do not grow well. The animal population is generally low and no mammals were present before contact. Such a limited-resource environment

Table 1. Location and land area of Southwestern Islands of Palau (after Engbring 1983).

Islands	Latitude (N)	Longitude (E)	Area (km²)
Sonsoror	5°20'	132°13'	1.36
Pulo Anna	4°40'	131°58'	0.5
Merir	4°19'	132°19'	0.9
Tobi	3°01'	131°11'	0.6
Helen Reef	2°59'	131°49'	0.25

is unlikely to have supported a large population (see Petersen 1999:398–399).

The ocean current around the Southwest Islands is called the Equatorial Countercurrent and flows from the west (near the southern Philippines and Halmahera) throughout the year. This current has to be crossed to navigate to Babeldaob, and it is necessary to navigate against this current when going to Southeast Asia. The navigational environment around the Southwest Islands does not favour navigation to any of the nearby resource-rich islands.

In contrast, it is easy to navigate from the Central Caroline Islands to Yap with the North Equatorial Current that flows from east to west. When a canoe gets lost, it is likely to end up in the Philippines.[1] It is very likely that one such drifted canoe ended up in the Southwest Islands, as described below.

The current delivers various kinds of flotsam to the Southwest Islands from Island Southeast Asia. During a visit to the Southwest Islands in 2002, a number of large bamboo poles were observed adrift on the beaches of some of the islands. There was even a bamboo raft adrift on the coast of Sonsorol, possibly from one of the Indonesian islands. This may indicate the possibility that humans could also have drifted from some of the islands of Southeast Asia to the Southwest Islands of Palau.

In the early 1900s, Kotondo Hasebe made body measurements of six males and two females from Tobi staying on Babeldaob. He pointed out that their physical characteristics, such as short height, long head and wide nose, were more similar to Malays than to other Southwest Islanders or Caroline Islanders (Hasebe 1928) (Figure 2).

Taro (*Cyrtosperma*) was planted in large cultivation pits that were dug down to the freshwater level in the central part of the islands. Banana and breadfruit trees were also cultivated. It is not clear whether any domesticated animals were kept on the islands.[2] As the islands are surrounded by the deep ocean, rich marine resources including migratory fishes are accessible.

History: Isolation and resource management

The Southwest Islands of Palau were recorded relatively early by the Europeans. After Magellan died in the Philippines, Espinosa directed the vessel *Trinidad* from Halmahera towards the Mariana Islands in 1522. Sonsorol was sighted and recorded for the first time on this voyage (Hezel and Valle 1972:26). However, the Palau mainland was not well known until 1710. Missionaries staying in the Philippines around the 17th and 18th centuries had heard about a number of small islands scattered east of the Philippines from Carolinians who had drifted ashore in the Philippines, and so desiring to evangelize them, they collected contributions and made requests to the Pope. Expedition ships were obtained from the Spanish king and were sent out several times to look for the Palau islands, but most of the expeditions failed.

In 1710, one of the three ships, the vessel *Santissima Trinidad* commanded by Francisco Padilla, finally found Sonsorol. Due to the fast current around the island, it took four days

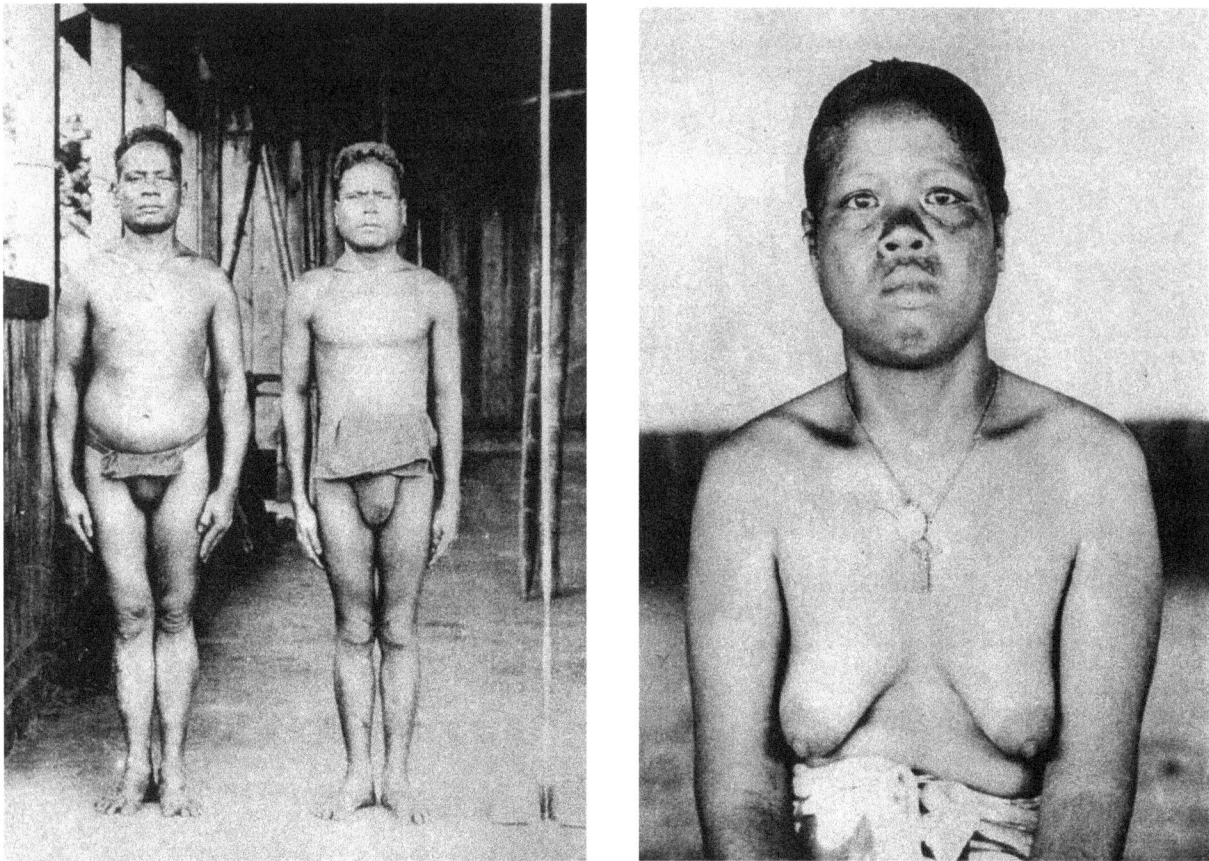

Figure 2. People of the Southwest Islands. Left to right: 2a and 2b, Tobi (after Hasebe 1928); Facing page, left to right: 2c, Merir (after Someki 1945); 2d, Pulo Anna (after Someki 1945).

to approach the reef before two missionaries were able to land. Before the two missionaries returned, the *Trinidad* had drifted away. While trying to go back to Sonsorol, *Trinidad* came upon Babeldaob and made a landing there. This visit demonstrates the speed of the ocean current around Sonsorol. The same difficulty was documented in the Japanese historical records (Hasebe 1928).

There were more records of sighting the other Southwest Islands in the late 18th and early 19th centuries. However, few records were made of daily life on the islands. By the early 19th century, Babeldaob had frequent contacts with European ships and obtained iron and guns which were used for internal warfare.

Palau became well known from the published record of the British ship *Antelope* that ran aground near Koror in 1783. The first direct record of the Southwest Islands was not, however, made until 1836, when Holden published a record of his experiences in Babeldaob and Tobi.

Holden was a seaman of the American whaling ship *Mentor* that ran aground at the western end of the reef surrounding Palau in 1832. Holden and other seamen landed on Babeldaob and built a large boat. They subsequently left for Canton with three Palauans, leaving three seamen behind as hostages. After several days, they were hit by a storm and started drifting. After nine days, they came close to Tobi and were attacked and captured by Tobians. In November 1834, the sole survivors, two Americans, were rescued by an English ship, *Britannia*. One of these two was Holden, who subsequently published an account of his experiences (Holden 1836).

According to Holden's description, the lives of hostages on Tobi were very harsh. All of their clothes and belongings were taken away and they were forced to work for the islanders. They had to dig the ground for taro planting with bare hands without tools. On top of this

harsh work and the violent treatment by the islanders, starvation from not eating proper food resulted in the deaths of most of the hostages. Food was extremely scarce on the island and the islanders, too, were described as starving. There were frequent fights over the insufficient coconuts and fish. Only five sea turtles were caught during the two years of Holden's stay. It is not clear whether these were normal living conditions on Tobi or whether that year was very unusual. Judging from the reasonably rich living conditions today, with plentiful coconuts and fish,[3] the severe situation of Holden's time could have been the result of either unusual climatic conditions or over population.

Conditions deteriorated during the two years of Holden's stay. The captured Americans were made to plant taro every day, but did not seem to be engaged for harvesting. It was repeatedly mentioned that food was extremely scarce. It is possible the taro cultivation pit was destroyed by natural hazards, such as typhoon or tidal wave. In fact, a large storm had stranded the *Mentor* on the reef the previous year, and several big storms hit the island while Holden was there. A number of coconut trees fell down and many coconuts were damaged. Holden also recorded that the taro cultivation pit was filled with sand. Taro does not tolerate saltwater. Once an island is devastated in this way, it takes considerable time for it to recover.

The hostages were made to dig the ground and mix humus with sandy soil by hand for planting taro. When a large storm hit the island, they were made to build a stone wall with large coral boulders to prevent trees from being washed out. It seems that land modification as a scheme for resource management was very active on the island (Figure 3). Visiting other islands for help was not mentioned in the record.

It is also unusual that fish were described as being scarce. This contradicts evidence provided by ethnographic and archaeological data. A number of fishing methods were described in the

Figure 3. A large taro cultivation pit on Tobi Island in 1909 (after Eilers 1936).

ethnographic data (Eilers 1936; Johannes 1981) and many pelagic fish remains were excavated on Tobi by Intoh and Ono (2007). It is possible, therefore, that there was a specific situation that brought about the poor resource conditions that Holden and others experienced.

It must be noted that the Palauan chiefs who came with Holden did not know about Tobi Island and did not understand the language. Cultural contacts between the Southwest Islands and the main islands of Palau must have been very limited. This situation was quite different from that which existed between Yap and the Central Caroline Islands, where close cultural contacts have been maintained, despite their language differences.

Language and ethnography: Palauan but not Palauan

The language of the Southwest Islands belongs to the Nuclear Micronesian subgroup of the Micronesian family of Oceanic languages. The language is distinct from that spoken in the main archipelago of Palau, which is classified as a Western Malayo-Polynesian language (Bender 1971; Kikusawa 2005). Although both languages belong to subgroups within the Austronesian family, they are mutually incomprehensible.

Micronesian languages are also found in the Central and Eastern Caroline Islands, including the outer islands of Yap, Chuuk, Pohnpei and Kosrae. The Southwest Islanders easily communicate with these Caroline Islanders. The reason behind this is linked to the colonisation history of the Southwest Islands (Ross 1989; Rehg 1995; Intoh 1997). According to oral tradition, the Southwest Islands were settled by groups of people from the Central Caroline Islands, especially from Fais and Ulithi.

The dispersal history of the Micronesian languages is complex. The Micronesian languages belong to the Oceanic subgroup, and were probably originally derived from languages associated with the Lapita expansion (Green 1997; Kirch 2000:98). These languages are believed to have split off from the southeastern Solomons or central and northern Vanuatu around 2000 years ago or earlier (Blust 1984; Pawley and Ross 1993). The western movement within Micronesia was made through the Central Caroline Islands and spread to the Southwest Islands of Palau. The date for this movement was between 1800 BP and 1000 BP (Intoh 1997).

The languages of the Southwest Islands and the Central Caroline Islands are similar, but the number of shared words is relatively low. Also, a dialectal discontinuity exists between them

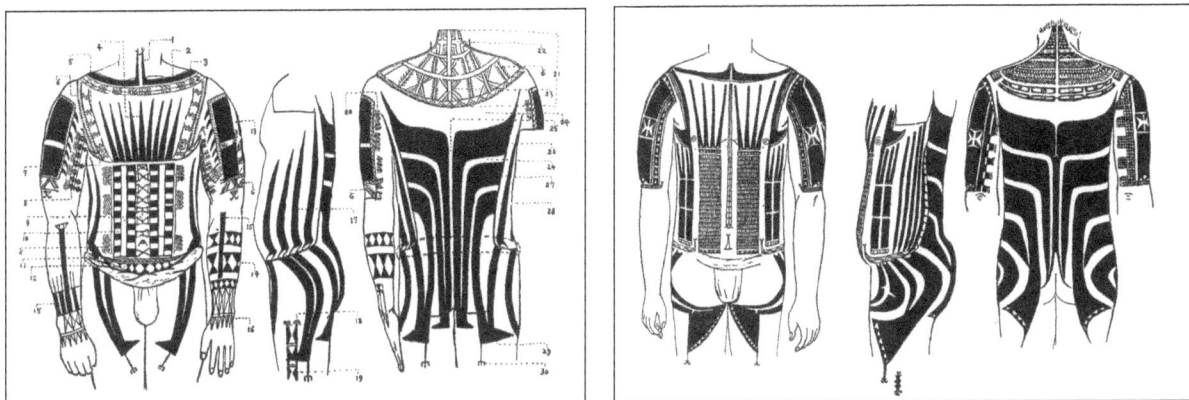

Figure 4. Tattoo designs in the Southwestern Islands of Palau and the Central Caroline Islands (after Hasebe 1928). Left to right: 4a, Sonsorol; 4b, Fais.

(Quackenbush 1968:108). This may indicate that these island groups did not have regular cultural contact after colonisation, which would be understandable, given the 600 km gap between Sonsorol and even the nearest Ngulu Atoll. On the other hand, there was a special relationship between the Southwest Islands and Ulithi. People from Ulithi once drifted to the Southwest Islands and as a result, they became relatives. Since then, whenever people from Ulithi have visited the Southwest Islands, they have been welcomed. However, the distance was too far to maintain regular contact (Lessa 1950). A similar relationship has been described between Fais and Tobi. These contacts were not more than accidental.

One of the cultural attributes shared between the Southwest Islanders and the Central Caroline Islanders was tattoo. The intricate design patterns covering almost the entire body recorded from both areas look very similar and indicate a shared tradition (Figure 4).

It is intriguing how people were able to continue to live on the Southwest Islands despite their resource-limited environment. There are no ethnographic records referring to a regular trade network like sawei between the main islands of Palau. This is verified by the scant pot sherds found from the Southwest Islands (Intoh and Ono 2007).

Loom weaving involves a set of sophisticated techniques that has a limited distribution in Oceania (Reisenberg and Gayton 1952). In the Central Caroline Islands, women wove their

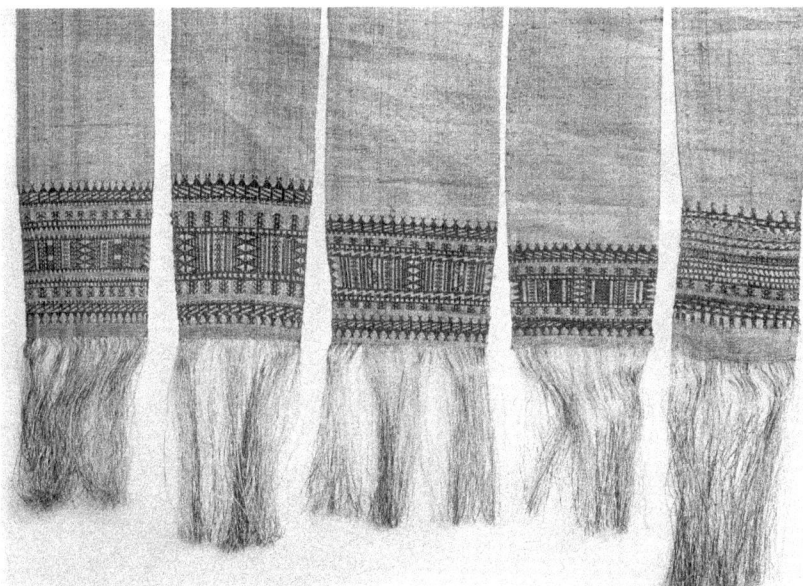

Figure 5. Woven cloth of Sonsorol (after Eilers 1935).

own cloth and made special clothes with very intricate designs. The material used for weaving was banana, a plant that also grows on coral islands. Importantly, woven cloth was one of the significant trading goods offered from coral islanders to the Yapese and was worn by Yapese men with high social status. However, the islands of western Micronesia (Yap and Palau) did not possess any weaving technology, and the people wore grass skirts.[4]

The textile designs made on Sonsorol and Tobi in the early 20th century are very similar to those made in the Central Caroline Islands (Figure 5), and it is very likely the weaving technology of both areas shares a common origin, as does their language.

In historic times, some Palauan influence can be observed from photographs taken in 1903 by the German South Seas Expedition (Eilers 1936). For example, grass skirts were worn on Pulo Anna and Merir, while woven cloth was worn on Sonsorol and Tobi.

How can we account for the grass skirts observed on Pulo Anna and Merir? The style of the grass skirts (long with a tied top) shown in the photograph is very stylised and is identical to that used in Palau. Moreover, the way grass skirts were put on, well below the belly with a shell or turtle-shell belt above the waist, is exactly the same style as used in Palau (Figure 6a) and is different from the way Yapese grass skirts were worn (Figure 6b). This similarity shows a definite influence from Palau, possibly in historic times, since the weaving technology on Pulo Anna is known from historic records (Riesenberg and Gayton 1952). Also, when Akira Someki visited the Southwest Islands in 1934, he observed two wooden beaters for weaving on Pulo Anna and noted that weaving was still periodically done on Merir (Someki 1945:273–296). Moreover, he did not observe any female wearing woven cloth on Sonsorol. The custom had changed over about 30 years. This demonstrates cultural influence from mainland Palau in historic times. The situation is quite different in the Central Caroline Islands, where the weaving tradition has been maintained to the present.

Figure 6. A woman wearing a grass skirt. Left to right: 6a, Pulo Anna (after Eilers 1935); 6b, Yap (photo by Intoh, 1983).

Prehistory: External relationships

The colonisation history of the main island group of Palau goes back more than 3000 years. Several archaeological sites have been excavated from raised coral islands surrounding Babeldaob. Dates associated with the sites are around 3000 BP (Fitzpatrick 2002; Clark 2005; Clark and Wright 2005; Liston 2005). The earliest people to settle the Palauan archipelago are believed to have come from somewhere in Island Southeast Asia or from New Guinea. Genetic studies suggest people in the main islands of Palau share several genetic traits with New Guinea populations (Lum and Cann 2000). The dispersal route is not clear, but dispersal is unlikely to have been through the Southwest Islands.

Three archaeological expeditions have been conducted in the Southwest Islands of Palau thus far.

The first expedition was conducted by Osborn in 1953 (Osborne 1966). This was limited to the observation of surface features and the collecting of some surface finds. A number of large and small mounds, possibly for dwellings, were recorded. A large dug-out taro cultivation pit and a large artificially built stone wall were documented on Tobi Island.

The second expedition was carried out by Rosalind Hunter-Anderson from Guam in 1992. Her research aimed to relocate the archaeological features recorded by Osborne and to make some test excavations (Hunter-Anderson 2000). She opened some test pits on Sonsorol, Pulo Anna, and Tobi. Most of the radiocarbon dates were less than 300 years before the present, except for one older date (about 1000 BP) obtained from Merir. This led Hunter-Anderson to conclude that the Southwest Islands were inhabited only in the very recent past.

The third expedition was carried out by Intoh and Ono in 2002. All the Southwest Islands except for Helen Reef were visited, and Tobi was chosen for a reconnaissance survey (Intoh and Ono 2006). A small number of Palauan pot sherds were observed on the ground surface and in private collections on Sonsorol and Pulo Anna. No pot sherds were found on Tobi from this research. However, as Hunter-Anderson obtained a few Palauan pot sherds from the surface, a few pots could have been imported from Palau.

The excavation was conducted in two places. One was at the infant burial ground associated with a women's house mound, and the other at a coastal deposit near the habitation area. Radiocarbon dates obtained from charcoal samples were 439±43 BP (AD 1400–1530) and 345±40 BP (AD 1450–1650) respectively (Intoh and Ono 2006:66–68). These dates are about 150 years older than those obtained by Hunter-Anderson. When other evidence, such as linguistic and ethnographic data, is considered, the Southwest Islands might have been colonised as early as AD 1400.

These dates correspond to the linguistic studies that indicate a relatively late colonisation. It is plausible that the movement from east to west of people speaking Micronesian languages had paused in the Central Caroline Islands before they dispersed to the Southwest Islands. Accidental contacts could have been one of the possible motivations for colonisation. The Southwest Islands are the last area in Micronesia where speakers of a Micronesian language settled.

A variety of artefacts were obtained from excavation and from the ground surface. These include

Figure 7. A *Tridacna gigas* shell adze/gouge (private collection on Tobi Island).

Tridacna sp. shell adzes, shell ornaments (bracelets and beads), fishing lures for trolling, and single fishhooks made of turtle carapace. The most distinctive artefact is a heavy shell adze made of *Tridacna gigas* (Figure 7). This has a curved blade and was likely used as a gouge in heavy woodworking. *Tridacna gigas* used to be found around the island, but is now extinct, due to over fishing. Islanders are known to have obtained sea turtles and *Tridacna gigas* from Helen Reef in historic times (Johansen 1981). Importing of resources from nearby islands was apparently practised.

Considering the reasonable number of *Tridacna gigas* shell adzes observed in private collections on the island, it would appear that they may have been manufactured on the island. This may be related to the fact that a large number of canoes were used on Tobi. A total of 78 canoe houses were recorded in 1903 by the German South Sea Expedition (Eilers 1936). When the ship carrying Holden was wrecked off Tobi, about 18 canoes came out from the shore. It was also recorded that whenever someone died on the island, the corpse was put in a canoe to be thrown into the ocean (Holden 1836). A photograph of a reasonably large canoe under construction was taken on Pulo Anna in 1903 (Figure 8).

A number of trolling lures made of mother-of-pearl were observed in private collections in the Southwest Islands (Figure 9). The range of head shape is within the variation found in the Central Caroline Islands. Due to the narrow lagoon and the deep sea surrounding the reef, fishing with lures was the major fishing method on the island (Johansen 1981).

Most of the artefacts described above are found generally in Oceania and no influence from Indonesia or New Guinea was detected except for weaving. Occasional accidental contacts were obvious. For example, drift bamboo was used for house building and making a huge basket for trap fishing (Eilers 1936) (Figure 10). The possibility cannot be ruled out that a drift raft, or a canoe with people aboard could have run aground on the island.

Discussion and conclusion

The Southwest Islands of Palau consist of four raised coral islands and a small atoll. These islands were settled by speakers of a Micronesian language who emigrated from the Central Caroline Islands about 450–600 years ago. Between the Southwest Islands and the main islands of Palau, there is a considerable cultural and linguistic gap. The main islands were colonised by an earlier

Figure 8. A large canoe under construction on Pulo Anna (after Eilers 1935).

human population from Island Southeast Asia or New Guinea more than 3000 years ago, but there is neither linguistic nor archaeological evidence that indicates any sign of prehistoric cultural contact between western Micronesia and Island Asia and New Guinea.

The Southwest Islands are in the vicinity of Micronesia, Melanesia and Island Southeast Asia and evidence of cultural interaction among these areas was expected. One of the cultural traits is weaving technology. The distribution of loom weaving was confined to the Southwest Islands of Palau, Central and Eastern Caroline Islands and the small islands of northern Melanesia (Lessa 1978).

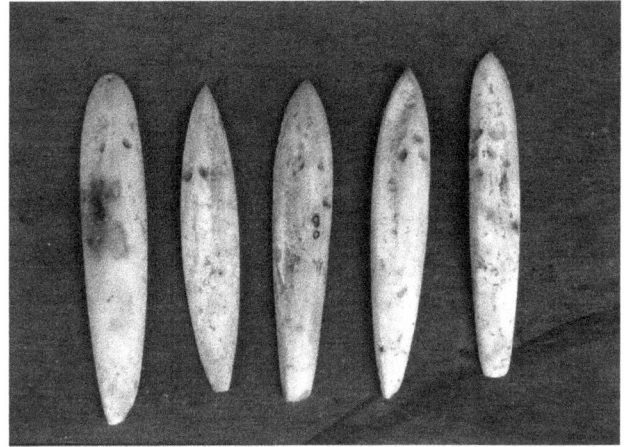

Figure 9. Trolling lures made of mother-of-pearl shell (private collection on Tobi).

Technological analysis suggests weaving was dispersed from Indonesia to the Caroline Islands and subsequently to Melanesia (Riesenberg and Gayton 1952). The direction is the opposite of that proposed by the linguistic model of human movement. It is possible that the central Caroline Islanders made accidental contacts with Indonesian islands and brought back weaving technology. However, it seems there was not a single one-way dispersal, but several, judging from the distribution of weaving in Melanesia. In any case, it is unclear whether introduction of weaving from Indonesia to Melanesia was direct, or whether the Southwestern Islands were the dispersal route.

However, it is difficult to understand how weaving technology could have spread all the way to Kosrae in the East Caroline Islands, since there was very little active interaction beyond Chuuk once permanent settlement was made. Perhaps Polynesian Outliers could have played a significant role in this cultural diffusion, since most of the Polynesian outliers had similar looms and weaving technology.

There is very limited evidence of contact between the Southwest Islands and the main island group of Palau, which contrasts with the close relationship between the Yapese and Central Caroline Islanders. A number of cultural attributes of the Southwest Islands, such as canoe types, tattoo designs, weaving techniques and design elements, show considerable similarities with the Central Caroline Islands from where colonisation probably began. There is little evidence showing cultural contact with the main islands of Palau. However, Palauan female fashions were introduced to some of the Southwest Islands by the end of 19th century.

Figure 10. Large basket bamboo fish traps on Tobi (after Eilers 1936).

In sum, the history of human habitation in the Southwest Islands of Palau is not extensive. The islands did not serve as stepping stones to colonise the main islands of Palau. The strong founding influence from the Central Caroline Islands (language and cultural traits) has been retained. External contacts for resource management seem not to have been active between the islands. Laborious land modifications were made for resource intensification, the techniques similar to those used in the Central Caroline Islands. The high frequency of shared words among the Southwest Islands could also indicate that cultural contact was maintained between the islands and that colonisation was probably relatively recent. Further work is needed to examine the role of the Southwest Islands in the introduction of loom-weaving to Micronesia.

Endnotes

1. It was recorded that about 30 drifted canoes were found on Samar in the Philippines in 1664 (Hezel 1983:40).
2. The distribution of the Austronesian domesticated animals, pig, dog and chicken, was irregular in Micronesia. Only Fais Island is known to have archaeological evidence of all (Intoh1986; Intoh and Shigehara 2004).
3. The recent population is much smaller, however. Only about 20 lived there in 2002, compared with 968 in 1909 (Black 1977). Overpopulation is also likely to explain such poor food conditions.
4. Weaving was practised in Yap by the outer islanders living in Yap. Yapese women did not themselves wear woven cloth.

Acknowledgements

Atholl Anderson made a strong impression on me when I was a student at Otago University. His active fieldwork and extensive writings were a great incentive to me and were valuable for my later academic career in Japan. My sincere thanks go to the people on Tobi, Palau, the Historic Preservation Office, and to Rintaro Ono for their help and enthusiasm during the archaeological research carried out on Tobi in 2003.

References

Alkire, W.H. 1978. *Coral Islanders*. Illinois: AHM Publishing.

Bender, B. 1971. Micronesian languages. In T.A Sebeok (ed), *Linguistics in Oceania*. Current Trends in Linguistics 8, pp. 426–465. The Hague: Mouton.

Black, P.W. 1977. Neo-Tobian culture. Unpublished PhD thesis, University of California.

Blust, R. 1984. Malaita-Micronesian: an Eastern Oceanic subgroup? *Journal of the Polynesian Society* 93(2):99–140.

Clark, G.R. 2005. A 3000-year culture sequence from Palau, Western Micronesia. *Asian Perspectives* 44(2):349–380.

Clark, G.R. and D. Wright 2005. On the periphery? Archaeological investigations at Ngelong, Angaur island, Palau. *Micronesica* 38(1):67–91.

Eilers, A. 1935. *Westkarolinen*. Ergebnisse der Südsee-Expedition 1908–1910, II.9i, Hamburg: Friederichsen de Gruyter.

Eilers, A. 1936. *Westkarolinen: Tobi und Ngulu*. Ergebnisse der Südsee-Expedition 1908–1910, II, B.9, ii. Hamburg: Friederichsen de Gruyter.

Fitzpatrick, S.M. 2002. A radiocarbon chronology of Yapese stone money quarries in Palau. *Micronesica* 34(2):227–242.

Green, R. 1997. Linguistic, biological, and cultural origins of the initial inhabitants of Remote Oceania. *New Zealand Journal of Archaeology* 17:5–27.

Hasebe, K. 1928. Togobei toumin ni tuite [On the islanders of Tobi]. *Jinruigaku Zasshi (Journal of the Anthropological Society of Nippon)* 43(2):63–70.

Hezel, F.X. 1983. *The First Taint of Civilization: A History of the Caroline and Marshall Islands in Pre-Colonial Days, 1521–1885*. Pacific Islands Monograph Series 1. Honolulu: University of Hawaii Press.

Hezel, F.X. and M.T.D. Valle 1972. Early European contact with the Western Carolines: 1525–1750. *Journal of Pacific History* 7:26–44.

Holden, H. 1836. *A Narrative of the Shipwreck, Captivity and Sufferings of Horace Holden and Benjamin H. Nute: who were cast away in the American ship Mentor, on the Pelew Islands, in the year 1832*. Boston: Russell Shattuck.

Hunter-Anderson, R.L. 2000. Ethnographic and archaeological investigations in the southwest islands of Palau. *Micronesia* 33(1/2):11–44.

Intoh, M. 1986. Pigs in Micronesia: introduction or re-introduction by the Europeans. *Man and Culture in Oceania* 2:1–26.

Intoh, M. 1997. Human dispersals into Micronesia. *Anthropological Science* 105(1):15–28.

Intoh, M. 2008. Introduction. In M. Intoh (ed), *Seitaishigen to Shouchouka [Natural Resources and Symbolization]*. Shigenjinruigaku [Anthropology of Resource Management] 7, pp.13–23. Kobundo, Tokyo.

Intoh, M. and R. Ono 2006. Reconnaissance Archaeological Research on Tobi Island, Palau. *People and Culture in Oceania* 22:53–83.

Intoh, M. and N. Shigehara 2004. Prehistoric pig and dog remains from Fais island, Micronesia. *Anthropological Science* 112:257–267.

Johannes, R.E. 1981. *Words of the Lagoon*. Berkeley: University of California Press.

Kikusawa, R. 2005. Mikuronesia no gengo [Languages of Micronesia]. In M. Intoh (ed), *Mikuronesiawo Sirutameno 58 Shou [58 Chapters to learn about Micronesia]*, pp. 48–52. Tokyo: Akashi Shoten Co.

Kirch, P.V. 2000. *On the Road of the Winds: An Archaeological History of the Pacific Islands before European Contact*. Berkeley: University of California Press.

Lessa, W.A. 1950. Ulithi and the outer native world. *American Anthropologist* 52:27–52.

Lessa, W.A. 1978. The Mapia islands and their affinities. In N.Gunson (ed), *The Changing Pacific: Essays in Honour of H.E. Maude*, pp. 228–245. Melbourne: Oxford University Press.

Liston, J. 2005. An assessment of radiocarbon dates from Palau, western Micronesia. *Radiocarbon* 47(2):295–354.

Lum, J.K. and R.L. Cann 2000. MtDNA lineage analyses: Origins and migrations of Micronesians and Polynesians. *American Journal of Physical Anthropology* 113:151–168.

Osborne, D. 1966. *The Archaeology of the Palau Islands: An Intensive Survey*. B.P. Bishop Museum Bulletin 230. Honolulu, Bishop Museum Press.

Pawley, A. and M. Ross 1993. Austronesian historical linguistics and culture history. *Annual Review of Anthropology* 22:425–459.

Petersen, G. 1999. Sociopolitical rank and conical clanship in the Caroline islands. *The Journal of the Polynesian Society* 108(4):367–410.

Riesenberg, S.H. and A.H. Gayton 1952. Caroline Island belt weaving. *Southwestern Journal of Anthropology* 8:342–375.

Rehg, K.L. 1995. The significance of linguistic interaction spheres in reconstructing Micronesian prehistory. *Oceanic Linguistics* 34:305–326.

Quackenbush, E.M. 1968. From Sonsorol to Truk: A dialect chain. Unpublished PhD thesis, Department of Anthropology, University of Michigan.

Ross, M.D. 1989. Early Oceanic linguistic prehistory. *Journal of Pacific History* 24(2):135–149.

Someki, A. 1945. *Nanyou no Fudo to Mingu [Environment and Material Culture of the South Seas]*. Tokyo,Shoko Shoin, Co.Ltd.

21

The historical archaeology of New Zealand's prehistory

Matthew Campbell

Anthropology Department, University of Auckland, New Zealand

mat.c@cfgheritage.com

Introduction

This paper began life as a review of *A Companion to Archaeology* (Bintliff 2006), a book intended as a broad overview of the discipline, though largely from a British perspective. The first section is called 'Thinking about archaeology' and contains two contrasting theoretical papers: one by Stephen Shennan ('Analytical archaeology'); and one by Julian Thomas ('The great dark book: archaeology, experience, and interpretation'). The most intriguing thing about reading these papers was that the theoretical concerns of these two British scholars did not seem particularly relevant to the archaeology that I do, and that Atholl Anderson does, the archaeology of New Zealand and the Pacific. We have largely received the theoretical and methodological basis of our archaeology from the Northern Hemisphere but our archaeology is very different from that of the European Neolithic with which Shennan and Thomas are concerned. So while the book hasn't been formally reviewed, it has been put to what I hope is a more interesting use, and one close to the editor's intentions; as a book of ideas, it has set me thinking about the basis of New Zealand archaeology (and Pacific archaeology, though this discussion is largely restricted to New Zealand). This paper doesn't deal with Shennan's and Thomas's ideas and their relevance; rather, it is about what sets our archaeology apart from theirs, because without understanding that it would be fruitless to apply their ideas uncritically.

This understanding of the relationship between imported ideas and New Zealand archaeology is not new; our archaeology *is* perceived to be different from British or American archaeology and naturally British or American ideas need to be adapted to local circumstances. But what makes the archaeology of neolithic Maori so different from the European Neolithic is not material culture, technology nor subsistence patterns, though clearly these differences are important. The main difference lies in the immediacy of Maori culture. Pre-European archaeology in New Zealand studies part of a living tradition, one that is recorded in great detail in a vast body of ethnography and traditional history. This requires a different approach to archaeological studies of the deep past such as the European Neolithic.

What I propose is that New Zealand 'prehistoric archaeology' is, in fact, a historical archaeology. This is not true, of course, in the narrowest senses of the term – pre-European Maori did not have writing. It is certain, however, that they had history and, what is more, that that history is accessible to us. When history and archaeology are used to supplement each other the result must be a historical archaeology.

A wide body of documentary sources is available to the New Zealand archaeologist: early European explorer's accounts; the letters, journals and writings of European missionaries and colonists; 19th and 20th century ethnographies; Maori manuscripts recording oral tradition, history and ritual; books, newspapers and other writings by Maori in both Maori and English; Land Court records; the output of Anthropology and Maori Studies Departments from New Zealand's major tertiary institutions; all these and more (including the archaeological record itself) constitute the historiography of the Maori. I refer in this paper to 'tradition' or the 'ethnographic record', which aren't really the same thing, though the ethnographic record contains much that is historical, and tradition much ethnography. This record has a long history of use in scholarship, including archaeology, though past misuse by scholars and archaeologists has led many archaeologists today to distrust it.

Tradition and archaeology in New Zealand

The early founders of the Polynesian Society turned to tradition in their attempts to formulate a coherent account of the whence of the Maori (most famously Smith 1910, 1913; see Simmons 1976 for a detailed account), which was formalised as the 'Great Fleet tradition'. This taught that Aotearoa (New Zealand) was discovered by Kupe and subsequently settled by the Great Fleet of canoes around AD 1350 (again Simmons 1976 gives a detailed account). Despite misgivings from some scholars (e.g. Golson 1960:397, quoted below), this account was the widely accepted conventional wisdom. Scholarly misgivings were substantiated in 1976 when Simmons published his critical account of the Fleet tradition, showing that much of it was a selective reinterpretation of selected sources (Simmons 1976:315), and, as Clayworth (2001) has subsequently demonstrated, in support of a preconceived theory. As Simmons (1976:321) makes clear, Maori tradition in the 19th century served to validate claims to mana, chieftainship and land for the corporate social groups which existed *at that time*; 'the social groups who took part in the original settlement no longer exist'. Subsequently, Orbell (1985) showed that the origin traditions were not valid historical accounts at all, though they were valid myths with valid social, political, religious and metaphysical significance.

Until 1976, however, it was still possible for serious scholars to accept the Fleet tradition, and to use methods similar to Smith's. Adkin (1960) formulated a rather fanciful New Zealand prehistory from traditional sources, and Keyes (1960) used tradition to outline the prehistory of D'Urville Island. These two papers provoked a swift response from Golson (1960) in which he demonstrated quite clearly that the origin traditions could not be validated by archaeology, or vice versa. Golson (1960:397–398) said he was 'not *necessarily* questioning the validity of the Toi and Fleet traditions, but only their usefulness for organising and interpreting the archaeological data of New Zealand prehistory … the traditions are *for these purposes* not sufficiently full, precise, or unambiguous, nor do they contain the right sort of information' (emphasis in original). Golson's argument is a critique of the historiography, not the utility of the ethnographic record.

Davidson (1990) later returned to this subject in her submission to the Waitangi Tribunal in the Te Roroa Claim Wai 38 on the place of Maori oral tradition in archaeology. Her specific concern was the expectations that the claimants may have had of archaeology, that it could be used to validate tradition. She concluded that generally archaeology and tradition refer to two very different understandings of the past, and neither can be used to validate the other, nor to disprove the other, though local tradition can provide a useful framework for interpreting archaeology.

Golson and Davidson were both responding to specific misunderstandings about the relationship between tradition and archaeology. Neither of them took the next step of outlining what the correct relationship/s might be. Golson, for instance, said our understanding of the culture of the first Maori 'is totally the result of archaeological research' (Golson 1960:386). This is simply not so, as Davidson (1990) makes clear. She noted that archaeology is not the same thing as prehistory, and prehistory draws on a number of disciplines in reconstructing pre-literate society. Archaeology is a set of specific techniques and methods for inquiry into the past; prehistory is a more broadly based discipline that combines and interprets data from several disciplines including archaeology. This distinction breaks down in practice however. Archaeologists are not just technicians whose job it is to generate data for others to use; they are prehistorians (or historical archaeologists) who gather data to interpret it themselves, in conjunction with data and knowledge from other disciplines. So while Davidson (1990) says that 'prehistory may be able to embrace the separate strands of archaeology and oral tradition in a way that archaeology alone cannot', this is precisely the sort of thing archaeologists do every day. The distinction between archaeology and prehistory is conceptually important, but is rarely carried through into everyday practice.

Davidson (1990), in fact, notes that archaeologists frequently draw on the descriptions of the early voyagers to help them understand 18th century Maori society (she refers to 'text-aided archaeology'). It is, after all, largely on the basis of their descriptions and collections that the archaeological 'Classic Maori culture' is defined. She then notes that archaeologists fail to appreciate the pitfalls of comparing the culture thus defined with the archaeologically defined 'Archaic' or 'Early Maori culture'. But she then goes on to say that 'Classic Maori culture ... [is] not so different from the earlier East Polynesian culture in New Zealand'.

I find this position ambivalent, an ambivalence that extends throughout New Zealand archaeology. It would be unfair to lay the situation at Golson's and Davidson's feet; their role has been merely to formalise a widely held view, and to incidentally provide me with convenient fodder. I am concerned to show that I am not raising a straw man – he is already there. In this paper, I will show that New Zealand archaeologists use textual sources on a daily basis. As I have outlined, the ethnographic record is a huge body of texts, many of which are historical. I largely agree with Golson's and Davidson's argument; we as archaeologists can't, and shouldn't even try to, prove that such-and-such an ancestor inhabited this pa or that kainga; we ought to merely accept it as true on its own terms. What we can do is *critically* examine the texts to generate understandings of pre-European Maori society that can help us interpret the archaeological record. This critical examination and analysis of texts lies at the heart of the historical methodology and the claim of any archaeology to be historical.

Archaeology, history and tradition

Archaeology is a historical science (this alone makes the idea of a separate historical archaeology problematic). The new archaeologists of the 1960s sought law-like regularity in their data (Trigger 1989:373). Historical sciences, on the other hand, recognise patterns in the particular and the contingent. This was one of the major failings of the processual project: choosing the wrong scientific model.

Contingency means that each historical situation is unique in its origins, its circumstances and its outcomes. Contingency obstructs the calculability of history (Kracauer 1969:45). To deal with contingency, history has developed methods for critically evaluating its data. Two questions, in particular, the researcher must ask of historical texts: are they credible, and are they reliable (Tosh 1984:51)? As Tosh (1984:58) says, sources are, by nature, 'inaccurate, incomplete or tainted by prejudice and self interest. The procedure is … to amass as many pieces as possible from a wide ranges of sources.' The historical method proceeds by inferring knowledge from evidence of past events to achieve an analytical, or explanatory, narrative, answering the questions 'why' or 'how'. Sufficient inferences in agreement with each other may be taken to constitute a proof (Lemon 1995).

Other sciences have embraced the historical method, particularly geology and evolutionary biology. The evolutionary biologist Gould (1986:65) claims that proofs are based on 'iterated pattern … on types of evidence so numerous and so diverse that no other coordinating interpretation could stand – even though any item, taken separately, could not provide conclusive proof'. Gould maintains that Darwin's unique contribution to science was not so much his theory of evolution, but the establishment of a methodology for deriving such a theory. 'Darwin was, above all, a historical methodologist … Darwin taught us why history matters and established the methodology for an entire second style of science' (Gould 1986:60). (Of course, this short two-paragraph summary does no justice to the richness of this method.)

This understanding of historical sciences is directly relevant to archaeology. Geertz (1983) pointed out more than 20 years ago that, as the social sciences have retreated from the search for law-like explanations, so they have turned to the arts for appropriate analytical analogies. Rather than making comparisons between social entities and biological organisms or systems, social scientists have made use of metaphors of drama or text. The analogy that post-processual archaeology developed in the mid 1980s was the textual analogy, implicit in the title of Hodder's (1991) seminal post-processual volume *Reading the Past* (and see also Bintliff 1991; Smith 1992; Patrik 1985). Such an understanding of archaeology implies the written document is just one of several sources of data that must be read together, with the same critical questions asked of them all: are they credible, and are they reliable?

There has been a tendency to generalise the stance that Golson and Davidson took against specific misuses or misunderstandings of tradition in archaeology across the whole relationship between archaeology and tradition. On the contrary, the relationship ought to be a far more positive one. And, in practice, it is. Despite believing at one level that archaeology and tradition don't mix, archaeologists in New Zealand happily mix the two every working day. Even to refer to a site as a pa is to make a value judgement, informed at many levels by the ethnographic record and tradition. The term 'pa' is not functionally neutral; it is an interpretation. We need to accept that this is what we do, to understand how and why we do it, and, more importantly, to adopt and adapt the methods of historical criticism to enable us to do it better. Archaeologists have little problem with integrating the data of physical sciences such as geology, biology or nuclear physics, but not the historical sciences. Perhaps this is because there is little appreciation of the scientific nature of history and how the methods of historical sciences differ from those of physical sciences.

Lightfoot (1995) argues for North America that the understanding of the contact and colonial period must be dependent on the study of prehistory. History is a continuum and European settlers, whether there or here, did not colonise a terra nullius, but a land that already had a history. Artificial divisions of archaeology into history and prehistory disguise continuities (Lightfoot 1995:202). Lightfoot calls for an end to the separation of history and prehistory, with their distinct research agendas, theories and methodologies, which are often kept separate in order to mark out academic territory. The result is that history-making before 1769 (in New Zealand) is no longer permissible.

This situation has partly come about through 'the erasure of local histories – one of the most cancerous products of international capitalism in both its colonial and metropolitan manifestations' (Schmidt and Patterson 1995:4). History-making (including archaeology), if not in the service of the politics of the day, is nonetheless part of the cultural and intellectual zeitgeist. Thus politically motivated distinctions like 'civilised/modern' versus 'primitive' find their echoes in the separation of historical and prehistoric archaeology. This dualism is as embedded in the discipline of archaeology as it is in the collective Western consciousness.

Overcoming this situation requires that tradition be accepted as a legitimate form of history. Historical archaeology must become more inclusive, and is potentially enriched by newly expanded horizons (Schmidt 2006:3). Schmidt, working with the oral traditions of Africa, calls for oral tradition to be used to supplement the archaeological record without the need a 'test of scientific proof for accuracy'. In other words, they may tell different, but still complementary, stories. Historical archaeology is not located only where tradition and archaeology overlap, but across the combined scope of both. If tradition and archaeology (and linguistics, geology, vegetation history, etc.) seem to contradict each other, then this is the opportunity for the process of history-making to develop a richer, more nuanced and more inclusive account (Schmidt 2006:28). Historians, too, are developing similar conceptual frameworks. Smail (2008:6–11) maintains that 'artifacts, fossils, vegetable remains, phonemes, and various forms of modern DNA ... like written documents, all these traces encode information about the past. Like written documents, they resist an easy reading and must be interpreted with care ... The archeologists, anthropologists, molecular biologists, and neuroscientists who study the deep past are also historians, regardless of the archives they consult.'

Historical archaeology revisited

Any attempt to rigidly define historical archaeology is bound to fail. Different practitioners of historical archaeology have different ideas of what it is and what its proper subject of study should be. All I can hope to do is outline the historical archaeology I am advocating for New Zealand, but in doing so, I necessarily tap into a wider international debate. Hicks and Beaudry (2006:1) refer merely to 'the archaeology of the period from around AD 1500 up to and including the present', but others are more specific. For Orser (2006:275), historical archaeology is the archaeological study of the 'expansion of Europeans into the non-European world'. For Leone and Potter (1988), it is the archaeology of capitalism. Hall and Silliman (2006) refer to 'the processes that have formed and shaped modernity, and the way the past is understood from the perspective of the present'. Together, these definitions amount to largely the same thing, an archaeology of modern capitalism with its roots in the Renaissance and European colonialism. Colonialism, capitalism and their international impacts are topics worthy of study, but these definitions of historical archaeology are primarily North American concepts (Funari 1999:37; Schmidt 2006:45). They derive from the early, formative work of Deetz (e.g. 1977) and the Annapolis project (e.g. Leone and Potter 1988); the latter, in particular, came to be associated with the study of North American capitalism. Historical archaeology as it is practised in Australasia closely follows the North American model. In Europe, Roman, Mediaeval and post-Mediaeval archaeologies have long depended on written documents. History there is a continuum and the development of post-processual or contextual archaeologies has further broken down the barriers between the disciplines of archaeology, anthropology and history (Funari 1999:40). As in North America, New Zealand lacks Mediaeval castles and the arrival of literate Europeans among the non-literate Maori seems to mark a clear-cut boundary separating prehistory from history.

Funari (1999:43–47) argues that these definitions rely on the apparently universal nature of modern capitalism, with its origins in European colonialism. Pre-capitalist societies, by contrast, are particularistic and so, then, is their archaeology. But capitalism was not universal; feudal modes of organisation continued well into the 19th century in many parts of Europe and Latin America, and North American plantation slavery is a non-capitalist mode of economic and social organisation. Historical archaeology, as defined above, comes out of a search for a global synthesis, but generalising the North American situation to a global definition fails to recognise that interest continues to lie in the particulars of local contexts (Johnson 1999:35).

> A world perspective would not confine historical archaeology to the study of European expansion ... nor to an all-encompassing capitalist system ... and would be concerned with the material culture of literate societies. Special attention would be paid to the relationship between artefacts and written documents in different societies, using texts and archaeological remains as complementary evidence ... as archaeological and documentary sources pose similar and related problems of interpretation ... and as apparent discrepancies between textual and archaeological sources must always be addressed by all scholars concerned with literate societies ... (Funari 1999:57).

It is this type of definition of historic archaeology, one that depends on the interplay of archaeological and written sources, and critically examines and compares all sources, that I am arguing for in New Zealand. The only issue I have with Funari's definition is that it continues to privilege the written word. Pre-European Maori had a sophisticated orality that functioned in many ways analogously to European literacy. Their history may have been of a different kind, but it was, and is, no less authentic. In the 19th century, Maori vigorously adopted writing and recorded their traditional knowledge in a remarkable outpouring (Orbell 1985), the study of which could keep all the university Departments of Maori Studies busy for a very long time to come. Tradition and the ethnographic record *in general* are valid sources of complementary material for archaeology, though each *specific* document must individually pass the tests of credibility and reliability.

A truly world perspective on historical archaeology would be concerned with the material culture of all peoples who have an accessible history, and any archaeology that applies the critical method of history to its readings is a historical archaeology.

Archaeology can rarely, if ever, provide a definitive, unfalsifiable proof of the historical record, or vice versa; this sort of validation is not the purpose of historical archaeology, nor a proper use of the ethnographic record. It was because Adkin (1960) attempted to use archaeology this way that Golson (1960) felt compelled to write his rebuttal. It was because of an expectation that it could be used this way that Davidson (1990) provided her submission to the Waitangi Tribunal. Two recent mitigation excavations in New Zealand provide examples (reports in preparation). The Mataraua site near Tauranga is associated in tradition with the Ngai Tamarawaho ancestor Mokoroa (Des Tata pers comm.). The archaeological evidence derived from our excavation would be quite unable to establish the connection between Mokoroa and Mataraua. Similarly, at the UCOL site in Wanganui, we excavated the house of Thomas Bamber, and similarly, the archaeological evidence derived from our excavation would be quite unable to establish the connection between Bamber and the house. In neither case was there anything in the archaeology to show who had lived at these places and we wouldn't expect to find it, though we have no reason to doubt the historical evidence connecting Mokoroa and Bamber to the respective sites. This kind of information comes entirely from non-archaeological sources.

It is the interplay between the two complementary kinds of data, documentary and archaeological, and the analysis of them in tandem that allows us to reach the conclusions we do, a historical proof of the kind advocated by Gould (1986:65, quoted above). Knowing, for instance, that Bamber was a blacksmith with his smithy on the adjacent lot allows us to interpret the rubbish pits full of waste iron as connected to his work; waste iron on its own doesn't demonstrate the presence of a blacksmith. The tradition of Mokoroa outlines the place of Mataraua in the local settlement pattern, which archaeology backs up and enlarges on.

At a slightly more complex level, the ethnographic record informs us about more subtle aspects of our archaeology. We know why a pa is a pa and can be quite confident in our judgement, even though that judgement is not a neutral interpretation. But at every stage we have to ask the question of the historical sources: are they credible, and are they reliable? Having established reliability and credibility, the ethnographic record provides a context for the archaeological record. By employing and critically evaluating multiple lines of evidence, the ethnographic record becomes more than just a simple analogue used to directly interpret the archaeology (Lightfoot 1995:205; Kepecs 1997:193). It is not only the ethnographic record that informs archaeology. European forms of history, and historical method, rely on change, development and explanation – they are more than just chronicles. Archaeology provides a time depth to the otherwise timeless record of the 'ethnographic present'.

The ethnographic record was made by chiefs, priests and colonial Europeans who brought their own social and cultural biases to their writings. The evidence of archaeology rarely indicates the predominance of hierarchy and ritual, however. Archaeology can serve as a balance to the biases inherent in the writings. A critical evaluation of the texts in light of who wrote them and why is essential. It must also be taken into account that Maori culture in the 19th century had already been changed by European contact (cf. Feinman 1997:373). A new literacy will have altered Maori attitudes to their own history; the ability to document the past means that a permanent record is created, and the resulting perspectives on the past will differ from those of an oral culture.

Historical archaeology in practice

Having made the claim that archaeologists use the ethnographic record every day, I need to emphasise that we do not necessarily do so critically. It is this critical analysis that defines historical archaeology. We unreflexively accept that a pa is a pa because we know one when we see one. Perhaps if we critically examined the ethnographic record on pa, including our own archaeological record, we might arrive at a new or expanded understanding of these sites. There are, however, several recent studies that have approached the ethnographic record critically and have produced a much richer and more nuanced account of prehistory.

East Polynesia

I have until now restricted this discussion to New Zealand archaeology, but some of the better examples of work in this field have taken place in Polynesia. First among these is the work of Kirch and Sahlins at Anahulu (Kirch 1992; Sahlins 1992). Kirch (Kirch 1992:1) describes 'an anthropological experiment that joined archival ethnography with field archaeology, so as to construct an integrated history of Anahulu Valley'. The ethnography derives primarily from the mid 19th century records of the Mahele land reforms. Ambitious in scope, this project has been inspirational to many that have followed it, although in the end, it failed to unite the two strands of ethnography and archaeology into a unified research programme with an integrated outcome.

Kirch and Green (2001) subsequently outlined the elements of an ethnography of an 'Ancestral Polynesian Society'. They used linguistics, archaeology and ethnography (they refer to the 'triangulation method') to push the timeframe for this historical archaeology back as far as perhaps 2500 BP (Kirch and Green 2001:1). This exploration of Ancestral Polynesian society has sparked considerable debate, but more importantly, has also acted as a springboard for archaeological and material-culture research, and a model against which new data can be tested. Burley and Shutler (2007), for instance, re-examine the archaeology of Ancestral Polynesian fishing gear from Tonga in light of Kirch and Green's conclusions, resulting in a more refined understanding of Ancestral Polynesian fishing strategies.

These approaches owe much to the historical anthropology in Polynesia of Sahlins (1981, 1985), among others. Kirch and Green (2001:Prologue) trace the rise and fall and rise again of these ideas through the 20th century; the notion that anthropology should not dwell in the timeless ethnographic present, but that its subjects, cultures and methods are products of history.

My own work in Rarotonga, in which I use tradition to contextualise the archaeology of the island, is also strongly influenced by Sahlins (Campbell 2002a, 2002b, 2006). My principal source has been the minute books of the Rarotongan Land Courts. These record the oral testimony of plaintiffs, respondents and witnesses in hearings to decide the ownership of parcels of land – it follows that they are inevitably partial. To make matters worse, any statements they make about prehistory are conditioned by 70 years of missionisation and colonialism. A critical analysis, disentangling the distortions of history and half-truth, is essential if the records are to be read with any confidence. Fortunately the records are sufficiently broad that several witnesses in unconnected cases can tell much the same story and a history of Rarotonga can be reconstructed for the last 200 years or so before European contact. Also, the most interesting and useful information for the archaeologist is usually peripheral to the main purpose of contesting land rights, so that even if the story told in court lacks reliability, the cultural logic behind it does not. The nature of land boundaries, relationships between chiefs and commoners, or conceptions of time and space are all topics that have been covered.

Papamoa

Returning now to New Zealand, the Papamoa dune plain east of Tauranga has been the focus of intensive archaeological mitigation investigation as the city has expanded rapidly along the coast. This previously largely intact archaeological landscape contained, primarily, shell middens with associated cooking features and occasional fish bone, occasional evidence of housing and kumara storage pits, and gardened soils. Swamps behind the foredune would have been an important source of various resources. Radiocarbon dates show this landscape was occupied between AD 1450 and 1750, that is, from the period of initial expansion out of a presumed early occupation around Tauranga harbour (early sites here are not well documented) until just before European contact. The first question is, why was this relatively productive environment abandoned? There is, for instance, no apparent environmental cause; later middens are essentially similar to earlier middens, so there is no immediate evidence of either anthropogenic or natural environmental degradation.

Tradition records that the people who lived at Papamoa were Waitaha a Hei. In the early 18th century, the area was invaded and conquered by Ngaiterangi from Opotiki (Stafford 1967:Chapter 21; Stokes 1980:Chapter 2; Ballara 2003:252). The change in settlement pattern we see with the abandonment of the Papamoa dunes does not have an environmental cause, nor does it reflect evolutionary change in the social structures of Tauranga Maori, the kinds of explanatory factors that traditional settlement archaeology is used to using. Rather, the cause, the Ngaiterangi conquest, is historical and contingent, unpredictable beforehand but clearly patterned in retrospect. The exposed and unprotected dune plains became too dangerous to occupy on any permanent basis.

Understanding this, it then becomes possible to ask the next question: what form did abandonment take? Exploitation of the dune plain may have continued, but in a fashion that left much less visible archaeological evidence. It would be difficult to explore this second question without having answered the first.

The Waihou river

Phillips (2000) examined the settlement archaeology of the Waihou river on the Hauraki Plains. As with my work in Rarotonga, she contextualised the archaeology using traditional accounts, principally from Land Court records. She examined history, landscape, environment, settlement, population and land use for the Waihou, integrating this data with the archaeological evidence. The context she provides is more a physical one than the social context I derived from the Rarotongan records – these records have the potential to provide a wide range of archaeologically useful information that has barely begun to be examined.

Southern Maori

My final example demonstrates a different approach to using the ethnographic record, but one fully in keeping with the historical archaeology I am advocating. Anderson and Smith (1996; see also Anderson 1998) examine the evidence for sedentary village settlement in southern New Zealand in both the early (14th century AD) and late (18th–early 19th centuries AD) periods. Late-period villages, largely known from ethnographic evidence, arose out of a combination of environmental, economic and political factors that resulted in a very mobile lifestyle with a fixed village base. A scarcity of resources meant that trade between villages was essential, and this trade also underscored the southern Maori polity. In contrast, early villages were characterised by a relative lack of mobility in an environment with very rich, though vulnerable, pockets of resources, in particular seals and moa. These villages were self-sufficient, though they did not outlast the depression or extirpation of local prey. Anderson and Smith have contrasted the archaeological and ethnographic records of either end of the span of human occupation in southern New Zealand to find complementary explanations for superficially similar settlement patterns.

Conclusion

I have proposed that the proper subject of historical archaeology is the archaeology of peoples with an accessible history, and that its appropriate core methodology is the critical methodology of history. It is the methodology, rather than any specific subject, that is crucial here.

Some of the arguments put forward for accepting the ethnographic record as credible and reliable might seem more political than scientific (for instance, the quote from Schmidt and Patterson, above). It is a post-modern truism that science is inevitably politicised, and this is particularly true for archaeology (Wylie 1992; Shanks 2006). It is, however, possible to put forward the simplest test for the usefulness of the ethnographic record in New Zealand archaeology. The strictly scientific approach would be to put forward the null hypothesis that 'the ethnographic record has nothing to contribute to archaeology'. I prefer to rephrase this as a simple question: 'Does the ethnographic record have a contribution to make?' The answer, as I think I have shown, is 'yes', in which case the methodology I have advocated here becomes essential.

Acknowledgements

This paper is offered to Atholl in acknowledgement of many years of friendship, teaching and inspiration. Janet Davidson and Ian Smith were kind enough to comment on an earlier version of this paper. Peter Clayworth provided an electronic copy of his thesis.

References

Adkin, G.L. 1960. An adequate cultural nomenclature for the New Zealand area. *Journal of the Polynesian Society* 69:228–238.

Anderson, A.J. 1998. *The Welcome of Strangers: An Ethnohistory of Southern Maori A.D. 1650–1850.* Dunedin: University of Otago Press.

Anderson, A.J. and I.W.G. Smith 1996. The transient village in Southern New Zealand. *World Archaeology* 27(3):359–371.

Ballara, A. 2003. *Taua:'Musket Wars', 'Land Wars' or Tikanga? Warfare in Maori Society in the Early Nineteenth Century.* Auckland: Penguin.

Bintliff, J. 1991. The Contribution of the *Annaliste*/Structural History Approach to Archaeology. In J. Bintliff (ed), *The Annales School and Archaeology*, pp. 1–33. Leicester University Press, Leicester.

Bintliff, J. (ed) 2006. *A Companion to Archaeology.* Blackwell, Malden MA.

Burley, D.V. and R. Shutler, Jr. 2007. Ancestral Polynesian fishing gear: archaeological insights from Tonga. In A. Anderson, K. Green and B.F. Leach (eds), *Vastly Ingenious: The Archaeology of Pacific Material Culture, in honour of Janet M. Davidson*, pp. 155–172. Dunedin: Otago University Press.

Campbell, M. 2002a. Ritual landscape in late pre-contact Rarotonga: a brief reading. *Journal of the Polynesian Society* 111(2):147–170.

Campbell, M. 2002b. History in prehistory: the oral traditions of the Rarotongan Land Court records. *Journal of Pacific History* 37(2):221–238.

Campbell, M. 2006. Memory and monumentality in the Rarotongan landscape. *Antiquity* 80:102–117.

Clayworth, P. 2001. An indolent and chilly folk: the development of the idea of the 'Moriori myth'. Unpublished PhD thesis, University of Otago.

Davidson, J.M. 1990. Maori archaeological traditions and archaeology. Unpublished report to the Crown Law Office, Wellington (Wai–38, Document #H6).

Deetz, J. 1977. *In Small Things Forgotten: The Archaeology of Early American Life.* Garden City: Anchor Press/Doubleday.

Feinman, G.M. 1997. Thoughts on new approaches to combining the archaeological and historical records. *Journal of Archaeological Method and Theory* 4(3/4):367–377.

Funari, P.P.A. 1999. Historical archaeology from a world perspective. In P.P.A. Funari, M. Hall and S. Jones (eds), *Historical Archaeology: Back from the Edge*, pp. 37–66. London: Routledge.

Geertz, C. 1983. Blurred genres: the reconfiguration of social thought. In C. Geertz (ed), *Local Knowledge: Further Essays in Interpretive Anthropology*, pp. 19–35. New York: Basic Books.

Golson, J. 1960. Archaeology, tradition, and myth in New Zealand prehistory. *Journal of the Polynesian Society* 69:380–402.

Gould, S.J. 1986. Evolution and the triumph of homology, or why history matters. *American Scientist* 74(1):60–69.

Hall, M. and S.W. Silliman 2006. Introduction: archaeology of the modern world. In M. Hall and S.W. Silliman (eds), *Historical Archaeology*, pp. 1–19. Malden: Blackwell.

Hicks, D. and M.C. Beaudry 2006. Introduction: the place of historical archaeology. In D. Hicks and M.C. Beaudry (eds), *The Cambridge Companion to Historical Archaeology*, pp. 1–9. Cambridge: Cambridge University Press.

Hodder, I. 1991. *Reading the Past: Current Approaches to Interpretation in Archaeology.* Cambridge: Cambridge University Press.

Johnson, M. 1999. Rethinking historical archaeology. In P.P.A. Funari, M. Hall and S. Jones (eds) *Historical Archaeology: Back from the Edge*, pp. 23–36. London: Routledge.

Kepecs, S. 1997. Introduction to new approaches to combining the archaeological and historical records. *Journal of Archaeological Method and Theory* 4(3/4):193–198.

Keyes, I.W. 1960. The cultural succession and ethnographic features of D'Urville Island. *Journal of the Polynesian Society* 69:239–265.

Kirch, P.V. 1992. The Archaeology of History. In P.V. Kirch and M.D. Sahlins (eds), *Anahulu: The Anthropology of History in the Kingdom of Hawaii*, Volume 2. Chicago: The University of Chicago Press.

Kirch, P.V. and R.C. Green 2001. *Hawaiki, Ancestral Polynesia: An Essay in Historical Anthropology.* Cambridge: Cambridge University Press.

Kracauer, S. 1969. *History: The Last Things Before the Last.* New York: Oxford University Press.

Lemon, M.C. 1995. *The Discipline of History and the History of Thought.* London: Routledge.

Leone, M. and P. Potter 1988. Introduction: issues in historical archaeology. In M. Leone and P. Potter (eds), *The Recovery of Meaning*, 1–22. Washington: Smithsonian Institution Press.

Lightfoot, K.G. 1995. Culture contact studies: redefining the relationship between prehistoric and historical archaeology. *American Antiquity* 60(2):199–217.

Orbell, M. 1985. *Hawaiki: A New Approach to Maori Tradition.* Christchurch: The University of Canterbury.

Orser, C.E. 2006. The archaeologies of recent history: historical, post-medieval, and modern-world. In J. Bintliff (ed), *A Companion to Archaeology*, pp. 272–290. Malden: Blackwell.

Patrik, L.E. 1985. Is there an archaeological record? In M.B. Schiffer (ed), *Advances in Archaeological Method and Theory*, pp. 27–62. Orlando: Academic Press.

Phillips, C. 2000. *Waihou Journeys: The Archaeology of 400 Years of Maori Settlement.* Auckland: Auckland University Press.

Sahlins, M.D. 1981. *Historical Metaphors and Mythical Realities: Structure in the Early History of the Sandwich Island Kingdom.* Ann Arbour: The University of Michigan Press.

Sahlins, M.D. 1985. *Islands of History.* Chicago: The University of Chicago Press.

Sahlins, M.D. 1992. Historical Ethnography. In P.V. Kirch and M. Sahlins (eds), *Anahulu: The Anthropology of History in the Kingdom of Hawaii*, Volume 1. Chicago: The University of Chicago Press.

Schmidt, P.R. 2006. *Historical Archaeology in Africa: Representation, Social Memory, and Oral Traditions.* Lanham: AltaMira Press.

Schmidt, P.R. and T.C. Patterson 1995. Introduction: from constructing to making alternative histories. In P.R. Schmidt and T.C. Patterson (eds), *Making Alternative Histories: The Practice of Archaeology and History in Non-Western Settings*, pp. 1–24. Sante Fe: School of American Research Press.

Shanks, M. 2006. Archaeology and politics. In J. Bintliff (ed), *A Companion to Archaeology*, pp. 490–508. Malden: Blackwell.

Shennan, S. 2006. Analytical archaeology. In J. Bintliff (ed), *A Companion to Archaeology*, pp. 1–20. Malden: Blackwell.

Simmons, D.R. 1976. *The Great New Zealand Myth: A Study of the Discovery and Origin Traditions of the Maori.* Wellington: A.H. and A.W. Reed.

Smail, D.L. 2008. *On Deep History and the Brain.* Berkeley: University of California Press.

Smith, C.D. 1992. The *Annales* for Archaeology? *Antiquity* 66:539–542.

Smith, S.P. 1910. *History and Traditions of the Maoris of the West Coast, North Island of New Zealand prior to 1840.* New Plymouth: T. Avery.

Smith, S.P. 1913. *The Lore of the Whare-wananga, or, Teachings of the Maori College on Religion, Cosmogony, and History: Written down by H.T. Whatahoro from the Teachings of Te Matorohanga and Nepia Pohuhu, Priest of the Whare-wananga of the East Coast, New Zealand.* New Plymouth: T. Avery.

Stafford, D.M. 1967. *Te Arawa: A History of the Arawa People.* Wellington: A.H. and A.W. Reed.

Stokes, E. 1980. *A History of Tauranga County.* Palmerston North: Dunmore Press.

Thomas, J. 2006. The great dark book: archaeology, experience, and interpretation. In J. Bintliff (ed), *A Companion to Archaeology*, pp. 21–36. Malden: Blackwell.

Tosh, J. 1984. *The Pursuit of History: Aims, Methods and New Directions in the Study of Modern History.* London: Longman.

Trigger, B.G. 1989. *A History of Archeological Thought.* Cambridge: Cambridge University Press.

Wylie, A. 1992. The interplay of evidential constraints and political interests: recent archaeological research on gender. *American Antiquity* 57(1):15–35.

22

Trans-Tasman stories: Australian Aborigines in New Zealand sealing and shore whaling

Nigel Prickett

Auckland War Memorial Museum, Auckland, New Zealand

nprickett@aucklandmuseum.com

Introduction

Soon after the establishment of the English convict settlement at Sydney in 1788, New Zealand's first sealers landed at Dusky Sound in 1792 (Smith 2002:11), alerted to the presence of seals there by the journal of Captain Cook who visited in 1773 during his second voyage to the Pacific (Beaglehole 1961:135). The first sealing on Bass Strait islands took place in 1798 (Ling 1999:327). Exploitation of subantarctic islands began in 1804 at the Antipodes group (Smith 2002:12). Everywhere, big early catches soon declined. Nonetheless, seal numbers in southern New Zealand were sufficient to maintain an industry into the early 1830s (Smith 2002:12), with gangs dropped off along the coast from vessels out of Sydney, or in the 1820s by boat from Foveaux Strait. As relationships developed with Maori, especially with Maori women, many sealers stayed on to make a new life in New Zealand.

The first shore whalers set up in New Zealand in the late 1820s at Preservation Inlet at the southwest of the South Island and at Tory Channel, Cook Strait. Many sealers who had made a home in New Zealand moved easily to the new industry. Throughout the 1830s and in the early 1840s, shore whaling was New Zealand's biggest industry, exporter and employer. New Zealand's early sealing and whaling industries were part of the commercial interests of Sydney merchants, who pursued anything that might turn a profit, also including New Zealand timber and flax (*Phormium tenax*), and beche-de-mer, sandalwood and pork from tropical Pacific islands. Sydney's ocean frontier was central to Australia's early commercial and capital development.

This paper derives from a historic-archaeology research project on New Zealand shore whaling, supported by the Marsden Fund of the Royal Society of New Zealand and carried out in collaboration with Ian Smith, of the Anthropology Department, University of Otago. The main research focus has been Banks Peninsula where the 1840s Oashore whaling station was excavated in January–February 2004, and the Hawke's Bay district (Hawke Bay) where Te Hoe on Mahia Peninsula was investigated in 2005. Shore whaling at these places was part of a sealing and whaling industry which played a significant role in early colonial economic and social history on both sides of the Tasman (Figure 1).

With Australia the source of most New Zealand shore whalers, it is not surprising that one and two generations after the First Fleet sailed into Port Jackson some were of Aboriginal descent. Their fathers were convicts or ex-convicts. Mothers came from the many tribes that lived at or near the Australian coast and were largely dispossessed and dispersed early in the process of colonisation. The best known among them was Thomas Chaseland, whose convict father arrived in New South Wales in 1792 and later settled in the Hawkesbury district near Sydney. Chaseland was sealing at Foveaux Strait from c. 1824 and later whaled at several southern stations. Notable Hawke's Bay whalers from the mixed-race sealing communities of Bass Strait and Kangaroo Island were George Morrison, Edward Tomlins and Samuel Harrington.

Thomas Chaseland

The father of the New Zealand sealer and whaler, also called Thomas Chaseland, was convicted at Middlesex, on October 26 1791, aged 19, for an offence given as 'Capital Respite' (Colonial Secretary, Convict Indents 1788 to 1798. COD/9, State Records NSW) – i.e. it was a capital offence (unstated) for which he received instead a life sentence. After time on a hulk, he arrived in Port Jackson on the *Royal Admiral* on October 7 1792 (Smee and Provis 1981). In July 1824, 'Thomas Chasling' applied for land not periodically flooded, as was his 30 acres at Lower Portland Head on the Hawkesbury River near Windsor (Colonial Secretary, Fiche No 3082:829, State Records NSW). He stated that he had arrived in the colony 'upwards of 31 years ago and [was] now settled upwards of 21 years', indicating he completed his sentence c. 1803.

Thomas Chaseland had several children with Margaret McMahon, beginning with John, born c. 1798 (reported as 30 years of age in the 1828 census, where the family is listed as 'Cheeseling', with 'Chaseling' under 'other surnames'; State Records NSW). There followed Ann, Jane, Thomas, Louisa and Charlotte (Smee and Provis 1981). Thomas and Margaret were married at St Matthew's Church, Windsor, on November 29 1812, with five of their children baptised the same day (McDougall pers comm. 2008). Margaret died in 1815 aged 38 (NSW Pioneers Index 1788–1988, State Records NSW). Thomas and Margaret's son Thomas was born in 1807 (Baptisms Index, NSW Registry of Births, Deaths and Marriages; State Records NSW), and is recorded in the 1828 census (State Records NSW) as 22 years of age and living at Lower

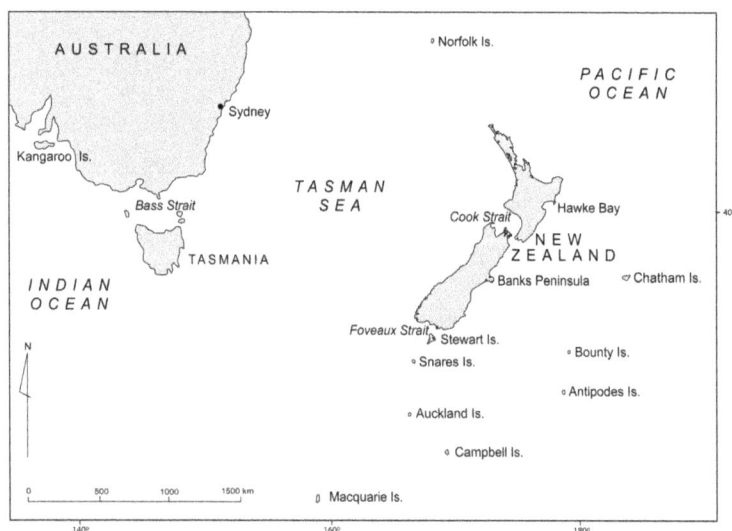

Figure 1. New Zealand and southeast Australia.

Portland Head (i.e. Windsor). Thomas senior died in 1847 at Wilberforce, New South Wales (Smee and Provis 1981). Thomas, born in 1807, died on October 30 1878 – at Wilberforce, like his father (Smee and Provis 1981).

The New Zealand Thomas Chaseland first appears in the crew list of the *Jupiter* (Captain Bunster), which left Sydney on August 6 1817 for Hobart, as 'Thomas Chaseling, son of a settler at Windsor by a native woman' (Cumpston 1970:44). The Society of Australian Genealogists (SAG) on-line 'NSW Ships' Musters 1816–1825' has Chaseland listed as a passenger on the *Frederick* and crew on the *King George*, both in 1818. 'Thomas Chaselin', 'Seaman', left Hobart for Port Dalrymple (Launceston) and Port Jackson on the *Governor Macquarie* on October 2 1819 (Crowther Port Certificate Book, L11, p. 71, Tasmanian State Archives). On October 7 1820 'Thomas Chaceland 23' left Sydney on the *Glory* for Port Dalrymple on a sealing voyage to the islands northwest of Australia (Cumpston 1970:54), which importantly gives his age. Ages are often given for younger seamen on crew lists at the time. Thomas was thus born c. 1797, 10 years before his half-brother of the same name, and a year before the birth of Thomas and Margaret's first child in 1798. The *Glory* returned to Sydney on January 13 1822 after 15 months, but details of the voyage and cargo are lacking (Cumpston 1970:54).

On April 9 1823, Chaseland left Sydney on the *St Michael* (Captain Beveridge) for New Zealand and Tonga (Cumpston 1970:70; Cumpston 1977:139; SAG on-line 'NSW Ships' Musters 1816–1825'). On January 25 1824, he sailed on the *Nereus* (Captain Emmett) from Sydney taking convicts to Port Dalrymple, arriving there on February 10 (Cumpston 1970:70, 1977:147; Nicholson 1983:94), and from there on a sealing voyage, because in May 1824 the *Nereus*, now under Captain Swindells, was back at George Town and Launceston with seal oil and skins from the 'Fishery/Sealing Is' (Cumpston 1970:70; Nicholson 1983:96), probably southern New Zealand. No later record of Chaseland has been found in crew or passenger lists out of Australian ports. Thus, although specific information is lacking, it is likely the *Nereus* left Chaseland at Foveaux Strait on this voyage. Important places in Chaseland's career in southern New Zealand are shown in Figure 2.

According to 1879 recollections of the whaler Edwin Palmer to Dunedin historian Dr T.M. Hocken, Chaseland was the headsman on sealing boats belonging to Sydney merchant (Robert) Campbell in Foveaux Strait in early 1826 (Begg and Begg 1979:300). On January 13 1827, Chaseland was on the *Glory*, in which Campbell had an interest, when it went ashore at Pitt Island in the Chathams (*The Australian* March 20 1827). Captain Swindells and some crew subsequently reached the Bay of Islands in a long boat. Chaseland and others reached New Zealand at Moeraki in an open sealing boat (Shortland 1851:153).

Herries Beattie, recorder of southern Maori lore, has accounts of the voyage from two Maori sources (given here from Church In press). An informant named Ellison states of Puna, wife of 'Tame Titirene' (Chaseland):

> Her husband and she went to Chatham Islands & were wrecked. They built a boat & put sufficient food on it & came back here. She was a great tohunga & pulled one of her hairs, said a karakia & put it in the sea, so they had a safe voyage and landed at Moeraki.

Mrs Walscott (Ema Karetai), told Beattie: 'Puna sat in the bow of his [Chaseland's] boat from Chatham Island karakia-ing to keep the storm down.' For southern Maori this was an important story about two notable individuals.

But Beattie (1919:219–220) has a less attractive story of Chaseland's relations with Maori when he and other sealers, provoked by a raid on their camp at Arnott Point in south Westland (Beattie has Arnett's Point) when one of their number was killed, attacked a Maori settlement in

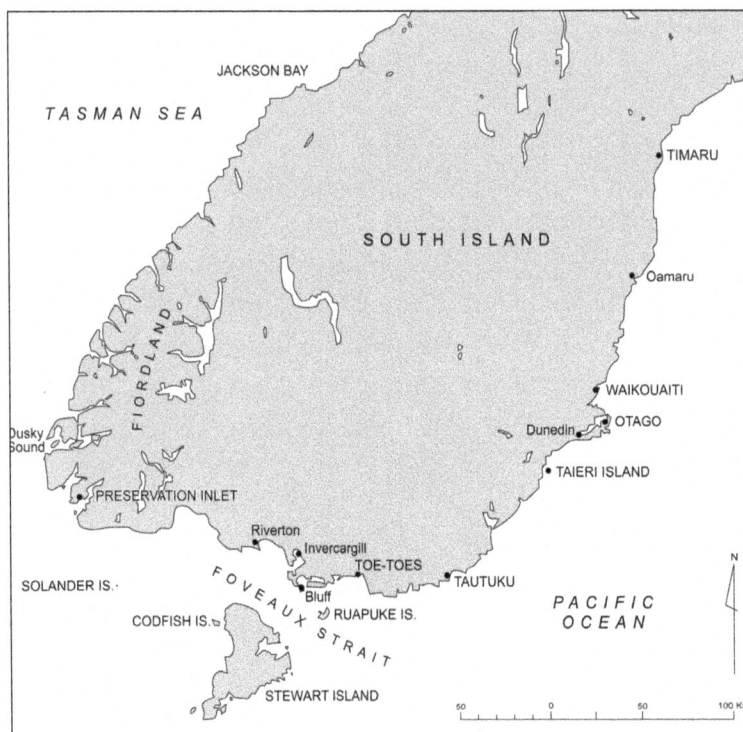

Figure 2. Southern New Zealand.

the vicinity of Okahu (Jackson Bay) or Arawhata. Several Maori were killed and a child named Ramirikiri, whose parents were killed, was left for dead by a berserk Chaseland who '... dashed her head on a rock'. But Ramirikiri survived and would later remind Chaseland of the event, who had nothing to say in reply. Another source has two sealers killed in the Maori raid and, from Chaseland's information on a map among papers of the survey ship HMS *Acheron*, an annotation that 30 Maori were killed in the reprisal (Starke 1986:xliv-xlv). The sealers then went to Anita Bay, Milford Sound, and attacked another Maori party, apparently killing all of them there or at Whareko, the next bay south. The Chaseland/*Acheron* map locates several tit-for-tat encounters between sealers and Maori in the 1820s.

On February 28 1831, Chaseland was among the first residents at Sealers Bay, Codfish Island (Whenuahou), after the island was set aside in the mid-1820s by Foveaux Strait chiefs for sealers and their Maori wives (Howard 1940:65; Anderson 1991:5; Middleton 2006:8–9). This was partly to help prevent just such conflict as described above between bands of sealers and Maori widely scattered around Foveaux Strait and northward. Doubtless it was useful for Maori to know where the sealers were, while sealers will have gained certainty for their settlement and security in numbers. This was important in 1833, when 200 Maori are said to have arrived on Codfish Island to 'exterminate' the sealers (Howard 1840:66–67). But the latter were warned by one of the Maori wives and met the war party on the beach armed with muskets, whereupon the sides agreed on peace, which was not broken afterwards.

On February 28 1831, Chaseland was one of three survivors of the *Industry* (Captain Wiseman), which left Codfish Island in a northerly gale for shelter and went down at Easy Harbour, Stewart Island (Howard 1940:85). Wiseman, 10 seamen and six Maori women were drowned (McNab 1913:86). The other survivors were Puna and George Moss who was living on Ruapuke Island. Howard says when the ship hit rocks entering the bay, Chaseland struggled to rescue Puna, but it was she who 'dragged the insensible Chaseland ashore', and the episode became the subject of a Maori song now lost. According to F. Hall-Jones (1944:157), Chaseland got Puna ashore then went back to rescue others, but hit his head on a rock, so Puna in turn rescued him. Differing accounts of the wreck and events leading to it are outlined by Middleton (2006:29–30). Also from his sealing days, Chaseland related how he was the only survivor of an attempted landing on one of two small islands (Green or Taieri) south of Cape Saunders (Shortland 1851:153–154).

When Sydney capitalists set up the first New Zealand whaling stations many Foveaux Strait sealers turned to the new industry. The first southern station was Bunn and Company's operation at Preservation Inlet from 1829 (Prickett 2002:19). Right whales calved in the bays and inlets of southern New Zealand from as early as April, the season continuing until about October. Chaseland had previous experience on sea-going whalers. The first record of his involvement in New Zealand is in 1835 when he and James Brown took 11 whales in 17 days from Toe-Toes at the mouth of the Mataura River (Shortland 1851:300). This was reported by Edward Shortland (1851:145) as 'the greatest feat of the kind ever performed in the country'. As there were no casks at the station, the oil was lost and the only product will have been whalebone. In 1836, Chaseland and Brown obtained 30 tuns (Shortland 1851:300), which is the last record of whaling at Toe-Toes.

In 1837, 'Chaseling' was 'chief headsman' at Preservation Inlet, where he was first to beat the boy Charles Denahan before Edward Palmer beat him with a rope's end, from which he died, leading to a manslaughter trial at Sydney (McNab 1913:204–220). In April 1838, Octavius Harwood, the Weller brothers' storekeeper at Otakou, issued Chaseland with whaling gear for the season, probably as manager at one of the harbour stations (Tod 1982:36). In September 1842, James Joss of Stewart Island wrote to Harwood that Chaseland had taken two boats to set up a 'new fishery' at Jackson Bay (Howard 1940:371), a locality he knew from sealing days. This suggests he was prospecting for the 1843 season, as unless the news was many months old, it was too late for 1842. There was a whaling station at Jackson Bay, but whether it was established as early as 1842 and whether Chaseland whaled there both need confirmation. He was not at Jackson Bay in 1843, as in March that year he signed an agreement to whale at Waikouaiti with Stephen Smith and Thomas Jones (Tod 1982:93), and was in Waikouaiti in August that year at the height of the whaling season for his marriage to Puna (see below). Later in 1843, Chaseland accompanied Shortland (1851:141–164) on Johnny Jones' *Scotia* from Waikouaiti in his survey of Foveaux Strait settlements.

In 1844, Chaseland managed a three-boat, 25-man station at Taieri Island for Johnny Jones, taking 45 tuns of oil and two tons of whalebone (*NZ Spectator and Cook's Straits Guardian* February 12 1845). Dr David Monro, of Nelson, who accompanied Frederick Tuckett's expedition looking for a site for a proposed Scottish settlement in southern New Zealand, wrote on May 1 1844 that the party was '... hospitably entertained by a Mr. Chasland, the head man on the island, while his active Maori wife acquitted herself most respectably of the household duties of cooking and bed-making' (Hocken 1898:247; see Hocken 1898:215 for Tuckett's comments). In 1846, the two-boat, 18-man Timaru station under 'Chesland' took 43 tuns of oil and two tons of whalebone (*NZ Spectator and Cook's Straits Guardian* February 3 1847). Joseph (1903) tells of Chaseland being a partner of Palmer at Tautuku. If so, he was there some time between 1839 and 1846, as William Palmer was set up at Tautuku by Johnny Jones in 1839 and said himself he was eight years there, 'until the whales became scarce' (*Evening Star* July 4 1881). This has confirmation from 1847, being the first year the station is not listed in New Zealand production data (*NZ Spectator and Cook's Straits Guardian* January 8 1848), indicating it was closed by then.

From the above information, of variable quality, Chaseland was whaling at Toe-Toes in

1835 and 1836, Preservation Inlet 1837, Otakou 1838, Jackson Bay 1842 (?), Waikouaiti 1843, Taieri Island 1844, Timaru 1846 and Tautuku in one or more of the missing years between 1839 and 1846. In 1851, he was taken on as pilot for HMS *Acheron's* survey of the West Coast sounds (Howard 1940:130).

Chaseland was renowned among Foveaux Strait sealing and whaling gangs for his 'great size and strength' and 'was considered the best whaler in New Zealand' (Shortland 1851:153). In 'Reminiscences of Early Days', published in *The Otago Witness* December 12 1906, L. Langlands says of Chaseland:

> … his mother being an Australian gin, from whom, probably, he inherited his wonderful sight, was a large, heavy, clumsy-looking man, but wonderfully light on his feet, and, despite his bulk, very active; when fast to a whale, on relinquishing the steer-oar to go to the bow of the boat to use the deadly lance, he would run along the gunnel as active as an acrobat.

There are stories of his extraordinary eyesight, such as seeing a whale invisible to the master of the *Amazon* who had the advantage of a telescope (Howard 1940:392). Church (In press:128) gives other claims by his contemporaries of an ability to see nearly a mile underwater. Shortland describes him as 'a universal favourite owing to his excellent temper; never being quarrelsome under any circumstances' (Shortland 1851:153). F. Hall-Jones (1944:157) writes of his 'eagle-eye, his uncanny knowledge of New Zealand waters, his almost super-human strength, courage, [and] prowess …'. In 1856, aged nearly 60, he offered to fight the first Bluff constable in a trial of manhood (F. Hall-Jones 1944:159).

The best-known story of the legendary Tommy Chaseland relates to the naming of the South Otago headland 'Chasland's Mistake' (the Maori name is Makati; or Makate, see Roberts 1909). One version has him mistaking it in fog for Cape Saunders, which Joseph (1903) rightly thinks unlikely, given his knowledge of the coast and famous eyesight. Chaseland himself said that it tells of an occasion when, against orders, his gang attacked seals as soon as they made their seasonal return to that part of the coast, rather than leave them alone until settled, and that most therefore fled and were lost. Another version has Chaseland landing one evening but leaving the seals for the morning, by which time they had gone (Beattie 1948:10; J. Hall-Jones 1990).

Another story is from Tautuku (Joseph 1903). Whales were sighted one foggy June morning and boats launched after them. But when Chaseland made fast to a whale he was towed into the fog, and when he got close enough to use the lance the whale lashed out and destroyed the boat. Two Maori and a Pakeha were killed and Chaseland, Sam Perkins and a third Maori were left clinging to wreckage. After nearly an hour in the water and hidden from the other boats by fog, Chaseland stripped off and swam for the shore six miles away. The other two were then rescued, although the Maori died afterwards from exposure. Despite a search, Chaseland was not found and the other boats returned to Tautuku to report the loss. But late in the afternoon, he was seen after his long swim in the cold southern ocean, walking along the beach to the station, where he was revived by dry clothes and a pannikin of rum.

In his appetite for alcohol, too, Chaseland was legendary. Shortland (1851:152) saw him at Ruapuke Island drunk on 'sour wine' from a wrecked cargo and lying 'like a cask' on the bottom of their boat. According to F. Hall-Jones (1945:76–77), it was actually rum, part of the cargo of the *Lunar* wrecked at Waipapa Point. It had been brought to Ruapuke, but when all the men were drunk at the same time, the rum was hidden by the Maori women. Chaseland apparently knew where it was. In another story, Captain Stevens of the Otago, who had engaged Chaseland for a whaling voyage, found him drunk in a Dunedin hotel and lured him into a whaleboat to be taken to the ship only by the promise of rum applied as required on the way out (Langlands

1906). When Stevens tried to ration the rum and told him to wait until they reached the next point in the harbour, Chaseland's reply was, 'Pull, and be ___ to you', the incident giving its name to Pulling Point below Port Chalmers. In his liking for alcohol, he was no different from most sealers and shore whalers at the time.

The marriage of 'Thomas Chaseling' and 'Mary Puna' was formalised at Waikouaiti on August 14 1843 by the Rev. James Watkin (J. Hall-Jones 1990). They had no children. Puna was a relation of the Otago chief Taiaroa (Joseph 1903; Howard 1940:85), or his sister, according to Tuckett, who met her at Taieri Island in May 1844 (Hocken 1898:215). Begg and Begg (1979:278) give a short whakapapa showing Taiaroa and Puna as brother and sister, but Shortland's (1851:Table F) more extensive genealogical table does not name Puna. Whatever the relationship, Puna's ritual ability to ensure a safe passage from the Chatham Islands reflects and proclaims her high birth. Chaseland and Puna were together as early as January 1827, when they were wrecked on Pitt Island, and probably in 1826, when he lived at Codfish with other sealers and Maori wives, if not earlier. Puna died of influenza and was buried on January 6 1849 at Waikouaiti, aged 42 (McDougall pers comm. 2008).

On August 15 1850 at Ruapuke Island, Chaseland, then resident at Bluff, married Pakauhatu/ Pakawhatu (Margaret Anthony in the marriage register), daughter of Anthony Remond and Esther Pura. The register has his age as 47 (he was probably 53) and hers as 15 (Wohlers Register of Marriages Nos 4 and 5, Hocken Library, Dunedin), although there is information giving her birth date as February 20 1837, and therefore 13 when she married (McDougall pers comm. 2008). They were to have six children: Maria born in 1852, Thomas 1854, John 1856, Caroline 1861, William Henry c. 1864 and Margaret 1866 (McDougall pers comm. 2008).

Thomas Chaseland died on Stewart Island on June 5 1869 (J. Hall-Jones 1990). His name is remembered in Chasland's Mistake and the associated Chaslands district, and by Chasland's Point on The Neck, Stewart Island, marked on Captain Wing's 1844 chart (Howard 1940:124, 126) and under Schoolhouse Point on the latest NZMS 260 map sheet. Chaseland also contributed to New Zealand science when he found a pair of moa feet at Waikouaiti, reported by Walter Mantell (1872:95). Mostly, however, he is remembered as a huge presence and character in the early contact period in southern New Zealand.

George Morrison

George Morrison was the son of Patrick Morrison, of County Tyrone, Ireland, who was convicted in March 1792, aged 19, and arrived in New South Wales on the *Boddington* on August 7 1793 on a seven-year sentence (Principal Superintendent of Convicts, Bound Indents, 1786–1799, State Records NSW). Patrick was one of many convicts who made for the sealing grounds when they finished their sentence. Having suffered for long under the often brutal and generally brutalising convict regime, they may have wished for nothing more than to go somewhere they would be left alone and where there was the prospect, at least, of earning a living, and possibly a great deal more. A generation later, whaling stations on both sides of the Tasman would offer the same attractions.

The younger Morrison was born on August 12 1817 on King Island, Bass Strait (Figure 3), and baptised with his brother Charles, older by one year, on October 9 1821 at St Johns, Launceston, when the family was living at Georgetown on the Tamar estuary (Baptisms in the Parish of St Johns, Launceston, Microfilm RGD 32/1, 1170/1821, Tasmanian State Archives). In the baptism register, their mother is named 'Elizabeth' and described simply as 'A Native'. Patrick Morrison is likely to be the same as buried at Launceston on March 19 1824 after drowning, although his age given as 54 does not quite match 19 years in 1792 (Register of

Burials, RGD 34/1, 1803–1838, 883/1824, Tasmanian State Archives). At the time, he is said to have been living at Launceston.

George Morrison may be the same as a Morrison in charge of a whaling party at Portland in 1837 (Townrow 1997:12), although he was 19 or 20 at the time, which is young for such a position. He first appears in New Zealand as whaling master at Macfarlane's fishery at Wairoa, Hawke's Bay (Figure 4), in its first seasons in 1844 and 1845 (*NZ Spectator and Cook's Straits Guardian* Febuary 22 1845, December 6 1845), possibly arriving to set up the station when men and stores were landed from Macfarlane's *Kate* in December 1843. This date is given as part of evidence in a court case arising from Morrison selling whalebone to a man named Crummer when the station's production rightfully belonged to Macfarlane as owner (*NZ Spectator and Cook's Straits Guardian* September 27 1845). Crummer and Morrison claimed that Morrison and others were at Wairoa setting up a 'share party' before Macfarlane first arrived at the end of 1843. If so, this did not change Macfarlane's ownership of the fishery, although it does leave open the date of Morrison's arrival. The court found for Macfarlane. Morrison was at Wairoa just two seasons (*NZ Spectator and Cook's Straits Guardian* February 22 1845, December 6 1845) before managing Perry's Waikokopu station in 1846 (Wakefield 1848:193). In August 1849, his schooner *Neptune* was wrecked at Long Point on Mahia Peninsula (Ingram 1984:37). Later records of his New Zealand career have not been found.

Edward Tomlins

Edward (Ned) Tomlins was born at Cape Barren in 1813 to Samuel Tomlins of Kangaroo Island (Plomley and Henley 1990:103) and a woman whose name George Robinson of the Tasmanian Aboriginal mission gives as POOL.RER.RE.NER, or BULL.RUB, BULLROE, BULRA and BOOLROI (Plomley 1966:1002). Edward was baptised at St John's, Launceston, on January 22 1819 (Tipping 1988:197; Plomley and Henley 1990:103). His father was aged 20 when sentenced to seven years' transportation, reaching Sydney in 1803 on the *Calcutta* and Hobart on January 1 1804 (Index to Tasmanian Convicts, Tasmanian State Archives; Tipping 1988:317; Plomley and Henley 1990:103). He was discharged in 1809 (Tipping 1988:197) and was soon on the sealing grounds between Australia and Van Diemen's Land (Figures 1 and 3). Samuel Tomlins drowned in 1819 when the *Jupiter* was anchored at the Bay of Shoals, Kangaroo Island (Cumpston 1970:45; Plomley and Henley 1990:103).

His son is also given as Tomlinson and 'Edward Hanson', although according to Plomley (1966:1016), the latter may be an error, since it appears only in part of Robinson's journal which relies on a copy and where there are several apparently incorrect names. Robinson describes Tomlins in 1830 at Hunter Island as 'a fine stout well-made young man about eighteen years of age' (Plomley 1966:179). Plomley and Henley (1990:103) say he was 5 ft 8 inches (1.73 m) in height and stoutly built. George Dunderdale ([1898]:13) in 'The Book of the Bush' states that 'Black Ned was a half-breed native of Kangaroo Island'. In 1830, he was living on Hunter Island with 'NICK.ER.UM.POW.WER.RER.TER', or 'Mary', of Leven River or Ben Lomond, Tasmania (Plomley 1966:1018).

When Robinson visited in June 1830, the 'head man' of four Hunter Island sealers was Bay of Islands Maori 'John Witieye' (Plomley 1966:179), also probably an error, as elsewhere Robinson has MYTYE, MYTEE and MYET.EYE (Plomley 1966:1014). The name may have been 'Maitai'. The other men were Robert Drew (Rew or Rue, see Plomley 1966:1015), David Kelly and 'the half-caste youth, named Edward Hanson' (Plomley 1966:180; but see above). In December 1830, Tomlins was one of five Hunter Island men marooned on the Clarke Island

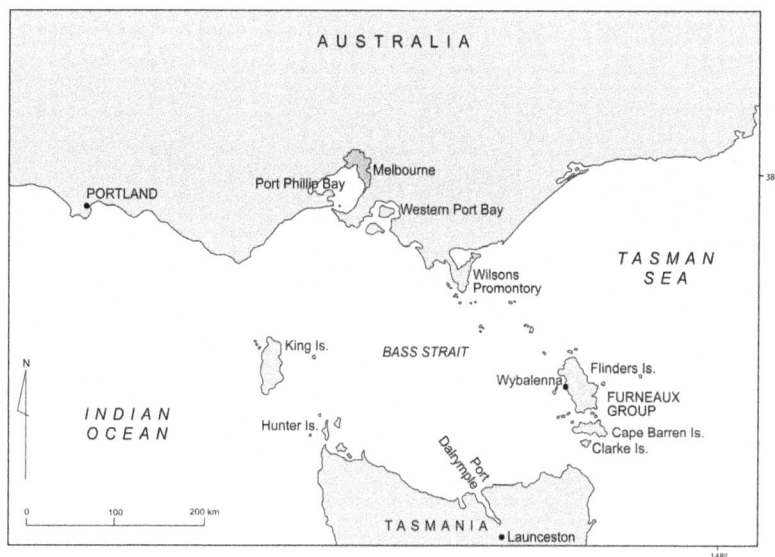

Figure 3. Bass Strait.

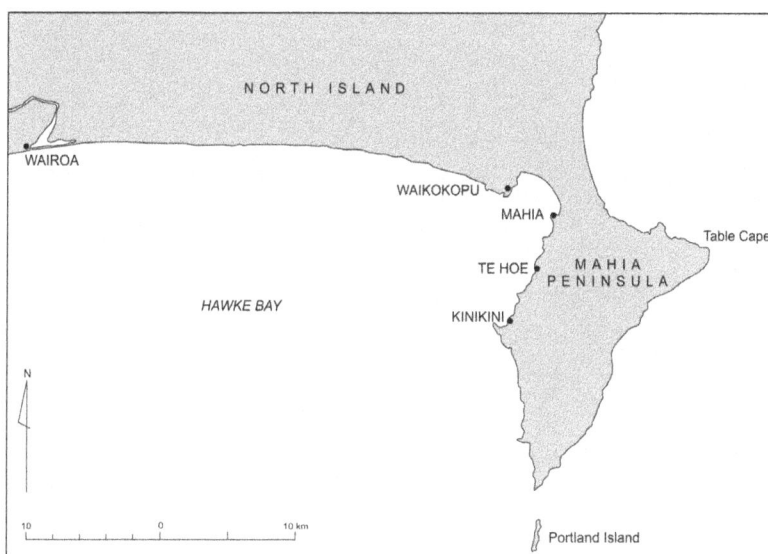

Figure 4. Northern Hawke's Bay.

reef when their boat was lost (Figure 3). Two disappeared trying to reach safety in a makeshift craft, the others living for eight days on seal meat and blood before being rescued (Plomley 1966:295–296).

In February 1832, Bulra arrived in Launceston from Kangaroo Island, where for years she had been living with a sealer named 'Young Scott' (Plomley 1966:801,1002). She went on to Hunter Island, probably because her son was there, but Edward left soon after on a whaling voyage to the 'western coast of New Holland', and may have sold or bartered his mother, who was soon living with John Dodson and then Robert 'Rew', both of them sealers and ex-convicts (Plomley 1966:1002). When Robinson returned to Hunter Island later in 1832, Bulra asked to be removed to the Aboriginal settlement on Flinders Island and was given up to him on August 17 (Plomley 1966:1002). At Flinders Island, she was probably at Lagoons until February 1833 and then at Wybalenna, when that settlement was established (see Birmingham 1992:129; Figure 3). In November 1832, Tomlins petitioned to have her returned to Hunter Island, but this was refused, Robinson advising: '… Tomlins is not a fit person to have charge of this woman he being wholly under the influence of the other sealers and himself addicted to drunkenness and immorality' (Plomley 1966:802). Bulra died on Flinders Island probably before September 1835 (Plomley 1966:1002).

Tipping (1988:317) states that Tomlins 'was an associate of William Dutton in the early days of whaling at Portland Bay and became a famous harpooner' (Figure 3). Nash (2003:91–92) has Dutton whaling for Launceston entrepreneurs Griffiths and Connolly in 1832 at Portland, which may have been the destination of Tomlins' whaling voyage early that year (see above). He is also likely to have been one of 24 men taken to Portland by the *Henry* in April 1833 (Cumpston 1970:120) for the second season. Dunderdale ([1898]:13) says that by 1835, Tomlins was 'looked upon as the best whaler in the colonies, and the smartest man ever seen in a boat'. On March 19 1836, he left Launceston as a passenger on the *Thistle* (Index to Departures 1817–1867, from an original record POL (Port of Launceston) 458/2, p. 21, Tasmanian State Archives), probably for the Portland fishery at that time of year. The *Thistle* was at Portland as early as 1834, initially to set up the Henty station in opposition to Dutton (Cumpston 1970:123–124).

On December 20 1836, 'Edward Tomlinson' was one of two headsmen on the barque *Socrates* (Captain Dutton), which left Launceston on a whaling voyage (POL 458/2, p. 56, Tasmanian State Archives). In early May 1836, the *Socrates* returned to Launceston from Portland with 23 tuns of sperm oil, with news that 'bay whaling' had commenced there (Chamberlain 1989:21). Thus, Tomlins at this time may have been whaling the year round, for sperm whales from the *Socrates* in summer and for right whales at Dutton's Portland station from autumn to October. Cumpston (1970:115–125) has an account of Griffiths and the productive Portland fisheries (see Nash 2003:91–94).

It is not known when Ned Tomlins arrived in Hawke's Bay. Information on his New Zealand career comes largely from 'An Old Colonist', thought to be F.W.C. Sturm, writing in the *Hawke's Bay Herald* in June 1868: 'Where all were drunkards, Ned Tomlins was notorious; he was a valuable man, and an able headsman.' In his 'Old Wairoa', Thomas Lambert (1925:368) describes Tomlins as 'said to be one of the best whalers that ever stepped into a boat' (apparently after Dunderdale), and recklessly generous, once giving away one of three sperm whales he had taken in exchange for a bucket of water. Lambert (1925:368) says he worked for Captain Mansfield and whaled out of Waikokopu and Kinikini. At Waikokopu, he probably whaled with Morrison, whom he may have known from Portland. Tomlins died there after a successful day's whaling. More drunk than others who were playing cards, he was turned out of a house, but insisted on trying to get back in. Finally, he was hit by the station owner, a man named Perry, and thrown from the door, later to be found dead outside. Perry himself read the burial service. This happened before Perry died of 'apoplexy' on the beach at Mahia in 1853.

Tomlins and Hipora Iwikatea of Mohaka had one son, also Edward Tomlins, who had three children, a girl Akenehi, a boy Tamati, and a second girl Hera. Hipora Iwikatea died on November 12 1900, her son Edward predeceasing her on December 15 1892 (Parsons pers comm. 2008).

Samuel Harrington

The Australian history of Samuel Harrington is more problematic. A published list of early 19th century sealer/Aboriginal liaisons in Tasmania has only one Harrington (Plomley and Henley 1990:64), who must logically be the same John Harrington said elsewhere in the same source to have lived in the Bass Strait islands with 'WORE.TER.NEEM.ME.RUM.NER.TAT.TE.YEN. NE', otherwise 'Bet Smith', who was abducted by him from Cape Portland as a child (Plomley

1966:1020). Harrington was, of course, a convict, who, two days after being discharged at Sydney on May 25 1820, sailed on the *Little Mary* for Port Dalrymple and Bass Strait (Plomley and Henley 1990:82–83) and the freedom of the sealing grounds. He drowned at Gun Carriage Island (now Vansittart Island, at the eastern end of the strait, which lies between Flinders and Cape Barren Islands) about December 1824, after which Bet Smith was 'seized' by Thomas Tucker, who sold her to Thomas Beadon (Plomley 1966:1020), or she was 'claimed' by John Williams (Plomley and Henley 1990:83). According to Robinson, Tucker was among those active in shooting Aboriginal men at their fires and then abducting their women (Plomley 1966:1017).

Although the partner of John Harrington in the Plomley and Henley (1990:64) list is said to be from Van Diemen's Land, rather than Australia (Cape Portland), this does not necessarily rule out Bet Smith or this particular Harrington. There is, however, a 'half-caste' Maria Harrington recorded twice by Plomley and Henley (1990:63): in 1827 aged 10 and living in the household of James Holman, and in an 1831 list of 'half-caste' children in Launceston, 'aged about 17, a vagrant'. Maria cannot have been the child of a man who reached Tasmania in 1820, so there was one other Harrington/Aborigine liaison at least. Another John Harrington in Tasmania early enough to be the father of Maria, and perhaps Samuel, is listed among convicts brought from Norfolk Island in 1808 (Nobbs 1988:195), probably reaching Hobart on the *City Of Edinburgh* on October 5 that year (Nash pers comm. 2008).

'T. McD.' in *The Lyttleton Times* (July 6 1885) refers to Harrington at the time of a visit to Wairoa by Bishop Selwyn, Church of England archbishop of New Zealand, as follows:

> One very powerful fellow, a half-caste Australian black, was known by the name of Shiloh. He was "cock of the walk" at the Wairoa, being a first-class boat-steerer, harpooner, fighter, fifty-two inches round the chest, and a hard drinker. These virtues retained him possession of the position he had gained.

The journal of Wairoa missionary the Reverend James Hamlin dates Selwyn's visit to December 1845 (Hamlin Journal, December 9 and 11 1845, Hocken Library). Harrington was thus under Morrison at Wairoa, raising the possibility that he and perhaps Tomlins as well, and other Australian whalers, all came with Morrison at the end of 1843, possibly from Portland. Lambert (1925:370) writes that Harrington was a 'Tasmanian half-caste' who whaled at Mahia, Kinikini and Waikokopu and for Joseph Carroll at Te Hoe.

Something of Harrington's style is told by a court case regarding an incident at Mahia in 1851, reported by boatsteerer Joseph Mason (Hawke's Bay Province, Donald McLean Papers, Folder 130A, Alexander Turnbull Library, Wellington). Harrington is said to have threatened and attacked his men, intending, it seems, to make them leave and break their contracts so he would not have to pay them out at the end of the season. This suggests he was owner of the station; otherwise, he presumably would not have had to bear the cost. Mason wrote to Donald McLean, as the only Justice of the Peace in the region, complaining that he had been 'most Barbarously ill treated and my life threatend by one Samuel Harrington in a most shoking maner and sent away without my wages'.

According to Mason, one day in October 1851, Harrington ordered the boat launched from his station with the purpose of going across the bay to Waikokopu for rum:

> Some time after we arrived there he was intoxicated about 12 o'clock at night he came down to the Boat Swearing in a most awfull maner and Enquiring where Hooper another whaler was the answer was lying on the grass where drunken people in general lay, he ordered us to launch the Boat which we did, when a short distance on the water he got up as one deprived of all reason and Seized a Boat Spade used to cut up the Whale's Blubber, and a most deadly instrument.

The boat with Harrington and two European and five Maori whalers aboard got home 'after a while and with much trouble'.

Next morning, Harrington:

> ... raving like a mad man took up an axx and threatening to kill all around. Struck one of the Natives on the Back but did not do him much hurt the Native runing at the time and he after him.

He then took up a tomahawk, swearing to kill anyone who opposed him. The whalers kept away from him, 'knowing that all our wages depended upon his honesty and being now to the amount of from £21 to £30 and upwards so that it appears that he did not wish to pay us ...'. Harrington then set fire to a house used by his Maori whalers.

The court case did not consider the violence, which was probably thought the business only of those involved. Instead, it set out to determine current whaling practice in order to establish the justice of Mason's claim. Four affidavits dated December 6 1851 are important in describing whaling practice in the bay at the time. The court's decision was for Mason to be paid out at a 1¼ share, although this may not have ended the matter, as among the case papers is a note: 'Mason agrees to take the share of 1 & ¼ which canot agree to pay', and initials which might be 'SWH'. Other cases heard the same day were Mason versus Carroll, seeking payment for the repair of a boat, and Stewart versus Mason for defamation and assault (McLean Journal, Vol. 4, p. 68, Alexander Turnbull Library), so Mason, too, may have been a difficult character.

Samuel John Harrington is listed in the 1858 Ahuriri and Hawke's Bay electoral roll as 'whaler' of Mohaka, in Hawke's Bay south of Wairoa, qualifying as a householder (*Hawke's Bay Herald* August 28 1858). He is listed under Mahia as a whaler in the first issue of *Wise's Directory*, published in 1875 (Feilding ed 1875). He died at Wairoa on December 15 1875 (*Hawke's Bay Herald* December 17 1875).

Aborigines in New Zealand sealing and shore whaling

In *Making Peoples*, historian James Belich (1996:131–132) notes the importance of the sealing industry to early Maori/Pakeha contact in southern New Zealand. He goes on, 'Sealing also pioneered a Tasman world', and he describes sealers, whalers and seamen who did not distinguish between two sides of the Tasman in their activities, with Bass and Foveaux Straits and the subantarctic islands all being referred to as the 'Sealing Islands', in 'a joint past historians in both countries seem reluctant to recognise'. Sydney was for long one of New Zealand's most important cities and New Zealand one of Sydney's most important hinterlands (Belich 1996:134). Sealing and whaling industries developed capital needed for Australia's early economic growth and were among New Zealand's first significant commercial activities (see Steven 1965; Hainsworth 1972).

Tomlins, Morrison and Harrington came from the mixed-race sealing communities of Bass Strait and Kangaroo Island. Robinson describes how sealers shot Aboriginal men as they sat around their fires, and then abducted the women (e.g. Plomley 1966:966). Or women were traded by Aborigines themselves, from their own tribes or others from which they had been abducted (Ryan 1977:30–31). At first, women were made available for the sealing season only, but as sealers began to stay on throughout the year, so too did their 'wives'. By 1816, sealers each might have two to five women for sexual and domestic purposes. Robinson refers to them as 'slaves' (Plomley 1966:1008). In 1830, Tomlins' headsman at Hunter Island, the Maori 'John Witieye', had two women (Plomley 1966:180). Coastal tribes were devastated, Robinson reporting just three women with 72 men in Tasmania's northeast, also in 1830 (Plomley 1966:966).

Chaseland had a very different early history in the Hawkesbury district near Sydney. His father also was a convict. Nothing is known of his mother, who was probably from a local tribe. He was born a year before his father's first child with his European wife. It seems he was then brought up at Windsor with step-brothers and step-sisters. He is said to have been illiterate (J. Hall-Jones 1990). Were his father's other children also illiterate? In 1807, a half-brother was also named Thomas after his father, who clearly was more pleased with his black son in 1797 than he was 10 years later. Chaseland almost certainly left home before the first available record on the 1817 *Jupiter* crew list when he was already 20.

In the best contemporary account of New Zealand shore whaling, Edward Jerningham Wakefield (1845 I:311) identifies the men as ex-seamen, runaway convicts from New South Wales and Van Diemen's Land, and their descendants whom he knew as 'currency lads' and whom he greatly admired. But this term did not include those discussed here. In the language of the day, they were Australian or Tasmanian half-castes or 'New Holland blacks' – that is, they were identified as being of mixed race or by their Aboriginal parentage. When Australia was naming and identifying with its colonial-born and the country they were making their own, such men were on the margins. Thomas Chaseland's half-brother of the same name was 'currency' that he could never be.

But if 'half-castes' felt excluded from the new Australia, the main reason for moving to New Zealand was undoubtedly economic. The opportunity of making a living, and even doing well, was an attraction in any industry first to exploit a new resource – grasslands and gold are other important Australasian examples. The men introduced here were experienced in sealing or whaling or both. Chaseland was probably a sealing headsman from his first arrival. His leading role at Toe-Toes in 1835 tells of previous whaling experience. Tomlins had a big reputation in Australian whaling, while Morrison must have been experienced to have begun in New Zealand as manager at Wairoa. Harrington was 'cock of the walk' in his first or second year at Wairoa and was later station manager at Mahia – or owner, since he planned to benefit from driving his men off to avoid paying them out. Hawke's Bay drew whalers from districts of declining production on both sides of the Tasman as the last significant whaling region to be developed, the first season probably being 1837 (Prickett 2002:103).

Other factors may have come into decisions to move to New Zealand. Chaseland may have met Puna on a previous visit, encouraging him to make the move. Also, such men were used to the freedom and opportunity of Sydney's ocean frontier and New Zealand would have appealed to those used to life beyond the reach of government at Bass Strait and Kangaroo Island. In July 1847, Hawke's Bay missionary William Colenso wrote of a Wairoa informant describing local whalers as 'runaway soldiers and man-of-warsmen, convicts from New South Wales and Van Dieman's Land, who openly boast of their defiance of the Government' (Dinwiddie 1916:28).

Other Aborigines in New Zealand include one of five sealers picked up in 1813 after several years stranded on the rock that is Solander Island at the western entrance to Foveaux Strait (McNab 1907:149–150), and a Kangaroo Island woman and two-year-old child who survived the killing of a sealing gang from the *General Gates* by Maori at Stewart Island, then to live on their own for eight months before being rescued and returned to Sydney in April 1824 (Cumpston 1970:66; Richards 1995:35). A 'Tasmanian half-caste' known only as 'Darkie Coon' whaled at Mahia and Wairoa, Hawke's Bay (Lambert 1925:371). There are records of several others.

Maori also left home on sealing and whaling voyages. On October 23 1813, five were on the *William and Ann* at Sydney (Cumpston 1970:36). On the *Glory* out of Sydney for Port Dalrymple and the seal fishery on October 30 1819 was 'Jacky Miti (Myty)' (Cumpston 1970:53), likely to be the same as Tomlins' headsman on Hunter Island in 1830 (see above).

Tahitians, too, were in Sydney's multi-racial crews. In 1816, four were on the Endeavour for Kangaroo Island (Cumpston 1970:42). When the *Perseverance* left for Kangaroo Island on July 21 1824, there were four Maori and two Tahitians in a crew of 21 (Cumpston 1970:69). In 1838, 30 Maori made up a third of the men in 15 whaleboat crews racing at Hobart, afterwards performing a haka for spectators (Morton 1982:169). For such men, the arrival of European commerce in the Pacific opened a new world of opportunity.

On both sides of the Tasman, the domestic comfort and sexual services provided by women was an important aspect of the relationship between native people and sealers and whalers. We have seen how adversely this impacted on Aborigines. There was also a major impact on Maori communities, although the trajectory of the native and newcomer relationship was very different. As in Bass Strait, Maori women were at first traded only for the sealing or whaling season, the men returning to Sydney in the off-season. Later, this changed to permanent relationships as men stayed throughout the year, cultivating gardens or living with their wives' relations. In 1844, Tuckett estimated that between Banks Peninsula and Riverton, 'two-thirds of the native women, who are not aged, are living with European men' (Hocken 1898:223). In northern Hawke's Bay, many of today's Maori families have whalers' names.

Tasmanian Aborigines were killed or removed from their land, and women bartered, sold or stolen (Ryan 1977). Maori tribes, on the other hand, remained on their land and in many cases incorporated the newcomers into tribal society and whakapapa, especially when women were from chiefly families, as in the case of Puna (see Anderson 1991:7). This is not to say that killings did not take place. Chaseland himself was involved, as we have seen, but where Maori could set aside Codfish Island as a home for sealers, or in Hawke's Bay insist on rent from whaling stations, they certainly had more power.

In the history of European expansion, men of Aboriginal descent working in the New Zealand sealing and whaling industries have personal histories at the edge of a fraught and often bloody European/native relationship. Yet in other ways, they were like the men they worked with, runaway or discharged convicts and their sons, ex-seamen who as likely as not had jumped ship, adventurers or men simply on the run from another life. All were looking for economic opportunity and many also escape from a past. All made their way in an environment new to them, where what counted were experience and skill and personal qualities. In shortcomings and achievements, Chaseland, Morrison, Tomlins and Harrington reflect sealer and whaler culture of the time. While they did not escape the labels 'half-caste' or 'black', they made the best of opportunities at Australasia's early maritime frontier, and so played a part in social, economic and ultimately political transformations of the time and place.

Acknowledgements

I would like especially to acknowledge and thank Atholl for his good company when we were students at Otago University in the early '70s. When the rest of us heard that typewriter clacking away into the small hours in the back office at Cumberland Street, we were not to know that his thesis on the Black Rocks middens was to begin a stellar contribution to New Zealand and Pacific archaeology and history.

This paper results from research on the New Zealand shore-whaling industry carried out with Ian Smith of the University of Otago and supported by the Royal Society of New Zealand's Marsden Fund. For particular help, I would like to thank: the late Terry Arnott, Heritage Branch,

South Australian Department of Environment and Heritage; Ian Church, Port Chalmers; John Hall-Jones, Invercargill; June McDougall, Dunedin; Tony Monteith and Patrick Parsons, Napier; Mike Nash, Parks and Wildlife Service, Tasmania; Lynette Russell, Monash University, Melbourne; Mark Staniforth, Flinders University, Adelaide; Auckland Museum library staff. Peter Quin prepared the figures.

References

Anderson, A.J. 1991. *Race Against Time*. Dunedin: Hocken Library.

Beaglehole, J.C. 1961. *The Journals of Captain James Cook on His Voyages of Discovery. The Voyage of the Resolution and Endeavour 1772–1775*. Cambridge: Cambridge University Press for the Hakluyt Society.

Beattie, H. 1919. Traditions and legends. Collected from the natives of Murihiku. (Southland, New Zealand). *Journal of the Polynesian Society* 28: 212–225.

Beattie, H. 1948. *Otago Place Names*. Dunedin: Otago Daily Times and Witness Newspapers.

Begg A.C. and N.C. Begg 1979. *The World of John Boultbee*. Christchurch: Whitcoulls.

Belich, J. 1996. *Making Peoples; a history of the New Zealanders*. Auckland: Allen Lane and Penguin.

Birmingham, J. 1992. *Wybalenna: the archaeology of cultural accommodation in nineteenth century Tasmania*. Sydney: Australian Society for Historical Archaeology.

Chamberlain, S. 1989. Sealing, whaling and early settlement of Victoria; an annotated bibliography of historical sources. *Victoria Archaeological Survey Occasional Report 29.*

Church, I. In Press. Gaining a foothold, historical records of the east Otago coast, 1770 to 1839.

Cumpston, J.S. 1970. *Kangaroo Island 1800–1836*. Canberra: Roebuck Society Publication No 1.

Cumpston, J.S. 1977. *Shipping Arrivals and Departures Sydney, 1788–1825*. Canberra: Roebuck Society Publication No 22.

Dinwiddie, W. 1916. *Old Hawkes Bay*. Napier: Dinwiddie, Walker and Co.

Dunderdale, G. [1898]. *The Book of The Bush*. London: Ward Lock.

Feilding, T.H. (ed) 1875. *Wise's Directory of New Zealand for the Years 1875–76*. Dunedin: Henry Wise and Co.

Hainsworth, D.R. 1972. *The Sydney Traders; Simeon Lord and his contemporaries 1788–1821*. Melbourne: Cassell Australia.

Hall-Jones, F.G. 1944. *Kelly of Inverkelly*. Invercargill: Southland Historical Committee and H. and J. Smith.

Hall-Jones, F.G. 1945. *Historical Southland*. Invercargill: Southland Historical Committee and H. and J. Smith.

Hall-Jones, J. 1990. Chaseland, Thomas. In *The Dictionary of New Zealand Biography* (Vol. 1), p. 80. Wellington: Allen and Unwin and the Department of Internal Affairs.

Hocken, T.M. 1898. *Contributions to the Early History of New Zealand (Settlement of Otago)*. London: Sampson Low, Marston.

Howard, B. 1940. *Rakiura; a history of Stewart Island, New Zealand*. Dunedin: Reed, for the Stewart Island Centennial Committee.

Ingram, C.W.N. 1984. *New Zealand Shipwrecks 1795–1982*, Sixth edition. Wellington: Reed.

Joseph, F.A. 1903. The old whaling station on Taieri Island. *The Otago Witness* 22 April 1903.

Lambert, T. 1925. *The Story of Old Wairoa*. Dunedin: Coulls, Somerville, Wilkie.

Langlands, L. 1906. Reminiscences of early days. *The Otago Witness* 12 December 1906.

Ling, J.K. 1999. Exploitation of fur seals and sea lions from Australian, New Zealand and adjacent subantarctic islands during the eighteenth, nineteenth and twentieth centuries. *Australian Zoologist* 31:323–350.

McNab, R. 1907. *Murihiku and the Southern Islands*. Invercargill: William Smith.

McNab, R. 1913. *The Old Whaling Days*. Wellington: Whitcombe and Tombs.

Mantell, W.B.D. 1872. On moa beds. *Transactions and Proceedings of the New Zealand Institute* 5:94–97.

Middleton, A. 2006. *Two Hundred Years on Codfish Island* (Whenuahou). Invercargill: Department of Conservation.

Morton, H. 1982. *The Whale's Wake*. Dunedin: University of Otago Press.

Nash, M. 2003. *The Bay Whalers; Tasmania's shore-based whaling industry*. Woden: Navarine Publishing.

Nicholson, I.H. 1983. *Shipping Arrivals and Departures, Tasmania, Vol. 1, 1803–1833*. Canberra: Roebuck Society Publication No 30.

Nobbs, R. 1988. *Norfolk Island and its First Settlement* 1788–1814. North Sydney: Library of Australian History.

Plomley, N.J.B. (ed) 1966. *Friendly Mission; the Tasmanian journals and papers of George Augustus Robinson 1829–1834*. Tasmania: Tasmanian Historical Research Association.

Plomley, N.J.B. and K.A. Henley 1990. The sealers of Bass Strait and the Cape Barren Island community. *Tasmanian Historical Research Association Papers and Proceedings* 37:37–127.

Prickett, N.J. 2002. *The Archaeology of New Zealand Shore Whaling*. Wellington: Department of Conservation.

Richards, R. 1995. *Murihiku Re-viewed; a revised history of southern New Zealand from 1804 to 1844*. Wellington: Lithographic Services.

Roberts. W.H.S. 1909. Maori nomenclature; early history of Otago. *The Otago Witness* 10 March 1909.

Ryan, L. 1996. *The Aboriginal Tasmanians*. Sydney: Allen and Unwin.

Shortland, E. 1851. *The Southern Districts of New Zealand*. London: Longman, Brown, Green and Longmans.

Smee, C.J. and J. S. Provis 1981. *The 1788–1820 Associations Pioneer Register*, 2nd edition, Vol. 1 (unpaginated). Sydney: The 1788–1820 Association.

Smith, I.W.G., 2002. *The New Zealand Sealing Industry*. Wellington: Department of Conservation.

Starke, J. (ed) 1986. *Journal of a Rambler; the journal of John Boultbee*. Auckland: Oxford University Press.

Steven, M. 1965. *Merchant Campbell 1769–1846*. Melbourne: Oxford University Press.

Tipping, M. 1988. *Convicts Unbound; the story of the Calcutta convicts and their settlement in Australia*. Ringwood: Viking O'Neil.

Tod, F. 1982. *Whaling in Southern Waters*. Dunedin: Published by the author.

Townrow, K. 1997. *An Archaeological Survey of Sealing and Whaling Sites in Victoria*. Heritage Victoria and Australian Heritage Commission.

Wakefield, E.J. 1845. *Adventure in New Zealand*. London: John Murray.

Wakefield, E.J. 1848. *The Hand-book for New Zealand*. London: John W. Parker.

23

Maori, Pakeha and Kiwi:
Peoples, cultures and sequence in
New Zealand archaeology

Ian Smith

Anthropology Department, University of Otago, New Zealand

ian.smith@stonebow.otago.ac.nz

Introduction

Archaeologists have generally constructed culture-history sequences within either a prehistoric or a historic time frame. As Lightfoot (1995) noted, this has constrained examination of the interface between these two periods. What is argued here is that this has also limited archaeology's contributions to understanding the modern world. Cultural interfaces and their dynamics dominate the 21st century world, yet archaeology generally deals only distantly, if at all, with the key elements of this. For example, the people typically identified as 'Polynesian' in modern New Zealand are not the descendants of the 'Polynesian settlement' of the country studied by archaeologists. The former are predominantly Samoan, Cook Island, Tongan and Niuean immigrants of the second half of the 20th century and their New Zealand-born offspring, while the latter concerns the arrival some 700 years earlier of ancestors of the indigenous Maori population. Although these groups have ancestral connections in biology, language and culture, they have quite different recent histories and distinctive identities in the modern world. Archaeology has played a significant role in documenting what these groups share, but it has contributed little to understanding the emergence of their distinctiveness.

This is not to say that archaeological study of New Zealand's past has not made important contributions to the ways in which the world today is understood. The long history of research into human interactions with fauna (e.g. Anderson 1989, 2002; Smith 2005; Leach 2006) and flora (McGlone 1989; McGlone and Wilmshurst 1999) have made New Zealand one of the foremost examples of the impact of human colonisation on island environments (Diamond 2000; Grayson 2001). Yet even here, the focus has been temporally constrained, with nearly all of the attention placed on the environmental impacts of prehistoric colonisation. In only a handful of cases has archaeological attention has been extended to encompass the environmental consequences of more recent colonisation (Diamond 1984; Smith 2005). The comparative perspective this enables has enhanced understanding of not only the specific cases under investigation, but also more general patterns of exploitation, response and outcomes.

This paper is a first attempt to construct an archaeological culture-history sequence that encompasses the whole of New Zealand's archaeological record. For the first two-thirds of this (c. 500 years), it draws on almost a century and a half of archaeological research into pre-European occupation. Archaeologically based sequences have been proposed since the 1870s (von Haast 1872; Duff 1956; Golson 1959; Green 1963; Davidson 1984). Although population replacement was initially posited as a driver of change, adaptation and innovation within a single cultural tradition has been preferred since 1959. Golson's terminology has been most persistent, although exactly what his Archaic and Classic terms mean in the light of recent chronometric shortening of New Zealand's human time scale (Anderson 1991a; McFadgen et al. 1994; Higham and Hogg 1997) has yet to be properly considered. Archaeology of the post–1769 era has been recorded since the 1920s, and especially during the past two decades (Smith 1991, 2004a). I am not aware of any archaeologically based sequences or models of change proposed for this era.

The approach offered here uses as its main driver three key phases of immigration: the initial Polynesian settlement; first European settlement; and subsequent multicultural immigration. Each brought new people, cultural forms and economic modes. They were also characterised by rapid adaptation to the New Zealand setting, making it appropriate to use indigenous terms adopted by or applied to the incomers as period names. **Maori**, derived from 'tangata maori' (ordinary people), was adopted by descendants of the initial settlers to distinguish themselves from the second wave of immigrants (Salmond 1997:21–22, 279). Of the various names Maori applied to these incomers, the most persistent was **Pakeha**, probably from 'pakepakeha' (pale-skinned people), and it soon became widely used (ibid). Although often extended to cover all non-Maori New Zealanders, its use here is restricted to those of European descent. Images of **Kiwi**, birds of the genus *Apteryx*, developed as a national emblem during the second half of the 19th century, and from the early 20th century, the name was adopted as a generic term for all New Zealanders (Phillips 2007). Its use as a period name here is extended back to the beginnings of the multicultural immigration phase. The implications of this approach for understanding the relationships of New Zealand's diverse peoples and cultures, and the nature of change throughout the archaeological sequence are considered below, after the main characteristics of each period are outlined.

Maori period

New Zealand was settled, near synchronously with other islands in southern Polynesia, about 1250–1300 AD (Anderson 2000; Higham and Jones 2004). Claims of earlier transient visits (Holdaway 1996; Holdaway et al. 2002) have not been corroborated (Anderson and Higham 2004; Wilmshurst and Higham 2004). Indeed, chronometric hygiene has reduced the timescale of human occupancy in New Zealand by about 25 percent, highlighting New Zealand's significance as a case study of human impact on the environment. Little attention has yet been given to the implications of a shortened timescale for understanding New Zealand's material or social culture, and preliminary consideration of this is given here.

The first settlers came from central eastern Polynesia. Archaeology, biology, linguistics and tradition all point towards the zone encompassing the Cook, Society and Marquesas islands as a homeland area (Walter 2004). Close similarities in material culture, economy and settlement pattern throughout this region make it difficult to define one or more specific island homes, but also give us a fairly good idea of the cultural patterns that would have existed there (Walter *et al.* 2006:275–277). Households were the primary unit of production and labour, located within sedentary villages as the main residential site type. These were situated so as to maximise access to major resource zones for an economy based around inshore fishing, root and tree-crop horticulture, husbandry of pigs, dogs and chickens, along with forest hunting and gathering. Smaller specialised sites indicate that the village communities integrated these activities through logistic mobility over relatively widespread territories. Key elements of the material-culture assemblage include adzes with quadrangular, triangular and trapezoidal sections, and sometimes a tanged lashing grip; shell fishing gear, dominated by trolling lures and one-piece bait hooks; and a range of ornament forms, including reels and whale-tooth pendants (Walter 1996).

Artefacts closely matching these patterns are found in early New Zealand sites, while some distinctly different forms were observed by the first European visitors (Davidson 1984:61). These, and other contrasts, have encouraged a polarised view of the Maori period, emphasising early hunting of now extinct moa and other 'big game', and later building of fortified pa, and formalised in material-culture terms by Golson's (1959) definition of Archaic and Classic phases. Although problems with this approach have been long recognised (Groube 1967; Davidson 1984:223; Furey 2004), the simple bipartite division has persisted.

The chronometric hygiene revolution has brought these problems into sharper relief, relegating to an 'undated' status many sites once considered to have been securely placed within the sequence. Only four of the sites Golson used to define the Archaic material-culture assemblage now have admissible dates, and his Classic phase was, from the outset, based on stratigraphically insecure collections and early European observations (Furey 2004). Most attempts to define more finely grained sequences of change within specific artefact classes (e.g. Crosby 1966; Hjarno 1967; Simmons 1973; Jacomb 1995) are equally lacking a secure chronological foundation. Nor can this problem be overcome by reliance on proxy indicators of age, as their evidential basis has also been undermined. A prime example is the use of evidence for hunting moa as an indicator of age. When Anderson (1989) reviewed data from more than 300 moa-hunting sites, some 73 were considered to have reliable radiocarbon ages, but application of rigorous criteria for acceptability culled this to just 15 (Schmidt 2000). While this does not overturn more than a century and a half of stratigraphic observations that moa remains are most commonly found in the earlier layers of multi-strata sites, it severely limits certainty about the time span of this activity and the usefulness of archaeological evidence of it for chronological placement of otherwise undated deposits.

Where sites have been sufficiently well dated to indicate a relatively short occupation span, and have had large artefact assemblages examined in detail, they have demonstrated the contemporaneity of some artefact forms once thought to be chronologically distinctive (Anderson *et al.* 1996; Furey 1996, 2002). This makes it difficult to view either the Archaic or Classic as discrete, monolithic assemblages, or to retain the common practice of using these terms to define chronological phases within the Maori period. There is now more than ever a critical need to reassess the nature and timing of cultural changes during the Maori period. Detailed assessment of this is beyond the scope of the present paper, but some initial propositions are offered towards this end.

It is clear that some aspects of tropical East Polynesian cultural systems were transformed rapidly on arrival in New Zealand. The most obvious example is the horticultural component of the economy, with only six of the tropical root and tree crops viable, their growth restricted to limited parts of the country, and new storage methods required (Furey 2006). New opportunities were also apparent, with much larger and more abundant resources available for hunting than was the case in the East Polynesian homeland. However, the inference that 'big game' hunting dominated early Maori economic activity cannot be sustained. There has been only one analysis undertaken of the relative contributions to prehistoric diets from all classes of fauna in a substantial nationwide sample of sites (Smith 2004b). This showed that marine animals were the most important sources of meat throughout the Maori period, even in areas where moa were hunted, with fish predominant in the north and marine mammals in central and southern regions. Nor was 'big game' hunting confined to the initial phase of settlement. Although seals had disappeared from the North Island by c. 1500 AD, they continued to be hunted in parts of the South Island until the end of the Maori period (Smith 2005). As already noted, it is difficult to define the period of moa hunting, and any regional variations in it. Transformations in material culture are also likely to have varied in pace, with the differing qualities of local materials influencing the rate of change from ancestral East Polynesian forms, and innovations arising sporadically. Detailed analysis of assemblages with radiocarbon dates that survive modern chronometric scrutiny will be required to document this and determine which, if any, artefact forms co-varied through time.

One aspect of change which has withstood the scrutiny of chronometric hygiene is the emergence of fortified pa about 1500 AD (Schmidt 1996). There have been widely varying interpretations of what this might reflect about changing social, settlement and subsistence patterns (Phillips and Campbell 2004). The interpretation preferred here is that pa are primarily defended versions of the residential villages, satellite camps and storage facilties that occurred in earlier times (Walter *et al.* 2006), and thus represent continuity, as much as change.

Most writers on the archaeology of the Maori period have drawn it to a close with the arrival of Cook in 1769. While this marks the first European footfall on New Zealand soil, and the major point of entry for Maori into the historical record (Salmond 1991, 1997), it is questionable how much impact it had on the archaeological record. Initial contact was confined in geographic extent, limited in duration, and followed by departure. A restricted range of items, such as iron nails, axes, beads and glass, may have been added in small numbers to the material inventory, but the only examples that can be securely provenanced to Cook's voyages are several medals distributed during his voyages (Jones 1984; Trotter and McCulloch 1989:97). Furthermore, archaeological investigations at initial-contact-phase sites have highlighted the continuity of Maori activities. Groube's (1965, 1966) attempt to uncover archaeologically what had been recorded by French explorers in 1772 showed this to have been substantially altered by subsequent Maori occupation. Likewise, recent investigation of gardens at Anaura Bay observed by Cook in 1769 disclosed a history of use beginning well before that time and continuing long after (Horrocks *et al.* In press). While 1769 might justifiably be considered to mark the onset of a protohistoric phase at the end of the Maori period, the near invisibility of this fleeting ethnohistoric moment in the archaeological record and the absence of any non-Maori settlers on New Zealand shores during the following two decades suggests it is of limited use in defining the beginning of a major new period in the long-term culture-history sequence.

Pakeha period

The Pakeha period began when the first Europeans were left behind by their ship on New Zealand shores in 1792. From this time forward, metal, glass and ceramic artefacts became increasingly common in the archaeological record. Also apparent were new forms of housing, typically with chimneys, and a new range of economic pursuits, many geared to markets beyond New Zealand's shores. The immigrant population grew very slowly, numbering only about 2000 people in 1839 (Adams 1977:28), or about 2.5 percent of the total, before the start of more rapid growth which saw the Maori population outnumbered by the end of the 1850s (Pool

1991:61). Immigrant activity is discussed here in four loosely defined phases, based on the initial occurrence of settlement patterns that appear to have distinctive archaeological characteristics and regional distributions. Consideration is also given to Maori sites of this period, and in particular, the cultural and economic changes they reflect. Importantly, there are also sites that cannot easily be characterised as either Maori or European.

In the first two decades of the Pakeha period, immigrants were sojourners, who spent short periods in residence on New Zealand shores before departing. The first were a gang of 11 men who lived at Luncheon Cove, Dusky Sound, for 11 months in 1792–93, hunting fur seals and building at least two houses and a 60-ton schooner. Archaeological traces of the settlement include remains of a forge, slag and ironwork from shipbuilding, and a few ceramic and glass fragments (Smith and Gillies 1997). A second, larger group occupied nearby Facile Harbour in 1795–1797, leaving a broader array of artefacts and the cobblestone floor and chimney of a house (Smith and Gillies 1998). In each case, the archaeological record was depleted by the acidic soils and high rainfall of the Fiordland coast, limiting what can be inferred about the nature of subsistence and other cultural patterns.

The most important category of sojourner sites are those associated with the commercial sealing industry, which flourished along the western and southern shores of the South Island and Stewart Island. Analysis of both archaeological and historical evidence of the commercial sealing industry has identified a small number of hut and cave sites used by sealing gangs either during the initial boom of 1803–1812 or in the following two decades (Smith 2002). Few of these have been excavated. Among those that have are three caves at Southport, Chalky Inlet, investigated by Coutts (1972), who interpreted European artefacts in their upper layers as evidence of contact between Maori occupants of the caves and European seamen. However, subsequently discovered historical evidence shows at least one of these caves was lived in by sealing gangs in the 1820s (Smith 2002:41), illustrating how difficult it is to distinguish the archaeological signature of European sojourners subsisting on local resources from that of contemporary Maori. Changes in southern South Island Maori subsistence and settlement patterns began to emerge after the introduction of European potatoes by sealers in 1808–09 (Anderson 1998:72–75).

Another important area of early European contact was in the northern North Island, where harbours were scouted for flax and timber during the early 1790s. Pelagic whaling ships operated offshore, and by 1802, were calling regularly at the Bay of Islands for food, water and fuel (Salmond 1997:321–325). Some sojourners are known to have lived ashore with Maori (Orchiston 1972), but there are no sites that can be associated with such settlements. Potatoes and pigs were introduced during this period and rapidly developed by Maori as trade products (Middleton 2007a). Potatoes were also incorporated into traditional horticultural production and spread rapidly throughout the North Island, well beyond direct European contact. Phillips' (2000) analysis of sites on the Waihou River suggests that despite rapid adoption of potatoes by Hauraki Maori, there was only limited incorporation of European material culture before 1820.

The second phase of the Pakeha period was inaugurated with the establishment of a permanent residential settlement by missionaries at Oihi, Bay of Islands, in 1814 (Middleton 2003). Archaeological investigation of its successor at Te Puna (Middleton 2005, 2008) shows the early New Zealand missions were small household-based enterprises that endeavoured to draw local populations towards Christianity through education in domestic, agricultural and industrial arts. At Kororareka, on the opposite side of the Bay of Islands, a permanent settlement had developed by 1827 (Earle 1966). It appears to have originated as a Maori village established to service visiting whaling ships, into which European mariners and traders settled.

Archaeological investigations have assisted in charting its transformation over two decades from a predominantly Maori settlement to a largely European one (Best 2002).

A residential settlement that cannot be classified easily as either Maori or European was established in 1825 at Sealers Bay, Codfish Island, in the far south. This was a small village occupied by a community of European men, mostly absconders from sealing gangs, Maori women, and their mixed-race children (Middleton 2007b). Excavation has disclosed remains of simple European-style housing, food remains that are mostly indigenous, and both an artefact assemblage and cooking-related features that reflect elements of each cultural tradition (Smith and Anderson 2007).

Expansion of residential settlement was slow, and confined almost entirely to the far north and far south of the country until the end of the 1820s. One consequence of this was geographical variation in Maori access to imported material culture, observed most dramatically in relation to muskets, first acquired by some northern iwi from about 1806 (Ballara 2003:183). Their incorporation into traditional warfare increased its lethality, and with greater access to them, northern tribes conducted devastating raids that precipitated temporary abandonment of some regions to the south. In archaeological terms, the most significant consequence was the adaptation of traditional Maori defensive structures to accommodate the new threat (Jones 1994:83–94).

Maori demand for trade goods and the quest by Sydney merchants for new resources to exploit stimulated the third phase of Pakeha settlement, which saw rapid dispersal of permanent settlement along the coast. This began with the harvesting of flax and timber in the Hokianga in 1826, and in the next five years isolated shore trading stations were established around the North Island, focused initially on procurement of flax (Stokes 2002). Missionary settlement also expanded around the North Island, but the most important driver of expanding settlement was the shore whaling industry. This began in 1829, and during the 1830s and 1840s, at least 72 shore whaling stations were established, nearly all along the east coast between Foveaux Strait in the south and Cape Runaway in the north. Of all these activities, it is shore whaling that has attracted most archaeological attention (Campbell 1994; Prickett 1998, 2002a). A key feature of the archaeological record is its diversity. At Oashore, on Banks Peninsula, housing, artefacts and fauna are almost exclusively European in character, while at Te Hoe on Mahia Peninsula, they exhibit distinctive Maori features (Smith and Prickett 2006, 2008). When contextualised with the historical record, however, both sites highlight the cultural, social and economic entanglement of Maori and a diverse range of immigrants within the communities that formed around whaling stations. They also illustrate adaptations in the technology of whaling and economy and settlement patterns as shore whaling declined in importance (Smith and Prickett nd).

There are a small number of excavated Maori sites with confirmed occupation during the 1830s. Puriri and Opita, on the Waihou River (Phillips 2000), and Papahinu, adjacent to Manukau Harbour (Foster and Sewell 1995), were reoccupied at this time, after being abandoned during warfare in the 1820s. They each exhibit fundamentally traditional cultural patterns into which imported material culture was incorporated very slowly. In parts of Northland and the East Coast of the North Island, Maori cultivation of maize expanded rapidly in the 1830s, predominantly as a trade crop (Hargreaves 1963:108; Petrie 2006). Although not precisely dated, archaeological correlates of this may include the ditch and bank fences and ploughed fields visible on the coastal flats at Nukutaurua, Mahia Peninsula (Jones 1994:251–255), and the maize pollen from cores at Anaura Bay (Horrocks et al. In press).

The final phase of the Pakeha period began in 1840 with the establishment of formal towns in Auckland, Wellington, Wanganui and Akaroa, soon followed by New Plymouth

(1841), Nelson (1842), Dunedin (1848), Christchurch (1850) and Napier (1851). Continuous occupation since first settlement often makes it difficult to identify archaeological traces of the first decade or two within urban settings. These have been identified most successfully in Auckland (Macready 1991), but are represented in as yet poorly reported excavations elsewhere. The year 1840 also marks the beginning of British colonial governance of New Zealand, and archaeological investigations have been undertaken at the first seat of government, at Okiato (Robinson 1995), and at the first parliament buildings in Auckland (Smith and Goodwyn 1990). Expanding colonial settlement and changing economic and political circumstances gave rise to sporadic conflict between the new government and some Maori. Archaeologically, this is reflected in the appearance of new styles of fortifications constructed by both Maori and European (Challis 1990; Smith 1989).

The 1840s and 1850s were a time of transition during which the principal settlement localities and economic pursuits that had sustained the Maori, European and mixed-race communities throughout the Pakeha period were marginalised by the burgeoning newly immigrant population and changes in economic focus. Pastoral farming, which had begun in the 1830s, expanded steadily through the Wairarapa, Hawkes Bay, Marlborough, Canterbury and Otago. Matanaka, in coastal Otago, is one of very few farmsteads established in this era to have been investigated by archaeological techniques (Knight and Coutts 1975). These decades were also the peak years of production for Maori agriculture, particularly the cultivation and milling of wheat, and for Maori engagement in the coastal trade that brought food and other products into the growing colonial towns (Petrie 2006). The changes this may have induced in settlement patterns have yet to be explored archaeologically. There are very few excavated Maori sites that can be confidently attributed to the 1840s or 1850s. The phase III occupation at Opita is one, and it shows a significantly greater presence of European artefacts than earlier Pakeha-period sites along the Waihou river (Phillips 2000).

Kiwi period

The year 1860 is used to define the beginning of the Kiwi period. It marks the first time since its arrival some 600 years earlier that the Maori population was outnumbered. In part, this reflects the steady decline in Maori numbers through the 19th century (Pool 1991), but the growth in immigrant numbers was a more important factor. This had become so rapid that the 1860s and 1870s was the only time since the late 13th century that people born overseas outnumbered those born in New Zealand (McKinnon 1997). The new immigrants were ethnically diverse. This was also true of the Pakeha period, although lack of data makes it impossible to document this, other than anecdotally, but the small, isolated, often pluralistic communities that dominated this era diminished its importance. The English made up probably just under half the new immigrants, followed by the Scottish, Irish and Australians, with Germans, Scandinavians, Chinese, Welsh and Americans making up much smaller groupings (Belich 1996:318).

The year 1860 also represents a major transition in ethnic politics, with rising immigrant demands for land and heightening Maori resistance to its loss giving rise to the first of a series of wars between various iwi and changing combinations of British, colonial and Maori forces. This stimulated two decades of fortification building throughout central regions of the North Island (Prickett 2002b), and led to massive alienation of land that displaced many Maori communities and disrupted their economic activities. Te Oropuriri, a small Taranaki village that spans the onset of the Kiwi period, shows that Maori housing retained much of its traditional character, but the material-culture inventory was dominated by ceramics, glassware and other European-made items (Holdaway and Gibbs 2006). There are very few excavated Maori sites from the

1860–1900 period, but where evidence is available, such as in the phase IV occupation at Opita (Phillips 2000) and at the Poutu and Te Rata settlements in the interior of the North Island (Newman 1988), imported artefacts are overwhelmingly dominant, suggesting widespread adoption of new cultural forms.

Of the new immigrant groups, only the Chinese have been subject to explicit archaeological scrutiny, which has shown they made a distinctive mark in the record following their arrival in 1865 (Ritchie 2003). Ceramics, food containers, opium-smoking paraphernalia and food preparation methods all provide clear indications of Chinese presence. While this reflects a distinct element of conservatism, adaptation to their new homeland is also evident in the adoption of locally available foods, beverages and building materials. Although no attempt has yet been made to explore this, it is expected other immigrant communities will be identified not so much through a distinct material signal, but through the integration of their oral and documentary histories with the archaeological record. It has been argued elsewhere that this approach to the analysis of community identity is one of the key challenges facing historical archaeology in New Zealand today (Smith 2004a).

At a more general level, there are several features of the artefactual record that characterise the period after 1860. Glass bottles appear in a wider range of types, but within each, they are more standardised in form. Nearly all embossing on bottles, other than some forms of base marks, date from after this time (Baugher-Perlin 1982). Ceramics include new decorative forms such as Japanese-themed central motifs (Samford 1997) and stand-alone banded rims (Brooks 2005:36). Further analysis will refine and expand this list.

The archaeological record of the first four decades of the Kiwi period is characterised by expansion in the geographic range of non-Maori settlement, the emergence of new economic pursuits, and the growth of urbanised settlements. It was the discovery of gold by Australian-born immigrant Gabriel Read in 1861 that sparked the first of a series of gold rushes that heightened the pace of immigration and transformed New Zealand's mid-19th century economy. This industry was almost certainly the largest single contributor to the making of New Zealand's archaeological landscape in terms of the acreage of land covered by sites (Ritchie 1991). It brought settlement to parts of the interior that had previously seen little other than transient Maori occupation, and left an archaeological record of fleeting camp sites (e.g. Bristow 1995) and permanent towns (e.g. Hamel 2004a). The wealth it generated, both directly and through mercantile support, transformed a number of towns into substantial cities. Excavations have shown that rebuilding of downtown areas variously destroyed and preserved older Pakeha-period parts of some cities (Petchey 2004), while those in foreshore reclamations have yielded substantial early Kiwi-period deposits (Bickler *et al.* 2004). Pastoral farming was another significant contributor to the emerging Kiwi economy. Initially, wool was its chief product and sheep numbers grew rapidly until the late 1860s, but its major growth took place after the development of refrigerated sea transport in the 1880s enabled large-scale meat production. Early development of the meat industry has been investigated archaeologically at Totara estate (Hamel 2004b), as has the changing importance of various farmed animals in 19th century diets and food supply networks (Watson 2000). Other large-scale industries, such as coal and coke production (Oliver and Wood 1981), emerged during this time, as did the road and rail infrastructure (Jacomb 2000) that for the first time in New Zealand's history reduced reliance on maritime communication and transport.

The foregoing discussion has been confined to the initial decades of the Kiwi period. To date, there has been only limited archaeological investigation of the transformations in economy, settlement pattern and material culture that occurred during the 20th century, but it is expected these will come under increasing scrutiny as the 21st century world impacts on the material remains of the 20th century.

Discussion

Maori, Pakeha and Kiwi are names used to refer to both groups of people and aspects of culture in New Zealand, and it is pertinent to set out what is intended by adopting them as period names in the sequence proposed here, and the relationships between these uses of the terms. They were employed as period names to emphasise that the advent of new peoples and their adaptation to this country were significant drivers of cultural change. As the foregoing review has illustrated, new forms of material culture, settlement pattern and economy emerged with each new phase of immigration, and these are recognisable through the archaeological record. In part, these new forms reflect the origins of the immigrants, in Polynesia, Europe or elsewhere. Artefact forms, styles of housing and modes of subsistence were transplanted from these homelands to New Zealand. However, the archaeological record shows that adaptation to the local setting was also an important contributor to change. For the first settlers, it was primarily differences in climate and resources that drove the process. For those that followed, adaptations also had to be made to the social and political world created by earlier arrivals. As indigenous names for successive waves of people, the terms Maori, Pakeha and Kiwi combine these concepts of advent and adaptation.

They are also intended to emphasise both the persistence and entanglement of peoples and cultures in the full sweep of New Zealand's history. It is obvious the people who became Maori and their culture were the only ones present in New Zealand during the Maori period. Their descendants and culture persist to this day, although transformed in many ways by biological and cultural entanglement with subsequent immigrants. As Anderson (1991b) has demonstrated, biological entanglement was rapid, and the resulting mixed-race communities followed diverse social and cultural trajectories. Archaeological evidence from the Pakeha and Kiwi periods provides a partial material record of such communities and has great potential to enhance understanding of both the persistence of traditional practices and the transformations through hybridisation that have shaped modern Maori culture.

Pakeha people and culture were defined, from the outset, by their entanglement with Maori. The small size and tenuous nature of their founding communities, coupled with the economic, political and numerical strength of Maori, encouraged interdependence, cooperation and intermarriage. Archaeology has begun to identify material evidence for the incorporation of Maori practices into early Pakeha culture. Like Maori, early Pakeha communities were transformed by the influx of immigrants in the 1860s. In their case, however, the majority of incomers were from a similar cultural tradition. This encouraged persistence of the term Pakeha despite a significant dilution of the early Maori influence. Nonetheless, fundamental aspects of Maori-Pakeha relations established during the Pakeha period have persisted or re-emerged as significant drivers of modern political, economic and cultural patterns in New Zealand.

Whereas Maori and Pakeha tend to be used as exclusive terms, Kiwi is inherently inclusive. When used to describe people, it refers to all those, including Maori, Pakeha, subsequent migrants and their diverse range of mixed-race offspring, who call New Zealand home. In a cultural sense, it includes the contributions of all resident communities. Modern Kiwi culture weaves together a plurality of strands. The dominant Pakeha strand, although originally derived largely from British and North American traditions, has a distinctive local flavour that distinguishes it from neighbouring Australia. Modern Maori culture retains ancestral elements from Polynesia shaped by seven centuries of adaptation, innovation, and borrowing from and hybridisation with subsequent immigrant cultures. In turn, it has influenced, but contrasts with, the hybrid Pasifika culture of the modern Polynesian migrants to New Zealand. Likewise, the descendants of late 19th and early 20th century immigrants from China have cultural patterns distinct from those of recent Chinese migrants. These, and many other examples that could be cited, demonstrate that each of strand of Kiwi culture has its own history. Archaeology has a significant role to play in charting these histories and discerning the processes that have shaped them. The long-term culture-history sequence proposed here provides a structure within which to achieve this.

Acknowledgments

The idea for this paper emerged while working with Atholl on the archaeology of Codfish Island/Whenua Hou, the southern New Zealand homeland of his Maori and Pakeha ancestors. Those investigations were funded by the Department of Conservation and the University of Otago. The paper also reflects a sustained period of research into the emergence of Pakeha culture supported by the Marsden Fund of the Royal Society of New Zealand. I am grateful for comments on the paper by Angela Middleton and an anonymous referee, and to Atholl for three decades of stimulating fieldwork, discussion and digression.

References

Adams, P. 1977. *Fatal Necessity: British Intervention in New Zealand, 1830–1847.* Auckland: Auckland University Press/Oxford University Press.

Anderson, A.J. 1989. *Prodigious Bird: Moas and Moa-hunting in Prehistoric New Zealand,* Cambridge: Cambridge University Press.

Anderson, A.J. 1991a. The chronology of colonisation in New Zealand. *Antiquity* 65:767–795.

Anderson, A.J. 1991b. *Race Against Time: The early Maori-Pakeha families and the development of the mixed-race population in southern New Zealand.* Dunedin, Hocken Library, University of Otago.

Anderson, A.J. 1998. *The Welcome of Strangers: an Ethnohistory of Southern Maori AD 1650–1850.* Dunedin: University of Otago Press.

Anderson, A.J. 2000. The advent chronology of south Polynesia. In P. Wallin and H. Martinsson-Wallin (eds), *Essays in Honour of Arne Skjolsvold,* pp. 73–82. The Kon Tiki Museum Occasional Papers 5.

Anderson, A.J. 2002. A fragile plenty: Pre-European Maori and the New Zealand environment. In E. Pawson and T. Brooking (eds), *Environmental Histories of New Zealand,* pp. 19–34. Melbourne: Oxford University Press.

Anderson, A.J., B.J. Allingham and I.W.G. Smith (eds) 1996. *Shag River Mouth: the Archaeology of an Early Southern Maori Village.* Research Papers in Archaeology and Natural History 27. Canberra: ANH Publications, RSPAS, The Australian National University.

Anderson, A.J. and T.F.G. Higham 2004. The age of rat introduction in New Zealand: Further evidence from Earthquakes #1, North Otago. *New Zealand Journal of Archaeology* 24:135–147.

Ballara, A. 2003. *Taua: 'Musket Wars', 'Land Wars' or 'Tikanga'? Warfare in Maori Society in the Early Nineteenth Century.* Auckland: Penguin Books.

Baugher-Perlin 1982. Analyzing glass bottles for chronology, function and trade networks. In R.S. Dickens (ed), *Archaeology of Urban America: The Search for Pattern and Process,* pp 259–290. New York: Academic Press.

Belich, J. 1996. *Making Peoples: A History of the New Zealanders from Polynesian Settlement to the end of the Nineteenth Century.* Auckland: Penguin.

Best, S.B. 2002. *Guns and Gods: The History and Archaeology of Rewa's Pa, Kororareka*. Whangarei: Department of Conservation.

Bickler, S., B. Bacquie and R. Clough 2004. Excavations at Britomart, Auckland. *Archaeology in New Zealand* 47(2):136–152.

Bristow, P. 1995. Excavation of a miner's hut (S143/226) in the Old Man Range. *Archaeology in New Zealand* 38:37–47.

Brooks, A. 2005. *An Archaeological Guide to British Ceramics in Australia, 1788–1901*. Melbourne: Australian Society for Historical Archaeology and La Trobe University Archaeology Program.

Campbell. M. 1994. Excavation of Weller's Rock tryworks, Otakou whaling station, Otago Harbour, New Zealand. *New Zealand Journal of Archaeology* 16:33–53.

Challis, A. 1990. The location of Heke's Pa, Te Kahika, Okaihau, New Zealand: A field analysis. New Zealand Journal of Archaeology 12:5–27.

Coutts, P.J.F. 1972. The emergence of the Foveaux Straits Maori from prehistory. Unpublished PhD dissertation, Anthropology, University of Otago.

Crosby, E.B.V. 1966 Maori Fishing Gear. A study of the development of Maori fishing gear, particularly in the North Island. Unpublished MA thesis, Anthropology, University of Auckland.

Davidson, J.M. 1984. *The Prehistory of New Zealand*. Auckland: Longman Paul.

Diamond, J. 1984. Historic extinctions: a Rosetta stone for understanding prehistoric extinctions. In P.S. Martin and R.G. Klein (eds), *Quaternary Extinctions: A Prehistoric Revolution*, pp. 824–826. Tucson: University of Arizona Press.

Diamond, J. 2000. Enhanced: Blitzkrieg against the moas. *Science* 287:2170–2171.

Duff, R.S. 1956 *The Moa-Hunter Period of Maori Culture*. 2nd edition. Wellington: Government Printer.

Earle, A. 1966. *Narrative of a Residence in New Zealand*. Oxford: Oxford University Press.

Foster, R. and B. Sewell 1995. *Papahinu: The Archaeology of an Early 19th Century Maori Settlement on the Bank of the Pukaki Creek, Manukau City*. Auckland: Department of Conservation.

Furey, L. 1996. *Oruarangi. The Archaeology and Material Culture of a Hauraki Pa*. Auckland Institute and Museum Bulletin 17.

Furey, L. 2002. *Hohoura. A Fourteenth Century Maori Village in Northland*. Auckland Museum Bulletin 19.

Furey, L. 2004. Material culture. In L. Furey and S. Holdaway (eds), *Change Through Time: 50 Years of New Zealand Archaeology*, pp. 29–54. New Zealand Archaeological Association Monograph 26.

Furey, L. 2006. *Maori Gardening: An Archaeological Perspective*. Wellington: Department of Conservation.

Golson, J. 1959. Culture change in prehistoric New Zealand. In J.D. Freeman and W.R. Geddes (eds), *Anthropology in the South Seas: Essays Presented to H. D. Skinner*, pp. 29–74. New Plymouth: Thomas Avery and Sons.

Grayson, D.K. 2001. The archaeological record of human impacts on animal populations. *Journal of World Prehistory* 15:1–68.

Green, R.C. 1963. *A Review of the Prehistoric Sequence in the Auckland Province*. Auckland Archaeological Society Publication 1 and New Zealand Archaeological Association Monograph 2. Auckland: University Bindery Press.

Groube, L.M. 1965. Excavations on Paeroa Village, Bay of Islands. *Historic Places Trust Newsletter* 9.

Groube, L.M. 1966. Rescue excavations in the Bay of Islands. *New Zealand Archaeological Association Newsletter* 9(3):108–114.

Groube, L.M. 1967. Models in prehistory: A consideration of the New Zealand evidence. *Archaeology and Physical Anthropology in Oceania* 2:1–27.

Hamel, J. 2004a. Potable water and sanitation in early Queenstown, New Zealand. *New Zealand Journal of Archaeology* 24:107–133.

Hamel, J. 2004b. *The Pig Pens at Totara*. Unpublished report to the NZ Historic Places Trust.

Hargreaves, R.P. 1963. Changing Maori agriculture in pre-Waitangi New Zealand. *Journal of the Polynesian Society* 72(2):101–117.

Higham, T.F.G. and A.G. Hogg 1997. Evidence for late Polynesian colonization of New Zealand: University of Waikato radiocarbon measurements. *Radiocarbon* 39(2):149–192.

Higham, T.F.G. and M. Jones 2004. Chronology and Settlement. In L. Furey and S. Holdaway (eds), *Change Through Time: 50 Years of New Zealand Archaeology*, pp. 215–234. New Zealand Archaeological Association Monograph 26.

Hjarno, J. 1967. Maori fish-hooks in southern New Zealand. *Records of the Otago Museum, Anthropology* 3.

Holdaway R.N. 1996. Arrival of rats in New Zealand. *Nature* 384:225–226.

Holdaway, R.N., R.G. Roberts, N.R. Beavan-Athfield, J.M. Olley and T.H. Worthy 2002. Optical dating of quartz sediments and accelerator mass spectrometry 14C dating of bone gelatin and moa eggshell: a comparison of age estimates for non-archaeological deposits in New Zealand. *Journal of the Royal Society of New Zealand* 32:463–506.

Holdaway, S. and R. Gibb 2006. *SH3 Stage Three Bell Block Archaeological Excavations at Te Oropuriri: Final Report*. Auckland: Auckland UniServices Ltd.

Horrocks, M., I.W.G. Smith, S.L. Nichol and R. Wallace In press. Sediment, soil and plant microfossil analysis of Maori gardens at Anaura Bay, eastern North Island, New Zealand: comparison with descriptions made in 1769 by Captain Cook's expedition. *Journal of Archaeological Science*.

Jacomb, C. 1995. Panau, periodisation, and north-east South Island prehistory. Unpublished MA thesis, Anthropology, University of Otago.

Jacomb, C. 2000. Bullock wagons and settlement patterns in a New Zealand pastoral landscape. *Australasian Historical Archaeology* 18:47–62.

Jones, K.L. 1984. A 1761 medalet from the East Coast, North Island, New Zealand: relic of Cook's first voyage. *Journal of the Polynesian Society* 93(3):315–320.

Jones, K.L. 1994. *Nga Tohuwhenua Mai Te Rangi: A New Zealand Archaeology in Aerial Photographs*. Wellington: Victoria University Press.

Knight, H. and P.J.F. Coutts 1975. *Matanaka*. Dunedin: McIndoe.

Leach, B.F. 2006. *Fishing in Pre-European New Zealand*. New Zealand Journal of Archaeology Special Publication, and Archaeofauna Vol 15.

Lightfoot, K.G. 1995. Culture contact studies: redefining the relationship between prehistoric and historical archaeology. *American Antiquity* 60(2):199–217.

Macready, S. 1991. A review of urban historical archaeology in Auckland to 1990. *Australasian Society of Historical Archaeology* 9:14–20.

McFadgen, B.G., F.B. Knox and T.R.L. Cole 1994. Radiocarbon calibration curve variations and their implications for the interpretation of New Zealand prehistory. *Radiocarbon* 36(2):221–236.

McGlone, M.S. 1989. The Polynesian settlement of New Zealand in relation to environmental and biotic changes. *New Zealand Journal of Ecology* 12 (Supplement):115–129.

McGlone, M.S. and J. Wilmshurst 1999. Dating initial Maori environmental impact in New Zealand. *Quaternary International* 59:5–16.

McKinnon, M. 1997. Colony and colonised: The Pakeha occupation and transformation of New Zealand. In M. McKinnon (ed), *New Zealand Historical Atlas*. Wellington: David Bateman in association with Department of internal Affairs.

Middleton, A. 2003. Maori and European landscapes at Te Puna, Bay of Islands, New Zealand, 1805–1850. *Archaeology in Oceania* 38:108–122.

Middleton, A. 2005. Te Puna: The archaeology and history of a New Zealand mission station, 1832–1874. Unpublished PhD thesis, Anthropology, University of Auckland.

Middleton, A. 2007a. Potatoes and muskets: Maori gardening at Kerikeri. In J. Binney (ed), *Te Kerikeri 1770–1850: The Meeting Pool*, pp. 33–39. Bridget Williams Books:

Middleton, A. 2007b. *Two Hundred Years on Codfish Island (Whenuahou): From Cultural Encounter to Nature Conservation.* Invercargill: Department of Conservation.

Middleton, A. 2008. *Te Puna: A New Zealand Mission Station.* New York: Kluwer Academic/Plenum Press.

Newman, M. 1988. *Archaeological Investigations in the Vicinity of Lake Rotoaira and the Lower Tongariro River, 1966–71.* Wellington: New Zealand Historic Places Trust Publication 21.

Oliver, R. and B. Wood 1981. Excavation at the Brunner coke ovens: January-February 1981. *New Zealand Archaeological Association Newsletter* 24(4):213–227.

Orchiston, D.W. 1972. George Bruce and the Maoris (1806–8). *Journal of the Polynesian Society* 8:248–254.

Petchey, P.G. 2004 *Beside the Swamp: The Archaeology of the Farmers Trading Company Site, Dunedin.* Dunedin: Southern Archaeology Ltd.

Petrie, H. 2006. *Chiefs of Industry: Maori Tribal Enterprise in Early Colonial New Zealand.* Auckland: Auckland University Press.

Phillips, C. 2000. *Waihou Journeys: The Archaeology of 400 Years of Maori Settlement.* Auckland: Auckland University Press.

Phillips, C. and M. Campbell 2004. From Settlement Patterns to Interdisciplinary Landscapes in New Zealand. In L. Furey and S. Holdaway (eds), *Change Through Time: 50 Years of New Zealand Archaeology*, pp. 85–104. New Zealand Archaeological Association Monograph 26.

Phillips, J. 2007. 'Kiwi' *Te Ara – the Encyclopaedia of New Zealand.* viewed 29 October 2007 <http://www.TeAra.govt.nz/TheBush/NativeBirdsAndBats/Kiwi/en>

Pool, I. 1991. *Te Iwi Maori: A New Zealand Population, Past, Present and Projected.* Auckland: Auckland University Press.

Prickett, N.J. 1998. The New Zealand shore whaling industry. In Lawrence, S. and M. Staniforth (eds), *The Archaeology of Whaling in Southern Australia and New Zealand*, pp. 48–54. Australasian Society for Historical Archaeology and the Australian Institute for Maritime Archaeology Special Publication 10.

Prickett, N.J. 2002a. *The Archaeology of New Zealand Shore Whaling.* Wellington: Department of Conservation.

Prickett, N.J. 2002b. *Landscapes of Conflict: A Field Guide to the New Zealand Wars.* Auckland: Random House.

Ritchie, N.A. 1991. Is there an optimum system?: the recording and assessment of historic mining sites. *The Australian Journal of Historical Archaeology* 9:47–54.

Ritchie, N.A. 2003. Traces of the past: Archaeological insights into the New Zealand Chinese experience in southern New Zealand. In M. Ip (ed), *Unfolding History, Evolving Identity. The Chinese in New Zealand.* Auckland: Auckland University Press.

Robinson, J. 1995. Recent excavations at the seat of New Zealand's first Colonial government: a preliminary report. Unpublished report, Department of Conservation, Whangarei.

Salmond, A. 1991. *Two Worlds: First Meetings Between Maori and Europeans 1642–1772.* Auckland: Viking.

Salmond, A. 1997. *Between Worlds: Early Exchanges Between Maori and Europeans 1773–1815.* Auckland: Viking.

Samford, P.M. 1997. Response to a market: Dating English underglaze transfer-printed wares. *Historical Archaeology* 31(2):1–30.

Schmidt, M.D. 2000. Radiocarbon dating the end of moa-hunting in New Zealand prehistory. *Archaeology in New Zealand* 43(4):314–329

Schmidt, M.D. 1996. The commencement of pa construction in New Zealand prehistory. *Journal of the Polynesian Society* 105:441–460.

Simmons, D.R. 1973 Suggested periods in South Island prehistory. *Records of the Auckland Institute and Museum* 10:1–58.

Smith, I.W.G. 1989. Fort Ligar: A colonial redoubt in central Auckland, New Zealand. *New Zealand Journal of Archaeology*. 11:117–141.

Smith, I.W.G. 1991. The development of historical archaeology in New Zealand 1921–1990. *Australasian Journal of Historical Archaeology* 9:6–13.

Smith, I.W.G. 2002. *The New Zealand Sealing Industry: History, Archaeology and Heritage Management.* Wellington: Department of Conservation.

Smith, I.W.G. 2004a. Archaeologies of identity: Historical archaeology for the 21st century. In L. Furey and S. Holdaway (eds), *Change Through Time: 50 Years of New Zealand Archaeology*, pp. 251–262. New Zealand Archaeological Association Monograph 26.

Smith, I.W.G. 2004b. Nutritional perspectives on prehistoric marine fishing in New Zealand. *New Zealand Journal of Archaeology* 24:5–31.

Smith, I.W.G. 2005. Retreat and resilience: Fur seals and human settlement in New Zealand. In G.G. Monks (ed), *The Exploitation and Cultural Importance of Sea Mammals*, pp. 6–18. Oxford: Oxbow Books.

Smith, I.W.G. and A.J. Anderson 2007. *Codfish Island/Whenua Hou Archaeological Project: Preliminary Report.* Otago Archaeological Laboratory Report 4, Anthropology Department, University of Otago, Dunedin.

Smith, I.W.G. and K.G. Gillies 1997. *Archaeological Investigations at Luncheon Cove, Dusky Sound, February 1997.* Report to New Zealand Historic Places Trust and Department of Conservation.

Smith, I.W.G. and K.G. Gillies 1998. *Archaeological Investigations at Facile Harbour, Dusky Sound, February 1998.* Report to New Zealand Historic Places Trust and Department of Conservation.

Smith, I.W.G. and J. Goodwyn 1990. Portable ceramics from the General Assembly site. *Archaeology in New Zealand* 33:21–39.

Smith, I.W.G. and N.J. Prickett 2006. *Excavations at the Oashore Whaling Station.* Otago Archaeological Laboratory Report 3, Anthropology Department, University of Otago, Dunedin.

Smith, I.W.G. and N.J. Prickett 2008. *Excavations at Te Hoe, Mahia Peninsula.* Otago Archaeological Laboratory Report 5, Anthropology Department, University of Otago, Dunedin.

Smith, I.W.G. and N.J. Prickett nd. The Historical Archaeology of Two New Zealand Shore Whaling Communities. Manuscript in preparation, Anthropology Department, University of Otago, Dunedin.

Stokes, E. 2002. Contesting resources: Maori, Pakeha and a tenurial revolution. In E. Pawson and T. Brooking (eds), *Environmental Histories of New Zealand*, pp. 35–51. Melbourne: Oxford University Press.

Trotter, M.M. and B. McCulloch 1989. *Unearthing New Zealand.* Wellington: GP Books.

von Haast, J. 1872. Moas and moahunters. Address to the Philosophical Institute of Canterbury. *Transactions and Proceedings of the New Zealand Institute.* 4:66–107.

Walter, R.K. 1996. What is the East Polynesian "Archaic"? A view from the Cook Islands. In J.M. Davidson, G.J. Irwin, B.F. Leach, A. Pawley and D. Brown (eds), *Oceanic Culture History: Essays in Honour of Roger Green*, pp. 513–529. New Zealand Journal of Archaeology Special Publication.

Walter, R.K. 2004. New Zealand Archaeology and its Polynesian Connections. In L. Furey and S. Holdaway (eds), *Change Through Time: 50 Years of New Zealand Archaeology*, pp. 125–146. New Zealand Archaeological Association Monograph 26.

Walter, R., I. Smith and C. Jacomb 2006. Sedentism, subsistence and socio-political organisation in prehistoric New Zealand *World Archaeology* 38(2):274–290.

Watson, K. 2000. Land of Plenty: Butchery Patterns and Meat Supply in Nineteenth Century New Zealand. Unpublished MA thesis, Anthropology, University of Otago.

Wilmshurst, J.M. and T.F.G. Higham 2004. Rat-gnawed seeds date the late arrival of Pacific rats and humans in New Zealand. *The Holocene* 14:801–806.

24

Translating the 18th century pudding

Helen Leach

Anthropology Department, University of Otago, New Zealand
helen.leach@stonebow.otago.ac.nz

Introduction

As Atholl Anderson has showed throughout his career, cross-cultural comparisons can improve our understanding of the origins and subsequent history of Pacific cultures. Comparative material can be sourced from within the Pacific basin, or from as far afield as Scandinavia and northern Europe. In this exercise in historical anthropology, offered in celebration of Atholl's valued contributions to cross-cultural studies, the comparison throws light on a feature of Polynesian and British culinary cultures in the 18th century: the pudding. I will argue that Captain Cook and his scientists' translation of dishes like the Tahitian mahi popoi as 'puddings' was not a trivial categorisation, but one based on a deep understanding of the roles that puddings played both in England and Tahiti.

European experience of Polynesian puddings

On each of Captain Cook's three voyages to the South Seas, the journals kept by the officers and scientists describe the preparation of special dishes by Polynesian cooks to which the observers commonly gave the name 'pudding'. One of the best accounts of a Tahitian dish of this type was provided by James Cook himself, on September 4 1777 during the third voyage:

> There was also a large pudding which I saw the whole process in making, it was made of Bread fruit, Ripe Plantains, Taro and Palm or Pandanes [pandanus] nuts, each rasped, scraped or beat up fine, and baked by it self, a quant[it]y of Juice express'd from Cocoa nut Kernels was put into a large tr[a]y or wooden Vessel, amongst it the other Articles pipeing hot as they were taken out of the Oven and a few hot stones just to keep the whole semmering; three or four men kept stiring the whole with sticks, till the several articles were incorporated one with a nother and the juice of the Cocoanut was turned to oil; so that the whole was about the consistency of hasty pudding (Beaglehole 1967:206–207).

Cook's description is valuable for the detail of both the ingredients and the process of preparation. He and some of his officers and scientists had previous experience with these dishes on which to draw. Soon after the *Endeavour* arrived at Tahiti on the first voyage, Sydney Parkinson saw several composite dishes being made. He recorded a dish made from starch extracted from the Polynesian arrowroot, mixed with coconut 'liquor', and thickened with hot stones 'till it formed a strong jelly: on tasting it we found it had an agreeable flavour, not unlike very good blanc-mange' (Parkinson 1972:17). Though he didn't equate this arrowroot dish with a pudding, he saw other dishes that were comparable:

> These people make up various kinds of paste, one of which, called Makey [*mahi*] Poe Poe [*popoi*], is made of fermented bread-fruit, and a substance called Meiya [*mei'a* – a type of banana], mixt with cocoa-nut milk, and baked, tastes very sweet. In making these pastes, they use a pestle made of a hard black stone, a kind of basaltes, with which they beat them in a wooden trough (Parkinson 1972:17; cf. Lepofsky 1994:79, 94).

As one of the expedition artists, Parkinson supplied an illustration and description of this heavy stone pestle (Parkinson 1972:76). For Parkinson, the terms paste and pudding overlapped in meaning, as is apparent in his vocabulary listing for Poe, as '*A paste, or pudding, made of the roots of arum* [taro]' (Parkinson 1972:75).

On the second voyage, again in Tahiti, George Forster recorded on April 23 1774 that his father had eaten 'a rich and most delicious kind of pudding, which is made of the kernel of coco-nuts and eddy-roots [taro], scraped very small, and mixed together' (Forster 2000:352). Tahiti was just one of several Polynesian islands where Cook's men encountered puddings. On July 11 1777 William Anderson summed up Tongan cookery with the following telling remark:

> They are as yet almost strangers to the thousand destructive luxurys which cookery has invented, but nevertheless have a few artificial dishes, such as a soft pudding made of Talo and other roots with Cocoa nut scrap'd into it, which gives an agreeable smoothness to every thing dress'd with it (Beaglehole 1967:942).

As missionaries and traders settled the other island groups inhabited by Polynesians, they found similar dishes, which differed from the usual chunks of baked fruit and vegetables that formed the daily diet of commoners. The distinguishing features were the amount of labour invested in achieving the paste-like consistency and the frequent addition of coconut cream. These dishes were served at feasts and notably to chiefs and important visitors. They were associated with valuable artefacts such as dressed basalt or calcite pounders, and large wooden vessels. As a component of feasts, puddings would also have been eaten by commoners, though such dishes were not made from the highest-ranked fruits or root crops (Leach 2003). It might be expected that on islands where society was less stratified than on Tahiti or Hawai'i, and fewer foods were proscribed for commoners, puddings marked feasts rather than the differential status of consumers. Nevertheless the inter-island similarities were such that it was not simply an English category name that grouped puddings together, but a Polynesian food concept that was clearly of some antiquity.

The elements and antiquity of Polynesian puddings

The appearance of what were obviously related dishes throughout West and East Polynesia stimulated To'aiga Su'a to investigate the history of this category in her Master's thesis in Anthropology (Su'a 1987). She assembled data on a large number of named dishes of this type and established that each had certain features in common:

- one (occasionally more) starchy foundation ingredient, either root crops such as yams, taro, or sweet potato, or fruit such as breadfruit or bananas;

- a softening, lubricating ingredient, usually coconut cream;

- a homogeneous texture achieved through the application of a consistent set of techniques, such as pounding, mashing, kneading, grating, and stirring.

In West Polynesian island groups, grating was a common technique for preparing the starchy base from a raw state. In East Polynesia, pounding was more prevalent. Where the base was pre-cooked, pounding was commonly practised, though it was not necessary to use a heavy stone pestle. If the pudding was made from a fermented starch paste, kneading might suffice. The desirable qualities of the pudding were its power to satiate the eater, the richness of flavour and aroma usually imparted by the coconut cream, and the smooth oily texture and correct viscosity for the particular dish (Su'a 1987:255–256).

There is no generic term for these dishes in Polynesia. They sometimes appear as binomials, combining the name of the foundation or emollient ingredient and the preparation technique. Among the range of names are some that have cognates in several island groups. These include fakakai (also fai'ai, feikai and fekei), loloi (also roroi), poke (po'e), (po)poi, (su)sua, tukituki, taufolo, and vaihalo (Leach 1989:133–134). Some of these terms relate to processing, such as poke, to mix, and tuki, to pound, while others refer to processing tools like graters. Others refer to preserved starch crop pastes, such as poi, that could also become the foundation of a dish. Based on the widespread use of these words, historical linguists have reconstructed many of them for the Proto-Polynesian language spoken up to three millennia ago and to Proto-Nuclear Polynesian in use in Western Polynesia 2000 years ago (Su'a 1987:193–209). For example, the Proto-Polynesian reconstruction *fai-kai is glossed as 'food cooked with coconut cream' and PPN *lolo-qi is glossed as 'to prepare food with coconut cream' (Kirch and Green 2001:158). Since ample archaeological evidence exists for the tools themselves, especially the heavy stone or calcite pounders, stone grating heads, and perforated shell peelers, we can confidently state that this category of dish was present in Pacific Island societies at the time that Polynesians separated into their major Western and Eastern divisions, and may even have been present when the Polynesians split from other Oceanic speakers of Austronesian languages.

Anthropologists are uniquely placed to conduct cross-cultural investigations. In the case of the smooth-paste pudding dishes seen in the Pacific, To'aiga Su'a (1987) examined their history, distribution, material culture, nomenclature, and social significance right through to the 20th century. But her study was focused on Polynesian cultures. There were people of other cultures present when the 18th century descriptions were made, and in choosing to call these dishes puddings, and specifically hasty puddings, they were making a cross-cultural comparison. The English officers and scientists were pudding eaters themselves. This paper will now examine the English pudding traditions that inspired the identification of these Polynesian dishes as puddings, and one in particular as a hasty pudding. But we cannot assume that what we mean by 'pudding' in the 21st century applied to the 18th century pudding. The English pudding of our ancestors needs almost as much effort in translation as that of the exotic cultures of Polynesia.

The English and North American 'hasty pudding'

What similarities did Cook have in mind in likening the Tahitian pudding to a hasty pudding? This question is best answered from the study of actual recipes. The earliest recipes for hasty puddings appear in the 17th century. In the revised 1665 edition of Robert May's *The Accomplisht Cook*, first published in 1660, there are three examples of hasty puddings. The first reveals by the wording of its title the origin of this pudding name – 'To make a Pudding in haste' (May

2000:179). The recipe calls for a pint of milk or cream, a handful each of raisins and currants, and a piece of butter. A handful of flour is stirred into it. The milk is brought to the boil, and bread and nutmeg grated in. After a quarter of an hour's boiling, it is dished up on beaten butter. The instructions are somewhat out of order and fail to note the problems of leaving a pot of thickened milk to boil. The second recipe is unlike most hasty puddings in that the flour-thickened cream is transferred to a floured cloth and boiled. The third recipe is more explicit and better arranged: two or three pints of thick cream are brought to the boil in a skillet. Then grated bread, flour, nutmeg, sugar and butter are added. The cook is instructed to 'stir them continual' (May 2000:181). Halfway through the cooking process the yolks of six eggs are stirred in. The finished hasty pudding is poured into a dish, decorated with thinly sliced candied orange peel, and enriched with some beaten butter and scrapings of loaf sugar.

Two of May's three recipes show features that were to characterise the 18th century hasty pudding:

- they were cooked quickly in a pot or pan, unlike other pudding types that were either boiled in a gut casing, cloth or wooden bowl for several hours, or baked in the oven for three-quarters of an hour, or longer;

- they were stirred continuously – though the rationale was not stated, this was to prevent the mixture burning on the bottom of the pot or forming lumps.

Many recipes have a long life in English cookery books, often of several centuries (for long-surviving soups see Leach 2006); however, as an increasingly popular style of dish, pudding types developed and diversified quite quickly over the 18th and 19th centuries. To determine what sorts of hasty puddings Captain Cook would have been familiar with, a century after Robert May's book appeared, we need to consult the popular recipe books used in 18th century kitchens. Apart from Sir Joseph Banks, it is unlikely that Cook's officers and scientists regularly dined in elite households; so we must choose cookbooks that contained dishes they would have known since childhood. In the first half of the 18th century, English recipe books fall into two groups: those presenting a fashionable cuisine strongly influenced by the French court, and those reproducing English cookery for middle-class households. Most of the former works were authored by male chefs, while the latter were predominantly compiled by women (Lehmann 1999a:277–279). Since the French had no dishes in their repertoire at that time that matched the English pudding, we can turn to female writers such as Eliza Smith (1734) and Hannah Glasse (1995 [1747]) for widely known examples of 18th century hasty puddings.

The first recipe for 'Hasty-Pudding' in Eliza Smith's *The Compleat Housewife* involved a different method of incorporating the flour into the boiling milk from that in the 17th century recipes. The flour was first mixed with an egg, then formed into a very stiff paste that was shredded into the milk, a bit like pasta, along with cinnamon, sugar and a knob of butter. Smith (1734:96) advised cooks to 'Keep it stirring all one way, till 'tis as thick as you would have it; and then stir in such another piece of Butter'. Her second recipe was for 'little Hasty-puddings' that started by boiling milk and flour 'into a smooth Hasty-pudding' (Smith 1734:105). The thickened mixture was sweetened, flavoured with nutmeg, and left to cool. Beaten eggs were then stirred into it and the mixture poured into custard cups, which were covered and boiled for more than half an hour. This recipe starts as a hasty pudding but is then processed as individual baked custards.

In 1747, Hannah Glasse offered three versions of hasty pudding: one thickened with wheat flour, one with oatmeal, and the third with the flour and egg paste employed in Eliza Smith's second recipe. In fact, the wording strongly suggests that it was copied directly from Smith. In the first recipe, egg yolks were mixed with cold milk, then hot milk infused with bay leaves was poured over them. The recipe continued with the instruction:

> then with a wooden Spoon in one Hand, and the Flower [sic] in the other, stir it in till it is of a good Thickness, but not too thick. Let it boil, and keep it stirring, then pour it into a Dish, and stick Pieces of butter here and there (Glasse 1995:80).

She noted that the eggs were optional, but in her opinion, an improvement.

Glasse's 'Oatmeal Hasty-Pudding' was a plainer dish. Water was brought to the boil, with a piece of butter and some salt added. Then Scotch oatmeal was stirred in progressively. When the mixture was thick, it was poured into the serving dish and dotted with butter. It could also be dressed with ale or wine and sugar, or with cream or new milk (Glasse 1995:80). A similarly plain hasty pudding was published by William Ellis in 1750, in a work addressed to country housewives. This 'common Farmers Hasty-pudding' combined milk (or milk diluted with water) and flour, stirred for quarter of an hour over the fire. Before serving, it too was enriched with butter and/or sugar (Ellis 1750:34).

From these and other examples, we can describe a generic hasty pudding from the mid-18th century as a liquid, usually milk, thickened with one or two starchy cereal products, usually wheat flour, and sometimes dressed before serving with a fat product such as butter or cream. Because it was not normally cooked in an oven or boiled in a cloth or bowl where the heat surrounds the mixture and cooks it evenly, special instructions were included in many hasty-pudding recipes: the mixture should be stirred continuously as it thickened. This prevented scorching and lumpiness.

When Captain Cook likened the Tahitian dish to a hasty pudding, he was probably aware they both shared a starchy base, a liquid ingredient, and the necessity for continuous stirring as the mixture thickened. He might also have drawn parallels between the oily coconut cream of the Polynesian pudding and the addition of butter to the hasty pudding. Before moving on to consider the wider constellation of 18th century puddings, it is interesting to note the later history of hasty puddings. In Britain, they made fewer appearances in 19th century cookbooks and were absent entirely from some of the most popular works, such as those by Isabella Beeton. Only the most extensive compilations, for example *Cassell's Dictionary of Cookery* (Anon c. 1875), offered more than a solitary recipe for hasty pudding. A few examples occurred early in the 20th century, but mainly in works recycling 19th century recipes, such as *Cassell's Shilling Cookery* (Payne 1916:268).

The situation was rather different in North America. Wheat-flour hasty puddings were essentially reproductions or modifications of British examples, while those based on maize meal look like a North American innovation. As an example of a modified hasty pudding, Eliza Leslie's 'Flour Hasty Pudding' (Leslie 1840:301), first published in 1837, replaced the bay leaves used by Hannah Glasse in her first recipe with peach leaves. Since bay laurel leaves were often confused with the true bay in English cookbooks, this substitution may have contributed the same desirable bitter-almond flavour just as readily as bay laurel. The stirring instructions closely follow Glasse's wording and appear to be an edited copy. Though wheat-flour hasty puddings are derivative, those utilising maize cornflour were distinctively American. In their simplest form, they involved stirring the cornmeal into boiling salted water then cooking it till very thick, as in Esther Howland's 'Indian Hasty Pudding' (Howland 1845:40), Catharine Beecher's 'Mush or Hasty Pudding' (Beecher 1850:108), and Elizabeth Lea's 'New England Hasty Pudding, or Stir-about' (Lea 1869:82). There is a suggestion in Lea's recipe that a special stirring stick developed for this dish, for she wrote 'stir well with a wooden stick kept for the purpose' (Lea 1869:82), while Fanny Gillette, author of the *White House Cook Book*, referred to a 'pudding-stick'. Her 'Corn-Meal Mush or Hasty Pudding' was thick enough to serve when the stick stood upright in the mixture (Gillette 1887:243). The name became rare in 20th century American cookbooks, being replaced by Indian Pudding, a modified recipe in which the cornmeal hasty pudding was prepared in a double boiler, then finished off by baking in an oven (Perkins 1949:551–552). It seems likely that an early adaptation of the 17th century English hasty pudding to the new cereal, maize, proved so acceptable in America that it flourished there while the English hasty pudding was losing ground. The pudding stick is thought to have been a stout piece of wood with a paddle-like end.

It is important to remember that before 18th century Polynesian puddings were likened to hasty puddings, they were categorised by the English observers as puddings in a more generic sense. The range of dishes called puddings in 18th century England included some, such as black puddings, that bore little resemblance to a stone-boiled coconut-cream concoction. However, there were others included in the recipe books that show significant similarities, not just in method or combination of food groups, but in social significance. Recipe books are not the only source of information on pudding characteristics, and indeed they are often silent on the context in which dishes were served or the sorts of people who might have been expected to eat them. Personal diaries and essays provide essential information, especially on the frequency of use of particular dishes and their place in the menu.

Parson Woodforde's puddings, 1767–1802

For the purpose of this study, the diaries of country parson (and gourmand), the Reverend James Woodforde of Weston Longville, Norfolk, provided important contextual detail. Woodforde was a farmer as well as a parson, and he also maintained an extensive orchard and kitchen garden. In consequence, there was much processing of primary produce, both animal and vegetable, by members of his household. From 1767, there are references in his diaries to puddings, as well as to the meat, fish, poultry and game dishes that provided the core of each of the two courses that constituted 18th century dinners. These entries increased as he settled in to life at Weston Parsonage in 1774–1775. From May 1 1791 he noted daily the chief dishes served at each dinner when at home or dining locally. Using John Beresford's selections from Woodforde's diaries, I tabulated 282 references to puddings over the period 1788–1802 (Beresford 1927, 1929, 1931). Although 57 simply referred to a pudding, or baked or boiled pudding, or plain or rich pudding, 225 entries specified the type of pudding eaten, sometimes with details of the course in which it was served (Table 1).

Plum puddings were by far the most common and the most prestigious, being served on formal occasions such as the day set aside for the tithe audit, in late November or early December, when the parson provided dinner for his tenant farmers, and on Christmas Day when the puddings were usually accompanied by mince pies. But they were not limited to such events: in 1792, for example, the household ate a baked plum pudding on May 2, and a boiled plum pudding on July 13; unspecified plum puddings were served on October 30 and November 4. Woodforde complained of the insufficient quantity of plum pudding when he ate at the King's Arms on May 18, but not when he dined there again on October 19. Four diary entries indicate that the plum puddings were served with the first course (April 17 1787; May 20 1791; July 13 1792; May 8 1797).

Of all the 18th century puddings, recipes for plum puddings are surprisingly rare. This cannot be because they were made infrequently. Since cooks were required to produce them on a regular basis, they may have known the recipe by heart. Mary Kettilby's (1714:89) 'An

Table 1. Number of entries for specific dishes called puddings in Parson Woodforde's diaries 1788–1802.

Dried fruit, e.g. 'plum', raisin	92
Fresh or preserved fruit, e.g. apple, apricot, gooseberry, plum, orange	42
Suet	28
Batter, including Norfolk, Yorkshire	26
Meat, game	10
Pease	10
Rice	9
Black	3
Custard	2
Potato	1
Bread	1
[Stuffing] in fish	1

excellent Plumb-Pudding' represents the plum pudding in its modest form: a pound of suet, finely shredded, a pound of stoned raisins, and four spoonfuls each of flour and sugar were mixed together. The yolks of five eggs and whites of three, beaten with a little salt, were then added. The mixture was tied tightly in a [floured] cloth and boiled for at least four hours. Hannah Glasse's 'A boiled Plumb Pudding' of 1747 had the same quantity of suet and raisins as Kettilby's, but had an extra pound of currants, more flour, grated breadcrumbs, three more eggs, a pint of milk, and a quantity of spice (nutmeg and ginger). It was boiled for five hours (Glasse 1995:69). Brandy was a common addition to this richer sort of plum pudding.

The puddings made from fresh or home-preserved fruit recorded in Woodforde's diaries were dominated by damson plums, apples and gooseberries. The damson puddings were eaten in September and October, when the fruit was freshly harvested, as well as in January and March, when it must have been preserved in some form. Hannah Glasse provided one recipe for preserving damsons whole within a damson jelly, and another for preserving them in a syrup with a paper cover and an oil layer to exclude air (Glasse 1995:154, 157). She supplied a recipe for a quince, apricot or white pear plum pudding that may have served as a template: the fruit was pre-cooked and then baked in a dish with a custard of cream and egg yolks (Glasse 1995:107). Alternatively, the damsons may have been cooked within a suet crust, tied in a cloth and boiled, a common method of making apple puddings. After describing this type of apple pudding, Glasse (1995:112) commented 'And thus you may make a Damson Pudding, or any sort of Plumbs, Apricots, Cherries, or Mulberries, and [these] are very fine'. Such fruit-pudding recipes increased in frequency during the second half of the 18th century and flourished in the 19th when the suet crust was especially common.

As for the gooseberry pudding, Elizabeth Raffald provided a recipe in which cooked gooseberry purée was beaten with sugar, butter, biscuit crumbs and eggs, and then baked for half an hour (Raffald 1970:182). Very similar recipes were published by Elizabeth Moxon (1769:84), Lydia Fisher (1788:37) and Edinburgh cookery teacher Mrs Frazer (1791:116–117). Parson Woodforde ate his gooseberry puddings between the third week in May and mid-July, so we can assume they were made from freshly picked fruit. However, we know that his neighbours, the Custances, preserved gooseberries, for they gave the parson a 'common Quart Bottle of preserved Gooseberries' on October 6 1792 (Beresford 1927:376). The damson pudding consumed on

March 7 1797 appears to have accompanied roast duck in the second course of dinner, but the parson did not provide information as to the course position of his other fruit puddings.

Parson Woodforde recorded another fruit-based pudding in his diaries during the 1770s, which on December 25 1773, was eaten with the first course. This was an orange pudding, which was so popular in the mid-18th century that Hannah Glasse (1995:105–106) provided four different recipes for it. Three of them required 16 egg yolks, and the fourth six. All beat the eggs with from half to one pound of butter, and from half to three-quarters of a pound of sugar. Cream was added in two of the recipes, along with grated Naples biscuits for extra body. The orange flavour was imparted by grating or pounding the rind of one to three Seville oranges. In two cases, the oranges were boiled in several changes of water to eliminate the characteristic bitterness, then pounded in a mortar before being added to the mixture. All four recipes instructed the cook to bake the pudding in a dish lined with puff pastry. These puddings were rich enough to justify inclusion at Christmas dinner. The one lemon pudding referred to on September 27 1796 may have been prepared in similar fashion.

Suet puddings were on the parsonage menu throughout the year, though a little more often over the colder months. They seem to have been viewed as a suitable accompaniment to boiled beef (May 20 1800; June 30 1802), roast beef (May 11 1796), as well as hashed mutton (August 30 1800), so they probably formed part of the first course. Hannah Glasse's recipe for 'A boiled Sewet Pudding' was a thick batter pudding made from eggs, flour and milk, with the suet adding a richness that is absent from the plain batter pudding. In keeping with its role as a savoury pudding, it was flavoured with ginger and pepper (Glasse 1995:69). Glasse's second suet pudding was placed in a chapter of her book addressed to sea captains. It is more like a basic plum pudding, containing dried fruit (currants and raisins), flour, and ginger, as well as the suet. But instead of eggs, it was mixed with salt water (Glasse 1995:124). Although this recipe offered the option of boiling or baking, most suet puddings were boiled in a well-buttered cloth.

In Woodforde's usage, batter puddings were either plain or sweet. Included in the plain type was Yorkshire pudding, which he invariably ate with roast beef during the first course of dinner (e.g. April 8 1783; July 19 1790; March 14 1797; September 4 1797). It is difficult to know whether by plain pudding, plain batter pudding and Norfolk plain batter pudding, he meant one and the same dish. These puddings were sometimes mentioned in association with roasted meat during the first course, and there is a diary entry for a batter pudding in the first course on June 18 1781. By contrast, one of several recorded 'sweet batter puddings' was served in the second course (April 8 1796), accompanied by red-currant jelly. As with plum puddings, batter-pudding recipes were so well known they were often omitted from recipe books. However in 1747, Hannah Glasse provided two, one with eggs and one without. The cook was instructed to mix six spoonfuls of flour with a little milk, some salt and ginger, then to add the rest of the quart of milk, six egg yolks and three whites. The batter was to be boiled for one and a quarter hours, and served with melted butter. In the eggless version, tincture of saffron was added (to compensate for the absence of bright yolks), and it was boiled for just one hour; dried fruit could be added if desired (Glasse 1995:108). But no instructions were supplied for preparing these puddings for cooking. Fortunately, Lydia Fisher (1788:36) was more explicit: 'you must take care your pudding is not thick; flour your cloth well. Three quarters of an hour will boil it.'

References to meat and game puddings included beef-steak, rabbit, pigeon, blackbird and sparrow puddings. The steak pudding was a clear predecessor of the steak and kidney pudding that appeared in the second half of the 19th century (Beeton 1869:288). The meat was seasoned and enclosed in a suet crust pastry. This was tied in a cloth and boiled for three to five hours depending on size. Hannah Glasse's 1747 recipe gives the impression that the development of this relatively new type of pudding was linked to the practice of cooking apple slices in a suet crust: 'make it up as you do an Apple-pudding … This is the best Crust for a Apple-pudding. Pigeons eat well this Way' (Glasse 1995:69).

William Ellis (1750:37) described a similar type (made with lard instead of suet) as 'Apple-pudding, the Hertfordshire Way' and implied that it was more economical than the cream and egg-yolk variety. In the absence of specific recipes for rabbit and small-bird puddings, we can only assume that they too were boiled within some sort of crust.

Pease pudding was a standard accompaniment to pork, and at Weston Parsonage, it was always served with a boiled leg of pork. On one occasion, James Woodforde suspected that it had made him ill (February 28 1782), but he continued to eat it with boiled pork till at least 1798. This simple pudding of dried split peas boiled in a cloth is often thought to be of medieval origin (Kelsey 1995:117); however the *Oxford English Dictionary* provides no examples of usage before the 18th century and no earlier recipes have been located. In contrast, pease pottage (an early form of soup) was common in the Middle Ages, and was cooked in a pot over the fire. The 18th century recipes for pease pudding recommended that split peas be boiled, loosely tied in a cloth, for one hour, then mixed with butter and seasoning, retied, and boiled for a further hour before serving (e.g. Frazer 1791:111).

In contrast, rice puddings were already of considerable antiquity by the 18th century, and so many recipes were in circulation that it is hard to know which ones were familiar to Woodforde and his household. He ate rice puddings both baked (e.g. June 30 1789; October 7 1794) and boiled (e.g. April 28 1790). He noted that on March 29 1792, the rice pudding formed part of the second course, while on April 20 1796, it was part of the first course. A century earlier, when Robert May's cookbook was in print, rice puddings were baked, boiled in cloths, or stuffed into the small intestines of pigs or sheep – probably the earliest form in which they were made (e.g. Murrell 1615). The rice was generally pre-boiled in milk or cream, then mixed with eggs, suet or bone marrow, grated bread, dried fruit, sugar, and flavourings such as rosewater, cinnamon, nutmeg or coriander (May 2000:21, 182). In 1747, Hannah Glasse (1995:108, 111, 124) gave recipes for nine different rice puddings. In these, the suet and marrow commonly used in the 17th century had been replaced by butter, and in the case of the baked rice puddings, milk was more common than cream for pre-boiling the rice. The simplest and cheapest rice puddings were composed of rice boiled in a cloth with or without some raisins, then dressed with melted butter before serving. By the 19th century, the suite of flavourings used in rice puddings had moved from nutmeg, mace and cinnamon to lemon and vanilla, and the majority were much less rich than their 17th century counterparts.

Potato puddings were a popular 18th century dish that lost ground during the 19th century. All began with pre-cooked mashed potatoes and butter. Other ingredients were added according to the richness desired: beaten eggs, sugar, cream, sack or brandy, currants, candied peel, or orange juice. The thick mixture could be boiled in a cloth, baked in a buttered dish, or poured into a pie dish lined with puff pastry (Glasse 1995:98, 105). On one occasion, James Woodforde ate 'a Rice and Potatoe Pudding' (October 4 1784), but potato puddings were infrequently served at the parsonage.

Two other pudding categories figured in Woodforde's diaries and these reflect the survival of the earliest forms of pudding from the late-medieval and early-modern period: puddings as stuffing for cavities in roasted birds, fish and larger animals (Austin 1888:41-42, 61), and puddings as stuffed intestines or paunches, or wrapped in membranes known as caul. The former lost the name 'pudding' towards the close of the 18th century, and became 'forcemeat' or 'farcing', and more recently 'stuffing'. The latter survive as the type of sausage we still call black and white puddings. The etymology of the word pudding has been subject to some debate, in particular as to whether the Middle English term poding shares the same root as 14th century Old French bodeyn, bowel (OED 2006–7). The antiquity of pudding recipes involving stuffing of gut portions supports the theory that the term was extended from the gut to the stuffing, and then to the stuffing by itself. Karen Hess summed up the subsequent evolution of the word and its glosses in 1981:

> … English puddings early on became ever more farinaceous, more porridgy, than their French counterparts, where such practice is regarded as adulteration. Most fifteenth-century pudding recipes already call for bread crumbs or *ote-mele*, and eventually, the *pudding-bag* became a surrogate maw or intestine for boiling the gutless – and meatless – sweet pudding (Hess 1981:102).

The process took several centuries, judging from the number of recipes in Robert May's 1685 cookbook for sweet puddings forced into lengths of gut. But 100 years later, the only sausage-like puddings made in Parson Woodforde's household were black puddings, prepared from a Somerset recipe obtained in 1786. This activity followed the annual killing of one of the household's own pigs in November or December. During the 19th century, recipes for black (blood) puddings were omitted from cookbooks addressed to urban housewives, as they no longer ate home-killed pork. They survived in Scottish recipe books into the 20th century (e.g. Guthrie Wright 1911:93).

Woodforde probably grew up hearing the stuffing in carcasses referred to as 'puddings'. For the majority of his diary entries he used this term. For example, he ate a pike 'rosted for dinner with a Pudding in his Belly' on June 4 1777, and again on March 6 1797. A 'Fowl rosted with a Pudding in its Breast' was part of the second course on May 8 1797. However, the modern term was already spreading and a 'fine Leveret rosted with stuffing in his Belly' was on the Parsonage menu on September 1, 1801, and 'a large Fowl … boiled … with Stuffing in his Breast' on November 17 1798 (Beresford 1931:17, 34, 147, 335).

Combining the details of pudding consumption from the long span of James Woodforde's diaries with the range of pudding recipes available from several of the most popular 18th century cookbooks has provided a picture of the types of puddings likely to have been familiar to members of Cook's expeditions. From this, we can single out several that shared the smoothness and richness of the Polynesian pudding: hasty puddings, batter puddings, pease puddings, and some of the sweet puddings where the starchy foundation ingredient was reduced to a paste, as in rice flour and potato puddings. In each case, extensive stirring, beating or mashing was required, just as in the South Seas puddings. The application of the term 'pudding' to the 18th century Polynesian dishes was both appropriate and instructive.

The iconic status of 18th century puddings

One more comparison needs to be made beyond the level of specific recipes and daily menus. We know that Polynesian puddings were served to chiefs and important guests, and that the dish was of such social and ceremonial significance that it had been an integral part of Polynesian feasts for several millennia. Did English puddings hold the same position? They did not have the same antiquity, at least not with the name 'pudding', but a case can be put that by the 18th century, puddings had achieved iconic status. This does not mean that all types of pudding were equally esteemed. Becoming an icon has more to do with symbolism and identity than with rank or status. An early clue that this was underway can be found in a change in the gloss for pudding between the third and fourth editions of Nathan Bailey's *An Universal Etymological*

English Dictionary. In the earlier (1726), a pudding was 'a Dish of Food well known; also Hog's-Puddings, &', while in the next (1728) and some later editions (e.g. the eighth of 1737), the entry read 'a sort of Food well known, chiefly in *England*, [such] as Hog's Puddings, &'. Can we identify a particular cause for this amendment? A few years before 1728, a paradoxical encomium had appeared, the work of either Henry Carey or Dr John Arbuthnot (Miller 1956:169fn), entitled *A Learned Dissertation On Dumpling; its dignity, antiquity, and excellence. With a word upon pudding...* (Carey 1726; Arbuthnot 1751). The encomium argued that flour and water dumplings evolved into puddings with the substitution of milk for water and the addition of marrow, butter, sugar and 'plumbs' (i.e. dried fruit). When eggs were introduced, 'the Pudding became a Pudding of Puddings' and 'From that Time the *English* became so famous for Puddings, that they are call'd Pudding-Eaters all over the World, to this Day' (Arbuthnot 1751:59). After demonstrating that virtually every food was a form of pudding, as well as many other things from bag-pipes to the human head, poetry, and kingdoms, and that even the universe is but a pudding of elements, the author concluded 'Let not *Englishmen* therefore be ashamed of the Name of *Pudding-Eaters*; but, on the contrary, let it be their Glory' (Arbuthnot 1751:70–71). Dr Arbuthnot may not have been the author of this encomium; however its resonance with his greatest literary character, the archetypal Englishman John Bull, is striking.

John Bull quickly became an icon of robust Englishness, along with the pudding. William Ellis introduced a pudding recipe in his 1750 book with the following affirmation of its national importance:

> Pudding is so necessary a part of an Englishman's food, that it and beef are accounted the victuals they most love. Pudding is so natural to our harvest-men, that without it they think they cannot make an agreeable dinner (Ellis 1750:33).

Another famous Englishman, Dr Johnson, may have been influenced by the Dissertation On Dumpling. On his tour with Boswell to the Hebrides, Johnson was so scornful of the Reverend James Hervey's *Meditations and Contemplations* that he created a parody, entitled 'Meditation on a Pudding', which also linked the ingredients of a pudding to universal themes (Chapman 1930:397–398). Whether Dr Johnson felt patriotic when presented with a steaming plum pudding is unclear.

The nationalistic associations of the English pudding need to be seen in their political context. As Gilly Lehmann (1999b:72–73, 75) has shown, from the late 17th century, French cooks were brought in to cook for the Whig elite, prompting a reaction by the Tory gentry which dismissed French dishes as ostentatious, disguised and expensive. Tories ate solid English fare epitomised by roast beef and pudding. Lehmann (1999b:80) quotes James Woodforde's condemnation of a meal he took at a grand house in August 1783, where 'most of the things [were] spoiled by being so frenchified in dressing'. In food at least, Woodforde's repertoire of puddings placed him as a Tory as well as an Englishman.

The iconic status of the pudding continued into the 19th century but seems to have become more focused, in particular on the plum pudding. William Kitchiner, author of *The Cook's Oracle*, emphasised that 'A little brandy...is an improvement to this excellent British Pudding, which is truly a British dish, [along] with roasted sirloin of beef...' (Kitchiner 1817:553). However, some writers began to adopt a less enthusiastic attitude, in parallel with the prints of the caricaturist James Gillray who from the 1790s began to depict John Bull as 'grotesquely ugly, moronic, [and] gullible' (Rogers 2003:163). Christian Johnstone, writing as Meg Dods on the subject of fruit puddings or charlottes, observed that the French did not esteem 'the solid, lumpy, and doughy English pudding...' (Johnstone 1826:282). The anonymous 'Lady' author of *Domestic*

Economy (Anon 1827) justified the omission of a 'great many puddings' in order to 'give room to other matter which appeared of more consequence, as pudding is a real national dish, and better understood than most other dishes' (Anon 1827:552fn). By the time Isabella Beeton was writing, the criticism of the English masses for their taste in puddings was less muted:

> Here [in Great Britain], from the simple suet-dumpling up to the most complicated Christmas production, the grand feature of substantiality is primarily attended to. Variety in the ingredients, we think, is held only of secondary consideration with the great body of the people, provided that the whole is agreeable and of sufficient abundance (Beeton 1869:620).

For the Polynesian pudding-eaters, substantiality was also a desirable quality of the pudding, and its power to create a feeling of satiation was specifically mentioned by informants (Su'a 1987:251).

What is clear is that during the 18th century, Englishmen saw the pudding as their national icon, a culinary offering for John Bull. They would not have shared its symbolic meaning lightly with non-English peoples. When they applied the word 'pudding' to Polynesian dishes, it was not just on the grounds of parallels in composition and method. They must have been conscious that in the South Seas these 'puddings' were more than a laboriously prepared dish, with a starch base and enriching 'cream'. Polynesian puddings epitomised the best of Polynesian culinary culture in all of the island groups they visited. The translation as 'puddings' of what they saw in preparation, and ate as honoured guests, reflected an impressive level of cross-cultural understanding.

Postscript: Puddings after the 18th century

The 19th century saw major changes in kitchen technology, in particular the spread of cast-iron ranges, and then gas stoves. New ingredients appeared, such as chemical raising agents, coconut and bananas. The number of pudding recipes exploded, with many given the names of important towns, or eminent people. The trend away from cooking puddings in gut casings that had been obvious through the 18th century, was now complete, and during the 19th century a similar shift affected puddings encased in cloths. The pudding cloth had been appropriate when mixtures such as pease or plain-batter puddings were cooked in large boilers at the same time as joints of meat. However, for the most delicate puddings, the rolling action of the boiling water was detrimental to their final appearance. Students at the National School of Cookery in 1876 were told that boiled puddings 'are lighter if boiled in a cloth, but easier to keep in shape if boiled in a basin' (Tegetmeier 1876:120). Manufacturers responded to this trend by patenting special pudding basins, including some that did away with the cloth tied over the top of the bowl. Judging from the frequent warnings about the importance of using a truly clean cloth, untainted by the flavour of soap, the task of maintaining the cloth in good condition after it was repeatedly floured or smothered in butter was onerous. The students were told 'It is most essential to keep a pudding cloth clean; it should be washed in two or three hot waters without soap immediately it is done with, wrung dry, and dried off quickly, or it will get a musty taste' (Tegetmeier 1876:120).

A new type of cooking method was adopted towards the end of the 19th century: steaming. This term was applied to two techniques. In the first, the pudding was cooked in a basin standing on a saucer within a pot, with the boiling water half way up the side; in the second, the pudding basin was placed on a rack above the boiling water or in the top half of a double saucepan. Though steamed puddings took longer to cook, their contents were protected from knocks, and if an inner paper cover was used, the cloth did not have to be floured or buttered. A smaller saucepan could be used, taking up less room on the stove top than a big iron boiler. Less boiling water was required, hence less fuel. However the risk of the pot boiling dry was acknowledged. Cooks were instructed to ensure that the level was maintained by additions from the boiling kettle. Steaming was the most suitable method of cooking a pudding on the top of a gas stove, where the burners delivered heat to small, circular areas.

In the first half of the 20th century, steaming and baking were the most popular methods of cooking hot puddings in New Zealand. In a study of the cooking methods applied to 885 dishes called puddings in a time series of 17 recipe books, the frequency of puddings cooked by steaming reached 50 percent in 1915, while those that were boiled in a cloth varied from a maximum of 15 percent in 1926 down to 2 percent in 1955. The only type of pudding boiled in a cloth from the 1950s was the highly traditional Christmas pudding (formerly known as Plum Pudding). After 1976, too few recipes retained the name pudding for reliable analysis. To understand the reason, we need to look at the category names applied to the different sweetened dishes through time.

As the 20th century approached, the term 'pudding' was applied more widely than ever before. It extended beyond the baked and boiled varieties, to gelled, frozen or iced dishes. However, the revolution in the structure of the English formal dinner placed the dish category names under pressure. Under the old system, referred to as *service à la française*, there were two main courses with a symmetrical arrangement of dishes. While fish and soup were always part of the first course, and game of the second, a pudding could appear in either, as we have seen from the Woodforde diaries. After the cloth had been removed, dessert (from French *desservir*) was placed on the table. It consisted of fruit, nuts and sweetmeats, and from the 18th century onwards, increasing numbers of jellies and creams. The adoption of *service à la russe* in the second half of the 19th century meant that a procession of dishes was brought to the table, raising questions as to the correct classification and position for the various types of puddings. While the hot sweet dishes retained the name pudding in Britain, the various creams and jellies were increasingly classified as 'cold sweets'. In North America, the preferred term was 'desserts'. Through the first half of the 20th century, the English ate hot puddings or cold sweets, while the Americans increasingly used 'desserts' as an umbrella term for all sweet dishes, whether hot or cold. Individual recipes might be called an Indian pudding, for example, but they were to be found in the desserts section of the cookbooks.

In New Zealand, where I have examined the terminology of both hot and cold sweet dishes in 855 New Zealand-published cookbooks (predominantly fundraisers) from 1888 to 1999, dessert sections make their first appearance in the 1930s and 1940s, unquestionably as a result of American influences. At first, the term was more acceptable as the category name for collections of cold sweet dishes, but from the 1970s, half of the recipe books classified hot sweet dishes as desserts, while the remainder clung to the name pudding. By the 1990s, only 15 percent of cookbooks used the category name pudding for hot sweet dishes (see Table 2). Individually, progressively fewer recipes carried the name pudding. A similar replacement of the pudding category name by dessert in England led to an editorial in *The Times* (February 3 1965), and an exchange of letters in 1971. To one correspondent who insisted that in Britain the course was known as 'the sweet', cookbook writer Robin McDouall replied 'Let him speak for himself: others call it pudding' (*The Times*, September 6 1971:15).

The collapse of the term 'pudding' for the sweet dishes eaten after the main course has been dramatic and may even lead to a complete loss of the generic term, to the point where no cookbook will have a section entitled 'puddings', though they will probably retain recipes for individual puddings, such as Christmas pudding. Does this mean that puddings will die out? It

Table 2. Changing category or section names for hot sweet dishes in 855 New Zealand cookbooks, 1888–1999.

Year	1880s	1890s	1900s	1910s	1920s	1930s	1940s	1950s	1960s	1970s	1980s	1990s
Sections n=848	2	1	14	19	35	61	51	81	129	171	189	95
Puddings	2	1	14	19	34	59	44	72	77	82	66	14
Sweets	0	0	0	0	0	0	3	3	6	4	5	7
Desserts	0	0	0	0	1	2	4	6	46	85	118	73
Afters	0	0	0	0	0	0	0	0	0	0	0	1

is worth remembering that Polynesian puddings never had a generic name, despite existence for two or three millennia. But to survive as an un-named category, the context of production has to be socially significant, which was the case in Polynesia. We cannot say the same of all English puddings. Eventually, consumers of the Christmas pudding may become as ignorant of its origins and history as they are today of the black pudding's. Nowadays, few people eat black pudding and even fewer know why it is called a pudding. It is possible that we will see the virtual extinction of 'pudding' both as category name and as part of an individual recipe's binomial within the next century. The dishes will continue to evolve, but under different names. But to my mind, dishes labelled 'afters' are much less desirable or enriched with historical associations than 'puddings'.

Acknowledgements

Some of the research for this paper was supported by the Marsden Fund of the Royal Society of New Zealand, and was part of a three-year project on the development of New Zealand's culinary traditions. Thanks are due to members of the research team who provided references and data, and especially to Jane Teal for comments. I must acknowledge To'aiga Su'a whose M.A. thesis (1987) provided the Polynesian foundation. I am also grateful to Peter Gathercole and Fiona Lucraft (UK) who attempted to find an answer to the question 'What is a Norfolk Pudding?' A shortened version of this paper was delivered to the David Nichol Smith Seminar in 18th-Century Studies XIII in Dunedin in April 2007.

References

Anon [A Lady] 1827. *Domestic Economy, and Cookery, for Rich and Poor*. London: Longman, Rees, Orme, Brown, and Green.

Anon [c. 1875]. *Cassell's Dictionary of Cookery*. London: Cassell Petter and Galpin.

Arbuthnot, J. 1751. *The Miscellaneous Works of the Late Dr. Arbuthnot*, Vol.1, James Carlile, Glasgow, viewed 30 March 2007, on Eighteenth Century Collections Online, <http://galenet.galegroup.com/servlet/ECCO>

Austin, T. (ed) 1888. *Two Fifteenth-Century Cookery-Books*, Oxford: Oxford University Press.

Bailey, N. 1726. *An Universal Etymological English Dictionary*, 3rd edition. London: J.Darby, viewed 30 March 2007, on Eighteenth Century Collections Online, <http://galenet.galegroup.com/servlet/ECCO>

Bailey, N. 1728. *An Universal Etymological English Dictionary*, 4th edition. London: J.Darby, viewed 30 March 2007, on Eighteenth Century Collections Online, <http://galenet.galegroup.com/servlet/ECCO>

Bailey, N. 1737. *An Universal Etymological English Dictionary*, 8th edition. London : D. Midwinter.

Beaglehole, J.C. (ed) 1967. *The Voyage of the Resolution and Discovery 1776–1780*. London: The Hakluyt Society.

Beecher, C.E. 1850. *Miss Beecher's Domestic Receipt Book*. New York: Harper, viewed 30 March 2007, <http://digital.lib.msu.edu/projects/cookbooks/html/project.html>

Beeton, I. 1869. *The Book of Household Management*, 2nd edition. London: Ward, Lock, and Tyler.

Beresford, J. (ed) 1927. *The Diary of a Country Parson: the Reverend James Woodforde, Vol. III 1788–1792*. London: Oxford University Press.

Beresford, J. (ed) 1929. *The Diary of a Country Parson: the Reverend James Woodforde, Vol. IV 1793–1796*. London: Oxford University Press.

Beresford, J. (ed) 1931. *The Diary of a Country Parson: the Reverend James Woodforde, Vol. V 1797–1802*. London: Oxford University Press.

Beresford, J. (ed) 1978. *The Diary of a Country Parson 1758–1802 by James Woodforde*. Oxford: Oxford University Press.

Carey, H. 1726. *A learned Dissertation on Dumpling; its dignity, antiquity, and excellence. With a word upon pudding...* 2nd edition. London : J. Roberts, viewed March 30 2007, on Eighteenth Century Collections Online, <http://galenet.galegroup.com/servlet/ECCO>

Chapman, R.W. (ed) 1930. *Johnson's Journey to the Western Islands of Scotland; and, Boswell's Journal of a Tour to the Hebrides with Samuel Johnson, LL.D*. London: Oxford University Press.

Ellis, W. 1750. *The Country Housewife's Family Companion*. London: James Hodges, viewed March 30 2007 on Eighteenth Century Collections Online, <http://galenet.galegroup.com/servlet/ECCO>

Fisher, L. 1788. *The Prudent Housewife, or, Compleat English Cook...* 24th ed., Women Advising Women, Part 6. Wiltshire: Adam Matthew Microfilms.

Forster, G. 2000. *A Voyage Round the World, Vol. 1.*, Nicholas Thomas and Oliver Berghof (eds). Honolulu: University of Hawaii Press,.

Frazer, Mrs. 1791. *The Practice of Cookery, Pastry, Pickling, Preserving*. Edinburgh: Peter Hill, viewed March 30 2007 on Eighteenth Century Collections Online, <http://galenet.galegroup.com/servlet/ECCO>

Gillette, F.L. 1887. *White House Cook Book: a selection of choice recipes...* Chicago: R.S. Peale and Co, viewed March 30 2007, <http://digital.lib.msu.edu/projects/cookbooks/html/project.html>

Glasse, H. 1995. *The Art of Cookery Made Plain and Easy, facsimile of 1st edition of 1747*. Devon: Prospect Books.

Guthrie W.C.E. 1911. *The School Cookery Book*. London: Macmillan.

Hess, K. 1981. *Martha Washington's Booke of Cookery*. New York: Columbia University Press.

Howland, E.A. 1845. *The New England Economical Housekeeper, and Family Receipt Book*. Cincinatti: H.W. Derby, viewed March 30 2007, <http://digital.lib.msu.edu/projects/cookbooks/html/project.html>

Johnstone, C.I. [Margaret Dods, pseudonym] 1826. *The Cook and Housewife's Manual*, Women and Victorian Values, 1837–1910, Part 7. Wiltshire: Adam Matthew Microfilms.

Kelsey, M.W. 1995. The Pudding Club and Traditional British Puddings. In H. Walker (ed), *Disappearing Foods. Studies in foods and dishes at risk. Proceedings of the Oxford Symposium on Food and Cookery 1994*, pp. 116–123. Devon: Prospect Books.

Kettilby, M. 1714. *A Collection of Above Three Hundred Receipts in Cookery, Physick and Surgery*, London: Richard Wilkin, viewed March 30 2007, on Eighteenth Century Collections Online, <http://galenet.galegroup.com/servlet/ECCO>

Kirch, P.V. and G. Roger 2001. Hawaiki, *Ancestral Polynesia. An essay in historical anthropology*. Cambridge: Cambridge University Press.

Kitchiner, W. 1817. *Apicius Redivivus; or, The Cook's Oracle*, Women Advising Women, Part 6. Wiltshire: Adam Matthew Microfilms.

Lea, E.E. 1869. *Domestic Cookery, Useful Receipts, and Hints to Young Housekeepers*. Baltimore: Cushings and Bailey, viewed March 30 2007, <http://digital.lib.msu.edu/projects/cookbooks/html/project.html>

Leach, H.M. 1989. The traditional background of Polynesian foods, *Proceedings of the Nutrition Society of New Zealand* 14:131–136.

Leach, H.M. 2003, Did East Polynesians have a concept of luxury foods?. *World Archaeology* 34(3):442–457.

Leach, H.M. 2006. From Dunoon to Dunedin - what two distant charitable cookbooks reveal about the British tradition of soups. *Petits Propos Culinaires* 80:33–59.

Lehmann, G. 1999a. English Cookery Books of the 18th Century. In A. Davidson (ed), *The Oxford Companion to Food*, pp. 277–279. Oxford: Oxford University Press.

Lehmann, G. 1999b. Politics in the Kitchen. *Eighteenth-Century Life* 23(2):71–83.

Lepofsky, D.S. 1994. Prehistoric agricultural intensification in the Society Islands, French Polynesia. PhD, University of California, Berkeley, University Microfilms International, Ann Arbor.

Leslie, E. 1840. *Directions for Cookery, in its Various Branches*. Philadelphia: E.L. Carey and Hart, viewed March 30 2007, <http://digital.lib.msu.edu/projects/cookbooks/html/project.html>

May, R. 2000. *The Accomplisht Cook, or the Art and Mystery of Cookery*, facsimile of 5th edition of 1685. Devon: Prospect Books.

Miller, H.K. 1956, The Paradoxical Encomium with Special Reference to its Vogue in England, 1600–1800. *Modern Philology* 53(3):145–178.

Moxon, E. 1769. *English Housewifery. Exemplified in above four hundred and fifty receipts...* 10th edition. Leeds: Griffith Wright, viewed March 30 2007, on Eighteenth Century Collections Online, <http://galenet.galegroup.com/servlet/ECCO>

Murrell, J. 1615. *A New Booke of Cookerie; London Cookerie*. London: John Browne, viewed March 30 2007, <http://homepage.univie.ac.at/thomas.gloning/tx/1615murr.htm>

Oxford English Dictionary Online 2006–7. Oxford: Oxford University Press, viewed March 30 2007, <http://dictionary.oed.com/entrance.dtl>

Parkinson, S. 1972. *A Journal of a Voyage to the South Seas, in His Majesty's Ship, the Endeavour*. Adelaide: Libraries Board of South Australia.

Payne, A.G. (ed) 1916. *Cassell's Shilling Cookery*. London, Cassell and Company.

Perkins, W.L. 1949. *The Boston Cooking-School Cook Book by Fannie Merritt Farmer*, 8th edition. London: George G. Harrap and Co.

Raffald, E. 1970. *The Experienced English Housekeeper*, facsimile of 8th edition of 1782. London: E and W Books.

Rogers, B. 2003. *Beef and Liberty. Roast beef, John Bull and the English nation*. London: Chatto and Windus.

Smith, E. 1734. *The Compleat Housewife*, 6th edition, Women Advising Women, Part 6. Wiltshire: Adam Matthew Microfilms.

Su'a, T.I. 1987. Polynesian pudding processes in West and East Polynesia. An ethnographic, linguistic and archaeological synthesis to study the antiquity of elaborate culinary concoctions in Polynesia, MA, University of Otago.

Tegetmeier, W.B. 1876. *The Scholars' Handbook of Household Management and Cookery*. London: Clay, Sons, and Taylor.

The Times Digital Archive 1785–1985, University of Otago Library, viewed March 30 2007, <http://infotrac.galegroup.com/itw/infomark/0/1/1/purl=rc6_TTDA?sw_aep=otago>

25

Boat images in the rock art of northern Australia with particular reference to the Kimberley, Western Australia

Sue O'Connor

Department of Archaeology and Natural History, Australian National University, Australia

sue.oconnor@anu.edu.au

Steve Arrow

12 Gregory Street, Broome, Western Australia, Australia

Introduction

Boats are a recurring motif in the rock art of northern Australia, particularly in the Northern Territory and the Kimberley region of Western Australia. They include Macassan praus, European vessels and a variety of smaller craft, which may be of local or Southeast Asian origin. Recent assessments of watercraft in rock-art assemblages have been undertaken for areas of Arnhem Land in the NT (including Groote Eylandt) and for the Kimberley, WA (Figure 1). These reviews indicate marked regional variation in the types of craft depicted, the style of depiction and the association of people with boats. For example, in Groote Eylandt art, Macassan praus dominate, whereas in the Mt Borradaile area of Western Arnhem Land and in the Kimberley, European vessels and simple canoes are numerically dominant (Bigourdan nd; Roberts 2004:21; Clark and Frederick 2006). It is argued here that these boat depictions are informative about the historical context and the nature of the relationships of contact in the different regions. This paper also describes three previously unrecorded boat images from the Kimberley coast and discusses these within the context of the known corpus of Kimberley boat images in the rock art.

Contact history and boat images in the rock art of northern Australia

Clarke and Frederick (2006) have recently documented the watercraft images on Groote Eylandt, the largest island in the Groote Eylandt archipelago on the western side of the Gulf of Carpentaria, Northern Territory. They analysed 23 depictions of boats, of which Indonesian praus represent 65 percent and European sailing boats 26 percent of all craft (two modern boats account for the rest) (Clarke and Frederick 2006:124, 2008). Most of the Macassan praus show

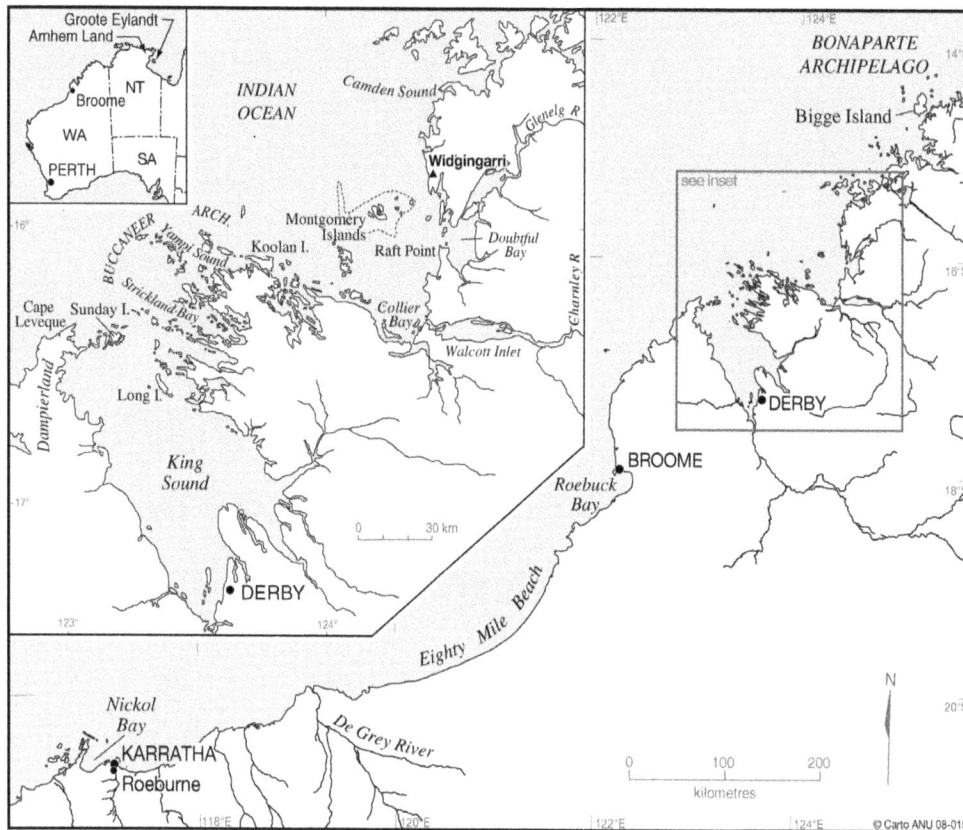

Figure 1. Map showing places and sites mentioned in the text.

people on board. Clarke and Frederick's (2008:2) aim was to examine 'archaeological signatures of art production to understand how cross-cultural engagements between Indigenous Groote Eylandters and non-Indigenous outsiders might be communicated through rock art'. They present a convincing case that the greater representation of Indonesian vessels over European craft, the intricacy of execution and use of multiple colours, and the detail shown on the praus probably reflect the greater frequency and duration of Macassan over European visitation. They also note that the presence of people on Macassan boats contrasts markedly with depictions of European boats, which rarely show people on board, and suggest this may indicate more familial relationships and cross-cultural understandings (Clarke and Frederick 2006).

From the mid 17th century until 1907, Indonesian fishing fleets sailed to the northern coast of Australia in search of edible trepang (also known as tripang, bêche de mer, sea cucumber (Eng.), *Holothurians* (L.)), which had a high value in the Chinese markets. They came predominantly from Macassar in southern Sulawesi (Udjung Pandang), hence are known as Macassans, but some also came from other parts of the Indonesian archipelago (Urry and Walsh 1981; Chaloupka 1996:131), including the islands of Timor, Roti and Aru. The trepang were processed, dried and smoked and the Macassans made large camps on protected areas of the coastline, within which they constructed their tripots, smokehouses and living quarters. Macknight (1976) provides a comprehensive account of the Macassan industry on northern Australian shores and only pertinent information will be outlined here.

The scale of the Macassan visitation to the NT is often not appreciated, although it is well documented historically. King, for example, met a fleet of 15 praus with 300 men on board near the Cobourg Peninsula and consequently named the spot Malay Bay (King 1827,I:77).

Large and regular fleets of praus, with up to two thousand men aboard, sailed in with the north-west monsoon each December. They spent the next four months ... gathering and curing trepang, and returned home with the south-east trade winds in March or April (Chaloupka 1996:132).

They worked sections of the coast in groups of five or six praus and each prau had a crew of 20 to 25 men (Chaloupka 1996:133), and was equipped with a suite of dugout canoes.

The regularity of the Macassan voyaging allowed the establishment of social and trade relationships and while trepang were the primary interest of the Macassans, they also collected a variety of other goods, such as pearl shell, pearls, minerals, sandalwood and turtle shell (Macknight 1976; Chaloupka 1996:131; Clarke and Frederick 2006:119). Local Aboriginal groups stockpiled these items in anticipation of the Macassan return the following season. It has been suggested that the Macassan presence had a significant effect on Aboriginal settlement patterns and exchange networks (Mitchell 1994; Clarke 2000:330–333).

> Members of the clan groups in whose estates Makassans established their camps and others from farther inland, attracted by availability of exotic goods, worked alongside the visitors, participating in all their endeavours. As payment they received dugout canoes, cloth, tobacco, spirits and treasured iron knives and tomahawks (Chaloupka 1996:132).

Aboriginal people adopted as a lingua franca a 'Macassar' pidgin which allowed them to communicate with the crews of the praus, as well as across Indigenous language groups (Urry and Walsh 1981:91–93). Each year, Aboriginal men sailed along the Arnhem Land coast into the Gulf of Carpentaria and some even undertook the return voyage to the port of Macassar or beyond (Earl 1841:116; Jukes 1847:259; Tindale 1926:130; Chaloupka 1996:138). Some may have been abducted, but the historical record indicates many went willingly and established close long-term relationships with families in the islands (Macknight 1976:86; Urry and Walsh 1981). In the 1870s, there were reportedly as many as 17 Aborigines in Macassar from Port Essington alone (Macknight 1976:86). The Macassan visits effectively ceased in 1907 when they were banned from fishing in Australian waters (Bain 1982:14).

The Macassan contact was recorded in Indigenous oral traditions, ceremonies, stone arrangements and rock and bark paintings. The paintings of Macassan praus demonstrate intimate knowledge of the workings of the boat, sails and rigging. The paintings on Groote Eylandt and many in Western Arnhem Land are executed in traditional x-ray style, enabling internal details and fittings within the hull to be shown (Chaloupka 1996:140).

Conversely, most contact paintings in western Arnhem land reflect European influence, but European influence from the later part of the 19th and the early 20th centuries (Roberts 2004). However, as Roberts (2004:41) has recently shown, while the artistic conventions used in the portrayal of Macassan and European craft may differ, the technical nautical knowledge displayed, and the accuracy of the transference of this knowledge into the paintings, is no less developed in the European boats than in the Macassan craft. In a review of the Mt Borradaile boat images, NT, Roberts (2004:26, 35) demonstrates that the paintings are concise enough with respect to rigging, sails and shape to be able to identify the types of craft depicted. They are mostly sloops, cutters, ketches and schooners, which would have been a common sight on the northern coastlines and rivers from about the 1870s to 1930s. These boats were used by buffalo hunters, European trepangers and others. Roberts (2004:39) describes the way in which the establishment of the buffalo-shooters' camps on the South and East Alligator floodplains generated non-traditional movements in western Arnhem Land as Indigenous people congregated around the hunters' camps. As well as direct contact with the Europeans, these changes, in turn, generated a different sort of 'contact'. The changed residential patterns stimulated by the attractions of the shooters' camps brought Indigenous groups into contact from regions far outside their traditional seasonal spheres of movement and interaction.

Contact history and boat images in the rock art of the Kimberley, Western Australia

Boat depictions are much rarer in the Kimberley than in the Northern Territory. A recent review of all known watercraft images in the Kimberley region prepared for the WA Department of Maritime Archaeology, Western Australian Museum, reports only 15 watercraft images from the Kimberley coast (Bigourdan nd). Of these, one may depict the outline of a prau (Crawford 1968), however this identification is uncertain as the image shows no detail of the boat construction or rigging. The remaining 14 boats are European craft (n=4) or canoes/small boats (n=10). The European boats include two sailing vessels, one rowboat with oars and rollocks, and one boat identified as 'a European craft' for which no further information is available. These small non-European boats may represent indigenous craft, or dugouts acquired from the Macassans. All of these small boats have people on board. Walsh (2000:32) has made a case that some small craft with high upswept prows and sterns are crewed by Bradshaw-style figures (Figure 2). Bradshaw figures have elsewhere been shown to have a minimum age of 17,000 years (Roberts *et al.* 1997).

Two of the European craft, the rowboat and one of the sailing boats, show people on board. Interestingly, the people in the rowboat are depicted in 'Wandjina-style' (Figure 3).

This paper focuses on three previously unrecorded paintings of European sailing boats recorded by the author in 2006 on the mainland coast adjacent to the Montgomery Islands (Figure 1). These provide enough technical detail to be able to assess their type, probable occupation and the approximate timeframe in which they were painted. This, in turn, may provide an insight into the history and relationships of contact in this region.

The absence of Macassan praus in the Kimberley-region rock art is puzzling. There is no doubt the Macassans were regular visitors to the Kimberley coast, which they called Kaju Djawa or Kai Jawa, although their visits are not as well documented as for the NT (Macknight 1972; Urry and Walsh 1981). Ian Crawford (1969) excavated a Macassan camp and processing site Tamarinda, near Kalumbura in the north Kimberley, and documents other camps and indications of Macassan visitation (Crawford 2001:72–75). We know from the presence of tamarind trees that the Macassans may have ventured as far south as Dampierland (O'Connor 1990:37). The prospector E.J. Stuart (1923:36) noted the remains of several Indonesian camp sites in Yampi Sound during his exploratory voyage up the Kimberley coast in 1917. In 1865, Scholl, the resident magistrate at Roebourne, reported seeing a fleet of praus in Camden Harbour and claimed they were engaged in slaving (Crawford 1968:61; Bain 1982:19), and there are documented cases of Aboriginals stolen by Macassan raiding parties being sold in slave markets in the port of Macassar (Shepherd 1975:32; Bain 1982:32).

This may account for the fact that the relationship between the local Indigenous groups and the Indonesian crews of the praus does not appear to have been as convivial as along the Arnhem Land coast. In fact, it appears the Kimberley Aboriginals were regarded by the Macassans as hostile (Urry and Walsh 1981:101; Bain 1982:14; Crawford 2001:71) (although Crawford (pers comm. in Choo 1994:8–9) reports that Aboriginal women were sent to the Macassan visitors by their husbands in exchange for goods such as metal and food). This may have led to less direct contact with the crews of the praus by Indigenous groups in the Kimberley and thus less familiarity with the working of their boats.

The first European voyages to the Kimberley were close in time to the earliest Macassan

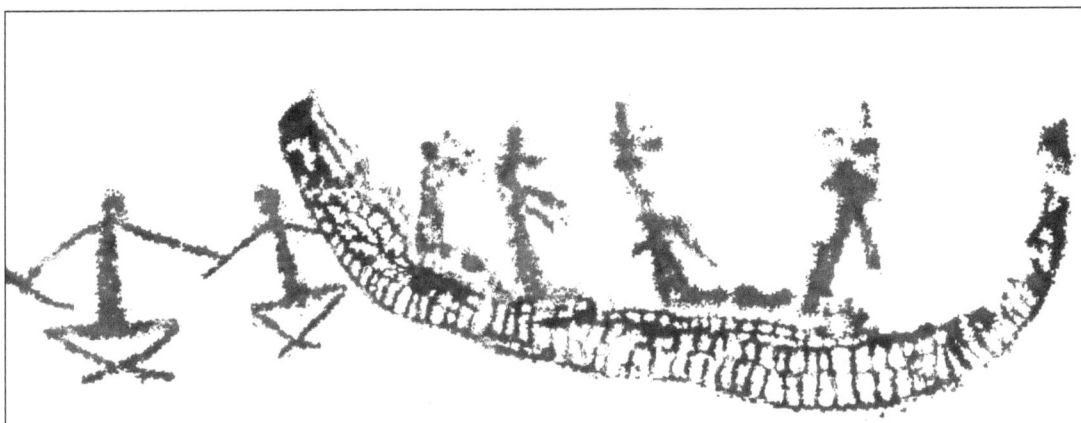

Figure 2. Small craft with upswept prau and stern that may be of bundle reed construction, crewed by Bradshaw-style figures (redrawn from Walsh 2000:32).

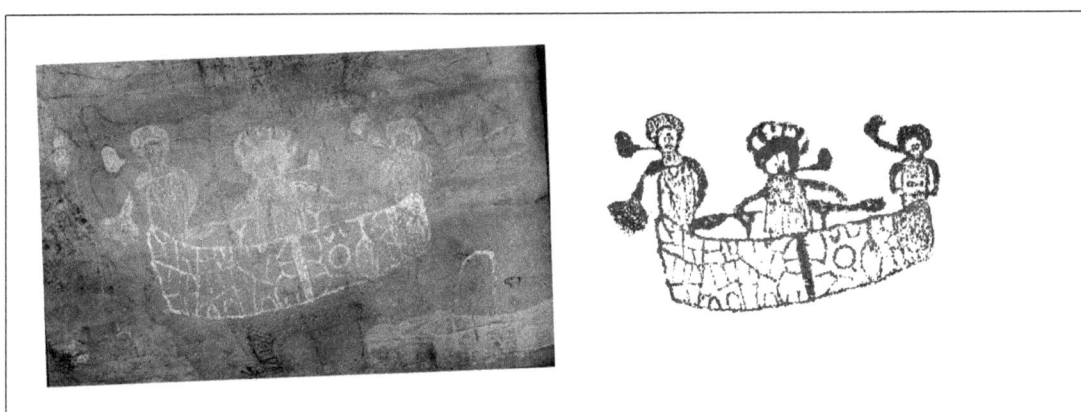

Figure 3. Painting of rowboat with rollocks and three 'Wandjina-style' figures from Bigge Island, Bonaparte Archipelago. Photo Pat Barker. This image was originally published by Ian Crawford (1968) in *The Art of the Wandjina*, with the permission of the traditional owners, and is reproduced here with the permission of the WA Museum.

visits. We know that in 1688, William Dampier, arriving in the *Cygnet*, spent time in King Sound repairing his boat. He was followed by the French explorers Baudin in 1803 and Freycinet in 1818. English explorations led by Philip Parker King and Lieutenants Stokes and Grey are known from their journals to have made contact with local Indigenous groups (O'Connor 1999:7–8). These events, however, appear to have gone unrecorded in the rock art of the region.

Boat paintings from the Kimberley coast, adjacent Montgomery Island

During fieldwork in 2006, three new images were added to the existing corpus of Kimberley painted craft.

Boat 1 Widgingarri

This boat is painted in simple red-brown outline over a white background that appears to have been applied using the traditional method of blowing the white pigment from the mouth. This provides a stark contrasting matt background against which to view the red boat. The boat overlies a fish in red outline with partial dotted infill also applied on to a white background, which in turn overlies a large kangaroo in yellow ochre with yellow dotted infill (Figure 4). Figure 5 shows an enlargement of Boat 1 and the outline extracted from the underlying images to better identify its features.

Both scale and detail of the rigging of this craft are very specific. The vessel shown in silhouette is gaff-rigged. It is not a pearling lugger per se, but rather a schooner. The defining characteristic is the dominant mizzen sail. The mizzen mast (the back one) is clearly the taller of the two masts and carries the larger sail. The artist has even drawn the cap spar, which connects the two masts together, and links the sail load to the clearly defined bowsprit and fore stay.

There is also no doubt the artist had good knowledge of the underwater structure of the boat. The depiction shows detail of the part of the hull that is ordinarily below the water line and not visible to the observer while afloat. This suggests it may be a recollection, in part, of the vessel as seen careened at low tide. These vessels were regularly careened to scrub the copper and caulk the garboard plank. They were probably careened every spring tide, or twice a month.

There appears to be detail of what is called the 'dead wood', or the space between the lower end of the keel and the termination of the garboard plank at the stern. This is where a rudder or a propeller shaft might protrude. There is a thickening of the line in this area, which may be the artist's attempt to show the rudder. Alternatively, the artist may be expressing the rudder as the small lobe extending out from the stern of the keel. In the alternative, this is an expression of the rudder pintle, the point where the rudder attaches to the keel.

Another interesting feature of Boat 1 is the pronounced stern extension above the water-line. This was typical of sailing vessels of this type and from that period. However, in the case of the Broome pearling vessels, there was a strong trend towards the popular counter stern. This was a semi-circular hemispherical or rounded shape that was separated from the deck by knees (usually three). The overhanging rim provided a good platform for controlling dive hoses, but perhaps more importantly, provided the ideal shape for use as a communal toilet (the overhang providing some degree of clearance from the lower stern hull and at ideal sitting height). The artist seems to be emphasising this shape. However, it is inverted vertically, so it does not read quite as you would see it. The rake of the bow is quite sheer, consistent with the form of the larger schooner-rigged ketches used at the time. There is accentuated roc or curve leading to the stern. Accentuated roc at the stern is a design feature particularly suited to strong following seas as it reduces the chances of broaching when a wave hits or drives against the stern.

Boat 1 is typical of the larger mother ships that supplied and serviced pearling fleets working off Broome in the last part of the 19th century and the early 20th century. Examples of this style of craft could be the *Sri Passir* (Streeter's schooner) or *The Mina* (Normans Schooner ex Beagle Bay).

In support of this interpretation is what appears to be a hafted axe or hatchet painted in outline and to the right of the schooner (Figure 4). The shape is unlike traditional stone axes/hatchets, but is strongly reminiscent of the shell-processing tomahawks that were used to

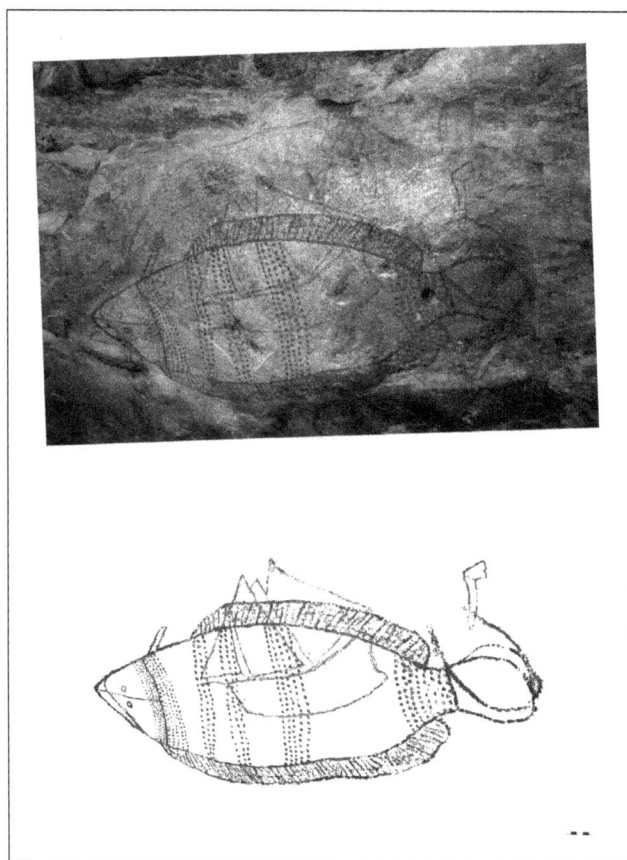

Figure 4. Boat 1 Widgingarri. Painting showing boat overlying fish and kangaroo paintings with possible tomahawk used for cleaning pearl shell to the right of this group (upper panel), and fish, boat and tomahawk extracted from background (lower panel).

clean away marine growth and chop the outer edge or growth process off the shell. This was the common way of removing the soft outer margin of the shell, which, unless removed, would shrink and crack the shell, affecting quality. The tomahawks were usually cut down so the operator had a short stump to wrap his hand around. The hatchet shown has the clearly defined wedge-shaped head and the arched hafting that is characteristic of the mount of the shell-processing tomahawks. Removing the edge of the shell created a neat open slit into which a knife was easily slid. A downward levering action would sever the abductor muscle and the pearl shell would spring open. Schooner mother ships sometimes acted as the processing point for the shell caught by satellite lugger fleets. There were two main reasons for this. Firstly, many of the early luggers were small vessels of about 40 feet. Deck space for processing and holding shell was limited. Handling bags of shell would have been difficult and cumbersome on an intra-vessel at sea basis. It was much easier for baskets of unprocessed shells to be lowered down to a collection dingy and transferred to the mother ship. The second reason was to maintain control over the shell-opening process by a trusted employee, therefore avoiding the potential loss of natural pearls by crew theft, something that was rife in the industry.

These schooners also carried an inventory of spares for the lugger fleets. It is likely they had an abundance of small steel-headed tomahawks. The artist may have stored the shelling tomahawks in the rock shelter while working on a lugger, or may have been given one in exchange for goods or services, or at the end of a period of work.

The detail of the sail plan, especially the detachment of the jib from bowsprit and the knowledge of hull structure below the waterline, indicates an intimate knowledge of the vessel. In summary, the artist is either an extraordinary observer, or has spent some time on this type of boat.

Boat 2 Widgingarri

Boat 2 is another very good example of a ketch-rigged vessel. It is painted in red pigment on to a traditionally applied white background (Figure 6). The hull is shown in solid red infill, as is the attached dinghy. The mast and sails are in red outline. This painting partly overlies a reclining Wandjina figure. The base of the hull of the boat has been painted over the right arm of the Wandjina, nestling closely into the body. Interestingly, this boat has been repainted and the mast configuration and hull shape have been changed at least once. Figure 6 shows the painting as it appears and the extracted outline of the boat, with the upper outline showing the earlier painted masts, as well as the most recent repainting, and the lower outline showing only the most recent painting of the masts. In the earlier configuration of Boat 2, the artist appears to have conformed to the style of Boat 1.

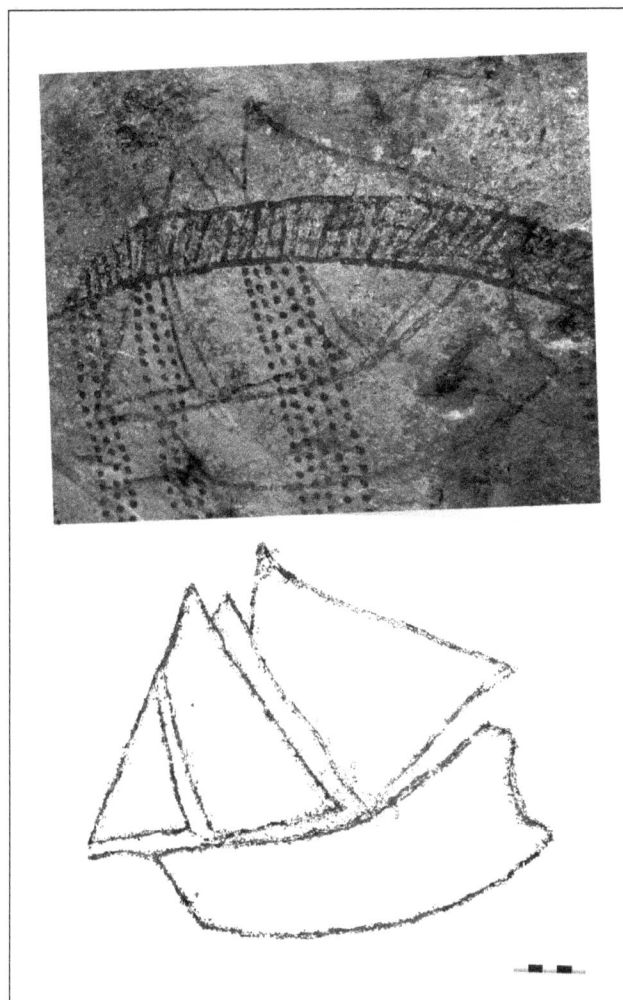

Figure 5. Boat 1 Widgingarri. Enlargement of boat and extracted outline.

Figure 6. Boat 2 Widgingarri. Original painting (upper panel), extracted image of boat (central panel) and extracted image showing only the most recent repainting of the sails (lower panel).

In particular, the mizzen mast and sail follows the trailing edge or luff of the foresail. In the repainting, the mizzen is straightened and separated.

The mizzen mast and sail appear to be either similar in size or larger than the foresail in the original painting. In the repainting, the mizzen mast is shorter than the foremast. It is possible this boat was originally painted as a schooner and later changed to reproduce the features of a lugger.

As in Boat 1, Boat 2 is painted in silhouette and details of the lower hull and counter are apparent. There is some interesting detail at the bow which does not appear on Boat 1. A connective line of dots emerging from the stem at the bow could be an anchor chain. In view of the strong ochre infill of the vessel hull, the careful separation of the dots suggests a deliberate choice on behalf of the artist to show the anchor chain.

The veering of the anchor was not always done when vessels were careened in a creek, mainly because the preference was to use the bases of mangrove trees as tie-off points. This gave the captain much more control over exactly where in the tidal gutter he would lay up his vessel. A single anchor off the bow could not ensure the vessel ended up exactly where it should sit for a good careening. It is possible, however, particularly in unfamiliar places with limited mangrove forest, that the anchor could be veered in order to hold the vessel for careening.

Figure 7. Boat 3 Widgingarri. Painting of small single-masted craft and extracted outline.

In other respects, the vessel seems to resemble Boat 1, but with extra detail. We see here also the inclusion of the bow sprit or bob stay chain. Again, the artist's knowledge of the vessel's rig and the way the sails are flying suggest a very good understanding of these boats. There appears to be an attempt at some structure emanating horizontally from the top of the mizzen mast. This could be an attempt to show the rope and pulley detail between the mast and the gaff, or it could be a flag. Often identification flags were flown from the top of the mizzen. This helped pearlers identify a specific fleet or vessels from a distance at sea.

The bow appears to have the classical elongation of the so-called fiddle bow, an early style that most probably came down with pearling vessels built in the Aru Islands.

It is interesting to note that unlike the ketch-rigged vessel, the dingy off the stern is shown as if it were floating in the water. No attempt has been made to show the detail below the waterline. The dingy has no mast nor rigging and therefore probably represents the standard clinker-hulled sculling vessel used to tender these vessels during the later part of the 18th century.

Boat 3 Widgingarri

Boat 3 is a small single-masted craft (Figure 7). It is painted in simple red outline and is very faded. It was probably executed on a blown white background, but the deteriorated condition of the painting makes this hard to determine. The faded condition of the red ochre and the greenish hue to the background suggests water damage is largely responsible for the deterioration.

This single-masted vessel could depict a cutter or a sloop. However, the length-to-depth ratio of the hull suggests it is a small boat. The small size of the craft and the little bump at the stern, which may be an attempt to indicate a rudder, suggest this is more likely to be a simple dinghy sail rig. Sailing dinghies were used as an alternative to sculling and rowing the various types of clinker-hull dinghies commonly used to tender luggers and schooners.

The following section provides the historical context for the three boats at Widgingarri.

The pearling industry and European sailing craft in the Kimberley

The first tentative pearling venture began in the Kimberley region at Nickol Bay about 200 km south of Broome in 1864 (Bain 1982:14). This was shore-based shell collection and was fairly

Figure 8. Pearling luggers and schooners in Roebuck Bay Broome (courtesy of the National Library of Australia).

short-lived, as shell supplies dwindled and it was quickly realised that pearl shell was more abundant in the deeper waters offshore. During the late 1860s to the mid 1880s, 'bare diving' took over from shore-based collection (Bailey 2001:22). Stripped naked, the divers went down holding their breath and returned with a bag of shell. The early years of the bare-diving phase involved mostly Aboriginal labour and as the profitability of pearling increased and labour requirements grew, Aboriginal labour was forcibly acquired by brutality and blackbirding (Bain 1982:20). The kidnapped Indigenous divers received no pay and at the end of their 'contract', or when they broke down, were often abandoned hundreds of kilometers from their traditional lands. Between 1871 and 1873, legislation was introduced aimed at improving the working conditions for Aboriginals on the luggers, prohibiting women from employment on board and stating that Aboriginals should be returned to their traditional lands at the end of their employment. Due to the remoteness of the Kimberley, there was little enforcement of this legislation (Bailey 2001:28).

Pearling began in Roebuck Bay in 1879 (Figure 8) and Broome was officially gazetted as a town in 1883 (Bailey 2001:29). The pearling industry based out of Roebuck Bay appears to have begun immediately with standard diving dress capabilities (Sam Male pers comm.), although some sources suggest that bare diving by Indigenous divers continued alongside suit-based collection through the 1880s and into the early 1890s (Bailey 2001:30–31). Suited diving was vastly more efficient in deeper water and was undertaken almost exclusively by Asian divers, mostly Japanese. Aboriginals employed in the industry after suit-based diving dominated were few, and were predominantly crew or shell cleaners (Bailey 2001:30–31; Shepherd 1975:178). By 1901, there were 232 pearling vessels working out of Broome, employing 132 whites, 1358

Asians and only 65 Aboriginals. Between 1908 and 1911, Aboriginal numbers had dwindled further, to between 20 and 29, while total Asian participation had risen to between 2094 and 2275 (Choo 1994:Appendix 2).

While the pearling industry was the major supplier of schooners, luggers and cutters along the Kimberley coast, examples of such boats operating between Broome and the north Kimberley coast engaged in less strictly commercial pursuits are numerous. Schooners were used as general supply boats and it is these that were engaged working the coast and supplying settlements between Broome and areas to the north.

The Port George the IV Mission was established on the mainland coast opposite Augustus Island about 1912 (O'Connor 1980:44) and later was moved a short distance inland and was renamed Kunmunya. A schooner regularly travelled between the mission and Broome, collecting and delivering mail and supplies (Stuart 1923:63). The missionary Love (1936:9) reports stopping his lugger on the way to and from Broome so his Indigenous crew could chat with friends or relations, drop off some tobacco, or collect turtle eggs to take back to their families at the mission.

The prospector E. J. Stuart travelled from Broome to Wyndham in 1917 in the schooner *Culwalla* and made observations of the many small maritime commercial operations and settlements using luggers dotting this coastline. For example, the self-styled missionary Hadley established a mission at Sunday Island at the turn of the century, and receiving no financial support from any source, he used small boats to collect trepang, *Trochus* and pearl shell. A highpoint in the calendar of mission life was the arrival of the schooner from Derby, which brought supplies such as flour every three months (Stuart 1923:18).

Harry Hunter, who lived with his large Indigenous family at Hunter Creek on the tip of Dampierland, was a lugger builder and trader and his family crewed his boat.

The Frenchman D'Antoine kept a small lugger at Tyri Island where he lived with a camp of more than 50 Indigenous people who assisted him in the enterprise of collecting trepang, bare diving for pearls and ferrying provisions (Stuart 1923:16). Most of these craft would have had Indigenous crew. For example, Stuart's crew included 'four black boys lent' to him by Hadley from the Sunday Island Mission, for the duration of his voyage (Stuart 1923:3).

In summary, while the historical records indicate that few Aboriginal people were directly engaged on pearling luggers working out of Roebuck Bay, they did work and crew on luggers and schooners working the waters north of Broome and there was no shortage of opportunities for them to observe these boats first hand. A close relationship with the workings of the boats is suggested by the technical accuracy of the rendering.

Conclusion

The three painted craft described here fit well into the artistic tradition of the paintings of traditional subjects in this region of the Kimberley. They are painted in red outline or combination outline and infill over a blown white background. As with most of the animals depicted in this style, they are shown in profile.

As Clarke and Frederick (2006) point out, the term 'contact' evokes the idea of an encounter with the unfamiliar. However, the 'idea that Aborigines regarded these subjects as exotic, foreign entities, existing outside the traditional Aboriginal experience, may be misleading' (Roberts 2004). While the boats represented are European and therefore are categorised as 'contact art', it is unlikely they were perceived as 'foreign' by the Indigenous people painting them. Like the paintings of European craft described by Roberts (2004) from western Arnhem Land, the three European boats described here would have been a common sight along this coast from the early

1900s until as late as the 1950s. The accuracy of observation and reproduction of the technical features of the craft suggests the artist(s) was intimately familiar, both from a technological and a social perspective, with the operation of the boats. Voyages on such boats may even have been part of the daily life of the artist(s) when working away from their traditional lands. They were, therefore, not painting scenes from somebody else's life, but a narrative of their own.

Acknowledgements

The trip to record the painting sites discussed was undertaken with Donny Woolagoodja, Adey Woolagoodja-Lane and Alfie Umbagai. Donny is a senior Worora elder and is thanked for his skill in getting us to this difficult section of coastline and for granting permission to record the art. The project was funded by the Australian Institute of Aboriginal and Torres Strait Islander Studies. Tony Barham assisted with the rock art and site recording. We would also like to acknowledge assistance from Paul Clark, Curator of Maritime Archaeology and History, Museum and Art Gallery of the Northern Territory. Adam Black undertook the extractions of the boat images in Figures 2, 3, 4, 5, 6 and 7. Moya Smith, Head, Anthropology Department, Western Australian Museum, assisted with information on the images of boats that were recorded by Ian Crawford from Bigge I. The WA Museum is thanked for granting permission to reproduce Figure 3 and the National Library of Australia for permission to reproduce Figure 8.

References

Bailey, J. 2001. *The White Divers of Broome: The True Story of a Fatal Experiment*. Sydney: Pan Macmillan.

Bain, M.A. 1982. *Full Fathom Five*. Perth: Artlook Books.

Bigourdan, N. nd. Aboriginal watercraft depictions in Western Australia. Unpublished Report Department of Maritime Archaeology Western Australian Museum, No 216.

Burningham, N. 1994. Aboriginal nautical art: A record of the Macassans and the pearling industry in northern Australia. *The Great Circle* 16(2):139–151.

Chaloupka, G. 1996. Praus in Marege: Makassan subjects in Aboriginal rock art of Arnhem Land, Northern territory, Australia. *Anthropologie* 34(1–2):131–142.

Choo, C. 1994. The impact of Asian-Aboriginal Australian contacts in Northern Australia, particularly the Kimberley, Western Australia. Unpublished manuscript (PMS 5328). AIATSIS collection, Canberra, AIATSIS.

Clarke, A. 2000. 'The Moormans Trousers': Macassan and Aboriginal interactions and the changing fabric of indigenous social life. In S. O'Connor and P. Veth (eds), *East of Wallace's Line: Studies of Past and Present Maritime Societies in the Indo-Pacific Region*, pp. 315–335. Modern Quaternary Research in Southeast Asia 16. Rotterdam: A. A. Balkema.

Clarke, A. and U. Frederick In press. The mark of marvellous ideas: Groote Eylandt rock art and performance of cross-cultural relations. In P. Veth, P. Sutton and M. Neale (eds), *Strangers on the shore: Early coastal contacts in Australia*, pp. 148–164. Canberra: National Museum of Australia.

Clarke, A and U. Frederick 2006. Closing the Distance: Interpreting Cross-Cultural Engagements through Indigenous Rock Art. In I. Lilley (ed), *Archaeology in Oceania, Australia and the Pacific Islands*, pp. 116–133. MA, USA: Blackwell.

Crawford, I.M. 1968. *The Art of the Wandjina*. London: Oxford University Press.

Crawford, I. 1969. Late prehistoric changes in Aboriginal cultures in Kimberley, Western Australia. Unpublished PhD thesis, London, University of London.

Crawford, I. 2001. *We won the victory: Aborigines and outsiders on the North West coast of the Kimberley.* Fremantle: Fremantle Arts Centre Press.

Earl, G.W. 1841. An account of a visit to Kisser, one of the Serawatti group in the Indian archipelago. *Journal of the Royal Geographical Society* 11:108–117.

Jukes, J.B. 1847. Narrative of the Surveying Voyage of H.M.S. Fly, commanded by Capt F.P. Blackwood, R.N. in *Torres Strait, New Guinea, and other islands of the Eastern Archipelago, during the years 1842-1846.* London: Ruols.

King, P.P. 1827. *Narrative of a Survey of the Intertropical and Western Coasts of Australia, Performed Between the Years 1818 and 1822,* Vol. I. London: John Murray.

Love, J.R.B. 1936. *Stone Age Bushman of Today: Life and Adventure Among a Tribe of Savages in North-Western Australia.* London: Blackie.

Macknight, C.C. 1972. Macassans and Aborigines. *Oceania* 42(4):183–321.

Macknight, C. 1976. *The Voyage to Marege, Macassan Tregangers in Northern Australia.* Melbourne: Melbourne University Press.

Mitchell, S. 1994. Stone exchange network in north-western Arnhem Land: Evidence for recent chronological change. In M. Sullivan, S. Brockwell and A. Webb (eds), *Archaeology in the North. Proceedings of the 1993 Australian Archaeological Conference*, pp. 188–200. Darwin: Northern Australian Research Unit, Australian National University.

O'Connor, S. 1990. 30,000 Years in the Kimberley. Unpublished PhD thesis, University of Western Australia.

O'Connor, S. 1999. 30,000 Years of Aboriginal Occupation, Kimberley North West Australia. *Terra Australis* 14. Department of Archaeology and Natural History and Centre for Archaeological Research, Canberra, Australian National University.

Roberts, D.A. 2004. Nautical themes in the Aboriginal Rock Paintings of Mount Borradaile, Western Arnhem Land. *The Great Circle* 26(1):19–50.

Roberts, R., G. Walsh, A. Murray, J. Olley, R, Jones, M. Morwood, C. Tuniz, E. Lawson, M. Macphail, D. Bowdery and I. Naumann 1997. Luminescence dating of rock art and past environments using mud-wasp nests in northern Australia. *Nature* 387:696–699.

Shepherd, B.W. 1975. A history of the pearling industry off the north-west coast of Australia from its origins until 1916. Unpublished MA thesis, University of Western Australia.

Stuart, E.J. 1923. *A Land of Opportunities: being an Account of the Author's recent Expedition to Explore the Northern Territories of Australia.* London: Bodley head.

Tindale, N. 1925–1926. Natives of Groote Eylandt and of the West Coast of the Gulf of Carpentaria. *Records of the South Australian Museum* 3:61–134.

Urry, J and M. Walsh 1981. The lost 'Macassar language' of northern Australia. *Aboriginal History* 5(2):91–109.

Walsh, G.L. 2000. *Bradshaw Art of the Kimberley*, Toowong: Takarakka Nowan Kas Publications.

26

The shifting place of Ngai Tahu rock art

Gerard O'Regan
Ngai Tahu Maori Rock Art Trust, 27 Strathallan Street, PO Box 983, Timaru, New Zealand
gerard.oregan@xtra.co.nz

Introduction

As Ngai Tahu's pre-eminent archaeologist, Atholl Anderson's contribution to southern Maori archaeology and historical research is well recognised, but less widely acknowledged is his involvement in the shaping of modern heritage-management directions within his tribe. During the early 1990s, Anderson was a founding member of Komiti Tuku Iho, the tribe's heritage committee, that among other things, articulated a tribal policy statement on human remains. This has resulted in the return to tribal care of all the relevant skeletal remains from museums within New Zealand (see O'Regan 2006). He was a primary author of Ngai Tahu's policy on the management of archaeological and rock-art sites, now regularly referred to in tribal resource-management plans and land-development consent processes, and with Brian Allingham, he founded the South Island Maori Rock Art Project, a survey project that was the genesis of the current Ngai Tahu Maori Rock Art Trust. This paper is an acknowledgement of Anderson's contribution to shaping Ngai Tahu's modern management of its heritage sites and their increasing relevance to expressions of tribal identity.

Wahi tapu are 'places held in reverence according to tribal custom and history' (Tau *et al.* 1992:s4:25). Associated with earlier generations, the most important among them are urupa (burials), as 'The dead are a link to the past and to the land' (Tau *et al.* 1992:s4:25). Today the term wahi tapu is attached to many places of historical and cultural significance to Maori (Mead 2003:69), including some places also categorised as archaeological and rock-art sites (see New Zealand Historic Places Trust 2004:45; Kai Tahu ki Otago 2005:63). The Historic Places Act (HPA) 1993 defines wahi tapu as a 'place sacred to Maori in the traditional, spiritual, religious, ritual, or mythological sense' (HPA 1993:s2) and makes provision for their registration. It defines archaeological sites as 'any place in New Zealand that – (a) either – (i) was associated with human activity that occurred before 1900; ... and (b) is or may be able through investigation by archaeological methods to provide evidence relating to the history of New Zealand' (HPA 1993:s2), and imposes restrictions on their uncontrolled modification. While a place may have both wahi tapu and archaeological values, each set of values is currently classed and protected separately under legislation.

There is provision in the HPA for Maori to be consulted on cultural values about proposed modifications to archaeological sites. Notwithstanding this, implicit in the legislation is a dichotomy of scientific archaeological values, on the one hand, and Maori cultural or spiritual values on the other. This undoubtedly reflects the historical backgrounds of the archaeological fraternity and Maori communities over the past century. A question can be asked, though, about whether such a clear-cut separation will persist into the future and, indeed, is it always quite so clear cut now? This paper explores this question through a case study of the reuse of southern Maori rock-art imagery and the recent tribal management of two rock-shelter sites in the Waitaki Valley, South Island.

Rock art is located in place

> Generally … it is meaningless to isolate paintings and engravings from their natural settings. They are not individual works on the walls of cliffs or on rocks, like paintings hanging on the walls of a museum. Their full meaning can only be appreciated in a broader context, in which water, cliffs, shelters, rocks, and weather – and the sacred stories attached to them – are every bit as significant as the images created by men and women (Clottes 2002:60).

Modern rock-art research places a great deal of emphasis on the placement of the art in important and permanent venues. This applies at the macro level of sites in the wider landscape, as well as at the micro level of images within a panel – where they are positioned in relation to different images and other parts of the site (Chippindale and Nash 2004:1). As the choice on where to position rock-art figures was determined by the world view of the artists, the meaning of rock art generally derives from an aggregate of factors, including religious practices, natural landscape formations and weather, which results, for example, in rock art in many arid regions of the world being linked to the presence of water (Clottes 2002:58). Drawing on studies of Hawaiian petroglyphs in relation to boundaries, trails and places of ritual, Lee (2002) argues that the place and marking of place is as important as the petroglyphs themselves, and that even though the exact meaning of motifs might not be determined, their relevance to the creators and users of them can be. Within individual sites, accumulations of rock art in some places and not in others show how the position of existing images influenced the placement of later figures. There are several clear examples of this in North Otago shelters, where deliberate but avoidable superimpositions appear to have made careful connections to pre-existing rock-art figures (O'Regan 2007). Such accumulations may result from a psychological response of one drawing leading to another, such as seen in graffiti, or it may be sanctification, a phenomenon in which an initial painting invests the rock wall with power that subsequent artistic additions look to benefit from and add to (Clottes 2002:73). In either case, the setting, the physical character of the rock surface and the presence of other art all contribute to how a rock-art figure is placed and shaped.

South Island Maori rock art has been explained as 'time-filling scribbles of storm-stayed travellers' (Duff 1950:7) and the results of a pleasurable pastime incidental to sheltering in rock shelters during hunting expeditions (Trotter and McCulloch 1981:81). On the other hand, Fomison concluded that the positioning of some art in uninhabitable places indicated the artists went to those places with a purposeful intent of drawing (Trotter and McCulloch 1981:16). Schoon (1947:6–7) described the rock-art figures as 'products of a dream life … [that] arise out of a religious concept which centred around a spirit-bearing world' and posited they reflected a positive function of artist-priests in the labyrinths of the South Island's limestone valleys. Whatever the case, common to all these explanations of the presence, purpose or meanings of southern Maori rock art, is some appreciation of the position of the art on the landscape.

There is a question as to what extent European contact-period rock art was a continuation of an earlier South Island tradition that dated to the time of moa hunting (see Trotter and McCulloch (1981:13, 81) and Anderson (1988) for contrasting views). Regardless, at the time of European contact, South Island Maori clearly knew of places in which rock art had been produced, and added to those places with images of European people, sailing ships and script in the Maori language. The process of Western colonisation shattered much of the traditional Maori world view within which the rock art had been created, and severed many of the relationships southern Maori communities had with the landscapes on which the art was positioned (O'Regan 2003). An appreciation of rock art in the landscape was not, then, something most Ngai Tahu throughout the 20th century would have experienced. If they encountered rock art at all, it would have most likely been in the form of images lifted from the landscape.

A shift in place

The first art to be graphically lifted from the landscape was images from the Takiroa site (NZAA SRS I40/9 in the New Zealand Archaeological Association Site Record Scheme) near Duntroon in the Waitaki Valley. Mantell's (1868:6–7) publication of a selection of paintings puts southern Maori rock art among the first aspects of the New Zealand archaeological record to have been formally recorded. While conducting a small archaeological excavation at Takiroa, Augustus Hamilton (1896) also photographed a number of the rock-art images there, as well as at the nearby Maerewhenua shelter (NZAA SRS I40/18). These glass-plate negatives survive in the Museum of New Zealand Te Papa Tongarewa photographic collection and provide a record of the figures before several were physically lifted from the sites for museum collections in about 1913 (Stevenson 1947:22). So it was that southern Maori rock art entered the New Zealand archaeological record. Its value as a resource for archaeological enquiry has been the focus of the attention it has received since.

It was in this light that from 1958 to 1960, archaeologists set about recording rock-art sites further up the Waitaki Valley before their flooding for the Benmore hydro-generation scheme (Ambrose 1970:384). Various shelters were excavated and the rock art was recorded in detail, including an image from Shepherd's Creek that is now widely interpreted as a juvenile kiwi in an egg or, more colloquially, 'the kiwi embryo'. The site had long been known to local farm residents and was recorded by Stevenson (1947:32–33), who described the setting and other rock-art figures there but made no mention of the kiwi embryo. The published archaeological reports (Ambrose and Davis 1958; Ambrose 1970) do present the image and discuss its spatial context (Figure 1). As it appeared the figure was painted by a person leaning down from a ledge, the earlier report suggested the figure should probably be examined upside down, and presented it as such (Ambrose and Davis 1958:17). The later report presented the figure the other way up (Ambrose 1970:428). It also noted that the survival of the kiwi embryo painting in an exposed place may

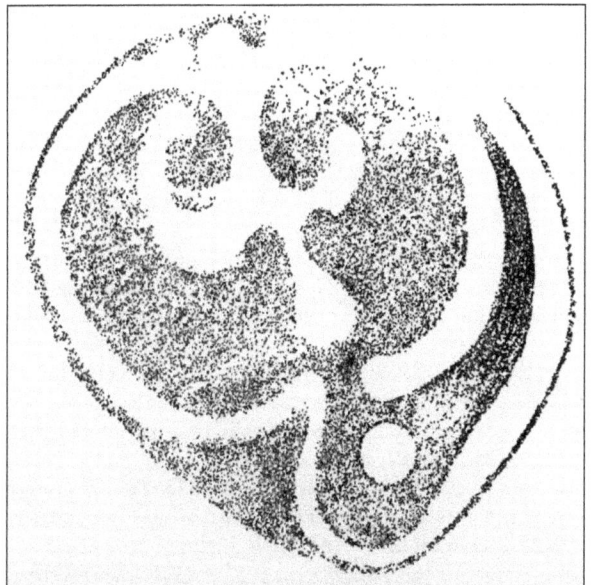

Figure 1. Archaeological recording of the kiwi-embryo rock-art figure by Wal Ambrose. In *Records of the Canterbury Museum* (1970) 8(5):428, Fig 22b (courtesy of the Canterbury Museum).

indicate its recent age relative to more sheltered rock-art figures that were more weathered (Ambrose 1970:429). The landscape, the figure's position within it, and the relationship of the kiwi embryo image to surrounding rock art were all, then, a fundamental part of the archaeological interpretation. The same is not so, however, for the subsequent reuse of the imagery drawn from the archaeological record.

A notable reuse of the kiwi-embryo image within archaeological circles is its reproduction as the cover emblem for the *New Zealand Journal of Archaeology*, produced by the New Zealand Archaeological Association. There, the image has been given defined edges and vertically flipped, making it more obviously an avian form than is readily apparent in Ambrose's 1970 reproduction. A gap in the outer rim of the motif has also been filled, completing the 'egg shell'. There is no accompanying imagery, nor note that indicates the image is rock art.

Brian Allingham (pers comm. 2007) recalls seeing a reference by Duff to an inaccurate rendition of a rock-art image in a South Island newspaper, possibly the kiwi-embryo motif. While such an article has not yet been identified by the author, it may explain a version of the motif that found its way, among other rock-art images, on to a series of peanut-butter jars (Figure 2). Although upside down and distorted, with the addition of a protruding lug, the image is undoubtedly based on the Shepherd's Creek rock-art figure. Anecdotal accounts suggest the empty jars became drinking vessels in many New Zealand homes, commonplace before mass plastic packaging. Surviving examples are valued by some as 'kiwiana'.

The image is similarly found as an emblem on the crockery at Rehua Marae in Christchurch, where the lugged version inspired artwork in the whare (meeting house) Te Whatu-Manawa Maoritanga o Rehua that opened in 1960 (Figure 3). When building the whare, the marae elders wanted to include a specifically South Island pattern and, following a visit to the Waitaki Valley, adopted the kiwi-embryo image (Terry Ryan pers comm. 2006). An entwined pair of the motif was used to create a 'Unique Ngai Tahu design showing the embryonic kiwi' (Tau

Figure 2. Rock-art images featured on a collector series of peanut-butter jars, now valued as examples of 'kiwiana'.

et al. 1992:s5:81) for some of the rafters in a very traditional Maori context and among other very traditional Maori kowhaiwhai (rafter paintings), carvings and tukutuku (woven panels) (Figure 4). That pattern was subsequently further stylised for similar use in the meeting house Aoraki at the Nga Hau e Wha national marae, also in Christchurch. Whereas these meeting houses are very traditional Maori spaces, the placement of multiple images on the inside of whare is far removed from the original rock-shelter context of the motif. Further, both houses are located some distance from Shepherd's Creek and numerous other rock-art images can be found closer to hand. The kiwi-embryo motif is again included in a contemporary mural on the wall of the whare Uenuku, North Otago. Te Runanga o Moeraki, the Maori community there, considers itself the guardian of the area in which the kiwi embryo was recorded and its use in that instance is as a marker of local identity. It is depicted on a rock, albeit a Moeraki boulder, which is another heritage icon of the area, found on the local beach.

Figure 3. Terry Ryan recalls that in the late 1950s the elders of Rehua Marae wanted to include a uniquely southern Maori image in the meeting house, Te Whatu-Manawa Maoritanga o Rehua, that was being built (photo with permission of Rehua Marae).

Figure 4. A unique Ngai Tahu design showing the embryonic kiwi, incorporated into the rafters of the meeting house (photo with permission of Rehua Marae).

The association of the motif with local identity is perhaps epitomised in its adaptation for a contemporary arts program commissioned by the tribal authority, Te Runanga o Ngai Tahu, in 2005. 'Pepeha in the City' was an initiative that sought to bring traditional Maori sayings to the fore in the Christchurch community. Artworks were commissioned and reproduced on cards distributed at community events. One of the artworks coupled several images of the kiwi-embryo figure with the traditional saying 'ka pakihi whakatekateka a waitaha [sic], the plains where waitaha [sic] strutted proudly' (Figure 5). This is a specific reference to the Canterbury plains and not associated with the locality at Shepherd's Creek in the Waitaki Valley.

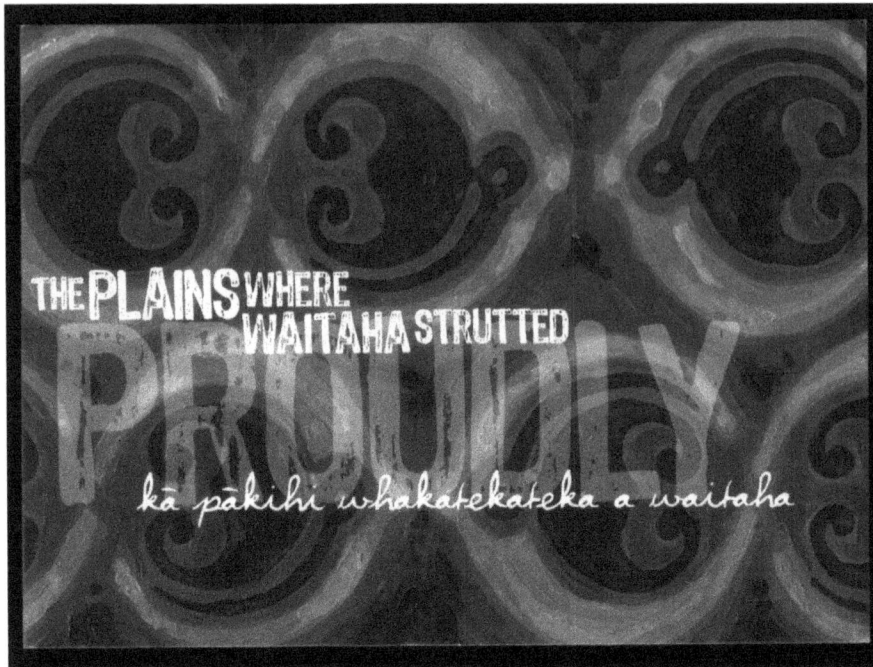

Figure 5. A card celebrating a southern Maori proverb associated with the Canterbury Plains. Designed by Frances Bryant (reproduced with permission of Te Runanga o Ngai Tahu).

The motif, as presented in the whare Rehua, was replicated as the corporate logo for the Ngai Tahu administration's Whakapapa Unit, which manages the genealogical records and registrations of the tribe. Terry Ryan (pers comm. 2006), the former manager of the unit explains its adoption as a symbol of reproduction and new growth. He points to others who shared that interpretation, such as Dunedin's Arai Te Uru cultural performance group, which incorporated it into the pari (bodices) of their performance costumes. Such use indicates that if there was a tapu (religious restriction) associated with the original placement of the art on the landscape, that was not perceived as a hindrance to wearing the motif on the body in the 1960s and 1970s.

Tribal discussions on rock art and other taonga (cultural treasures), such as the 2005 Ngai Tahu cultural symposium held at Huirapa, Karitane, quickly turn to concerns about the non-tribal abuse of tribal intellectual and cultural property. The commercial exploitation of rock-art designs, including reproductions on T-shirts for sale, is considered a misappropriation of cultural imagery and widely looked upon with disdain within the tribe. Recently, the Ngai Tahu Maori Rock Art Trust proposed producing a series of T-shirts, one of which incorporated the kiwi embryo, as a fundraiser. The local marae communities that maintain tribal authority over the rock-art images permitted the use, as sales were to be restricted to tribal members. Although permission was later granted for public sales, to increase returns for the protection of rock art, the marae's initial position reflected the idea that only tribal members should proudly wear the works of the ancestors. This expression of tribal pride exhibited through the rock-art imagery has extended to its incorporation in body art in the current ta moko (tattooing) renaissance. Among its other reuses, the kiwi embryo is permanently inked into the arms of the Kamo family of Canterbury (Figure 6).

This brief survey of the reuse of the kiwi-embryo image is far from comprehensive. Nor is the morphing of the images – from rock art on the landscape, to archaeological records, commercial misappropriation, kiwiana, meeting houses, contemporary artworks, corporate logos, group emblems and tattoos on the bodies of young Ngai Tahu – a unique story. The

Figure 6. Ward Kamo shares the kiwi-embryo motif as a ta moko with his siblings. The design both connects them to their tribal landscape and celebrates their whanau (family) time at Rehua Marae.

same tale can be told about the eagle images from Te Manunui (Frenchmans Gully, NZAA SRS J39/17) and the renowned Opihi (NZAA SRS J38/75) taniwha images. Indeed, there are hundreds of examples of the modern use of southern Maori rock-art imagery. Each case reflects how the art has intrigued and inspired different people and groups, and how they have sought, albeit in their own ways, to celebrate it. The point of this review is to illustrate that the place of the kiwi-embryo image in Ngai Tahu culture has shifted, from rock art, on the one hand, to body art on the other. That is to say, it has undergone a transition from an artwork fixed in place in a landscape full of meaning, to what is at one extreme a taonga (treasure) ingrained in a person wherever in the world the person happens to be.

There are a number of factors to note in this transition. First, of the approximately 40,000 Ngai Tahu people today, none has seen the now flooded kiwi embryo image, and relatively few have seen other rock-art images in a landscape context. Second, it follows that as an appreciation of the location of the art in the landscape is fundamental to explanations of its meaning, purpose or presence, then these are largely lost in the reuse of the images, which are the limit of most people's experience of the art. Third, whereas Ngai Tahu generally disapproves of the use by others of tribal rock-art imagery in personal clothing, corporate logos, contemporary art and souvenir pieces, these are all things the tribe does itself, and sometimes for a wider market. This suggests the tribal position is less about what is being done, and more a question of who is doing it, and under whose *mana* (authority). These factors lead to a recognition of the new place of southern Maori rock art as a tribal heritage art form promoted as a statement of tribal identity. A relationship to a landscape is implicit in this, but it is to a wider *rohe* (tribal area), rather than to a specific rock shelter.

Treasured sites

Tracking the reuse of the rock-art imagery and its place in the modern tribe is interesting in terms of contemporary tribal arts and statements of identity. It is also of interest in understanding the rationale behind Ngai Tahu's management of some archaeological sites, including the aforementioned Takiroa and Maerewhenua rock-art shelters.

On the side of State Highway 83 and with at least 35,000 visitors a year, Takiroa is perhaps the most accessible and highly visited rock-art site in the country. The rock art extends along an interconnected series of shelters that undercut a large limestone bluff. Despite the removal of some figures for museum collections, the subsequent erosion and the ongoing weathering of the art, a large number of figures are still clearly visible, including some particularly large, bold, red paintings. The shelters were set aside as a historic reserve in 1981. An initial fence protected the main concentration of surviving figures. Further art is located beyond the area originally fenced and beyond the boundary of the reserve, which extends only a few metres in front of the main painted part of the shelter wall. In the mid 1990s, the Historic Places Trust developed a management plan for the site, which resulted in more extensive fencing covering more of the rock-art images, interpretive guide boards and a paved access route. The path crosses private farmland that has been actively grazed, resulting in the regular fouling of the path by cattle.

Four kilometres southeast of Takiroa, the Maerewhenua shelter is in the upper levels of a large limestone outcrop at the juncture of the Waitaki and Maerewhenua River valleys. From a side road a few hundred metres off State Highway 83, access to the shelter was by way of a stile over a farm fence and then up what can be described as a steep 'goat track' that climbed across private farmland directly to the shelter front. Despite a protective wire cage across the front of the shelter, the rock art concentrated on the rear wall is still readily visible to visitors. The historic reserve boundaries put in place in 1980 extend only as far as the shelter itself.

Both sites have archaeological evidence dating from the time of moa hunting. At the foot of the talus slope in front of the Maerewhenua shelter, Hamilton (1896:173) noted many moa bones, some of which were fragmented and cut. Allingham (nd) recorded moa bone from a small oven feature in front of the Takiroa shelter, and during his excavation at the site, Hamilton (1896:172–173) found a moa feather among the other avian remains above the 'Maori level', which contained lumps of kokowai (red iron oxide), which was used, among other purposes, for painting rock art. The character of the deposits found at both sites suggests they were used for short visits, rather than long-term occupation. There are only limited ethnohistorical references to southern Maori rock art, and none that explain the meaning of the art at Takiroa and Maerewhenua, nor why it was put there.

As historic reserves, both sites were managed by the New Zealand Historic Places Trust, mostly through its North Otago Branch Committee. As a result of the increase in interest in rock art following the tribe's 1993 adoption of the South Island Maori Rock Art Project survey, Te Runanga o Moeraki moved to increase tribal authority over the Takiroa site (O'Regan 1994). This eventually came about with the transfer of the management of the Maerewhenua and Takiroa sites to the tribe as part of cultural redress in the 1998 settlement of Ngai Tahu's historic land claim to the Waitangi Tribunal. The management is vested in the tribal council, Te Runanga o Ngai Tahu, with the local management responsibility being delegated to Te Runanga o Moeraki. Takiroa and Maerewhenua are the only two rock-art sites in North Otago managed directly by the tribe. Whereas Te Runanga o Moeraki supported the Historic Places Trust's previous efforts to improve visitor facilities at Takiroa, it remained dissatisfied with the state of presentation of the flagship sites. Accordingly, with the support of the Ngai Tahu Maori Rock Art Trust, it embarked on a site upgrade for each.

With the support of the landowners, the areas in front of the shelters were set aside and fenced from stock. Palisade-style fencing was erected, along with posts reminiscent of pou whenua (landmark posts) that carried new interpretation panels. These present more impressive entrances to the sites and extend the perceived spaces visited outwards from the shelter walls (Figure 7). At Maerewhenua, a properly stepped path of limestone chips in keeping with the natural environment now zigzags up the slope and eases the climb. The tired and patched caging was replaced and the path from which the art is viewed was levelled. Native species were planted at both sites, and will, with time, further distinguish the sites from the farmland. Following these upgrades, Transit New Zealand has arranged the purchase of neighbouring land to build a safe car-parking area for visitors to Takiroa. An on-site event marked the completion of the redevelopments in December 2007 (Figure 8). The two sites previously presented as caged shelters of archaeological interest in the middle of farm paddocks have been transformed into cared-for places that are distinctly recognisable as being of cultural significance to Maori.

Conclusions

The site developments at Takiroa and Maerewhenua have been warmly applauded in the community. There is little doubt the rock-art visitor experience at both sites is now more accessible, and enhanced with a stronger sense of 'old-time Maori'. Yet, how 'authentic' is the message imparted? The modern paths, particularly the steep frontal approach at Maerewhenua, may not reflect the way the artists accessed the sites (O'Regan 2007:138–139). Nor is there anything to suggest these sites ever had palisades, gateways or pou whenua. In themselves, the upgrades have done little to advance understanding of the meaning of the rock art or to directly contribute to its better conservation. Instead, the upgrades reflect the current place of rock art within Ngai Tahu culture as an expression of pride in the past, rather than a reiteration of that past. The efforts have been focused squarely on reflecting the rock art as something treasured. Emerging from this is the suggestion that the rationale behind the tribal reclamation of the management of the Takiroa and Maerewhenua sites and the recent upgrades is a concern for showing that the places are treasured and who is doing the treasuring, rather than a concern

Figure 7. Along with the palisade-style fencing, native planting will increasingly shift the perspective of Maerewhenua away from being a caged archaeological site in the middle of a farm paddock (courtesy of Ellen Andersen).

Figure 8. The local Maori community, Te Runanga o Moeraki, share its pride in the Takiroa rock art-site with other community members at the launch of the new visitor facilities, December 2007 (courtesy of Ellen Andersen).

for the presentation of archaeological or historical 'truths'. This is perhaps the fundamental difference in New Zealand between managing a place as an 'archaeological site' and managing it as a 'wahi tapu'.

Such developments are not unique to rock-art sites. The same phenomenon is demonstrated by the carved gateway at Huriawa pa site at Karitane, the interpretations and pou (posts) at Otatara Pa in Hawke's Bay, and numerous other places throughout New Zealand where pou whenua (posts that mark significant localities) have been set in place. Unlike pa sites, though, that often have detailed and significant tribal histories for which wahi tapu values can be easily recognised, at Takiroa and Maerewhenua it is the rock art itself, the archaeology of the site, that underpins the treatment of the places as wahi tapu. In these two cases, the distinction between the archaeological values and the wahi tapu values are blurred. The case also demonstrates that the archaeology of the sites is dynamic, with the story still unfolding.

As it stands today, southern Maori record wahi tapu, and some of these places may have archaeological values (Kai Tahu ki Otago 2005:63). Archaeologists record archaeological sites, but note they may have other values to Maori (Walton 1999:10). While the current legislative environment implies archaeological values are distinct from the Maori cultural values that underpin recognition of a place as a wahi tapu, the above discussion suggests that in regard to rock art at least, such a distinction is more perceived than actual. This blurring of values can be graphically tracked through the shifting place of rock art in Ngai Tahu culture. As we track the resultant shift in the modern management of rock-art sites, at least in so far as his own tribe's heritage is concerned, we can see the hand of Atholl Anderson from the outset.

References

Allingham, B. pers comm. Telephone discussion regarding the kiwi embryo motif, December 2007.

Allingham, B. nd. Takiroa, Waitaki Valley, South Island Maori Rock Art Project Te Kaupapa i nga Tuhituhi Tawhito o Te Wai Pounamu, Vol. 4, unpublished report, Te Runanga o Ngai Tahu, Christchurch.

Ambrose, W. 1970. Archaeology and rock drawings from the Waitaki Gorge, Central South Island. *Records of the Canterbury Museum* 8(5):383–437.

Ambrose, W. and F. Davis 1958. Interim report on the recording of Maori rock shelter art at Benmore. *Report of the National Historic Places Trust for the year ended 31 March 1958*, pp. 11–23. Wellington: Government Printer.

Anderson, A. 1988. The art of concealment: Some thoughts on South Island Maori rock drawings. National Museum of New Zealand Te Whare Taonga o Aotearoa and Manawatu Art Gallery, *Ka Tuhituhi o Nehera, The Drawings of Ancient Times*. National Museum of New Zealand Te Whare Taonga o Aotearoa and Manawatu Art Gallery.

Chippindale, C. and G. Nash 2004. Pictures in place: Approaches to the figured landscapes of rock-art. In C. Chippindale and G. Nash (eds), *Pictures in Place: The Figured Landscapes of Rock-Art*, pp.1–36. Cambridge: Cambridge University Press.

Clottes, J. 2002. *World Rock Art*. Los Angeles: The Getty Conservation Institute.

Duff, R. 1950. Maori art in rock drawings. *Arts Year Book* 6:6–11.

Hamilton, A. 1896. On some paintings on the walls of rock-shelters in the Waitaki Valley. *Transactions and Proceedings of the New Zealand Institute* 29:169–174.

Kai Tahu ki Otago 2005. *Kai Tahu ki Otago Natural Resource Management Plan 2005*. Dunedin: Kai Tahu ki Otago Ltd.

Lee, G. 2002. Wahi Pana: Legendary places on Hawai'i Island. In B. David and M. Wilson (eds), *Inscribed Landscapes: Marking and Making Place*, pp. 79–92. Honolulu: University of Hawai'i Press.

Mantell, W. 1868. Abstract of address on the Moa. *Transactions and Proceedings of the New Zealand Institute* 1:5–7.

Mead, H.M. 2003. *Tikanga Maori: Living by Maori Values*. Wellington: Huia Publishers.

New Zealand Historic Places Trust 2004. *Heritage Management Guidelines for Resource Management Practitioners*. Wellington: New Zealand Historic Places Trust.

O'Regan, G. 1994. Caring for rock art. *New Zealand Historic Places* 50:27–28.

O'Regan, G. 2003. The history and future of New Zealand Maori Rock Art – A Tribal Perspective. Before Farming: The archaeology and anthropology of hunter-gatherers 2003/1(9), viewed 1 August 2007, <http://www.waspress.co.uk>.

O'Regan, G. 2006. Regaining Authority: Setting the agenda in Maori Heritage through the control and shaping of data. *Public History Review* 13:95–107.

O'Regan, G. 2007. Wahi tapu and rock art: an intra-site analysis of two Southern Maori rock art shelters. Unpublished MA thesis, Department of Anthropology, University of Auckland.

Ryan, T. pers comm. Email regarding the reuse of the kiwi embryo image, April 2006.

Schoon, T. 1947. New Zealand's oldest art galleries. *New Zealand Listener*, September 12:6–7.

Stevenson, G.B. 1947. *Maori and Pakeha in North Otago*. Wellington: A.H. and A.W. Reed.

Tau, Te M., A. Goodall, D. Palmer and R. Tau 1992. *Te Whakatau Kaupapa: Ngai Tahu Resource Management Strategy for the Canterbury Region*. Wellington: Aoraki Press.

Trotter, M. and B. McCulloch 1981. *Prehistoric Rock Art of New Zealand*. Auckland: Longman Paul Ltd.

Walton, T. 1999. *Accessing the archaeological values of historic places: procedures, methods and field techniques*. Science and Research Internal Report 167, Department of Conservation, Wellington.

27

Phosphates and bones: An analysis of the courtyard of marae Manunu, Huahine, Society Islands, French Polynesia

Paul Wallin
Department of Archaeology and Osteology, Gotland University, Sweden
Paul.Wallin@hgo.se

Inger Österholm
Department of Archaeology and Osteology, Gotland University, Sweden

Sven Österholm
Gotland Community College, Sweden

Reidar Solsvik
Kon-Tiki Museum, Oslo, Norway

Introduction

The investigations at marae Manunu (Figure 1) were part of an archaeological project called 'Local development and regional interactions', a collaboration between the Kon-Tiki Museum, B.P. Bishop Museum, Oslo University, and the Service de la Culture et du Patrimoine, Tahiti, French Polynesia. The project was conducted from 2001 to 2004 on the island of Huahine in the Society Islands. One team from the B.P. Bishop Museum in Hawai'i, led by Dr Y.H. Sinoto and E. Komori, investigated a submerged coastal habitation site on the base of the slope of Mata'ire'a hill behind Maeva Village. Another team from the Kon-Tiki Museum, led by the first author, investigated marae sites around Maeva village, as well as several other marae on the island.

The excavation of the marae Manunu took place in August 2003 and has been reported in detail elsewhere (Wallin *et al.* 2004; Wallin and Solsvik 2005a, b, 2006a, b). In this paper, we report the results of a phosphate analysis made in the courtyard of marae Manunu and along the ahu wall. The purpose of the study was to see whether ritual activity at marae, such as animal

Figure 1. Front view of marae Manunu, Huahine (photo by Paul Wallin).

and human sacrifice, feasting and the presentation of food stuffs to deities, left behind phosphate residues. Areas with high and low phosphate were excavated to see whether archaeological data, particularly the amount of bone remains, correlated with the phosphate readings.

The setting

The district of Maeva comprises the north and northeastern part of Huahine Nui that surrounds the sacred mountain of Moua Tapu. A small village is on a strip of land along the lagoon and just behind the Maeva village, the hill of Mata'ire'a rises steeply to about 60 m above sea level. Along the slopes and on top of this hill, there are house foundations, terraces and about 40 marae structures. The most important temple on the island is marae Mata'ire'a Rahi, on the summit of Mata'ire'a. Across the lagoon from Maeva village on Motu Ovarei is the huge marae of Manunu-i-te-ra'i.

The settlement at Maeva consists of three distinct components. First, there are the 10 marae structures built along the shores of the lagoon-lake Fauna Nui that provided a range of marine foods in prehistory. These marae are the classic Leeward Island coastal marae type and comprised the ritual and ceremonial centre of Huahine during the proto-historic period. The most important of these marae, Orohahaa, is located in the grounds of the local church and has been destroyed. In conjunction with, and close to, these temples are large concave stone platforms with round-ended house curbing, located along the inland side of the modern road. Given the size and number of these house platforms, they probably represent chiefly dwelling platforms belonging to the late proto-historic era.

The settlement on the slopes and top of Mata'ire'a hill makes up the second component of the chiefly centre of Maeva. Test-excavation of house foundations in the upper parts of the Te Ana land division by Sinoto and Komori (Sinoto 1996) showed that settlement in this part of Mata'ire'a was underway by AD 1300–1400. Our investigations of marae structures on this same land division found, in several cases, evidence of habitation stratigraphically below marae platforms.

The third element of settlement at Maeva are the two marae structures which have island-wide religious significance; marae Mata'ire'a Rahi and marae Manunu. These two temples were of paramount importance in the ritual cycle of Huahine. Without them, a new paramount chief could not be invested in his position, nor could the life-giving pa'i atua ceremony take place. Marae Mata'ire'a Rahi is on the summit of the hill and marae Manunu has its ahu rear wall oriented towards the open sea. At these two marae all the ritual ceremonies necessary for annual growth and the maintenance of order were held. As part of the ritual cycle, the god Tane was carried from one marae to the next as the ritual calendar dictated.

A detailed settlement history for Mata'ire'a hill has not yet been proposed. Sinoto (1996) suggested the main settlement on the hill, inland from marae Tefano, marae Mata'ire'a Rahi and marae Tamata Uporu, was not in use during the proto-historic period. It was suggested that Mata'ire'a had been abandoned in favour of the settlement on the coastal flat close to the marae along the edge of the lagoon. Sinoto's argument was based on a morphological change in marae architecture from an 'Inland Type 2' to the classic 'Coastal Type' (Sinoto 1996:549–550, 2002). The marae seaward of marae Tefano (marae Mata'ire'a Rahi and marae Temata Uporu) had been rebuilt as the classic 'Coastal Type'. During our resurvey and excavation of marae Mata'ire'a Rahi, it became evident that the marae had been rebuilt from a Leeward Coastal Type to an Intermediate Type (Wallin *et al.* 2004; Wallin and Solsvik 2005a). The consequence of this rebuilding for the settlement sequence of Mata'ire'a remains to be determined. At present we know that: (1) settlements without marae were established on Mata'ire'a around AD 1300–1400; (2) sometime after AD 1450–1500 marae were constructed within these settlements; and (3) some of these settlements were in use up to historic times c. AD 1817.

The two national marae of Maeva

According to the missionary Orsmond, marae Manunu was the national temple of Huahine Nui and dedicated to the god Tane (Henry 1928). Tane was also the god honoured on marae Mata'ire'a Rahi and here the god had his earthly home in a small house built on stilts on a terrace just north of the great marae. That the abode of Tane was on marae Mata'ire'a Rahi and not on marae Manunu, might be interpreted to mean that Manunu was subordinate to Mata'ire'a Rahi in the religious hierarchy of Maeva. It is possible there existed a third temple, marae Orohahaa, in this ritual hierarchy that encompassed these two great temples.

Investigations at marae Manunu

Marae Manunu was restored by Y.H. Sinoto in 1967 and has been repaired several times since. The gigantic size of the ahu made it difficult from a practical perspective to excavate inside and underneath the ahu. We decided to concentrate our efforts, therefore, on the courtyard in front of the ahu. A local coordinate system was established in front of the ahu and c. 10 m right of the northwest corner of the ahu. Nine test units were excavated along three transect lines, spaced 10 m apart in the direction ENE and WSW. The units were excavated in 10 cm spits down to a well-defined sterile sand layer, usually reached at a depth of 20 cm to 30 cm below surface, after which the NW half of each unit was taken down with a shovel to 50–75 cm depth. After establishing the general stratigraphy, three areas containing bones were extended into area excavations. From these excavations we recovered 379 pieces of bone and charcoal, along with a piece of iron and a blue glass bead. The last two items may have been obtained from early European contacts.

Radiocarbon dating marae Manunu

Marae Manunu appears to have become the new ritual centre of Maeva after marae Mata'ire'a Rahi lost its importance. We wanted to see whether the transition in marae use that was attested in oral traditions could be identified by radiocarbon dating marae Manunu. Two samples, both on fragments of pig bone, have been analysed to date marae Manunu at the Waikato Laboratory in New Zealand. The first age result (Wk-14603) was on a fragment of pig jaw (Figure 2) found at a depth of about 35 cm on top of sterile beach sand and stratigraphically below a standing slab forming the ahu front wall (Wallin *et al.* 2004:76–83; Wallin and Solsvik 2005a). The bone sample gave a conventional radiocarbon age (CRA) of 306±42 BP (Wk-14603, ^{13}C -18.8±0.2‰). Another piece of pig bone was found under a slab of the ahu rear wall (Wallin *et al.* 2004), where it was probably deposited just before the wall slab was erected. This sample returned an age of 296±34 BP (Wk-16790, ^{13}C -17.3±0.2). Both of these dates when calibrated have a two-sigma span of AD 1650 to 1950. We conclude that the construction of marae Manunu occurred sometime after AD 1650 and probably well before European discovery of Tahiti in the 18th century.

Phosphate analysis

We systematically collected earth samples during excavations to test the feasibility of phosphate analysis for investigating ritual practices at Polynesian temple sites (Figure 3 and Figure 4). The aim was to identify locations which had detectable phosphate levels that might be the result of prehistoric activities around, or on, marae. Such investigations to our knowledge have not been carried out on marae courtyards and surroundings previously.

The spot-test method

There are several phosphate-analysis methods used in archaeological investigations. The technique goes back to the well-known work of Olof Arrhenius in the 1930s (Arrhenius 1931, 1934, 1938). However, his sole interest was to map the phosphate requirements of Swedish arable land. His method used a citric-acid solution to release phosphates. After adding a reagent, the content of dissolved phosphates was recorded with a photometer in phosphate degrees (P°). When doing his survey, Arrhenius soon noted that both prehistoric and medieval settlements could be identified by their higher phosphate content, and he pointed out the potential for phosphate surveys as an archaeological aid. The 'Arrhenius' method is laboratory based and

time consuming. Instead, we used the so-called spot-test method that can be used in the field. The test was developed by Gundlach (1961). It has been tested extensively by the authors at Neolithic settlement sites on Gotland Island in Sweden, and has also been used at megalith graves sites in Ireland since the end of the 1970s. The method has been tested in both field and laboratory situations (Wallin 1984; I. Österholm 1989; I. Österholm and S. Österholm 1997).

The method has been proven useful for detecting or delimiting prehistoric settlements or other human activities, since phosphates that emanate from animal/human bones, fish and meat waste etc. are bound to soil particles and are very stable and insoluble in water, and are therefore ideal as indicators of prehistoric activities. An important source of phosphates is, of course, human and animal excrement, but since the marae is a ritual space, excrement is not likely to be found there, which means the phosphates detected in this investigation may derive from different sacrifices or ritual feasting (Hayden 1996:141).

Figure 2. Detail of location of radiocarbon-dated pig jaw (photo by Paul Wallin).

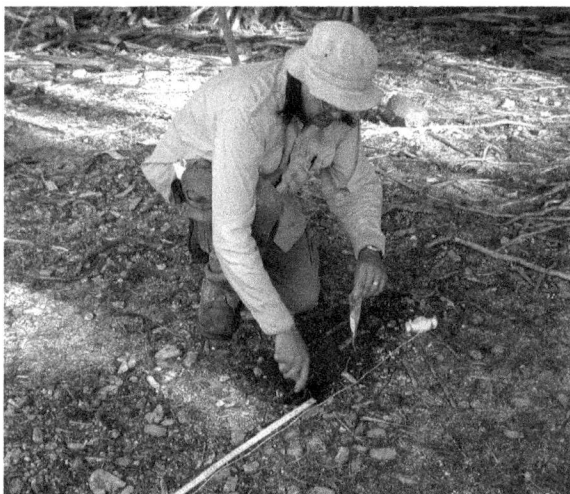

Figure 3. Systematic collection of earth samples for the phosphate analysis (photo by Reidar Solsvik).

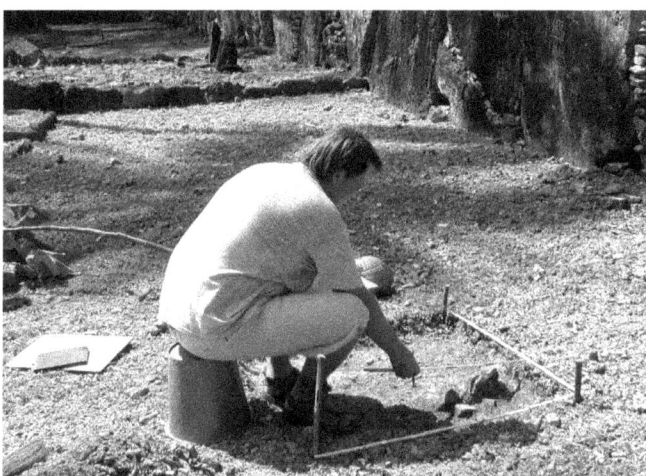

Figure 4. Earth samples collected during excavation (photo by Paul Wallin).

This is supported by finds of human and animal bones in the courtyard during our excavations. The phosphates bound in the soil can easily be released with the help of a strong acid. The principle of the spot-test method is that the phosphates in a small earth sample placed on a filter paper are extracted with the help of a strong acid and further indicated by amoniumheptamolybdate and ascorbic acid. The phosphates are indicated by a blue spot that spreads out from the earth sample, which varies in size depending on the phosphate content (Österholm and Österholm 1997:138).

Gundlach (1961) recommended the following liquids and analysis procedure:

Solution 1: 5 g amoniumheptamolybdate/$(NH_4)_6Mo_7O_{24}$/ is dissolved in 100 ml cold water and mixed with 35 ml diluted nitric acid (17.5 ml conc. HNO_3 + 17.5 ml H_2O).

Solution 2: 0.5 g ascorbic acid ($C_6H_8O_6$) is dissolved in 100 ml cold water.

Method: A pinch of soil (c. 50 mg) is placed on a piece of filter paper and a few drops of solution 1 are added from a drop bottle. After 30 seconds, a few drops of solution 2 are added. After a further 30 seconds, a blue spot will have radiated from the soil sample if it contains phosphates. The blueness is proportional to the degree of phosphates in the sample (Österholm and Österholm 1997:139). A graded phosphate scale (I–V) is shown in Figure 5.

When using the liquids in hot climates, as in Polynesia, it is important to keep them in a cool place, and only freshly mixed liquids should be used to obtain useful results.

The marae Manunu samples were collected from a rhombus area divided into a grid with

I. No or insignificant blue colouring.

II. Blue colouring surrounding the edge of the soil.

III. Blue colouring surrounding the edge of the soil with a tendency to radiating beams.

IV. Yellow colouring already after solution 1, blue colouring after solution 2, radiating beams all around.

V. As IV, but with more intensive colouring and radiation.

Phosphate value

• = I
• = II
● = III
● = IV
● = V

N

ScH-2-18
Marae Manunu
27 August 2003
P. Wallin / R. Solsvik

5 m

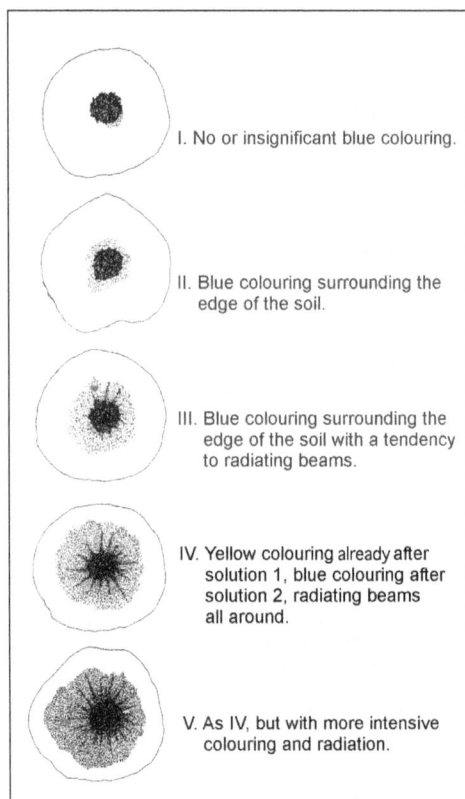

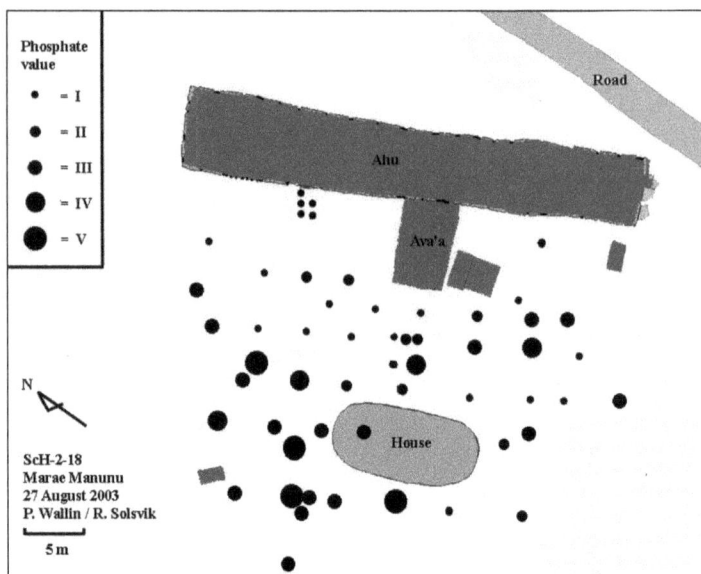

Figure 5 (left). Illustration of phosphate values (after Österholm and Österholm 1997:145).

Figure 6 (right). Results of the phosphate analysis plotted on the site plan.

5 m spacing. In the areas where large-scale excavations were conducted, additional samples were collected. Samples were taken from the bottom of the cultural deposit, since phosphates are washed into the ground. Since most of the activities took place on the present surface, the sample depth was 5–10 cm. Small holes were dug with a trowel and samples were collected in plastic bags.

Phosphate analysis results

After plotting the result of the phosphate analysis on the map, several areas containing higher phosphate levels were identified (Figure 6). Phosphate values with a range of I and II, indicate limited phosphate-generating activity. Phosphate values in the III to V range suggest phosphate production from, for example, the decomposition of human and/or animal sacrifices has taken place in the past.

In the area directly in front of the ahu and between 15 m and 20 m into the courtyard, the samples returned phosphate values in the range I and II. Hence, we can say with some confidence that no offerings, either of animals or humans, have been left to decompose in this area. Around the ahu, in a strip 5–6 m wide, white coral sand has been deposited, marking the area in front of the ahu as clean and probably tapu. The low phosphate results in this area are in accord with the evidence of use in marae architecture.

An area at the northwestern corner of the courtyard about 15 m x 25 m in size and oriented in a north-south direction also stood out in the phosphate spot test, giving consistently high phosphate values of III, IV and V. This area may have had some kind of offering structure or altar. Another smaller area about 5 m x 15 m, on the southeast part of the courtyard and oriented in a northwest to southeast direction, returned medium to high phosphate values of III and IV. The phosphate values suggest there was less decomposition here than in the northwest corner of the courtyard. A few phosphate samples in other parts of the courtyard returned values

Table 1. Osteological analysis of the bone remains, indicating MNI and NISP, at marae Manunu.

Species	Adult (MNI)	Juvenile (MNI)	Infant (MNI)	MNI Total	NISP
Human	1	1	0	2	7
Pig	1	1	1	3	297
Polynesian rat	3	0	0	3	3
Bird	1	0	0	1	6
Fish	2	0	0	2	9
Sheep/goat	1	0	0	1	1
Cat	1	0	0	1	1

of III–IV. An oval-shaped house on the west side of the court is also associated with the high-phosphate area in the northwestern part of the marae courtyard.

Bone remains

The bones collected during excavation of the marae in 2003 were brought to the osteological research laboratory at Gotland University, Sweden. The bones were cleaned and dried in the field and packed in labelled plastic bags, and each bone was identified to species, element, side and age. Age determination of human remains was based on criteria outlined by Bass (1971). There were four individuals represented by the human remains: infant I (0–4 years); infant II (5–12 years); juvenile (13–17 years) and adult (18–60 years) (Sjövold 1978).

Age determination of the animal bones followed Silver (1963). Infant animal bones were those with diaphyseal surfaces and an overall size much smaller than juvenile bones. Juvenile bones were represented by remains with incomplete and loose epiphyses. Adult individuals had fully fused epiphyses and fully erupted permanent dentition. Bone remains from human, pig, rat, bird, fish, sheep or goat and cat were identified. The NISP (number of identified specimens) and MNI for each species is shown in Table 1, and the number of bone fragments collected from excavations is shown in Figure 7.

In the western part of the courtyard, there was a relatively high frequency of pig bone, with elements from the entire skeleton recorded (43 fragments/m²). A test unit located inside the round-ended house platform had the highest frequency of bones, with 157 fragments in a single 1 m² unit. The remains were the most varied in terms of species, and were from pig, Polynesian rat, fish, bird, sheep/goat and cat. Human bones were also found in the excavations, but not within any of the high-phosphate areas. They were located in a trench excavated directly in front of the ahu, and in a trench in a central part of the courtyard in front of the ava'a. In these two trenches there was a low bone frequency (6–9 fragments/m²), including pig bone, a single bone from the Polynesian rat, and a fish bone. Pig bone was also present in the high phosphate area in the southeast part of the courtyard.

Taken together, the phosphate and the osteological analyses reveal several interesting results (Figure 7). There are three areas of the courtyard, where different activities appear to have been carried out (Figure 8). The low-phosphate area, in front of and close to the ahu, as well as on the central parts of the courtyard, also had small amounts of bone. However, this area is where the human bones were found. This might mean the area was kept relatively clean of sacrificial debris. The diverse bone remains found within the perimeter of the house may be the result of consumption of ritual meals. The area located on the western corner of the marae courtyard

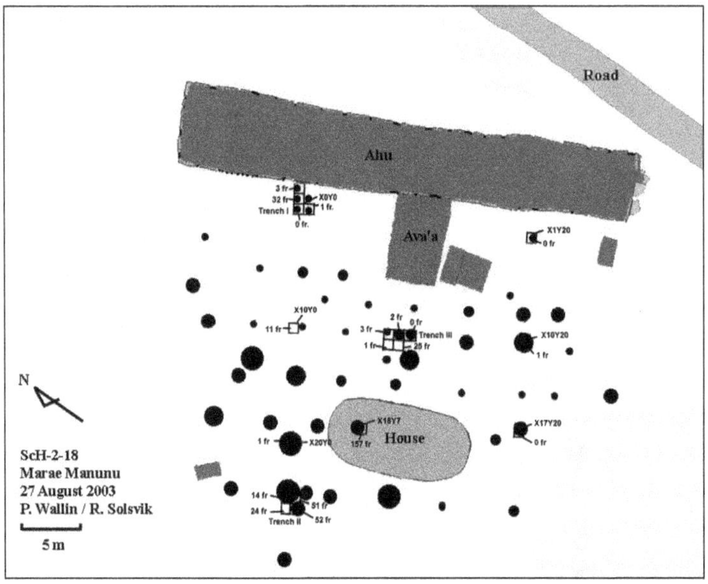

Figure 7. Excavated test pits/trenches and number of bone fragments.

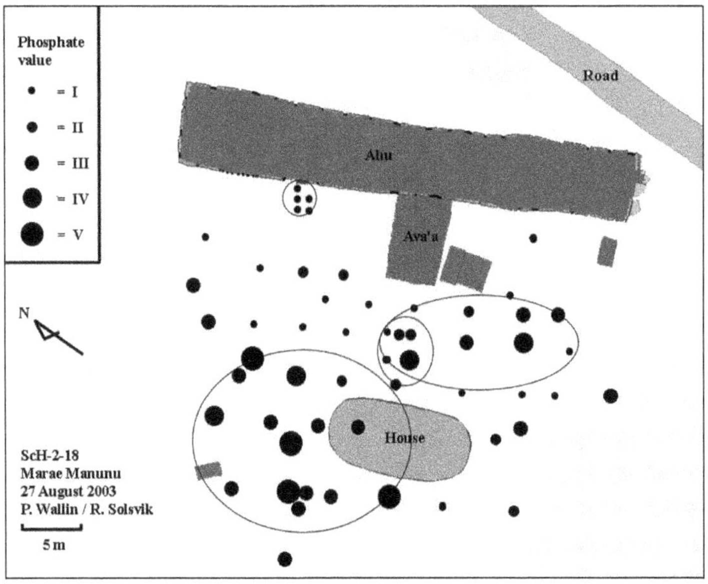

Figure 8. Interpretation of phosphate mapping.

outside the house could have been the main sacrificial area for pigs, judging by the amount of pig bone recovered. The smaller area on the southeast part of the courtyard could be a smaller sacrificial area in front of the ahu.

The western part of the courtyard is hypothesised to be the location of a large sacrificial altar. These altars, called fata (Figure 9), were an important structure at every marae. They were normally constructed of rows of wooden posts with a height of about 2–3 m, and a length of up to about 12 m. The top of the fata platform was covered with matting. The offerings on such altars consisted of pigs, dogs, fish and fruit (Wallin 1998:12–13). When the offerings on the platform rotted, highly organic debris would drop and seep from the platform into the ground below, creating the high phosphate values. The pig bones recovered probably represent sacrifices to the gods, as well as ritual food for the persons participating in different ceremonial events. Pigs from all different age groups were present, but most bones came from small suckling pigs up to individuals six to nine months old, although some teeth indicate adult pigs were offered/consumed (Wallin 2003).

The round-ended house in the marae courtyard is likely to be a priest house or fare ia ma-naha (Figure 10). The function of the fare ia manaha was to house sacred objects, such as the

Figure 9. A fata, or offering altar, at a Tahitian marae, with pigs placed on top of the structure (detail from engraving in Wilson 1799).

Figure 10. Priest house situated in connection with a Tahitian marae (detail from Wilson 1799).

Figure 11. Human sacrifice and a smaller fata, or offering altar, recorded from Tahiti in the 1770s (from J. Cook 1818).

drums, dresses and shell trumpets used in different marae ceremonies. The house was also the place where the priests dressed and prepared themselves for ceremonial activity (Henry 1928:161–164). The sheep and cat found in the trench inside the house platform are clearly post-European in age. However, these remains were found under gravel and were mixed with the remains of pig, rat, bird and fish. The sheep and cat bones both came from the heads of the animals. Captain Cook gave sheep/goats and cats as gifts on his visits to Tahiti (Ellis 1833:72), and it is feasible the bones represent European animals sacrificed at this huge marae in the late 18th century or early 19th century.

In the courtyard close to the ahu, human remains, mainly teeth, were recovered. However, phosphate samples analysed in this area were low, indicating limited decomposition had taken place at these spots. In the engraving of a human sacrifice from Tahiti made during Captain Cook's second voyage, the body is seen being treated at this location in the marae courtyard (Figure 11). In the same engraving, there are human crania visible on the ahu itself. The crania and long bones of sacrificed individuals were sometimes displayed on the marae or deposited in the ahu. It is possible the decomposition of the body took place at a special house outside the marae, and the bones were taken afterwards to the marae for display. In Figure 11, a small fata, or sacrificial altar, with pigs on it can be seen in front of the ahu. Such an altar may have been located within the southeastern area that registered high phosphate values at marae Manunu. A priest house may also be seen to the left in the picture (Figure 10).

Conclusion

The investigation of phosphate residues in prehistoric sites in tandem with a zooarchaeological analysis of bone remains demonstrates that locations with high phosphate levels also contained higher quantities of bone. Based on our initial study, it appears that a phosphate analysis carried out before excavation will be a useful tool for identifying ritual activity areas associated with Polynesian marae and ritual structures in other parts of the Pacific.

Acknowledgements

Our warmest thanks to Dr Yosi Sinoto for inviting us to collaborate with him, and for so generously sharing his knowledge on the Maeva site with us. Special thanks to all the local helpers in the field, and to the families of Maeva, who were patient with us through the years of excavating their marae. Finally, we are deeply sad to say that one of the authors of this paper, Dr. Inger Österholm, passed away before she could see the result of her last phosphate analysis in print.

References

Arrhenius, O. 1931. *Markanalysen i arkeologins tjänst.* Geologiska föreningens Förhandlingar, Stockholm.

Arrhenius, O. 1934. Fosfathalten i skånska jordar. *Sveriges Geologiska Undersökning.* Årsbok 28. No. 3. Stockholm.

Arrhenius, O. 1938. *Markundersökning och arkeologi.* Fornvännen Årg. 30, Stockholm.

Arrhenius, O. 1950. *Förhistoriska bebyggelser antydda genom kemisk analys. Fornvännen.* Årg. 45, Stockholm.

Bass, W.M. 1971. *Human Osteology: A Laboratory and Field Manual.* Missouri: Special Publications Missouri Archaeological Society.

Cook, J. 1818. *A Voyage to the Pacific Ocean; Undertaken by the Command of His Majesty, for making Discoveries in the Northern Hemisphere; performed under the Direction of Captains Cook, Clerke, and Gore, in the Years 1776, 1777, 1778, 1779, 1780.* Compiled from the Various Accounts of that Voyage hitherto published. Volume I. Philadelphia: Robert Desilver.

Ellis, W. 1833. *Polynesian researches, during a residence of nearly six years in the South Sea Islands, including descriptions of the natural history and scenery of the Islands, with remarks on the history, mythology, traditions, government, arts, manners, and customs of the inhabitants.* New York: J and J. Harper.

Gundlach, H. 1961. Tüpfelmethode auf Phosphat, angewandt in prähistorischer Forschung (als Feldmethode). *Mikrochimica Acta* 5:735–737.

Hayden, B. 1996. Feasting in Prehistoric and Traditional Societies. In P. Wiessner and W. Schiefenhövel (eds), *Food and the Status Quest. An Interdisciplinary Perspective,* pp. 127–147. Providence: Berghahn Books.

Henry, T. 1928. *Ancient Tahiti.* Bernice P. Bishop Museum Bulletin 48, Honolulu: Bishop Museum Press.

Österholm, I. 1989. *Bosättningsmönstret på Gotland under stenåldern. En analys av fysisk miljö, ekonomi och social struktur.* Theses and Papers in Archaeology 3. Department of Archaeology, Stockholm University.

Österholm, I. and S. Österholm 1982. *Spot test som metod för fosfatanalys i fält – praktiska erfarenheter.* Riksantikvarieämbetets Gotlandsundersökningar Nr 6.

Österholm, I. and S. Österholm 1997. Spot tests as a phosphate survey method in the field: practical experiences. In G. Burenhult (ed), Remote sensing Vol. 1. *Theses and Papers in North-European Archaeology* 13:a 137–152.

Silver, I.A. 1963. The Ageing of Domestic Animals. In D. Brothwell and E. Higgs (eds), *Science in Archaeology,* pp. 250–268. London: Thames and Hudson.

Sinoto, Y.H. 1996. Mata'ire'a Hill, Huahine. A Unique Settlement, and a Hypothetical Sequence of Marae Development in the Society Islands. In J. Davidson, G. Irwin, B.F. Leach, A. Pawley, and D. Brown (eds), *Oceanic Culture History Essays in Honour of Roger C. Green,* pp. 541–553. *New Zealand Journal of Archaeology Special Publication.* Dunedin, New Zealand Journal of Archaeology.

Sinoto, Y.H. 2002. A Case Study of Marae Restorations in the Society Islands. In C.M. Stevenson, G. Lee, and F.J. Morin (eds), *Pacific 2000. Proceedings of the Fifth International Conference on Easter Island and the Pacific,* pp. 253–265. Los Osos: Easter Island Foundation.

Sjövold, T. 1978. Inference Concerning the Age Distribution of Skeletal Population and some Consequences for Paleodemography. *Anthropologie Kozlemenyek* 22:99–114.

Wallin, P. 1984. Den gropkeramiska boplatsen Hemmor i När socken på Gotland. En studie av topografi, resursområde och fyndmaterial. Uppsats i påbyggnadskurs i arkeologi vid, unpublished BA Thesis, Stockholms Universitet.

Wallin, P. 1998. *The Symbolism of Polynesian Temple Rituals.* Kon-Tiki Museum Occasional Papers, Volume 4. Oslo: Kon-Tiki Museum.

Wallin, P. 2003. Osteological Analysis of Bone Remains from marae Manunu and Marae Matairea Rahi. Unpublished report in possession of the authors.

Wallin, P., E. Komori and R. Solsvik 2004. Excavations of One Habitation Site and Various Marae Structures on Land Fareroi, Te Ana, Tehu'a, Tearanu'u, and Tetuatiare, in Maeva, Huahine, Society Islands, French Polynesia, 2003. Report from the Project 'Local Developments - Regional Interactions' to the Service de la Culture et du Patrimoine, Punaauia, Tahiti. Unpublished report in the Archives of the Institute for Pacific Archaeology and Cultural History, Oslo.

Wallin, P. and R. Solsvik 2005a. Historical Records and Archaeological Excavations of Two 'National' Marae Complexes on Huahine, Society Islands, French Polynesia: A Preliminary Report. *Rapa Nui Journal* 19(1):13–24.

Wallin, P. and R. Solsvik 2005b. Radiocarbon Dates from Marae Structures in the District of Maeva, Huahine, Society Islands, French Polynesia. *Journal of the Polynesian Society* 114(4):375–383.

Wallin, P. and R. Solsvik 2006a. Dating Ritual Structures in Maeva, Huahine. Assessing the development of marae structures in the Leeward Society Islands, French Polynesia. *Rapa Nui Journal* 20(1):9–30.

Wallin, P. and R. Solsvik 2006b. Report from Archaeological Investigations of Marae Structures in the District of Maeva, Huahine, 2003. In H. Marchesi (ed), *Bilan de la recherche archéologique en Polynésie francaise 2003–2004*. Dossier d'Archéologie polynésienne, Vol. 3. Punaauia: Ministère de la Culture de Polynésie francaise, Service de la Culture et du Patrimoine.

Wilson, J. 1799. *A Missionary Voyage to the South Pacific Ocean, Performed on the Years 1796, 1797, 1798, on the Ship Duff, Commanded by Captain James Wilson Under the Direction of the Missionary Society*. London: T. Chapman.

28

The physical and mineralogical characteristics of pottery from Mochong, Rota, Mariana Islands

Foss Leach
Honorary Research Associate, Museum of New Zealand Te Papa Tongarewa, Wellington, New Zealand
Foss.Leach@University-of-Ngakuta.ac.nz

Janet Davidson
Honorary Research Associate, Museum of New Zealand Te Papa Tongarewa, Wellington, New Zealand

Graeme Claridge
33 Kotari Rd, Days Bay, Lower Hutt, New Zealand

Graeme Ward
Australian Institute of Aboriginal and Torres Island Studies, Canberra, Australia

John Craib
Bonhomme Craig and Associates, Mudgeeraba, Queensland, Australia

Introduction

In a reflective paper about the relationship between archaeometry and archaeology, Atholl observed that 'whereas most archaeological data arise from direct observation or the use of simple equipment, archaeometrical data are characteristically created by complex machinery, the use of which is sometimes taken as a rule-of-thumb guide to the limits of the subject' (Anderson 1987:3). He identified a gulf between the two disciplines which is only briefly bridged when archaeologists themselves colonise one attractive new methodological patch created by archaeometrists before moving on to the next (ibid:13). We hope that Atholl will appreciate our attempt here to occupy a new patch using bucket chemistry and only simple equipment with no flashing lights and fancy dials, in an effort to learn a little more from tiny scraps of apparently insignificant pot sherds.

Studies of Marianas pottery have generally focused on variables such as rim form, surface treatment, temper type, and sherd thickness (e.g. Moore 1983; Sant and Lebestki 1988). A classification based on temper was already established (Reinman 1977; Leidemann 1980; Ray 1981; Moore 1983) when the present study was initiated and has since been further developed (Dickinson *et al.* 2001:831; Dickinson 2006:40). More recent studies have also explored clay pastes (e.g. Graves *et al.* 1990; Dickinson *et al.* 2001). Changes in vessel form have been identified (e.g. Moore and Hunter-Anderson 1999). However, it is thought that there was 'a single evolving Mariana ceramic tradition forming a continuum that spans Pre-Latte and Latte times' (Dickinson *et al.* 2001:829). The present study aimed to explore physical and technological aspects of Marianas pottery through water-absorption tests, differential thermal analysis, and mineralogical description.

In 1983, Ward and Craib (1983) carried out excavations at Mochong on the northeast coast of the island of Rota (Figure 1). The excavation consisted of a series of squares (TP1–TP8) on a 150 m long transect. TP8, from which the analysed pottery samples were taken, was on the inland side of a latte structure (ML13) in a part of the site in which relatively early deposits were known to exist. It was also the least disturbed part of the site. Five radiocarbon dates from TP8 range from 540 to 2450 years BP (Leach *et al.* 1988:47). Pottery was common in the excavations.

At Mochong, there was a clear stratigraphic separation of the earlier CST (calcareous sand tempered) and later VST (volcanic sand tempered) sherds. However, pottery identified as MST (mixed sand tempered) occurred at several levels in the excavation. It was decided to select samples from two chronological periods to see whether any significant change in pottery technology could be detected. Details of the samples analysed are given in Table 1. In each case, 25 sherds were selected for analysis. These were grab samples, subjectively chosen as representing the range of pottery available in each category.

Stratum IIa, from which Assemblages A and C derive, is associated with the latte feature ML13 and has a radiocarbon date of 540±60 (Beta-9651), confirming the latte association. Stratum IIb, from which Assemblage B derives, has two dates of 2240±60 (Beta-7155) and 2110±80 (Beta-9652), placing this material firmly in the Intermediate Pre-Latte Period, which is now thought to date between 2500 and 1600 BP (Moore and Hunter-Anderson 1999). Assemblage D derives from the underlying Stratum IV, which is undated but bracketed between the two previous dates and a basal date of 2450±90 (Beta-9653). Assemblage D probably also dates to the Intermediate Pre-Latte Period. Takayama and Intoh (1976:21) obtained a date of

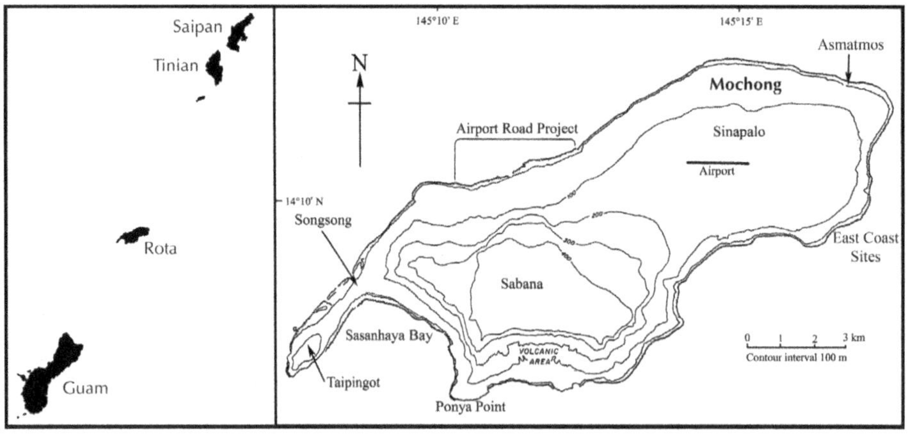

Figure 1. The island of Rota in the Mariana Islands showing the location of the Mochong site. Dickinson *et al.* (2001) sampled sherds from Mochong, Asmatmos and five east coast sites.

Table 1. Pottery samples analysed from TP8 at Mochong.

Assemblage	Stratum	Spits	Temper type	Period
A	IIa	3 and 4	MST	Latte
B	IIb	7 and 8	MST	IPL
C	IIa	3 and 4	VST	Latte
D	IV	9, 10 and 11	CST	IPL

IPL = Intermediate Pre-Latte Period.

2590±85 BP for a layer near the base of their earlier excavation in the Mochong site, and some Early Pre-Latte material was recovered in their excavations.

Physical characteristics

Water-absorption tests were carried out using the method described by Intoh (1982). These tests reveal physical characteristics of pottery, and are very helpful in discerning similarities and differences in the pottery technology of different prehistoric groups. Special standard tiles were used to check on reproducibility of results. The basic results of these tests are given in Appendix 1, which lists the percentage water absorption (WA), apparent porosity (AP), bulk density (BD), and specific gravity (SG) for each sherd. For each assemblage, summary statistics are given, including the mean and its associated standard error, the standard deviation and its standard error, the skewness and kurtosis statistics (G1 and G2, see Geary and Pearson 1938; Geary 1947), and the associated normalised deviates (W1 and W2, see Rao 1952:219).

The clearest differences revealed by these analyses concern the CST and VST pottery types. For example, the mean porosity is considerably higher in the case of CST pottery (45.3 percent cf. 37.0 percent, t=5.4 with 42 degrees of freedom, which is significant p=.001). Similar, but less marked, differences are found in the case of bulk density and specific gravity. The CST pottery has a lower bulk density and a higher specific gravity. Another interesting feature is that there is significant negative skewness in the case of VST apparent porosity. This is largely due to three very low values for sherds AT606, AT607 and AT613. The remainder of the VST values form a fairly tight distribution about the mean figure. This may indicate that included in the VST pottery assemblage are some unusual sherds, perhaps from a different source than the majority of sherds in this assemblage. In this analysis, the two MST assemblages are similar to each other and to the VST pottery.

In Figure 2, the positions of a wide range of prehistoric pottery assemblages from the Pacific are plotted, using the mean figures for apparent porosity and specific gravity. The original study on which this information is based was carried out by Intoh (1982). There are several interesting features in Figure 2. It will be noticed, for example, that the Mochong MST and VST pottery has an unusually low specific gravity, making it rather distinct from other Pacific Island traditions. The Mochong calcareous pottery, on the other hand, plots out quite close to Palau plain ware (#15), Fefan Island calcareous ware (#22), and the two Marianas samples studied by Intoh, characterised as Marianas plain ware (#18) and Marianas red ware (#19). The only other calcareous pottery available for comparison was from the Yap Islands (#17). This has a similarly high apparent porosity, but significantly higher specific gravity.

Thin-section characteristics

Thin sections were prepared at Otago University and were examined with optical microscopy by Claridge and Mr A.V. Weatherhead. Mineral grain and calcite contents were estimated by

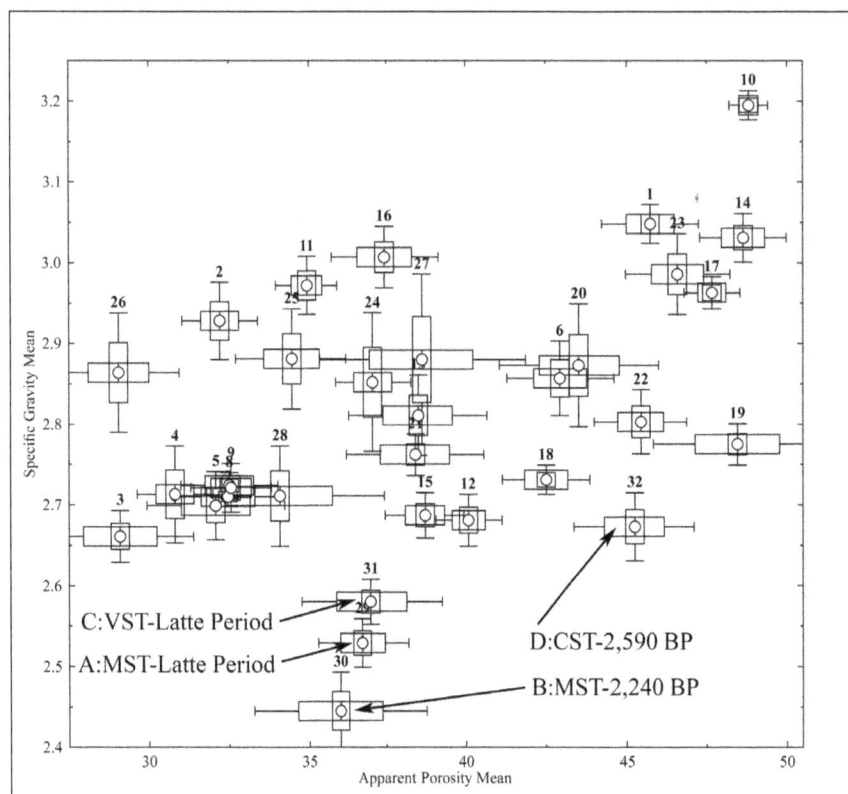

Figure 2. Physical characteristics of Pacific Island prehistoric pottery.
1=Reef Islands Lapita, 2=Vailele thick coarse ware, 3=Yanuca early-Lapita decorated ware, 4=Yanuca early plain ware, 5=Yanuca late plain ware, 6=Yap late laminated ware, 7=Yanuca middle-period paddle-impressed (parallel-rib), 8=Yanuca middle-period paddle-impressed (cross-hatch), 9=Yanuca middle-period plain ware, 10=Sasoa`a thin fine ware, 11=Sasoa`a thick coarse ware, 12=Taumako andesitic ware, 13=Taumako pyroxenic ware, 14=Yap middle-period unlaminated ware, 15=Palau plain ware, 16=Mulifanua Lapita ware, 17=Yap early calcareous ware, 18=Marianas plain ware, 19=Marianas red ware, 20=Ngulu Island ware, 21=Banks Islands ware, 22=Fefan Island calcareous ware, 23=Nan Madol plain ware, 24=Lakeba Lapita ware, 25=Natunuku Lapita ware, 26=Natunuku paddle-impressed ware and late incised, 27=Sigatoka paddle-impressed ware, 28=Lakeba paddle-impressed ware and late plain, 29=Mochong Assemblage A MST, 30=Mochong Assemblage B MST, 31=Mochong Assemblage C VST, 32=Mochong Assemblage D CST.

comparison with reference charts and are quoted on an area basis. Mineral species were identified by their optical properties, confirmed in one case by separation of the heavy mineral fraction from crushed material and X-ray diffraction analysis. The composition of the mineral fraction was estimated visually. The colour of the section was determined from the appearance of the slide in the microscope, viewed in reflected light. Colours are Munsell colour notation. The detailed descriptions are given in Appendix 2.

The cracking parallel to the axis of the sherds, evident on most of the sections, is probably due to shrinkage of the clay matrix during drying before firing. In some cases the cracks were clearly infilled with mounting medium and were present before sectioning, while in others they may have been produced during preparation of the section, as infillings were not obviously present. This question could probably be resolved by SEM observation of broken faces of the sherds. Cracking perpendicular to the axis or random cracking may be a result of deterioration of the sherd by weathering.

Mineral content varies widely, but in general, appears low. The composition of the mineral fraction also varies. In some cases, quartz is dominant; in others, feldspar or ferromagnesians are dominant. It was concluded that the non-calcareous sand-size grains were present in the original clay, and were not added deliberately. Where calcite is present, this has been added in considerable amounts and the addition must have been deliberate. The sand appears to be a fine-grained beach deposit formed from coral and marine shells.

The mineral content is consistent with a clay formed from strongly weathered soils from andesitic parent materials, which have been transported as alluvium or colluvium, as the sand grains are in many cases sharp and angular. However, the variation in composition of the mineral fraction points to different sources for the clay. These differences may correspond to those in deliberately added temper sands identified by Dickinson *et al.* (2001), who have shown that significant quartz content is typical of temper originating on Saipan, while olivine and high ferromagnesian content is typical of temper originating on Guam. However, they report restricted exposures of andesitic rock on Rota (ibid: 834, 836), and Dickinson (2006:42) reports some temper so far unique in the Marianas in sherds he studied from Mochong. It seems likely that at least some of the pottery found at Mochong was made locally.

The multi-coloured aspect of the Mochong sherds is due partly to mixing of clays during preparation of the body, partly to differential weathering, and partly to variation in penetration of the firing heat into the clay. Many of the sherds show a red colour on the outside and a darker colour inside, as if temperatures on the inside of the fired article did not rise sufficiently high to burn out the organic constituents of the clay. However, such an effect can also be the result of a small soak time, typical of flash firing at low temperature, with a reducing atmosphere inside the pot.

In other cases, the sections show the presence of reddish globules, which appear to be iron-rich clay, produced by weathering of ferromagnesian minerals. This may be important in considering whether the absence of ferromagnesians is significant in assessing the origin of the clay.

Evidence of low firing temperature in some sherds is the presence of birefringence in the matrix arising from preferred orientation of clay particles. Its presence in these thin sections indicates that the clay structure is still largely present and therefore that firing temperatures did not rise sufficiently high for the structure to be destroyed. This can be expected to begin between 500 and 600C. Some birefringence is present in a Latte Period sherd (AT624) as well as in an early CST tempered sherd (AT633) (see Appendix 2).

There are some interesting differences between the assemblages, notably between the two MST assemblages. The sherds examined from Assemblage A contained no calcite, whereas those from Assemblage B all contained significant amounts. In this analysis, Assemblage A (MST) looks very like Assemblage C (VST). Assemblage B (MST) looks like Assemblage D (CST). There is also at least one difference in mineral content that may be significant. The mineral content of all the sherds from Assemblage B is high in quartz (estimated at 90 percent in all five sherds), whereas quartz is low in Assemblage A (averaging 12.5 percent). The quartz content is variable in the other two assemblages.

These characteristics are summarised in Table 2. The high quartz content of all analysed sherds in Assemblage B is similar to that of some sherds of CQT (quartz-calcite) temper from predominantly Pre-Latte contexts, including one from Rota, in the study of Dickinson *et al.* (2001:843, Table VI). Dickinson *et al.* state that Saipan origin can be confidently inferred for any sherd with quartz content higher than 1–2 percent. This would indicate that almost all of the Mochong sherds studied originated on Saipan. However, the presence in at least one

Table 2. Mineral and calcite content of Mochong sherds examined in thin section, and amount of quartz in mineral content.

Assemblage	Sherd	Mineral(%)	Calcite(%)	Quartz
A MST	AT554	20	—	low
A MST	AT556	1–2	—	low
A MST	AT557	5	—	low
A MST	AT559	2	—	low
B MST	AT581	10	10	high
B MST	AT583	1	20	high
B MST	AT584	10	30	high
B MST	AT598	5	40	high
B MST	AT602	15	15	high
C VST	AT605	10	—	low
C VST	AT619	15	—	low
C VST	AT620	5	—	medium
C VST	AT623	10	5–10	high
C VST	AT624	5	—	low
D CST	AT628	>1	50	high
D CST	AT629	5	5	low
D CST	AT630	2	20	medium
D CST	AT633	5	30	medium
D CST	AT643	5	20	high

High = 80% or more, medium = 40-50%, low = 25% or less.

Mochong sherd (AT629) of both quartz and olivine (the latter identified by Dickinson *et al.* as typical of Guam rather than Saipan tempers) indicates the picture is probably more complex.

Differential thermal analysis

Differential thermal analysis (DTA) is a valuable tool for estimating the maximum firing temperature a pot has reached. A powdered sample of the pottery is used, along with a control sample of inert material. Both are placed in an aluminium block and heated at a controlled rate in an electric furnace. A differential thermocouple is used to measure the temperature difference between the pottery and the control, and this is plotted against the pottery temperature during refiring. If the pottery temperature is higher than the control at any point, this is due to exothermic reactions taking place inside the pottery. If it is lower, this is due to endothermic reactions taking place (Tite 1972:295ff.).

The presence of an endothermic peak for a known mineral in the pottery indicates that the pot has never been fired to this temperature before. Conversely, the absence of such a peak indicates that the pot has been fired to at least this temperature previously. Some well-known peaks are as follows:

1. 100–200C: a broad endothermic peak in this range is due to the loss of absorbed water in the sample. This peak should be present in virtually all samples.

2. 250–500C: a broad exothermic peak in this range is due to the combustion of organic material in the pottery. Its presence depends on the amount of organic material in the pottery.

3. 550–600C: an endothermic peak here indicates the loss of chemically combined hydroxyl water by clay minerals such as kaolin. When this peak is present, it shows the pottery has not been heated above this temperature previously; when it is absent, the pottery has been fired above this temperature.

4. 800–900C: an endothermic peak here indicates the decomposition of calcite. When this peak is present, it shows the pottery has not been heated above this temperature previously; when is it absent, the pottery has been fired above this temperature.

5. 900–1000C: an exothermic peak in this range is due to the formation of various high-temperature mineral phases from clay. When this peak is present, it shows the pottery has not been heated above this temperature previously. When this peak is absent, there can be several reasons: (i) the pottery had not previously been fired above this temperature; (ii) a large endothermic calcite peak is concealing the smaller exothermic peak; (iii) kaolin was not present in the original pottery paste.

Five samples from each assemblage were examined by DTA; the curves of each of these samples are shown in Figures 3 and 4.

The sherds in Figure 3 are from early contexts in the Mochong site, dating to about 2200 years BP and earlier. Both the earliest CST type and the stratigraphically slightly later MST type have strong endothermic peaks between 800 and 900C, showing that calcite had not been fired to this temperature previously. The lack of significant endothermic peaks at 550–600C suggests that clay minerals had previously been dehydroxylated by being fired above this temperature. Sherd AT629 shows a small peak at 550C, attributable to kaolin. This pot must have been fired at a temperature either close to or not exceeding this value. It is interesting that this pot has very little calcite in it (c. 5 percent, see Table 2) and this is reflected in an equally small calcite endothermic peak. Sherd AT581 shows a very strong exothermic peak due to organic matter in the pottery. It also has a fairly low abundance of calcite (c. 10 percent), once again reflected in the lack of a pronounced calcite peak. It is concluded that both the CST and MST pottery, dating to at and before about 2200 years BP, were fired above 550–600C and below 800–900C; that is, between 600 and 800C. The presence of the small peak at 550C on one of the pots suggests the firing temperatures were probably closer to the bottom end of this range, perhaps 650–700C.

The DTA curves for the later MST and VST pottery samples (Figure 4), dating to the Latte period, are very different from the earlier ones, and quite similar to each other. They are relatively featureless, suggesting higher original firing temperatures than in the earlier pottery. There are signs of organic material in most of the curves. None of the curves show endothermic peaks around 550–600C, suggesting that clay minerals had previously been dehydroxylated by firing above this temperature. Only AT623 possessed calcite in thin section (Table 2), yet the DTA curve shows no sign of the 800–900C endothermic peak associated with the decomposition of calcite. Therefore, this sherd would have been fired above this temperature. Unfortunately, none of the other sherds contained enough calcite to prove that this firing temperature applied to them as well. However, clearly the technology did exist to fire at or above this temperature, so it is a reasonable inference that other pots were fired at least this high too. Further evidence for this is provided by only small indications of the exothermic peak between 900–1000C

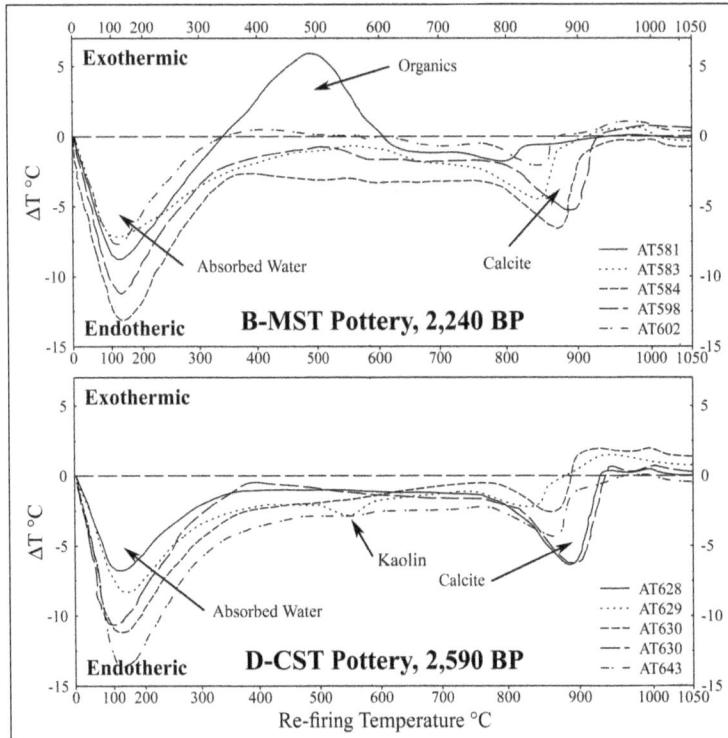

Figure 3. Differential thermal analysis of the two early assemblages of pottery from Mochong. A firing temperature of 650–700C is indicated.

associated with formation of clay minerals such as mullite. The absence of an endothermic peak at 800–900C and the diminutive exothermic peak at 900–1000C suggest an original firing temperature between these two values, about 900C, for these two Latte-period pottery types.

Discussion

Pottery is a common artefact in the Mariana Islands, and has been studied and classified by many previous workers. Spoehr (1957:108–122), on the basis of his investigations in Saipan, Tinian and Rota, defined two main types, Marianas Plain and Marianas Red. Marianas Plain and related decorated wares were associated with the Latte phase of Marianas prehistory, and Marianas Red with the earlier, Pre-Latte phase. Subsequent workers have had difficulty with the category of Marianas Red, particularly, although Spoehr's two basic chronological divisions – pottery associated with the Latte and Pre-Latte phases – have continued to be used and further defined.

Ray (1981) and Reinman (1977), studying pottery from Guam, a short distance south of Rota, independently recognised the significance of temper as a criterion for classifying pottery from the Marianas. Reinman (1977:62–66) analysed sherds from excavations at five sites in southern Guam and established the categories of CST and VST pottery for the Pre-Latte and Latte-phase pottery respectively. He recognised that his CST pottery contained mixed tempers as well as purely calcareous temper.

Leidemann (1980) used Reinman's classification in her study of spatial and temporal variation at Ypao Beach on Guam, but established a separate category, MST, for the mixed temper which Reinman had included in his CST category.

Ray recovered nearly 5000 sherds of pre-Latte pottery from two adjacent excavations at Tarague Beach in northern Guam, as well as a quantity of later pottery. He called the earlier

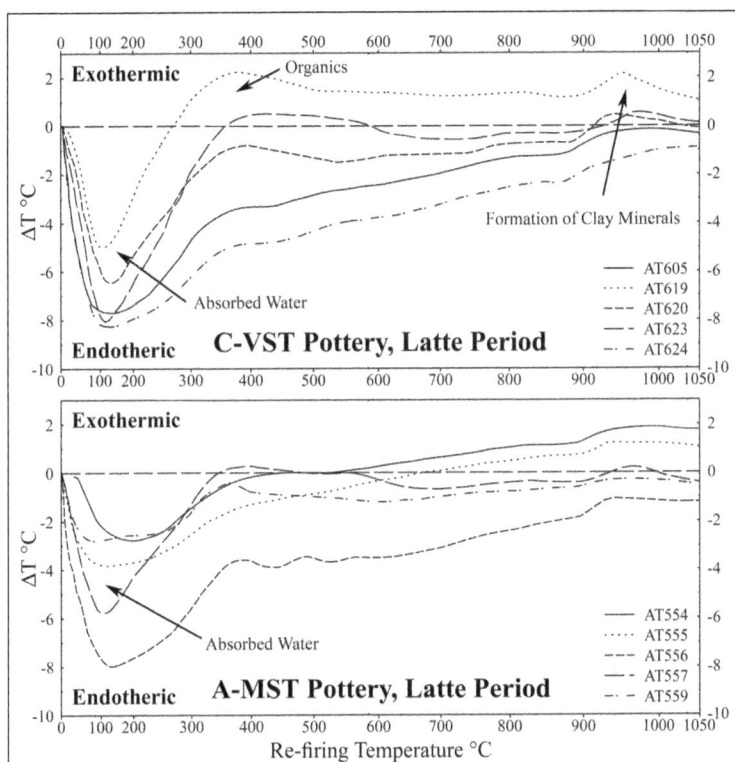

Figure 4. Differential thermal analysis of the two Latte-period assemblages from Mochong. A firing temperature of 900C is indicated.

pottery Mariana Red (not the same as Spoehr's Marianas Red) and defined it in some detail (Ray 1981:111–112). In this early pottery, he identified seven temper types (one having two variants), which he subsequently placed into four groups, calcareous sand (CST), volcanic sand (VST), mixed sand (MST) and rare or exotic (no acronym) (ibid:80–83, 115–122). One of his rare temper types consisted of 70 percent to 100 percent crystalline quartz. Ray demonstrated a decline in CST sherds and an increase in MST sherds in the four strata at Tarague from which he recovered his early pottery. He also proposed a possible trend from an early use of 'fat' or pure clay, to later use of clay with more natural inclusions, perhaps because the earlier sources had been depleted (ibid:79, 143). In his later Marianas Plain pottery, VST sherds comprised 15 percent, but MST, CST and exotic sherds each represented only 1 percent or less. Other temper types identified were crushed rock, 'trashy' appearing, and sparse, but Ray found the distinctions less clear cut than in the earlier pottery (ibid:143–145).

Further excavations were carried out at Tarague in 1980 (Kurashina and Clayshulte 1983) and the pottery was studied in detail by Moore (1983). She also recognised the significance of temper, but found that it was a 'temporally ambiguous attribute for determining fine temporal intervals' (ibid:172). Moore's study of temper was restricted by the facilities and resources available to her and she therefore based her analysis on the previously recognised categories of CST, VST and MST, with the addition of limonite and crushed limestone. However, she noted that clay from Mt Santa Rosa on Guam's northern plateau contained natural mineral inclusions, and that this clay, tempered with CST, would produce pottery that looked like her MST category. She also suggested that some VST pottery could have been made from untempered clay with natural mineral inclusions. The addition of CST, however, was probably deliberate (ibid:77–78).

Subsequent studies have shown that quartz is a significant component of some Mariana sand tempers. Variants of VST tempers include volcanic-quartz temper (VQT or VSQT) where quartz is prominent, and quartz temper (QT) where quartz is dominant. A separate category of quartz-calcite tempers (CQT, QCT or CSQT) has been established for variants of mixed sand tempers consisting of admixtures of quartz grains from volcanic bedrock and calcareous grains of reef detritus (Dickinson *et al.* 2001:831). As noted above, all quartz tempers are attributed to Saipan (Dickinson *et al.* 2001).

The results presented here add to our knowledge of pottery technology in the Mariana Islands. Firstly, the suggestion made by Moore (1983:77–78) that mineral inclusions in some of the pottery from Guam were natural rather than deliberately added is supported. At least in the Mochong pottery, the minerals do not appear to have been deliberately added, but are probably part of the original clays collected for making pottery. This is contrary to the findings of Dickinson *et al.* (2001:837), who found 'distinct size differences between the smallest temper grains and the largest silt grains enclosed within clay pastes'. However, they did not include any sherds from Tarague in their study (ibid:836).

It may be that in some places in the Mariana Islands, particular clays were deliberately chosen because of their mineral composition – that is, they possessed natural grit which functioned as a tempering material to minimise thermal shock during firing. A similar conclusion was arrived at for the potteries on the Yap Islands, some 740 km south of Guam. It was argued that in the case of the highly characteristic laminated ware from this island, the mineral content is natural (Intoh and Leach 1985:73), while in the case of the plain ware, some vessels were formed with deliberately added mineral tempering (ibid:81). As at Mochong, there is also a calcareous sand tempered ware, and these inclusions are certainly deliberate.

The sequence of change in temper type in Marianas pottery is supported at a gross level by the pottery from Mochong. Calcareous sand temper is present only in negligible amounts in later pottery associated with the Latte phase, as other workers have found (Moore 1983:87, 172). Only one of the VST sherds (AT623) from Stratum IIa that were examined in thin section contained calcite and this was low (5–10 percent). None of the sherds from Stratum IIa classified as MST and examined in thin section contained calcite.

None of the sherds studied from Mochong can be regarded as pure CST, rather than MST, since all contain some minerals. It is possible that early potters on Guam used 'purer' clay than their colleagues on Rota, and that the use of some Guam clays with CST additions produced the true CST pottery recognised by archaeologists working in Guam. The category of CST pottery from Mochong appears to contain naturally occurring minerals and deliberately added calcareous sand temper. If pottery was made at the same time on both Rota and Guam, one might expect variations in mineral content due to the use of different clay sources.

The Mochong sherds could now be classified as various kinds of quartz-tempered pottery, since all those examined in thin section contain varying amounts of quartz, ranging from five percent to 95 percent. The Latte-period Assemblages A and C (with the exception of sherd AT623) appear to be volcanic-quartz temper (variously labelled VQT or VSQT). Assemblages B and D have quartz-calcite tempers (CQT, QCT or CSQT). Sherd AT623 is, in this respect, closer to quartz-calcite temper.

The separate identity of MST pottery from Mochong is not clear. As indicated above, there is a definite difference between the two MST assemblages. All sherds in the earlier Assemblage B contain both calcite and minerals; however, none of the sherds from the later Assemblage A contains calcite. The classification of this assemblage as MST is therefore questionable on mineralogical grounds. In this respect, the MST (A) and VST (C) assemblages from the Latte period appear indistinguishable.

The porosity analysis reveals a difference between the assemblages containing calcite:

Table 3. Apparent Porosity of calcareous sand tempered sherds from Mochong.

Assemblage	Sherd	Calcite	Minerals	Apparent Porosity
B	AT581	10%	10%	27.0%
B	AT583	20%	1%	27.5%
B	AT584	30%	10%	30.1%
B	AT598	40%	5%	39.1%
A	AT602	15%	15%	33.7%
C	AT623	10%	5–10%	37.1%
D	AT628	50%	>1%	46.4%
D	AT629	5%	5%	43.3%
D	AT630	20%	2%	46.7%
D	AT633	30%	5%	49.2%
D	AT643	20%	5%	45.8%

the early CST pottery of Assemblage D and the slightly later MST pottery of Assemblage B. Table 3 shows the calcite and mineral content and the apparent porosity of all the sherds with calcareous temper identified in thin section. The single calcareous sherd from Assemblage C is indistinguishable from those in Assemblage B.

The water-absorption tests show that the CST pottery of Assemblage D has a consistently high porosity, as high as 52.1 percent in one case. The tendency of these sherds to disintegrate easily parallels Moore's experience with her early CST pottery from Tarague. She found that sherds disintegrated during washing in the laboratory, and attributed this to poor firing (1983:78). The porosity values of Assemblages A, B and C range widely, but have almost identical ranges and means (see Appendix 1). In this respect, they form a group apart from the early CST pottery of Assemblage D.

It is not surprising there should be a difference between the two assemblages at Mochong in which calcareous temper is present. Although both assemblages can be attributed to the Intermediate Pre-Latte period on the basis of radiocarbon dates, they are stratigraphically separated within this period. The difference appears to be one of several technological changes in the course of the Marianas pottery tradition.

The Mochong results highlight the complexity of the Marianas pottery sequence, both between islands and within individual islands and even individual sites. Dickinson *et al.* (2001:838, Table II) analysed eight sherds from an earlier excavation at Mochong by Takayama and Intoh (1976) attributed to the Early Pre-Latte, Intermediate Pre-Latte and Latte periods, and identified three as VST and five as MST. There is no mention of quartz, although the present study found quartz in all Mochong sherds examined. Dickinson *et al.* (ibid) do report VQT and CQT sherds from Latte-period sites on the east coast of Rota.

Dickinson *et al.* (2001) provide guidelines for attributing temper sands in some sherds to either Saipan or Guam. Using their results, it could be argued that Assemblage B pottery at Mochong was imported from Saipan. The other assemblages, however, are not so easily attributed, as some sherds contain both quartz in significant amounts (Saipan) and olivine or ferromagnesians (Guam). This raises the possibility that there are, or were, on Mochong clays suitable for pottery manufacture without temper addition and/or sands suitable for temper. Dickinson *et al.* point to the need for further research on temper, which this study strongly endorses.

The differential thermal analysis indicated a clear difference between the early (B and D) and later (A and C) assemblages. The earlier pottery was fired between 600C and 800C, probably in

Table 4. Changes through time in Mochong pottery.

Assemblage	Period	Calcite	Quartz	Porosity Firing Mean	Temperature
A	Latte	absent	low	36.7 ± 0.7	higher
C	Latte	rare	low-medium	37.0 ± 1.1	higher
B	IPL	present	high	36.0 ± 1.4	lower
D	IPL	present	low-high	45.3 ± 0.9	lower

IPL = Intermediate Pre-Latte.

the lower part of this range, perhaps 650–700C. The later pottery was probably fired at around 900C. Elsewhere in the Pacific, technological aspects of Lapita pottery, including firing, have recently been reviewed by Ambrose (1997:529–530). Low firing temperatures are common in early Pacific pottery (e.g. Intoh 1982:135; Clough 1992:189). Rye (1976) documented the problems that calcareous sand tempers can produce in firing. In the Mochong pottery, the early assemblages, which incorporate calcareous sand temper, were low-fired, while the later assemblages were fired at higher temperatures. It is notable, however, that the single sherd with calcite from the later Assemblage C also appears to have been fired at a higher temperature.

Conclusions

Several changes took place in the technology of the pottery used by the people who lived at Mochong. These are summarised in Table 4.

The earliest pottery studied was highly porous; the three subsequent assemblages had lower porosity. Both the earlier assemblages consistently contained deliberately added calcareous sand temper and both were low-fired. In the two later assemblages, most pots were fired at a higher temperature and calcareous temper was present rarely and in small amounts. The two end points of this sequence are the CST and the VST pottery types. On the evidence available for this study, the earlier MST pottery (Assemblage B) is a distinct entity, intermediate between CST and VST. However, the later MST pottery (Assemblage A) is essentially the same as the contemporary VST pottery.

All sherds analysed contain quartz, but the amounts are consistently high only in Assemblage B. This may reflect a specific source for this assemblage. The minerals in the Mochong sherds and the probability that they were, for the most part, present in the clay, rather than deliberately added, suggest that at least some of the Mochong pottery was made on the island, rather than imported from Saipan and Guam.

This study did not include any of the very early pottery known in the Marianas. Even so, the Mochong sequence covers a period of some 2000 years, during which there were significant changes and improvements in pottery technology. The earlier potters coped with the problem of thermal shock by adding significant amounts of calcareous sand temper to the paste and firing at a low temperature. Later potters leaned how to fire their pots successfully at a higher temperature, producing a more durable ware. An important challenge for future research is to see how these changes in technology correlate with the changes in vessel form and possible changes in vessel function discussed by Moore and Hunter-Anderson (1999). There is much still to be learned about how pottery was made, distributed, and used during 3000 years of prehistory in the Mariana Islands.

References

Ambrose, W.R. 1997. Contradictions in Lapita pottery, a composite clone. *Antiquity* 71:525–538.

Anderson, A.J. 1987. Supertramp science: some thoughts on archaeometry and archaeology in Oceania. In W.R. Ambrose and J.M.J. Mummery (eds), *Archaeometry: Further Australasian studies*, pp. 3–18. Research School of Pacific Studies, Australian National University, Canberra.

Clough, R. 1992. Firing temperatures and the analysis of Oceanic ceramics: a study of Lapita ceramics from Reef/Santa Cruz, Solomon Islands. In J.-C. Galipaud (ed), *Poterie Lapita et Peuplement*, pp. 177–92. Nouméa: ORSTOM.

Dickinson, W.R. 2006. *Temper Sands in Prehistoric Oceanian Pottery: Geotectonics, Sedimentology, Petrography, Provenance*. Geological Society of America Special Paper 406.

Dickinson, W.R., B.M. Butler, D.R. Moore and M. Swift 2001. Geologic sources and geographic distribution of sand tempers in prehistoric potsherds from the Mariana Islands. *Geoarchaeology* 16(8):827–854.

Geary, R.C. 1947. Testing for normality. *Biometrika* 34:209.

Geary, R.C. and E.S. Pearson 1938. *Tests of Normality*. London: Biometrika Office, University College.

Graves, M.W., T.L. Hunt and D. Moore 1990. Ceramic production in the Mariana Islands: explaining change and diversity in prehistoric interaction and exchange. *Asian Perspectives* 29:211–233.

Intoh, M. 1982. The Physical Analysis of Pacific Pottery. Unpublished MA thesis, Anthropology Department, University of Otago.

Intoh, M. and B.F. Leach 1985. *Archaeological Investigations in the Yap Islands, Micronesia*. British Archaeological Reports S277.

Kurashina, H. and R.N. Clayshulte 1983. *Site Formation Processes and Cultural Sequence at Tarague, Guam*. Tarague Archaeology Special Paper 1. Micronesian Area Research Center, Guam.

Leach, F., M. Fleming, J. Davidson, G. Ward and J. Craib 1988. Prehistoric fishing at Mochong, Rota, Mariana Islands. *Man and Culture in Oceania* 4:31–62.

Leidemann, H. 1980. Intrasite Variation at Ypao Beach, Guam: a Preliminary Assessment. Unpublished MA thesis, Behavioral Sciences, University of Guam.

Moore, D. 1983. Measuring Change in Marianas Pottery: the Sequence of Pottery Production at Tarague, Guam. Unpublished MA thesis, Behavioral Sciences, University of Guam.

Moore, D.R. and R.L. Hunter-Anderson 1999. Pots and pans in the Intermediate Pre-Latte (2500–1600 bp) Mariana Islands, Micronesia. In J.-C. Galipaud and I. Lilley (eds), *Le Pacifique de 5000 à 2000 avant le Présent: Supplements à l'Histoire d'une Colonisation*, pp. 487–503. Paris: Institut de Recherche pour le Développement.

Rao, C.R. 1952. *Advanced Statistical Methods in Biometric Research*. London: John Wiley.

Ray, E. 1981. The Material Culture of Prehistoric Tarague Beach, Guam. Unpublished MA thesis, Anthropology Department, Arizona State University, Tempe.

Rye, O.S. 1976. Keeping your temper under control: materials and manufacture of Papuan pottery. *Archaeology and Physical Anthropology in Oceania* 11(2):105–137.

Reinman, F. 1977. *An Archaeological Survey and Preliminary Test Excavations on the Island of Guam, Mariana Islands, 1965–1966*. Miscellaneous Publication 1, Micronesian Area Research Centre, University of Guam.

Sant, M.B. and N. Lebetski 1988. Ceramics. In B.M. Butler (ed), *Archaeological Investigations on the North Coast of Rota, Mariana Islands*, pp. 179–253. Southern Illinois University at Carbondale Center for Archaeological Investigations Occasional Paper 8. Carbondale.

Spoehr, A. 1957. *Marianas Prehistory: Archaeological Survey and Excavations on Saipan, Tinian and Rota*. Fieldiana: Anthropology 48. Chicago: Field Museum of Natural History.

Takayama, J. and M. Intoh 1976. *Archaeological Excavation of Latte Site (M–13), Rota, in the Marianas*. Reports of Pacific Archaeological Survey IV, Tokai University.

Tite, M.S. 1972. *Methods of Physical Examination in Archaeology*. London: Seminar Press.

Ward, G.K. and J.L. Craib 1983. Mochong Archaeological Research 1983. Report to CNMI Historic Preservation Office, Saipan.

Appendix 1
Results of water-absorption tests

Assemblage A: MST, Spits 3 and 4

Sherd AT566 disintegrated during analysis. The results for sherd AT560 are possibly suspect, as the final dry weight was 7% different from the first determination.

ACC	WA	AP	BD	SG
AT553	24.20	38.87	1.61	2.63
AT554*	19.63	34.02	1.73	2.63
AT555	24.05	37.08	1.54	2.45
AT556*	20.81	33.56	1.61	2.43
AT557*	21.12	34.86	1.65	2.53
AT558	21.31	35.23	1.65	2.55
AT559*	22.13	35.52	1.60	2.49
AT560	19.66	33.91	1.73	2.61
AT561	25.57	39.30	1.54	2.53
AT562	16.33	28.85	1.77	2.48
AT563	19.37	32.68	1.69	2.51
AT564	24.84	38.48	1.55	2.52
AT565	20.61	34.45	1.67	2.55
AT567	23.36	36.76	1.57	2.49
AT568	25.07	38.80	1.55	2.53
AT569	26.86	40.61	1.51	2.55
AT570	21.52	34.23	1.59	2.42
AT571	24.64	37.21	1.51	2.40
AT572	25.97	40.48	1.56	2.62
AT573	23.42	37.06	1.58	2.51
AT574	33.68	47.34	1.41	2.67
AT575	24.81	39.11	1.58	2.59
AT576	23.24	35.88	1.54	2.41
AT577	22.85	37.24	1.63	2.60
Disperson statistics				
Mean	23.13 ± .69	36.73 ± .72	1.60 ± .02	2.53 ± .02
SD	3.37 ± .49	3.55 ± .51	0.08 ± .01	0.07 ± .01
G1/W1	0.92/2.17	0.69/1.87	0.09/0.69	-0.02/0.33
G2/W2	5.47/3.67	5.04/3.10	3.10/0.46	2.25/0.69

* indicates sherd examined in thin section.

Final sample size = 24.

Assemblage B: MST, Spits 7 and 8

Sherd AT580 disintegrated during analysis. The results for sherd AT599 are suspect, as the final dry weight was 21% different from the first determination, showing that some of the sherd disintegrated during analysis.

ACC	WA	AP	BD	SG
AT578	22.24	34.67	1.56	2.39
AT579	22.54	35.52	1.58	2.44
AT581*	16.36	27.02	1.65	2.26
AT582	32.54	44.37	1.36	2.45
AT583*	15.60	27.50	1.76	2.43
AT584*	17.51	30.13	1.72	2.46
AT585	19.01	31.72	1.67	2.44
AT586	29.62	43.02	1.45	2.55
AT587	29.24	41.97	1.44	2.47
AT588	35.62	47.77	1.34	2.57
AT589	14.41	25.35	1.76	2.36
AT590	34.72	46.78	1.35	2.53
AT591	15.11	26.95	1.78	2.44
AT592	20.66	32.12	1.55	2.29
AT593	29.48	42.59	1.45	2.52
AT594	29.64	42.74	1.44	2.52
AT595	21.94	35.08	1.60	2.46
AT596	22.58	34.24	1.52	2.31
AT597	20.43	33.80	1.65	2.50
AT598*	26.12	39.08	1.50	2.46
AT599	27.30	43.34	1.59	2.80
AT600	19.45	30.31	1.56	2.24
AT601	22.08	34.43	1.56	2.38
AT602*	21.13	33.73	1.60	2.41
Disperson statistics				
Mean	23.55 ± 1.27	36.01 ± 1.37	1.56 ± .03	2.44 ± .02
SD	6.22 ± .90	6.69 ± .97	0.13 ± .02	0.12 ± .02
G1/W1	0.38/1.40	0.17/0.94	0.01/0.27	0.78/2.00
G2/W2	2.11/0.88	1.87/1.21	2.19/0.78	4.78/2.74

* indicates sherds examined in thin section.
Final sample size = 24.

Assemblage C: VST, Spits 3 and 4

One of the original sample of 25 sherds was too small for analysis.

ACC	WA	AP	BD	SG
AT603	25.18	39.43	1.57	2.59
AT604	23.39	38.06	1.63	2.63
AT605*	26.33	40.86	1.55	2.62
AT606	13.87	25.55	1.84	2.48
AT607	13.31	24.66	1.85	2.46
AT608	21.65	35.62	1.64	2.55

continued overleaf

ACC	WA	AP	BD	SG
AT609	16.70	29.76	1.78	2.54
AT610	21.20	33.89	1.60	2.42
AT611	21.85	36.10	1.65	2.59
AT612	22.45	36.96	1.65	2.61
AT613	13.92	25.67	1.84	2.48
AT614	29.24	43.41	1.48	2.62
AT615	30.89	44.32	1.43	2.58
AT616	23.91	38.45	1.61	2.61
AT617	26.08	40.98	1.57	2.66
AT618	27.02	41.59	1.54	2.63
AT619*	24.96	39.65	1.59	2.63
AT620*	27.30	41.72	1.53	2.62
AT621	23.53	36.99	1.57	2.49
AT622	23.12	37.44	1.62	2.59
AT623*	22.74	37.08	1.63	2.59
AT624*	26.07	41.00	1.57	2.67
AT625	26.21	40.28	1.54	2.57
AT626	23.35	38.52	1.65	2.68
Disperson statistics				
Mean	23.10 ± 0.94	37.00 ± 1.12	1.62 ± 0.02	2.58 ± 0.01
SD	4.63 ± 0.67	5.48 ± 0.79	0.11 ± 0.02	0.07 ± 0.01
G1/W1	-0.80/2.03	-1.11/2.39	0.87/2.11	-0.74/1.95
G2/W2	3.10/0.46	3.33/0.77	3.18/0.57	1.36/1.89

Final sample size = 24.

Assemblage D: CST, Spits 9, 10 and 11

Sherds AT631, AT646, AT649, and AT650 disintegrated during analysis. The results for sherd AT629 are possibly suspect, as the final dry weight was 6.5% different from the first determination. One of the original sample of 25 sherds was too small for analysis.

ACC	WA	AP	BD	SG
AT627	33.68	48.06	1.43	2.75
AT628*	33.14	46.44	1.40	2.62
AT629*	29.66	43.25	1.46	2.57
AT630*	32.07	46.72	1.46	2.73
AT632	25.21	39.77	1.58	2.62
AT633*	35.44	49.16	1.39	2.73
AT634	34.28	48.59	1.42	2.76
AT635	31.83	47.10	1.48	2.80
AT636	22.77	36.73	1.61	2.55
AT637	35.90	49.38	1.38	2.72
AT638	31.53	44.66	1.42	2.56
AT639	27.81	42.41	1.53	2.65
AT640	34.82	48.42	1.39	2.70
AT641	32.69	46.21	1.41	2.63

continued on facing page

ACC	WA	AP	BD	SG
AT642	27.73	42.85	1.54	2.70
AT643*	30.92	45.82	1.48	2.74
AT644	38.18	51.21	1.34	2.75
AT645	33.58	48.81	1.45	2.84
AT647	29.67	43.46	1.46	2.59
AT648	22.55	35.90	1.59	2.48
Disperson statistics				
Mean	31.17 ± 0.95	45.25 ± 0.93	1.46 ± 0.02	2.67 ± 0.02
SD	4.23 ± 0.67	4.16 ± 0.66	0.08 ± 0.01	0.09 ± 0.01
G1/W1	-0.63/1.68	-0.87/1.97	0.58/1.60	-0.24/1.04
G2/W2	2.70/0.01	2.98/0.35	2.47/0.32	2.11/0.79

Final sample size = 20.

Appendix 2
Descriptions of thin sections

Assemblage A: MST, Spits 3 and 4

AT554. Mineral content 20%, moderately rounded to subangular grains, up to 1 mm, 60% andesine-labradorite, somewhat weathered, 10% quartz and 10% rock fragments (quartzo-feldspathic). Matrix brownish yellow (10YR 6/8) with pale reddish orange (2.5YR 7/4) inclusions, compact, few voids, shows flow structure.

AT556. Mineral content 1–2%, angular grains, up to 0.4 mm, 70% andesine, 20% magnetite, 5% quartz and 5% augite. Matrix pinkish grey (7.5YR 7/3), mottled orange (2.5YR 7/8) and light reddish brown (2.5YR 6/4), shows vague flow structure and about 30% voids. Some voids may have been occupied by mineral grains, some reddish nodules may represent weathered ferromagnesians.

AT557. Mineral content 5%, small semiangular grains, up to 0.5 mm, 60% andesine, 20% magnetite, 10% augite and 10% quartz. Matrix brownish yellow (10YR 6/8) with red (7.5R 4/8) blotches, shows flow structure, many elongated voids and some rounded vesicles filled with clay which may represent weathered ferromagnesians.

AT559. Mineral content 2%, small angular grains, up to 0.15 mm, composition of mineral fraction 50% augite, 25% labradorite and 25% quartz. Matrix brownish yellow (10YR 7/3) with some pink (7.5YR 7/4) and reddish yellow (7.5YR 6/6) nodules, fine silty texture, irregularly fractured.

Assemblage B: MST, Spits 7 and 8

AT581. Mineral content 10%, angular fragments up to 0.75 mm, 90% quartz, and 10% magnetite, no ferromagnesians or feldspars seen. Calcite 10%, stained rounded fragments without shell structure, 0.4 mm. Matrix reddish yellow (5YR 7/8) and black (5YR 2/1), banded, many lenticular cracks parallel to axis of sherd.

AT583. Mineral content 1%, angular fragments, up to 0.75 mm, 90% quartz, 10% magnetite. Calcite 20%, shell fragments, 0.5 mm. Matrix yellowish red (5YR 5/6) with few light red (10R 6/8) mottles, compact, few lenticular voids.

AT584. Mineral content 10%, angular grains, some up to 1 mm, 90% quartz, 10% magnetite.

Calcite 30%, as rounded shell fragments, 0.5 mm. Matrix strong brown (7.5YR 4/8), many lenticular cracks parallel to surface of sherd.

AT598. Mineral content 5%, up to 1 mm, 90% quartz, 10% magnetite. Calcite 40%, rounded shell fragments, up to 1 mm. Matrix banded red (10R 5/8) and dusky red (10R 3/3).

AT602. Mineral content 15%, up to 1 mm, 90% quartz, 5% andesine, 5% magnetite. Calcite 15%, shell fragments, up to 1 mm. Matrix red (10R 4/6) to light red (10R 6/8), banded with globules of red clay present, many lenticular cracks parallel to axis of sherd.

Assemblage C: VST, Spits 3 and 4

AT605. Mineral content 10%, 90% andesine, 5% quartz and 5% augite. Matrix orange (2.5YR 7/8) with red (10R 5/8) mottles, compact, many fine lenticular voids.

AT619. Mineral content 15%, small angular grains, 0.5 mm, 50% labradorite, 25% rock fragments, 10% augite, 5% quartz. Matrix reddish yellow (5YR 7/8) to red (10R 5/8), pleochroic due to oriented clay particles, few large cracks parallel to axis of sherd.

AT620. Mineral content 5%, fragments up to 0.5 mm, 50% quartz, 50% augite. Matrix reddish yellow (5YR 7/8) with strong brown (7.5YR 5/8) to reddish yellow (7.5YR 6/8) mottles, fine globular structure, broken into small fragments with many voids.

AT623. Mineral content 10%, angular, 0.25 mm, 80% quartz and 20% magnetite. Calcite 5–10%, rounded shell fragments, 0.5 mm. Matrix reddish brown (5YR 5/4), compact, about 5–10% globular clay aggregates which may have been weathered feldspars or ferromagnesians, compact, thin lenticular voids parallel to axis of sherd.

AT624. Mineral content 5%, fragments 0.3 mm, 70% andesine, 15% quartz and 15% augite. Matrix red (10R 5/8), birefringent and shows flow structure of clay aggregates, some globules may be altered feldspars or ferromagnesians, compact, many fine lenticular cracks.

Assemblage D: CST, Spits 9, 10 and 11

AT628. Mineral content <1%, quartz only, 0.2 mm. Calcite 50%, shell fragments, 0.3 mm. Matrix light red (10R 6/8), clay shows flow structures around shell fragments, many cracks perpendicular and parallel to axis.

AT629. Mineral content 5%, fragments 0.2 mm, 40% labradorite, 20% quartz, 20% magnetite, 10% olivine and 10% augite. Calcite 5%, rounded grains, very strongly weathered, shell structure not visible, 0.5 mm. Matrix reddish yellow (5YR 7/8) and red (10R 5/8), pleochroic, no preferred orientation shown, some large cracks parallel to axis of sherd.

AT630. Mineral content 2%, fragments 0.25 mm, 40% quartz, 40% oligoclase, 15% magnetite and 5% horneblende. Calcite 20%, rounded shell fragments, 0.3 mm. Matrix red (10R 5/8), shows pleochroic flow structures, many cracks parallel to axis of sherd and many large voids which may be due to plucking of grains during grinding.

AT633. Mineral content 5%, fragments 0.2 mm, 40% quartz, 40% andesine, 15% magnetite and 5% horneblende. Calcite 30%, shell fragments, 1 mm. Matrix yellowish red (5YR 4/6), birefringent but does not show prominent flow structures, many fine cracks parallel to axis of sherd.

AT643. Mineral content 5%, angular fragments, up to 0.5 mm, 95% quartz, 5% magnetite. Calcite 20%, rounded fragments without obvious shell structure, 0.5 mm. Matrix mottled light red (10R 6/8) and reddish brown (5YR 4/4), many fine cracks with no apparent preferred orientation.

29

The dry and the wet: The variable effect of taphonomy on the dog remains from the Kohika Lake Village, Bay of Plenty, New Zealand

Graeme Taylor

c/o Anthropology Department, University of Auckland, New Zealand

GTaylor@adhb.govt.nz

Geoffrey Irwin

Anthropology Department, University of Auckland, New Zealand

Introduction

Since the mid 1980s, there have been several detailed taphonomic studies on New Zealand faunal assemblages, summarised by Allen and Nagaoka (2004:207–209), and these, not surprisingly given the breadth of his zooarchaeological publications, have included a contribution by Atholl Anderson (Anderson *et al.* 1996). However, most of these studies have been concerned with bones recovered from dry-land sites, whereas bone preserved under very different conditions in wetland archaeological sites has received little consideration.

This paper examines the dog-bone assemblages recovered from the site of Kohika V15/80 during three Auckland University excavations between 2005 and 2007. Kohika was a 17th century Maori lake village on a low island near the southern shore of Lake Kohika in the Bay of Plenty, New Zealand. It was abandoned after a flood and fortuitously preserved in peat, and then remained undisturbed until agricultural drainage in 1974. Excavations were carried out at the site between 1974 and 1981, and the diversity of the evidence uncovered and the specialist analysis done on the material revealed extensive information about the economic, domestic and social activities of a community that existed well before the advent of the pakeha (Irwin 2004a). Although the site is best known for its well-preserved wooden and fibre artefacts, these first excavations also recovered almost 200 dog bones, which Clark (1995:272) described as the most complete and best-preserved collection of dog remains from any site in the country.

The more recent excavations have doubled the size of this assemblage and the collection now includes a significant number of bones from both the wetland and dry-land parts of the site. In this paper, the dog bones from these different parts of Kohika, especially those recovered since 2005, are compared. This intra-site comparison not only provides an insight into the variable taphonomic processes operating at Kohika, but also provides a window into the taphonomic effects which may have been operating at many other New Zealand sites with less optimal bone-preservation conditions.

The island of Kohika is shown in Figure 1, and its core is a remnant of the 2000 BP shoreline left stranded by a prograding coast. At the time of occupation, the site was surrounded by swamp and a shallow fresh-water lake, and lightly defended with a palisade. There were households located around the shore, typically with houses, raised pataka storehouses and miscellaneous shelters. Canoes were drawn up at the shore and excavations have revealed formed landing places beside entrances through the palisade. Figure 2 shows the bay on the northern side of the site, which was an area of concentrated activity in prehistory. Since 2005, the excavations at Kohika have been mainly in two areas, known as Area D and Area E. Area D was located in the former lake, as it was during the occupation of the village, and many wooden and fibre artefacts, and other ecofacts were recovered from an anaerobic environment of peat and lacustrine silt. In contrast, Area E was located on dry land on the adjacent shore and generally inside the palisade. Figure 2 shows one house, a carefully constructed marae structure and other buildings. The deposit of Area E was aerobic and composed largely of marine dune sand and reworked tephra, and it yielded large numbers of artefacts of obsidian, pounamu greenstone and bone. Figure 2 also shows the location of the Area D excavations of the 1970s, where much of the deposit also consisted of peat of the former lake, but there were artificially laid sand platforms of a former household as well (Irwin 2004a).

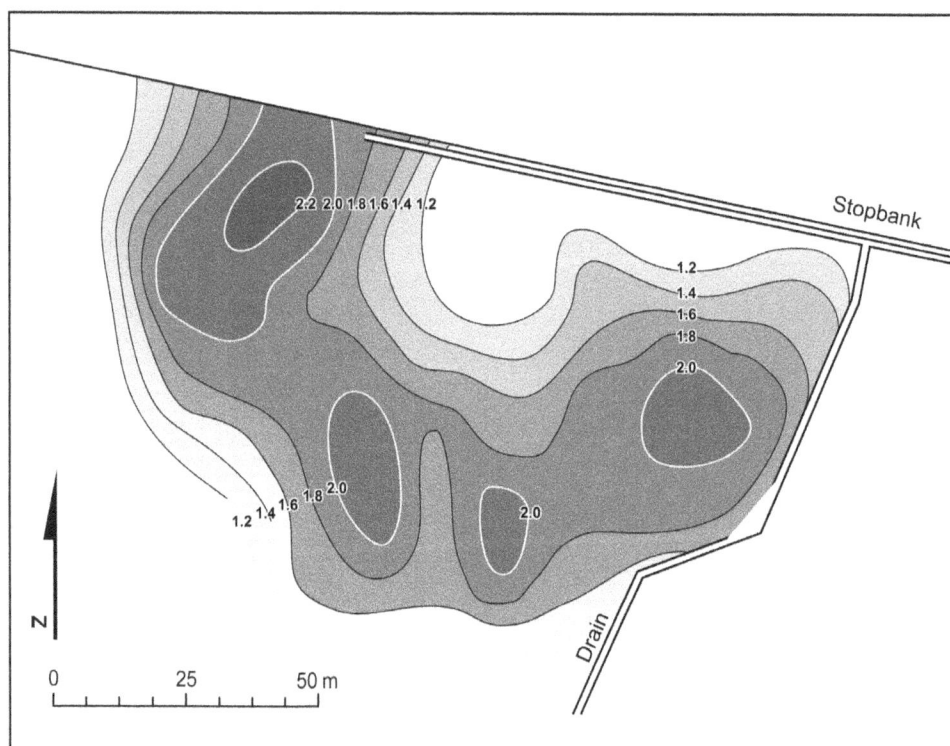

Figure 1. Kohika was a low island surrounded by shallow lake and swamp in the fork of the Rangitaiki and Tarawera rivers, which entered the sea through a common river mouth nearby. Its location gave easy access by canoe to local resources, and good communications into the central North Island of New Zealand and along the Bay of Plenty coast.

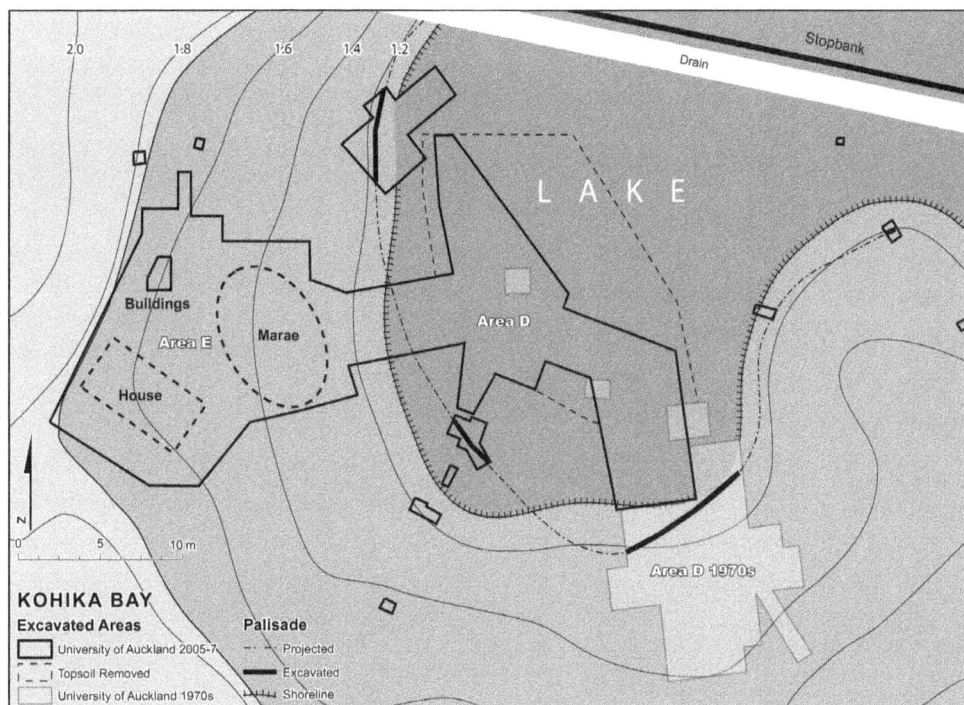

Figure 2. Excavations 2005–2007 were concentrated around a former bay on the north of the island. Area D consisted of waterlogged deposits in the area of the former lake. Area E revealed a household on the adjacent dry shore. There were formed canoe landings at the lake edge and entrances through a light palisade. The locations of the Area D excavations of the 1970s are also shown.

Methods

The provenience of each bone or bone artefact recovered during the 2005–2007 excavations was recorded with a total station. After being cleaned and dried, each of these bones and bone artefacts was identified by element (where possible), using the zooarchaeological comparative collection housed in the Auckland University Anthropology Department. In addition, each bone specimen was examined for evidence of dog or rat gnawing, weathering and cultural modifications, including cut, saw or chop marks, drill holes, filing and burning. For the dog remains, skeletal maturity was assessed using the criteria established by Clark (1995:62–64) for mandibles and crania, by Clark (1997:205) for long bones, and by Allo (1970:34) for tooth eruption.

The number of identified specimens (NISP) was defined as any element or any parts of a single element which could be refitted, with a single shot number (as recorded by the total station). This definition allowed for any bone breakage during and subsequent to excavation. The minimum number of elements (MNE) was determined by calculating the most frequently occurring part of an element. For example, dog tibiae were divided into proximal and distal ends and shafts for both the right and left sides. If the collection of right dog tibiae consisted of seven proximal ends, six shafts and five distal ends, then the MNE for right dog tibiae was seven. If a similar calculation for left tibiae gave an MNE of five, the total MNE for dog tibiae was 12. The minimum number of individuals (MNI) was represented by either the MNE for unpaired elements or the largest MNE for paired elements. Using the dog-tibiae example, the MNI for dogs would be seven based on the presence of seven right tibiae. However, it was sometimes possible to increase the MNI by considering mature and immature specimens. For example, if all seven right proximal tibiae came from mature dogs but two of the five left proximal tibiae came from immature dogs, then the MNI would be nine (seven right proximal tibiae, plus two unmatched immature left proximal tibiae).

Results

Dog remains recovered from Areas D and E from 2005–2007

Table 1 shows that the minimum number of dogs identified in the Kohika excavations from 2005 to 2007 is 20, based on left mandibles. To get an idea of the relative frequency with which some dog-bone elements have been recovered compared with others it is useful to graph the MNIs derived from each element, as shown in Figure 3.

Both Table 1 and Figure 3 show there is significant variation in the frequency with which particular dog bones have been recovered. Mandibles were at least two to three times more likely to have been recovered than crania, any of the long bones, the pelves, or the first and second cervical vertebrae. A third group of bones, including scapulae, ribs, vertebrae other than C1 or C2, and the small bones of the feet, were under-represented to an even greater extent.

Comparison of dog bones from Areas D and E

In addition to comparing the relative frequencies of various elements across the whole site, it is useful to compare the MNE for each element in Area D and Area E, given that Area D was in the lake and the bones from this part of the site were recovered from anaerobic peat, while the bones from Area E were located inside the village palisade in an aerobic and often sandy environment. The MNE for the various dog elements in Areas D and E are presented in Table 2 and Figure 4.

As shown, there is a pronounced difference in the proportions of the various dog bones found in Areas D and E, even though these two areas were of approximately equal size (Table 2 and Figure 4). Only mandibles, radii and the C1 and C2 cervical vertebrae were found in greater numbers in Area E, and of these, mandibles were three times as frequent as any other single element. In contrast, all the scapulae and ribs and virtually all the crania, pelves and vertebrae, other than C1 and C2 vertebrae, were found in Area D. Moreover, with the exception of radii, long bones were at least twice as likely to be recovered from Area D as Area E. Although mandibles were relatively frequent in Area D, they were not as dominant as in Area E, and the MNIs derived from mandibles, pelves and crania in Area D were roughly equivalent (MNI respectively 10, 9 and 8).

The differences in bone-recovery patterns between Areas D and E are also highlighted by the proportion of whole or near-whole bones (greater than 90 percent of the element intact) identified within the two areas, as outlined in Table 3.

As illustrated by Table 3, the great majority of whole or near-whole bones was found in Area D and whole bones were almost six times more likely to have come from this part of the site than from Area E. Furthermore, of the whole or near-whole bones identified in Area E, just over half were mandibles.

The proportions of mature and immature dog bones identified in Areas D and E can also be compared. Twenty osteologically immature dog bones were recovered, and all 20 came from Area D, including eight bones found together from a single individual of about six months of age. No immature dog bones were found in Area E.

Aside from contrasting the frequencies of different elements and the proportions of whole bones and immature bones within the two areas, the extent to which the bones from Areas D and E were weathered and gnawed by animals can be evaluated.

Bone-weathering patterns have been described by Behrensmeyer (1978), who proposed six weathering stages. The main changes, in the approximate order they occur, include: hair-line cracks on the bone surface perpendicular to the long axis of the bone, flaking of the cortical surface, and cracks through the full thickness of the cortex, after which the bones fall apart. The proportion of weathered bones in Areas D and E is shown in Table 4.

Table 4 shows a significant proportion of the bones from Area E was weathered, whereas virtually none of the bones from Area D was affected. Moreover, the single weathered bone from Area D was only lightly weathered, whereas a small proportion of the Area E bones were so weathered they were falling apart (Figure 5). Across the whole site, 15 percent of bones were weathered.

In addition to weathering, bone attrition as a consequence of animal gnawing is an important taphonomic variable. In the setting of New Zealand prehistory, the gnawing of bones by dogs and Polynesian rats has been most thoroughly examined by M. Taylor (1984) in reference to the bone assemblage from Twilight Beach in Northland. Dogs prefer to chew the epiphyseal ends of long bones and gnawed bones characteristically demonstrate crenulated edges, tooth puncture marks and irregular scratches and pits where the teeth have been dragged across the bone surface. In contrast to dogs, rats prefer to gnaw bone diaphyses (shafts) and leave a series of parallel, closely spaced, flat-bottomed grooves. The proportions of dog and rat-gnawed bones from Areas D and E are outlined in Table 5.

Although Table 5 shows there was little difference in the proportions of dog-gnawed bones in Area D and Area E, the extent to which bones had been reduced as a result of dog gnawing did differ. Most dog-gnawed bones in Area D were relatively intact (see Figure 6 and Figure 7), however, with the exception of mandibles, many dog-gnawed bones in Area E had been quite markedly reduced (see Figures 8–12). Rat gnawing was also exclusively found on bones from Area E. Across the whole site, 24 percent of bones showed evidence of dog gnawing and 7 percent demonstrated rat gnawing.

In addition to the proportion of dog-gnawed bones, another notable feature of the assemblage was the consistent pattern of dog gnawing found on particular elements. As noted by Taylor (1984:92), the epiphyseal ends of long bones were certainly favoured (Figure 8), but specific gnawing patterns were also identified on mandibles, crania and pelves. For example, dog-gnawed mandibles were frequently broken through the canine cavity. These irregular breaks contrasted sharply with the pattern of sawing and breakage associated with purposeful removal of the canines by humans (Figure 12). A number of dog-gnawed, but relatively preserved, pelves and crania found in Area D also showed consistent patterns of damage. The gnawed pelves were invariably missing the medial end of the pubis and the cranial end of the ilium (Figure 6), while the gnawed crania were often missing the rostral end of the snout and the zygomatic arches (Figure 7).

A further taphonomic variable which can be compared between Areas D and E is the modification of dog bones by human sawing. Although evidence of burning, chopping and drilling were also sought, there was only a single burnt dog bone, one drilled canine and a single femur with a chop mark, so these factors are not further considered. Moreover, cut marks, which were present on 20 percent of dog bones across both areas, are not considered further either, as they have little influence on the rates of bone survival. Saw marks are defined as deep grooves made by repeatedly moving a blade back and forth in the same cut (Taylor 1984:100). There is usually a set of shallower, parallel striations adjacent to the main saw mark where the blade has jumped out of its intended track when the sawing process began.

Table 1. Dog bones recovered from Kohika 2005–2007.

Element	NISP	MNE	MNI	Side used for MNI
Crania	15	9	9	
Mandibles	49	35	20	left
Humeri	13	12	7	right
Radii	10	9	6	right
Ulnae	15	14	9	left
Femora	14	12	7	right
Tibiae	14	10	8	left*
Pelves	17	17	9	right
Scapulae	6	6	4	left
Ribs	7	7	1	
C1 (atlas)	7	7	7	
C2 (axis)	6	6	6	
Other cervical vertebrae	6	6	2	
Thoracic vertebrae	3	3	1	
Lumbar vertebrae	6	6	1	
Caudal vertebrae	1	1	1	
Metapodials	6	6	1	
Calcaniae	1	1	1	
Canines	11	11	3	

*MNI for tibiae consisted of six left tibiae plus two unmatched immature right tibiae

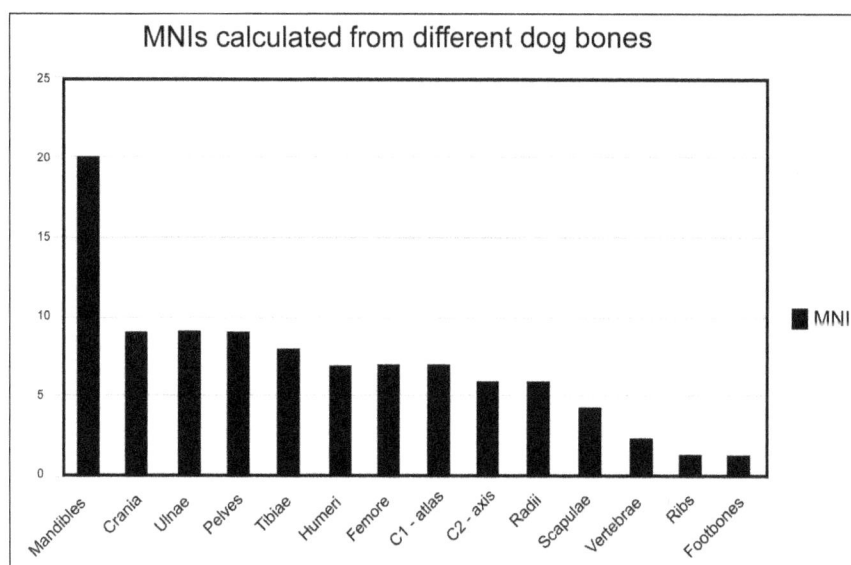

Figure 3. Comparison of MNIs derived from different dog bones, Kohika 2005-2007.

Table 2. MNE for different dog bones in Area D versus Area E.

Element	MNE Area D	MNE Area E
Crania	8	1
Mandibles	17	18
Humeri	10	2
Radii	3	6
Ulnae	10	4
Femora	8	4
Tibiae	8	4
Pelves	16	1
C1 and C2 vertebrae	6	7
Other vertebrae	15	1
Scapulae	6	0
Ribs	7	0
Distal limb bones	5	2

Table 3. Number of whole or near-whole bones from Area D versus Area E.

Element	Area D	Area E
Crania	5	0
Mandibles	15	8
Humeri	10	0
Radii	3	0
Ulnae	8	0
Femora	7	1
Tibiae	5	0
Pelves	6	0
C1and C2 vertebrae	6	4
Other vertebrae	11	0
Scapulae	5	0
Ribs	2	0
Distal limb bones	5	2
Total	**88**	**15**

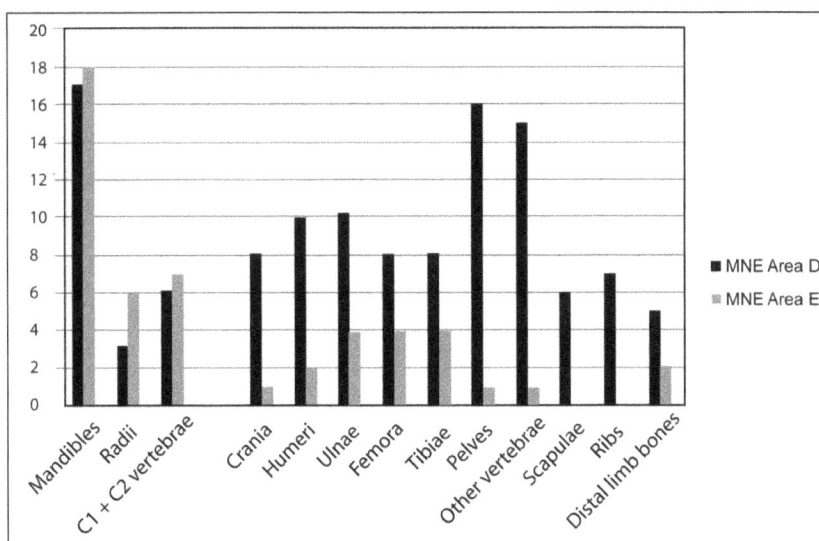

Figure 4. MNE for different dog bones in Area D versus Area E.

Table 4. Number of weathered bones Area D versus Area E.

Element	NISP Area D	No. weathered	NISP Area E	No. weathered
Crania	11	0	4	0
Mandibles	17	0	32	8
Humeri	10	0	3	2
Radii	3	0	7	1
Ulnae	10	1	5	3
Femora	9	0	5	3
Tibiae	8	0	6	2
Pelves	16	0	1	1
C1/C2 vertebrae	6	0	7	4
Other vertebrae	15	0	1	0
Scapulae	6	0	0	0
Ribs	7	0	0	0
Distal limb bones	5	0	2	0
Canines	2	0	9	7
Total	**125**	**1(0.8%)**	**82**	**31(38%)**

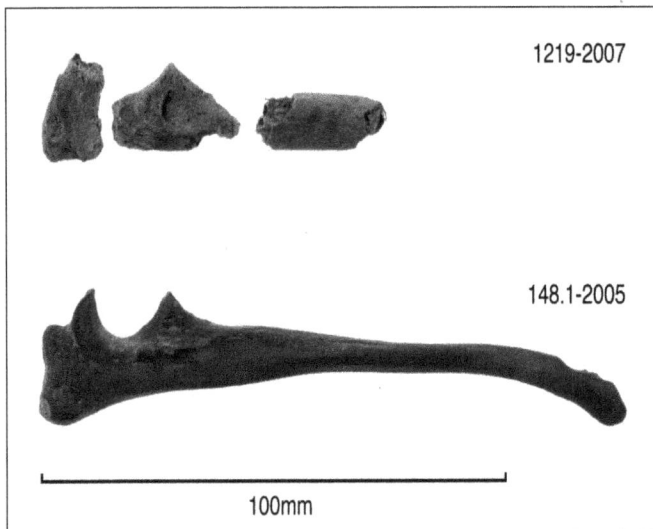

Figure 5. Two dog ulnae showing the effect of weathering on bones in Area E compared with Area D. The lower ulna comes from Area D and is typical of the non-weathered bones from this part of the site. The upper ulna, from Area E, is markedly weathered and is falling apart.

Table 5. Number of dog and rat-gnawed bones Area D versus Area E.

Element	NISP Area D	No. dog gnawed	No. rat gnawed	NISP Area E	No. dog gnawed	No. rat gnawed
Crania	11	6	0	4	2	0
Mandibles	17	2	0	32	9	4
Humeri	10	0	0	3	2	2
Radii	3	1	0	7	0	0
Ulnae	10	1	0	5	0	1
Femora	9	0	0	5	3	2
Tibiae	8	4	0	6	1	1
Pelves	16	11	0	1	1	0
C1/C2 vertebrae	6	0	0	7	3	2
Other vertebrae	15	0	0	1	0	0
Scapulae	6	2	0	0	0	0
Ribs	7	1	0	0	0	0
Small limb bones	5	0	0	2	0	0
Canines	2	0	0	9	0	3
Totals	**125**	**28 (22%)**	**0(0%)**	**82**	**21(26%)**	**15(18%)**

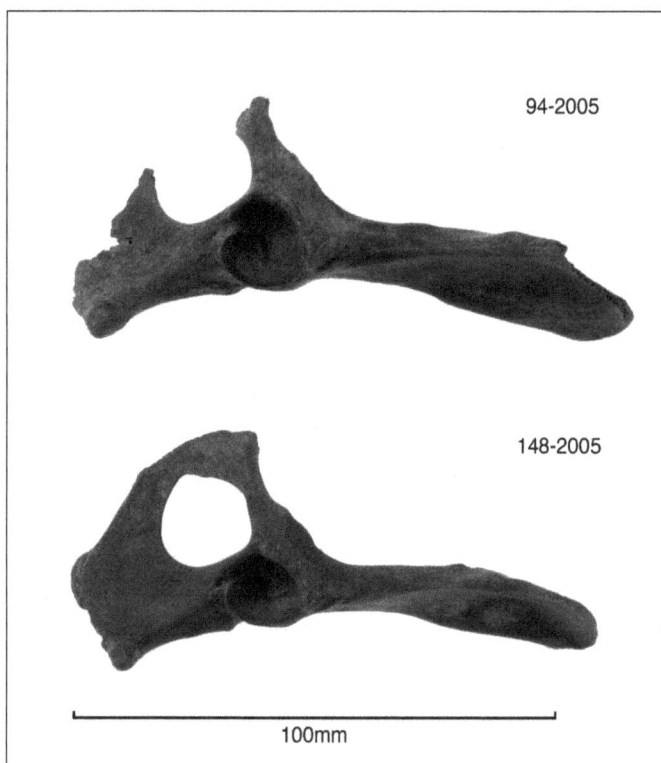

Figure 6. An intact dog hemipelvis from Area D on the bottom and a dog-gnawed hemipelvis from Area D on the top. Note the typical loss of the medial end of the pubis and the cranial end of the ilium in the latter specimen.

Table 6. Number of dog bones with saw marks in Area D versus Area E.

Element	Area D NISP	No. with saw marks	Area E NISP	No. with saw marks	Percentage worked (both Areas)
Crania	11	0	4	0	0%(0/15)
Mandibles	17	2	32	10	24% (12/49)
Humeri	10	0	3	1	8% (1/13)
Radii	3	0	7	6	60% (6/10)
Ulnae	10	0	5	0	0% (0/15)
Femora	9	0	5	2	14% (2/14)
Tibiae	8	0	6	4	29% (4/14)
Pelves	16	0	1	0	0% (0/17)
Vertebrae	21	0	8	0	0% (0/29)
Scapulae	6	0	0	0	0% (0/6)
Ribs	7	0	0	0	0% (0/7)
Small limb bones	5	0	2	0	0% (0/7)
Canines	2	0	9	1 (+1)	18% (2/11)
Total	**125**	**2 (1.6%)**	**82**	**24 (29%)**	**13% (26/207)**

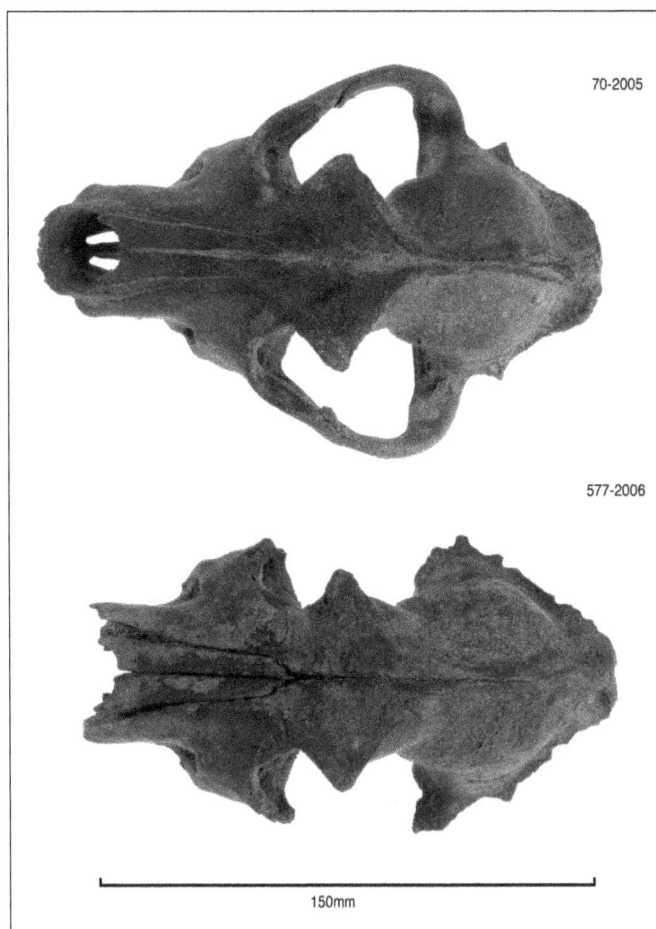

Figure 7. An intact cranium from Area D on the top and a dog-gnawed cranium from Area D on the bottom. The loss of the rostral end of the snout and the zygomatic arches in the latter specimen were often identified in dog-gnawed crania.

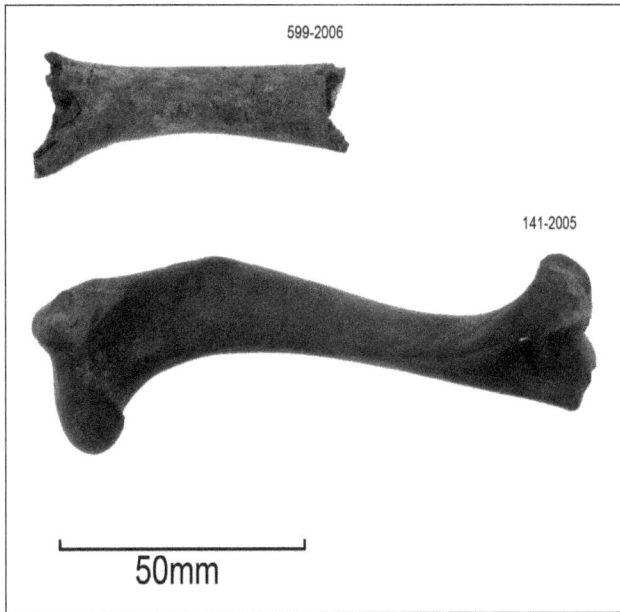

Figure 8. A completely intact dog humerus from Area D on the bottom compared with a dog-gnawed humerus from Area E on the top. The latter shows the characteristic loss of both epiphyseal ends and also represents the largest fragment of humerus found in Area E.

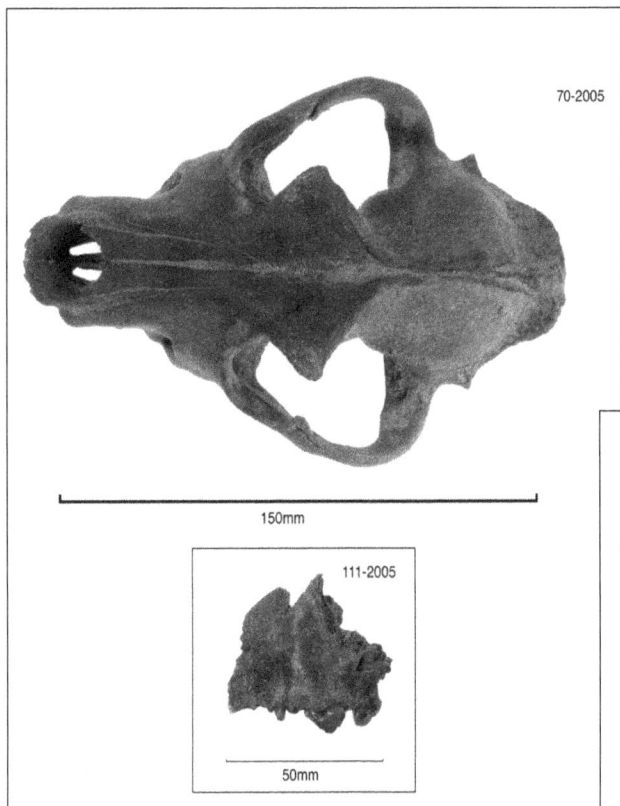

Figure 9 (left). The cranium on the top is the best-preserved example of a dog skull from Area D, whereas the dog-gnawed fragment of left maxilla on the bottom represents one of the two largest cranial fragments found in Area E (compare with the dog-gnawed crania in Area D, as shown in Figure 7).

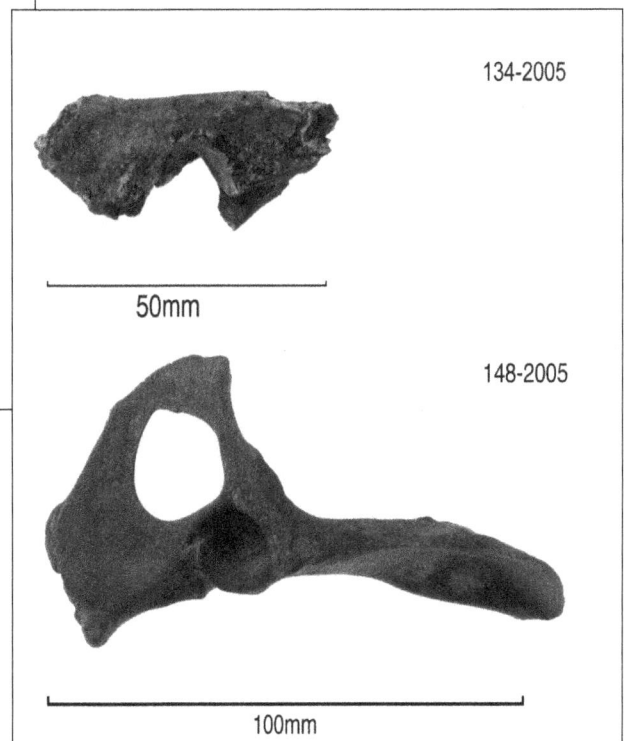

Figure 10 (right). On the bottom is a completely intact hemipelvis from Area D, while the fragment on the top, which includes part of the left acetabulum, is dog gnawed and weathered and represents the only fragment of pelvis found in Area E (compare with the dog-gnawed pelves in Area D as shown in Figure 6).

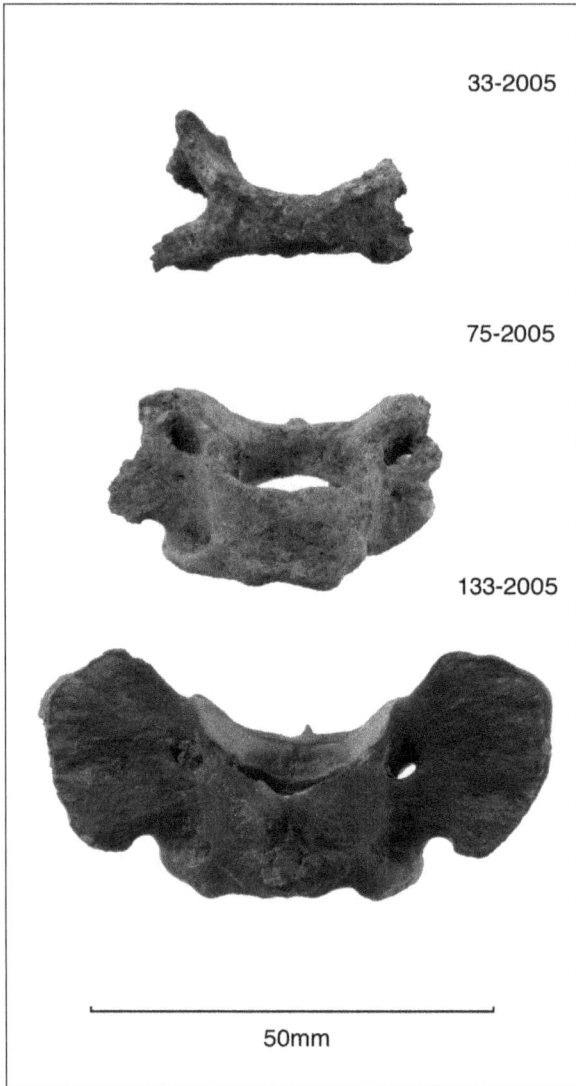

Figure 11. Three C1 cervical vertebrae (axes). The bottom bone is intact and comes from Area D, whereas the top two are both dog gnawed and weathered and come from Area E.

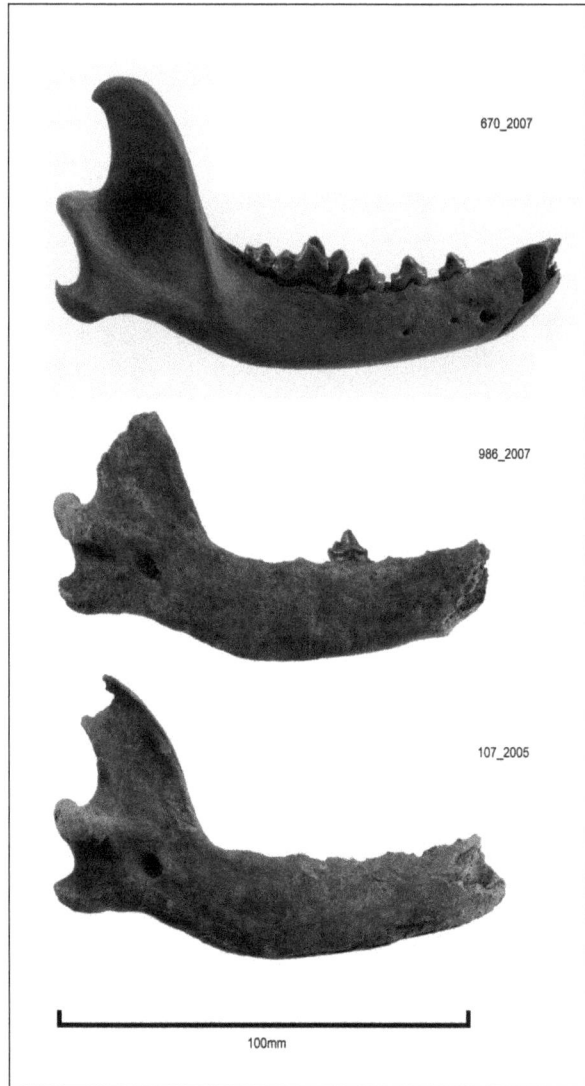

Figure 12. One right (top) and two left dog mandibles. The top mandible is from Area D and shows a saw mark below the empty canine cavity, in keeping with purposeful removal of the canine. The bottom two, from Area E, are broken through the canine cavity as a result of dog gnawing but are nonetheless relatively intact.

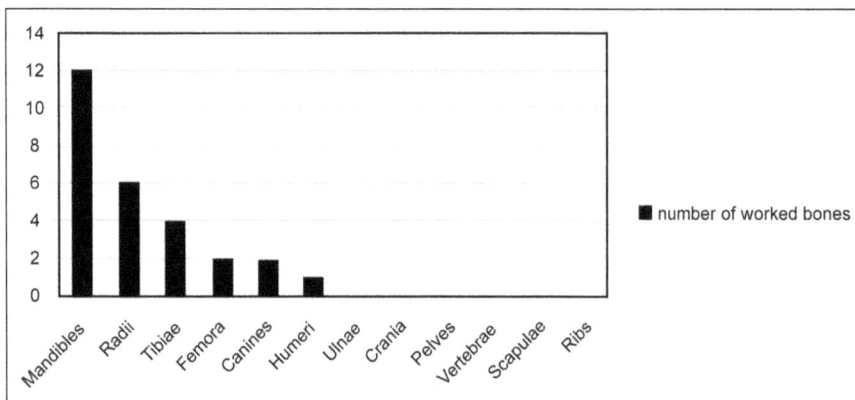

Figure 13. Total number of worked bones provided by each dog element.

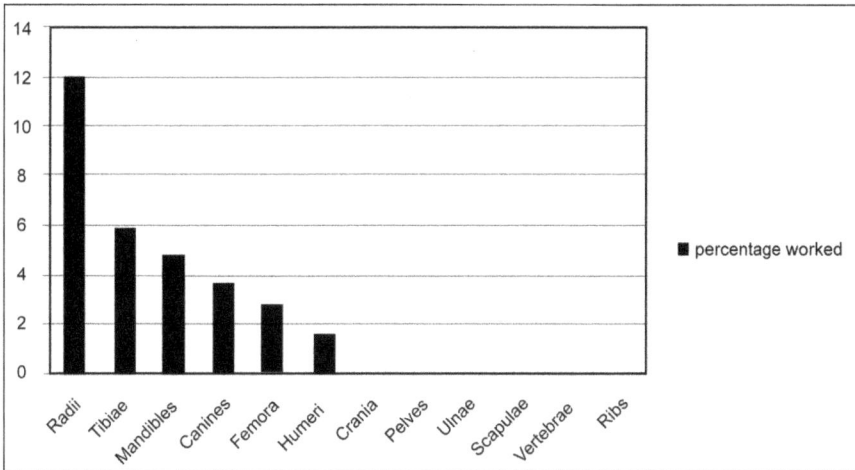

Figure 14. Percentage of each dog element that had been worked.

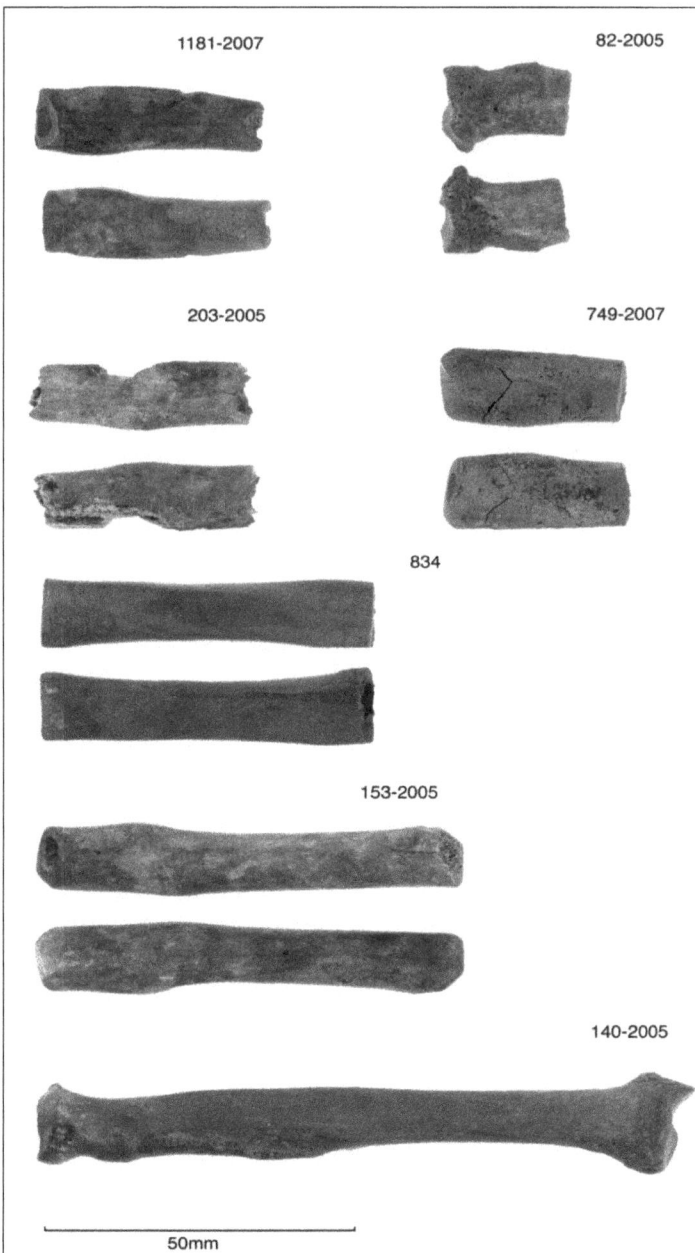

Figure 15. Dog radii. The bottom specimen (140-2005) is an intact radius for comparison. The six top specimens are all sawn and were found in Area E. 82-2005 in the top right corner is the sawn distal end of a radius, while the other five represent sawn lengths of radial shaft.

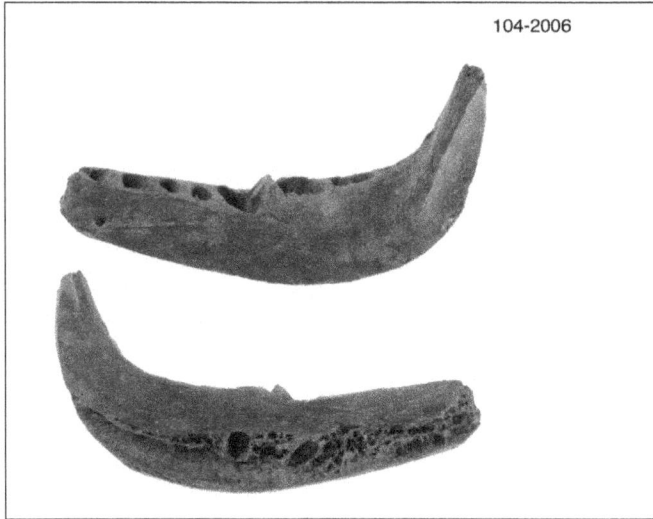

104-2006

Figure 16. A 'dog jaw point' found in Area D showing the dorsal (top) and ventral (bottom) aspects of the artefact. This is part of a two-piece fishhook made from a dog mandible by sawing off the ventral margin and the cranial end of the ascending ramus. The teeth have also been sawn out (see Figure 17) and the tooth sockets filed flat.

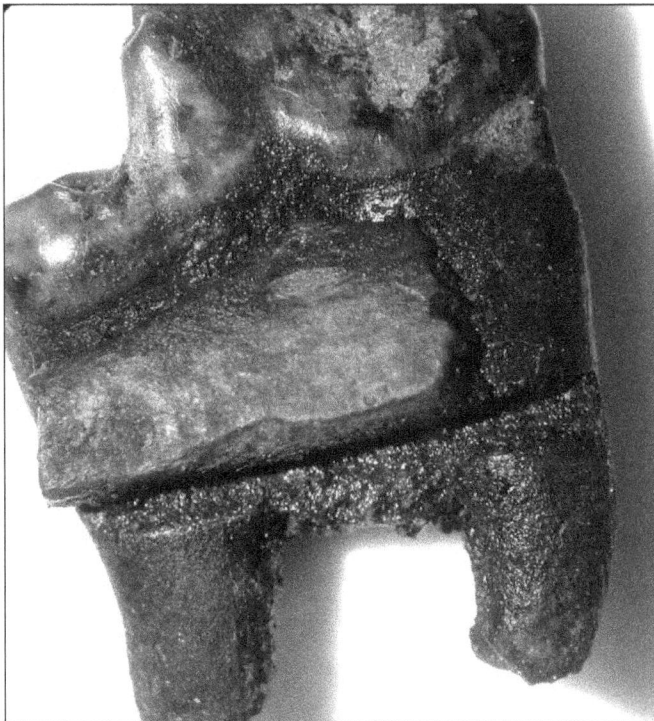

Figure 17. A sawn M1 dog molar (1178-2007) from Area E. The horizontal sawing groove is clearly identified just below the centre of the picture.

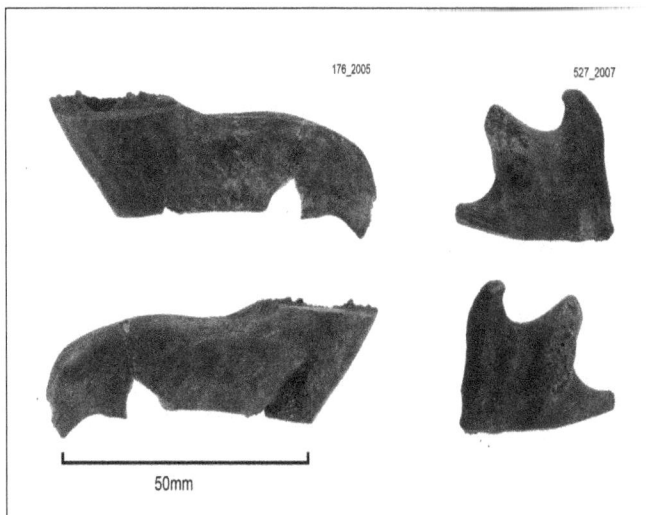

176_2005   527_2007

50mm

Figure 18. Two sawn fragments of dog mandible from Area E. The left specimen includes the coronoid process and is sawn at the rostral and cranial ends. The right specimen includes the articular and angular processes and is sawn only at the rostral end.

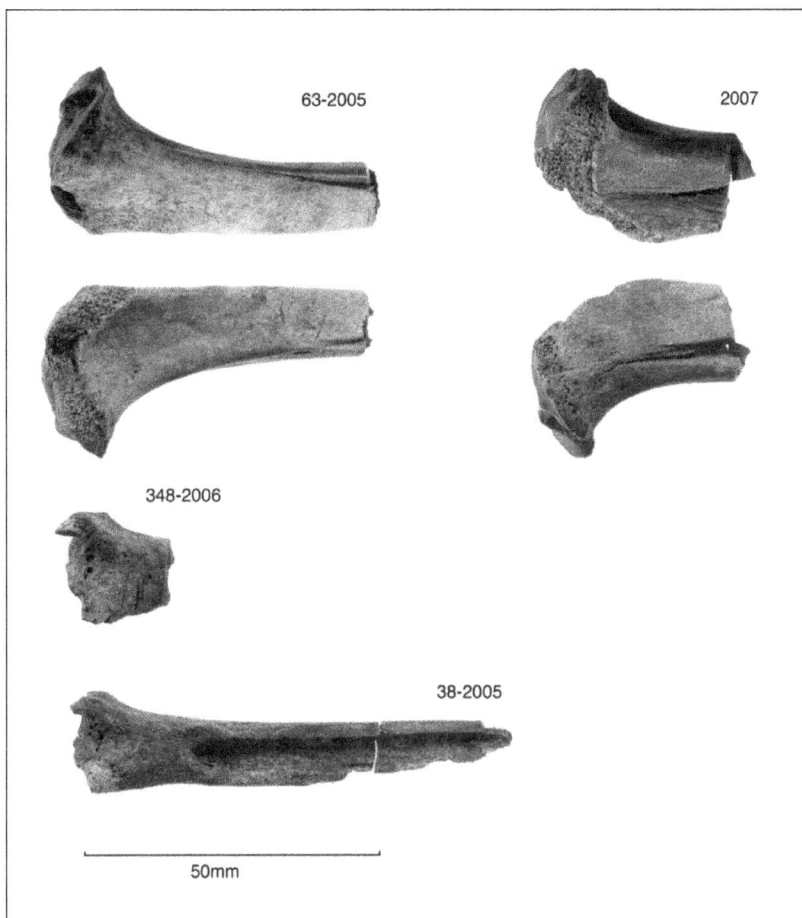

Figure 19. Sawn fragments of dog tibia from Area E. The top two specimens (63-2005 and 2007) are both proximal ends that have been sawn transversely and also have longitudinal grooves on the lateral and medial aspects, suggesting the manufacture of a consistent artefact, perhaps a chisel. 348-2006 (second from bottom) is the distal end of a tibia which has been sawn off. 38-2005 (at the bottom) is a rather poorly preserved chisel, also made from the distal end.

In general, the sawing at Kohika only proceeded to a certain depth and then the bone was snapped along the sawn groove. This sawing and snapping technique has been previously noted at other later-period Maori sites, such as Oruarangi (Furey 1996:162). Because it is most cost-efficient for prehistoric peoples with stone tools to cut through joints and around bones, rather than through bones, when butchering an animal, sawing is more likely be indicative of bone-tool manufacture than butchery (Lyman 1987:263). Therefore, in combination with drilling and filing, the proportion of sawn bone is effectively a measure of the amount of worked bone at Kohika.

Table 6 records the number of dog bones with saw marks in Areas D and E and the proportion of each element which had been sawn. The proportion of each element which had been worked (either sawn, or in the case of one canine, drilled) is demonstrated graphically in Figure 13, while Figure 14 compares the actual number of worked items for each element.

Table 6 shows that virtually all sawn bone was found in Area E. The only two worked bones found in Area D were a mandible, which had had the canine purposely sawn out (Figure 12), and a 'dog jaw point' (Figure 16), which appeared incompletely finished and may have been accidentally lost in the lake.

Figure 13 shows that in terms of the proportion worked compared with the number found, the element most commonly worked was the radius (Figure 15 shows examples of sawn radii). However, Figure 14 demonstrates that in terms of the actual numbers of worked items, there were more worked mandibles than any other element (Figures 16–18 show various examples of sawn mandibles and mandibular molars). Figures 13 and 14 both show other relatively sought-after bones were the tibiae (Figure 19), femora and canines.

Summary of results

The NISP for all dog bone recovered from Kohika from 2005 to 2007 was 207; the MNE was 178; and the MNI was 20, based on left mandibles. Compared with the number of mandibles identified, there was a paucity of bones from other parts of the dog, and in particular, scapulae, ribs, vertebrae other than C1 and C2, and the small bones of the distal limbs were markedly under-represented.

There were also a number of differences in the dog bones retrieved from Area D, which was situated in Lake Kohika at the time of site occupation, and those recovered from Area E, which was on dry land during the same period. Greater proportions of all bones were found in Area D, with the exception of mandibles, radii and C1 and C2 vertebrae, and furthermore, all immature dog bones were found in Area D. Moreover, a far higher number of whole or near-whole bones were retrieved from Area D, whereas bones from Area E were more likely to be weathered and fragmented. Although an approximately equal number of dog-gnawed bones was found in both areas, bones had been reduced by dogs to a far greater extent in Area E, and furthermore, rat-gnawed bones were only found in Area E.

In addition, sawn bone, which is the most effective archaeological measure of worked bone at Kohika, was almost exclusively found in Area E. The elements most frequently sawn were mandibles and radii, but tibiae and canines were also relatively sought after.

In summary, dog bones in Area E were more weathered, more worked and more gnawed than dog bones in Area D, which were more likely to be intact and more representative of a greater proportion of the dog skeleton.

Comparison of the dog assemblage from 2005–2007 with the 1970s dog assemblage

The bones recovered from Kohika during the 1970s have been reported by Irwin *et al.* (2004), and the principal analyst of the dog was M. Taylor. The MNI of 20 derived from the current assemblage is similar to the MNI of 16 calculated from the 1975–1977 excavations, although the latter was based on crania, rather than left mandibles (Irwin et al. 2004:200). When the two assemblages are combined, the MNI is 32, based on left mandibles. Aside from the mandibles, crania are relatively frequent, with a combined MNI of 25.

In addition to being dominated by mandibles and crania, the two assemblages have other similarities. In both, long bones are relatively under-represented, by a factor of two to three, while ribs, vertebrae, scapulae and small limb bones are under-represented by an even greater factor (Irwin *et al.* 2004:200). Furthermore, in both assemblages, the proportions of weathered and gnawed bones are similar (Irwin *et al.* 2004:201). Overall, 29 percent of dog bones from the 1975–1977 excavations were dog gnawed (55 bones in total), compared with 24 percent in the current assemblage (49 bones in total), and in both, dog-gnawed bones were distributed through all parts of the site. Rat-gnawed bones made up just over 6 percent of the 1970s collection (12 bones in total), versus 7 percent of the 2005–2007 collection (15 bones in total). In the 1970s assemblage, rat-gnawed bones were found in all parts of the site, including Area D, while they were restricted to Area E in the current assemblage. However, parts of Area D during the 1970s were composed of artificially laid dry-sand floors, whereas all of Area D in the later excavations was situated in the lake (see Figure 1).

Weathering was identified on 11 percent of the dog bones found in the 1970s, although 22 percent of the bones from the Whakatane Historical Society site were weathered, whereas this was a feature of only 3 percent of Area D bones. The 2005–2007 assemblage had a similar overall proportion of weathered bones (15 percent) and once again, bones from Area D showed little evidence of weathering (less than 1 percent) compared with bones from Area E (38 percent).

The ages of the dogs in the two assemblages were also comparable. Based on 15 crania, Irwin *et al.* (2004:201) identified 12 adult dogs, two adolescent dogs and one juvenile dog within the 1970s assemblage, and the bones recovered since 2005 confirm most dogs at Kohika were killed after reaching maturity. On the basis of the mandibles and tooth-eruption patterns, there were a minimum of 18 dogs aged more than seven months, one dog aged about six months, and two dogs aged fewer than than four months in this latter assemblage.

These comparisons show the two Kohika assemblages, although taken from different parts of the village site, have many features in common. However one taphonomic variable which does differ between the two collections is the amount of sawn bone. Within Area E, 29 percent of dog bone recovered since 2005 had been sawn, which is a far greater proportion than the amount of sawn bone found in any area during the 1970s. In contrast, the amount of sawn bone in Area D is comparable (3.5 percent of bone from the 1970s assemblage and 1.6 percent of dog bone from the later collection).

Discussion

Why are there so many dog mandibles at Kohika and what has happened to the remainder of the dog skeletons?

One feature shared by both the Kohika dog-bone assemblages is a relatively high proportion of mandibles and, to a lesser extent, crania, while the remainder of the skeleton is under-represented. Of the dog bones recovered since 2005, this predominance of mandibles is especially noticeable in the drier parts of the site, as represented by Area E. In contrast, long bones are only half as frequent as they should be and there are even fewer bones from the majority of the axial skeleton. Based on the 1970s assemblage, Irwin and colleagues (2004:200) suggested three possible causes for this relative absence of trunk and limb bones, including dog gnawing with associated bone destruction, the loss of bones selected for industrial purposes, or 'the sharing of dog carcasses' through either trade or gift exchange. A fourth possibility, raised by Smith (1996:193) in relation to the dog remains from Shag River Mouth, is intra-site variability in the discard of certain parts of the butchered dog carcasses.

These alternatives are considered in turn.

Hypothesis 1: *There has been a selective loss of the bones used for industrial purposes*

Of the alternatives noted above, the loss of specific dog bones through their use in artefact manufacture is perhaps the least satisfactory explanation for the absence of parts of the dog skeleton. As the results show, mandibles were the most common element identified, but more mandibles than any other element had also been worked (Figure 6). Furthermore, in the less protected environment of Area E, two of the three elements found in greater proportions than Area D, namely mandibles and radii, were two of the elements which appeared to have been in the greatest demand for tool manufacture. In contrast, those bones mostly absent from Area E, such as pelves, scapulae, vertebrae, ribs and crania, seem never to have been worked. Therefore, rather than the industrial use of certain dog bones leading to the loss of particular skeletal remains, the Kohika results suggest the opposite might be true; the selection of certain bones for artefact manufacture may have actually assisted in their survival. The reasons bones selected for tool manufacture may have enjoyed preferential survival include the purposeful protection of these potentially useful elements from carnivore gnawing and weathering, and the intentional use of bones with the greatest density and therefore the greatest potential for survival for tool manufacture.

Hypothesis 2: *There was intra-site variability in the discard of different parts of the dog carcass*

At the 14th century Shag River Mouth site in East Otago, Smith (1996:193) has noted variation in the proportional representation of dog body parts in different parts of the site. Body parts with higher food value, including the forelimbs, predominated in the Swamp and upper layers of the Dune areas, whereas lower-value body parts, including the head, trunk and hind limbs, predominated in the lower Dune layers. Smith believed the lower Dune assemblages represented waste from initial carcass preparation, whereas the forelimb-dominated assemblages represented waste from human food consumption. He considered variation in bone discard was more likely to account for these assemblage differences than taphonomic processes.

The patterns identified by Smith at Shag River Mouth do not appear to account for the disparities between Areas D and E at Kohika. The lake was probably a dumping ground for food and bone waste from the adjacent household (see below). However, both forelimb and hind-limb bones remain half as frequent as expected, compared with mandibles, crania and pelves, and there is also a relative paucity of scapulae, vertebrae and ribs. This assemblage does not appear to represent a consistent assemblage of dog bones with low food value, as many of the bones from the trunk, limb extremities and hind limbs are missing. Since the bones in the lake are well preserved, some of these missing bones must have been discarded elsewhere. Similarly, it is not a forelimb-dominated assemblage, as might be anticipated in a midden predominately composed of human food waste.

In Area E, there is also no clear pattern of high or low food-value bones. The Area E assemblage is dominated by mandibles, but C1 and C2 cervical vertebrae and radii are also more frequent than other bones. In contrast to the Shag River Mouth remains, these elements do not form a coherent collection of either butchery-waste or food-waste bones.

Hypothesis 3: *Parts of the dog carcasses have been removed from the site*

The possibility dog carcasses were sometimes moved off-site, perhaps through gifting or exchange, was raised by Smith (1981) as a possible explanation for the differential representation of body parts at the early-period Pig Bay site on Motutapu Island. Dog remains were prominent at Pig Bay, and as with Kohika, the MNI based on mandibles and crania was approximately twice that of all the long bones and about four times that derived from ribs and scapulae. Since there was no evidence that the limb bones, or any other dog bones, were being used to make tools, Smith believed the relative absence of long bones could indicate that the forelimbs and hind limbs were often detached from carcasses and shared or traded. He reported a historical account of dog carcasses being used as an exchange item, and the hypothesis receives possible support from some of the ethnohistorical accounts of Maori dogs collected by Allo (1970), which record how dog meat was considered a highly esteemed delicacy consumed on important occasions by priests and tattooists and prepared at feasts for distinguished visitors (Allo 1970:153–155). Certainly, it is conceivable that such a valued item was sometimes gifted, although the application of these ethnohistorical accounts for early-period sites such as Pig Bay may be questionable.

Although dog carcasses could have been removed from Pig Bay and Kohika, there are some problems with the hypothesis. The importance of dog gnawing as a taphonomic variable was not fully realised by New Zealand archaeologists until M. Taylor's 1984 thesis on bone remains at Twilight Beach highlighted the effect dogs could have on faunal assemblages. A second problem arises from the similarity of the MNIs derived from each element at both Kohika and Pig Bay, where mandibles and crania dominated both assemblages, were twice as common as limb bones and were at least four times as common as scapulae and ribs. While this similarity may indicate the same body parts were being removed, it might also indicate similar taphonomic issues at the two sites. That this latter possibility is worth bearing in mind is underscored by a consideration of dog bones found in other New Zealand sites. Clark (1995:250–279) summarised dog-bone remains by skeletal element from 34 early and late-period sites from throughout the country and found mandibles were the most frequent element at 19 of these sites and crania the most frequent at another 10. Allo (1970:171–174) also identified crania and mandibles as the most common dog bones recovered from most New Zealand sites, especially from the Archaic period.

The Clark (1995) and Allo (1970) studies show Kohika and Pig Bay are not alone in being relatively rich in dog crania and mandibles compared with other dog bones. Are these similarities a reflection of analogous cultural practices or could they represent similar taphonomic processes? This latter possibility is now considered.

Hypothesis 4: *Selective bone loss is attributable to taphonomic processes*

Comparison of the dog bones from the protected anaerobic environment of Area D and the aerobic sandy environment of Area E shows weathering and animal gnawing were having a significant effect on the survival of dog bones at Kohika. But the comparison also shows these taphonomic variables did not affect all elements equally. For example, based on the remains from Area D, the MNI derived from crania, pelves and mandibles is quite similar (eight for crania, nine for pelves and 10 for mandibles), but the MNIs for these three elements in Area E are quite different (one for crania, one for pelves and 10 for mandibles). Figures 9 and 10 illustrate the marked effect of dog gnawing and weathering on crania and pelves in Area E compared with the preservation of these same elements in the lacustrine environment of Area D. In contrast, Figure 12 shows mandibles in Area E were relatively resistant to both weathering and dog gnawing. The same taphonomic processes affecting crania and pelves also acted on long bones and vertebrae, as shown in Figures 5, 8 and 11, and for the same reason, it is no surprise that relatively fragile bones such as scapulae, ribs and most vertebrae were completely absent from Area E.

The reason mandibles are more resistant to the taphonomic processes operating in Area E than most other dog bones is likely to be attributable to their greater density. Dog skeletons are adapted for mobility, and their bones, although strong, are relatively light and thin-walled (Taylor 1984:12–13). In fact, small elements can occasionally be difficult to distinguish from bird bones. As a result, dog bones are quite vulnerable to animal gnawing (Taylor 1984:172). Taylor (1984:23, 91) has described how modern dogs can completely destroy certain elements such as vertebrae and even sheep and pig-sized long bones, and it is likely kuri would have had a similar potential to destroy dog bones. The one exception is the dog mandible, which is adapted to crushing and gnawing bone and is the strongest and most dense element in the skeleton (Taylor 1984:13, 171). As noted by Binford (1981:217) and Taylor (1984:24), bone survival is directly related to bone density, as it increases resistance to both weathering and animal gnawing, and it is probably this property which explains why mandibles are more likely to survive in archaeological sites. These same properties of bone density and strength also explain why Maori frequently selected the dog mandible for artefact manufacture.

However, weathering, dog gnawing and bone density are not the only factors to consider at Kohika. Firstly, the amount of gnawing in any assemblage will be dictated by the size of the carnivore population. Given the number of dog bones and coprolites recovered from Kohika, the dog population in this village was possibly quite large and this also would have been an important variable. Secondly, the degree to which bones are reduced by animal gnawing is proportional to the time bones are exposed (Taylor 1984:24). Comparison of Areas D and E is again of interest in this regard, as it is clear the bones in Area D were exposed to dogs for a shorter period than the bones in Area E. As shown in Figures 6 and 7, dog-gnawed bones in Area D were still largely intact compared with gnawed bones in Area E (Figures 8–11). Furthermore, rat gnawing was only identified in Area E. Unlike dogs, which will only gnaw relatively fresh bones, it has been suggested rats will gnaw old bones, including sub-fossil bones (Taylor 1984:24, 26–27). Taken together, this suggests the bones in Area E were exposed to animal gnawing for prolonged periods, whereas the gnawed bones in Area D were transferred into the lake while still relatively fresh, having only been partly gnawed by dogs and not yet gnawed by rats. This dumping of relatively fresh, partly gnawed dog bones, especially larger bones such as crania, pelves and mandibles, into the lake was more likely to have been initiated by humans than dogs and suggests some form of tidying of the site by its occupants. This process may also account for the relative excess of crania, mandibles and pelves in Area D, which is otherwise unexpected, given this area was protected from the taphonomic variables operating in Area E. Further proof the lake was used as a general rubbish dump is highlighted by the presence of numerous ungnawed whole dog elements in Area D, which must have been discarded while relatively fresh and perhaps still covered in soft tissues, and by the discovery of multiple bones from the same individual in one place, which was never identified in Area E. For example, the body of a virtually entire albatross, minus the wings, was found in the lake, as were eight long bones from a single immature dog.

A further factor which probably dictated both bone survival and the potential for recovery during archaeological excavations was bone size. Small bones generally survive destructive processes such as weathering and animal gnawing less well than large bones. Archaeological recovery techniques can compound this issue, and this could be relevant at Kohika where only selected parts of the deposit were sieved. Together, these two factors were probably at least partly responsible for the poor representation of smaller dog bones such as vertebrae, ribs and the small bones of the distal limbs.

In summary, there is no doubt taphonomic variables including animal gnawing, weathering, bone density, bone size and archaeological recovery techniques had a profound influence on the make up of the dog-bone remains in the drier parts of Kohika, as represented by Area E. Some of these factors are particularly well highlighted by comparing the dog assemblage in Area E with the wetland assemblage from Area D. Furthermore, it is likely these taphonomic processes are a significant part of the reason why dog mandibles were found so much more frequently than any other element in Area E. In contrast, the bones in Area D were in a protected environment, and weathering, animal gnawing, bone density and bone size were less relevant to the make up of this assemblage. Instead, it is likely that human bone dumping and tidying practices determined the survival of dog remains in this part of Kohika.

Conclusion

The large dog-bone assemblage from the late 17th century Maori lake village of Kohika provides a unique opportunity to compare the taphonomic processes affecting bones deposited in anaerobic wetland and aerobic dry-land environments. About half the dog bones recovered from

Kohika between 2005 and 2007 came from an area that would have been located within the lake and outside the village palisade during occupation of the site. Most of these bones tended to be well preserved and were frequently completely intact, even if small and from immature dogs. Some elements, such as crania, pelves, scapulae, ribs and non-cervical vertebrae, were almost exclusively found in this part of the site. The remainder of the dog-bone assemblage came from inside the village palisade and was deposited in a dry and often sandy environment where the bones were exposed to weathering, human modification and prolonged dog and rat gnawing. Mandibles dominated this dry-land assemblage, which probably reflects the greater density of these elements compared with other dog bones and their relative resistance to weathering and dog gnawing. However, the preferential selection of certain bones, such as mandibles and radii, for tool manufacture may have also contributed to the greater frequency of these bones in the dry-land areas. Other bones, such as the remaining long bones, crania and most of the bones of the trunk, were infrequent in this part of the site, and this was most likely because they had been heavily reduced by gnawing and weathering, rather than because dog carcasses were being routinely moved from the village. Overall, the Kohika dog bones highlight the importance of considering taphonomy when assessing faunal remains, and moreover, the dry-land assemblage suggests taphonomic variables are likely to account for many of the discrepancies in dog body-part representation in other dry-land New Zealand archaeological sites.

Acknowledgements

We are grateful for assistance from the landowners and farmers Dennis and Mary Sax and Cees Bruyn, and support from Ngati Awa, Te Whare Wanaga Awanuiarangi, the Whakatane and District Historical Society, and the Whakatane Museum and Gallery. Research funds were provided by the Marsden Fund.

References

Allen, M. and L. Nagaoka 2004. In the footsteps of Von Haast "… the discoveries something grand": the emergence of zooarchaeology in New Zealand. In L. Furey and S. Holdaway (eds), *Change Through Time: 50 years of New Zealand Archaeology*, pp. 193–214. Auckland: New Zealand Archaeological Association,.

Allo, J. 1970. The Maori dog: a study of the Polynesian dog of New Zealand. Unpublished MA, University of Auckland.

Anderson, A., T. Worthy and R. McGovern-Wilson 1996. Moa remains and taphonomy. In A. Anderson, B. Allingham and I. Smith (eds), *Shag River mouth: the archaeology of an early Southern Maori village*, pp. 200–213. Canberra: ANH publications, Australian National University.

Behrensmeyer, A. 1978. Taphonomic and ecologic information from bone weathering. *Paleobiology* 4:150–162.

Binford, L. 1981. *Bones: ancient men and modern myths*. New York: Academic Press.

Clark, G. 1995. The kuri in prehistory: a skeletal analysis of the extinct Maori dog. Unpublished MA, University of Otago.

Clark, G. 1997. Maori subsistence change: zooarchaeological evidence from the prehistoric dog of New Zealand. *Asian Perspectives*, 36:200–219.

Furey, L. 1996 Oruarangi: *the archaeology and material culture of a Hauraki pa*. Auckland: Auckland Institute and Museum.

Irwin, G. 2004a. Kohika as a late northern Maori lake village. In G. Irwin (ed), *Kohika: the archaeology of la late Maori lake village*, pp. 239–248. Auckland: Auckland University Press.

Irwin, G. 2004b. Excavations and site history at Kohika. In G. Irwin (ed), *Kohika: the archaeology of a late Maori lake village*, pp. 45–75. Auckland: Auckland University Press.

Irwin, G., R. Nichol, M. Taylor, T. Worthy and I. Smith 2004. Faunal remains from Kohika. In G. Irwin (ed), *Kohika: the archaeology of a late Maori lake village*, pp. 198–216. Auckland: Auckland University Press.

Lyman, R. 1987. Archaeofaunas and butchery studies: a taphonomic perspective. *Advances in Archaeological Method and Theory* 10:249–337.

Smith, I. 1981. Mammalian fauna from an Archaic site on Motutapu Island, New Zealand. *Records of the Auckland Institute and Museum*, 18:95–105.

Smith, I. 1996. The mammal remains. In A. Anderson, B. Allingham and I. Smith (eds), *Shag River mouth: the archaeology of an early Southern Maori village*, pp. 185–199. Canberra: ANH publications, Australian National University.

Taylor, M. 1984. Bone refuse from Twilight Beach. Unpublished MA, University of Auckland.

30

Taphonomic analysis of the Twilight Beach seals

Lisa Nagaoka
Department of Geography, University of North Texas, USA
lnagaoka@unt.edu

Steve Wolverton
Department of Geography, University of North Texas, USA

Ben Fullerton
Department of Geography, University of North Texas, USA

Introduction

Taphonomic studies have become an integral part of zooarchaeological research over the past 30 years. Understanding the processes that led to the samples of animal remains found in archaeological sites is crucial for evaluating the validity of interpretations of these datasets (Klein and Cruz-Uribe 1984; Lyman 1994a). It is important to recognise that taphonomic analysis, 'as the science of the laws of embedding or burial' (Lyman 1994a:1), is not done for its own sake, but to solve problems in zooarchaeological research (e.g. Gifford-Gonzalez 1991; Lyman 1994a; Stiner 2005). The purpose of this paper is to highlight the importance of taphonomic analyses, and provide an example of a detailed taphonomic analysis of a fauna – the Twilight Beach fauna – related to particular research questions in New Zealand.

One of the earliest taphonomic studies in New Zealand was Michael Taylor's (1982) work on the Twilight Beach fauna. Since then, taphonomic and zooarchaeological methodology has changed considerably. For example, detailed syntheses of quantitative methods in zooarchaeology have been published (Grayson 1984; Lyman 1994b, 2008). As important experimental studies of carnivore ravaging of bone assemblages have been undertaken (Marean and Spencer 1991; Marean et al. 1992), density-related preservation and destruction of bone has been studied extensively (Lyman 1994a; Lam et al. 2003; see also Darwent and Lyman 2002), the effects of differential recovery of remains on zooarchaeological analyses are better understood (Shaffer 1992; Gordon 1993; Shaffer and Sanchez 1994; Nagaoka 1994, 2005a), and fragmentation has been explored as a proxy of several taphonomic processes, including the use of within-bone nutrients (marrow and grease) by humans (Marean and Kim 1998; Wolverton 2002; Munro and Bar-Oz 2005; Nagaoka 2005b, 2006). In addition, comprehensive syntheses on taphonomy have been published (e.g. Lyman 1994a; Fisher 1995). Finally, extensive analyses that incorporate taphonomy in subsistence zooarchaeology are becoming more commonplace (e.g. Broughton 1999; Munro 2004; Stiner 1994, 2005).

Taphonomic analyses are somewhat under-utilised in Pacific Island archaeology, and there is ample room for expanding their depth and breadth in New Zealand. The most important goal of taphonomic analysis is to evaluate the suitability of faunal samples for answering particular research questions. Taphonomic analysis helps answer the question: 'Are we studying what we think we are studying?' We use our re-analysis of the Twilight Beach seal assemblage to illustrate how this question can be addressed. Although a taphonomic study of the Twilight Beach sample was done previously (Taylor 1982), the research was primarily descriptive and methodological and did not focus on particular archaeological or ecological research questions.

Taphonomic analysis in practice often lacks a theoretical perspective (but see Lyman 1994a), and our opinion is that failure to use conceptual guide posts has produced variability in what it means to assess a zooarchaeological assemblage taphonomically (compare Marean and Kim 1998 and Pickering *et al.* 2003 to Stiner 2002). George Gaylord Simpson's (1963) distinction between immanent and configurational properties of phenomena in the historical sciences is deeply relevant to studies that incorporate taphonomic analysis (Lyman 1994a). The two concepts, immanence and configuration, provide structure and direct goals for taphonomy in zooarchaeology. Simpson (1963:24–25) defines the two properties in the following manner:

> The unchanging properties of matter and energy [for example, those of chemistry, physics, and mechanics] and the likewise unchanging processes and principles arising therefrom are *immanent* in the material universe. They are nonhistorical, even though they occur and act in the course of history. The actual state of the universe or of any part of it at a given time, its configuration, is not immanent and is constantly changing. It is *contingent* ... or *configurational* ... History may be defined as configurational change through time.

Immanent properties are those that are the same in all places and times, and for which we can derive 'law-like' statements. For example, the taphonomic effect of bone struck with a certain amount of force in a particular direction will be the same whether the taphonomic agent is a bison trampling the bone, or a human flaking the bone, or a river rock striking the bone during saltation. The physics of flaking bones (or stones) is unchanging across time and space. On the other hand, configurational properties are contingent on historical circumstances. In other words, they are unique to a particular situation. For example, each faunal assemblage will have its own taphonomic history that is configurational (unique because of the specific circumstances in which the assemblage was created, preserved and recovered). Often in taphonomic studies we record the magnitude or severity with which immanent properties occur in order to document configurational properties. For example, burning is an immanent property because it produces a specific pattern on bone that is different from other taphonomic processes. When we record the degree of burning on bone, we are examining the configurational properties of burning for a bone or an assemblage. We are unable to derive laws about what temperature the different categories of burning represent, except in only the broadest sense (e.g. calcined bone; Lyman 1994a:386).

This distinction between immanent and configurational properties is important because only immanent properties hold to the uniformitarian principles we tout as the basis for taphonomy. When we confuse configurational properties for immanent ones, we are saying that the magnitude and pattern of taphonomic damage on bone caused by a particular taphonomic agent should be the same across time and space, which clearly is not the case, despite statements to the contrary (e.g. Marean and Cleghorn 2003 in reference to laws of carnivore damage). In addition, it is important to recognise that studying taphonomic configurational properties provides us with the taphonomic history of an assemblage, which is crucial for evaluating the ability of faunal data to address particular research questions. That configurational history of change (or lack thereof) will include spatio-temporal contingencies in which destructive or preservational processes occurred.

In this study, we provide documentation of the taphonomic configuration of the Twilight Beach fur-seal faunal assemblage to determine whether or not the fauna can be used to adequately address questions related to prehistoric exploitation and prehistoric biogeographic distribution of seals.

This study is designed to examine destructive agents, such as carnivore damage, butchery, weathering, and other processes that influence survival of skeletal parts, and how they affect data used to address larger-scale research questions regarding exploitation of seal carcasses and demographic patterns of seals exploited. For example, recent studies of carcass exploitation highlight that density-mediated attrition, element fragmentation and diagenetic processes can radically alter assemblages (Lyman 1994a; Stiner *et al.* 1995, 2005). Thus, it is necessary to evaluate the taphonomic history of the assemblage and how it has impacted skeletal element representation and bone fragmentation, both of which are variables used to understand carcass exploitation. In addition, the demographic data gathered from the seal remains will be used to determine whether seals were being exploited from haul outs and/or rookeries in the far northern reaches of New Zealand. The taphonomic analysis is important here because it can determine whether or not low-density, easily destroyed pup remains are under-represented by evaluating the destructive formation processes (see Schiffer 1987; see also Wolverton 2001, 2006) important in the fauna accumulation history at the site. Understanding the demographic profile represented in the assemblage can help inform seal conservation efforts that use past breeding distributions to model future trends (e.g. Bradshaw *et al.* 2000, 2002).

Twilight Beach

The Twilight Beach site is located on the northwestern tip of the North Island of New Zealand (Figure 1). This peninsula of land is flanked by the Pacific Ocean to the east and the Tasman Sea to the west. The region is composed of a sequence of sand dunes that have formed within the past 50,000 years (Taylor 1982). Before human occupation, these sand dunes were covered by light vegetation, which acted to stabilise the sediment and minimise erosion. According to wood, pollen and charcoal data, the region was covered by mixed podocarp-broadleaf forest and scrub before and during initial occupation at Twilight Beach (Taylor 1982). The site was occupied during the early period of human colonisation at about 1005 BP (NZ6579 in Coster 1989:56).

After deposition and burial of the Twilight Beach site, the far north region of New Zealand was stripped bare of vegetation as a result of widespread burning by early Polynesian settlers. The effect of this widespread burning and the associated decrease in vegetation was to expose the sand dunes to long-term wind erosion, which continued

Figure 1. The location of the Twilight Beach site (N1+2/976).

until the site was excavated. This wind erosion resulted in the exposure and movement of parts of the Twilight Beach deposits, which covered an area of 6 m by 1.5 m, with a depth of more than 1 m. The southeastern slope was littered with eroded shell debris and some of the deposits were observed falling down the steep northern slope when the site was discovered. Atop the pinnacle of the sand dune was the consolidated portion of the shell midden that could be observed only from the eastern slope.

When it was recognised that the site would be destroyed by ongoing erosion, it was decided it should be investigated (Taylor 1982). The remaining intact deposits were removed in 25 cm by 25 cm by 5 cm slices and about 80 percent of the eroded midden debris covering the surface of the southeastern slope was collected. All matrix recovered was returned to the University of Auckland, where it was screened through nested sieves of 4 mm, 2 mm and 0.5 mm.

The stratigraphy of the site is characterised by five main layers. Level 5, at the base of the deposits, is a weathered Pleistocene sand layer devoid of cultural materials. This layer was not included in the excavated portions. Above this was a yellow dune-sand layer about 1 m thick that included some charcoal and shell bioturbated from preceding layers. This layer contained a nearly complete moa skeleton, but the skeleton was not fully excavated. Layer 3 formed the bulk of the deposit and it varied in composition across the site. At the northern end of the site, Layer 3 was characterised by charcoal-stained sediment with sparse cultural deposits. At the southern end, Layer 3 was characterised by a dense matrix of shell, bone and other artefacts. Layer 2 was composed of compact yellow-grey sand and contained very few cultural remains. Finally, Layer 1, at the top of the site, was composed of a thin, black topsoil with sparse vegetation.

The site produced a large assemblage of animal remains, including remains of shellfish, fish, birds, dogs, seals and cetaceans. Taylor (1982) examined all taxa except the bird sample, which has never been fully analysed. The assemblage has been important in many other faunal studies. The dog remains were used as part of Clark's (1995, 1997a, 1997b) comprehensive morphometric analysis of kuri in New Zealand. The assemblage was also used as part of larger studies examining fish exploitation in the region (Nichol 1988; Leach *et al.* 1997), which documented a dominance of snapper (*Pagrus auratus*). Taylor's analysis concentrated mainly on the mammal assemblage, particularly on the seals. Like Taylor's work, our analysis focused on the Twilight Beach fur-seal assemblage. We chose to emphasise fur seals because our larger research questions deal with fur-seal exploitation and because fur seals are the most abundant mammalian taxon, with 2880 identified specimens (NISP), and an MNI of 67 (Taylor (1982). Thus, the fur-seal assemblage is ideal for examining how taphonomic processes can affect faunal data sets.

Taphonomic analysis

The Twilight Beach seal assemblage was examined for taphonomic factors that could be relevant to carcass exploitation and mortality analysis. Specifically, we examined differential fragmentation, fragmentation patterns, carnivore damage, weathering, burning and cut marks. These taphonomic factors were documented across skeletal elements and body parts (in the manner of Stiner 1994, 2002) to determine whether particular skeletal parts were differentially affected, and if so, why.

Differential attrition of skeletal parts

While researchers have long recognised that bone mineral density is likely to be an important factor in skeletal element representation (Guthrie 1967; Brain 1969), Lyman (1984) was the first to evaluate this assumption quantitatively. He used photon-densitometry to estimate bone

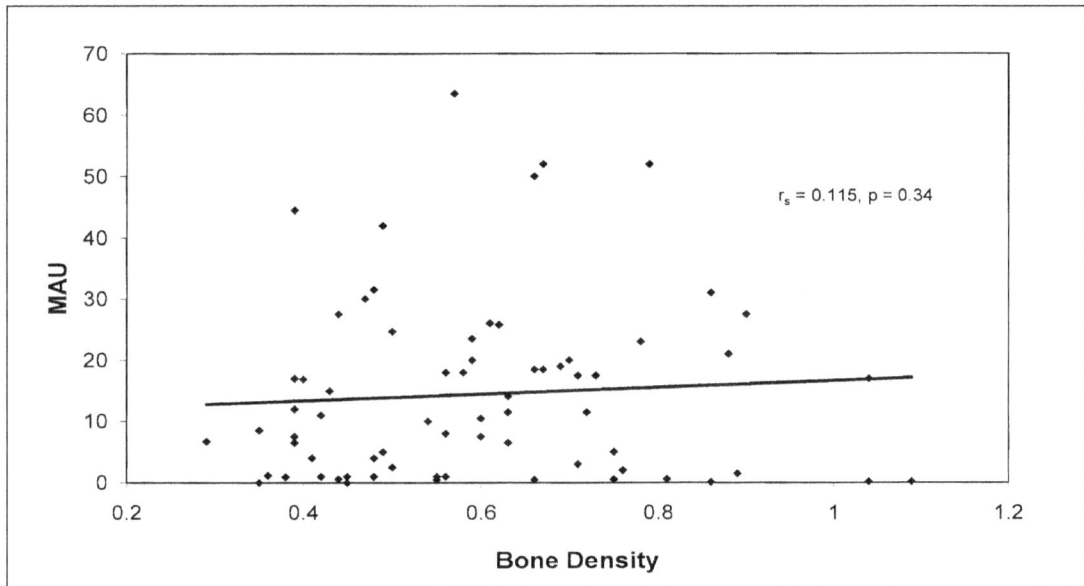

Figure 2. Correlation analysis between bone mineral density and skeletal element representation (MAU) across individual scan sites for Twilight Beach fur-seal remains. The line provides a visual representation of the relationship.

density for several points or scan sites across each skeletal element. Since then, bone-density values for several different vertebrate taxa have been generated (Chambers 1992; Kreutzer 1992; Lyman *et al.* 1992; Butler and Chatters 1994; Hindelang and Ann 1997; Lam *et al.* 1999; Pavao and Stahl 1999; Stahl 1999; Dirrigl 2001; Pickering and Carlson 2002; Cruz and Elkins 2003; Ioannidou 2003; Izeta 2005; Novecosky and Popkin 2005), using different techniques (Lam *et al.* 1998, 2003; Symmons 2004). It has become common practice to assess whether differential attrition of skeletal parts has played a role in the formation of the faunal assemblage.

To determine whether elemental representation of the Twilight Beach fur-seal assemblage has been affected by differential attrition, minimal animal unit (MAU, Binford 1984) by scan site was compared with bone density per scan site (Lyman 1994a). The analysis shows there is no significant correlation nor visual relationship between fur-seal skeletal-element representation at Twilight Beach and seal bone density (Figure 2). Therefore, the assemblage as a whole does not appear to be affected by density-mediated attrition. In other words, overall, denser portions of skeletal elements are not significantly over-represented and less dense portions are not significantly under-represented.

Fragmentation analysis methods

Analysis of skeletal-element fragmentation has become important for determining how elements have been modified through either cultural or natural processes. In general, the more fragmented an assemblage, the more likely that one or more taphonomic processes have been at work on the elements in the assemblage. While there are numerous ways to measure fragmentation (Marean and Spencer 1991; Lyman 1994a), it is important to make the distinction between measuring the extent and the intensity of fragmentation (Lyman 1994a, 1994c; Wolverton 2002). Extent of fragmentation refers to the proportion of broken elements in an assemblage. Fragmentation extent is often determined using the percentage of whole elements (% whole) (Todd and Rapson 1988; Lyman 1994b; Wolverton 2002). An assemblage with very few whole elements has a greater extent of fragmentation than one comprised mainly of complete elements. Fragmentation intensity, on the other hand, examines the degree to which an element is fragmented. Several different measures have been used to document intensity of fragmentation. Since an element that is more fragmented has a greater number of fragments and those fragments are smaller, measures of intensity have examined both fragment numbers and fragment size (e.g. Marean and Spencer 1991; Lyman 1994b; Wolverton 2002; Outram 2004; Stiner et al. 2005; Nagaoka 2006).

For this study, we used several measures of fragmentation intensity, including the ratio of NISP to MNE (NISP:MNE), the average percent of total scan sites represented per specimen (shortened to 'average percent scan site'), and the average fragment size. NISP:MNE is a measure commonly used to indicate fragment number (Lyman 1994a, c). It takes the total number of specimens identified to a particular element (NISP) and divides that value by the minimum number of elements calculated, based on the most common portion of the element represented. NISP:MNE answers the question: 'Of the elements (MNE) represented in an assemblage, how many specimens (NISP) occur?' In this analysis, we recorded portions of elements by documenting the bone density scan sites represented (Chambers 1992, Lyman 1994a). The value for the most common scan site is the MNE.

Another measure of fragmentation records the zones or portions of an element represented by a specimen (Todd and Rapson 1988), to estimate fragment size. For this assemblage, we used the average percent scan site. For each specimen, the bone density scan sites represented are recorded. The number of scan sites recorded is then divided by the total possible number of scan sites for that element. For example, the humerus has five scan sites. If a humerus specimen has two of the five scan sites present, then that specimen represents 40 percent of that element. The values for all humerus specimens are then averaged to get the average percent scan site for that element in an assemblage.

One limitation of this measure is that the minimum fragment size is determined by the number of scan sites. That is, scan-site coverage is relative to particular elements, and the more scan sites an element has, the smaller a fragment can be. For humeri, the minimum fragment size is 20 percent, since there are five scan sites for this element. If the number of scan sites for an element is three, the minimum size is 33.3 percent; if it is 10, the minimum size is 10 percent. Thus, the lower threshold of this measure varies across skeletal elements. As a result, the measure may not be appropriate for highly fragmented assemblages. On the other hand, this problem may be mitigated by the fact that as fragment size decreases, there is a corresponding decline in identifiability (Marshall and Pilgram 1991; Lyman 1994a; Wolverton 2002). If the minimum identifiable size range corresponds to the minimum scan site percentage, this may not be a problem. Further, average percent scan site can be scaled across elements such that the lowest common scan-site coverage is used, and if data are treated at ordinal scale, fragmentation can then be described as low, medium or high intensity.

Our final measure of fragmentation is an absolute measure. Each specimen was measured with a digital caliper to the nearest 0.01 mm to obtain the length of the maximum dimension of each fragment (as in Stiner et al. 2005). For this assemblage, we measured the maximum fragment length for just a few elements (humerus, radius, ulna, femur) as an experiment, to evaluate the utility of this method for New Zealand seal assemblages. The measurements of fragmented specimens for each skeletal element were then averaged.

Fragmentation analysis results

For the Twilight Beach seal assemblage, the extent of fragmentation is high. Only 1.3 percent of the seal remains are complete (Table 1). For most elements, none of the specimens are complete (Figure 3). There are no whole crania, vertebrae, scapulae, radii, innominates, nor tibiae. Fragmentation is least extensive for the lower limb bones. About 30 percent of metapodials

Table 1. Occurrence of taphonomic processes on the Twilight Beach seal assemblage.

Taphonomic process	Assemblage total
Extent of fragmentation (% Whole)	1.3
Intensity of fragmentation (NISP:MNE)	2.9
Weathering (% NISP)	13.6
Carnivore damage (% NISP)	9.0
Rodent gnawing (% NISP)	0.3
Cut marks (% NISP)	3.2
Burning (% NISP)	4.2

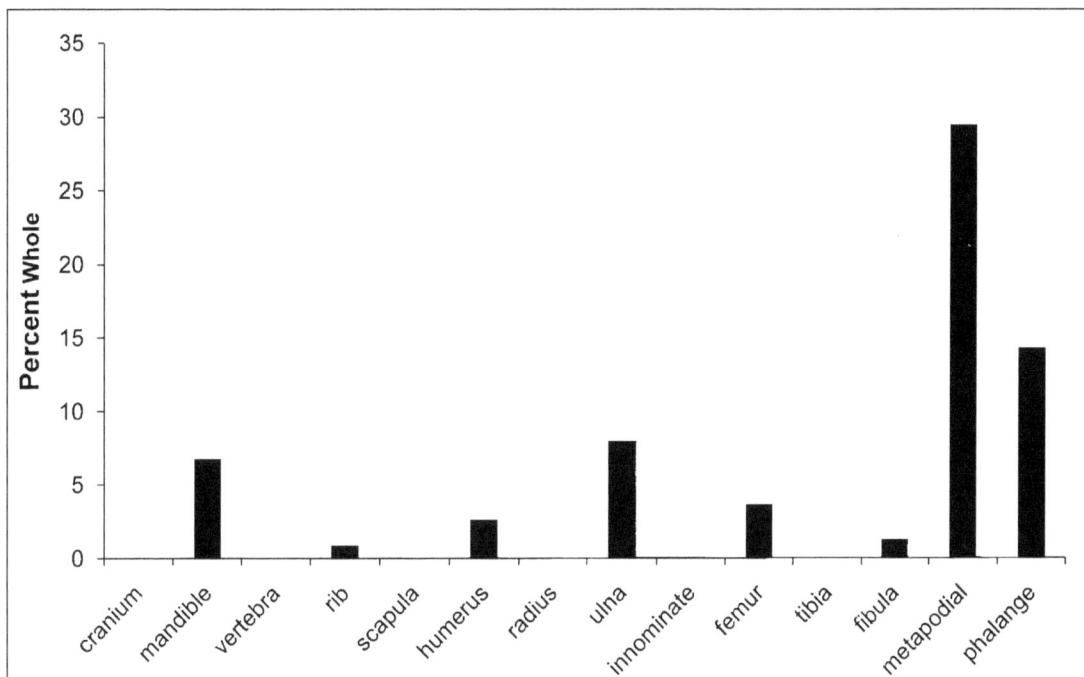

Figure 3. Percentage of whole elements.

and 15 percent of phalanges are complete. Often the percentage of whole long bones is low in studies that focus on terrestrial mammals because these elements are fractured for marrow extraction (Munro and Bar-Oz 2005). However, seals do not have large marrow cavities in their long bones, like terrestrial mammals. The paucity of whole long bones at Twilight Beach more likely reflects the predominance of unfused juvenile specimens. Very few of the ends of long-bone elements that are present are fused. Further, those elements that exhibit a relatively high percentage of whole bones tend to be from flippers (metapodial phalanges), the structure of which may have offered some protection from fragmentation processes (e.g. human fracturing for within-bone nutrients).

Although most specimens are fragmented (low %whole), the intensity of fragmentation is relatively low for all measures. For NISP:MNE, the fragmentation rate across elements is about two fragments or fewer per element (Figure 4). Most elements have an average percent scan site that falls between 30 percent and 60 percent (Table 2, Figure 5), supporting the NISP:MNE results and the interpretation that elements are fragmented into only two or three pieces. In fact,

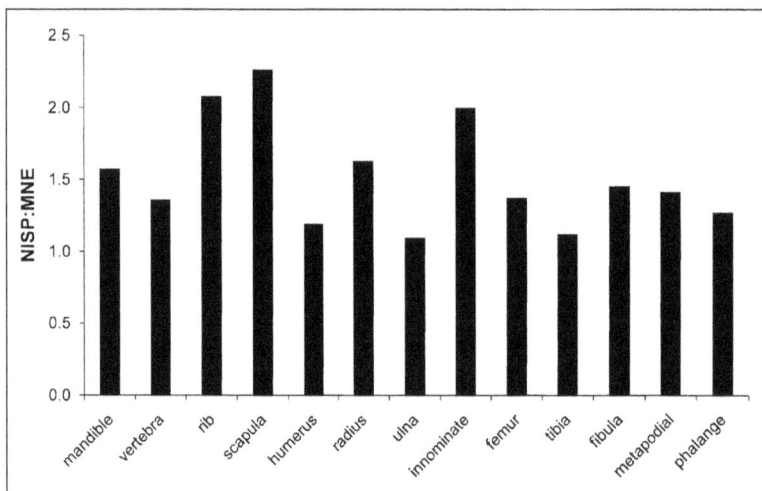

Figure 4. Ratio of specimen fragments (NISP) to the minimum number of elements (MNE).

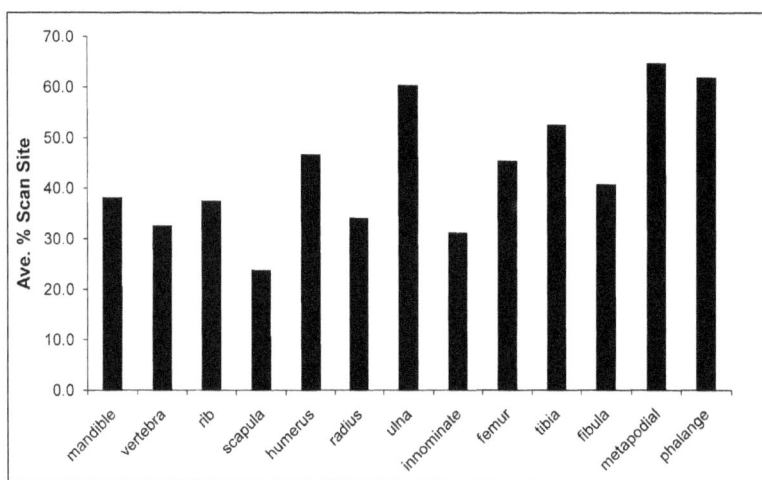

Figure 5. Average percent scan site across elements.

Table 2. Number of scan sites and the average percent scan site for each element.

Element	Nunber of scan sites	Average % scan site
Mandible	6	38.2
Vertebrae	3	32.7
Rib	5	29.3
Scapula	8	23.9
Humerus	5	46.8
Radius	5	34.2
Ulna	4	60.4
Innominate	7	31.3
Femur	6	45.5
Tibia	5	52.6
Fibula	5	40.8
Metapodial	3	64.7
Phalange	3	61.9

when the two measures are compared with one another, there is a negative correlation (Figure 6, rs= -0.89, p <0.001). As expected, the larger the fragment, as represented by increasing average percent scan site values, the fewer the fragments, as seen in the lower NISP:MNE values.

Average scan site data can be directly compared with NISP:MNE by calculating the expected number of fragments, based on the scan sites represented. For example, the humerus has five scan sites; dividing 100 percent by the average percent scan site of 46.8 percent gives an expected number of fragments per humerus (expected NISP:MNE) of 2.14. This can be compared with the actual NISP:MNE per element from the assemblage to determine how well average percent scan site measures fragmentation intensity. When the actual NISP:MNE values are compared with the values derived from the scan-site information, the scan-site data consistently overestimate fragmentation relative to NISP:MNE (Figure 7). It is likely the overestimation of fragment size is because the average scan site is constrained by the number of scan sites, as discussed earlier. A more detailed evaluation will require analysis of fragment size metrically on fragments of specimens from same-age/sex individuals, which we are unable to do using the Twilight Beach fauna. What is important here is that NISP:MNE and average percent scan site positively correlate, indicating that both measure fragmentation size/intensity at ordinal scale.

Fragment size for humeri, ulnae, radii and femora specimens were measured in their longest dimension to the nearest 0.01 mm to provide another reference point for the intensity of fragmentation (Lyman and O'Brien 1987; Outram 2001). Figure 8 shows the frequency distribution of the size data across elements. The graphs for the humeri, ulnae, radii and femora show a unimodal distribution of fragment size, indicating that in this assemblage, most long-bone fragments are medium in size, with some small and a few large. In general, few large fragments can indicate that %whole is low; however, few small fragments reflects either that there truly is a low representation of small fragments or that an identifiability threshold exists in a highly fragmented assemblage. If the latter is the case, then below a certain fragment size, specimens become unidentifiable to element (e.g. Marshall and Pilgram 1991; see also Marean and Kim 1998). For Twilight Beach, NISP:MNE is low, indicating low fragmentation intensity, which supports the conclusion that small fragments are rare in the assemblage and the distributions of fragment size are not related to identifiability. Further, the distribution for radii is bimodal; the mode at the lower end represents proximal epiphyses, which comprise about one-third of the sample of radii. This pattern suggests that

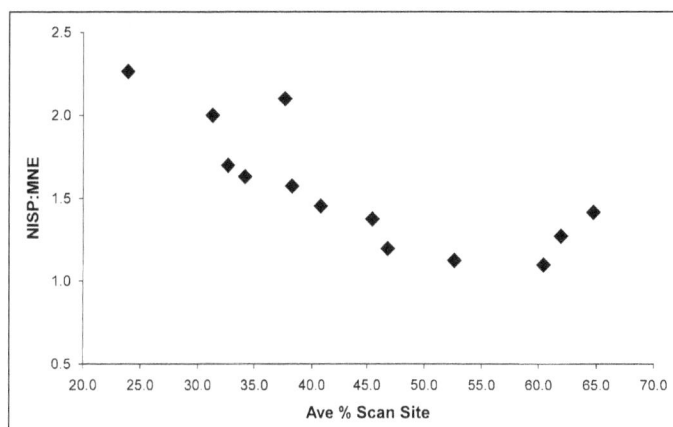

Figure 6. Scatter plot between average percent scan site and NISP:MNE.

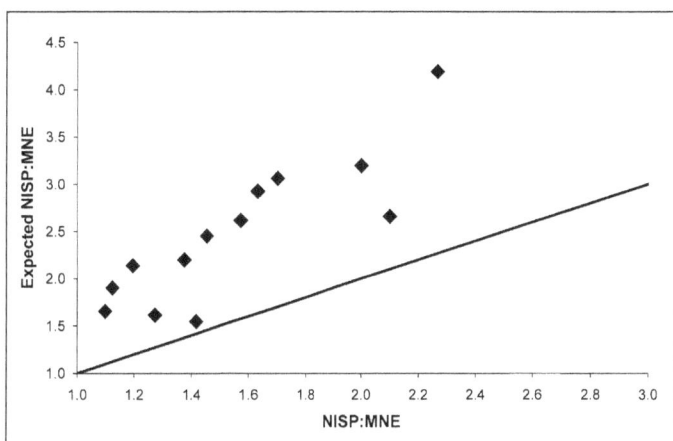

Figure 7. Comparison of expected NISP:MNE as measured by average percent scan site and the actual NISP:MNE values. The line represents the expected values if scan-site data accurately estimate the NISP:MNE value.

Table 3. Modern size range elements and the average fragment size of the Twilight Beach seal remains.

Element	Size range (mm)	Average fragment size (mm)	Average % scan site
Humerus	67-150+	64.6	46.8%
Radius	71-152	47.7	34.2%
Femur	38-95	43.4	45.5%
Ulna	na	82.9	60.4%

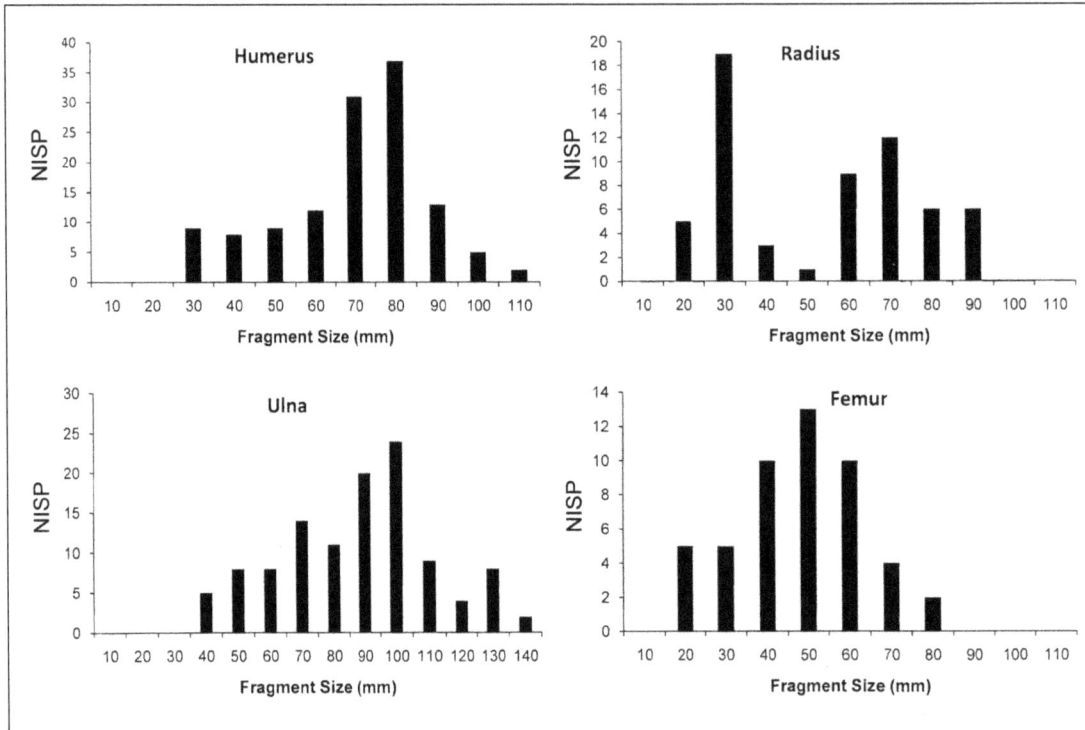

Figure 8. Frequency graphs of fragment size for several long-bone elements.

even when small portions – in this case unfused epiphyses – are present, they are identifiable.

Average percent scan site is theoretically an approximation of fragment size; in order to evaluate this relationship empirically, fragment-size measurements are compared with the scan-site data (Table 3). The size range for each skeletal element varies considerably because fur seals grow until they are six to 10 years old, depending on the sex. Thus, the lower end of the range represents pups, while the upper end is adult males. As a result, it is not possible to convert the fragment-size data into the proportion of the element that is represented. However, at ordinal scale, the two measures appear to be comparable. The element with the largest average fragment size is the ulna and it is also the element with the greatest average percent scan site represented. A sample of fragment-size data across a larger range of elements is needed to fully understand how well percent scan site reflects fragment size for fur seals. While determining how these measurements of fragmentation relate to one another is tentative for this sample, they are very useful as ordinal scale measures when making comparisons across assemblages.

Weathering

Weathering is a taphonomic process that occurs when bone is left exposed on the surface. The bone often becomes bleached and cracked. Behrensmeyer (1978) developed several weathering stages that focused mainly on the physical breakdown of bone in the form of cracking. For this analysis, however, we recorded only the presence or absence of cracking or bleaching. Weathering was the most common taphonomic process represented in the seal assemblage, with more than 13 percent of the bones showing signs (Table 1). Most specimens were not highly weathered (Figure 9), and probably fall into Stage 1 of Behrensmeyer's (1978) weathering stages. Weathered bones should be expected, given that the faunal material was eroding out of the dunes. In fact, the provenance of the weathered bone is telling; a significant percentage comes from the surface contexts (Table 4). Thus, most of the weathering probably occurred recently. The low weathering percentage for bones from non-surface contexts supports Taylor's

Table 4. Number of weathered specimens and the percentage of those weathered specimens found in surface contexts.

Element	# weathered specimens	% specimens surface recovered
Cranium	5	60.0
Mandible	15	53.3
Vertebrae	7	100.0
Ribs	426	47.7
Scapula	6	100.0
Humerus	14	92.9
Radius	8	75.0
Ulna	12	66.7
Innominate	1	100.0
Femur	4	100.0
Tibia	5	100.0
Metapodial	3	100.0
Phalange	1	0.0

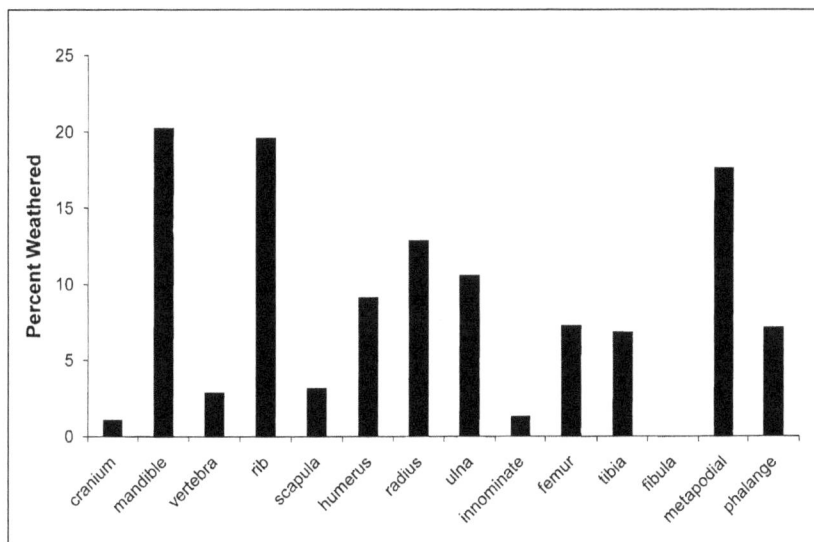

Figure 9. Percentage of weathered specimens across elements.

(1982:199) interpretation that the site was formed as a result of rapid deposition. For purposes of this general taphonomic study, the fact that the weathering is light and only occurs on a small proportion of the assemblage indicates it was not an important destructive agent that would have removed low-density skeletal parts in the Twilight Beach fauna's accumulation history.

Animal damage

Animal damage includes rodent gnawing and carnivore gnawing. Only a small fraction of the seal bones exhibits any evidence of rodent gnawing (Table 1). In mild contrast, nine percent of the seal assemblage is carnivore gnawed. The elements displaying the most damage are the long bones, with about 50 percent or more of these elements exhibiting evidence of carnivore gnawing (Figure 10). Carnivore damage tends to occur on the ends of long bones because the proximal and distal ends contain more fat in cancellous bone, making them more attractive than shafts to carnivores (Marean and Spencer 1991; Marean and Kim 1998; Pickering *et al.* 2003). In addition, these ends tend to be less dense than shafts and thus are likely to be sensitive to any type of taphonomic agent. As a result, carnivore gnawing (and other processes) can differentially affect the sample of long-bone ends in faunal assemblages (Klein 1975; Marean and Kim 1998; Pickering *et al.* 2003).

To examine whether or not carnivore gnawing played a role in the attrition of long-bone ends, we analyse the proportional abundance of carnivore gnaw marks relative to the distribution of density between proximal and distal ends (as in Binford 1981). It is expected that the 'spongier' ends (Bunn 1986) – or lower-density ends (Lyman 1984) – are more susceptible to damage by carnivores. In addition, cancellous bone contains more grease, which may make epiphyseal ends more attractive to carnivores. As a result, we assume that dogs preferentially gnawed on low-density ends and thus those portions should exhibit a higher proportion of gnaw marks. Table 5 shows the density values for proximal and distal ends of seal long bones. As expected, the proximal ends of tibiae and the distal ends of radii, ulnae and metapodials are more frequently gnawed than the denser ends (Table 5). However, for humeri and femora, proximal and distal ends are evenly gnawed. In fact, of the long bones examined, more than 50 percent of the specimens for these two elements are carnivore-gnawed at both ends, supporting the even pattern of gnaw marks across these elements (Table 6). Femora still follow the less dense/more gnawed pattern, but the difference between the two ends is minimal. Even though the difference in density between proximal and distal ends of humeri is one of the largest for long bones in seals, the presence of gnaw marks in the Twilight Beach sample is the same for both ends. This indicates that in those cases in which carnivores gnawed on femora and humeri (roughly 50 percent), they showed no preference about which end.

To determine whether gnawing preference affects the presence of ends in the assemblage, we consider whether or not ends are under-represented compared with shafts, using a ratio of shafts to ends for long bones in the Twilight Beach assemblage (Table 7). MNEs for shafts and ends are tabulated using scan-site counts across portions. If ends and shafts are equally represented, then the ratio should be 0.5 (i.e. one shaft per two ends). As Table 7 shows, only metapodials have an even representation of shafts to ends. Radii and ulnae exhibit about three times as many shafts as expected, given the number of proximal and distal ends, while humeri, femora and tibiae have five to six times as many shafts as ends. Since skeletal-element fragmentation related to marrow extraction and other processes is minimal (see above), these data suggest a substantial proportion of proximal and distal long-bone ends have been lost to carnivore gnawing. The ends of humeri, femora and tibiae are larger and likely contain more fat than those of radii, ulnae and metapodials, making them more attractive to carnivores.

The distribution of carnivore gnawing across elements at Twilight Beach is not straightforward and highlights the need not to treat any particular taphonomic process simplistically. It is commonly stated that expectations regarding carnivore gnawing effects on long-bone ends are uniform across faunas in a 'law-like' (immanent) manner (Marean and Cleghorn 2003; Pickering

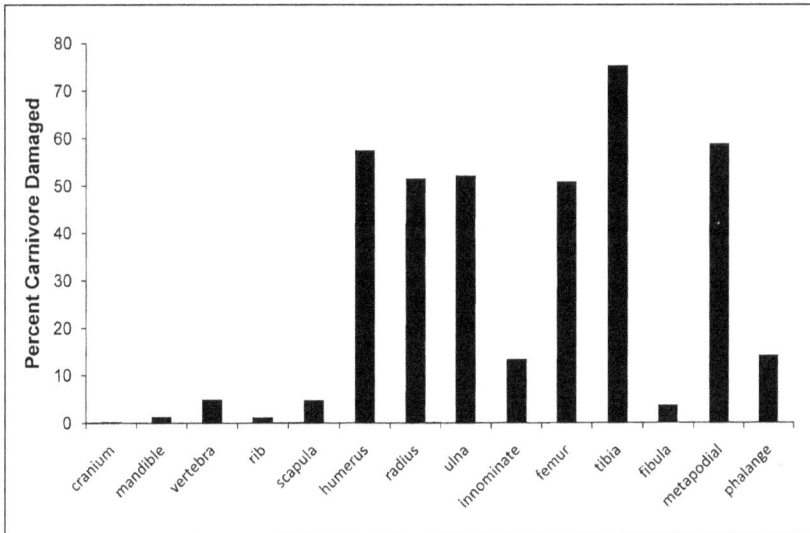

Figure 10. Percentage of carnivore- damaged specimens across elements.

Table 5. Distribution of carnivore gnaw marks across proximal and distal ends of the most commonly damaged limb elements, and the bone mineral densities for the proximal and distal ends of those elements (Chambers 1992). The underlined values are the ends that are less gnawed and those with higher bone densities.

Element	No. of gnawed Specimens	Percentage		Density	
		Proximal	Distal	Proximal	Distal
Humerus	88	77.3	77.3	0.43	0.60
Radius	32	40.6	87.5	0.63	0.45
Ulna	59	25.4	47.5	0.44	0.35
Femur	28	78.6	75.0	0.50	0.57
Tibia	55	85.5	56.4	0.39	0.48
Metapodial	10	40.0	80.0	no data	no data

Table 6. Percentage of carnivore-damaged long bones gnawed at both ends.

Element	% Carnivore gnaw marks at both ends
Humerus	54.5
Radius	28.1
Ulna	15.3
Femur	53.6
Tibia	41.8
Metapodial	20.0

Table 7. Proportion of long-bone shafts to proximal and distal ends.

Element	Shaft:Ends
Humerus	2.8
Radius	1.7
Ulna	1.5
Femur	3.1
Tibia	2.6
Metapodial	0.6

et al. 2003). Our study accentuates that taphonomic histories related to multiple processes need to be examined on an assemblage by assemblage basis, and the effects of any particular process are expected to be diverse across faunas, related to distinctive contingencies relevant to particular taphonomic histories (Lyman 1994a; Stiner 1994).

Cut marks

Cut marks have been an important part of taphonomic studies, particularly for research examining the question of hominid subsistence practices (e.g. Bunn 1981; Bunn and Kroll 1986; Lyman 1987). Research on cut marks has focused on identifying cut marks as distinguished from natural taphonomic effects (e.g. Olsen and Shipman 1988), documenting the distribution of cut marks across a carcass to reconstruct butchering patterns (e.g. Lupo and O'Connell 2002; Lyman 2005), and using the number or density of cut marks to indicate intensity of butchering (e.g. Abe *et al.* 2002; Egeland 2003). For example, in Taylor's (1982) original analysis of the Twilight Beach seals, he documented where cut marks tended to occur to reconstruct the butchery process. In other research, a high frequency of cut marks at different locations on the skeleton has been used to suggest that foragers were processing carcasses more intensively. However, recent experimental work has shown that the number of cut marks left on a bone is accidental and often does not correlate with the number of cutting strokes, nor butchering intensity (Egeland 2003). Thus, cut marks may best be used to indicate that butchering has occurred and to determine which elements were removed, or had meat removed from them.

For the Twilight Beach fur-seal assemblage, cut marks were found on fewer than five percent of the specimens. Most elements, except metapodials, exhibit some cut marks. Mandibles and humeri have the highest proportions of cut marks, followed by femora and phalanges (Figure 11). Since cut marks are left when muscle or elements are being removed from a carcass, they contribute to understanding carcass exploitation at the Twilight Beach site. For example, the cut marks on humeri are found mainly on the proximal end of the element, on muscle attachments such as the greater tuberosity, the lesser tuberosity and the deltoid ridge, suggesting either that meat was being removed from the shoulder area, or that humeri were being detached from scapulae. In contrast, lower forelimb elements have fewer cut marks, suggesting these portions were less commonly butchered. However, caution must be taken when using these data because sample sizes are relatively small. For most elements, the number of specimens with cut marks is fewer than 10. Thus, any patterns in cut-mark location may be products of sampling error, which may result in spurious conclusions. In addition, given the loss of long-bone ends to carnivore damage, cut marks that potentially occurred on these ends as a result of element disarticulation are missing.

Burning

Burning was recorded only as present or absent for the Twilight Beach seal assemblage; no attempt was made to record the degree or extent of burning. Only 4.2 percent of the fur-seal remains exhibit signs of burning. Most of the burning is found on the lower limbs, particularly the phalanges and metapodials (Figure 12). It is possible these elements were burned as anatomical units (that is, as whole flippers, rather than individual elements). Burned bone can be an indication of cooking; however, bone can also be burned incidentally as a result of other cultural or natural processes (Stiner *et al.* 2005). There are few ethnographic descriptions of how seals were cooked, and each seems to describe a different method (Anderson 1994; Smith 1996). Seal carcasses could have been butchered and cooked in underground ovens, or the meat could have been preserved in fat and stored in kelp bags, or they could have been smoked. So

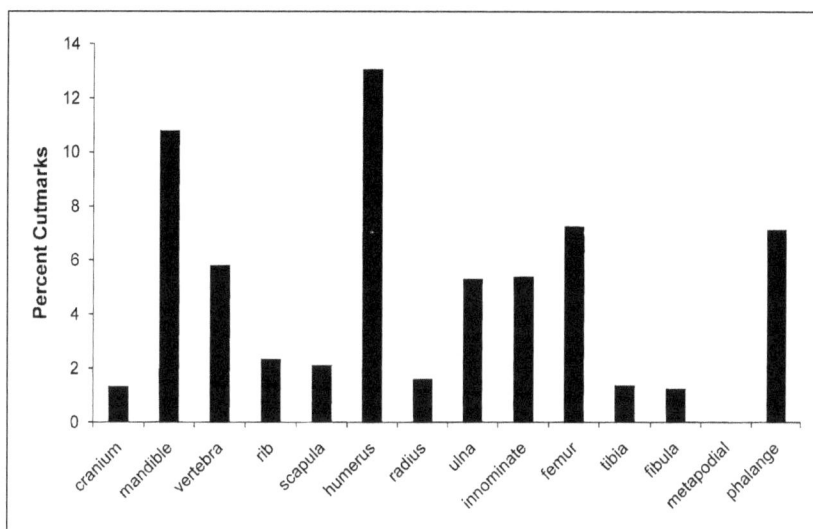

Figure 11. Percentage of specimens with cut marks across elements.

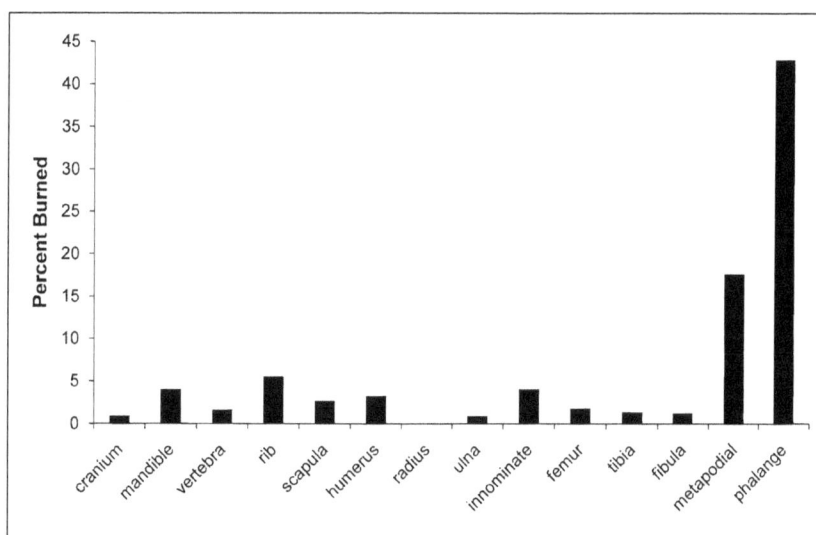

Figure 12. Percentage of burned specimens across elements.

it is unclear what to expect for cooked bone in New Zealand sites, particularly from early sites, where processing and cooking methods may have differed from those described historically. What we do know is there are no cut marks on metapodials and few on phalanges, so it does not appear that flippers were being disarticulated during butchery. There is a significant amount of carnivore damage on metapodials but not on phalanges, so dogs may have had differential access to them, or a preference for one over the other. However, like the cut-mark data, the frequency of burning is so low that caution must be taken when trying to extract patterns from the data and when relating those patterns to past human actions.

Summary

In general, the taphonomic history of the Twilight Beach fauna suggests that several processes had minimal effects on frequencies of skeletal parts represented. Low-density skeletal parts are as likely to be preserved as high-density ones, despite the carnivore gnawing on a small portion of the seal remains. Carnivore damage on long bones, however, indicates that in many cases ends were destroyed by gnawing, and this pattern tended to affect long bones with larger epiphyseal

Table 8. Values for seal food utility (FUI), skeletal element representation (%MAU) and percent carnivore damage for each element. Food utility data (FUI) from Savelle *et al.* (1996).

Element	FUI	%MAU	% Carnivore damage
Cranium/mandible	27.4	38.21	0.7
Cervical	35.9	10.73	7.6
Thoracic	24.9	3.66	4.2
Lumbar	32.9	0.97	9.1
Ribs	100.0	41.95	2.2
Scapula	19.8	68.29	7.1
Humerus	10.7	100.00	42.2
Radius/ulna	4.8	84.55	18.5
Innominate	44.5	30.08	12
Femur	4.5	32.52	17.9
Tibia/fibula	16.5	50.41	29.3
Flipper	5.0	1.63	37.5

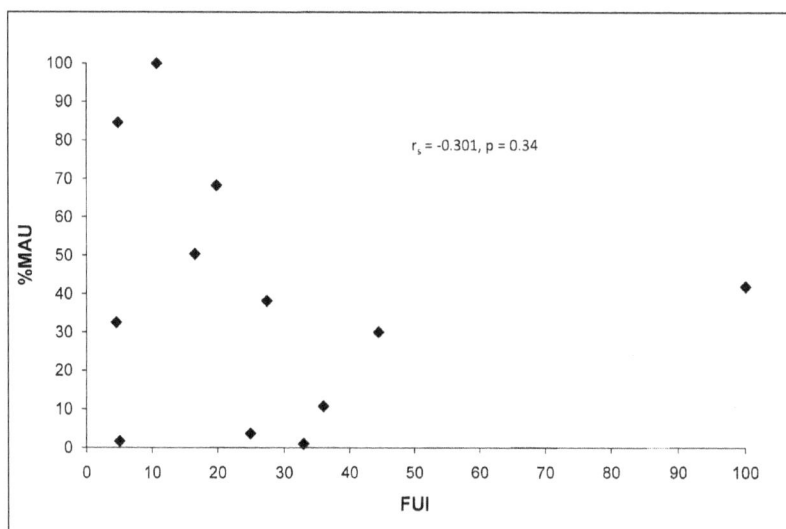

Figure 13. Scatter plot of the values for seal food utility (FUI) and skeletal element representation (%MAU) for each element.

ends. Carnivore gnawing, though one of the relatively important processes in the Twilight Beach fauna's taphonomic history, did not render long bones unidentifiable and thus had a minimal impact on skeletal part frequencies overall. Along similar lines, evidence of light weathering occurs on parts of the assemblage, but this indicates remains were rapidly buried, which is likely to have enhanced preservation. Burning and butchery are apparent in the assemblage, but probably simply reflect that the assemblage was cultural. However, the occurrence of either process is relatively low, thus study of their effects is limited in terms of detailed analysis of human behaviour.

Implications for subsistence and semographic interpretations

The ultimate goals of studying the Twilight Beach seal assemblage are to understand early seal-carcass exploitation and to determine the demographic profile of harvested seals. This taphonomic analysis has an impact on our ability to use the assemblage to address these questions.

Carcass exploitation

Foraging theory has been very useful in understanding the human decision-making process regarding carcass exploitation (e.g. O'Connell *et al.* 1988; Bartram 1993; Zeanah 2000; Lupo 2001; Cannon 2003). If foraging efficiency declined as a result of resource depression, the pattern of carcass exploitation would be expected to change. In particular, the kinds of skeletal elements found at archaeological sites are predicted to vary depending on their nutritional returns or 'utility' (Binford 1981; Metcalfe and Jones 1989). Elements transported to sites are affected by the transport costs involved (Cannon 2003; Nagaoka 2006). If transport distance and thus transport costs increase, then the mean utility or net returns of the skeletal elements transported should also increase. In other words, foragers will focus on transporting higher-utility elements when transport costs increase. However, in settings in which people exploited local resources and transport costs are low, a broader range of elements should have been taken back to the site, with declining foraging efficiency. That is, with low transport costs, it is advantageous to intensify carcass exploitation, with a decline in resource availability.

Analysis of carcass exploitation related to foraging efficiency relies on skeletal-part representation data. Thus, it is important to evaluate the taphonomic history of an assemblage to understand whether the patterns in skeletal-part frequencies are due to past butchery and transport practices or to taphonomic processes. For example, to examine whether carcass parts were being transported back to the site based on their nutritional value, we can compare the relative skeletal abundance (%MAU) of each element with its utility (FUI, Savelle *et al.* 1996). Analysis of the Twilight Beach fur-seal data shows that skeletal-element abundance is not correlated with food utility at an ordinal level (r_s = -0.301, p = 0.34; without outlier r_s = -0.409, p = 0.21). Thus, it appears that instead of transporting elements preferentially, based on nutritional returns, humans transported most parts of seal carcasses to the site (Figure 13, Table 8). Overall, the taphonomic history appears to have been minimally important in forming the assemblage. The bone-density analysis suggests the distribution of elements is not due to differential attrition of low-density parts. In addition, there is little weathering across the assemblage and the intensity of fragmentation is low. However, carnivore damage could have played a significant role in the preservation of skeletal elements.

To determine whether carnivore gnawing affected element abundances in the Twilight Beach seal assemblage, we compared carnivore damage with food utility across elements. There is a significant negative correlation between the percent of carnivore damage and FUI (Figure 14, r_s = -0.643, p=0.24; Table 8), suggesting that dogs (*Canis familiaris*) primarily had access to and were gnawing on relatively low-utility skeletal parts. Thus, in an analysis of carcass exploitation, low-utility elements may be under-represented, due to carnivore damage. However, our analysis of carnivore gnawing suggests that when dogs had access to long bones, they tended to destroy ends, and long bones were not sufficiently damaged to render them unidentifiable and analytically absent from the fauna. The low frequency of carnivore damage across the assemblage, the fact that most destructive damage occurred in long-bone ends, and the fact that end-damage did not render elements unidentifiable indicate the effect of carnivore damage on skeletal-part frequencies is limited.

Perhaps the most important taphonomic variable, fragmentation, relates to multiple processes. However, given that non-cultural processes appear to have only mildly affected the fauna during its taphonomic history, fragmentation patterns are likely to reflect carcass exploitation by humans for use of within-bone nutrients (see Nagaoka 2005b, 2006). As a result, the intensity and extent of fragmentation can be used to examine whether the use of within-bone nutrients intensified or declined through time, which can be related to a broader study of carcass-part transport and exploitation related to foraging efficiency.

Mortality analysis

Previous research on the Twilight Beach seal fauna suggests people exploited seals from a rookery near the site (Smith 1985). Given fur seals no longer breed in the region, identifying prehistoric rookeries is important for understanding changes in seal distribution, as well as providing information to conservation biologists about possibilities for expanding modern seal breeding grounds. Morphometric data on prehistoric fur-seal remains are important for identifying the population structure of exploited seals. In particular, the presence of pre-weaned pups and the paucity of sub-adult males can indicate that rookeries, rather than haul outs, were exploited, as indicated by Smith (1985). Pups do not travel far from rookeries early in their lives and sub-adult males are excluded from adult-male territories.

Two taphonomic problems relate to the abundance of individuals in these two age/sex cohorts at Twilight Beach. First, our taphonomic analysis suggests sub-adult male remains might be under-identified in this assemblage because long-bone ends are preferentially destroyed by carnivores. It is the presence of large, unfused long-bone ends that allows identification of members of this age/sex cohort. However, based on those long bones that are well preserved, large, unfused specimens (sub-adult males) are uncommon, indicating a rookery was exploited (Figure 15).

Second, while the presence of pups can be used to indicate exploitation of rookeries, the larger the sample of pup remains, the more convincing the argument. However, skeletal elements of pups are low in density, and thus are more likely to be destroyed by taphonomic processes (see Symmons 2005; Wolverton 2001, 2006 for similar discussions). Therefore, it is important to examine the taphonomic history of the sample to determine whether pups are rare or

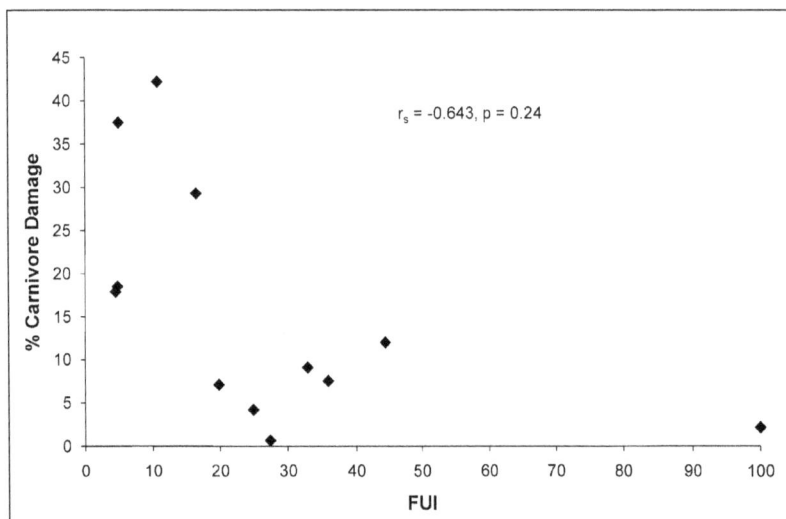

The scatter plot shows % Carnivore Damage (y-axis, 0 to 45) versus FUI (x-axis, 0 to 100). The annotation reads $r_s = -0.643$, $p = 0.24$.

Figure 14. Scatter plot of the rank order of seal food utility and percentage of carnivore-damaged specimens for each element.

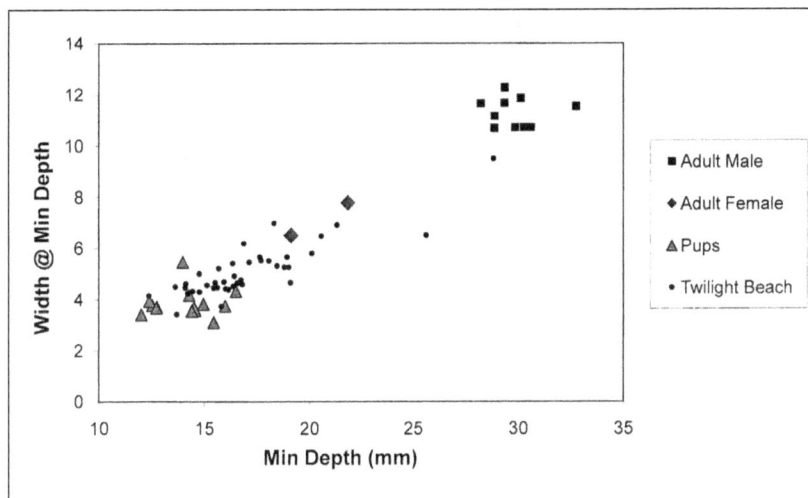

Figure 15. Comparison of modern seal mandible measurements with those from Twilight Beach to illustrate the demographic composition of the seals from the site.

absent because of exploitation patterns or preservation. Our analysis suggests density-mediated destruction of remains and related taphonomic processes did not cause substantial damage to the Twilight Beach fauna. As a result, we suggest the abundance of pup remains is representative of the demographic structure of seal hunting by prehistoric foragers at Twilight Beach.

Conclusions

Taphonomic analysis is not undertaken in a vacuum, but helps shed light on broader research problems. Nonetheless, there is apparent fission in modern zooarchaeology about the role taphonomic analysis and quantification should play (compare Marean and Kim 1998 with Stiner 1998, and Pickering *et al.* 2003 with Stiner 2002). Our position is that taphonomic histories vary by assemblage and appropriate quantitative analysis should vary by research problem. Acknowledging a conceptual framework for taphonomy (e.g. Gifford-Gonzalez 1991; Lyman 1994a) that recognises the different roles that immanent and configurational properties play in taphonomic analysis highlights that diversity in taphonomic effects is to be expected. Although it is tempting to treat the effects of particular taphonomic processes, such as the role of carnivore damage in density-mediated attrition, as uniform (e.g. Marean and Cleghorn 2003; Pickering *et al.* 2004), contingencies of accumulation histories might as easily and uniformly be expected to vary through time and across space. As a result, any particular assemblage must be evaluated on an individual basis for the analytical role it can play in a particular research question. Taphonomic methods should be creative and diverse to account for the myriad permutations and magnitudes that attritional agents can play in taphonomic histories of archaeological faunas.

Acknowledgements

We thank Michael Taylor for access to data, samples and related materials from Twilight Beach. The Department of Anthropology at the University of Auckland provided laboratory space for analysis and access to the collections. This research was funded by NSF Grant BCS-0408963 and Research Experience for Undergraduate (REU) supplement.

References

Abe, Y., W.M. Curtis, J.N. Peter, A. Zelalem and C.E Stone 2002. The analysis of cutmarks on archaeofauna: A review and critique of quantification procedures and a new image-analysis GIS approach. *American Antiquity* 67:643–663.

Anderson, A.J. (ed) 1994, *Traditional Lifeways of the Southern Maori*. Dunedin: University of Otago

Bartram, L.E. Jr. 1993. Perspectives on skeletal part profiles and utility curves from eastern Kalahari ethnoarchaeology. In J. Hudson (ed), *From Bones to Behavior: Ethnoarchaeological and Experimental Contributions to the Interpretation of Faunal Remains*, pp. 115–137. Southern Illinois University, Carbondale: Center for Archaeological Investigations.

Behrensmeyer, A.K. 1978. Taphonomic and ecologic information from bone weathering. *Paleobiology* 4:150–162.

Binford, L.R. 1981. *Bones: Ancient Men and Modern Myths*. New York: Academic.

Binford, L.R. 1984. *Faunal Remains from Klasies River Mouth*. New York: Academic.

Bradshaw, C.J.A., S.D. Lloyd, P. Martin, Z. Qingqing and L.B George 2002. Using artificial neural networks to model the suitability of coastline for breeding by New Zealand fur seals (*Arctocephalus forsteri*). *Ecological Modelling* 148:111–131.

Bradshaw, C.J.A., L. Chris and M.T. Caryn 2000. Clustering of colonies in an expanding population of New Zealand fur seals (*Arctocephalus forsteri*). *Journal of Zoology* 250:105–112.

Brain, C.K. 1969. The contribution of the Namib Desert Hottentots to an understanding of Australopithecine bone accumulations. *Scientific Papers of the Namib Desert Research Station* 39:13–22.

Broughton, J.M. 1999. *Resource Depression and Intensification during the Late Holocene, San Francisco Bay: Evidence from the Emeryville Shellmound*. University of California, Anthropological Records Volume 32.

Bunn, H.T. 1981. Archaeological evidence for meat-eating by Plio-Pleistocene hominids from Koobi Fora and Olduvai Gorge. *Nature* 291:574–477.

Bunn, H.T. 1986. Patterns of skeletal representation and hominid subsistence activities at Olduvai Gorge, Tanzania, and Koobi Fora, Kenya. *Journal of Human Evolution* 15:673–690.

Bunn, H.T. and E.M. Kroll 1986. Systematic butchery by Plio-Pleistocene hominds at Olduvai Gorge, Tanzania. *Current Anthropology* 27:431–452.

Butler, V.L. and C.C. James 1994. The role of bone density in structuring prehistoric salmon bone assemblages. *Journal of Archaeological Science* 21:413–424.

Cannon, M.D. 2003. A model of central place forager prey choice and an application to faunal remains from the Mimbres Valley, New Mexico. *Journal of Anthropological Archaeology* 22:1–25.

Chambers, A. 1992. Seal Bone Mineral Density: Its Effect on Specimen Survival in Archaeological Sites. Unpublished BA Honors Thesis, University of Missouri.

Clark, G.R. 1995. The *Kuri* in Prehistory. Unpublished MA thesis, University of Otago.

Clark, G. 1997a. Osteology of the kuri Maori: The prehistoric dog of New Zealand. *Journal of Archaeological Science* 24:113–126.

Clark, G.R. 1997b. Maori subsistence change: Zooarchaeological evidence from the prehistoric dog of New Zealand. *Asian Perspectives* 36:200–219.

Coster, J. 1989. Dates from the dunes: A sequence for the Aupouri Peninsula, Northland New Zealand. *New Zealand Journal of Archaeology* 11:51–75.

Cruz, I. and E. Dolores 2003. Structural Bone Density of the Lesser Rhea (Pterocnemia pennata) (Aves: Rheidae). Taphonomic and Archaeological Implications. *Journal of Archaeological Science* 30:37–44.

Darwent, C.M. and R.L. Lyman 2002. Detecting the postburial fragmentation of carpals, tarsals, and phalanges. In W.D. Haglund and M.H. Sorg (eds), *Advances in forensic taphonomy: Method, theory and archaeological perspectives*, pp. 356–377. Boca Raton: CRC Press.

Dirrigl, F.J. 2001. Bone Mineral Density of Wild Turkey (Meleagris gallopavo) Skeletal Elements and its Effect on Differential Survivorship. *Journal of Archaeological Science* 28:817–832.

Egeland, C.P. 2003. Carcass processing intensity and cutmark creation: An experimental approach. *Plains Anthropologist* 48:39–51.

Fisher, J.W. Jr. 1995. Surface modification of bone. *Journal of Archaeological Method and Theory* 2:7–68.

Gifford-Gonzalez, D.P. 1991. Bones are not enough: Analogues, knowledge, and interpretive strategies in zooarchaeology. *Journal of Anthropological Archaeology* 10:215–254.

Gordon, E.A. 1993. Screen size and differential faunal recovery: A Hawaiian example. *Journal of Field Archaeology* 20:453–460.

Grayson, D.K. 1984. *Quantitative Zooarchaeology*. New York: Academic.

Guthrie, R.D. 1967. Differential preservation and recovery of Pleistocene large mammal remains in Alaska. *Journal of Paleontology* 41:243–246.

Hindelang, M. and L.M. Ann 1997. Bone density determination of moose skeletal remains from Isle Royale National Park using digital image enhancement and quantitative computed tomography (QCT). *International Journal of Osteoarchaeology* 7:193–201.

Ioannidou, E. 2003. Taphonomy of animal bones: Species, sex, age and breed variability of sheep, cattle and pig bone density. *Journal of Archaeological Science* 30:355–365.

Izeta, A.D. 2005. South American camelid bone structural density: What are we measuring? Comments on data sets, values, their interpretation and application. *Journal of Archaeological Science* 32:1159–1168.

Klein, R.G. 1975. Paleoanthropological implications of the nonarchaeological bone assemblage from Swartklip I, south-western Cape Province, South Africa. *Quaternary Research* 5:275–288.

Klein, R.G. and K. Cruz-Uribe 1984. *The Analysis of Animal Bones from Archaeology Sites*. Chicago: University of Chicago Press.

Kreutzer, L.A. 1992. Bison and deer bone mineral densities: Comparisons and implications for the interpretation of archaeological faunas. *Journal of Archaeological Science* 19:271–294.

Lam, Y.M., C. Xingbin, W.M. Curtis and J.F Carol 1998. Bone density and long bone representation in archaeological faunas: Comparing results from CT and photon densitometry. *Journal of Archaeological Science* 25:559–570.

Lam, Y.M., C. Xingbin and O.M. Pearson 1999. Intertaxonomic variability in patterns of bone density and the differential representation of bovid, cervid, and equid elements in the archaeological record. *American Antiquity* 64:343–362.

Lam, Y.M., O.M. Pearson, W.M Curtis and C. Xingbin 2003. Bone density studies in zooarchaeology. *Journal of Archaeological Science* 30:1701–1708.

Leach, B.F., J.M Davidson and L.M. Horwood 1997. Prehistoric Maori fishermen at Kokohuia, Hokianga Harbour, Northland, New Zealand. *Man and Culture in Oceania* 13:99–116.

Lupo, K.D. 2001. Archaeological skeletal part profiles an differential transport: An ethnoarchaeological example from Hadza bone assemblages. *Journal of Anthropological Archaeology* 20:361–378.

Lupo, K.D. and J.F. O'Connell 2002. Cut and tooth mark distributions on large animal bones: ethnoarchaeological data from the Hadza and their implications for current ideas about early human carnivory. *Journal of Archaeological Science* 29:85–109.

Lyman, R.L. 1984. Bone density and differential survivorship of fossil classes. *Journal of Anthropological Archaeology* 3:259–299.

Lyman, R.L. 1987. Archaeofaunas and butchery studies: A taphonomic perspective. In M.B. Schiffer (ed), *Advances in Archaeological method and theory Vol. 10*, pp. 249–337. San Diego: Academic Press.

Lyman, R.L. 1994a. *Vertebrate Taphonomy*. Cambridge: Cambridge University.

Lyman, R.L. 1994b. Quantitative units and terminology in zooarchaeology. *American Antiquity* 59:36–71.

Lyman, R.L. 1994c. Relative abundances of skeletal specimens and taphonomic analysis of vertebrate remains. *Palaios* 9:288–298.

Lyman, R.L. 2005. Analyzing cut marks: lessons from artiodactyl remains in the northwestern United States. *Journal of Archaeological Science* 32:1722–1732.

Lyman, R.L. 2008. *Quantitative Paleozoology*. Cambridge: Cambridge University Press.

Lyman, R.L and M.J. O'Brien 1987. Plow-zone zooarchaeology: Fragmentation and identifiability. *Journal of Field Archaeology* 14:493–498.

Lyman, R.L., L.E. Houghton and A.L. Chambers 1992. The effect of structural density on marmot skeletal part representation in archaeological sites. *Journal of Archaeological Science* 19:557–573.

Marean, C.W. 1991. Measuring the post-depositional destruction of bone in archaeological assemblages. *Journal of Archaeological Science* 18:677–694.

Marean, C.W. and N. Cleghorn 2003. Large mammal skeletal element transport: Applying foraging theory in a complex taphonomic system. *Journal of Taphonomy* 1:15–42.

Marean, C.W. and S.Y. Kim 1998. Mousterian large-mammal remains from Kobeh Cave. Comments/ Reply. *Current Anthropology* 39:S79.

Marean, C.W. and L.M. Spencer 1991. Impact of carnivore ravaging on zooarchaeoloigcal measures of element abundance. *American Antiquity* 56: 645–658.

Marean, C.W., L.M. Spencer, R.J. Blumenschine and S.D. Capaldo 1992. Captive hyaena bone choice and destruction, the Schlepp effect and *Olduvai archaeofaunas*. *Journal of Archaeological Science* 19:101–121.

Marshall, F. and T. Pilgram 1991. Meat versus within-bone nutrients: Another look at the meaning of body part representation in archaeological sites. *Journal of Archaeological Science* 18:149–163.

Metcalfe, D. and K.T. Jones 1988. A reconsideration of animal body-part utility indices. *American Antiquity* 53:486–504.

Munro, N.D. 2004. Zooarchaeological measures of hunting pressure and occupation intensity in the Natufian. *Current Anthropology* 45(Supplement):S5-S33.

Munro, N.D. and G. Bar-Oz 2005. Gazelle bone fat processing in the Levantine Epipaleolithic. *Journal of Archaeological Science* 32:223–239.

Nagaoka, L. 1994. Differential recovery of Pacific Island fish remains: Evidence from the Moturakau Rockshelter, Aitutaki, Cook Islands. *Asian Perspectives* 33:1–17.

Nagaoka, L. 2005a. Differential recovery of Pacific Island fish remains. *Journal of Archaeological Science* 32:941–955.

Nagaoka, L. 2005b. Declining foraging efficiency and moa carcass exploitation in southern New Zealand. *Journal of Archaeological Science* 32:1328–1338.

Nagaoka, L. 2006. Prehistoric seal carcass exploitation at the Shag Mouth site, New Zealand. *Journal of Archaeological Science* 33:1474–1481.

Nichol, R. 1988. Tipping the Feather Against the Scale: Archaeozoology from the Tail of a Fish. Unpublished PhD thesis, University of Auckland.

Novecosky, B.J. and P.R.W. Popkin 2005. Canidae volume bone mineral density values: An application to sites in western Canada. *Journal of Archaeological Science* 32:1677–1690.

O'Connell, J.F., K. Hawkes and N.B. Jones 1988. Hadza hunting, butchering, and bone transport and their archaeological implications. *Journal of Anthropological Research* 44:113–161.

Olsen, S.L. and P. Shipman 1988. Surface modification on bone: Trampling versus butchery. *Journal of Archaeological Science* 15:535–553.

Outram, A.K. 2001. A new approach to identifying bone marrow and grease exploitation: Why the 'indeterminate' fragments should not be ignored. *Journal of Archaeological Science* 28:401–410.

Outram, A.K. 2004. Applied models and indices vs. high-resolution, observed data: Detailed fracture and fragmentation analyses for the investigation of skeletal part abundance patterns. *Journal of Taphonomy* 2:167–184.

Pavao, B. and P.W. Stahl 1999. Structural density assays of leporid skeletal elements with implications for taphonomic, actualistic and archaeological research. *Journal of Archaeological Science* 26:53–66.

Pickering, T.R. and K.J. Carlson 2002. Baboon bone mineral densities: Implications for the taphonomy of primate skeletons in South African cave sites. *Journal of Archaeological Science* 29:883–896.

Pickering, T.R., C.W. Marean and M. Dominguez-Rodrigo 2003. Importance of limb bone shaft fragments in zooarchaeology: A response to 'On in situ attrition and vertebrate body part profiles' (2002), by M.C. Stiner. *Journal of Archaeological Science* 30:1469–1482.

Pickering, T.R., M. Dominguez-Rodrigo, C.P. Egeland and C.K. Brain 2004. Beyond leopards: Tooth marks and the contribution of multiple carnivore taxa to the accumulation of the Swartkrans Member 3 fossil assemblage. *Journal of Human Evolution* 46:595–604.

Savelle, J.M., T.M. Friesen and R.L. Lyman 1996. Derivation and application of an otariid utility index. *Journal of Archaeological Science* 23:705–712.

Schiffer, M.B. 1987. *Formation Processes of the Archaeological Record*. Albuquerque: University of New Mexico.

Shaffer, B.S. 1992. Quarter-inch screening: Understanding biases in recovery of vertebrate faunal remains. *American Antiquity* 57:129–136.

Shaffer, B.S. and J.L.J. Sanchez 1994. Comparison of 1/8'- and 1/4'-mesh recovery of controlled samples of small- to medium-sized mammals. *American Antiquity* 59:525–530.

Simpson, G.G. 1963. Historical science. In C.C. Albritton (ed), *The fabric of geology*, pp. 24–48. Reading: Addison-Wesley.

Smith, I.W.G. 1985. Sea Mammal Hunting and Prehistoric Subsistence in New Zealand. Unpublished PhD thesis, University of Otago.

Smith, I.W.G. 1996, Historical documents, archaeology and 18th century seal hunting in New Zealand. In J.M. Davidson, G. Irwin, B.F. Leach, A. Pawley and D. Brown (eds), *Oceanic culture history. Essays in honour of Roger Green*, pp. 675–688. New Zealand Journal of Archaeology Special Publication.

Stahl, P.W. 1999. Structural density of domesticated South American camelid Skeletal elements and the archaeological investigation of prehistoric Andean Ch'arki. *Journal of Archaeological Science* 26:1347–1368.

Stiner, M.C. 1994. *Honor Among Thieves: A Zooarchaeological Study of Neanderthal Ecology*. Princeton: Princeton University.

Stiner, M.C. 1998. Comment on Marean and Kim, Mousterian large-mammal remains from Kobeh Cave: Behavioral implications. *Current Anthropology* 39:s98–s103.

Stiner, M.C. 2002. On in-situ attrition and vertebrate body part profiles. *Journal of Archaeological Science* 29:979–991.

Stiner, M.C. 2005. *The Faunas of Hayonim Cave, Israel: A 200,000-Year Record of Paleolithic Diet, Demography and Society*. New Haven: Peabody Museum.

Stiner, M.C., S.L. Kuhn, S. Weiner and O. Bar-Yosef 1995. Differential Burning, Recrystallization, and Fragmentation of Archaeological Bone. *Journal of Archaeological Science* 22:223–237.

Stiner, M. C., O. Bar-Yosef, S.L. Kuhn and S. Weiner 2005. Experiments in fragmentation and diagenesis of bone and shell. In M.C. Stiner (ed), *The faunas of Hayonim Cave, Israel: A 200,000-year record of paleolithic diet, demography and society*, pp. 39–58. American School of Prehistoric Research, Bulletin 48.

Symmons, R. 2004. Digital photodensitometry: a reliable and accessible method for measuring bone density. *Journal of Archaeological Science* 31:711–719.

Symmons, R. 2005. New density data for unfused and fused sheep bones, and a preliminary discussion on the modelling of taphonomic bias in archaeofaunal age profiles. *Journal of Archaeological Science* 32:1691–1698.

Taylor, M. 1982. Bone Refuse from Twilight Beach. Unpublished MA thesis, University of Auckland.

Todd, L.C. and D.J. Rapson 1988. Long bone fragmentation and interpretation of faunal assemblages: Approaches to comparative analysis. *Journal of Archaeological Science* 15:307–325.

Wolverton, S. 2001. Caves, ursides and artifacts: a natural-trap hypothesis. *Journal of Ethnobiology* 21:55–72.

Wolverton, S. 2002. NISP:MNE and % whole in analysis of prehistoric carcass exploitation. *North American Archaeologist* 23:85–100.

Wolverton, S. 2006. Natural-trap ursid mortality and the Kurten Response. *Journal of Human Evolution* 50:540–551.

Zeanah, D.W. 2000. Transport costs, central-place foraging, and hunter-gatherer alpine land-use strategies. In D.B. Madsen and M.D. Metcalf (eds), *Intermountain Archaeology*, pp. 1–14. Salt Lake City: University of Utah Press.

31

A new genus and species of pigeon (Aves: Columbidae) from Henderson Island, Pitcairn Group

Trevor H. Worthy

Department of Earth and Environmental Sciences, University of Adelaide, Australia

trevor.worthy@adelaide.edu.au

Graham M. Wragg

Department of Zoology, Oxford University, United Kingdom

Introduction

An extensive fossil record of birds has now been described from many islands in the Pacific, as comprehensively reviewed by Steadman (2006a). In recurrent cases across the breadth of the Pacific, up to half the birds are extinct (Steadman 2006a) – for example, extinct-bird remains have been found in New Caledonia (Balouet and Olson 1989), Fiji (Worthy 2000, 2001), the Tongan and Cook Island groups (Steadman 1989a, 1993, 1995), Samoa (Steadman 1994), Niue (Steadman *et al.* 2000), Society Islands (Steadman 1989a), Marquesas (Steadman 1989a; Steadman and Rolett 1996), Hawaii (James and Olson 1991; Olson and James 1991), and Easter Island (Steadman 1995). Among the extinct taxa are many species of columbids (Balouet and Olson 1987, 1989; Steadman 1989a, 1989b, 1992, 1997, 2006a, 2006b; Worthy 2001; Worthy and Wragg 2003; Wragg and Worthy 2006).

Henderson Island of the Pitcairn Group is one of the most remote islands in Oceania (see Figure 1 in Wragg and Worthy 2006). It is located about 177 km east-northeast of the high volcanic island of Pitcairn, at 24o22' S, 128o18' W. It is a relatively small raised atoll, with an area of about 37 km², and is low, with a maximum elevation of 33 m. Fossil birds were first recorded from Henderson Island by Steadman and Olson (1985), who studied 303 bird bones recovered from Sinoto's excavations (Fosberg *et al.* 1983; Sinoto 1983). These were dominated by sea birds, but among the few land birds, they reported two species of pigeon. They considered nine incomplete wing bones were inseparable from *Ducula aurorae* or *D. pacifica,* and two partial tibiotarsi and a mandibular fragment similar to *Ducula galeata.* This interpretation was challenged by Bourne and David (1986), who considered it more likely that these bones represented just one species with reduced wings. Despite examination of a further 2795 bird bones by Schubel and Steadman (1989), this issue was not resolved, although they did record the presence of a *Gallicolumba* species, based on a tarsometatarsus.

In 1991–1992, the large multidisciplinary Sir Peter Scott Commemorative Expedition to the Pitcairn Islands (Spencer and Benton 1995) included extensive archaeological and some palaeontological investigations (Weisler 1994, 1995; Wragg 1995a, b; Wragg and Weisler 1994). During these investigations, some 42 one metre square test pits were excavated in 11 archaeological and one natural site, resulting in a collection of some 42,213 bird bones (Wragg 1995a). Among four extinct land birds, Wragg and Weisler (1994) and Wragg (1995a) listed Columbidae n. gen et n. sp., *Ducula* n. sp., and *Gallicolumba* n. sp.. Steadman (1997, 2006a) continued to list *Ducula aurorae* and *D. galeata* from Henderson Island, while admitting that the taxonomy of the extinct columbids was unresolved. Subsequently, Worthy and Wragg (2003) have described *G. leonpascoi,* and Wragg and Worthy (2006) *Ducula harrisoni*. It is the purpose of the present contribution to describe the new genus and species Wragg and Weisler (1994) revealed.

Methods

Site terminology and excavation

The locations of the sites are shown in Weisler (1995:Figure 2) and Wragg (1995b:Figure 2.1) and we follow the site nomenclature used therein here and on specimen labels. During excavations, all sediment was sieved through 6.4 mm mesh sieves and selected samples fine-screened with 1.5 or 3.2 mm meshes (Wragg and Weisler 1994). Weisler initially sorted the bird bones from the recovered materials, and initial identification of these was made by Wragg (Wragg and Weisler 1994; Wragg 1995a, b). THW is responsible for the comparisons reported here.

Abbreviations

The following abbreviations are used in the text.

Institution: AIM, Auckland Institute and Museum, Auckland, New Zealand (NZ); AM, Australian Museum, Sydney, NSW, Australia; AMNH, American Museum of Natural History, New York, United States of America; BMNH, Natural History Museum, London, United Kingdom (formerly British Museum (Natural History)); CM, Canterbury Museum, Christchurch, NZ; FM, Fiji Museum, Suva, Fiji; LACM, Natural History Museum, Los Angeles County, California, USA; NMNZ, Museum of New Zealand Te Papa Tongarewa, Wellington (formerly National Museum of New Zealand, Dominion Museum, and Colonial Museum), NZ; MVZ, Museum of Vertebrate Zoology, University of California, Berkeley, California, USA; OM, Otago Museum, Dunedin, NZ; SAM, South Australia Museum, Adelaide, South Australia, Australia; USNM, United States National Museum, Smithsonian Institution, Washington D.C., USA; UWBM, Burke Museum, University of Washington, Seattle, Washington, USA.

Skeletal elements and descriptive terms used: Anatomical nomenclature for specific bone landmarks follows Baumel and Witmer (1993). Some common terms are abbreviated as follows: *proc.* for *processus*; *artic.* for *articularis*. Element abbreviations: cor, coracoid; cmc, carpometacarpus; phal. dig., digital phalanx; hum, humerus; pt, part; tib, tibiotarsus. The following abbreviations apply to single and plural usage of the elements. When listing material, bones are sometimes identified as left (L) or right (R) elements. L or R prefixed by 'p' or 'd' indicates 'proximal' or 'distal' part of the element respectively, e.g. dR tib means the distal part of a right tibiotarsus. TP for test pit.

Measurements

Measurements were made with Tesa® dial callipers and rounded to 0.1 mm. TL: greatest length, except for the coracoid, which was measured down the medial side (ML). PW: proximal width in the lateromedial plane; DW: distal width.

Comparative material

All material is from modern skeletons unless stated otherwise. Extinct taxa are indicated †.

Goura cristata (Pallas, 1764), western crowned pigeon, CM Av7110; SAM B.4997; SAM B.5057; SAM B.11546; SAM B.11551. *Microgoura meeki* (Rothschild, 1904), Choiseul pigeon †, AMNH 24959, cast R tmt, cast dR tt from skin AMNH 616460, Choiseul Island, Solomon Islands. *Didunculus strigirostris* (Jardine, 1845), tooth-billed pigeon, CM Av7160, Samoa; AM O.303. *Caloenas nicobarica* (Linnaeus, 1758), Nicobar pigeon, NMNZ 22475; USNM 292221; USNM 557085; UWBM 38797; SAM B.5056; SAM B.36831; SAM B.51203. *Otidiphaps nobilis* (Gould, 1870), pheasant pigeon, USNM 614236. *Gallicolumba stairi* (G. R. Gray, 1856), friendly ground dove, BMNH S/1975.3.3. Fossil bones: NMNZ S38223, 54 bones 6 individuals, Vatulele Island, Fiji. *G. rubescens* (Vieillot, 1818), MVZ 46017. *G. luzonica* (Scopoli, 1786), MVZ 53804; LACM 89051; LACM 89050. *G. rufigula* (Pucheran, 1853), LACM 106368. *G. criniger* (Pucheran, 1853), LACM 89052. *G. beccarii* (Salvadori, 1876), AMNH 7718; USNM 615012; UWBM 43037. *G. jobiensis* (A. B. Meyer, 1875), AM O.64814; AMNH 6753. *Columba vitiensis* (Quoy and Gaimard, 1830), white-throated pigeon, AM O.7921; FM 26. *Columba leucomela* (Temminck, 1821), white-headed pigeon, SAM B.31352; AM O.58907. *Columba livia* (Gmelin, 1789), rock pigeon, SAM B.46041; SAM B.46044; SAM B.46046. *Streptopelia chinensis* (Scopoli, 1786), spotted dove, AIM B5632; SAM B.48177; SAM B.49668. *Phaps chalcoptera* (Latham, 1790), common bronzewing, CM Av7129; SAM B.46373; SAM B.48297. *Phaps elegans*, (Temminck, 1810), brush bronzewing, SAM B.37405; SAM B.47648. *Ocyphaps lophotes* (Temminck, 1882), crested pigeon, SAM B.48075; SAM B.48078. *Chalcophaps indica* (Linnaeus, 1758), emerald dove, SAM B.31777; SAM B.37059; SAM B.38758. *Macropygia phasianella* (Temminck, 1821), large brown cuckoo dove, SAM B.38504; SAM B.38757. *Leucosarcia melanoleuca* (Latham, 1801), Wonga pigeon, SAM B.5090; SAM B.10598. *Ptilinopus perousii* (Peale, 1848), many-coloured fruit dove, FM 31; FM23. *Ptilinopus victor* (Gould, 1871), orange dove, FM unreg.; BMNH S/1975.3.1. *Ptilinopus porphyraceus* (Temminck, 1821), crimson-coloured fruit dove, NMNZ 16391. *Ptilinopus magnificus* (Temminck, 1821), magnificent fruit dove, SAM B.21929; SAM B.46569. *Ptilinopus regina* (Swainson, 1825), pink-capped fruit dove, SAM B.37060. *Ducula goliath* (G. R. Gray, 1859), New Caledonian imperial pigeon, NMNZ 22839, 3 mixed individuals. *Ducula pacifica* (Gmelin, 1789), Pacific pigeon, AM O.7919; NMNZ 16389A; NMNZ 25350; NMNZ 25351; NMNZ 25352; NMNZ 25353; AIM 7233; AIM 7262. *Ducula latrans* (Peale, 1848), Peale's imperial pigeon, FM 28; BMNH S/1975.3.4; BMNH S/1975.3.2; MVZ 51372. *Ducula galeata* (Bonaparte, 1855), Marquesan imperial pigeon, BMNH S/1975.9.5; NMNZ 26971, cast of selected elements BMNH S/1975.9.5. *Ducula bicolor* (Scopoli, 1786), pied imperial pigeon, AM O.68476. *Ducula melanochroa* (Sclater, 1878), Bismarck imperial pigeon, USNM 615013. *Ducula pistrinaria* (Bonaparte, 1854), island imperial pigeon. *D. pistrinaria pistrinaria*, UWBM 60203. *Ducula rubricera* (Bonaparte, 1854), red-knobbed imperial pigeon. *D. rubricera rufigula*, UWBM 63088. *Ducula spilorrhoa* (G.R. Gray, 1858), Australian pied imperial pigeon, SAM B.23902. *Hemiphaga novaeseelandiae* (Gmelin, 1789), New Zealand pigeon, OM Av1851, many NMNZ specimens.

Fossil specimens compared: *Gallicolumba leonpascoi* – NMNZ specimens listed in Worthy and Wragg (2003), but especially coracoids S.40776, R; S.40804, pR; S.40831, L; carpometacarpi S.40786, L; S.40816, R; S.40828, R; and humeri S.40793, dR; S.40796, pR; S.40826, R; S.40828, L; S.40833, 2L; S.40843, 1L1dL. S.40847, R; and tibiotarsus S.40842, dL.

Ducula harrisoni – NMNZ specimens listed in Wragg and Worthy (2006), but especially coracoids S.41618, R, S.41639, L; S.41640, R; S.41728, R; S.41758, L; tibiotarsi S.41717, 1sL2dR; humeri S.41641, 2pL; S.41649, dR; S.41722, dL; carpometacarpi S.41617, L; S.41684, R; and S.41760, sternum.

Systematic palaeontology

Class Aves
Order Columbiformes
Family Columbidae
The fossils described here are referred to Columbidae as they have the following combination of characters. Coracoid elongate; *cotyla scapularis* (scapular cotyla) flat, not forming deep cup-like depression; *proc. acrocoracoideus* (acrocoracoid) large, overhangs medial margin of shaft; *proc. procoracoideus* (procoracoid) lacks foramen; *impressio m. sternocoracoidei* (sternocoracoidal impression) contains at least one area of pneumatic foramina. Humerus: caudo-cranially inflated; *crista deltopectoralis* (deltoid crest) short, robust, triangular; *tub. dorsale* (dorsal tubercle) elongate, merges into *caput humeri* (head) medially; head markedly convex proximally; *fossa pneumotricipitalis ventralis* (ventral pneumotricipital fossa) large, pneumatic; no dorsal pneumotricipital fossa; and no *impressio coracobrachialis* (bicipital furrow).

Bountyphaps new genus

Type species. *Bountyphaps obsoleta* nov. gen. et sp.

Etymology. For both the ship *Bounty* on which Europeans discovered the Pitcairn Group, and for the former bounty this bird provided re food; and 'phaps' Greek, feminine noun for wild pigeon.

Diagnosis. A genus of pigeon slightly larger than *Ducula latrans* characterised by the following unique combination of coracoidal characters: 1, large pneumatic foramina penetrating acrocoracoid from supracoracoidal sulcus; 2, sternocoracoidal impression separated from medial margin by broad ridge, pneumatic foramina located centromedially; 3, tip of procoracoid not extending as lobe craniad of scapular cotyla; 4, *facies artic. clavicularis* (clavicle facet) notched, distinct ventral and dorsal lobes; 5, ventral lobe of clavicle facet hooked sternally; 6, base of procoracoid short relative to shaft length; 7, deep depression at distal end humeral articular facet on lateral facies of shaft.

Comparisons

Compared especially to Pacific pigeon genera, *Bountyphaps* is larger than any species of *Phaps*, *Chalcophaps, Ocyphaps, Macropygia, Ptilinopus* (with single exception of *P. magnificus* of Australia), *Drepanoptila, Gallicolumba* and *Didunculus*. It is similar in size to larger species of *Columba* and *Ducula*, although smaller than *Ducula galeata* and *D. goliath*. It is markedly smaller than *Natunaornis, Goura* and *Caloenas*, but perhaps not much smaller than *Microgoura*. The diagnostic characters, whose distributions within columbid genera are given in Table 1, differentiate *Bountyphaps* from other genera as follows. Presence of a large pneumatic foramen under the acrocoracoid is only found in *Ptilinopus, Macropygia, Goura, Caloenas* (variably present e.g.

Table 1. Distribution of coracoidal characters across various columbid taxa.

Taxon	Pneumatic foramina under acrocoracoid	Sterno-coracoidal impression location	Procoracoid lobe extends craniad of scap cotyla	Clavicle facet notched	Clavicle facet ventral notch hooked sternally	Base of procoracoid elongate	Deep depression distad of humeral facet on shaft lateral facies	Medial angle acute/obtuse	Dorsal clavicle facet overhangs scap cotyla	Ventral pt corpus coracoideum convex opposite scap. cotyla
Bountyphaps obsoleta	Y large	centromedial	N	Y	Y	N	Y	acute	weakly	N
Didunculus	Y small	centromedial	Y	Y	Y	Y	Y	acute	weakly	Y
Gallicolumba stairi, beccarii, rubescens, leonpascoi	N	medial	N	Y	Y	N	Y	acute	Y	N
Gallicolumba jobiensis	N	medial	N	Y	Y	N	Y	near obtuse	Y	Y
Gallicolumba luzonica, criniger, rufigula	N	medial	Y	Y	Y	N	?	obtuse	Y	N
Ptilinopus	Y large	medial	weakly	N	Y	N	N	acute	weakly	N
Ducula	N or Y small	medial	weakly	Y	Y	N	N	acute	weakly	N
Columba	N or Y small	medial/central	Y	Y	Y	N	N	acute	Y	N
Hemiphaga	Y	medial	N	N	N	N	N	acute	weakly	N
Otidiphaps	?	medial	N	?	Y	N	?	?	?	?
Phaps	N	medial	Y	Y	Y	N	Y	acute	Y	N
Chalcophaps	N or Y small	medial	Y	Y	Y	N	Y	acute	Y	weakly
Goura	Y	centromedial	Y extreme	Y	Y	Y	Y	obtuse	Y	N
Natunaornis	Y	centromedial	?	?Y	N	N	Y	acute	?	?
Caloenas	N or Y	centromedial	Y extreme	Y	Y	N	Y	obtuse	Y	weakly
Macropygia	Y large	medial	Y	Y	Y	N	Y	acute	Y	weakly
Streptopelia	N	medial	Y	Y	Y	N	Y	acute	Y	weakly
Leucosarcia	N	medial	Y	Y	Y	N	Y	acute	Y	N
Ocyphaps	N	centromedial	Y	Y	Y	N	Y	acute	Y	weakly

Abbreviations: Y=yes, N=no.

USNM 292221 is pneumatic, and USNM 557085 is not), and *Natunaornis*. In all other genera, either pneumatic foramina are absent, e.g. *Phaps*, *Gallicolumba*, or may be present or absent, but if present are very small (e.g. *Didunculus*, *Ducula*, *Hemiphaga*, *Columba*, *Chalcophaps*). The region of pneumatic foramina in the sternocoracoidal impression is located towards the centre of the bone similar to *Goura*, *Caloenas*, *Natunaornis* and *Didunculus*, thereby differing from *Ducula*, *Hemiphaga*, *Columba*, *Ptilinopus*, *Macropygia* and *Gallicolumba* in which it is medially located. In *Otidiphaps* coracoids, the sternocoracoidal impression is relatively much larger and deeper, even more so than in *Goura* and *Caloenas*, and it is pneumatic medially, rather than centrally. That the tip of the procoracoid does not extend as a lobe above the scapular cotyla towards clavicle facet differs greatly from *Goura* and *Caloenas*, where there is extreme cranial development of the procoracoid tip to nearly reach the clavicle facet and does enclose a canal through the supracoracoidal sulcus. Many other genera, including *Didunculus*, have significant extension of the procoracoid towards the acrocoracoid (Table 1). This character is variable in *Gallicolumba*, as in taxa from Oceania the procoracoid is relatively small and does not extend craniad of the scapular cotyla, but in taxa from the western Pacific, e.g. *G. luzonica*, *G. criniger* and *G. rufigula*, the procoracoid is relatively enlarged cranially. A notched clavicle facet further distinguishes *Bountyphaps* from *Ptilinopus*, which lacks such a notch. A sternally hooked ventral lobe of the clavicle facet distinguishes *Bountyphaps* from *Natunaornis* and *Hemiphaga*, where such a hook is absent. A short base to the procoracoid distinguishes *Bountyphaps* from *Goura*, where the juncture with the shaft is very elongate, comprising about 30 percent of length from the scapular cotyla to the medial angle, and to a lesser extent from *Didunculus* (24 percent) and *Caloenas* (c. 15 percent). The fossil has a distinct elongate fossa immediately distad of the humeral facet on the lateral facies. This feature, noted by Steadman (2006b), is shared with the Pacific columbids *Didunculus*, *Gallicolumba*, *Goura* and *Caloenas*, thus differentiating it from other Pacific columbids including *Ptilinopus*, *Ducula* and *Columba*. Steadman (2006) noted that a convex humero-ventral portion of the *corpus coracoideum*, which we interpret as the ventral facies adjacent to the humeral facet and opposite the scapular cotyla, was a feature of *Didunculus*. We found this feature difficult to interpret in smaller taxa, but in most pigeon genera the shaft is flattened in this area. In NMNZ S.44246, it is flattened, unlike *Didunculus*, *Gallicolumba jobiensis* and *Caloenas*.

In *Bountyphaps*, the sternocoracoidal impression is bound medially by a ridge that is not closer than 2 mm from the medial edge, diverges from the medial margin cranially, and extends nearly to mid-length, where it is centred on the dorsal facies. In *Didunculus* and *Ducula*, this ridge tends to converge on the medial margin cranially, but in *Columba* and *Gallicolumba* remains separated from it. The *angulus medialis* is acute with the profile of the medial margin evenly concave towards the tip in *Bountyphaps* (as in *Gallicolumba stairi*), rather than convex in profile towards the tip as is characteristic of *Didunculus*, *Ptilinopus* and *Columba*, but also some *Gallicolumba* e.g. *G. jobiensis*. It lacks a flange-like ridge leading proximally along the margin from the medial angle, which when present creates a convex profile of the medial margin above the angle, e.g. as in *Ptilinopus*, *Columba* and *Didunculus*. The sternal articulation has large dorsal and ventral facets. The profile of the sternal margin is shallowly concave, not markedly concave, as *Ducula* species.

In summary, *Bountyphaps* has more features in common with *Didunculus* than other taxa, yet it differs considerably as follows: procoracoid with shorter base and tip not hooked cranially, larger pneumatic foramina in supracoracoidal sulcus, sternocoracoidal impression more widely separated from the medial margin, and the medial angle is more acute and lacks a convex medial margin.

Bountyphaps obsoleta nov. gen. et sp. (Figures 1 and 2)

Holotype. NMNZ S.44246, R coracoid, near complete, but part of the mid-shaft region ventrally, the tip of the *proc. lateralis* (lateral angle), and the extreme tip of the procoracoid are lost.

Etymology. Latin, feminine, adjective for extinct or forgotten about.

Diagnosis. As for genus.

Measurements of the holotype.

Medial length 42.7 mm, least shaft width 3.8 mm, length scapular cotyla to tip of acrocoracoid 14.3 mm, length scapular cotyla to cranial end of humeral facet 9.6 mm.

Type Locality. Henderson Island, site 5, test pit 10, spit 6; collected by M. Weisler and G. Wragg during the Pitcairn Islands Scientific Expedition 1991–1992.

Paratypes. All from Henderson Island and collected by M. Weisler and G. Wragg during the Pitcairn Islands Scientific Expedition 1991–1992. NMNZ S.44256, dR tib, site 5, unit 6, spit 2; S.44247, pL hum, site 5, unit 15, spit 4; S.44244, L cmc, site 5, unit 2, spit 12; S.44259, dL tib, site 5, unit 8, spit 3.

Referred Material. All from Henderson Island and collected by M. Weisler and G. Wragg during the Pitcairn Islands Scientific Expedition 1991–1992. NMNZ S.41737, dR hum, site 5, unit 16, spit 3; S.41753, dL hum, site 5, unit 16, spit 50; S.44242, R phal. dig. major (prox.), site 1, unit 2, spit 1; S.44243, R phal. dig. major (prox.), site 5, unit 7, spit 2; S.44245, sternal pt R coracoid, site 5, unit 7, spit 1; S.44248, L metatarsal, site 5, unit 5, spit 3; S.44249, L metatarsal, site 11, unit 5, spit 4; S.44250, L scap, site 5, unit 5, spit 4; S.44251, L scap, site 5, unit 7, spit 2; S.44252, L scap, site 6, unit 3, spit 3; S.44253, anterior sternum, site 5, unit 8, spit 3; S.44257, sL tib, site 5, unit 8, spit 3; S.44258, pR ulna, site 5, unit 1, spit 14.

All these specimens are referred to *Bountyphaps obsoleta,* as they are pigeon bones, but are not *Ducula harrisoni* nor *Gallicolumba leonpascoi,* and are too large to be referred to *Ptilinopus insularis.*

In addition to the characters discussed under the generic diagnosis, the coracoid has the following features (Figure 1). The dorsal lobe of the clavicle facet is expanded dorsally so that medially it overhangs the scapular cotyla, however this is accentuated by an apparent pathology on the dorsal side of this facet. The shaft in dorsal view widens caudally, that is, lacks a section with parallel sides, as in for example *Gallicolumba.* The ventral margin of the *facies artic. humeralis* extends ventrally as a prominent ridge over the shaft ventro-laterally.

Bountyphaps obsoleta is easily distinguished from coracoids of other columbids on Henderson Island. It is markedly larger than those of *Ptilinopus insularis* and *Gallicolumba leonpascoi.* While of similar size to those of *Ducula harrisoni* (Table 2), it is distinguished by a relatively more robust cranial end, the presence of pneumatic foramina in the supracoracoidal sulcus and a centromedially placed sternocoracoidal impression. In *D. harrisoni,* the impression is deepest and pneumatic closest to the medial margin and its defining ridge medially is narrowly separated from and converges on the medial margin cranially.

Humerus. The pL humerus S.44247 (Figure 2) is of typical columbid form, but is distinguished from all genera except *Didunculus, Goura, Caloenas* and *Gallicolumba* by the presence of a marked tuberosity located caudally on the distal margin of the caput at the end of the capital groove and above the pneumotricipital fossa. It is smaller than specimens attributed to *Ducula harrisoni* (Table 2).

Carpometacarpus. The L carpometacarpus NMNZ S.44244 (Figure 2), length 33.8 mm,

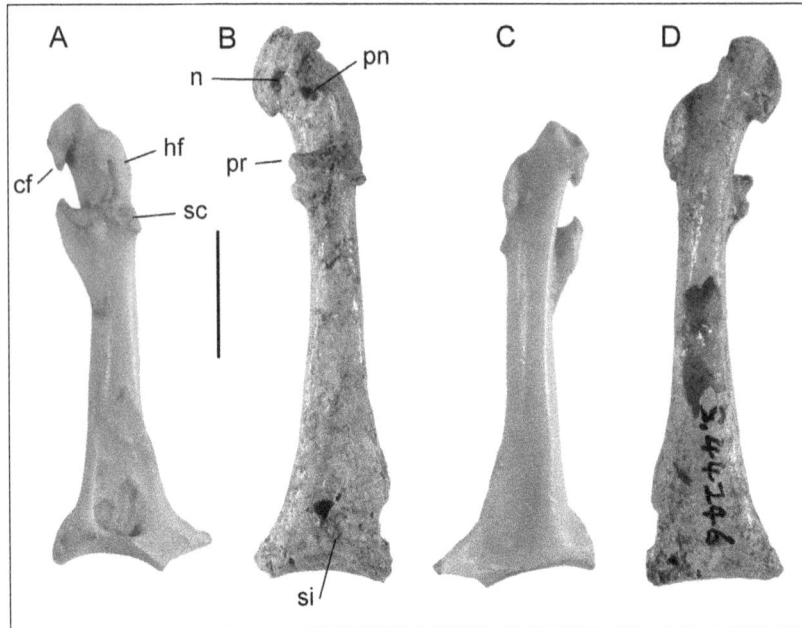

Figure 1. Right coracoids of *Didunculus strigirostris* AM S303 (A, C) and *Bountyphaps obsoleta* NMNZ S.44246 (B, D) in dorsal aspect (A, B) and ventral aspect (C, D). Scale bar is 10 mm. Abbreviations: cf, clavicle facet; hf, humeral facet; n, notch; pn, pneumatic foramen; pr, procoracoid; sc, scapular cotyla; si, sternocoracoidal impression.

Table 2. Measurements of selected elements of *Bountyphaps obsoleta* compared with the formerly sympatric columbids *Gallicolumba leonpascoi* and *Ducula harrisoni*.

Measurement	Coracoid ML	L scapula cotyla - tip acrocor	Hum PW ex dorsal tubercle	Tib DW	L cmc
Bountyphaps obsoleta	42.7	14.3	15.7	8.2, 9.2	33.8
G. leonpascoi	28.4	-	9.9–10.8	7.5–7.8	21.9–24.2
D. harrisoni	41.6–42.2	12.0–13.3	16.5–17.6	10.6–10.8	39.1–39.6

Abbreviations: as in Methods, and acrocor, acrocoracoid.

is very similar in length to that of *Didunculus* (AM S.303) 33.7 mm, and *Columba vitiensis* (AM O.7921) 34.1 mm, and so smaller than specimens referred to *Ducula harrisoni* (Table 2). The Henderson fossil has a less inflated *trochlea carpalis* than does *Columba vitiensis*, and a very shallow *fossa infratrochlearis*, shallower than in *Didunculus Ducula* and *Columba*. It is further distinguished from *Didunculus* by a lack of a fossa at the base of the *os metacarpalis alulae* on the dorsal facies and from *Columba*, *Ducula* and *Didunculus* by a stouter, less cranially directed extensor process.

Tibiotarsus. The specimens NMNZ S.44256 and S.44259 (Figure 2) allow determination of the arrangement of ligamental attachment points on the distal tibiotarsus in *Bountyphaps obsoleta*, which differ markedly between columbid taxa (Worthy 2001). 1. The tuberosity for the proximal attachment of the *retinaculum extensorium tibiotarsi* (ptRET) is prominent and is separated from the *condylus medialis* by a distance less than the height of the medial condyle (as in *Goura, Microgoura, Natunaornis, Caloenas, Didunculus, Gallicolumba, Otidiphaps, Ocyphaps* and *Phaps*), but differing markedly from *Ducula, Columba, Hemiphaga* and *Ptilinopus* where the ptRET is located farther proximally. 2. The distal attachment point for the *retinaculum extensorium tibiotarsi* (dtRET) is a marked prominence on the *pons supratendineus* (as in *Didunculus, Gallicolumba, Ocyphaps, Phaps, Natunaornis, Goura, Microgoura, Caloenas*), but is shifted proximally to merge into a ridge on the lateral side of the *sulcus extensorius* in *Ducula,*

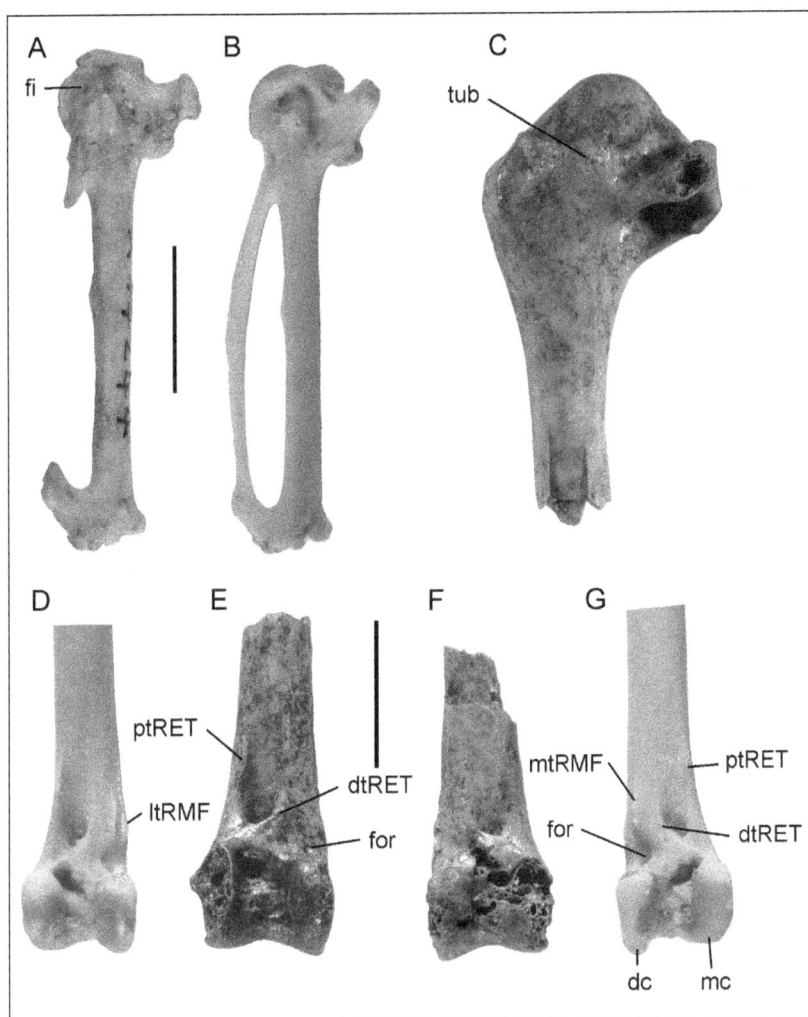

Figure 2. Carpometacarpi (A, B) in ventral aspect, proximal left humerus in caudal aspect (C), and distal tibiotarsi in anterior aspect (D-G) of *Bountyphaps obsoleta* (A, NMNZ S.44244; C, S.44247; E, left, S.44259; F, right, S.44256) and *Didunculus strigirostris* AM S303 (B, D, H). B is a mirror image of the right element. Scale bar is 10 mm. Abbreviations: dc, dorsal condyle; dtRET, distal attachment *retinaculum extensorium tibiotarsi*; fi *fossa infratrochlearis*; for, foramen; ltRMF, lateral attachment *retinaculum muscularis fibularis*; mc, medial condyle; mtRMF, medial attachment retinaculum m. fibularis; ptRET, proximal attachment *retinaculum extensorium tibiotarsi*; tub tubercle.

Columba, Hemiphaga and *Ptilinopus*. 3. The lateral margin of the extensor sulcus proximal to the *pons supratendineus* is rounded (as in *Goura, Microgoura, Caloenas, Didunculus, Gallicolumba, Ocyphaps* and *Phaps*), so differing markedly from e.g. *Natunaornis, Ducula, Columba, Hemiphaga* and *Ptilinopus*, in which the sulcus has a sharp crest laterally. 4. There is no prominent medial attachment point for the *retinaculum m. fibularis* (mtRMF) laterad of the *pons supratendineus*, as in *Natunaornis, Goura, Microgoura, Caloenas, Ducula, Columba* and *Ptilinopus*. In contrast, *Didunculus, Gallicolumba, Otidiphaps, Ocyphaps*, and *Phaps*, have a prominent mtRMF attachment point. 5. The *retinaculum m. fibularis* (ltRMF) is positioned on the lateral facies and is aligned anterocaudally rather than parallel to the shaft, as in *Natunaornis, Goura, Microgoura, Caloenas, Ocyphaps* and *Phaps*. In *Didunculus* and *Gallicolumba*, the ltRMF is plainly visible in anterior aspect and is aligned parallel to the shaft. In *Ducula, Columba, Hemiphaga*, and *Ptilinopus*, the ltRMF is on the lateral facies and aligned parallel to the shaft. 6. A foramen penetrates the corpus at the anterior margin of the *condylus lateralis* distad of the mtRMF, as in

Natunaornis, Goura, Caloenas, Ocyphaps, Phaps and *Hemiphaga*. A similar, but larger foramen is present in *Microgoura, Didunculus* and *Gallicolumba*. There is no such foramen in *Ducula, Columba* and *Ptilinopus*. 7. The width across the distal condyles is narrower posteriorly than anteriorly, as in *Natunaornis, Goura, Microgoura, Caloenas, Didunculus, Gallicolumba, Ocyphaps, Otidiphaps* and *Phaps*, rather than equal, as in *Ducula, Columba, Hemiphaga* and *Ptilinopus*. 8. The depth of the medial condyle is greater than the distal condylar width (as in *Natunaornis, Goura, Microgoura, Caloenas, Didunculus, Gallicolumba, Otidiphaps, Ocyphaps* and *Phaps*) but these values are about equal in *Ducula, Columba, Hemiphaga* and *Ptilinopus*. This feature can be otherwise expressed in terms of overall width and depth: in the former group of taxa the depth of the condyles is about equal to or deeper than condylar width, whereas in the latter group, condylar width is greater than their depth. The Henderson tibiotarsi thus differ markedly from *Ducula, Columba, Hemiphaga* and *Ptilinopus*. They are most similar to *Goura, Microgoura*, and *Caloenas* (share eight characters), then *Natunaornis, Ocyphaps* and *Phaps* (seven characters), but also have significant similarity with *Didunculus* and *Gallicolumba* (six characters). We interpret these similarities as homoplasy due to a terrestrial habit for all of these taxa. Measurements of distal width are less than those of *Ducula harrisoni* (Table 2).

Discussion

Wragg and Weisler (1994) and Wragg (1995a) recorded the presence of a distinct undescribed genus and species of pigeon on Henderson Island. Here we have described this taxon as *Bountyphaps obsoleta* based on 18 bones from four archaeological sites (1, 5, 6 and 11). Both sites five and six contained prehistoric material mixed into the archaeological sequence by the burrowing activities of sea birds, as evidenced by dates on bones up to 13,420[14]C yrs BP (OxA-5910), with this oldest date being on bones of *Gallicolumba leonpascoi* (Hedges *et al.* 1997; Wragg 1995b). However, the deposition of most specimens was in Polynesian middens (Wragg 1995b). Polynesians occupied Henderson for about 600 years, commencing sometime in the period 1300–1000[14]C yrs BP, but certainly by about AD 1050 (Weisler 1995).

Bountyphaps obsoleta was the largest of the four columbids formerly extant on Henderson Island, and like *Ducula harrisoni* and *Gallicolumba leonpascoi* (Worthy and Wragg 2003; Wragg and Worthy 2006), it went extinct following the colonisation of Henderson Island by people. Only *Ptilinopus* survives today. The affinities of *Bountyphaps obsoleta* are obscure at present, and would be facilitated by the discovery of tarsometatarsi. Its relationships are currently perhaps partly confounded by homoplasy related to convergence to a terrestrial habit, but these initial comparisons suggest it is most closely related to *Didunculus* and *Caloenas*. Both taxa have relict distributions in the Pacific now with extinct taxa on widely separated islands (Steadman 2006a, b). In particular, *Caloenas nicobarica* has a modern distribution in New Guinea, the Bismarck Archipelago, Palau and the Solomon Islands (Steadman 2006a), but the fossil taxon *C. canacorum* (Balouet and Olson 1989) is found in New Caledonia and Tonga (Steadman 2006a).

The few available specimens indicate *Bountyphaps obsoleta* had relatively reduced wings for its body size, as indicated by its coracoid length compared with the sympatric *Ducula*. This suggests *B. obsoleta* was a comparatively weaker flier, but as the legs are not relatively larger than *D. harrisoni*, it probably was not flightless.

Steadman (2006a) detailed the distribution of extant and prehistoric columbids throughout the Pacific Ocean, finding them the most taxonomically diverse family of land birds in the region. He listed 10 described and four undescribed extinct taxa in seven genera. *Bountyphaps obsoleta* adds to this diversity and shows yet again how multiple pigeon genera coexisted on Pacific islands. The listing of *Ducula aurorae* and *D. galeata* in the former Henderson fauna (e.g. Steadman 2006a) is no longer tenable, as the bones these taxa were listed from together are *Ducula harrisoni* (Wragg and Worthy 2006). The description of *B. obsoleta* completes the description of the extinct Henderson Island columbids. In prehistoric times, this small island had four genera and species (*B. obsoleta*, *Gallicolumba leonpascoi*, *Ducula harrisoni* and *Ptilinopus insularis*), of which only the latter survives. Doubtless, as shown by the data in Steadman (2006a), further genera and species of pigeon will be described from Pacific fossil avifaunas. Large and unique forms certainly await discovery on islands impacted by humans for which palaeofaunas are so far lacking.

Acknowledgements

We are pleased to acknowledge Marshall Weisler, who led the archaeological investigations that were part of the Sir Peter Scott Commemorative Expedition to the Pitcairn Islands 1991–1992, and whose work thus is primarily responsible for recovery of the specimens described here. GW also thanks the people of Pitcairn for the hospitality given to him and other expedition members at that time.

This study was much advanced by the patient assistance of the curators and collections managers in the following institutions: AIM – Brian Gill; AM – Walter Boles; AMNH – Paul Sweet, Allison Andors, Christine Blake; BMNH – Joanne Cooper for measurements of specimens; CM – Paul Scofield and for associated data; FM – Tarisi Sorovi-Vunidilo, Sagale Buadromo; LACM – Christina Couroux; NMNZ – Alan Tennyson, Sandy Bartle; MVZ – Carla Cicero; USNM – Storrs Olson, Phil Angle; UWBM – Robert C. Faucett.

References

Balouet, J.C. and S.L. Olson 1987. An extinct species of giant pigeon (Columbidae: *Ducula*) from archaeological deposits on Wallis (Uvea) Island, South Pacific. *Proceedings of the Biological Society of Washington* 100(4):769–775.

Balouet J.C. and S.L. Olson 1989. Fossil birds from late Quaternary deposits in New Caledonia. *Smithsonian Contributions to Zoology* 469:1–38.

Baumel, J.J. and L.M. Witmer 1993. Osteologia. In J.J. Baumel, A.S. King, J.E. Breazile, H.E. Evans and J.C. Vanden Berge (eds), *Handbook of avian anatomy: Nomina Anatomica Avium*, Second Edition. *Publications of the Nuttall Ornithological Club* 23, pp. 45–132, figs 4.1–4.18.Cambridge: Massachusetts.

Bourne, W.R.P. and A.C.F. David. 1986. Henderson Island. *Nature* 322:302.

Fosberg, F.R., M.-H. Sachet and D.R. Stoddart 1983. Henderson Island (Southeastern Polynesia): Summary of current knowledge. *Atoll Research Bulletin* 272, 1–47.

Hedges, R.E.M., P. B. Pettitt, C.B. Ramsay and G.L. Van Klinken 1997. Radiocarbon dates from the Oxford AMS system: Archaeometry datelist 24. *Archaeometry* 39:445–471.

James, H.F. and S.L. Olson 1991. Descriptions of thirty-two new species of birds from the Hawaiian Islands: Part 2. Passeriformes. *Ornithological Monographs* 46:1–88.

Olson, S. L. and H.F. James 1991. Descriptions of thirty-two new species of birds from the Hawaiian Islands: Part 1. Non-Passeriformes. *Ornithological Monographs* 45:1–88.

Schubel, S.E. and D.W. Steadman 1989. More bird bones from archaeological sites on Henderson Island, Pitcairn Group, South Pacific. *Atoll Research Bulletin* 325:1–13.

Sinoto, Y. 1983. An analysis of Polynesian migrations based on the archaeological assessments. *Journal de la Société des Océanistes* 39:57–67.

Spencer, T. and T.G.Benton 1995. The Sir Peter Scott Commemorative Expedition to the Pitcairn Islands 1991–1992. In T.G. Benton and T. Spencer (eds), *The Pitcairn Islands: biogeography, ecology and prehistory*, pp 1–5. London: Academic Press Ltd.

Steadman, D.W. 1989a. Extinction of birds in Eastern Polynesia: a review of the record, and comparisons with other Pacific Island groups. *Journal of Archaeological Science* 16:177–205.

Steadman, D.W. 1989b. New species and records of birds (Aves: Megapodiidae, Columbidae) from an archaeological site on Lifuka, Tonga. *Proceedings of the Biological Society of Washington* 102(3):537–552.

Steadman, D.W. 1992. New species of *Gallicolumba* and *Macropygia* (Aves: Columbidae). *Los Angeles County Museum of Natural History, Science Series* 36:329–348.

Steadman, D.W. 1993. Biogeography of Tongan birds before and after human impact. *Proceedings of the National Academy of Sciences U.S.A.* 90:818–822.

Steadman, D.W. 1994. Bird bones from the To'aga site, Ofu, American Samoa: prehistoric loss of seabirds and megapodes. *University of California Archaeological Research Facility, Contributions* 51:217–228.

Steadman, D.W. 1995. Prehistoric extinctions of Pacific island birds: Biodiversity meets zooarchaeology. *Science* 267:1123–1131.

Steadman, D.W. 1997. The historic biogeography and community ecology of Polynesian pigeons and doves. *Journal of Biogeography* 24:737–753.

Steadman, D.W. 2006a. *Extinction and Biogeography of tropical Pacific birds*. Chicago: University of Chicago Press.

Steadman, D.W. 2006b. An extinct species of tooth-billed pigeon (*Didunculus*) from the Kingdom of Tonga, and the concept of endemism in insular land birds. *Journal of Zoology* 268:233–241.

Steadman D.W. and S.L. Olson 1985. Bird remains from an archaeological site on Henderson Island, South Pacific: man-caused extinctions on an 'uninhabited' island. *Proceedings of the National Academy of Sciences, USA* 82:6191–6195.

Steadman, D.W. and B. Rolett 1996. A chronostratigraphic analysis of landbird extinction on Tahuata, Marquesas Islands. *Journal of Archaeological Science* 23:81–94.

Steadman, D.W., T.H. Worthy, A.J. Anderson and R. Water 2000. New species and records of birds from prehistoric sites on Niue, Southwest Pacific. *Wilson Bulletin* 112(2):165–186.

Weisler, M.I. 1994. The settlement of remote Polynesia: new evidence from Henderson Island. *Journal of Field Archaeology* 21:83–102.

Weisler, M.I. 1995. Henderson Island prehistory: colonisation and extinction on a remote Polynesian island. In T.G. Benton and T. Spencer (eds), *The Pitcairn Islands: biogeography, ecology and prehistory*, pp. 377–404. London: Academic Press Ltd.

Worthy, T.H. 2000. The fossil megapodes (Aves: Megapodiidae) of Fiji with descriptions of a new genus and two new species. *Journal of the Royal Society of New Zealand* 30:337–364.

Worthy, T.H. 2001. A giant flightless pigeon gen. et sp. nov. and a new species of *Ducula* (Aves: Columbidae), from Quaternary deposits in Fiji. *Journal of the Royal Society of New Zealand* 31:763–794.

Worthy, T.H. and G.M Wragg 2003. A new species of *Gallicolumba*: Columbidae from Henderson Island, Pitcairn Group. *Journal of the Royal Society of New Zealand* 33:769–793.

Wragg, G.M. 1995a. The fossil birds of Henderson Island, Pitcairn Group: natural turnover and human impact, a synopsis. In T.G. Benton, T. Spencer (eds), *The Pitcairn Islands: biogeography, ecology band prehistory*, pp. 405–414. London: Academic Press Ltd.

Wragg, G.M. 1995b. The fossil birds of Henderson Island, Pitcairn Group, South Pacific: a chronology of human-caused extinctions. Unpublished D.Phil, University of Oxford.

Wragg, G.M. and M.I. Weisler 1994. Extinctions and new records of birds from Henderson Island, Pitcairn Group, South Pacific Ocean. *Notornis* 41:61–70.

Wragg, G.M. and T.H. Worthy 2006. A new species of extinct imperial pigeon (*Ducula*: Columbidae) from Henderson Island, Pitcairn Group. *Historical Biology* 18(2):127–140.

www.ingramcontent.com/pod-product-compliance
Lightning Source LLC
Chambersburg PA
CBHW051308270326

41929CB00029B/3453